Actuarial Mathematics for Life Contingent Risks

How can actuaries best equip themselves for the products and risk structures of the future? In this ground-breaking textbook, three leaders in actuarial science give a modern perspective on life contingencies.

The book begins with actuarial models and theory, emphasizing practical applications using computational techniques. The authors then develop a more contemporary outlook, introducing multiple state models, emerging cash flows and embedded options. This expanded edition contains more examples and exercises designed to help with exam preparation as well as developing up-to-date expertise. There are brand new sections and chapters on discrete time Markov processes, on models involving joint lives and on Universal Life insurance and participating traditional insurance.

Balancing rigour with intuition, and emphasizing applications, this textbook is ideal for university courses, for qualified actuaries wishing to renew and update their skills and for individuals preparing for the professional actuarial examinations of the Society of Actuaries or Institute and Faculty of Actuaries. The book covers the entire SOA MLC syllabus and will be especially valuable for students preparing for the new, long answer exam questions.

DAVID C. M. DICKSON is Professor of Actuarial Studies in the Department of Economics at the University of Melbourne. He is a Fellow of the Faculty of Actuaries and of the Institute of Actuaries of Australia. He has twice been awarded the H. M. Jackson Prize of the Institute of Actuaries of Australia, most recently for his book *Insurance Risk and Ruin* (Cambridge University Press, 2005).

MARY R. HARDY holds the CIBC Chair in Financial Risk Management at the University of Waterloo, Ontario. She is a Fellow of the UK Institute and Faculty of Actuaries and of the Society of Actuaries. She is a past Vice President of the Society of Actuaries. In 2013 she was awarded the Finlaison Medal of the Institute and Faculty of Actuaries for services to the actuarial profession, in research, teaching and governance.

HOWARD R. WATERS is Professor in the Department of Actuarial Mathematics and Statistics at Heriot-Watt University, Edinburgh. He is a Fellow of the Institute and Faculty of Actuaries, by whom he was awarded the Finlaison Medal for services to the actuarial profession in 2006.

INTERNATIONAL SERIES ON ACTUARIAL SCIENCE

The *International Series on Actuarial Science*, published by Cambridge University Press in conjunction with the Institute and Faculty of Actuaries, contains textbooks for students taking courses in or related to actuarial science, as well as more advanced works designed for continuing professional development or for describing and synthesizing research. The series is a vehicle for publishing books that reflect changes and developments in the curriculum, that encourage the introduction of courses on actuarial science in universities, and that show how actuarial science can be used in all areas where there is long-term financial risk.

A complete list of books in the series can be found at www.cambridge.org/statistics. Recent titles include the following:

Solutions Manual for Actuarial Mathematics for Life Contingent Risks (2nd Edition)
David C.M. Dickson, Mary R. Hardy & Howard R. Waters

Actuarial Mathematics for Life Contingent Risks (2nd Edition)
David C.M. Dickson, Mary R. Hardy & Howard R. Waters

Risk Modelling in General Insurance
Roger J. Gray & Susan M. Pitts

Financial Enterprise Risk Management
Paul Sweeting

Regression Modeling with Actuarial and Financial Applications
Edward W. Frees

Nonlife Actuarial Models
Yiu-Kuen Tse

Generalized Linear Models for Insurance Data
Piet De Jong & Gillian Z. Heller

Market-Valuation Methods in Life and Pension Insurance
Thomas Møller & Mogens Steffensen

ACTUARIAL MATHEMATICS FOR LIFE CONTINGENT RISKS

SECOND EDITION

DAVID C. M. DICKSON

University of Melbourne

MARY R. HARDY

University of Waterloo, Ontario

HOWARD R. WATERS

Heriot-Watt University, Edinburgh

CAMBRIDGE
UNIVERSITY PRESS

CAMBRIDGE
UNIVERSITY PRESS

University Printing House, Cambridge CB2 8BS, United Kingdom

Cambridge University Press is part of the University of Cambridge.

It furthers the University's mission by disseminating knowledge in the pursuit of education, learning and research at the highest international levels of excellence.

www.cambridge.org
Information on this title: www.cambridge.org/9781107044074

First published 2009
6th printing 2012
Second edition 2013
4th printing 2016

Printed in the United States of America by Sheridan Books, Inc.

A catalogue record for this publication is available from the British Library

Dickson, D. C. M. (David C. M.), 1959–
Actuarial mathematics for life contingent risks / David C M Dickson, Mary R Hardy, Howard R Waters. – 2nd edition.
pages cm
Includes bibliographical references.
ISBN 978-1-107-04407-4 (Hardback)
1. Insurance–Mathematics.   2. Risk (Insurance)–Mathematics.   I. Hardy, Mary, 1958–
II. Waters, H. R. (Howard Richard)   III. Title.
HG8781.D528 2013
368′.01–dc23   2013013708

ISBN 978-1-107-04407-4 Hardback

*To
Carolann,
Vivien
and Phelim*

Contents

Preface to the second edition

Life insurance has undergone enormous change in the last two to three decades. New and innovative products have been developed at the same time as we have seen vast increases in computational power. In addition, the field of finance has experienced a revolution in the development of a mathematical theory of options and financial guarantees, first pioneered in the work of Black, Scholes and Merton, and actuaries have come to realize the importance of that work to risk management in actuarial contexts.

In this book we have adapted the traditional approach to the mathematics of life contingent risk to be better adapted to the products, science and technology that are relevant to current and future actuaries, taking into consideration both demographic and financial uncertainty. The material is presented with a certain level of mathematical rigour; we intend for readers to understand the principles involved, rather than to memorize methods or formulae. The reason is that a rigorous approach will prove more useful in the long run than a short-term utilitarian outlook, as theory can be adapted to changing products and technology in ways that techniques, without scientific support, cannot. However, this is a very practical text. The models and techniques presented are versions, a little simplified in parts, of the models and techniques in use by actuaries in the forefront of modern actuarial management.

The first seven chapters set the context for the material, and cover traditional actuarial models and theory of life contingencies, with modern computational techniques integrated throughout, and with an emphasis on the practical context for the survival models and valuation methods presented. Through the focus on realistic contracts and assumptions, we aim to foster a general business awareness in the life insurance context, at the same time as we develop the mathematical tools for risk management in that context.

From Chapter 8, we move into more modern theory and methods.

In Chapter 8 we introduce multiple state models, which generalize the life–death contingency structure of previous chapters. Using multiple state models allows a single framework for a wide range of insurance, including income replacement insurance where benefits and premiums depend on the health status of the policyholder; critical illness insurance, which pays a benefit on diagnosis of certain serious medical disorders, and some insurance policies which pay additional benefits in the case of accidental death.

In Chapter 9 we apply the models and results from multiple state models to insurance involving two lives, typically domestic partners. It is common for partners to purchase life insurance cover or annuity income products where the benefits depend on both lives, not on a single insured life.

In Chapter 10 we apply the theory developed in the earlier chapters to problems involving pension benefits. Pension mathematics has some specialized concepts, particularly in funding principles, but in general this chapter is an application of the theory in the preceding chapters.

In Chapter 11 we move to a more sophisticated view of interest rate models and interest rate risk. In this chapter we explore the crucially important difference between diversifiable and non-diversifiable risk.

In Chapter 12 we introduce a general algorithm for projecting the emerging surplus of insurance policies, by considering the year-to-year net cash flows. One of the liberating aspects of the computer revolution for actuaries is that we are no longer required to summarize complex benefits in a single actuarial value; we can go much further in projecting the cash flows to see how and when surplus will emerge. This is much richer information that the actuary can use to assess profitability and to better manage portfolio assets and liabilities. In life insurance contexts, the emerging cash flow projection is often called 'profit testing'.

In Chapter 13 we follow up on the cash flow projections of Chapter 12 to show how profit testing can be used to design and assess products for which policyholders share profits with the insurer. The first type of policy examined is a traditional with-profits policy, where profits are distributed as cash dividends, or as additional life insurance benefit. The second type is the Universal Life policy, which is very popular in North America.

In Chapter 14 we use the emerging cash flow approach to assess equity-linked contracts, where a financial guarantee is commonly part of the contingent benefit. The real risks for such products can only be assessed taking the random variation in potential outcomes into consideration, and we demonstrate this with Monte Carlo simulation of the emerging cash flows.

The products that are explored in Chapter 14 contain financial guarantees embedded in the life contingent benefits. Option theory is the mathematics of valuation and risk management of financial guarantees. In Chapter 15 we introduce the fundamental assumptions and results of option theory.

In Chapter 16 we apply option theory to the embedded options of financial guarantees in insurance products. The theory can be used for pricing and for determining appropriate reserves, as well as for assessing profitability.

The material in this book is designed for undergraduate and graduate programmes in actuarial science, for those self-studying for professional actuarial exams, and for practitioners interested in updating their skill set. The content has been designed primarily to prepare readers for practical actuarial work in life insurance and pension funding and valuation. The text covers all the most recent syllabus requirements for the MLC exam of the Society of Actuaries and for the CT5 exam of the UK Institute and Faculty of Actuaries. Some of the topics in this book are not currently covered by those professional exams, and many of the topics that are in the exams are covered in significantly more depth in this book, particularly where we believe the content will be valuable beyond the exams.

Students and other readers should have sufficient background in probability to be able to calculate moments of functions of one or two random variables, and to handle conditional expectations and variances. We assume familiarity with the binomial, uniform, exponential, normal and lognormal distributions. Some of the more important results are reviewed in Appendix A. We also assume that readers have completed an introductory level course in the mathematics of finance, and are aware of the actuarial notation for interest, discount and annuities-certain.

Throughout, we have opted to use examples that liberally call on spreadsheet-style software. Spreadsheets are ubiquitous tools in actuarial practice, and it is natural to use them throughout, allowing us to use more realistic examples, rather than having to simplify for the sake of mathematical tractability. Other software could be used equally effectively, but spreadsheets represent a fairly universal language that is easily accessible. To keep the computation requirements reasonable, we have ensured that every example and exercise can be completed in Microsoft Excel, without needing any VBA code or macros. Readers who have sufficient familiarity to write their own code may find more efficient solutions than those that we have presented, but our principle was that no reader should need to know more than the basic Excel functions and applications. It will be very useful for anyone working through the material of this book to construct their own spreadsheet tables as they work through the first seven chapters, to generate mortality and actuarial functions for a range of mortality models and interest rates. In the worked examples in the text, we have worked with greater accuracy than we record, so there will be some differences from rounding when working with intermediate figures.

One of the advantages of spreadsheets is the ease of implementation of numerical integration algorithms. We assume that students are aware of the principles of numerical integration, and we give some of the most useful algorithms in Appendix B.

The material in this book is appropriate for two one-semester courses. The first seven chapters form a fairly traditional basis, and would reasonably constitute a first course. Chapters 8–16 introduce more contemporary material. Chapter 15 may be omitted by readers who have studied an introductory course covering pricing and delta hedging in a Black–Scholes–Merton model. Chapter 10, on pension mathematics, is not required for subsequent chapters, and could be omitted if a single focus on life insurance is preferred.

Changes from the first edition

The major changes are listed here.

- The material on joint life models has been substantially expanded, and placed in a separate chapter. In the first edition, the joint life material was incorporated in Chapter 8.
- The material on profit sharing and Universal Life, in Chapter 13, is new. Some of this has been adapted from the monograph 'Supplementary Notes for Actuarial Mathematics for Life Contingent Risks', previously available as a free supplement to the first edition.
- Additional content in Chapter 7 (policy values) covers modified premium valuation and its relationship to deferred acquisition costs and net premium valuation. This content is relevant for any readers who need to understand US valuation methods, and may be omitted by those who do not.
- More short, examination-style questions, which do not require spreadsheets, have been added to the exercises in many of the chapters. The questions are designed to help students prepare for exams as well as develop understanding. To support these questions, we have included some exam-style tables in Appendix D.
- Other, smaller changes include new sections on mortality reduction factors, discrete time Markov chains, and construction of multiple decrement models.

Acknowledgements

We acknowledge all the colleagues and students who provided comment and feedback during the writing of the first edition of the text. Special thanks go to Carole Bernard, Phelim Boyle, Johnny Siu-Hang Li, Ana Maria Mera, Kok Keng Siaw and Matthew Till.

Many friends and colleagues have provided feedback on the first edition, and we thank all those who helped us to shape the new material. We are particularly grateful to Chris Groendyke, who assisted with the Universal Life material, and to Mike Xiaobai Zhu, for his careful review of much of the final manuscript.

We are grateful to the Society of Actuaries for permission to reproduce questions from their MLC exams, for which they own copyright. The relevant questions are noted in the text.

The authors gratefully acknowledge the contribution of the Departments of Statistics and Actuarial Science, University of Waterloo, Actuarial Mathematics and Statistics, Heriot-Watt University, and the Department of Economics, University of Melbourne, in welcoming the non-resident authors for short visits to work on this book.

Finally, thanks to Carolann Waters, Vivien Dickson and Phelim Boyle, to whom this book is dedicated, for their unstinting support and generosity.

David Dickson
University of Melbourne

Mary Hardy
University of Waterloo

Howard Waters
Heriot-Watt University

1

Introduction to life insurance

1.1 Summary

Actuaries apply scientific principles and techniques from a range of other disciplines to problems involving risk, uncertainty and finance. In this chapter we set the context for the mathematics of later chapters, by describing some of the background to modern actuarial practice in life insurance, followed by a brief description of the major types of life insurance products that are sold in developed insurance markets. Because pension liabilities are similar in many ways to life insurance liabilities, we also describe some common pension benefits. We give examples of the actuarial questions arising from the risk management of these contracts. How to answer such questions, and solve the resulting problems, is the subject of the following chapters.

1.2 Background

The first actuaries were employed by life insurance companies in the early eighteenth century to provide a scientific basis for managing the companies' assets and liabilities. The liabilities depended on the number of deaths occurring amongst the insured lives each year. The modelling of mortality became a topic of both commercial and general scientific interest, and it attracted many significant scientists and mathematicians to actuarial problems, with the result that much of the early work in the field of probability was closely connected with the development of solutions to actuarial problems.

The earliest life insurance policies provided that the policyholder would pay an amount, called the **premium**, to the insurer. If the named life insured died during the year that the contract was in force, the insurer would pay a predetermined lump sum, the **sum insured**, to the policyholder or his or her estate. So, the first life insurance contracts were annual contracts. Each year the premium would increase as the probability of death increased. If the insured life became very ill at the renewal date, the insurance might not be renewed, in which case no benefit would be paid on the life's subsequent death. Over a large number of contracts, the premium income each year should approximately match the claims outgo. This method of matching income and outgo annually, with no attempt to smooth or balance the premiums over the years, is called **assessmentism**. This method is still used for group life insurance, where an employer purchases life insurance cover for its employees on a year-to-year basis.

The radical development in the later eighteenth century was the level premium contract. The problem with assessmentism was that the annual increases in premiums discouraged policyholders from renewing their contracts. The level premium policy offered the policyholder the option to lock-in a regular premium, payable perhaps weekly, monthly, quarterly or annually, for a number of years. This was much more popular with policyholders, as they would not be priced out of the insurance contract just when it might be most needed. For the insurer, the attraction of the longer contract was a greater likelihood of the policyholder paying premiums for a longer period. However, a problem for the insurer was that the longer contracts were more complex to model, and offered more financial risk. For these contracts actuarial techniques had to develop beyond the year-to-year modelling of mortality probabilities. In particular, it became necessary to incorporate financial considerations into the modelling of income and outgo. Over a one-year contract, the time value of money is not a critical aspect. Over, say, a 30-year contract, it becomes a very important part of the modelling and management of risk.

Another development in life insurance in the nineteenth century was the concept of **insurable interest**. This was a requirement in law that the person contracting to pay the life insurance premiums should face a financial loss on the death of the insured life – an insurance payout should not leave the beneficiary financially better off than if the insured life had not died. The insurable interest requirement ended the practice where individuals would insure persons (often public figures) with no connection to the purchaser, as a form of gambling. It also, importantly, removed the incentive for a policyholder to hasten the death of the insured life. Subsequently, insurance policies tended to be purchased by the insured life, and in the rest of this book we use the convention that the policyholder who pays the premiums is also the life insured, whose survival or death triggers the payment of the sum insured under the conditions of the contract.

The earliest studies of mortality include life tables constructed by John Graunt and Edmund Halley. A life table summarizes a survival model by specifying the proportion of lives that are expected to survive to each age. Using London mortality data from the early seventeenth century, Graunt proposed, for example, that each new life had a probability of 40% of surviving to age 16, and a probability of 1% of surviving to age 76. Edmund Halley, famous for his astronomical calculations, used mortality data from the city of Breslau in the late seventeenth century as the basis for his life table, which, like Graunt's, was constructed by proposing the average ('medium' in Halley's phrase) proportion of survivors to each age from an arbitrary number of births. Halley took the work two steps further. First, he used the table to draw inference about the conditional survival probabilities at intermediate ages. That is, given the probability that a newborn life survives to each subsequent age, it is possible to infer the probability that a life aged, say, 20, will survive to each subsequent age, using the condition that a life aged zero survives to age 20. The second major innovation was that Halley combined the mortality data with an assumption about interest rates to find the value of a whole life annuity at different ages. A whole life annuity is a contract paying a level sum at regular intervals while the named life (the annuitant) is still alive. The calculations in Halley's paper bear a remarkable similarity to some of the work still used by actuaries in pensions and life insurance.

This book continues in the tradition of combining models of mortality with models in finance to develop a framework for pricing and risk management of long-term policies in life insurance. Many of the same techniques are relevant also in pensions mathematics. However, there have been many changes since the first long-term policies of the late eighteenth century.

1.3 Life insurance and annuity contracts

1.3.1 Introduction

The life insurance and annuity contracts that were the object of study of the early actuaries were very similar to the contracts written up to the 1980s in all the developed insurance markets. Recently, however, the design of life insurance products has radically changed, and the techniques needed to manage these more modern contracts are more complex than ever. The reasons for the changes include:

- Increased interest by the insurers in offering combined savings and insurance products. The original life insurance products offered a payment to indemnify (or offset) the hardship caused by the death of the policyholder. Many modern contracts combine the indemnity concept with an opportunity to invest.
- More powerful computational facilities allow more complex products to be modelled.
- Policyholders have become more sophisticated investors, and require more options in their contracts, allowing them to vary premiums or sums insured, for example.

- More competition has led to insurers creating increasingly complex products in order to attract more business.
- Risk management techniques in financial products have also become increasingly complex, and insurers have offered some benefits, particularly financial guarantees, that require sophisticated techniques from financial engineering to measure and manage the risk.

In the remainder of this section we describe some of the most important modern insurance contracts, which will be used as examples in later chapters. Different countries have different names and types of contracts; we have tried to cover the major contract types in North America, the United Kingdom and Australia.

The basic transaction of life insurance is an exchange; the policyholder pays premiums in return for a later payment from the insurer which is life contingent, by which we mean that it depends on the death or survival or possibly the state of health of the policyholder. We usually use the term '**insurance**' when the benefit is paid as a single lump sum, either on the death of the policyholder or on survival to a predetermined **maturity date**. (In the UK it is common to use the term 'assurance' for insurance contracts involving lives, and insurance for contracts involving property.) An **annuity** is a benefit in the form of a regular series of payments, usually conditional on the survival of the policyholder.

1.3.2 Traditional insurance contracts

Term, whole life and endowment insurance are the traditional products, providing cash benefits on death or maturity, usually with predetermined premium and benefit amounts. We describe each in a little more detail here.

Term insurance pays a lump sum benefit on the death of the policyholder, provided death occurs before the end of a specified term. Term insurance allows a policyholder to provide a fixed sum for his or her dependents in the event of the policyholder's death.

Level term insurance indicates a level sum insured and regular, level premiums.

Decreasing term insurance indicates that the sum insured and (usually) premiums decrease over the term of the contract. Decreasing term insurance is popular in the UK where it is used in conjunction with a home mortgage; if the policyholder dies, the remaining mortgage is paid from the term insurance proceeds.

Renewable term insurance offers the policyholder the option of renewing the policy at the end of the original term, without further evidence of the policyholder's health status. In North America, Yearly Renewable

Term (YRT) insurance is common, under which insurability is guaranteed for some fixed period, though the contract is written only for one year at a time.

Convertible term insurance offers the policyholder the option to convert to a whole life or endowment insurance at the end of the original term, without further evidence of the policyholder's health status.

Whole life insurance pays a lump sum benefit on the death of the policyholder whenever it occurs. For regular premium contracts, the premium is often payable only up to some maximum age, such as 80. This avoids the problem that older lives may be less able to pay the premiums.

Endowment insurance offers a lump sum benefit paid either on the death of the policyholder or at the end of a specified term, whichever occurs first. This is a mixture of a term insurance benefit and a savings element. If the policyholder dies, the sum insured is paid just as under term insurance; if the policyholder survives, the sum insured is treated as a maturing investment. Endowment insurance is obsolete in many jurisdictions. Traditional endowment insurance policies are not currently sold in the UK, but there are large portfolios of policies on the books of UK insurers, because until the late 1990s, endowment insurance policies were often used to repay home mortgages. The policyholder (who was the home owner) paid interest on the mortgage loan, and the principal was paid from the proceeds on the endowment insurance, either on the death of the policyholder or at the final mortgage repayment date.

Endowment insurance policies are becoming popular in developing nations, particularly for 'micro-insurance' where the amounts involved are small. It is hard for small investors to achieve good rates of return on investments, because of heavy expense charges. By pooling the death and survival benefits under the endowment contract, the policyholder gains on the investment side from the resulting economies of scale, and from the investment expertise of the insurer.

Participating insurance

Also part of the traditional design of insurance is the division of business into 'participating' or 'par' business, also known as 'with-profit', and 'nonparticipating', or 'non-par', also known as 'without profit'. Under participating insurance, the profits earned on the invested premiums are shared with the policyholders. In North America, the profit share often takes the form of cash dividends or reduced premiums. In the UK and in Australia the traditional approach is to use the profits to increase the sum insured, through bonuses called '**reversionary bonuses**' and '**terminal bonuses**'. Reversionary bonuses are awarded during the term of the contract; once a reversionary bonus is awarded it is guaranteed. Terminal bonuses are awarded when the policy matures, either through the death of the insured, or when an endowment policy reaches the end of the term. Reversionary bonuses may be expressed as a percentage of the total of the previous sum insured plus bonus, or as a percentage of the original sum insured plus a different percentage of the previously declared bonuses. Reversionary and terminal bonuses are determined by the insurer based on the investment performance of the invested premiums.

Participating insurance is used to offer policyholders a savings element with their life insurance. However, the traditional participating contract was designed primarily for the life insurance cover, with the savings aspect a secondary feature.

1.3.3 Modern insurance contracts

In recent years insurers have provided more flexible products that combine the death benefit coverage with a significant investment element, as a way of competing for policyholders' savings with other institutions, for example, banks or open-ended investment companies (e.g. mutual funds in North America, or unit trusts in the UK). Additional flexibility also allows policyholders to purchase less insurance when their finances are tight, and then increase the insurance coverage when they have more money available.

In this section we describe some examples of modern, flexible insurance contracts.

- **Universal Life insurance** combines investment and life insurance. The policyholder determines a premium and a level of life insurance cover. Premiums are flexible, as long as the accumulated value of the premiums is sufficient to pay for the designated sum insured under the term insurance part of the contract. Universal Life is a common insurance contract in North America.
- **Unitized with-profit** is a UK insurance contract; it is an evolution from the conventional with-profit policy, designed to be more transparent than the original. Premiums are used to purchase units (shares) of an investment fund, called the with-profit fund. As the fund earns investment return, the shares increase in value (or more shares are issued), increasing the benefit entitlement as reversionary bonus. The shares will not decrease in value. On death or maturity, a further terminal bonus may be payable depending on the performance of the with-profit fund.

  After some poor publicity surrounding with-profit business, and, by association, unitized with-profit business, these product designs were withdrawn from the UK and Australian markets in the early 2000s. However, they will remain important for many years as many companies carry very large portfolios of with-profit (traditional and unitized) policies issued during the second half of the twentieth century.

• **Equity-linked insurance** has a benefit linked to the performance of an investment fund. There are two different forms. The first is where the policyholder's premiums are invested in an open-ended investment company style account; at maturity, the benefit is the accumulated value of the premiums. There is a guaranteed minimum death benefit payable if the policyholder dies before the contract matures. In some cases, there is also a guaranteed minimum maturity benefit payable. In the UK and most of Europe, these are called **unit-linked** policies, and they rarely carry a guaranteed maturity benefit. In Canada they are known as **segregated fund** policies and always carry a maturity guarantee. In the USA these contracts are called **variable annuity** contracts; maturity guarantees are increasingly common for these policies. (The use of the term 'annuity' for these contracts is misleading. The benefits are designed with a single lump sum payout, though there will be an option to convert the lump sum to an annuity.)

The second form of equity-linked insurance is the **Equity-Indexed Annuity** (EIA) in the USA. Under an EIA the policyholder is guaranteed a minimum return on their premium (minus an initial expense charge). At maturity, the policyholder receives a proportion of the return on a specified stock index, if that is greater than the guaranteed minimum return.

EIAs are generally rather shorter in term than unit-linked products, with seven-year policies being typical; variable annuity contracts commonly have terms of 20 years or more. EIAs are much less popular with consumers than variable annuities.

1.3.4 Distribution methods

Most people find insurance dauntingly complex. Brokers who connect individuals to an appropriate insurance product have, since the earliest times, played an important role in the market. There is an old saying amongst actuaries that 'insurance is sold, not bought', which means that the role of an intermediary in persuading potential policyholders to take out an insurance policy is crucial in maintaining an adequate volume of new business.

Brokers, or other financial advisors, are often remunerated through a **commission system**. The commission would be specified as a percentage of the premium paid. Typically, there is a higher percentage paid on the first premium than on subsequent premiums. This is referred to as a **front-end load**. Some advisors may be remunerated on a fixed-fee basis, or may be employed by one or more insurance companies on a salary basis.

An alternative to the broker method of selling insurance is **direct marketing**. Insurers may use television advertising or other telemarketing methods to sell direct to the public. The nature of the business sold by direct marketing methods tends to differ from the broker-sold business. For example, often the sum insured is smaller. The policy may be aimed at a niche market, such as older lives concerned with insurance to cover their own funeral expenses (called **pre-need** insurance in the USA). Another mass marketed insurance contract is loan or credit insurance, where an insurer might cover loan or credit card payments in the event of the borrower's death, disability or unemployment.

1.3.5 Underwriting

It is important in modelling life insurance liabilities to consider what happens when a life insurance policy is purchased. Selling life insurance policies is a competitive business and life insurance companies (also known as life offices) are constantly considering ways in which to change their procedures so that they can improve the service to their customers and gain a commercial advantage over their competitors. The account given below of how policies are sold covers some essential points but is necessarily a simplified version of what actually happens.

For a given type of policy, say a 10-year term insurance, the life office will have a schedule of premium rates. These rates will depend on the size of the policy and some other factors known as **rating factors**. An applicant's risk level is assessed by asking them to complete a **proposal form** giving information on relevant rating factors, generally including their age, gender (where legislation permits), smoking habits, occupation, any dangerous hobbies, and personal and family health history. The life insurer may ask for permission to contact the applicant's doctor to enquire about their medical history. In some cases, particularly for very large sums insured, the life insurer may require that the applicant's health be checked by a doctor employed by the insurer.

The process of collecting and evaluating this information is called **underwriting**. The purpose of underwriting is, first, to classify potential policyholders into broadly homogeneous risk categories, and secondly to assess what additional premium would be appropriate for applicants whose risk factors indicate that standard premium rates would be too low.

On the basis of the application and supporting medical information, potential life insurance policyholders will generally be categorized into one of the following groups:

- **Preferred lives** have very low mortality risk based on the standard information. The preferred applicant would have no recent record of smoking;

no evidence of drug or alcohol abuse; no high-risk hobbies or occupations; no family history of disease known to have a strong genetic component; no adverse medical indicators such as high blood pressure or cholesterol level or body mass index.

The preferred life category is common in North America, but has not yet caught on elsewhere. In other areas there is no separation of preferred and normal lives.

- **Normal lives** may have some higher rated risk factors than preferred lives (where this category exists), but are still insurable at standard rates. Most applicants fall into this category.

- **Rated lives** have one or more risk factors at raised levels and so are not acceptable at standard premium rates. However, they can be insured for a higher premium. An example might be someone having a family history of heart disease. These lives might be individually assessed for the appropriate additional premium to be charged. This category would also include lives with hazardous jobs or hobbies which put them at increased risk.

- **Uninsurable lives** have such significant risk that the insurer will not enter an insurance contract at any price.

Within the first three groups, applicants would be further categorized according to the relative values of the various risk factors, with the most fundamental being age, gender and smoking status. Note, however, that gender-based premiums are no longer permitted in some jurisdictions, including the European Union countries. Most applicants (around 95% for traditional life insurance) will be accepted at preferred or standard rates for the relevant risk category. Another 2–3% may be accepted at non-standard rates because of an impairment, or a dangerous occupation, leaving around 2–3% who will be refused insurance.

The rigour of the underwriting process will depend on the type of insurance being purchased, on the sum insured and on the distribution process of the insurance company. Term insurance is generally more strictly underwritten than whole life insurance, as the risk taken by the insurer is greater. Under whole life insurance, the payment of the sum insured is certain, the uncertainty is in the timing. Under, say, 10-year term insurance, it is assumed that the majority of contracts will expire with no death benefit paid. If the underwriting is not strict there is a risk of **adverse selection** by policyholders – that is, that very high-risk individuals will buy insurance in disproportionate numbers, leading to excessive losses. Since high sum insured contracts carry more risk than low sum insured, high sums insured would generally trigger more rigorous underwriting.

The distribution method also affects the level of underwriting. Often, direct marketed contracts are sold with relatively low benefit levels, and with the attraction that no medical evidence will be sought beyond a standard questionnaire. The insurer may assume relatively heavy mortality for these lives to compensate for potential adverse selection. By keeping the underwriting relatively light, the expenses of writing new business can be kept low, which is an attraction for high-volume, low sum insured contracts.

It is interesting to note that with no third party medical evidence the insurer is placing a lot of weight on the veracity of the policyholder. Insurers have a phrase for this – that both insurer and policyholder may assume 'utmost good faith' or '*uberrima fides*' on the part of the other side of the contract. In practice, in the event of the death of the insured life, the insurer may investigate whether any pertinent information was withheld from the application. If it appears that the policyholder held back information, or submitted false or misleading information, the insurer may not pay the full sum insured.

1.3.6 Premiums

A life insurance policy may involve a single premium, payable at the outset of the contract, or a regular series of premiums payable provided the policyholder survives, perhaps with a fixed end date. In traditional contracts the regular premium is generally a level amount throughout the term of the contract; in more modern contracts the premium might be variable, at the policyholder's discretion for investment products such as equity-linked insurance, or at the insurer's discretion for certain types of term insurance.

Regular premiums may be paid annually, semi-annually, quarterly, monthly or weekly. Monthly premiums are common as it is convenient for policyholders to have their outgoings payable with approximately the same frequency as their income.

An important feature of all premiums is that they are paid at the start of each period. Suppose a policyholder contracts to pay annual premiums for a 10-year insurance contract. The premiums will be paid at the start of the contract, and then at the start of each subsequent year provided the policyholder is alive. So, if we count time in years from $t = 0$ at the start of the contract, the first premium is paid at $t = 0$, the second is paid at $t = 1$, and so on, to the tenth premium paid at $t = 9$. Similarly, if the premiums are monthly, then the first monthly instalment will be paid at $t = 0$, and the final premium will be paid at the start of the final month at $t = 9\frac{11}{12}$ years. (Throughout this book we assume that all months are equal in length, at $\frac{1}{12}$ years.)

1.3.7 Life annuities

Annuity contracts offer a regular series of payments. When an annuity depends on the survival of the recipient, it is called a 'life annuity'. The recipient is called an annuitant. If the annuity continues until the death of the annuitant, it is called a **whole life annuity**. If the annuity is paid for some maximum period it is called a **term life annuity**.

Annuities are often purchased by older lives to provide income in retirement. Buying a whole life annuity guarantees that the income will not run out before the annuitant dies.

- **Single Premium Deferred Annuity (SPDA)** Under an SPDA contract, the policyholder pays a single premium in return for an annuity which commences payment at some future, specified date. The annuity is 'life contingent', by which we mean the annuity is paid only if the policyholder survives to the payment dates. If the policyholder dies before the annuity commences, there may be a death benefit due. If the policyholder dies soon after the annuity commences, there may be some minimum payment period, called the guarantee period, and the balance would be paid to the policyholder's estate.
- **Single Premium Immediate Annuity (SPIA)** This contract is the same as the SPDA, except that the annuity commences as soon as the contract is effected. This might, for example, be used to convert a lump sum retirement benefit into a life annuity to supplement a pension. As with the SPDA, there may be a guarantee period applying in the event of the early death of the annuitant.
- **Regular Premium Deferred Annuity (RPDA)** The RPDA offers a deferred life annuity with premiums paid through the deferred period. It is otherwise the same as the SPDA.
- **Joint life annuity** A joint life annuity is issued on two lives, typically a married couple. The annuity (which may be single premium or regular premium, immediate or deferred) continues while both lives survive, and ceases on the first death of the couple.
- **Last survivor annuity** A last survivor annuity is similar to the joint life annuity, except that payment continues while at least one of the lives survives, and ceases on the second death of the couple.
- **Reversionary annuity** A reversionary annuity is contingent on two lives, usually a couple. One is designated as the annuitant, and one the insured. No annuity benefit is paid while the insured life survives. On the death of the insured life, if the annuitant is still alive, the annuitant receives an annuity for the remainder of his or her life.

1.4 Other insurance contracts

The insurance and annuity contracts described above are all contingent on death or survival. There are other life contingent risks, in particular involving short-term or long-term disability. These are known as morbidity risks.

- **Income protection insurance** When a person becomes sick and cannot work, their income will, eventually, be affected. For someone in regular employment, the employer may cover salary for a period, but if the sickness continues the salary will be decreased, and ultimately will stop being paid at all. For someone who is self-employed, the effects of sickness on income will be immediate. Income protection policies replace at least some income during periods of sickness. They usually cease at retirement age.
- **Critical illness insurance** Some serious illnesses can cause significant expense at the onset of the illness. The patient may have to leave employment, or alter their home, or may incur severe medical expenses. Critical illness insurance pays a benefit on diagnosis of one of a number of severe conditions, such as certain cancers or heart disease. The benefit is usually in the form of a lump sum.
- **Long-term care insurance** This is purchased to cover the costs of care in old age, when the insured life is unable to continue living independently. The benefit would be in the form of the long-term care costs, so is an annuity benefit.

1.5 Pension benefits

Many actuaries work in the area of pension plan design, valuation and risk management. The pension plan is usually sponsored by an employer. Pension plans typically offer employees (also called pension plan members) either lump sums or annuity benefits or both on retirement, or deferred lump sum or annuity benefits (or both) on earlier withdrawal. Some offer a lump sum benefit if the employee dies while still employed. The benefits therefore depend on the survival and employment status of the member, and are quite similar in nature to life insurance benefits – that is, they involve investment of contributions long into the future to pay for future life contingent benefits.

1.5.1 Defined benefit and defined contribution

Defined Benefit (DB) pensions offer retirement income based on service and salary with an employer, using a defined formula to determine the pension. For example, suppose an employee reaches retirement age with n years of service (i.e. membership of the pension plan), and with pensionable salary averaging

S in, say, the final three years of employment. A typical **final salary** plan might offer an annual pension at retirement of $B = Sn\alpha$, where α is called the **accrual rate,** and is usually around 1–2%. The formula may be interpreted as a pension benefit of, say, 2% of the final average salary for each year of service.

The defined benefit is funded by contributions paid by the employer and (usually) the employee over the working lifetime of the employee. The contributions are invested, and the accumulated contributions must be enough, on average, to pay the pensions when they become due.

Defined Contribution (DC) pensions work more like a bank account. The employee and employer pay a predetermined contribution (usually a fixed percentage of salary) into a fund, and the fund earns interest. When the employee leaves or retires, the proceeds are available to provide income throughout retirement. In the UK most of the proceeds must be converted to an annuity. In the USA and Canada there are more options – the pensioner may draw funds to live on without necessarily purchasing an annuity from an insurance company.

1.5.2 Defined benefit pension design

The **age retirement pension** described in the section above defines the pension payable from retirement in a standard final salary plan. **Career average salary** plans are also common in some jurisdictions, where the benefit formula is the same as the final salary formula above, except that the average salary over the employee's entire career is used in place of the final salary.

Many employees leave their jobs before they retire. A typical **withdrawal benefit** would be a pension based on the same formula as the age retirement benefit, but with the start date deferred until the employee reaches the normal retirement age. Employees may have the option of taking a lump sum with the same value as the deferred pension, which can be invested in the pension plan of the new employer.

Some pension plans also offer **death-in-service** benefits, for employees who die during their period of employment. Such benefits might include a lump sum, often based on salary and sometimes service, as well as a pension for the employee's spouse.

1.6 Mutual and proprietary insurers

A **mutual** insurance company is one that has no shareholders. The insurer is owned by the with-profit policyholders. All profits are distributed to the with-profit policyholders through dividends or bonuses.

A **proprietary** insurance company has shareholders, and usually has with-profit policyholders as well. The participating policyholders are not owners, but have a specified right to some of the profits. Thus, in a proprietary insurer, the profits must be shared in some predetermined proportion, between the shareholders and the with-profit policyholders.

Many early life insurance companies were formed as mutual companies. More recently, in the UK, Canada and the USA, there has been a trend towards demutualization, which means the transition of a mutual company to a proprietary company, through issuing shares (or cash) to the with-profit policyholders. Although it would appear that a mutual insurer would have marketing advantages, as participating policyholders receive all the profits and other benefits of ownership, the advantages cited by companies who have demutualized include increased ability to raise capital, clearer corporate structure and improved efficiency.

1.7 Typical problems

We are concerned in this book with developing the mathematical models and techniques used by actuaries working in life insurance and pensions. The primary responsibility of the life insurance actuary is to maintain the solvency and profitability of the insurer. Premiums must be sufficient to pay benefits; the assets held must be sufficient to pay the contingent liabilities; bonuses to policyholders should be fair.

Consider, for example, a whole life insurance contract issued to a life aged 50. The sum insured may not be paid for 30 years or more. The premiums paid over the period will be invested by the insurer to earn significant interest; the accumulated premiums must be sufficient to pay the benefits, on average. To ensure this, the actuary needs to model the survival probabilities of the policyholder, the investment returns likely to be earned and the expenses likely to be incurred in maintaining the policy. The actuary may take into consideration the probability that the policyholder decides to terminate the contract early. The actuary may also consider the profitability requirements for the contract. Then, when all of these factors have been modelled, they must be combined to set a premium.

Each year or so, the actuary must determine how much money the insurer or pension plan should hold to ensure that future liabilities will be covered with adequately high probability. This is called the valuation process. For with-profit insurance, the actuary must determine a suitable level of bonus.

The problems are rather more complex if the insurance also covers morbidity risk, or involves several lives. All of these topics are covered in the following chapters.

The actuary may also be involved in decisions about how the premiums are invested. It is vitally important that the insurer remains solvent, as the contracts are very long-term and insurers are responsible for protecting the financial security of the general public. The way the underlying investments are selected can increase or mitigate the risk of insolvency. The precise selection of investments to manage the risk is particularly important where the contracts involve financial guarantees.

The pensions actuary working with defined benefit pensions must determine appropriate contribution rates to meet the benefits promised, using models that allow for the working patterns of the employees. Sometimes, the employer may want to change the benefit structure, and the actuary is responsible for assessing the cost and impact. When one company with a pension plan takes over another, the actuary must assist with determining the best way to allocate the assets from the two plans, and perhaps how to merge the benefits.

1.8 Notes and further reading

A number of essays describing actuarial practice can be found in Renn (ed.) (1998). This book also provides both historical and more contemporary contexts for life contingencies.

The original papers of Graunt and Halley are available online (and any search engine will find them). Anyone interested in the history of probability and actuarial science will find these interesting, and remarkably modern.

1.9 Exercises

Exercise 1.1 Why do insurers generally require evidence of health from a person applying for life insurance but not for an annuity?

Exercise 1.2 Explain why an insurer might demand more rigorous evidence of a prospective policyholder's health status for a term insurance than for a whole life insurance.

Exercise 1.3 Explain why premiums are payable in advance, so that the first premium is due now rather than in one year's time.

Exercise 1.4 Lenders offering mortgages to home owners may require the borrower to purchase life insurance to cover the outstanding loan on the death of the borrower, even though the mortgaged property is the loan collateral.

(a) Explain why the lender might require term insurance in this circumstance.
(b) Describe how this term insurance might differ from the standard term insurance described in Section 1.3.2.
(c) Can you see any problems with lenders demanding term insurance from borrowers?

Exercise 1.5 Describe the difference between a cash bonus and a reversionary bonus for participating whole life insurance. What are the advantages and disadvantages of each for (a) the insurer and (b) the policyholder?

Exercise 1.6 It is common for insurers to design whole life contracts with premiums payable only up to age 80. Why?

Exercise 1.7 Andrew is retired. He has no pension, but has capital of $500 000. He is considering the following options for using the money:

(a) Purchase an annuity from an insurance company that will pay a level amount for the rest of his life.
(b) Purchase an annuity from an insurance company that will pay an amount that increases with the cost of living for the rest of his life.
(c) Purchase a 20-year annuity-certain.
(d) Invest the capital and live on the interest income.
(e) Invest the capital and draw $40 000 per year to live on.

What are the advantages and disadvantages of each option?

2

Survival models

2.1 Summary

In this chapter we represent the future lifetime of an individual as a random variable, and show how probabilities of death or survival can be calculated under this framework. We then define an important quantity known as the force of mortality, introduce some actuarial notation, and discuss some properties of the distribution of future lifetime. We introduce the curtate future lifetime random variable. This is a function of the future lifetime random variable which represents the number of complete years of future life. We explain why this function is useful and derive its probability function.

2.2 The future lifetime random variable

In Chapter 1 we saw that many insurance policies provide a benefit on the death of the policyholder. When an insurance company issues such a policy, the policyholder's date of death is unknown, so the insurer does not know exactly when the death benefit will be payable. In order to estimate the time at which a death benefit is payable, the insurer needs a model of human mortality, from which probabilities of death at particular ages can be calculated, and this is the topic of this chapter.

We start with some notation. Let (x) denote a life aged x, where $x \geq 0$. The death of (x) can occur at any age greater than x, and we model the future lifetime of (x) by a continuous random variable which we denote by T_x. This means that $x + T_x$ represents the age-at-death random variable for (x).

Let F_x be the distribution function of T_x, so that

$$F_x(t) = \Pr[T_x \leq t].$$

Then $F_x(t)$ represents the probability that (x) does not survive beyond age $x + t$, and we refer to F_x as the **lifetime distribution** from age x. In many life

17

insurance problems we are interested in the probability of survival rather than death, and so we define S_x as

$$S_x(t) = 1 - F_x(t) = \Pr[T_x > t].$$

Thus, $S_x(t)$ represents the probability that (x) survives for at least t years, and S_x is known as the **survival function**.

Given our interpretation of the collection of random variables $\{T_x\}_{x \geq 0}$ as the future lifetimes of individuals, we need a connection between any pair of them. To see this, consider T_0 and T_x for an individual who is now aged x. The random variable T_0 represented the future lifetime at birth for this individual, so that, at birth, the individual's age at death would have been represented by T_0. This individual could have died before reaching age x – the probability of this was $\Pr[T_0 < x]$ – but has survived. Now that the individual has survived to age x, so that we know that $T_0 > x$, her future lifetime is represented by T_x and her age at death is now $x + T_x$. If she dies within t years from now, then $T_x \leq t$ and $T_0 \leq x + t$. Loosely speaking, we require the events $[T_x \leq t]$ and $[T_0 \leq x + t]$ to be equivalent, given that the individual survives to age x. We achieve this by making the following assumption for all $x \geq 0$ and for all $t > 0$

$$\boxed{\Pr[T_x \leq t] = \Pr[T_0 \leq x + t \mid T_0 > x].} \tag{2.1}$$

This is an important relationship.

Now, recall from probability theory that for two events A and B

$$\Pr[A \mid B] = \frac{\Pr[A \text{ and } B]}{\Pr[B]},$$

so, interpreting $[T_0 \leq x + t]$ as event A, and $[T_0 > x]$ as event B, we can rearrange the right-hand side of (2.1) to give

$$\Pr[T_x \leq t] = \frac{\Pr[x < T_0 \leq x + t]}{\Pr[T_0 > x]},$$

that is,

$$F_x(t) = \frac{F_0(x + t) - F_0(x)}{S_0(x)}. \tag{2.2}$$

Also, using $S_x(t) = 1 - F_x(t)$,

$$\boxed{S_x(t) = \frac{S_0(x + t)}{S_0(x)},} \tag{2.3}$$

which can be written as

$$\boxed{S_0(x + t) = S_0(x)\, S_x(t).} \tag{2.4}$$

This is a very important result. It shows that we can interpret the probability of survival from birth to age $x + t$ as the product of

(1) the probability of survival to age x from birth, and
(2) the probability, having survived to age x, of further surviving to age $x + t$.

Note that $S_x(t)$ can be thought of as the probability that (0) survives to at least age $x + t$ given that (0) survives to age x, so this result can be derived from the standard probability relationship

$$\Pr[A \text{ and } B] = \Pr[A|B]\Pr[B]$$

where the events here are $A = [T_0 > x + t]$ and $B = [T_0 > x]$, so that ·

$$\Pr[A|B] = \Pr[T_0 > x + t | T_0 > x],$$

which we know from (2.1) is equal to $\Pr[T_x > t]$.

Similarly, any survival probability for (x), for, say, $t + u$ years can be split into the probability of surviving the first t years, and then, given survival to age $x + t$, subsequently surviving another u years. That is,

$$S_x(t + u) = \frac{S_0(x + t + u)}{S_0(x)}$$
$$\Rightarrow S_x(t + u) = \frac{S_0(x + t)}{S_0(x)} \frac{S_0(x + t + u)}{S_0(x + t)}$$
$$\Rightarrow S_x(t + u) = S_x(t) S_{x+t}(u). \tag{2.5}$$

We have already seen that if we know survival probabilities from birth, then, using formula (2.4), we also know survival probabilities for our individual from any future age x. Formula (2.5) takes this a stage further. It shows that if we know survival probabilities from any age x (≥ 0), then we also know survival probabilities from any future age $x + t (\geq x)$.

Any survival function for a lifetime distribution must satisfy the following conditions to be valid.

Condition 1 $S_x(0) = 1$; that is, the probability that a life currently aged x survives 0 years is 1.

Condition 2 $\lim_{t \to \infty} S_x(t) = 0$; that is, all lives eventually die.

Condition 3 The survival function must be a non-increasing function of t; it cannot be more likely that (x) survives, say 10.5 years than 10 years, because in order to survive 10.5 years, (x) must first survive 10 years.

These conditions are both necessary and sufficient, so that any function S_x which satisfies these three conditions as a function of t (≥ 0), for a fixed

x (≥ 0), defines a lifetime distribution from age x, and, using formula (2.5), for all ages greater than x.

For all the distributions used in this book, we make three additional assumptions:

Assumption 2.1 $S_x(t)$ *is differentiable for all* $t > 0$. *Note that together with Condition 3 above, this means that* $\frac{d}{dt}S_x(t) \leq 0$ *for all* $t > 0$.

Assumption 2.2 $\lim_{t \to \infty} t\, S_x(t) = 0$.

Assumption 2.3 $\lim_{t \to \infty} t^2\, S_x(t) = 0$.

These last two assumptions ensure that the mean and variance of the distribution of T_x exist. These are not particularly restrictive constraints – we do not need to worry about distributions with infinite mean or variance in the context of individuals' future lifetimes. These three extra assumptions are valid for all distributions that are feasible for human lifetime modelling.

Example 2.1 Let

$$F_0(t) = \begin{cases} 1 - (1 - t/120)^{1/6} & \text{for } 0 \leq t \leq 120 \\ 1 & \text{for } t > 120 \end{cases}.$$

Calculate the probability that

(a) a newborn life survives beyond age 30,
(b) a life aged 30 dies before age 50, and
(c) a life aged 40 survives beyond age 65.

Solution 2.1 (a) The required probability is

$$S_0(30) = 1 - F_0(30) = (1 - 30/120)^{1/6} = 0.9532.$$

(b) From formula (2.2), the required probability is

$$F_{30}(20) = \frac{F_0(50) - F_0(30)}{1 - F_0(30)} = 0.0410.$$

(c) From formula (2.3), the required probability is

$$S_{40}(25) = \frac{S_0(65)}{S_0(40)} = 0.9395.$$

$\square$

We remark that in the above example, $S_0(120) = 0$, which means that under this model, survival beyond age 120 is not possible. In this case we refer to 120 as the limiting age of the model. In general, if there is a limiting age, we use the Greek letter ω to denote it. In models where there is no limiting age, it is often practical to introduce a limiting age in calculations, as we will see later in this chapter.

2.3 The force of mortality

The force of mortality is an important and fundamental concept in modelling future lifetime. We denote the force of mortality at age x by μ_x and define it as

$$\mu_x = \lim_{dx \to 0^+} \frac{1}{dx} \Pr[T_0 \leq x + dx \mid T_0 > x]. \tag{2.6}$$

From equation (2.1) we see that an equivalent way of defining μ_x is

$$\mu_x = \lim_{dx \to 0^+} \frac{1}{dx} \Pr[T_x \leq dx],$$

which can be written in terms of the survival function S_x as

$$\mu_x = \lim_{dx \to 0^+} \frac{1}{dx} \left(1 - S_x(dx)\right). \tag{2.7}$$

Note that the force of mortality depends, numerically, on the unit of time; if we are measuring time in years, then μ_x is measured per year.

The force of mortality is best understood by noting that for very small dx, formula (2.6) gives the approximation

$$\mu_x \, dx \approx \Pr[T_0 \leq x + dx \mid T_0 > x]. \tag{2.8}$$

Thus, for very small dx, we can interpret $\mu_x \, dx$ as the probability that a life who has attained age x dies before attaining age $x + dx$. For example, suppose we have a life aged exactly 50, and that the force of mortality at age 50 is 0.0044 per year. A small value of dx might be a single day, or 0.00274 years. Then the approximate probability that the life dies on his 50th birthday is $0.0044 \times 0.00274 = 1.2 \times 10^{-5}$.

We can relate the force of mortality to the survival function from birth, S_0. As

$$S_x(dx) = \frac{S_0(x + dx)}{S_0(x)},$$

formula (2.7) gives

$$\begin{aligned} \mu_x &= \frac{1}{S_0(x)} \lim_{dx \to 0^+} \frac{S_0(x) - S_0(x + dx)}{dx} \\ &= \frac{1}{S_0(x)} \left(-\frac{d}{dx} S_0(x)\right). \end{aligned}$$

Thus,

$$\boxed{\mu_x = \frac{-1}{S_0(x)} \frac{d}{dx} S_0(x).} \tag{2.9}$$

From standard results in probability theory, we know that the probability density function for the random variable T_x, which we denote f_x, is related to the distribution function F_x and the survival function S_x by

$$f_x(t) = \frac{d}{dt} F_x(t) = -\frac{d}{dt} S_x(t).$$

So, it follows from equation (2.9) that

$$\boxed{\mu_x = \frac{f_0(x)}{S_0(x)}.}$$

We can also relate the force of mortality function at any age $x + t$, $t > 0$, to the lifetime distribution of T_x. Assume x is fixed and t is variable. Then $d(x + t) = dt$ and so

$$\mu_{x+t} = -\frac{1}{S_0(x + t)} \frac{d}{d(x + t)} S_0(x + t)$$

$$= -\frac{1}{S_0(x + t)} \frac{d}{dt} S_0(x + t)$$

$$= -\frac{1}{S_0(x + t)} \frac{d}{dt} (S_0(x) S_x(t))$$

$$= -\frac{S_0(x)}{S_0(x + t)} \frac{d}{dt} S_x(t)$$

$$= \frac{-1}{S_x(t)} \frac{d}{dt} S_x(t).$$

Hence

$$\mu_{x+t} = \frac{f_x(t)}{S_x(t)}. \tag{2.10}$$

This relationship gives a way of finding μ_{x+t} given $S_x(t)$. We can also use equation (2.9) to develop a formula for $S_x(t)$ in terms of the force of mortality function. We use the fact that for a function h whose derivative exists,

$$\frac{d}{dx} \log h(x) = \frac{1}{h(x)} \frac{d}{dx} h(x),$$

so from equation (2.9) we have

$$\mu_x = -\frac{d}{dx} \log S_0(x),$$

and integrating this identity over $(0, y)$ yields

$$\int_0^y \mu_x dx = -\left(\log S_0(y) - \log S_0(0) \right).$$

As $\log S_0(0) = \log \Pr[T_0 > 0] = \log 1 = 0$, we obtain

$$S_0(y) = \exp\left\{-\int_0^y \mu_x dx\right\},$$

from which it follows that

$$\boxed{S_x(t) = \frac{S_0(x+t)}{S_0(x)} = \exp\left\{-\int_x^{x+t} \mu_r dr\right\} = \exp\left\{-\int_0^t \mu_{x+s} ds\right\}.}$$

(2.11)

This means that if we know μ_x for all $x \geq 0$, then we can calculate all the survival probabilities $S_x(t)$, for any x and t. In other words, the force of mortality function fully describes the lifetime distribution, just as the function S_0 does. In fact, it is often more convenient to describe the lifetime distribution using the force of mortality function than the survival function.

Example 2.2 As in Example 2.1, let

$$F_0(x) = 1 - (1 - x/120)^{1/6}$$

for $0 \leq x \leq 120$. Derive an expression for μ_x.

Solution 2.2 As $S_0(x) = (1 - x/120)^{1/6}$, it follows that

$$\frac{d}{dx} S_0(x) = \tfrac{1}{6}(1 - x/120)^{-5/6}\left(-\tfrac{1}{120}\right),$$

and so

$$\mu_x = \frac{-1}{S_0(x)}\frac{d}{dx} S_0(x) = \tfrac{1}{720}(1 - x/120)^{-1} = \frac{1}{720 - 6x}.$$

As an alternative, we could use the relationship

$$\mu_x = -\frac{d}{dx}\log S_0(x) = -\frac{d}{dx}\left(\frac{1}{6}\log(1 - x/120)\right) = \frac{1}{720(1 - x/120)}$$

$$= \frac{1}{720 - 6x}.$$

□

Example 2.3 Let $\mu_x = Bc^x$, $x > 0$, where B and c are constants such that $0 < B < 1$ and $c > 1$. This model is called **Gompertz' law of mortality**. Derive an expression for $S_x(t)$.

Solution 2.3 From equation (2.11),

$$S_x(t) = \exp\left\{-\int_x^{x+t} Bc^r dr\right\}.$$

Writing c^r as $\exp\{r \log c\}$,

$$\int_x^{x+t} Bc^r dr = B \int_x^{x+t} \exp\{r \log c\} dr$$

$$= \frac{B}{\log c} \exp\{r \log c\} \Big|_x^{x+t}$$

$$= \frac{B}{\log c} \left(c^{x+t} - c^x \right),$$

giving

$$S_x(t) = \exp\left\{ \frac{-B}{\log c} c^x (c^t - 1) \right\}.$$

$\square$

The force of mortality under Gompertz' law increases exponentially with age. At first sight this seems reasonable, but as we will see in the next chapter, the force of mortality for most populations is not an increasing function of age over the entire age range. Nevertheless, the Gompertz model does provide a fairly good fit to mortality data over some age ranges, particularly from middle age to early old age.

Example 2.4 Calculate the survival function and probability density function for T_x using Gompertz' law of mortality, with $B = 0.0003$ and $c = 1.07$, for $x = 20$, $x = 50$ and $x = 80$. Plot the results and comment on the features of the graphs.

Solution 2.4 For $x = 20$, the force of mortality is $\mu_{20+t} = Bc^{20+t}$ and the survival function is

$$S_{20}(t) = \exp\left\{ \frac{-B}{\log c} c^{20} (c^t - 1) \right\}.$$

The probability density function is found from (2.10):

$$\mu_{20+t} = \frac{f_{20}(t)}{S_{20}(t)} \Rightarrow f_{20}(t) = \mu_{20+t} S_{20}(t) = Bc^{20+t} \exp\left\{ \frac{-B}{\log c} c^{20} (c^t - 1) \right\}.$$

Figure 2.1 shows the survival functions for ages 20, 50 and 80, and Figure 2.2 shows the corresponding probability density functions. These figures illustrate some general points about lifetime distributions.

First, we see an effective limiting age, even though, in principle, there is no age to which the survival probability is exactly zero. Looking at Figure 2.1, we see that although $S_x(t) > 0$ for all combinations of x and t, survival beyond age 120 is very unlikely.

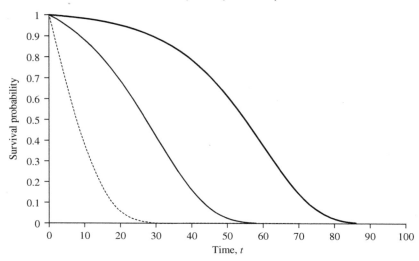

Figure 2.1 $S_x(t)$ for $x = 20$ (bold), 50 (solid) and 80 (dotted).

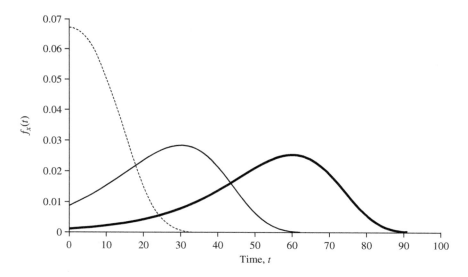

Figure 2.2 $f_x(t)$ for $x = 20$ (bold), 50 (solid) and 80 (dotted).

Second, we note that the survival functions are ordered according to age, with the probability of survival for any given value of t being highest for age 20 and lowest for age 80. For survival functions that give a more realistic representation of human mortality, this ordering can be violated, but it usually holds at ages of interest to insurers. An example of the violation of this ordering is that $S_0(1)$ may be smaller than $S_x(1)$ for $x \geq 1$, as a result of perinatal mortality.

Looking at Figure 2.2, we see that the densities for ages 20 and 50 have similar shapes, but the density for age 80 has a quite different shape. For ages 20 and 50, the densities have their respective maximums at (approximately) $t = 60$ and $t = 30$, indicating that death is most likely to occur around age 80. The decreasing form of the density for age 80 also indicates that death is more likely to occur at age 80 than at any other age for a life now aged 80. A further point to note about these density functions is that although each density function is defined on $(0, \infty)$, the spread of values of $f_x(t)$ is much greater for $x = 20$ than for $x = 50$, which, as we will see in Table 2.1, results in a greater variance of future lifetime for $x = 20$ than for $x = 50$. $\qquad\square$

2.4 Actuarial notation

The notation used in the previous sections, $S_x(t)$, $F_x(t)$ and $f_x(t)$, is standard in statistics. Actuarial science has developed its own notation, **International Actuarial Notation**, that encapsulates the probabilities and functions of greatest interest and usefulness to actuaries. The force of mortality notation, μ_x, comes from International Actuarial Notation. We summarize the relevant actuarial notation in this section, and rewrite the important results developed so far in this chapter in terms of actuarial functions. The actuarial notation for survival and mortality probabilities is

$$\boxed{{}_t p_x = \Pr[T_x > t] = S_x(t),} \tag{2.12}$$

$$\boxed{{}_t q_x = \Pr[T_x \leq t] = 1 - S_x(t) = F_x(t),} \tag{2.13}$$

$$\boxed{{}_{u|t} q_x = \Pr[u < T_x \leq u + t] = S_x(u) - S_x(u + t).} \tag{2.14}$$

That is

${}_t p_x$ is the probability that (x) survives to at least age $x + t$,

${}_t q_x$ is the probability that (x) dies before age $x + t$,

${}_{u|t} q_x$ is the probability that (x) survives u years, and then dies in the subsequent t years, that is, between ages $x + u$ and $x + u + t$.

We may drop the subscript t if its value is 1, so that p_x represents the probability that (x) survives to at least age $x + 1$. Similarly, q_x is the probability that (x) dies before age $x + 1$. In actuarial terminology q_x is called the **mortality rate** at age x. We call ${}_{u|t} q_x$ a **deferred mortality probability**, because it is the probability that death occurs in the interval of t years, following a deferred period of u years.

The relationships below follow immediately from the definitions above and the previous results in this chapter:

$$_tp_x + {}_tq_x = 1,$$

$$_{u|t}q_x = {}_up_x - {}_{u+t}p_x,$$

$$_{t+u}p_x = {}_tp_x \, {}_up_{x+t} \quad \text{from (2.5),} \tag{2.15}$$

$$\mu_x = -\frac{1}{{}_xp_0}\frac{d}{dx}{}_xp_0 \quad \text{from (2.9).} \tag{2.16}$$

Similarly,

$$\mu_{x+t} = -\frac{1}{{}_tp_x}\frac{d}{dt}{}_tp_x \Rightarrow \frac{d}{dt}{}_tp_x = -{}_tp_x\,\mu_{x+t}, \tag{2.17}$$

$$\mu_{x+t} = \frac{f_x(t)}{S_x(t)} \Rightarrow f_x(t) = {}_tp_x\,\mu_{x+t} \quad \text{from (2.10),} \tag{2.18}$$

$$_tp_x = \exp\left\{-\int_0^t \mu_{x+s}ds\right\} \quad \text{from (2.11).} \tag{2.19}$$

As F_x is a distribution function and f_x is its density function, it follows that

$$F_x(t) = \int_0^t f_x(s)ds,$$

which can be written in actuarial notation as

$$_tq_x = \int_0^t {}_sp_x\,\mu_{x+s}ds. \tag{2.20}$$

This is an important formula, which can be interpreted as follows. Consider time s, where $0 \le s < t$. The probability that (x) is alive at time s is ${}_sp_x$, and the probability that (x) dies between ages $x + s$ and $x + s + ds$, having survived to age $x+s$, is (loosely) $\mu_{x+s}ds$, provided that ds is very small. Thus $_sp_x\,\mu_{x+s}ds$ can be interpreted as the probability that (x) dies between ages $x + s$ and $x + s + ds$. Now, we can sum over all the possible death intervals s to $s + ds$ – which requires integrating because these are infinitesimal intervals – to obtain the probability of death before age $x + t$.

We can illustrate this event sequence using the time-line diagram shown in Figure 2.3.

This type of interpretation is important as it can be applied to more complicated situations, and we will employ the time-line again in later chapters.

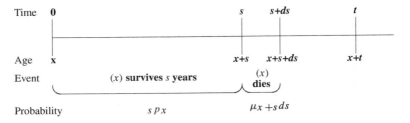

Figure 2.3 Time-line diagram for $_tq_x$.

In the special case when $t = 1$, formula (2.20) becomes

$$q_x = \int_0^1 {_sp_x}\, \mu_{x+s} ds.$$

When q_x is small, it follows that p_x is close to 1, and hence $_sp_x$ is close to 1 for $0 \le s < 1$. Thus

$$q_x \approx \int_0^1 \mu_{x+s} ds \approx \mu_{x+1/2},$$

where the second relationship follows by the mid-point rule for numerical integration.

Example 2.5 As in Examples 2.1 and 2.2, let

$$F_0(x) = 1 - (1 - x/120)^{1/6}$$

for $0 \le x \le 120$. Calculate both q_x and $\mu_{x+1/2}$ for $x = 20$ and for $x = 110$, and comment on these values.

Solution 2.5 We have

$$p_x = \frac{S_0(x+1)}{S_0(x)} = \left(1 - \frac{1}{120 - x}\right)^{1/6},$$

giving $q_{20} = 0.00167$ and $q_{110} = 0.01741$, and from the solution to Example 2.2, $\mu_{20\frac{1}{2}} = 0.00168$ and $\mu_{110\frac{1}{2}} = 0.01754$. We see that $\mu_{x+1/2}$ is a good approximation to q_x when the mortality rate is small, but is not such a good approximation, at least in absolute terms, when the mortality rate is not close to 0.   □

2.5 Mean and standard deviation of T_x

Next, we consider the expected future lifetime of (x), $\mathrm{E}[T_x]$, denoted in actuarial notation by $\overset{\circ}{e}_x$. We call this the **complete expectation of life**. In order to evaluate $\overset{\circ}{e}_x$, we note from formulae (2.17) and (2.18) that

$$f_x(t) = {}_t p_x \, \mu_{x+t} = -\frac{d}{dt} {}_t p_x. \tag{2.21}$$

From the definition of an expected value, we have

$$\overset{\circ}{e}_x = \int_0^\infty t \, f_x(t) dt$$

$$= \int_0^\infty t \, {}_t p_x \, \mu_{x+t} dt.$$

We can now use (2.21) to evaluate this integral using integration by parts as

$$\overset{\circ}{e}_x = -\int_0^\infty t \left(\frac{d}{dt} {}_t p_x\right) dt$$

$$= -\left(t \, {}_t p_x \Big|_0^\infty - \int_0^\infty {}_t p_x dt \right).$$

In Section 2.2 we stated the assumption that $\lim_{t \to \infty} t \, {}_t p_x = 0$, which gives

$$\boxed{\overset{\circ}{e}_x = \int_0^\infty {}_t p_x dt.} \tag{2.22}$$

Similarly, for $E[T_x^2]$, we have

$$E[T_x^2] = \int_0^\infty t^2 \, {}_t p_x \, \mu_{x+t} dt$$

$$= -\int_0^\infty t^2 \left(\frac{d}{dt} {}_t p_x\right) dt$$

$$= -\left(t^2 \, {}_t p_x \Big|_0^\infty - \int_0^\infty {}_t p_x \, 2t \, dt \right)$$

$$= 2 \int_0^\infty t \, {}_t p_x \, dt. \tag{2.23}$$

So we have integral expressions for $E[T_x]$ and $E[T_x^2]$. For some lifetime distributions we are able to integrate directly. In other cases we have to use numerical integration techniques to evaluate the integrals in (2.22) and (2.23). The variance of T_x can then be calculated as

$$V[T_x] = E\left[T_x^2\right] - \left(\overset{\circ}{e}_x\right)^2.$$

Example 2.6 As in Example 2.1, let

$$F_0(x) = 1 - (1 - x/120)^{1/6}$$

for $0 \le x \le 120$. Calculate $\overset{\circ}{e}_x$ and $V[T_x]$ for (a) $x = 30$ and (b) $x = 80$.

Solution 2.6 As $S_0(x) = (1 - x/120)^{1/6}$, we have

$$_t p_x = \frac{S_0(x+t)}{S_0(x)} = \left(1 - \frac{t}{120 - x}\right)^{1/6}.$$

Now recall that this formula is valid for $0 \leq t \leq (120 - x)$, because, under this model, survival beyond age 120 is impossible. Technically, we have

$$_t p_x = \begin{cases} \left(1 - \frac{t}{120-x}\right)^{1/6} & \text{for } x + t \leq 120, \\ 0 & \text{for } x + t > 120. \end{cases}$$

So the upper limit of integration in equation (2.22) is $120 - x$, and

$$\overset{\circ}{e}_x = \int_0^{120-x} \left(1 - \frac{t}{120 - x}\right)^{1/6} dt.$$

We make the substitution $y = 1 - t/(120 - x)$, so that $t = (120 - x)(1 - y)$, giving

$$\overset{\circ}{e}_x = (120 - x) \int_0^1 y^{1/6} dy$$

$$= \tfrac{6}{7}(120 - x).$$

Then $\overset{\circ}{e}_{30} = 77.143$ and $\overset{\circ}{e}_{80} = 34.286$.

Under this model the expectation of life at any age x is 6/7 of the time to age 120.

For the variance we require $E[T_x^2]$. Using equation (2.23) we have

$$E\left[T_x^2\right] = 2\int_0^{120-x} t\, _t p_x dt$$

$$= 2\int_0^{120-x} t \left(1 - \frac{t}{120 - x}\right)^{1/6} dt.$$

Again, we substitute $y = 1 - t/(120 - x)$ giving

$$E\left[T_x^2\right] = 2(120 - x)^2 \int_0^1 (y^{1/6} - y^{7/6})\, dy$$

$$= 2(120 - x)^2 \left(\frac{6}{7} - \frac{6}{13}\right).$$

Then

$$V[T_x] = E[T_x^2] - \left(\overset{\circ}{e}_x\right)^2 = (120 - x)^2 \left(2(6/7 - 6/13) - (6/7)^2\right)$$

$$= (120 - x)^2 (0.056515) = ((120 - x)(0.23773))^2.$$

So $V[T_{30}] = 21.396^2$ and $V[T_{80}] = 9.509^2$.

Table 2.1 *Values of* $\overset{\circ}{e}_x$, $SD[T_x]$ *and expected age at death for the Gompertz model with* $B = 0.0003$ *and* $c = 1.07$.

x	$\overset{\circ}{e}_x$	$SD[T_x]$	$x + \overset{\circ}{e}_x$
0	71.938	18.074	71.938
10	62.223	17.579	72.223
20	52.703	16.857	72.703
30	43.492	15.841	73.492
40	34.752	14.477	74.752
50	26.691	12.746	76.691
60	19.550	10.693	79.550
70	13.555	8.449	83.555
80	8.848	6.224	88.848
90	5.433	4.246	95.433
100	3.152	2.682	103.152

Since we know under this model that all lives will die before age 120, it makes sense that the uncertainty in the future lifetime should be greater for younger lives than for older lives.   □

A feature of the model used in Example 2.6 is that we can obtain formulae for quantities of interest such as $\overset{\circ}{e}_x$, but for many models this is not possible. For example, when we model mortality using Gompertz' law, there is no explicit formula for $\overset{\circ}{e}_x$ and we must use numerical integration to calculate moments of T_x. In Appendix B we describe in detail how to do this.

Table 2.1 shows values of $\overset{\circ}{e}_x$ and the standard deviation of T_x (denoted $SD[T_x]$) for a range of values of x using Gompertz' law, $\mu_x = Bc^x$, where $B = 0.0003$ and $c = 1.07$. For this survival model, $_{130}p_0 = 1.9 \times 10^{-13}$, so that using 130 as the maximum attainable age in our numerical integration is accurate enough for practical purposes.

We see that $\overset{\circ}{e}_x$ is a decreasing function of x, as it was in Example 2.6. In that example $\overset{\circ}{e}_x$ was a linear function of x, but we see that this is not true in Table 2.1.

We are sometimes interested in the future lifetime random variable subject to a cap of n years, which is represented by the random variable $\min(T_x, n)$. For example, suppose that (x) is entitled to a benefit payable continuously for a maximum of n years, conditional on survival. Then $\min(T_x, n)$ would represent the payment period for the benefit. We derive the mean and variance of this random variable, using a similar approach to the derivation of the mean and variance of T_x. The expected value of $\min(T_x, n)$ is denoted $\overset{\circ}{e}_{x:\overline{n}|}$, and is called the **term expectation of life.**

$$E[\min(T_x, n)] = \overset{\circ}{e}_{x:\overline{n}|} = \int_0^n t \, {}_t p_x \, \mu_{x+t} \, dt + \int_n^\infty n \, {}_t p_x \, \mu_{x+t} \, dt$$

$$= \int_0^n t \left(-\frac{d}{dt} \, {}_t p_x \right) dt + n \, {}_n p_x$$

$$= -\left(t \, {}_t p_x \Big|_0^n - \int_0^n {}_t p_x \, dt \right) + n \, {}_n p_x$$

$$\Rightarrow \overset{\circ}{e}_{x:\overline{n}|} = \int_0^n {}_t p_x \, dt \,.$$

The $\overline{n}|$ notation is used to denote a period of n years (just as in annuity-certain notation), and is used extensively in later chapters.

2.6 Curtate future lifetime

2.6.1 K_x and e_x

In many insurance applications we are interested not only in the future lifetime of an individual, but also in what is known as the individual's curtate future lifetime. The **curtate future lifetime** random variable is defined as the integer part of future lifetime, and is denoted by K_x for a life aged x. If we let $\lfloor \ \rfloor$ denote the floor function, we have

$$K_x = \lfloor T_x \rfloor.$$

We can think of the curtate future lifetime as the number of whole years lived in the future by an individual. As an illustration of the importance of curtate future lifetime, consider the situation where a life aged x at time 0 is entitled to payments of 1 at times 1, 2, 3, ... provided that (x) is alive at these times. Then the number of payments made equals the number of complete years lived after time 0 by (x). This is the curtate future lifetime.

We can find the probability function of K_x by noting that for $k = 0, 1, 2, \ldots$, $K_x = k$ if and only if (x) dies between the ages of $x + k$ and $x + k + 1$. Thus for $k = 0, 1, 2, \ldots$

$$Pr[K_x = k] = Pr[k \le T_x < k + 1]$$

$$= {}_{k|}q_x$$

$$= {}_k p_x - {}_{k+1} p_x$$

$$= {}_k p_x - {}_k p_x \, p_{x+k}$$

$$= {}_k p_x \, q_{x+k}.$$

The expected value of K_x is denoted by e_x, so that $e_x = \mathrm{E}[K_x]$, and is referred to as the **curtate expectation of life** (even though it represents the expected curtate lifetime). So

$$\mathrm{E}[K_x] = e_x$$

$$= \sum_{k=0}^{\infty} k \Pr[K_x = k]$$

$$= \sum_{k=0}^{\infty} k \, (_k p_x - {}_{k+1} p_x)$$

$$= (_1 p_x - {}_2 p_x) + 2(_2 p_x - {}_3 p_x) + 3(_3 p_x - {}_4 p_x) + \cdots$$

$$= \sum_{k=1}^{\infty} {}_k p_x. \tag{2.24}$$

Note that the lower limit of summation is $k = 1$.

Similarly,

$$\mathrm{E}[K_x^2] = \sum_{k=0}^{\infty} k^2 \, (_k p_x - {}_{k+1} p_x)$$

$$= (_1 p_x - {}_2 p_x) + 4(_2 p_x - {}_3 p_x) + 9(_3 p_x - {}_4 p_x) + 16(_4 p_x - {}_5 p_x) + \cdots$$

$$= 2 \sum_{k=1}^{\infty} k \, {}_k p_x - \sum_{k=1}^{\infty} {}_k p_x$$

$$= 2 \sum_{k=1}^{\infty} k \, {}_k p_x - e_x.$$

As with the complete expectation of life, there are a few lifetime distributions that allow $\mathrm{E}[K_x]$ and $\mathrm{E}[K_x^2]$ to be calculated analytically. For more realistic models, such as Gompertz', we can calculate the values easily using Excel or other suitable software. Although in principle we have to evaluate an infinite sum, at some age the survival probability will be sufficiently small that we can treat it as an effective limiting age.

Analogous to the random variable $\min(T_x, n)$ we have the random variable $\min(K_x, n)$. For example, if a life aged x is entitled to payments of 1 at times $1, 2, 3, \ldots, n$, where n is an integer, then $\min(K_x, n)$ represents the number of payments made. An important difference between these two random variables is that $\min(T_x, n)$ is a mixed random variable (with a density over $(0, n)$ and a mass of probability at n), whereas $\min(K_x, n)$ is a discrete random variable since K_x is a discrete random variable. The expected value of $\min(K_x, n)$ is denoted $e_{x:\overline{n}|}$, and when n is an integer is given by

$$e_{x:\overline{n}|} = \sum_{k=1}^{n} {}_k p_x.$$

The proof of this result is set as Exercise 2.16.

2.6.2 *The complete and curtate expected future lifetimes, $\overset{\circ}{e}_x$ and e_x*

As the curtate future lifetime is the integer part of future lifetime, it is natural to ask if there is a simple relationship between $\overset{\circ}{e}_x$ and e_x. We can obtain an approximate relationship by writing

$$\overset{\circ}{e}_x = \int_0^\infty {}_t p_x \, dt = \sum_{j=0}^{\infty} \int_j^{j+1} {}_t p_x \, dt.$$

If we approximate each integral using the trapezium rule for numerical integration (see Appendix B), we obtain

$$\int_j^{j+1} {}_t p_x \, dt \approx \tfrac{1}{2} \left({}_j p_x + {}_{j+1} p_x \right),$$

and hence

$$\overset{\circ}{e}_x \approx \sum_{j=0}^{\infty} \tfrac{1}{2} \left({}_j p_x + {}_{j+1} p_x \right) = \tfrac{1}{2} + \sum_{j=1}^{\infty} {}_j p_x.$$

Thus, we have an approximation that is frequently applied in practice, namely

$$\overset{\circ}{e}_x \approx e_x + \tfrac{1}{2}. \tag{2.25}$$

In Chapter 5 we will meet a refined version of this approximation. Table 2.2 shows values of $\overset{\circ}{e}_x$ and e_x for a range of values of x when the survival model is Gompertz' law, with $B = 0.0003$ and $c = 1.07$. Values of e_x were calculated by applying formula (2.24) with an upper limit of summation of $130 - x$, and values of $\overset{\circ}{e}_x$ are as in Table 2.1. This table illustrates that formula (2.25) is a very good approximation in this particular case for younger ages, but is less accurate at very old ages. This observation is true for most realistic survival models.

2.7 Notes and further reading

Although laws of mortality such as Gompertz' law are appealing due to their simplicity, they rarely represent mortality over the whole span of human ages.

Table 2.2 *Values of e_x and $\overset{\circ}{e}_x$*
for Gompertz' law with
$B = 0.0003$ and $c = 1.07$.

x	e_x	$\overset{\circ}{e}_x$
0	71.438	71.938
10	61.723	62.223
20	52.203	52.703
30	42.992	43.492
40	34.252	34.752
50	26.192	26.691
60	19.052	19.550
70	13.058	13.555
80	8.354	8.848
90	4.944	5.433
100	2.673	3.152

A simple extension of Gompertz' law is **Makeham's law** (Makeham, 1860), which models the force of mortality as

$$\mu_x = A + Bc^x. \tag{2.26}$$

This is very similar to Gompertz' law, but adds a fixed term that is not age related, that allows better for accidental deaths. The extra term tends to improve the fit of the model to mortality data at younger ages. See Exercise 2.11.

In recent times, the Gompertz–Makeham approach has been generalized further to give the GM(r, s) (Gompertz–Makeham) formula,

$$\mu_x = h_r^1(x) + \exp\{h_s^2(x)\},$$

where h_r^1 and h_s^2 are polynomials in x of degree r and s, respectively. A discussion of this formula can be found in Forfar *et al.* (1988). Both Gompertz' law and Makeham's law are special cases of the GM formula.

In Section 2.3, we noted the importance of the force of mortality. A further significant point is that when mortality data are analysed, the force of mortality is a natural quantity to estimate, whereas the lifetime distribution is not. The analysis of mortality data is a huge topic and is beyond the scope of this book. An excellent summary article on this topic is Macdonald (1996). For more general distributions, the quantity $f_0(x)/S_0(x)$, which actuaries call the force of mortality at age x, is known as the **hazard rate** in survival analysis and the **failure rate** in reliability theory.

2.8 Exercises

Exercise 2.1 Let $F_0(t) = 1 - (1 - t/105)^{1/5}$ for $0 \le t \le 105$. Calculate

(a) the probability that a newborn life dies before age 60,
(b) the probability that a life aged 30 survives to at least age 70,
(c) the probability that a life aged 20 dies between ages 90 and 100,
(d) the force of mortality at age 50,
(e) the median future lifetime at age 50,
(f) the complete expectation of life at age 50,
(g) the curtate expectation of life at age 50.

Exercise 2.2 The function

$$G(x) = \frac{18\,000 - 110x - x^2}{18\,000}$$

has been proposed as the survival function $S_0(x)$ for a mortality model.

(a) What is the implied limiting age ω?
(b) Verify that the function G satisfies the criteria for a survival function.
(c) Calculate $_{20}p_0$.
(d) Determine the survival function for a life aged 20.
(e) Calculate the probability that a life aged 20 will die between ages 30 and 40.
(f) Calculate the force of mortality at age 50.

Exercise 2.3 Calculate the probability that a life aged 0 will die between ages 19 and 36, given the survival function

$$S_0(x) = \frac{1}{10}\sqrt{100 - x}, \quad 0 \le x \le 100 \, (= \omega).$$

Exercise 2.4 Let

$$S_0(x) = \exp\left\{-\left(Ax + \frac{1}{2}Bx^2 + \frac{C}{\log D}D^x - \frac{C}{\log D}\right)\right\}$$

where A, B, C and D are all positive.

(a) Show that the function S_0 is a survival function.
(b) Derive a formula for $S_x(t)$.
(c) Derive a formula for μ_x.
(d) Now suppose that

$$A = 0.00005, \quad B = 0.0000005, \quad C = 0.0003, \quad D = 1.07.$$

(i) Calculate $_t p_{30}$ for $t = 1, 5, 10, 20, 50, 90$.
(ii) Calculate $_t q_{40}$ for $t = 1, 10, 20$.

(iii) Calculate $_t|_{10}q_{30}$ for $t = 1, 10, 20$.
(iv) Calculate e_x for $x = 70, 71, 72, 73, 74, 75$.
(v) Calculate $\overset{\circ}{e}_x$ for $x = 70, 71, 72, 73, 74, 75$, using numerical integration.

Exercise 2.5 Let $F_0(t) = 1 - e^{-\lambda t}$, where $\lambda > 0$.

(a) Show that $S_x(t) = e^{-\lambda t}$.
(b) Show that $\mu_x = \lambda$.
(c) Show that $e_x = (e^\lambda - 1)^{-1}$.
(d) What conclusions do you draw about using this lifetime distribution to model human mortality?

Exercise 2.6 Given $p_x = 0.99$, $p_{x+1} = 0.985$, $_3p_{x+1} = 0.95$ and $q_{x+3} = 0.02$, calculate

(a) p_{x+3},
(b) $_2p_x$,
(c) $_2p_{x+1}$,
(d) $_3p_x$,
(e) $_1|_2q_x$.

Exercise 2.7 Given

$$F_0(x) = 1 - \frac{1}{1+x} \quad \text{for } x \geq 0,$$

find expressions for (a), (b), (c) below, simplifying as far as possible,

(a) $S_0(x)$,
(b) $f_0(x)$,
(c) $S_x(t)$,

and calculate:

(d) p_{20}, and
(e) $_{10}|_5q_{30}$.

Exercise 2.8 Given

$$S_0(x) = e^{-0.001 x^2} \quad \text{for } x \geq 0,$$

find expressions for (a) and (b), simplifying as far as possible,

(a) $f_0(x)$, and
(b) μ_x.

Exercise 2.9 Show that

$$\frac{d}{dx} {}_tp_x = {}_tp_x \left(\mu_x - \mu_{x+t} \right).$$

Exercise 2.10 Suppose that Gompertz' law applies with $\mu_{30} = 0.000130$ and $\mu_{50} = 0.000344$. Calculate $_{10}p_{40}$.

Exercise 2.11 A survival model follows Makeham's law, so that

$$\mu_x = A + Bc^x \qquad \text{for } x \geq 0.$$

(a) Show that under Makeham's law

$$_tp_x = s^t g^{c^x(c^t-1)}, \tag{2.27}$$

where $s = e^{-A}$ and $g = \exp\{-B/\log c\}$.

(b) Suppose you are given the values of $_{10}p_{50}$, $_{10}p_{60}$ and $_{10}p_{70}$. Show that

$$c = \left(\frac{\log(_{10}p_{70}) - \log(_{10}p_{60})}{\log(_{10}p_{60}) - \log(_{10}p_{50})} \right)^{0.1}.$$

Exercise 2.12 (a) Construct a table of p_x for Makeham's law with parameters $A = 0.0001$, $B = 0.00035$ and $c = 1.075$, for integer x from age 0 to age 130, using Excel or other appropriate computer software. You should set the parameters so that they can be easily changed, and you should keep the table, as many exercises and examples in future chapters will use Makeham's law.

(b) Use the table to determine the age last birthday at which a life currently aged 70 is most likely to die.

(c) Use the table to calculate e_{70}.

(d) Using a numerical approach, calculate $\overset{\circ}{e}_{70}$.

Exercise 2.13 A life insurer assumes that the force of mortality of smokers at all ages is twice the force of mortality of non-smokers.

(a) Show that, if $*$ represents smokers' mortality, and the 'unstarred' function represents non-smokers' mortality, then

$$_tp_x^* = (_tp_x)^2.$$

(b) Calculate the difference between the life expectancy of smokers and non-smokers aged 50, assuming that non-smokers mortality follows Gompertz' law, with $B = 0.0005$ and $c = 1.07$.

(c) Calculate the variance of the future lifetime for a non-smoker aged 50 and for a smoker aged 50 under Gompertz' law.

Hint: You will need to use numerical integration for parts (b) and (c).

Exercise 2.14 (a) Show that

$$\overset{\circ}{e}_x \le \overset{\circ}{e}_{x+1} + 1.$$

(b) Show that

$$\overset{\circ}{e}_x \ge e_x.$$

(c) Explain (in words) why

$$\overset{\circ}{e}_x \approx e_x + \frac{1}{2}.$$

(d) Is $\overset{\circ}{e}_x$ always a non-increasing function of x?

Exercise 2.15 (a) Show that

$$\overset{o}{e}_x = \frac{1}{S_0(x)} \int_x^{\infty} S_0(t)dt,$$

where $S_0(t) = 1 - F_0(t)$, and hence, or otherwise, prove that

$$\frac{d}{dx}\overset{o}{e}_x = \mu_x \overset{o}{e}_x - 1.$$

Hint: $\dfrac{d}{dx}\left\{ \displaystyle\int_a^x g(t)dt \right\} = g(x)$. What about $\dfrac{d}{dx}\left\{ \displaystyle\int_x^a g(t)dt \right\}$?

(b) Deduce that

$$x + \overset{o}{e}_x$$

is an increasing function of x, and explain this result intuitively.

Exercise 2.16 Show that for integer n,

$$e_{x:\overline{n}|} = \sum_{k=1}^{n} {}_k p_x .$$

Answers to selected exercises

2.1 (a) 0.1559
(b) 0.8586
(c) 0.1394
(d) 0.0036
(e) 53.28
(f) 45.83
(g) 45.18

2.2 (a) 90

(c) 0.8556

(d) $1 - 3x/308 - x^2/15\,400$

(e) 0.1169

(f) 0.021

2.3 0.1

2.4 (d) (i) 0.9976, 0.9862, 0.9672, 0.9064, 0.3812, 3.5×10^{-7}

(ii) 0.0047, 0.0629, 0.1747

(iii) 0.0349, 0.0608, 0.1082

(iv) 13.046, 12.517, 12.001, 11.499, 11.009, 10.533

(v) 13.544, 13.014, 12.498, 11.995, 11.505, 11.029

2.6 (a) 0.98

(b) 0.97515

(c) 0.96939

(d) 0.95969

(e) 0.03031

2.7 (d) 0.95455

(e) 0.08218

2.10 0.9973

2.12 (b) 73

(c) 9.339

(d) 9.834

2.13 (b) 6.432

(c) 125.89 (non-smokers),   80.11 (smokers)

3

Life tables and selection

3.1 Summary

In this chapter we define a life table. For a life table tabulated at integer ages only, we show, using fractional age assumptions, how to calculate survival probabilities for all ages and durations.

We discuss some features of national life tables from Australia, England & Wales and the United States.

We then consider life tables appropriate to individuals who have purchased particular types of life insurance policy and discuss why the survival probabilities differ from those in the corresponding national life table. We consider the effect of 'selection' of lives for insurance policies, for example through medical underwriting. We define a select survival model and we derive some formulae for such a model.

We discuss briefly how mortality rates change over time, and illustrate one way to allow for mortality trends in a survival model.

3.2 Life tables

Given a survival model, with survival probabilities $_t p_x$, we can construct the **life table** for the model from some initial age x_0 to a maximum age ω. We define a function $\{l_x\}$ for $x_0 \leq x \leq \omega$ as follows. Let l_{x_0} be an arbitrary positive number (called the **radix** of the table) and, for $0 \leq t \leq \omega - x_0$, define

$$l_{x_0+t} = l_{x_0} \, _t p_{x_0}.$$

From this definition we see that for $x_0 \leq x \leq x + t \leq \omega$,

$$l_{x+t} = l_{x_0} \, _{x+t-x_0} p_{x_0}$$
$$= l_{x_0} \, _{x-x_0} p_{x_0} \, _t p_x$$
$$= l_x \, _t p_x,$$

so that

$$\boxed{\,_t p_x = l_{x+t}/l_x.}$$ (3.1)

For any $x \geq x_0$, we can interpret l_{x+t} as the expected number of survivors at age $x + t$ from l_x independent individuals aged x. This interpretation is more natural if l_x is an integer, and follows because the number of survivors to age $x + t$ is a random variable with a binomial distribution with parameters l_x and $_t p_x$. That is, suppose we have l_x independent lives aged x, and each life has a probability $_t p_x$ of surviving to age $x + t$. Then the number of survivors to age $x + t$ is a binomial random variable, $\mathbf{L}_t$, say, with parameters l_x and $_t p_x$. The expected value of the number of survivors is then

$$E[\mathbf{L}_t] = l_x \,_t p_x = l_{x+t}.$$

We always use the table in the form l_y/l_x which is why the radix of the table is arbitrary – it would make no difference to the survival model if all the l_x values were multiplied by 100, for example.

From (3.1) we can use the l_x function to calculate survival probabilities. We can also calculate mortality probabilities. For example,

$$q_{30} = 1 - \frac{l_{31}}{l_{30}} = \frac{l_{30} - l_{31}}{l_{30}}$$ (3.2)

and

$$_{15|30}q_{40} = \,_{15}p_{40} \,_{30}q_{55} = \frac{l_{55}}{l_{40}}\left(1 - \frac{l_{85}}{l_{55}}\right) = \frac{l_{55} - l_{85}}{l_{40}}.$$ (3.3)

In principle, a life table is defined for all x from the initial age, x_0, to the limiting age, ω. In practice, it is very common for a life table to be presented, and in some cases even defined, at integer ages only. In this form, the life table is a useful way of summarizing a lifetime distribution since, with a single column of numbers, it allows us to calculate probabilities of surviving or dying over integer numbers of years starting from an integer age.

It is usual for a life table, tabulated at integer ages, to show the values of d_x, where

$$\boxed{d_x = l_x - l_{x+1},}$$ (3.4)

in addition to l_x, as these are used to compute q_x. From (3.4) we have

$$d_x = l_x\left(1 - \frac{l_{x+1}}{l_x}\right) = l_x(1 - p_x) = l_x \, q_x.$$

Table 3.1 *Extract from a life table.*

x	l_x	d_x
30	10 000.00	34.78
31	9 965.22	38.10
32	9 927.12	41.76
33	9 885.35	45.81
34	9 839.55	50.26
35	9 789.29	55.17
36	9 734.12	60.56
37	9 673.56	66.49
38	9 607.07	72.99
39	9 534.08	80.11

We can also arrive at this relationship if we interpret d_x as the expected number of deaths in the year of age x to $x + 1$ from a group of l_x lives aged exactly x, so that, using the binomial distribution again

$$\boxed{d_x = l_x \, q_x .}$$ (3.5)

Example 3.1 Table 3.1 gives an extract from a life table. Calculate

(a) l_{40},

(b) $_{10}p_{30}$,

(c) q_{35},

(d) $_5q_{30}$, and

(e) the probability that a life currently aged exactly 30 dies between ages 35 and 36.

Solution 3.1 (a) From equation (3.4),

$$l_{40} = l_{39} - d_{39} = 9\,453.97.$$

(b) From equation (3.1),

$$_{10}p_{30} = \frac{l_{40}}{l_{30}} = \frac{9\,453.97}{10\,000} = 0.94540.$$

(c) From equation (3.5),

$$q_{35} = \frac{d_{35}}{l_{35}} = \frac{55.17}{9\,789.29} = 0.00564.$$

(d) Following equation (3.2),

$$_5q_{30} = \frac{l_{30} - l_{35}}{l_{30}} = 0.02107.$$

(e) This probability is $_5|q_{30}$. Following equation (3.3),

$$_5|q_{30} = \frac{l_{35} - l_{36}}{l_{30}} = \frac{d_{35}}{l_{30}} = 0.00552.$$

□

3.3 Fractional age assumptions

A life table $\{l_x\}_{x \geq x_0}$ provides exactly the same information as the corresponding survival distribution, S_{x_0}. However, a life table tabulated at integer ages only does not contain all the information in the corresponding survival model, since values of l_x at integer ages x are not sufficient to be able to calculate probabilities involving non-integer ages, such as $_{0.75}p_{30.5}$. Given values of l_x at integer ages only, we need an additional assumption or some further information to calculate probabilities for non-integer ages or durations. Specifically, we need to make some assumption about the probability distribution for the future lifetime random variable between integer ages.

We use the term **fractional age assumption** to describe such an assumption. It may be specified in terms of the force of mortality function or the survival or mortality probabilities.

In this section we assume that a life table is specified at integer ages only and we describe the two most useful fractional age assumptions.

3.3.1 Uniform distribution of deaths

The uniform distribution of deaths (UDD) assumption is the most common fractional age assumption. It can be formulated in two different, but equivalent, ways as follows.

UDD1
For integer x, and for $0 \leq s < 1$, assume that

$$\boxed{_sq_x = s\,q_x.} \tag{3.6}$$

UDD2
Recall from Chapter 2 that K_x is the integer part of T_x, and define a new random variable R_x such that

$$T_x = K_x + R_x.$$

The UDD2 assumption is that, for integer x, $R_x \sim U(0, 1)$, and R_x is independent of K_x.

The equivalence of these two assumptions is demonstrated as follows. First, assume that UDD1 is true. Then for integer x, and for $0 \leq s < 1$,

$$\Pr[R_x \leq s] = \sum_{k=0}^{\infty} \Pr[R_x \leq s \text{ and } K_x = k]$$

$$= \sum_{k=0}^{\infty} \Pr[k \leq T_x \leq k + s]$$

$$= \sum_{k=0}^{\infty} {}_kp_x \, {}_sq_{x+k}$$

$$= \sum_{k=0}^{\infty} {}_kp_x \, s \, (q_{x+k}) \quad \text{using UDD1}$$

$$= s \sum_{k=0}^{\infty} {}_kp_x \, q_{x+k}$$

$$= s \sum_{k=0}^{\infty} \Pr[K_x = k]$$

$$= s.$$

This proves that $R_x \sim U(0, 1)$. To prove the independence of R_x and K_x, note that

$$\Pr[R_x \leq s \text{ and } K_x = k] = \Pr[k \leq T_x \leq k + s]$$

$$= {}_kp_x \, {}_sq_{x+k}$$

$$= s \, {}_kp_x \, q_{x+k}$$

$$= \Pr[R_x \leq s] \Pr[K_x = k]$$

since $R_x \sim U(0, 1)$. This proves that UDD1 implies UDD2.

To prove the reverse implication, assume that UDD2 is true. Then for integer x, and for $0 \leq s < 1$,

$$_sq_x = \Pr[T_x \leq s]$$

$$= \Pr[K_x = 0 \text{ and } R_x \leq s]$$

$$= \Pr[R_x \leq s] \Pr[K_x = 0]$$

as K_x and R_x are assumed independent. Thus,

$$_sq_x = s \, q_x \, . \tag{3.7}$$

Formulation UDD2 explains why this assumption is called the Uniform Distribution of Deaths, but in practical applications of this assumption, formulation UDD1 is the more useful of the two.

An immediate consequence is that

$$\boxed{l_{x+s} = l_x - s\, d_x} \qquad (3.8)$$

for $0 \le s < 1$. This follows because

$$_s q_x = 1 - \frac{l_{x+s}}{l_x}$$

and substituting $s\, q_x$ for $_s q_x$ gives

$$s\, \frac{d_x}{l_x} = \frac{l_x - l_{x+s}}{l_x}.$$

Hence

$$l_{x+s} = l_x - s\, d_x$$

for $0 \le s \le 1$. Thus, we assume that l_{x+s} is a linearly decreasing function of s.

Differentiating equation (3.6) with respect to s, we obtain

$$\frac{d}{ds}\, _s q_x = q_x, \quad 0 \le s < 1$$

and we know that the left-hand side is the probability density function for T_x at s, because we are differentiating the distribution function. The probability density function for T_x at s is $_s p_x\, \mu_{x+s}$ so that under UDD

$$\boxed{q_x = {}_s p_x\, \mu_{x+s}} \qquad (3.9)$$

for $0 \le s < 1$.

The left-hand side does not depend on s, which means that the density function is a constant for $0 \le s < 1$, which also follows from the uniform distribution assumption for R_x.

Since q_x is constant with respect to s, and $_s p_x$ is a decreasing function of s, we can see that μ_{x+s} is an increasing function of s, which is appropriate for ages of interest to insurers. However, if we apply the approximation over successive ages, we obtain a discontinuous function for the force of mortality, with discontinuities occurring at integer ages, as illustrated in Example 3.4. Although this is undesirable, it is not a serious drawback.

Example 3.2 Given that $p_{40} = 0.999473$, calculate $_{0.4}q_{40.2}$ under the assumption of a uniform distribution of deaths.

Solution 3.2 We note that the fundamental result in equation (3.7), that for fractions of a year s, $_s q_x = s\, q_x$, requires x to be an integer. We can manipulate the required probability $_{0.4}q_{40.2}$ to involve only probabilities from integer ages as follows

$$_{0.4}q_{40.2} = 1 - {}_{0.4}p_{40.2} = 1 - \frac{l_{40.6}}{l_{40.2}}$$
$$= 1 - \frac{_{0.6}p_{40}}{_{0.2}p_{40}} = 1 - \frac{1 - 0.6q_{40}}{1 - 0.2q_{40}}$$
$$= 2.108 \times 10^{-4}. \qquad \square$$

Example 3.3 Use the life table in Example 3.1 above, with the UDD assumption, to calculate (a) $_{1.7}q_{33}$ and (b) $_{1.7}q_{33.5}$.

Solution 3.3 (a) We note first that

$$_{1.7}q_{33} = 1 - {}_{1.7}p_{33} = 1 - (p_{33}) \, (_{0.7}p_{34}).$$

We can calculate p_{33} directly from the life table as $l_{34}/l_{33} = 0.995367$ and $_{0.7}p_{34} = 1 - 0.7 \, q_{34} = 0.996424$ under UDD, so that $_{1.7}q_{33} = 0.008192$.
(b) To calculate $_{1.7}q_{33.5}$ using UDD, we express this as

$$_{1.7}q_{33.5} = 1 - {}_{1.7}p_{33.5}$$
$$= 1 - \frac{l_{35.2}}{l_{33.5}}$$
$$= 1 - \frac{l_{35} - 0.2d_{35}}{l_{33} - 0.5d_{33}}$$
$$= 0.008537. \qquad \square$$

Example 3.4 Under the assumption of a uniform distribution of deaths, calculate $\lim_{t \to 1^-} \mu_{40+t}$ using $p_{40} = 0.999473$, and calculate $\lim_{t \to 0^+} \mu_{41+t}$ using $p_{41} = 0.999429$.

Solution 3.4 From formula (3.9), we have $\mu_{x+t} = q_x/{_t}p_x$ for $0 \leq t < 1$. Setting $x = 40$ yields

$$\lim_{t \to 1^-} \mu_{40+t} = q_{40}/p_{40} = 5.273 \times 10^{-4},$$

while setting $x = 41$ yields

$$\lim_{t \to 0^+} \mu_{41+t} = q_{41} = 5.71 \times 10^{-4}. \qquad \square$$

Example 3.5 Given that $q_{70} = 0.010413$ and $q_{71} = 0.011670$, calculate $_{0.7}q_{70.6}$ assuming a uniform distribution of deaths.

Solution 3.5 As deaths are assumed to be uniformly distributed between ages 70 and 71 and ages 71 and 72, we first write the probability as

$$_{0.7}q_{70.6} = {}_{0.4}q_{70.6} + (1 - {}_{0.4}q_{70.6}) \, _{0.3}q_{71}.$$

Following the same arguments as in Solution 3.3, we obtain

$$_{0.4}q_{70.6} = 1 - \frac{1 - q_{70}}{1 - 0.6q_{70}} = 4.191 \times 10^{-3},$$

and as $_{0.3}q_{71} = 0.3q_{71} = 3.501 \times 10^{-3}$, we obtain $_{0.7}q_{70.6} = 7.678 \times 10^{-3}$. $\square$

3.3.2 Constant force of mortality

A second fractional age assumption is that the force of mortality is constant between integer ages. Thus, for integer x and $0 \leq s < 1$, we assume that μ_{x+s} does not depend on s, and we denote it μ_x^*. We can obtain the value of μ_x^* by using the fact that

$$p_x = \exp\left\{-\int_0^1 \mu_{x+s} ds\right\}.$$

Hence the assumption that $\mu_{x+s} = \mu_x^*$ for $0 \leq s < 1$ gives $p_x = e^{-\mu_x^*}$ or $\mu_x^* = -\log p_x$. Further, under the assumption of a constant force of mortality, for $0 \leq s < 1$ we obtain

$$_sp_x = \exp\left\{-\int_0^s \mu_x^* du\right\} = e^{-\mu_x^* s} = (p_x)^s.$$

Similarly, for $t, s > 0$ and $t + s < 1$,

$$_sp_{x+t} = \exp\left\{-\int_0^s \mu_x^* du\right\} = (p_x)^s.$$

Thus, under the constant force assumption, the probability of surviving for a period of $s < 1$ years from age $x + t$ is independent of t provided that $s + t < 1$.

The assumption of a constant force of mortality between integer ages leads to a step function for the force of mortality over successive years of age, whereas we would expect the force of mortality to increase smoothly. However, if the true force of mortality increases slowly over the year of age, the constant force of mortality assumption is reasonable.

Example 3.6 Given that $p_{40} = 0.999473$, calculate $_{0.4}q_{40.2}$ under the assumption of a constant force of mortality.

Solution 3.6 We have $_{0.4}q_{40.2} = 1 - {}_{0.4}p_{40.2} = 1 - (p_{40})^{0.4} = 2.108 \times 10^{-4}$. $\square$

Example 3.7 Given that $q_{70} = 0.010413$ and $q_{71} = 0.011670$, calculate $_{0.7}q_{70.6}$ under the assumption of a constant force of mortality.

Solution 3.7 As in Solution 3.5 we write

$$_{0.7}q_{70.6} = {}_{0.4}q_{70.6} + (1 - {}_{0.4}q_{70.6})\,_{0.3}q_{71},$$

where $_{0.4}q_{70.6} = 1 - (p_{70})^{0.4} = 4.178 \times 10^{-3}$ and $_{0.3}q_{71} = 1 - (p_{71})^{0.3} = 3.515 \times 10^{-3}$, giving $_{0.7}q_{70.6} = 7.679 \times 10^{-3}$. □

Note that in Examples 3.2 and 3.5 and in Examples 3.6 and 3.7 we have used two different methods to solve the same problems, and the solutions agree to five decimal places. It is generally true that the assumptions of a uniform distribution of deaths and a constant force of mortality produce very similar solutions to problems. The reason for this can be seen from the following approximations. Under the constant force of mortality assumption

$$q_x = 1 - e^{-\mu^*} \approx \mu^*$$

provided that μ^* is small, and for $0 < t < 1$,

$$_t q_x = 1 - e^{-\mu^* t} \approx \mu^* t.$$

In other words, the approximation to $_t q_x$ is t times the approximation to q_x, which is what we obtain under the uniform distribution of deaths assumption.

3.4 National life tables

Life tables based on the mortality experience of the whole population of a country are regularly produced for many countries in the world. Separate life tables are usually produced for males and for females and possibly for some other groups of individuals, for example on the basis of smoking habits.

Table 3.2 shows values of $q_x \times 10^5$, where q_x is the probability of dying within one year, for selected ages x, separately for males and females, for the populations of Australia, England & Wales and the United States. These tables are constructed using records of deaths in a particular year, or a small number of consecutive years, and estimates of the population in the middle of that period. The relevant years are indicated in the column headings for each of the three life tables in Table 3.2. Data at the oldest ages are notoriously unreliable. For this reason, the United States Life Tables do not show values of q_x for ages 100 and higher.

For all three national life tables and for both males and females, the values of q_x follow exactly the same pattern as a function of age, x. Figure 3.1

Table 3.2 *Values of $q_x \times 10^5$ from some national life tables.*

	Australian Life Tables 2000–02		English Life Table 15 1990–92		US Life Tables 2002	
x	Males	Females	Males	Females	Males	Females
0	567	466	814	632	764	627
1	44	43	62	55	53	42
2	31	19	38	30	37	28
10	13	8	18	13	18	13
20	96	36	84	31	139	45
30	119	45	91	43	141	63
40	159	88	172	107	266	149
50	315	202	464	294	570	319
60	848	510	1 392	830	1 210	758
70	2 337	1 308	3 930	2 190	2 922	1 899
80	6 399	4 036	9 616	5 961	7 028	4 930
90	15 934	12 579	20 465	15 550	16 805	13 328
100	24 479	23 863	38 705	32 489	–	–

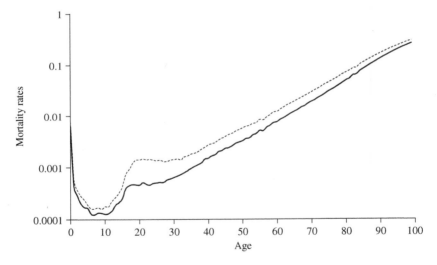

Figure 3.1 US 2002 mortality rates, male (dotted) and female (solid).

shows the US 2002 mortality rates for males and females; the graphs for England & Wales and for Australia are similar. (Note that we have plotted these on a logarithmic scale in order to highlight the main features. Also, although the information plotted consists of values of q_x for $x = 0, 1, \ldots, 99$, we have plotted a continuous line as this gives a clearer representation.) We note the following points from Table 3.2 and Figure 3.1.

- The value of q_0 is relatively high. Mortality rates immediately following birth, *perinatal mortality*, are high due to complications arising from the later stages of pregnancy and from the birth process itself. The value of q_x does not reach this level again until about age 55. This can be seen from Figure 3.1.

- The rate of mortality is much lower after the first year, less than 10% of its level in the first year, and declines until around age 10.

- In Figure 3.1 we see that the pattern of male and female mortality in the late teenage years diverges significantly, with a steeper incline in male mortality. Not only is this feature of mortality for young adult males common for different populations around the world, it is also a feature of historical populations in countries such as the UK where mortality data have been collected for some time. It is sometimes called the accident hump, as many of the deaths causing the 'hump' are accidental.

- Mortality rates increase from age 10, with the accident hump creating a relatively large increase between ages 10 and 20 for males, a more modest increase from ages 20 to 40, and then steady increases from age 40.

- For each age, all six values of q_x are broadly comparable, with, for each country, the rate for a female almost always less than the rate for a male of the same age. The one exception is the Australian Life Table, where q_{100} is slightly higher for a female than for a male. According to the Australian Government Actuary, Australian mortality data indicate that males are subject to lower mortality rates than females at very high ages, although there is some uncertainty as to where the cross-over occurs due to small amounts of data at very old ages.

- The Gompertz model introduced in Chapter 2 is relatively simple, in that it requires only two parameters and has a force of mortality with a simple functional form, $\mu_x = Bc^x$. We stated in Chapter 2 that this model does not provide a good fit across all ages. We can see from Figure 3.1 that the model cannot fit the perinatal mortality, nor the accident hump. However, the mortality rates at later ages are rather better behaved, and the Gompertz model often proves useful over older age ranges. Figure 3.2 shows the older ages US 2002 Males mortality rate curve, along with a Gompertz curve fitted to the US 2002 Table mortality rates. The Gompertz curve provides a pretty close fit – which is a particularly impressive feat, considering that Gompertz proposed the model in 1825.

A final point about Table 3.2 is that we have compared three national life tables using values of the probability of dying within one year, q_x, rather than the force of mortality, μ_x. This is because values of μ_x are not published for any ages for the US Life Tables. Also, values of μ_x are not published for age 0 for

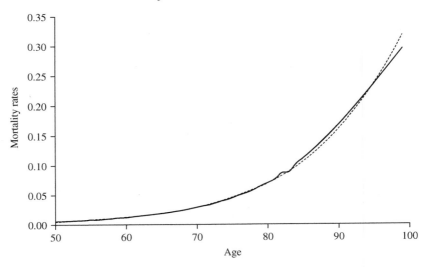

Figure 3.2 US 2002 male mortality rates (solid), with fitted Gompertz mortality rates (dotted).

the other two life tables – there are technical difficulties in the estimation of μ_x within a year in which the force of mortality is changing rapidly, as it does between ages 0 and 1.

3.5 Survival models for life insurance policyholders

Suppose we have to choose a survival model appropriate for a man, currently aged 50 and living in the UK, who has just purchased a 10-year term insurance policy. We could use a national life table, such as English Life Table 15, so that, for example, we could assume that the probability this man dies before age 51 is 0.00464, as shown in Table 3.2. However, in the UK, as in some other countries with well-developed life insurance markets, the mortality experience of people who purchase life insurance policies tends to be different from the population as a whole. The mortality of different types of life insurance policyholders is investigated separately, and life tables appropriate for these groups are published.

Table 3.3 shows values of the force of mortality ($\times 10^5$) at two-year intervals from age 50 to age 60 taken from English Life Table 15, Males (ELTM 15), and from a life table prepared from data relating to term insurance policyholders in the UK in 1999–2002 and which assumes the policyholders *purchased their policies at age 50*. This second set of values comes from Table A14 of a 2006 working paper of the Continuous Mortality Investigation in the UK. Hereafter

Table 3.3 *Values of the force of mortality* $\times 10^5$.

x	ELTM 15	CMI A14
50	440	78
52	549	152
54	679	240
56	845	360
58	1057	454
60	1323	573

we refer to this working paper as CMI, and further details are given at the end of this chapter. The values of the force of mortality for ELTM 15 correspond to the values of q_x shown in Table 3.2.

The striking feature of Table 3.3 is the difference between the two sets of values. The values from the CMI table are very much lower than those from ELTM 15, by a factor of more than 5 at age 50 and by a factor of more than 2 at age 60. There are at least three reasons for this difference.

(a) The data on which the two life tables are based relate to different calendar years; 1990–92 in the case of ELTM 15 and 1999–2002 in the case of CMI. Mortality rates in the UK, as in many other countries, have been decreasing for some years so we might expect rates based on more recent data to be lower (see Section 3.11 for more discussion of mortality trends). However, this explains only a small part of the differences in Table 3.3. An interim life table for England & Wales, based on male population data from 2002–2004, gives $\mu_{50} = 391 \times 10^{-5}$ and $\mu_{60} = 1008 \times 10^{-5}$. Clearly, mortality in England & Wales has improved over the 12-year period, but not to the extent that it matches the CMI values shown in Table 3.3. Other explanations for the differences in Table 3.3 are needed.

(b) A major reason for the difference between the values in Table 3.3 is that ELTM 15 is a life table based on the *whole male population* of England & Wales, whereas CMI Table A14 is based on the experience of males who are *term insurance policyholders*. Within any large group, there are likely to be variations in mortality rates between subgroups. This is true in the case of the population of England and Wales, where social class, defined in terms of occupation, has a significant effect on mortality. Put simply, the better your job, and hence the wealthier you are likely to be, the lower your mortality rates. Given that people who purchase term insurance policies are likely to be among the better paid people in the population, we have an explanation for a large part of the difference between the values in Table 3.3.

(c) The third reason, which is the most significant, arises from the selection process which policyholders must complete before the insurer will issue the insurance policy. The selection, or underwriting process ensures that people who purchase life insurance cover are healthy at the time of purchase, so the CMI figures apply to lives who were all healthy at age 50, when the insurance was purchased. The ELT tables, on the other hand, are based on data from both healthy and unhealthy lives. This is an example of **selection**, and we discuss it in more detail in the following section.

3.6 Life insurance underwriting

The values of the force of mortality in Table 3.3 are based on data for males who purchased term insurance at age 50. CMI Table A14 gives values for different ages at the purchase of the policy ranging from 17 to 90. Values for ages at purchase 50, 52, 54 and 56 are shown in Table 3.4.

There are two significant features of the values in Table 3.4, which can be seen by considering the rows of values for ages 56 and 62.

(a) Consider the row of values for age 56. Each of the four values in this row is the force of mortality at age 56 based on data from the UK over the period 1999–2002 for males who are term insurance policyholders. The only difference is that they purchased their policies at different ages. The more recently the policy was purchased, the lower the force of mortality. For

Table 3.4 *Values of the force of mortality* $\times 10^5$
from CMI Table A14.

	Age at purchase of policy			
x	50	52	54	56
50	78	—	—	—
52	152	94	—	—
54	240	186	113	—
56	360	295	227	136
58	454	454	364	278
60	573	573	573	448
62	725	725	725	725
64	917	917	917	917
66	1159	1159	1159	1159

example, for a male who purchased his policy at age 56, the value is 0.00136, whereas for someone of the same age who purchased his policy at age 50, the value is 0.00360.

(b) Now consider the row of values for age 62. These values, all equal to 0.00725, do not depend on whether the policy was purchased at age 50, 52, 54 or 56.

These features are due to life insurance underwriting, which we described in Chapter 1. Recall that the life insurance underwriting process evaluates medical and lifestyle information to assess whether the policyholder is in normal health.

The important point for this discussion is that the mortality rates in the CMI tables are based on individuals accepted for insurance at normal premium rates, that is, individuals who have passed the required health checks. This means, for example, that a man aged 50 who has just purchased a term insurance at the normal premium rate is known to be in good health (assuming the health checks are effective) and so is likely to be much healthier, and hence have a lower mortality rate, than a man of age 50 picked randomly from the population. When this man reaches age 56, we can no longer be certain he is in good health – all we know is that he was in good health six years ago. Hence, his mortality rate at age 56 is higher than that of a man of the same age who has just passed the health checks and been permitted to buy a term insurance policy at normal rates. This explains the differences between the values of the force of mortality at age 56 in Table 3.4.

The effect of passing the health checks at issue eventually wears off, so that at age 62, the force of mortality does not depend on whether the policy was purchased at age 50, 52, 54 or 56. This is point (b) above. However, note that these rates, 0.00725, are still much lower than μ_{62} ($=0.01664$) from ELTM 15. This is because people who buy term life insurance in the UK tend to have lower mortality than the general population. In fact the population is made up of many heterogeneous lives, and the effect of initial selection is only one area where actuaries have tried to manage the heterogeneity. In the US, there has been a lot of activity recently developing tables for 'preferred lives', who are assumed to be even healthier than the standard insured population. These preferred lives tend to be from higher socio-economic groups. Mortality and wealth are closely linked.

3.7 Select and ultimate survival models

A feature of the survival models studied in Chapter 2 is that probabilities of future survival depend only on the individual's current age. For example, for a given survival model and a given term t, $_tp_x$, the probability that an individual currently aged x will survive to age $x + t$, depends only on the current age x. Such survival models are called **aggregate survival models**, because lives are all aggregated together.

The difference between an aggregate survival model and the survival model for term insurance policyholders discussed in Section 3.6 is that in the latter case, probabilities of future survival depend not only on current age but also on how long ago the individual entered the group of policyholders, i.e. when the policy was purchased.

This leads us to the following definition. The mortality of a group of individuals is described by a **select and ultimate survival model**, usually shortened to **select survival model**, if the following statements are true.

(a) Future survival probabilities for an individual in the group depend on the individual's current age *and* on the age at which the individual joined the group.

(b) There is a positive number (generally an integer), which we denote by d, such that if an individual joined the group more than d years ago, future survival probabilities depend only on current age. The initial selection effect is assumed to have worn off after d years.

We use the following terminology for a select survival model. An individual who enters the group at, say, age x, is said to be **selected**, or just **select**, at age x. The period d after which the age at selection has no effect on future survival probabilities is called the **select period** for the model. The mortality that applies to lives after the select period is complete is called the **ultimate** mortality, so that the complete model comprises a select period followed by the ultimate period.

Going back to the term insurance policyholders in Section 3.6, we can identify the 'group' as male term insurance policyholders in the UK. A select survival model is appropriate in this case because passing the health checks at age x indicates that the individual is in good health and so has lower mortality rates than someone of the same age who passed these checks some years ago. There are indications in Table 3.4 that the select period, d, for this group is less than or equal to six years. See point (b) in Section 3.6. In fact, the select period is five years for this particular model. Select periods typically range from one year to 15 years for life insurance mortality models.

For the term insurance policyholders in Section 3.6, being selected at age x meant that the mortality rate for the individual was lower than that of a term insurance policyholder of the same age who had been selected some years earlier. Selection can occur in many different ways and does not always lead to lower mortality rates, as Example 3.8 shows.

Example 3.8 Consider men who need to undergo surgery because they are suffering from a particular disease. The surgery is complicated and there is a probability of only 50% that they will survive for a year following surgery. If they do survive for a year, then they are fully cured and their future mortality follows the Australian Life Tables 2000–02, Males, from which you are given the following values:

$$l_{60} = 89\,777, \quad l_{61} = 89\,015, \quad l_{70} = 77\,946.$$

Calculate

(a) the probability that a man aged 60 who is just about to have surgery will be alive at age 70,
(b) the probability that a man aged 60 who had surgery at age 59 will be alive at age 70, and
(c) the probability that a man aged 60 who had surgery at age 58 will be alive at age 70.

Solution 3.8 In this example, the 'group' is all men who have had the operation. Being selected at age x means having surgery at age x. The select period of the survival model for this group is one year, since if they survive for one year after being 'selected', their future mortality depends only on their current age.

(a) The probability of surviving to age 61 is 0.5. Given that he survives to age 61, the probability of surviving to age 70 is

$$l_{70}/l_{61} = 77\,946/89\,015 = 0.8757.$$

Hence, the probability that this individual survives from age 60 to age 70 is

$$0.5 \times 0.8757 = 0.4378.$$

(b) Since this individual has already survived for one year following surgery, his mortality follows the Australian Life Tables 2000–02, Males. Hence, his probability of surviving to age 70 is

$$l_{70}/l_{60} = 77\,946/89\,777 = 0.8682.$$

(c) Since this individual's surgery was more than one year ago, his future mortality is exactly the same, probabilistically, as the individual in part (b). Hence, his probability of surviving to age 70 is 0.8682. □

Selection is not a feature of national life tables since, ignoring immigration, an individual can enter the population only at age zero. It is an important feature of many survival models based on data from, and hence appropriate to, life insurance policyholders. We can see from Tables 3.3 and 3.4 that its effect on the force of mortality can be considerable. For these reasons, select survival models are important in life insurance mathematics.

The select period may be different for different survival models. For CMI Table A14, which relates to term insurance policyholders, it is five years, as noted above; for CMI Table A2, which relates to whole life and endowment policyholders, the select period is two years.

In the next section we introduce notation and develop some formulae for select survival models.

3.8 Notation and formulae for select survival models

A select survival model represents an extension of the ultimate survival model studied in Chapter 2. In Chapter 2, survival probabilities depended only on the current age of the individual. For a select survival model, probabilities of survival depend on current age and (within the select period) age at selection, i.e. age at joining the group. However, the survival model for those individuals all selected at the same age, say x, depends only on their current age and so fits the assumptions of Chapter 2. This means that, provided we fix and specify the age at selection, we can adapt the notation and formulae developed in Chapter 2 to a select survival model. This leads to the following definitions:

$_t p_{[x]+s} =$ Pr[a life currently aged $x + s$ who was select at age x survives to age $x + s + t$],

$_t q_{[x]+s} =$ Pr[a life currently aged $x + s$ who was select at age x dies before age $x + s + t$],

$\mu_{[x]+s}$ is the force of mortality at age $x + s$ for an individual who was select at age x,

$$\mu_{[x]+s} = \lim_{h \to 0^+} \left(\frac{1 - {_h p_{[x]+s}}}{h} \right).$$

From these definitions we can derive the following formula

$$_t p_{[x]+s} = \exp \left\{ -\int_0^t \mu_{[x]+s+u} \, du \right\}.$$

This formula is derived precisely as in Chapter 2. It is only the notation which has changed.

For a select survival model with a select period d and for $t \geq d$, that is, for durations at or beyond the select period, the values of $\mu_{[x-t]+t}$, $_s p_{[x-t]+t}$ and $_{u|s} q_{[x-t]+t}$ do not depend on t, they depend only on the current age x. So, for $t \geq d$ we drop the more detailed notation, $\mu_{[x-t]+t}$, $_s p_{[x-t]+t}$ and $_{u|s} q_{[x-t]+t}$, and write μ_x, $_s p_x$ and $_{u|s} q_x$. For values of $t < d$, we refer to, for example, $\mu_{[x-t]+t}$ as being in the **select** part of the survival model and for $t \geq d$ we refer to $\mu_{[x-t]+t}$ ($\equiv \mu_x$) as being in the **ultimate** part of the survival model.

3.9 Select life tables

For an ultimate survival model, as discussed in Chapter 2, the life table $\{l_x\}$ is useful since it can be used to calculate probabilities such as $_{t}|_u q_x$ for non-negative values of t, u and x. We can construct a **select life table** in a similar way but we need the table to reflect duration as well as age, during the select period. Suppose we wish to construct this table for a select survival model for ages at selection from, say, x_0 (≥ 0). Let d denote the select period, assumed to be an integer number of years.

The construction in this section is for a select life table specified at all ages and not just at integer ages. However, select life tables are usually presented at integer ages only, as is the case for ultimate life tables.

First we consider the survival probabilities of those individuals who were selected at least d years ago and hence are now subject to the ultimate part of the model. The minimum age of these people is $x_0 + d$. For these people, future survival probabilities depend only on their current age and so, as in Chapter 2, we can construct an ultimate life table, $\{l_y\}$, for them from which we can calculate probabilities of surviving to any future age.

Let l_{x_0+d} be an arbitrary positive number. For $y \geq x_0 + d$ we define

$$l_y = {}_{(y-x_0-d)}p_{x_0+d}\, l_{x_0+d}. \tag{3.10}$$

Note that $_{(y-x_0-d)}p_{x_0+d} = {}_{(y-x_0-d)}p_{[x_0]+d}$, because d years after selection at age x_0, the probability of future survival depends only on the current age, $x_0 + d$. From this definition we can show that for $y > x \geq x_0 + d$

$$l_y = {}_{y-x}p_x\, l_x. \tag{3.11}$$

This follows because

$$
\begin{aligned}
l_y &= \left({}_{(y-x_0-d)}p_{x_0+d}\right) l_{x_0+d} \\
&= \left({}_{y-x}p_{[x_0]+x-x_0}\right) \left({}_{(x-x_0-d)}p_{[x_0]+d}\right) l_{x_0+d} \\
&= \left({}_{y-x}p_x\right) \left({}_{(x-x_0-d)}p_{x_0+d}\right) l_{x_0+d} \\
&= {}_{y-x}p_x\, l_x.
\end{aligned}
$$

This shows that within the ultimate part of the model we can interpret l_y as the expected number of survivors to age y out of l_x lives currently aged x ($< y$), who were select at least d years ago.

Formula (3.10) defines the life table within the ultimate part of the model. Next, we need to define the life table within the select period. We do this for a life select at age x by 'working backwards' from the value of l_{x+d}. For $x \geq x_0$ and for $0 \leq t \leq d$, we define

$$l_{[x]+t} = \frac{l_{x+d}}{{}_{d-t}p_{[x]+t}} \tag{3.12}$$

which means that if we had $l_{[x]+t}$ lives aged $x + t$, selected t years ago, then the expected number of survivors to age $x + d$ is l_{x+d}. This defines the select part of the life table.

Example 3.9 For $y \geq x + d > x + s > x + t \geq x \geq x_0$, show that

$$_{y-x-t}p_{[x]+t} = \frac{l_y}{l_{[x]+t}} \tag{3.13}$$

and

$$_{s-t}p_{[x]+t} = \frac{l_{[x]+s}}{l_{[x]+t}}. \tag{3.14}$$

Solution 3.9 First,

$$
\begin{aligned}
_{y-x-t}p_{[x]+t} &= {}_{y-x-d}p_{[x]+d} \times {}_{d-t}p_{[x]+t} \\
&= {}_{y-x-d}p_{x+d} \times {}_{d-t}p_{[x]+t} \\
&= \frac{l_y}{l_{x+d}} \frac{l_{x+d}}{l_{[x]+t}} \\
&= \frac{l_y}{l_{[x]+t}},
\end{aligned}
$$

which proves (3.13). Second,

$$
\begin{aligned}
_{s-t}p_{[x]+t} &= \frac{_{d-t}p_{[x]+t}}{_{d-s}p_{[x]+s}} \\
&= \frac{l_{x+d}}{l_{[x]+t}} \frac{l_{[x]+s}}{l_{x+d}} \\
&= \frac{l_{[x]+s}}{l_{[x]+t}},
\end{aligned}
$$

which proves (3.14).   □

This example, together with formula (3.11), shows that our construction preserves the interpretation of the ls as expected numbers of survivors within both the ultimate and the select parts of the model. For example, suppose we have $l_{[x]+t}$ individuals currently aged $x + t$ who were select at age x. Then, since $_{y-x-t}p_{[x]+t}$ is the probability that any one of them survives to age y, we can see from formula (3.13) that l_y is the expected number of survivors to age y. For $0 \leq t \leq s \leq d$, formula (3.14) shows that $l_{[x]+s}$ can be interpreted as the expected number of survivors to age $x + s$ out of $l_{[x]+t}$ lives currently aged $x + t$ who were select at age x.

Example 3.10 Write an expression for $_{2|6}q_{[30]+2}$ in terms of $l_{[x]+t}$ and l_y for appropriate x, t and y, assuming a select period of five years.

Solution 3.10 Note that $2|6q_{[30]+2}$ is the probability that a life currently aged 32, who was select at age 30, will die between ages 34 and 40. We can write this probability as the product of the probabilities of the following events:

- a life aged 32, who was select at age 30, will survive to age 34, and,
- a life aged 34, who was select at age 30, will die before age 40.

Hence,

$$
\begin{aligned}
2|6q_{[30]+2} &= {}_2p_{[30]+2}\, {}_6q_{[30]+4} \\
&= \frac{l_{[30]+4}}{l_{[30]+2}}\left(1 - \frac{l_{[30]+10}}{l_{[30]+4}}\right) \\
&= \frac{l_{[30]+4} - l_{40}}{l_{[30]+2}}.
\end{aligned}
$$

Note that $l_{[30]+10} \equiv l_{40}$ since 10 years is longer than the select period for this survival model. □

Table 3.5 *Extract from US Life Tables, 2002.*

x	l_x
70	80 556
71	79 026
72	77 410
73	75 666
74	73 802
75	71 800

Example 3.11 A select survival model has a select period of three years. Its ultimate mortality is equivalent to the US Life Tables, 2002, Females. Some l_x values for this table are shown in Table 3.5.

You are given that for all ages $x \geq 65$,

$$ p_{[x]} = 0.999, \qquad p_{[x-1]+1} = 0.998, \qquad p_{[x-2]+2} = 0.997. $$

Calculate the probability that a woman currently aged 70 will survive to age 75 given that

(a) she was select at age 67,
(b) she was select at age 68,
(c) she was select at age 69, and
(d) she is select at age 70.

Solution 3.11 (a) Since the woman was select three years ago and the select
period for this model is three years, she is now subject to the ultimate
part of the survival model. Hence the probability she survives to age 75 is
l_{75}/l_{70}, where the ls are taken from US Life Tables, 2002, Females. The
required probability is

$$_5p_{70} = 71\,800/80\,556 = 0.8913.$$

(b) We have

$$_5p_{[68]+2} = \frac{l_{[68]+2+5}}{l_{[68]+2}} = \frac{l_{75}}{l_{[68]+2}} = \frac{71\,800}{l_{[68]+2}}.$$

We calculate $l_{[68]+2}$ by noting that

$$l_{[68]+2} \times p_{[68]+2} = l_{[68]+3} = l_{71} = 79\,026.$$

We are given that $p_{[68]+2} = 0.997$. Hence, $l_{[68]+2} = 79\,264$ and so

$$_5p_{[68]+2} = 0.9058.$$

(c) We have

$$_5p_{[69]+1} = \frac{l_{[69]+1+5}}{l_{[69]+1}} = \frac{l_{75}}{l_{[69]+1}} = \frac{71\,800}{l_{[69]+1}}.$$

We calculate $l_{[69]+1}$ by noting that

$$l_{[69]+1} \times p_{[69]+1} \times p_{[69]+2} = l_{[69]+3} = l_{72} = 77\,410.$$

We are given that $p_{[69]+1} = 0.998$ and $p_{[69]+2} = 0.997$. Hence, $l_{[69]+1} = 77\,799$ and so

$$_5p_{[69]+1} = 0.9229.$$

(d) We have

$$_5p_{[70]} = \frac{l_{[70]+5}}{l_{[70]}} = \frac{l_{75}}{l_{[70]}} = \frac{71\,800}{l_{[70]}}.$$

Proceeding as in (b) and (c),

$$l_{[70]} \times p_{[70]} \times p_{[70]+1} \times p_{[70]+2} = l_{[70]+3} = l_{73} = 75\,666,$$

giving

$$l_{[70]} = 75\,666/(0.997 \times 0.998 \times 0.999) = 76\,122.$$

Hence

$$_5p_{[70]} = 0.9432.$$

$\square$

Table 3.6 *CMI Table A5: male non-smokers who have whole life or endowment policies.*

Age, x	Duration 0 $q_{[x]}$	Duration 1 $q_{[x-1]+1}$	Duration 2+ q_x
60	0.003469	0.004539	0.004760
61	0.003856	0.005059	0.005351
62	0.004291	0.005644	0.006021
63	0.004779	0.006304	0.006781
⋮	⋮	⋮	⋮
70	0.010519	0.014068	0.015786
71	0.011858	0.015868	0.017832
72	0.013401	0.017931	0.020145
73	0.015184	0.020302	0.022759
74	0.017253	0.023034	0.025712
75	0.019664	0.026196	0.029048

Example 3.12 CMI Table A5 is based on UK data from 1999 to 2002 for male non-smokers who are whole life or endowment insurance policyholders. It has a select period of two years. An extract from this table, showing values of $q_{[x-t]+t}$, is given in Table 3.6. Use this survival model to calculate the following probabilities:

(a) $_4p_{[70]}$,

(b) $_3q_{[60]+1}$, and

(c) $_2|q_{73}$.

Solution 3.12 Note that CMI Table A5 gives values of $q_{[x-t]+t}$ for $t = 0$ and $t = 1$ and also for $t \geq 2$. Since the select period is two years $q_{[x-t]+t} \equiv q_x$ for $t \geq 2$. Note also that each row of the table relates to a man *currently* aged x, where x is given in the first column. Select life tables, tabulated at integer ages, can be set out in different ways – for example, each row could relate to a fixed age at selection – so care needs to be taken when using such tables.

(a) We calculate $_4p_{[70]}$ as

$$
\begin{aligned}
_4p_{[70]} &= p_{[70]}\, p_{[70]+1}\, p_{[70]+2}\, p_{[70]+3} \\
&= p_{[70]}\, p_{[70]+1}\, p_{72}\, p_{73} \\
&= (1 - q_{[70]})\, (1 - q_{[70]+1})\, (1 - q_{72})\, (1 - q_{73}) \\
&= 0.989481 \times 0.984132 \times 0.979855 \times 0.977241 \\
&= 0.932447.
\end{aligned}
$$

(b) We calculate $_3q_{[60]+1}$ as

$$_3q_{[60]+1} = q_{[60]+1} + p_{[60]+1}\, q_{62} + p_{[60]+1}\, p_{62}\, q_{63}$$
$$= q_{[60]+1} + (1 - q_{[60]+1})\, q_{62} + (1 - q_{[60]+1})\,(1 - q_{62})\, q_{63}$$
$$= 0.005059 + 0.994941 \times 0.006021$$
$$+ 0.994941 \times 0.993979 \times 0.006781$$
$$= 0.017756.$$

(c) We calculate $_2|q_{73}$ as

$$_2|q_{73} = {}_2p_{73}\, q_{75}$$
$$= (1 - q_{73})\,(1 - q_{74})\, q_{75}$$
$$= 0.977241 \times 0.974288 \times 0.029048$$
$$= 0.027657. \qquad \Box$$

Example 3.13 A select survival model has a two-year select period and is specified as follows. The ultimate part of the model follows Makeham's law, so that

$$\mu_x = A + Bc^x$$

where $A = 0.00022$, $B = 2.7 \times 10^{-6}$ and $c = 1.124$. The select part of the model is such that for $0 \le s \le 2$,

$$\mu_{[x]+s} = 0.9^{2-s} \mu_{x+s}.$$

Starting with $l_{20} = 100\,000$, calculate values of

(a) l_x for $x = 21, 22, \ldots, 82$,
(b) $l_{[x]+1}$ for $x = 20, 21, \ldots, 80$, and,
(c) $l_{[x]}$ for $x = 20, 21, \ldots, 80$.

Solution 3.13 First, note that

$$_tp_x = \exp\left\{ -At - \frac{B}{\log c} c^x (c^t - 1) \right\}$$

and for $0 \le t \le 2$,

$$_tp_{[x]} = \exp\left\{ -\int_0^t \mu_{[x]+s} ds \right\}$$
$$= \exp\left\{ 0.9^{2-t} \left(\frac{1 - 0.9^t}{\log(0.9)} A + \frac{c^t - 0.9^t}{\log(0.9/c)} Bc^x \right) \right\}. \qquad (3.15)$$

(a) Values of l_x can be calculated recursively from

$$l_x = p_{x-1} l_{x-1} \quad \text{for} \quad x = 21, 22, \ldots, 82.$$

Table 3.7 *Select life table with a two-year select period, Example 3.13.*

x	$l_{[x]}$	$l_{[x]+1}$	l_{x+2}	$x+2$	x	$l_{[x]}$	$l_{[x]+1}$	l_{x+2}	$x+2$
			100 000.00	20	50	98 552.51	98 450.67	98 326.19	52
			99 975.04	21	51	98 430.98	98 318.95	98 181.77	53
20	99 995.08	99 973.75	99 949.71	22	52	98 297.24	98 173.79	98 022.38	54
21	99 970.04	99 948.40	99 923.98	23	53	98 149.81	98 013.56	97 846.20	55
22	99 944.63	99 922.65	99 897.79	24	54	97 987.03	97 836.44	97 651.21	56
⋮	⋮	⋮	⋮	⋮	⋮	⋮	⋮	⋮	⋮
47	98 856.38	98 778.94	98 684.88	49	79	77 465.70	75 531.88	73 186.31	81
48	98 764.09	98 679.44	98 576.37	50	80	75 153.97	73 050.22	70 507.19	82
49	98 663.15	98 570.40	98 457.24	51					

(b) Values of $l_{[x]+1}$ can be calculated from

$$l_{[x]+1} = l_{x+2}/p_{[x]+1} \quad \text{for} \quad x = 20, 21, \ldots, 80.$$

(c) Values of $l_{[x]}$ can be calculated from

$$l_{[x]} = l_{x+2}/{}_2p_{[x]} \quad \text{for} \quad x = 20, 21, \ldots, 80.$$

Sample values are shown in Table 3.7. The full table up to age 100 is given in Table D.1 in Appendix D. □

This model is used extensively throughout this book for examples and exercises. We call it the **Standard Select Survival Model** in future chapters.

The ultimate part of the model, which is a Makeham model with $A = 0.00022$, $B = 2.7 \times 10^{-6}$ and $c = 1.124$, is also used in many examples and exercises where a select model is not required. We call this the **Standard Ultimate Survival Model**.

3.10 Some comments on heterogeneity in mortality

We noted in Section 3.5 the significant difference between the mortality of the population as a whole, and the mortality of insured lives. It is worth noting, further, that there is also considerable variability when we look at the mortality experience of different groups of insurance company customers and pension plan members. Of course, male and female mortality differs significantly, in shape and level. Actuaries will generally use separate survival models for men and women when this does not breach discrimination laws. Smoker and non-smoker mortality differences are very important in whole life and term insurance; smoker mortality is substantially higher at all ages for both sexes, and separate smoker/non-smoker mortality tables are in common use.

In addition, insurers will generally use product-specific mortality tables for different types of contracts. Individuals who purchase immediate or deferred annuities may have different mortality from those purchasing term insurance. Insurance is sometimes purchased under group contracts, for example by an employer to provide death-in-service insurance for employees. The mortality experience from these contracts will generally be different from the experience of policyholders holding individual contracts. The mortality experience of pension plan members may differ from the experience of lives who purchase individual pension policies from an insurance company. Interestingly, the differences in mortality experience between these groups will depend significantly on country. Studies of mortality have shown, though, that the following principles apply quite generally.

◇ Wealthier lives experience lighter mortality overall than less wealthy lives.

◇ There will be some impact on the mortality experience from self-selection; an individual will only purchase an annuity if he or she is confident of living long enough to benefit. An individual who has some reason to anticipate heavier mortality is more likely to purchase term insurance. While underwriting can identify some selective factors, there may be other information that cannot be gleaned from the underwriting process (at least not without excessive cost). So those buying term insurance might be expected to have slightly heavier mortality than those buying whole life insurance, and those buying annuities might be expected to have lighter mortality.

◇ The more rigorous the underwriting, the lighter the resulting mortality experience. For group insurance, there will be minimal underwriting. Each person hired by the employer will be covered by the insurance policy almost immediately; the insurer does not get to accept or reject the additional employee, and will rarely be given information sufficient for underwriting decisions. However, the employee must be healthy enough to be hired, which gives some selection information.

All of these factors may be confounded by tax or legislative systems that encourage or require certain types of contracts. In the UK, it is very common for retirement savings proceeds to be converted to life annuities. In other countries, including the USA, this is much less common. Consequently, the type of person who buys an annuity in the USA might be quite a different (and more self-select) customer than the typical individual buying an annuity in the UK.

3.11 Mortality trends

A challenge in developing and using survival models is that survival probabilities are not constant over time. Commonly, mortality experience gets lighter over time. In most countries, for the period of reliable records, each generation, on average, lives longer than the previous generation. This can be explained by advances in health care and by improved standards of living. Of course, there are exceptions, such as mortality shocks from war or from disease, or declining life expectancy in countries where access to health care worsens, often because of civil upheaval. The changes in mortality over time are sometimes separated into three components: trend, shock and idiosyncratic. The trend describes the gradual reduction in mortality rates over time. The shock describes a short-term jump in mortality rates from war or pandemic disease. The idiosyncratic risk describes year to year random variation that does not come from trend or shock, though it is often difficult to distinguish these changes.

While the shock and idiosyncratic risks are inherently unpredictable, we can often identify trends in mortality by examining mortality patterns over a number of years. We can then allow for mortality improvement by using a survival model which depends on both age and calendar year. A common model for projecting mortality is to assume that mortality rates at each age are decreasing annually by a constant factor, which depends on the age and sex of the individual. That is, suppose $q(x, Y)$ denotes the mortality rate for a life aged x in year Y, so that $q(x, 0)$ denotes the mortality rate at age x for a baseline year, $Y = 0$. Then, the estimated one-year mortality probability for a life aged x at time $Y = s$ is

$$q(x, s) = q(x, 0)\, r_x^s \quad \text{where} \quad 0 < r_x \leq 1.$$

The r_x terms are called mortality **reduction factors**, and typical values are in the range 0.95 to 1, where the higher values (implying less reduction) tend to apply at older ages. Using $r_x = 1$ for the oldest ages reflects the fact that, although many people are living longer than previous generations, there is little or no increase in the maximum age attained; the change is that a greater proportion of lives survive to older ages. In practice, the reduction factors are applied for integer values of s.

Figure 3.3 shows reduction factors for females based on mortality in Australia in the 25 years prior to the production of Australian Life Tables 2000–02. This shows the greatest reduction in mortality rates has occurred at the youngest ages, that mortality rates have not fallen greatly from mid-teens to late thirties, and that as age increases from around age 60, reduction factors are increasing.

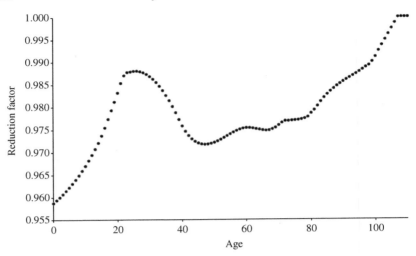

Figure 3.3 Reduction factors, r_x, based on Australian female mortality.

Given a baseline survival model, with mortality rates $q(x, 0) = q_x$, say, and a set of age-based reduction factors, r_x, we can calculate survival probabilities from the baseline year, $_t p(x, 0)$, say, as

$$_t p(x, 0) = p(x, 0)\, p(x + 1, 1) \ldots p(x + t - 1, t - 1)$$
$$= (1 - q_x)\,(1 - q_{x+1}\, r_{x+1})\left(1 - q_{x+2}\, r_{x+2}^2\right) \ldots \left(1 - q_{x+t-1}\, r_{x+t-1}^{t-1}\right).$$
$$(3.16)$$

Some survival models developed for actuarial applications implicitly contain some allowance for mortality improvement. When selecting a survival model to use for valuation and risk management, it is important to verify the projection assumptions.

The use of reduction factors allows for predictable improvements in life expectancy. However, if the improvements are underestimated, then mortality experience will be lighter than expected, leading to losses on annuity and pension contracts. This risk, called longevity risk, is of great recent interest, as mortality rates have declined in many countries at a much faster rate than anticipated. As a result, there has been increased interest in stochastic mortality models, where the force of mortality in future years follows a stochastic process which incorporates both predictable and random changes in longevity, as well as pandemic-type shock effects.

Table 3.8 shows the effect of reduction factors on the calculation of expectation of life. In this table we show values of e_x under two scenarios. The

Table 3.8 *Values of e_x without and with reduction factors.*

x	Scenario 1 e_x	Scenario 2 e_x	x	Scenario 1 e_x	Scenario 2 e_x
0	82.36	94.97	50	34.01	38.80
10	72.86	84.18	60	24.94	28.06
20	63.00	72.84	70	16.57	18.26
30	53.22	61.47	80	9.48	10.15
40	43.51	50.06	90	4.83	5.03

first scenario is that no reduction factors apply to the female mortality rates of Australian Life Tables 2000–02, and the second scenario is that the reduction factors shown in Figure 3.3 apply, with survival probabilities calculated according to formula (3.16).

The values in Table 3.8 show that the application of reduction factors to mortality rates can have a significant effect on expected future lifetime, particularly at younger ages. However, the values in this table should be treated with caution. The key underlying assumption in the calculations is that mortality rates will continue to reduce in the future, and this assumption is questionable. Nevertheless, the table does illustrate the basic fact that allowing for mortality improvement may have a significant effect on expectation of life.

3.12 Notes and further reading

The mortality rates in Section 3.4 are drawn from the following sources:

- Australian Life Tables 2000–02 were produced by the Australian Government Actuary (2004).

- English Life Table 15 was prepared by the UK Government Actuary and published by the Office for National Statistics (1997).

- US Life Tables 2002 were prepared in the Division of Vital Statistics of the National Center for Health Statistics in the US – see Arias (2004).

The Continuous Mortality Investigation in the UK has been ongoing for many years. Findings on mortality and morbidity experience of UK policyholders are published via a series of formal reports and working papers. In this chapter we have drawn on CMI (2006).

In Section 3.5 we noted that there can be considerable variability in the mortality experience of different groups in a national population. Coleman and Salt (1992) give a very good account of this variability in the UK population.

The paper by Gompertz (1825), who was the Actuary of the Alliance Insurance Company of London, introduced the force of mortality concept.

See, for example, Lee and Carter (1992), Li *et al.* (2010) or Cairns *et al.* (2009) for more detailed information about stochastic mortality models.

3.13 Exercises

Exercise 3.1 Sketch the following as functions of age x for a typical (human) population, and comment on the major features.

(a) μ_x,

(b) l_x, and

(c) d_x.

Exercise 3.2 You are given the following life table extract.

Age, x	l_x
52	89 948
53	89 089
54	88 176
55	87 208
56	86 181
57	85 093
58	83 940
59	82 719
60	81 429

Calculate

(a) $_{0.2}q_{52.4}$ assuming UDD (fractional age assumption),

(b) $_{0.2}q_{52.4}$ assuming constant force of mortality (fractional age assumption),

(c) $_{5.7}p_{52.4}$ assuming UDD,

(d) $_{5.7}p_{52.4}$ assuming constant force of mortality,

(e) $_{3.2|2.5}q_{52.4}$ assuming UDD, and

(f) $_{3.2|2.5}q_{52.4}$ assuming constant force of mortality.

Exercise 3.3 Table 3.9 is an extract from a (hypothetical) select life table with a select period of two years. Note carefully the layout – each row relates to a fixed age at selection.

Table 3.9 *Extract from a (hypothetical)
select life table.*

x	$l_{[x]}$	$l_{[x]+1}$	l_{x+2}	$x+2$
75	15 930	15 668	15 286	77
76	15 508	15 224	14 816	78
77	15 050	14 744	14 310	79
⋮	⋮	⋮	⋮	⋮
80			12 576	82
81			11 928	83
82			11 250	84
83			10 542	85
84			9 812	86
85			9 064	87

Table 3.10 *Mortality rates for female non-smokers with term insurance.*

Age, x	Duration 0 $q_{[x]}$	Duration 1 $q_{[x-1]+1}$	Duration 2 $q_{[x-2]+2}$	Duration 3 $q_{[x-3]+3}$	Duration 4 $q_{[x-4]+4}$	Duration 5+ q_x
69	0.003974	0.004979	0.005984	0.006989	0.007994	0.009458
70	0.004285	0.005411	0.006537	0.007663	0.008790	0.010599
71	0.004704	0.005967	0.007229	0.008491	0.009754	0.011880
72	0.005236	0.006651	0.008066	0.009481	0.010896	0.013318
73	0.005870	0.007456	0.009043	0.010629	0.012216	0.014931
74	0.006582	0.008361	0.010140	0.011919	0.013698	0.016742
75	0.007381	0.009376	0.011370	0.013365	0.015360	0.018774
76	0.008277	0.010514	0.012751	0.014988	0.017225	0.021053
77	0.009281	0.011790	0.014299	0.016807	0.019316	0.023609

Use this table to calculate

(a) the probability that a life currently aged 75 who has just been selected will survive to age 85,

(b) the probability that a life currently aged 76 who was selected one year ago will die between ages 85 and 87, and

(c) $_{4|2}q_{[77]+1}$.

Exercise 3.4 CMI Table A23 is based on UK data from 1999 to 2002 for female non-smokers who are term insurance policyholders. It has a select period of five years. An extract from this table, showing values of $q_{[x-t]+t}$, is given in Table 3.10.

Use this survival model to calculate

(a) $_2p_{[72]}$,
(b) $_3q_{[73]+2}$,
(c) $_{1|}q_{[65]+4}$, and
(d) $_7p_{[70]}$.

Table 3.11 *Mortality rates for female smokers with term insurance.*

Age x	Duration 0 $q_{[x]}$	Duration 1 $q_{[x-1]+1}$	Duration 2 $q_{[x-2]+2}$	Duration 3 $q_{[x-3]+3}$	Duration 4 $q_{[x-4]+4}$	Duration 5+ q_x
70	0.010373	0.013099	0.015826	0.018552	0.021279	0.026019
71	0.011298	0.014330	0.017362	0.020393	0.023425	0.028932
72	0.012458	0.015825	0.019192	0.022559	0.025926	0.032133
73	0.013818	0.017553	0.021288	0.025023	0.028758	0.035643
74	0.015308	0.019446	0.023584	0.027721	0.031859	0.039486
75	0.016937	0.021514	0.026092	0.030670	0.035248	0.043686
76	0.018714	0.023772	0.028830	0.033888	0.038946	0.048270
77	0.020649	0.026230	0.031812	0.037393	0.042974	0.053262

Exercise 3.5 CMI Table A21 is based on UK data from 1999 to 2002 for female smokers who are term insurance policyholders. It has a select period of five years. An extract from this table, showing values of $q_{[x-t]+t}$, is given in Table 3.11. Calculate

(a) $_7p_{[70]}$,
(b) $_{1|2}q_{[70]+2}$, and
(c) $_{3.8}q_{[70]+0.2}$ assuming UDD.

Exercise 3.6 A select survival model has a select period of three years. Calculate $_3p_{53}$, given that

$$q_{[50]} = 0.01601, \quad _2p_{[50]} = 0.96411,$$
$$_{2|}q_{[50]} = 0.02410, \quad _{2|3}q_{[50]+1} = 0.09272.$$

Exercise 3.7 When posted overseas to country A at age x, the employees of a large company are subject to a force of mortality such that, at exact duration t years after arrival overseas ($t = 0, 1, 2, 3, 4$),

$$q^A_{[x]+t} = (6 - t)q_{x+t}$$

where q_{x+t} is on the basis of US Life Tables, 2002, Females. For those who have lived in country A for at least five years the force of mortality at each age

Table 3.12 *An extract
from the United States
Life Tables, 2002,
Females.*

Age, x	l_x
30	98 424
31	98 362
32	98 296
33	98 225
34	98 148
35	98 064
⋮	⋮
40	97 500

is 50% greater than that of US Life Tables, 2002, Females, at the same age.
Some l_x values for this table are shown in Table 3.12.

Calculate the probability that an employee posted to country A at age 30 will survive to age 40 if she remains in that country.

Exercise 3.8 A special survival model has a select period of three years. Functions for this model are denoted by an asterisk, *. Functions without an asterisk are taken from the Canada Life Tables 2000–02, Males. You are given that, for all values of x,

$$p^*_{[x]} = 4p_{x-5}; \quad p^*_{[x]+1} = 3p_{x-1}; \quad p^*_{[x]+2} = 2p_{x+2}; \quad p^*_x = p_{x+1}.$$

A life table, tabulated at integer ages, is constructed on the basis of the special survival model and the value of l^*_{25} is taken as 98 363 (i.e. l_{26} for Canada Life Tables 2000–02, Males). Some l_x values for this table are shown in Table 3.13.

(a) Construct the $l^*_{[x]}$, $l^*_{[x]+1}$, $l^*_{[x]+2}$, and l^*_{x+3} columns for $x = 20, 21, 22$.
(b) Calculate $_{2|38}q^*_{[21]+1}$, $_{40}p^*_{[22]}$, $_{40}p^*_{[21]+1}$, $_{40}p^*_{[20]+2}$, and $_{40}p^*_{22}$.

Exercise 3.9 (a) Show that a constant force of mortality between integer ages implies that the distribution of R_x, the fractional part of the future life time, conditional on $K_x = k$, has the following truncated exponential distribution for integer x, for $0 \le s < 1$ and for $k = 0, 1, \dots$

$$\Pr[R_x \le s \mid K_x = k] = \frac{1 - \exp\{-\mu^*_{x+k}s\}}{1 - \exp\{-\mu^*_{x+k}\}} \tag{3.17}$$

where $\mu^*_{x+k} = -\log p_{x+k}$.

Table 3.13 *Canada
Life Tables 2000–02,
Males.*

Age, x	l_x
15	99 180
16	99 135
17	99 079
18	99 014
19	98 942
20	98 866
21	98 785
22	98 700
23	98 615
24	98 529
25	98 444
26	98 363
$\vdots$	$\vdots$
62	87 503
63	86 455
64	85 313
65	84 074

(b) Show that if formula (3.17) holds for $k = 0, 1, 2, \ldots$ then the force of mortality is constant between integer ages.

Exercise 3.10 Verify formula (3.15).

Answers to selected exercises

3.2 (a) 0.001917
   (b) 0.001917
   (c) 0.935422
   (d) 0.935423
   (e) 0.030957
   (f) 0.030950
3.3 (a) 0.66177
   (b) 0.09433
   (c) 0.08993
3.4 (a) 0.987347
   (b) 0.044998
   (c) 0.010514
   (d) 0.920271
3.5 (a) 0.821929

(b) 0.055008

(c) 0.065276

3.6 0.90294

3.7 0.977497

3.8 (a) The values are as follows:

x	$l^*_{[x]}$	$l^*_{[x]+1}$	$l^*_{[x]+2}$	l_{x+3}
20	99 180	98 942	98 700	98 529
21	99 135	98 866	98 615	98 444
22	99 079	98 785	98 529	98 363

(b) 0.121265,   0.872587,   0.874466,   0.875937,   0.876692.

4

Insurance benefits

4.1 Summary

In this chapter we develop formulae for the valuation of traditional insurance benefits. In particular, we consider whole life, term and endowment insurance. For each of these benefits we identify the random variables representing the present values of the benefits and we derive expressions for moments of these random variables. The functions we develop for traditional benefits will also be useful when we move to modern variable contracts.

We develop valuation functions for benefits based on the continuous future lifetime random variable, T_x, and the curtate future lifetime random variable, K_x, from Chapter 2. We introduce a new random variable, $K_x^{(m)}$, which we use to value benefits which depend on the number of complete periods of length $1/m$ years lived by a life (x). We explore relationships between the expected present values of different insurance benefits.

We also introduce the actuarial notation for the expected values of the present value of insurance benefits.

4.2 Introduction

In the previous two chapters, we have looked at models for future lifetime. The main reason that we need these models is to apply them to the valuation of payments which are dependent on the death or survival of a policyholder or pension plan member. Because of the dependence on death or survival, the timing and possibly the amount of the benefit are uncertain, so the present value of the benefit can be modelled as a random variable. In this chapter we combine survival models with time value of money functions to derive the distribution of the present value of an uncertain, life contingent future benefit.

We generally assume in this chapter (and in the following five chapters) that the interest rate is constant and fixed. This is appropriate, for example, if the premiums for an insurance policy are invested in risk-free bonds, all yielding the same interest rate, so that the term structure is flat. In Chapter 11 we introduce more realistic term structures, and consider some models of interest that allow for uncertainty.

For the development of present value functions, it is generally easier, mathematically, to work in continuous time. In the case of a death benefit, working in continuous time means that we assume that the death payment is paid at the exact time of death. In the case of an annuity, a continuous benefit of, say, $1 per year would be paid in infinitesimal units of dt in every interval $(t, t + dt)$. Clearly both assumptions are impractical; it will take time to process a payment after death, and annuities will be paid at most weekly, not every moment (though the valuation of weekly payments is usually treated as if the payments were continuous, as the difference is very small). In practice, insurers and pension plan actuaries work in discrete time, often with cash flow projections that are, perhaps, monthly or quarterly. In addition, when the survival model being used is in the form of a life table with annual increments (that is, l_x for integer x), it is simplest to use annuity and insurance present value functions that assume payments are made at integer durations only. We work in continuous time in the first place because the mathematical development is more transparent, more complete and more flexible. It is then straightforward to adapt the results from continuous time analysis to discrete time problems.

4.3 Assumptions

To perform calculations in this chapter, we require assumptions about mortality and interest. We use the term **basis** to denote a set of assumptions used in life insurance or pension calculations, and we will meet further examples of bases when we discuss premium calculation in Chapter 6, policy values in Chapter 7 and pension liability valuation in Chapter 10.

Throughout this chapter we illustrate the results with examples using the following survival model which was introduced in Example 3.13.

The Standard Ultimate Survival Model

$$\text{Makeham's law with} \quad A = 0.00022$$
$$B = 2.7 \times 10^{-6}$$
$$c = 1.124.$$

We call this an ultimate model to differentiate it from the standard select model that we will use in later chapters.

We also assume that interest rates are constant. As discussed above, this interest assumption can be criticized as unrealistic. However, it is a convenient assumption from a pedagogical point of view, is often accurate enough for

practical purposes (but not always) and we relax the assumption in later
chapters.

It is convenient to work with interest theory functions that are in common
actuarial and financial use. We review some of these here.

Given an effective annual rate of interest i, we use $v = 1/(1 + i)$, so that the
present value of a payment of S which is to be paid in t years' time is Sv^t. The
force of interest per year is denoted δ where

$$\delta = \log(1 + i), \quad 1 + i = e^\delta, \quad \text{and} \quad v = e^{-\delta};$$

δ is also known as the continuously compounded rate of interest. In financial
mathematics and corporate finance contexts, and in particular if the rate of
interest is assumed risk free, the common notation for the continuously compounded rate of interest is r.

The nominal rate of interest compounded p times per year is denoted $i^{(p)}$
where

$$i^{(p)} = p\left((1 + i)^{1/p} - 1\right) \Leftrightarrow 1 + i = \left(1 + i^{(p)}/p\right)^p.$$

The effective rate of discount per year is d where

$$d = 1 - v = iv = 1 - e^{-\delta},$$

and the nominal rate of discount compounded p times per year is $d^{(p)}$ where

$$d^{(p)} = p\left(1 - v^{1/p}\right) \Leftrightarrow (1 - d^{(p)}/p)^p = v.$$

4.4 Valuation of insurance benefits

4.4.1 Whole life insurance: the continuous case, $\bar{A}_x$

For a whole life insurance policy, the time at which the benefit will be paid is
unknown until the policyholder actually dies and the policy becomes a claim.
Since the present value of a future payment depends on the payment date, the
present value of the benefit payment is a function of the time of death, and
is therefore modelled as a random variable. Given a survival model and an
interest rate we can derive the distribution of the present value random variable
for a life contingent benefit, and can therefore compute quantities such as the
mean and variance of the present value.

We start by considering the value of a benefit of amount \$1 payable fol-
lowing the death of a life currently aged x. Using a benefit of \$1 allows us
to develop valuation functions per unit of sum insured, then we can multiply
these by the actual sum insured for different benefit amounts.

We first assume that the benefit is payable immediately on the death of (x). This is known as the continuous case since we work with the continuous future lifetime random variable T_x. Although in practice there would normally be a short delay between the date of a person's death and the time at which an insurance company would actually pay a death benefit (due to notification of death to the insurance company and legal formalities) the effect is slight and we will ignore that delay here.

For our life (x), the present value of a benefit of \$1 payable immediately on death is a random variable, Z, say, where

$$Z = v^{T_x} = e^{-\delta T_x}.$$

We are generally most interested in the expected value of the present value random variable for some future payment. We refer to this as the Expected Present Value or EPV. It is also commonly referred to as the Actuarial Value or Actuarial Present Value.

The EPV of the whole life insurance benefit payment with sum insured \$1 is $E[e^{-\delta T_x}]$. In actuarial notation, we denote this expected value by $\bar{A}_x$, where the bar above A denotes that the benefit is payable immediately on death.

As T_x has probability density function $f_x(t) = {}_t p_x \mu_{x+t}$, we have

$$\bar{A}_x = E[e^{-\delta T_x}] = \int_0^\infty e^{-\delta t} {}_t p_x \mu_{x+t} dt. \qquad (4.1)$$

It is worth looking at the intuition behind this formula. In Figure 4.1 we use the time-line format that was introduced in Section 2.4.

Consider time s, where $x \le x + s < \omega$. The probability that (x) is alive at time s is ${}_s p_x$, and the probability that (x) dies between ages $x + s$ and $x + s + ds$, having survived to age $x + s$, is, loosely, $\mu_{x+s} ds$, provided that ds is very small. In this case, the present value of the death benefit of \$1 is $e^{-\delta s}$.

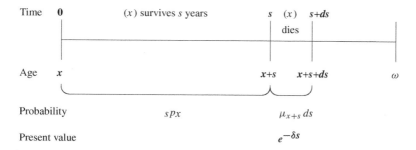

Figure 4.1 Time-line diagram for continuous whole life insurance.

Now we can integrate (that is, sum the infinitesimal components of) the product of present value and probability over all the possible death intervals s to $s + ds$ to obtain the EPV of the death benefit that will be paid in exactly one of these intervals.

Similarly, the second moment (about zero) of the present value of the death benefit is

$$E[Z^2] = E[(e^{-\delta T_x})^2] = E[e^{-2\delta T_x}]$$
$$= \int_0^\infty e^{-2\delta t} \, _tp_x \, \mu_{x+t} dt$$
$$= {}^2\bar{A}_x \tag{4.2}$$

where the superscript ^{2} indicates that the calculation is at force of interest 2δ, or, equivalently, at rate of interest j, where $1 + j = e^{2\delta} = (1 + i)^2$.

The variance of the present value of a unit benefit payable immediately on death is

$$V[Z] = V[e^{-\delta T_x}] = E[Z^2] - E[Z]^2 = {}^2\bar{A}_x - (\bar{A}_x)^2. \tag{4.3}$$

Now, if we introduce a more general sum insured, S, say, then the EPV of the death benefit is

$$E[SZ] = E[Se^{-\delta T_x}] = S\bar{A}_x$$

and the variance is

$$V[SZ] = V[Se^{-\delta T_x}] = S^2 \left({}^2\bar{A}_x - \bar{A}_x^2\right).$$

In fact we can calculate any probabilities associated with the random variable Z from the probabilities associated with T_x. Suppose we are interested in the probability $\Pr[Z \leq 0.5]$, for example. We can rearrange this into a probability for T_x:

$$\Pr[Z \leq 0.5] = \Pr[e^{-\delta T_x} \leq 0.5]$$
$$= \Pr[-\delta T_x \leq \log(0.5)]$$
$$= \Pr[\delta T_x > -\log(0.5)]$$
$$= \Pr[\delta T_x > \log(2)]$$
$$= \Pr[T_x > \log(2)/\delta]$$
$$= {}_u p_x$$

where $u = \log(2)/\delta$. We note that low values of Z are associated with high values of T_x. This makes sense because the benefit is more expensive to the insurer if it is paid early, as there has been little opportunity to earn interest. It is less expensive if it is paid later.

4.4.2 Whole life insurance: the annual case, A_x

Suppose now that the benefit of \$1 is payable at the end of the year of death of (x), rather than immediately on death. To value this we use the curtate future lifetime random variable, K_x, introduced in Chapter 2. Recall that K_x measures the number of complete years of future life of (x). The time to the end of the year of death of (x) is then $K_x + 1$. For example, if (x) lived for 25.6 years from the issue of the insurance policy, the observed value of K_x would be 25, and the death benefit payable at the end of the year of death would be payable 26 years from the policy's issue.

We again use Z to denote the present value of the whole life insurance benefit of \$1, so that Z is the random variable

$$Z = v^{K_x+1}.$$

The EPV of the benefit, $E[Z]$, is denoted by A_x in actuarial notation.

In Chapter 2 we derived the probability function for K_x, $\Pr[K_x = k] = {}_{k|}q_x$, so the EPV of the benefit is

$$A_x = E\left[v^{K_x+1}\right] = \sum_{k=0}^{\infty} v^{k+1} {}_{k|}q_x = vq_x + v^2 {}_{1|}q_x + v^3 {}_{2|}q_x + \cdots. \quad (4.4)$$

Each term on the right-hand side of this equation represents the EPV of a death benefit of \$1, payable at time k conditional on the death of (x) in $(k-1, k]$.

In fact, we can always express the EPV of a life contingent benefit by considering each time point at which the benefit can be paid, and summing over all possible payment times the product of

(1) the amount of the benefit,
(2) the appropriate discount factor, and
(3) the probability that the benefit will be paid at that time.

We will justify this more rigorously in Section 4.6. We illustrate the process for the whole life insurance example in Figure 4.2.

The second moment of the present value is

$$\sum_{k=0}^{\infty} v^{2(k+1)} {}_{k|}q_x = \sum_{k=0}^{\infty} (v^2)^{(k+1)} {}_{k|}q_x = (v^2)q_x + (v^2)^2 {}_{1|}q_x + (v^2)^3 {}_{2|}q_x + \cdots.$$

Just as in the continuous case, we can calculate the second moment about zero of the present value by an adjustment in the rate of interest from i to $(1+i)^2 - 1$.

Figure 4.2 Time-line diagram for discrete whole life insurance.

We define

$$^{2}A_{x} = \sum_{k=0}^{\infty} v^{2(k+1)} \, _{k}|q_{x}, \tag{4.5}$$

and so the variance of the present value of a benefit of S payable at the end of the year of death is

$$S^{2}\left(^{2}A_{x} - (A_{x})^{2}\right). \tag{4.6}$$

4.4.3 Whole life insurance: the 1/mthly case, $A_{x}^{(m)}$

In Chapter 2 we introduced the random variable K_{x}, representing the curtate future lifetime of (x), and we saw in Section 4.4.2 that the present value of an insurance benefit payable at the end of the year of death can be expressed in terms of K_{x}.

We now define the $1/m$thly curtate future lifetime random variable $K_{x}^{(m)}$, where $m > 1$ is an integer, to be the future lifetime of (x) in years rounded to the lower $\frac{1}{m}$th of a year. The most common values of m are 2, 4 and 12, corresponding to half years, quarter years and months. Thus, for example, $K_{x}^{(4)}$ represents the future lifetime of (x), rounded down to the lower 1/4.

Symbolically, if we let $\lfloor \, \rfloor$ denote the integer part (or floor) function, then

$$K_{x}^{(m)} = \frac{1}{m} \lfloor mT_{x} \rfloor. \tag{4.7}$$

For example, suppose (x) lives exactly 23.675 years. Then

$$K_{x} = 23, \ K_{x}^{(2)} = 23.5, \ K_{x}^{(4)} = 23.5, \text{ and } K_{x}^{(12)} = 23\tfrac{8}{12} = 23.6667.$$

Note that $K_{x}^{(m)}$ is a discrete random variable. $K_{x}^{(m)} = k$ indicates that the life (x) dies in the interval $[k, k + 1/m)$, for $k = 0, \frac{1}{m}, \frac{2}{m}, \ldots$

The probability function for $K_{x}^{(m)}$ can be derived from the associated probabilities for T_{x}. For $k = 0, \frac{1}{m}, \frac{2}{m}, \ldots,$

Figure 4.3 Time-line diagram for $1/m$thly whole life insurance.

$$\Pr[K_x^{(m)} = k] = \Pr\left[k \le T_x < k + \tfrac{1}{m}\right] = {}_{k|\frac{1}{m}}q_x = {}_kp_x - {}_{k+\frac{1}{m}}p_x.$$

In Figure 4.3 we show the time-line for the $1/m$thly benefit. At the end of each $1/m$ year period, we show the amount of benefit due, conditional on the death of the insured life in the previous $1/m$ year interval, the probability that the insured life dies in the relevant interval, and the appropriate discount factor.

Suppose, for example, that $m = 12$. A whole life insurance benefit payable at the end of the month of death has present value random variable Z where

$$Z = v^{K_x^{(12)}+1/12}.$$

We let $A_x^{(12)}$ denote the EPV of this benefit, so that

$$E[Z] = A_x^{(12)} = v^{1/12} \, {}_{\frac{1}{12}}q_x + v^{2/12} \, {}_{\frac{1}{12}|\frac{1}{12}}q_x + v^{3/12} \, {}_{\frac{2}{12}|\frac{1}{12}}q_x$$
$$+ v^{4/12} \, {}_{\frac{3}{12}|\frac{1}{12}}q_x + \cdots.$$

Similarly, for any m,

$$A_x^{(m)} = v^{1/m} \, {}_{\frac{1}{m}}q_x + v^{2/m} \, {}_{\frac{1}{m}|\frac{1}{m}}q_x + v^{3/m} \, {}_{\frac{2}{m}|\frac{1}{m}}q_x + v^{4/m} \, {}_{\frac{3}{m}|\frac{1}{m}}q_x + \cdots \quad (4.8)$$

$$= \sum_{k=0}^{\infty} v^{\frac{k+1}{m}} \, {}_{\frac{k}{m}|\frac{1}{m}}q_x. \quad (4.9)$$

As for the continuous and annual cases, we can derive the variance of the present value of the $1/m$thly whole life benefit by adjusting the interest rate for the first term in the variance. We have

$$E[Z^2] = E[v^{2(K_x^{(12)}+1/12)}] = E[(v^2)^{K_x^{(12)}+1/12}] = {}^2A_x^{(12)},$$

so the variance is

$$ {}^2A_x^{(12)} - (A_x^{(12)})^2.$$

4.4.4 Recursions

In practice, it would be very unusual for an insurance policy to provide the death benefit at the end of the year of death. Nevertheless, the annual insurance function A_x is still useful. We are often required to work with annual life tables, such as those in Chapter 3, in which case we would start by calculating the annual function A_x, then adjust for a more appropriate frequency using the relationships and assumptions we develop later in this chapter.

Using the annual life table in a spreadsheet, we can calculate the values of A_x using **backwards recursion**. To do this, we start from the highest age in the table, ω. We assume all lives expire by age ω, so that $q_{\omega-1} = 1$. If the life table does not have a limiting age, we choose a suitably high value for ω so that $q_{\omega-1}$ is as close to 1 as we like. This means that any life attaining age $\omega - 1$ may be treated as certain to die before age ω, in which case we know that $K_{\omega-1} = 0$ and so

$$A_{\omega-1} = \mathrm{E}\big[v^{K_{\omega-1}+1}\big] = v.$$

Now, working from the summation formula for A_x we have

$$
\begin{aligned}
A_x &= \sum_{k=0}^{\omega-x-1} v^{k+1} \,_k p_x \, q_{x+k} \\
&= v\, q_x + v^2 \, p_x \, q_{x+1} + v^3 \,_2 p_x \, q_{x+2} + \cdots \\
&= v\, q_x + v\, p_x \left(v\, q_{x+1} + v^2 \, p_{x+1}\, q_{x+2} + v^3 \,_2 p_{x+1}\, q_{x+3} + \cdots \right),
\end{aligned}
$$

giving the important recursion formula

$$\boxed{A_x = v\, q_x + v\, p_x\, A_{x+1}.} \tag{4.10}$$

This formula can be used in spreadsheet format to calculate A_x backwards from $A_{\omega-1}$ back to A_{x_0}, where x_0 is the minimum age in the table.

The intuition for equation (4.10) is that we separate the EPV of the whole life insurance into the value of the benefit due in the first year, followed by the value at age $x + 1$ of all subsequent benefits, multiplied by p_x to allow for the probability of surviving to age $x + 1$, and by v to discount the value back from age $x + 1$ to age x.

We can use the same approach for $1/m$thly benefits; now the recursion will give $A_x^{(m)}$ in terms of $A_{x+\frac{1}{m}}^{(m)}$. Again, we split the benefit into the part payable in the first period – now of length $1/m$ years – followed by the EPV of the insurance beginning after $1/m$ years. We have

$$
\begin{aligned}
A_x^{(m)} &= v^{1/m} \,_{\frac{1}{m}} q_x + v^{2/m} \,_{\frac{1}{m}} p_x \,_{\frac{1}{m}} q_{x+\frac{1}{m}} + v^{3/m} \,_{\frac{2}{m}} p_x \,_{\frac{1}{m}} q_{x+\frac{2}{m}} + \cdots \\
&= v^{1/m} \,_{\frac{1}{m}} q_x + v^{1/m} \,_{\frac{1}{m}} p_x \left(v^{1/m} \,_{\frac{1}{m}} q_{x+\frac{1}{m}} + v^{2/m} \,_{\frac{1}{m}} p_{x+\frac{1}{m}} \,_{\frac{1}{m}} q_{x+\frac{2}{m}} + \cdots \right),
\end{aligned}
$$

Table 4.1 *Sample values of A_x using the Standard Ultimate Survival Model, Example 4.1.*

x	A_x	x	A_x	x	A_x
30	0.07698	50	0.18931	98	0.85177
31	0.08054	51	0.19780	99	0.86153
32	0.08427	52	0.20664	100	0.87068
$\vdots$	$\vdots$	$\vdots$	$\vdots$	$\vdots$	$\vdots$

giving the recursion formula

$$A_x^{(m)} = v^{1/m} \, {}_{\frac{1}{m}}q_x + v^{1/m} \, {}_{\frac{1}{m}}p_x \, A_{x+\frac{1}{m}}^{(m)}.$$

Example 4.1 Using the Standard Ultimate Survival Model from Section 4.3, and an interest rate of 5% per year effective, construct a spreadsheet of values of A_x for $x = 20, 21, \ldots, 100$. Assume that $A_{129} = v$.

Solution 4.1 The survival model for the Standard Ultimate Survival Model is the ultimate part of the model used in Example 3.13 and so values of ${}_t p_x$ can be calculated as explained in the solution to that example. The value of q_{129} is 0.99996, which is indeed close to 1. We can use the formula

$$A_x = vq_x + vp_x A_{x+1}$$

to calculate recursively $A_{128}, A_{127}, \ldots, A_{20}$, starting from $A_{129} = v$. Values for $x = 20, 21, \ldots, 80$, are given in Appendix D, Table D.3. Some excerpts are shown in Table 4.1. □

Example 4.2 Using the Standard Ultimate Survival Model from Section 4.3, and an interest rate of 5% per year effective, develop a spreadsheet of values of $A_x^{(12)}$ for x starting at age 20, in steps of $1/12$.

Solution 4.2 For this example, we follow exactly the same process as for the previous example, except that we let the ages increase by $1/12$ year in each row. We construct a column of values of ${}_{\frac{1}{12}}p_x$ using

$$ {}_{\frac{1}{12}}p_x = \exp\left\{-A/12 - Bc^x(c^{1/12} - 1)/\log(c)\right\}.$$

We again use 130 as the limiting age of the table. Then set $A_{129\frac{11}{12}}^{(12)} = v^{1/12}$, and for all the other values of $A_x^{(12)}$ use the recursion

$$A_x^{(12)} = v^{1/12} \, {}_{\frac{1}{12}}q_x + v^{1/12} \, {}_{\frac{1}{12}}p_x \, A_{x+\frac{1}{12}}^{(12)}.$$

Table 4.2 *Sample values of $A_x^{(12)}$ using the Standard Ultimate Survival Model, Example 4.2.*

x	$\frac{1}{12}p_x$	$\frac{1}{12}q_x$	$A_x^{(12)}$
20	0.999979	0.000021	0.05033
$20\frac{1}{12}$	0.999979	0.000021	0.05051
$20\frac{2}{12}$	0.999979	0.000021	0.05070
$20\frac{3}{12}$	0.999979	0.000021	0.05089
$\vdots$	$\vdots$	$\vdots$	$\vdots$
50	0.999904	0.000096	0.19357
$50\frac{1}{12}$	0.999903	0.000097	0.19429
$\vdots$	$\vdots$	$\vdots$	$\vdots$
$129\frac{10}{12}$	0.413955	0.586045	0.99427
$129\frac{11}{12}$			0.99594

The first and last few lines of the spreadsheet are reproduced in Table 4.2. □

It is worth making a remark about the calculations in Examples 4.1 and 4.2. In Example 4.1 we saw that $q_{129} = 0.99996$, which is sufficiently close to 1 to justify us starting our recursive calculation by setting $A_{129} = v$. In Example 4.2, our recursive calculation started from $A_{129\frac{11}{12}} = v^{1/12}$. If we calculate $\frac{1}{12}q_{129\frac{11}{12}}$ we find its value is 0.58960, which is certainly not close to 1.

What is happening in these calculations is that, for Example 4.1, we are replacing the exact calculation

$$A_{129} = v\left(q_{129} + p_{129}\,A_{130}\right)$$

by $A_{129} = v$, which is justifiable because A_{130} is close to 1, meaning that $v(q_{129} + p_{129}\,A_{130})$ is very close to v. Similarly, for Example 4.2, we replace the exact calculation

$$A_{129\frac{11}{12}}^{(12)} = v^{1/12}\left(\tfrac{1}{12}q_{129\frac{11}{12}} + \tfrac{1}{12}p_{129\frac{11}{12}}\,A_{130}^{(12)}\right)$$

by $A_{129\frac{11}{12}}^{(12)} = v^{1/12}$. As the value of $A_{130}^{(12)}$ is very close to 1, it follows that

$$v^{1/12}\left(\tfrac{1}{12}q_{129\frac{11}{12}} + \tfrac{1}{12}p_{129\frac{11}{12}}\,A_{130}^{(12)}\right)$$

can by approximated by $v^{1/12}$.

Example 4.3 Using the Standard Ultimate Survival Model, and an interest rate of 5% per year effective, calculate the mean and standard deviation of the

Table 4.3 *Mean and standard deviation of the present value of a whole life insurance benefit of $100 000, for Example 4.3.*

Age, x	Continuous (a)		Monthly (b)		Annual (c)	
	Mean	St. Dev.	Mean	St. Dev.	Mean	St. Dev.
20	5 043	5 954	5 033	5 942	4 922	5 810
40	12 404	9 619	12 379	9 600	12 106	9 389
60	29 743	15 897	29 683	15 865	29 028	15 517
80	60 764	17 685	60 641	17 649	59 293	17 255
100	89 341	8 127	89 158	8 110	87 068	7 860

present value of a benefit of $100 000 payable (a) immediately on death, (b) at the end of the month of death, and (c) at the end of the year of death for lives aged 20, 40, 60, 80 and 100, and comment on the results.

Solution 4.3 For part (a), we must calculate $100 000 \bar{A}_x$ and

$$100 000 \sqrt{^2\bar{A}_x - (\bar{A}_x)^2}$$

for $x = 20, 40, 60$ and 80, where $^2\bar{A}_x$ is calculated at effective rate of interest $j = 10.25\%$. For parts (b) and (c) we replace each $\bar{A}_x$ by $A_x^{(12)}$ and A_x, respectively. The values are shown in Table 4.3. The continuous benefit values in the first column are calculated by numerical integration, and the annual and monthly benefit values are calculated using the spreadsheets from Examples 4.1 and 4.2.

We can make the following observations about these values. First, values for the continuous benefit are larger than the monthly benefit, which are larger than the annual benefit. This is because the death benefit is payable soonest under (a) and latest under (c). Second, as x increases the mean increases for all three cases. This occurs because the smaller the value of x, the longer the expected time until payment of the death benefit. Third, as x increases, the standard deviation decreases relative to the mean, in all three cases. And further, as we get to very old ages, the standard deviation decreases in absolute terms, as the possible range of payout dates is reduced significantly.

It is also interesting to note that the continuous and monthly versions of the whole life benefit are very close. That is to be expected, as the difference arises from the change in the value of money in the period between the moment of death and the end of the month of death, a relatively short period. □

4.4.5 Term insurance

The continuous case, $\bar{A}^{\,1}_{x:\overline{n}|}$

Under a term insurance policy, the death benefit is payable only if the policy-holder dies within a fixed term of, say, n years.

In the continuous case, the benefit is payable immediately on death. The present value of a benefit of $1, which we again denote by Z, is

$$
Z = \begin{cases} v^{T_x} = e^{-\delta T_x} & \text{if } T_x \leq n, \\ 0 & \text{if } T_x > n. \end{cases}
$$

The EPV of this benefit is denoted $\bar{A}^{\,1}_{x:\overline{n}|}$ in actuarial notation. The bar above A again denotes that the benefit is payable immediately on death, and the 1 above x indicates that the life (x) must die before the term of n years expires in order for the benefit to be payable.

Then

$$
\boxed{\bar{A}^{\,1}_{x:\overline{n}|} = \int_0^n e^{-\delta t}\,_t p_x \mu_{x+t} dt}
\tag{4.11}
$$

and, similarly, the expected value of the square of the present value is

$$
{}^2\bar{A}^{\,1}_{x:\overline{n}|} = \int_0^n e^{-2\delta t}\,_t p_x \mu_{x+t} dt
$$

which, as with the whole life case, is calculated by a change in the rate of interest used.

The annual case, $A^{\,1}_{x:\overline{n}|}$

Next, we consider the situation when a death benefit of 1 is payable at the end of the year of death, provided this occurs within n years. The present value random variable for the benefit is now

$$
Z = \begin{cases} v^{K_x+1} & \text{if } K_x \leq n - 1, \\ 0 & \text{if } K_x \geq n. \end{cases}
$$

The EPV of the benefit is denoted $A^{\,1}_{x:\overline{n}|}$ so that

$$
\boxed{A^{\,1}_{x:\overline{n}|} = \sum_{k=0}^{n-1} v^{k+1}\,_k|q_x.}
\tag{4.12}
$$

Table 4.4 *EPVs of term insurance benefits.*

x	$\bar{A}^{\,1}_{x:\overline{10}|}$	$A^{(4)\,1}_{x:\overline{10}|}$	$A^{\,1}_{x:\overline{10}|}$
20	0.00214	0.00213	0.00209
40	0.00587	0.00584	0.00573
60	0.04356	0.04329	0.04252
80	0.34550	0.34341	0.33722

The 1/$m$thly case, $A^{(m)\,1}_{x:\overline{n}|}$

We now consider the situation when a death benefit of 1 is payable at the end of the 1/mth year of death, provided this occurs within n years. The present value random variable for the benefit is

$$
Z = \begin{cases} v^{K_x^{(m)}+\frac{1}{m}} & \text{if } K_x^{(m)} \le n - \frac{1}{m}, \\ 0 & \text{if } K_x^{(m)} \ge n. \end{cases}
$$

The EPV of the benefit is denoted $A^{(m)\,1}_{x:\overline{n}|}$ so that

$$
A^{(m)\,1}_{x:\overline{n}|} = \sum_{k=0}^{mn-1} v^{(k+1)/m} \; {}_{\frac{k}{m}|\frac{1}{m}}q_x. \tag{4.13}
$$

Example 4.4 Using the Standard Ultimate Survival Model as specified in Section 4.3, with interest at 5% per year effective, calculate $\bar{A}^{\,1}_{x:\overline{10}|}$, $A^{(4)\,1}_{x:\overline{10}|}$ and $A^{\,1}_{x:\overline{10}|}$ for $x = 20, 40, 60$ and 80 and comment on the values.

Solution 4.4 We use formula (4.11) with $n = 10$ to calculate $\bar{A}^{\,1}_{x:\overline{10}|}$ (using numerical integration), and formulae (4.13) and (4.12), with $m = 4$ and $n = 10$ to calculate $A^{(4)\,1}_{x:\overline{10}|}$ and $A^{\,1}_{x:\overline{10}|}$.

The values are shown in Table 4.4, and we observe that values in each case increase as x increases, reflecting the fact that the probability of death in a 10-year period increases with age for the survival model we are using. The ordering of values at each age is the same as in Example 4.3, for the same reason – the ordering reflects the fact that any payment under the continuous benefit will be paid earlier than a payment under the quarterly benefit. The end year benefit is paid later than the quarterly benefit, except when the death occurs in the final quarter of the year, in which case the benefit is paid at the same time. □

4.4.6 Pure endowment

Pure endowment benefits are conditional on the survival of the policyholder at a policy maturity date. For example, a 10-year pure endowment with sum insured $10 000, issued to (x), will pay $10 000 in 10 years if (x) is still alive at that time, and will pay nothing if (x) dies before age $x + 10$. Pure endowment benefits are not sold as stand-alone policies, but may be sold in conjunction with term insurance benefits to create the endowment insurance benefit described in the following section. However, pure endowment valuation functions turn out to be very useful.

The pure endowment benefit of $1, issued to a life aged x, with a term of n years has present value Z, say, where:

$$Z = \begin{cases} 0 & \text{if } T_x < n, \\ v^n & \text{if } T_x \geq n. \end{cases}$$

There are two ways to denote the EPV of the pure endowment benefit using actuarial notation. It may be denoted $A_{x:\overline{n}|}^{\ 1}$. The '1' over the term subscript indicates that the term must expire before the life does for the benefit to be paid. This notation is consistent with the term insurance notation, but it can be cumbersome, considering that this is a function which is used very often in actuarial calculations. A more convenient standard actuarial notation for the EPV of the pure endowment is $_nE_x$.

If we rewrite the definition of Z above, we have

$$Z = \begin{cases} 0 & \text{with probability } 1 - {}_np_x, \\ v^n & \text{with probability } {}_np_x. \end{cases} \tag{4.14}$$

Then we can see that the EPV is

$$\boxed{A_{x:\overline{n}|}^{\ 1} = {}_nE_x = v^n\, {}_np_x \ .} \tag{4.15}$$

Note that because the pure endowment will be paid only at time n, assuming the life survives, there is no need to specify continuous and discrete time versions; there is only a discrete time version.

We will generally use the more direct notation $v^n\, {}_np_x$ or $_nE_x$ for the pure endowment function, rather than the $A_{x:\overline{n}|}^{\ 1}$ notation.

4.4.7 Endowment insurance

An endowment insurance provides a combination of a term insurance and a pure endowment. The sum insured is payable on the death of (x) should (x) die within a fixed term, say n years, but if (x) survives for n years, the sum insured is payable at the end of the nth year.

Traditional endowment insurance policies were popular in Australia, North America and the UK up to the 1990s, but are rarely sold these days in these markets. However, as with the pure endowment, the valuation function turns out to be quite useful in other contexts. Also, companies operating in these territories will be managing the ongoing liabilities under the policies already written for some time to come. Furthermore, traditional endowment insurance is still relevant and popular in some other insurance markets.

We first consider the case when the death benefit (of amount 1) is payable immediately on death. The present value of the benefit is Z, say, where

$$Z = \begin{cases} v^{T_x} = e^{-\delta T_x} & \text{if } T_x < n, \\ v^n & \text{if } T_x \geq n \end{cases}$$
$$= v^{\min(T_x, n)} = e^{-\delta \min(T_x, n)}.$$

Thus, the EPV of the benefit is

$$E[Z] = \int_0^n e^{-\delta t} {}_t p_x \mu_{x+t} dt + \int_n^\infty e^{-\delta n} {}_t p_x \mu_{x+t} dt$$
$$= \int_0^n e^{-\delta t} {}_t p_x \mu_{x+t} dt + e^{-\delta n} {}_n p_x$$
$$= \bar{A}_{x:\overline{n}|}^{1} + A_{x:\overline{n}|}^{1}$$

and in actuarial notation we write

$$\boxed{\bar{A}_{x:\overline{n}|} = \bar{A}_{x:\overline{n}|}^{1} + A_{x:\overline{n}|}^{1}.} \tag{4.16}$$

Similarly, the expected value of the squared present value of the benefit is

$$\int_0^n e^{-2\delta t} {}_t p_x \mu_{x+t} dt + e^{-2\delta n} {}_n p_x$$

which we denote ${}^2\bar{A}_{x:\overline{n}|}$.

In the situation when the death benefit is payable at the end of the year of death, the present value of the benefit is

$$Z = \begin{cases} v^{K_x+1} & \text{if } K_x \leq n - 1, \\ v^n & \text{if } K_x \geq n \end{cases}$$
$$= v^{\min(K_x+1, n)}.$$

The EPV of the benefit is then

$$\sum_{k=0}^{n-1} v^{k+1} {}_{k|}q_x + v^n P[K_x \geq n] = A_{x:\overline{n}|}^{1} + v^n {}_n p_x, \tag{4.17}$$

Table 4.5 *EPVs of endowment
insurance benefits.*

x	$\bar{A}_{x:\overline{10}|}$	$A^{(4)}_{x:\overline{10}|}$	$A_{x:\overline{10}|}$
20	0.61438	0.61437	0.61433
40	0.61508	0.61504	0.61494
60	0.62220	0.62194	0.62116
80	0.68502	0.68292	0.67674

and in actuarial notation we write

$$A_{x:\overline{n}|} = A^{1}_{x:\overline{n}|} + A_{x:\overline{n}|}^{1}. \tag{4.18}$$

Similarly, the expected value of the squared present value of the benefit is

$$^{2}A_{x:\overline{n}|} = \sum_{k=0}^{n-1} v^{2(k+1)} \, {}_{k|}q_x + v^{2n} \, {}_np_x.$$

Finally, when the death benefit is payable at the end of the $1/m$th year of death, the present value of the benefit is

$$Z = \begin{cases} v^{K_x^{(m)}+\frac{1}{m}} & \text{if } K_x^{(m)} \leq n - \frac{1}{m}, \\ v^n & \text{if } K_x^{(m)} \geq n \end{cases}$$

$$= v^{\min(K_x^{(m)}+\frac{1}{m}, n)}.$$

The EPV of the benefit is

$$\sum_{k=0}^{mn-1} v^{(k+1)/m} \, {}_{\frac{k}{m}|\frac{1}{m}}q_x + v^n \, P[K_x^{(m)} \geq n] = A^{(m)1}_{x:\overline{n}|} + v^n \, {}_np_x,$$

and in actuarial notation we write

$$A^{(m)}_{x:\overline{n}|} = A^{(m)1}_{x:\overline{n}|} + A_{x:\overline{n}|}^{1}. \tag{4.19}$$

Example 4.5 Using the Standard Ultimate Survival Model as specified in Section 4.3, with interest at 5% per year effective, calculate $\bar{A}_{x:\overline{10}|}$, $A^{(4)}_{x:\overline{10}|}$ and $A_{x:\overline{10}|}$ for $x = 20, 40, 60$ and 80 and comment on the values.

Solution 4.5 We can obtain values of $\bar{A}_{x:\overline{10}|}$, $A^{(4)}_{x:\overline{10}|}$ and $A_{x:\overline{10}|}$ by adding $A_{x:\overline{10}|}^{1} = v^{10} \, {}_{10}p_x$ to the values of $\bar{A}^{1}_{x:\overline{10}|}$, $A^{(4)1}_{x:\overline{10}|}$, and $A^{1}_{x:\overline{10}|}$ in Example 4.4. The values are shown in Table 4.5.

The actuarial values of the 10-year endowment insurance functions do not vary greatly with x, unlike the values of the 10-year term insurance functions. The reason for this is that the probability of surviving 10 years is large ($_{10}p_{20} = 0.9973$, $_{10}p_{60} = 0.9425$) and so for each value of x, the benefit is payable after 10 years with a high probability. Note that $v^{10} = 0.6139$, and as time 10 years is the latest possible payment date for the benefit, the values of $\bar{A}_{x:\overline{10}|}$, $A^{(4)}_{x:\overline{10}|}$ and $A_{x:\overline{10}|}$ must be greater than this for any age x.

$\square$

4.4.8 Deferred insurance benefits

Deferred insurance refers to insurance which does not begin to offer death benefit cover until the end of a deferred period. Suppose a benefit of $1 is payable immediately on the death of (x) provided that (x) dies between ages $x + u$ and $x + u + n$. The present value random variable is

$$Z = \begin{cases} 0 & \text{if } T_x < u \text{ or } T_x \geq u + n, \\ e^{-\delta T_x} & \text{if } u \leq T_x < u + n. \end{cases}$$

This random variable describes the present value of a deferred term insurance. We can, similarly, develop random variables to value deferred whole life or endowment insurance.

The actuarial notation for the EPV of the deferred term insurance benefit is $_{u|}\bar{A}^{1}_{x:\overline{n}|}$. Thus

$$_{u|}\bar{A}^{1}_{x:\overline{n}|} = \int_{u}^{u+n} e^{-\delta t}\, {}_{t}p_x \mu_{x+t} dt. \tag{4.20}$$

Changing the integration variable to $s = t - u$ gives

$$_{u|}\bar{A}^{1}_{x:\overline{n}|} = \int_{0}^{n} e^{-\delta(s+u)}\, {}_{s+u}p_x\, \mu_{x+s+u}\, ds$$

$$= e^{-\delta u}\, {}_{u}p_x \int_{0}^{n} e^{-\delta s}\, {}_{s}p_{x+u}\, \mu_{x+s+u}\, ds$$

$$= e^{-\delta u}\, {}_{u}p_x\, \bar{A}^{1}_{x+u:\overline{n}|} = v^{u}\, {}_{u}p_x\, \bar{A}^{1}_{x+u:\overline{n}|} = {}_{u}E_x\, \bar{A}^{1}_{x+u:\overline{n}|}. \tag{4.21}$$

A further expression for $_{u|}\bar{A}^{1}_{x:\overline{n}|}$ is

$$\boxed{_{u|}\bar{A}^{1}_{x:\overline{n}|} = \bar{A}^{1}_{x:\overline{u+n}|} - \bar{A}^{1}_{x:\overline{u}|}} \tag{4.22}$$

which follows from formula (4.20) since

$$\int_{u}^{u+n} e^{-\delta t}\, {}_{t}p_x \mu_{x+t} dt = \int_{0}^{u+n} e^{-\delta t}\, {}_{t}p_x \mu_{x+t} dt - \int_{0}^{u} e^{-\delta t}\, {}_{t}p_x \mu_{x+t} dt.$$

Thus, the EPV of a deferred term insurance benefit can be found by differencing the EPVs of term insurance benefits for terms $u + n$ and u.

Note the role of the pure endowment term $_uE_x = v^u \, _up_x$ in equation (4.21). This acts similarly to a discount function. If the life survives u years, to the end of the deferred period, then the EPV at that time of the term insurance is $\bar{A}^1_{x+u:\overline{n}|}$. Multiplying by $v^u \, _up_x$ converts this to the EPV at the start of the deferred period.

Our main interest in this EPV is as a building block. We observe, for example, that an n-year term insurance can be decomposed as the sum of n deferred term insurance policies, each with a term of one year, and we can write

$$\bar{A}^1_{x:\overline{n}|} = \int_0^n e^{-\delta t} \, _tp_x\mu_{x+t}dt$$

$$= \sum_{r=0}^{n-1} \int_r^{r+1} e^{-\delta t} \, _tp_x\mu_{x+t}dt$$

$$= \sum_{r=0}^{n-1} {_{r|}}\bar{A}^1_{x:\overline{1}|}. \tag{4.23}$$

A similar decomposition applies to a whole life insurance policy and we can write

$$\bar{A}_x = \sum_{r=0}^{\infty} {_{r|}}\bar{A}^1_{x:\overline{1}|}.$$

We can derive similar results for the deferred benefit payable at the end of the year of death, with EPV denoted $_{u|}A^1_{x:\overline{n}|}$.

In particular, it is useful to note that

$$\boxed{A_x = A^1_{x:\overline{n}|} + {_{n|}}A_x}$$

where $_{n|}A_x$ is the EPV of a benefit of 1 payable at the end of the year of death of (x) if death occurs after time n, so that

$$A^1_{x:\overline{n}|} = A_x - {_{n|}}A_x$$

$$= A_x - v^n \, _np_x \, A_{x+n}.$$

This relationship can be used to calculate $A^1_{x:\overline{n}|}$ for integer x and n given a table of values of A_x and l_x.

4.5 Relating $\bar{A}_x$, A_x and $A_x^{(m)}$

We mentioned in the introduction to this chapter that, even though insurance contracts with death benefits payable at the end of the year of death are very unusual, functions like A_x are still useful. The reason for this is that we can approximate $\bar{A}_x$ or $A_x^{(m)}$ from A_x, and we might wish to do this if the only

Table 4.6 *Ratios of $A_x^{(4)}$ to A_x and $\bar{A}_x$ to A_x, Standard Ultimate Survival Model.*

x	$A_x^{(4)}/A_x$	$\bar{A}_x/A_x$
20	1.0184	1.0246
40	1.0184	1.0246
60	1.0184	1.0246
80	1.0186	1.0248
100	1.0198	1.0261
120	1.0296	1.0368

information we had was a life table, with integer age functions only, rather than a formula for the force of mortality that could be applied for all ages.

In Table 4.6 we show values of the ratios of $A_x^{(4)}$ to A_x and $\bar{A}_x$ to A_x, using the Standard Ultimate Survival Model from Section 4.3, with interest at 5% per year effective.

We see from Table 4.6 that, over a very wide range of ages, the ratios of $A_x^{(4)}$ to A_x and $\bar{A}_x$ to A_x are remarkably stable, giving the appearance of being independent of x. In the following section we show how we can approximate values of $A_x^{(m)}$ and $\bar{A}_x$ using values of A_x.

4.5.1 Using the uniform distribution of deaths assumption

The difference between $\bar{A}_x$ and A_x depends on the lifetime distribution between ages y and $y + 1$ for all $y \geq x$. If we do not have information about this, for example, because we have mortality information only at integer ages, we can approximate the relationship between the continuous function $\bar{A}_x$ and the discrete function A_x using the fractional age assumptions that we introduced in Section 3.3. The most convenient fractional age assumption for this purpose is the uniform distribution of deaths assumption, or UDD.

Recall, from equation (3.9), that under UDD, we have for $0 \leq s < 1$, and for integer y, $_s p_y\, \mu_{y+s} = q_y$. Using this assumption

$$
\bar{A}_x = \int_0^\infty e^{-\delta t}\, {}_t p_x\, \mu_{x+t}\, dt
$$

$$
= \sum_{k=0}^\infty \int_k^{k+1} e^{-\delta t}\, {}_t p_x\, \mu_{x+t}\, dt
$$

$$
= \sum_{k=0}^\infty {}_k p_x\, v^{k+1} \int_0^1 e^{(1-s)\delta}\, {}_s p_{x+k}\, \mu_{x+k+s}\, ds
$$

$$= \sum_{k=0}^{\infty} {}_k p_x \, q_{x+k} v^{k+1} \int_0^1 e^{(1-s)\delta} \, ds \quad \text{using UDD}$$

$$= A_x \frac{e^\delta - 1}{\delta}.$$

Because $e^\delta = 1 + i$, under the assumption of UDD we have

$$\bar{A}_x = \frac{i}{\delta} A_x. \tag{4.24}$$

This exact result under the UDD assumption gives rise to the approximation

$$\boxed{\bar{A}_x \approx \frac{i}{\delta} A_x.} \tag{4.25}$$

The same approximation applies to term insurance and deferred insurance, which we can show by changing the limits of integration in the proof above.

We may also want to derive a $1/m$thly death benefit EPV, such as $A_x^{(m)}$, from the annual function A_x.

Under the UDD assumption we find that

$$\boxed{A_x^{(m)} = \frac{i}{i^{(m)}} A_x,} \tag{4.26}$$

and the right-hand side is used as an approximation to $A_x^{(m)}$. The proof of formula (4.26) is left as an exercise for the reader.

We stress that these approximations apply only to death benefits. The endowment insurance combines the death and survival benefits, so we need to split off the death benefit before applying one of the approximations. That is, under the UDD approach,

$$\boxed{\bar{A}_{x:\overline{n}|} \approx \frac{i}{\delta} A^{\,1}_{x:\overline{n}|} + v^n \, {}_n p_x.} \tag{4.27}$$

4.5.2 *Using the claims acceleration approach*

The claims acceleration approach is a more heuristic way of deriving an approximate relationship between the annual death benefit EPV, A_x, and the $1/m$thly or continuous EPVs, $A_x^{(m)}$ and $\bar{A}_x$. The only difference between these benefits is the timing of the payment. Consider, for example, A_x and $A_x^{(4)}$. The insured life, (x), dies in the year of age $x + K_x$ to $x + K_x + 1$. Under the end year of death benefit (valued by A_x), the sum insured is paid at time $K_x + 1$. Under the end of quarter-year of death benefit (valued by $A_x^{(4)}$), the benefit will be paid either at $K_x + 1/4$, $K_x + 2/4$, $K_x + 3/4$ or $K_x + 1$ depending on the quarter year in which the death occurred. If the deaths occur evenly over the year (the same assumption as we use in the UDD approach), then, on average, the benefit is paid at time $K_x + 5/8$, which is $3/8$ years earlier than the end of year of death benefit.

Similarly, suppose the benefit is paid at the end of the month of death. Assuming deaths occur uniformly over the year, then on average the benefit is paid at $K_x + 13/24$, which is $11/24$ years earlier than the end year of death benefit.

In general, for an $1/m$thly death benefit, assuming deaths are uniformly distributed over the year of age, the average time of payment of the death benefit is $(m + 1)/2m$ in the year of death.

So we have the resulting approximation

$$A_x^{(m)} \approx q_x v^{\frac{m+1}{2m}} + {}_1|q_x v^{1+\frac{m+1}{2m}} + {}_2|q_x v^{2+\frac{m+1}{2m}} + \cdots$$

$$= \sum_{k=0}^{\infty} {}_k|q_x v^{k+\frac{m+1}{2m}}$$

$$= (1 + i)^{\frac{m-1}{2m}} \sum_{k=0}^{\infty} {}_k|q_x v^{k+1}.$$

That is

$$\boxed{A_x^{(m)} \approx (1 + i)^{\frac{m-1}{2m}} A_x.} \tag{4.28}$$

For the continuous benefit EPV, $\bar{A}_x$, we let $m \to \infty$ in equation (4.28), to give the approximation

$$\boxed{\bar{A}_x \approx (1 + i)^{1/2} A_x.} \tag{4.29}$$

This is explained by the fact that, if the benefit is paid immediately on death, and lives die uniformly through the year, then, on average, the benefit is paid half-way through the year of death, which is half a year earlier than the benefit valued by A_x.

As with the UDD approach, these approximations apply only to death benefits. Hence, for an endowment insurance using the claims acceleration approach we have

$$\boxed{\bar{A}_{x:\overline{n}|} \approx (1 + i)^{1/2} A_{x:\overline{n}|}^{\,1} + v^n \, {}_n p_x.} \tag{4.30}$$

Note that both the UDD and the claims acceleration approaches give values for $A_x^{(m)}$ or $\bar{A}_x$ such that the ratios $A_x^{(m)}/A_x$ and $\bar{A}_x/A_x$ are independent of x. Note also that for $i = 5\%$, $i/i^{(4)} = 1.0186$ and $i/\delta = 1.0248$, whilst $(1 + i)^{3/8} = 1.0185$ and $(1 + i)^{1/2} = 1.0247$. The values in Table 4.6 show that both approaches give good approximations in these cases.

4.6 Variable insurance benefits

For all the insurance benefits studied in this chapter the EPV of the benefit can be expressed as the sum over all the possible payment dates of the product of three terms:

- the amount of benefit paid,
- the appropriate discount factor for the payment date, and
- the probability that the benefit will be paid at that payment date.

This approach works for the EPV of any traditional benefit – that is, where the future lifetime is the sole source of uncertainty. It will not generate higher moments or probability distributions.

The approach can be justified technically using **indicator random variables**. Consider a life contingent event E – for example, E is the event that a life aged x dies in the interval $(k, k + 1]$. The indicator random variable is

$$I(E) = \begin{cases} 1 & \text{if } E \text{ is true,} \\ 0 & \text{if } E \text{ is false.} \end{cases}$$

In this example, $\Pr[E \text{ is True}] = {}_{k|}q_x$, so the expected value of the indicator random variable is

$$\mathrm{E}[I(E)] = 1({}_{k|}q_x) + 0(1 - {}_{k|}q_x) = {}_{k|}q_x,$$

and, in general, the expected value of an indicator random variable is the probability of the indicator event.

Consider, for example, an insurance that pays \$1000 after 10 years if (x) has died by that time, and \$2000 after 20 years if (x) dies in the second 10-year period, with no benefit otherwise.

We can write the present value random variable as

$$1\,000\, I(T_x \leq 10)v^{10} + 2\,000\, I(10 < T_x \leq 20)v^{20}$$

and the EPV is then

$$1\,000\, {}_{10}q_x\, v^{10} + 2\,000\, {}_{10|10}q_x\, v^{20}.$$

Indicator random variables can also be used for continuous benefits. Here we consider indicators of the form

$$I(t < T_x \leq t + dt)$$

for infinitesimal dt, with associated probability

$$\begin{aligned} \mathrm{E}[I(t < T_x \leq t + dt)] &= \Pr[t < T_x \leq t + dt] \\ &= \Pr[T_x > t]\Pr[T_x < t + dt | T_x > t] \\ &\approx {}_t p_x\, \mu_{x+t}\, dt. \end{aligned}$$

Consider, for example, an increasing insurance policy with a death benefit of T_x payable at the moment of death. That is, the benefit is exactly equal to the number of years lived by an insured life from age x to his or her death. This is a continuous whole life insurance under which the benefit is a linearly increasing function.

To find the EPV of this benefit, we note that the payment may be made at any time, so we consider all the infinitesimal intervals $(t, t + dt)$, and we sum over all these intervals by integrating from $t = 0$ to $t = \infty$.

First, we identify the amount, discount factor and probability for a benefit payable in the interval $(t, t + dt)$. The amount is t, the discount factor is $e^{-\delta t}$. The probability that the benefit is paid in the interval $(t, t+dt)$ is the probability that the life survives from x to $x + t$, and then dies in the infinitesimal interval $(t, t + dt)$, which gives an approximate probability of $_t p_x \, \mu_{x+t} \, dt$.

So, we can write the EPV of this benefit as

$$\int_0^\infty t \, e^{-\delta t} \,_t p_x \, \mu_{x+t} dt. \tag{4.31}$$

In actuarial notation we write this as $(\bar{I}\bar{A})_x$. The I here stands for 'increasing' and the bar over the I denotes that the increases are continuous.

An alternative approach to deriving equation (4.31) is to identify the present value random variable for the benefit, denoted by Z, say, in terms of the future lifetime random variable,

$$Z = T_x \, e^{-\delta T_x}.$$

Then any moment of Z can be found from

$$\mathrm{E}[Z^k] = \int_0^\infty \left(t \, e^{-\delta t} \right)^k \,_t p_x \, \mu_{x+t} \, dt.$$

The advantage of the first approach is that it is very flexible and generally quick, even for very complex benefits.

If the policy term ceases after a fixed term of n years, the EPV of the death benefit is

$$(\bar{I}\bar{A})^{\,1}_{x:\overline{n}|} = \int_0^n t \, e^{-\delta t} \,_t p_x \, \mu_{x+t} dt.$$

There are a number of other increasing or decreasing benefit patterns that are fairly common. We present several in the following examples.

Example 4.6 Consider an n-year term insurance policy issued to (x) under which the death benefit is $k+1$ if death occurs between ages $x+k$ and $x+k+1$, for $k = 0, 1, 2, \ldots, n - 1$. Assume that the benefit is paid at the end of the year of death.

(a) Derive a formula for the EPV of the benefit using the first approach described, that is multiplying together the amount, the discount factor and the probability of payment, and summing for each possible payment date.

(b) Derive a formula for the variance of the present value of the benefit.

Solution 4.6 (a) If the benefit is paid at time $k+1$, the benefit amount is $(k+1)$ and the discount factor is v^{k+1}. The probability that the benefit is paid at that date is the probability that the policyholder died in the year $(k, k+1]$, which is $_k|q_x$, so the EPV of the death benefit is

$$\sum_{k=0}^{n-1} v^{k+1}(k+1) \,_k|q_x.$$

In actuarial notation the above EPV is denoted $(IA)^1_{x:\overline{n}|}$.

If the term n is infinite, so that this is a whole life version of the increasing annual policy, with benefit $k+1$ following death in the year k to $k+1$, the EPV of the death benefit is denoted $(IA)_x$ where

$$(IA)_x = \sum_{k=0}^{\infty} v^{k+1}(k+1) \,_k|q_x.$$

(b) We must go back to first principles. First, we identify the random variable as

$$Z = \begin{cases} (K_x + 1)v^{K_x+1} & \text{if } K_x < n, \\ 0 & \text{if } K_x \geq n. \end{cases}$$

So

$$E[Z^2] = \sum_{k=0}^{n-1} v^{2(k+1)}(k+1)^2 \,_k|q_x,$$

and the variance is

$$V[Z] = \sum_{k=0}^{n-1} v^{2(k+1)}(k+1)^2 \,_k|q_x - \left((IA)^1_{x:\overline{n}|}\right)^2.$$

$\square$

Example 4.7 A whole life insurance policy offers an increasing death benefit payable at the end of the quarter year of death. If (x) dies in the first year of the contract, then the benefit is 1, in the second year it is 2, and so on. Derive an expression for the EPV of the death benefit.

Solution 4.7 First, we note that the possible payment dates are 1/4, 2/4, 3/4, ... Next, if (x) dies in the first year, then the benefit payable is 1, if death occurs in the second year the benefit payable is 2, and so on. Third, corresponding to the possible payment dates, the discount factors are $v^{1/4}$, $v^{2/4}$, ...

The probabilities associated with the payment dates are $\frac{1}{4}q_x$, $\frac{1}{4}|\frac{1}{4}q_x$, $\frac{2}{4}|\frac{1}{4}q_x$, $\frac{3}{4}|\frac{1}{4}q_x$, ...

Hence, the EPV, which is denoted $(IA^{(4)})_x$, can be calculated as

$$\frac{1}{4}q_x\, v^{\frac{1}{4}} + \frac{1}{4}|\frac{1}{4}q_x\, v^{\frac{2}{4}} + \frac{2}{4}|\frac{1}{4}q_x\, v^{\frac{3}{4}} + \frac{3}{4}|\frac{1}{4}q_x\, v^1$$

$$+ 2\left(1|\frac{1}{4}q_x\, v^{1\frac{1}{4}} + 1\frac{1}{4}|\frac{1}{4}q_x\, v^{1\frac{2}{4}} + 1\frac{2}{4}|\frac{1}{4}q_x\, v^{1\frac{3}{4}} + 1\frac{3}{4}|\frac{1}{4}q_x\, v^2 \right)$$

$$+ 3\left(2|\frac{1}{4}q_x\, v^{2\frac{1}{4}} + 2\frac{1}{4}|\frac{1}{4}q_x\, v^{2\frac{2}{4}} + 2\frac{2}{4}|\frac{1}{4}q_x\, v^{2\frac{3}{4}} + 2\frac{3}{4}|\frac{1}{4}q_x\, v^3 \right) + \cdots$$

$$= A^{(4)1}_{x:\overline{1}|} + 2\,_1|A^{(4)1}_{x:\overline{1}|} + 3\,_2|A^{(4)1}_{x:\overline{1}|} + \cdots .$$

□

We now consider the case when the amount of the death benefit increases in geometric progression. This is important in practice because compound reversionary bonuses will increase the sum insured as a geometric progression.

Example 4.8 Consider an n-year term insurance issued to (x) under which the death benefit is paid at the end of the year of death. The benefit is 1 if death occurs between ages x and $x + 1$, $1 + j$ if death occurs between ages $x + 1$ and $x + 2$, $(1 + j)^2$ if death occurs between ages $x + 2$ and $x + 3$, and so on. Thus, if death occurs between ages $x + k$ and $x + k + 1$, the death benefit is $(1 + j)^k$ for $k = 0, 1, 2, \ldots, n - 1$. Derive a formula for the EPV of this death benefit.

Solution 4.8 The amount of benefit is 1 if the benefit is paid at time 1, $(1 + j)$ if the benefit is paid at time 2, $(1 + j)^2$ if the benefit is paid at time 3, and so on, up to time n. The EPV of the death benefit is then

$$v\,q_x + (1 + j)v^2\,_1|q_x + (1 + j)^2\,v^3\,_2|q_x + \cdots + (1 + j)^{n-1}\,v^n\,_{n-1}|q_x$$

$$= \sum_{k=0}^{n-1} v^{k+1}(1 + j)^k\,_k|q_x$$

$$= \frac{1}{1+j}\sum_{k=0}^{n-1} v^{k+1}(1 + j)^{k+1}\,_k|q_x$$

$$= \frac{1}{1+j}A^1_{x:\overline{n}|i*} \qquad (4.32)$$

where

$$i^* = \frac{1+i}{1+j} - 1 = \frac{i-j}{1+j}.$$

□

The notation $A^{1}_{x:\overline{n}|i^*}$ indicates that the EPV is calculated using the rate of interest i^*, rather than i. In most practical situations, $i > j$ so that $i^* > 0$.

Example 4.9 Consider an insurance policy issued to (x) under which the death benefit is $(1+j)^t$ if death occurs at age $x+t$, with the death benefit being payable immediately on death.

(a) Derive an expression for the EPV of the death benefit if the policy is an n-year term insurance.
(b) Derive an expression for the EPV of the death benefit if the policy is a whole life insurance.

Solution 4.9 (a) The present value of the death benefit is $(1+j)^{T_x} v^{T_x}$ if $T_x < n$, and is zero otherwise, so that the EPV of the death benefit is

$$\int_0^n (1+j)^t v^t \; {}_tp_x \mu_{x+t} dt = \bar{A}^{1}_{x:\overline{n}|i^*}$$

where

$$i^* = \frac{1+i}{1+j} - 1.$$

(b) Similarly, if the policy is a whole life insurance rather than a term insurance, then the EPV of the death benefit would be

$$\int_0^\infty (1+j)^t v^t \; {}_tp_x \mu_{x+t} dt = (\bar{A}_x)_{i^*}$$

where

$$i^* = \frac{1+i}{1+j} - 1.$$

□

4.7 Functions for select lives

Throughout this chapter we have developed results in terms of lives subject to ultimate mortality. We have taken this approach simply for ease of presentation. All of the above development equally applies to lives subject to select mortality.

For example, $\bar{A}_{[x]}$ denotes the EPV of a benefit of 1 payable immediately on the death of a select life (x). Similarly, $A_{[x]:\overline{n}|}$ denotes the EPV of a benefit of 1 payable at the end of the year of death within n years, of a newly selected life age x, or at age $x+n$ if (x) survives.

4.8 Notes and further reading

The Standard Ultimate Survival Model incorporates Makeham's law as its survival model. A feature of Makeham's law is that we can integrate the force of mortality analytically and hence we can evaluate, for example, $_tp_x$ analytically, as in Exercise 2.11. This in turn means that the EPV of an insurance benefit payable immediately on death, for example $\bar{A}_x$, can be written as an integral where the integrand can be evaluated directly, as follows

$$\bar{A}_x = \int_0^\infty e^{-\delta t}\, {}_tp_x\, \mu_{x+t}\, dt.$$

This integral cannot be evaluated analytically but can be evaluated numerically. In many practical situations, the force of mortality cannot be integrated analytically, for example if μ_x is a GM(r, s) function with $s \geq 2$, from Section 2.7. In such cases, $_tp_x$ can be evaluated numerically but not analytically. Functions such as $\bar{A}_x$ can still be evaluated numerically but, since the integrand has to be evaluated numerically, the procedure may be a little more complicated. See Exercise 4.22 for an example. The survival model in Exercise 4.22 has been derived from data for UK whole life and endowment insurance policyholders (non-smokers), 1999–2002. See CMI (2006, Table 1).

4.9 Exercises

Exercise 4.1 You are given the following table of values for l_x and A_x, assuming an effective interest rate of 6% per year.

x	l_x	A_x
35	100 000.00	0.151375
36	99 737.15	0.158245
37	99 455.91	0.165386
38	99 154.72	0.172804
39	98 831.91	0.180505
40	98 485.68	0.188492

Calculate

(a) $_5E_{35}$,

(b) $A^1_{35:\overline{5}|}$,

(c) $_{5|}A_{35}$, and

(d) $\bar{A}_{35:\overline{5}|}$ assuming UDD.

Exercise 4.2 Using tables in Appendix D and interest at 5% per year effective, calculate

(a) $A^{1}_{30:\overline{20}|}$,

(b) $\bar{A}_{40:\overline{20}|}$ assuming UDD,

(c) $_{10|}A_{25}$.

Exercise 4.3 Assuming a uniform distribution of deaths over each year of age, show that $A^{(m)}_x = (i/i^{(m)})A_x$.

Exercise 4.4 A whole life insurance policy issued to a life aged exactly 30 has an increasing sum insured. In the tth policy year, $t = 1, 2, 3, \ldots$, the sum insured is $\$100\,000\,(1.03^{t-1})$. Using the Standard Ultimate Survival Model, with interest at 5% per year, calculate the EPV of this benefit.

Exercise 4.5 (a) Show that

$$A_{x:\overline{n}|} = \sum_{k=0}^{n-2} v^{k+1}\,_k|q_x + v^n\,_{n-1}p_x.$$

(b) Compare this formula with formula (4.17) and comment on the differences.

Exercise 4.6 Show that

$$(IA^{(m)})_x = A^{(m)}_x + vp_x A^{(m)}_{x+1} + v^2\,_2p_x A^{(m)}_{x+2} + \cdots$$

and explain this result intuitively.

Exercise 4.7 (a) Derive the following recursion formula for an n-year increasing term insurance:

$$(IA)^{1}_{x:\overline{n}|} = vq_x + vp_x\left((IA)^{1}_{x+1:\overline{n-1}|} + A^{1}_{x+1:\overline{n-1}|}\right).$$

(b) Give an intuitive explanation of the formula in part (a).

(c) You are given that $(IA)_{50} = 4.99675$, $A^{1}_{50:\overline{1}|} = 0.00558$, $A_{51} = 0.24905$ and $i = 0.06$. Calculate $(IA)_{51}$.

Exercise 4.8 You are given that $A_x = 0.25$, $A_{x+20} = 0.40$, $A_{x:\overline{20}|} = 0.55$ and $i = 0.03$. Calculate $10\,000\bar{A}_{x:\overline{20}|}$ using

(a) claims acceleration, and

(b) UDD.

Exercise 4.9 Show that

$$(IA)^1_{x:\overline{n}|} = (n+1)A^1_{x:\overline{n}|} - \sum_{k=1}^{n} A^1_{x:\overline{k}|}$$

and explain this result intuitively.

Exercise 4.10 Assuming a uniform distribution of deaths over each year of age, find an expression for $(\bar{I}\bar{A})_x$ in terms of A_x and $(IA)_x$.

Exercise 4.11 Show that $\bar{A}_x$ is a decreasing function of i, and explain this result by general reasoning.

Exercise 4.12 Calculate A_{70} given that

$$A_{50:\overline{20}|} = 0.42247, \quad A^1_{50:\overline{20}|} = 0.14996, \quad A_{50} = 0.31266.$$

Exercise 4.13 Under an endowment insurance issued to a life aged x, let X denote the present value of a unit sum insured, payable at the moment of death or at the end of the n-year term.

Under a term insurance issued to a life aged x, let Y denote the present value of a unit sum insured, payable at the moment of death within the n-year term.

Given that

$$V[X] = 0.0052, \quad v^n = 0.3, \quad _np_x = 0.8, \quad E[Y] = 0.04,$$

calculate $V[Y]$.

Exercise 4.14 Show that if $v_y = -\log p_y$ for $y = x, x+1, x+2, \ldots$, then under the assumption of a constant force of mortality between integer ages,

$$\bar{A}_x = \sum_{t=0}^{\infty} v^t \, _tp_x \, \frac{v_{x+t}(1 - vp_{x+t})}{\delta + v_{x+t}}.$$

Exercise 4.15 Let Z_1 denote the present value of an n-year term insurance benefit, issued to (x). Let Z_2 denote the present value of a whole of life insurance benefit, issued to the same life.

Express the covariance of Z_1 and Z_2 in actuarial functions, simplified as far as possible.

Exercise 4.16 You are given the following excerpt from a select life table.

$[x]$	$l_{[x]}$	$l_{[x]+1}$	$l_{[x]+2}$	$l_{[x]+3}$	l_{x+4}	$x+4$
[40]	100 000	99 899	99 724	99 520	99 288	44
[41]	99 802	99 689	99 502	99 283	99 033	45
[42]	99 597	99 471	99 268	99 030	98 752	46
[43]	99 365	99 225	99 007	98 747	98 435	47
[44]	99 120	98 964	98 726	98 429	98 067	48

Assuming an interest rate of 6% per year, calculate

(a) $A_{[40]+1:\overline{4}|}$,
(b) the standard deviation of the present value of a four-year term insurance, deferred one year, issued to a newly selected life aged 40, with sum insured $100 000, payable at the end of the year of death, and
(c) the probability that the present value of the benefit described in (b) is less than or equal to $85 000.

Exercise 4.17 (a) Describe **in words** the insurance benefits with the present values given below.

$$\text{(i)} \qquad Z_1 = \begin{cases} 20\,v^{T_x} & \text{if } T_x \le 15, \\ 10\,v^{T_x} & \text{if } T_x > 15. \end{cases}$$

$$\text{(ii)} \qquad Z_2 = \begin{cases} 0 & \text{if } T_x \le 5, \\ 10\,v^{T_x} & \text{if } 5 < T_x \le 15, \\ 10\,v^{15} & \text{if } T_x > 15. \end{cases}$$

(b) Write down in integral form the formula for the expected value for (i) Z_1 and (ii) Z_2.
(c) Derive expressions in terms of standard actuarial functions for the expected values of Z_1 and Z_2.
(d) Derive an expression in terms of standard actuarial functions for the covariance of Z_1 and Z_2.

Exercise 4.18 (a) Describe in words the insurance benefits with present value given by

$$Z = \begin{cases} T_{30}\,v^{T_{30}} & \text{if } T_{30} \le 25, \\ 25\,v^{T_{30}} & \text{if } T_{30} > 25. \end{cases}$$

(b) Write down an expression in terms of standard actuarial functions for E[Z].

Exercise 4.19 Using the tables in Appendix D and interest at 5% per year effective, calculate the standard deviation of the present value of a payment of $100 000 at the end of the year of death of a life now aged 30 who is subject to ultimate mortality, if payment is contingent on death occurring

(a) at any age, and

(b) before age 50.

Exercise 4.20 Suppose that Makeham's law applies with $A = 0.0001$, $B = 0.00035$ and $c = 1.075$. Assume also that the effective rate of interest is 6% per year.

(a) Use Excel and backward recursion in parts (i) and (ii).
  (i) Construct a table of values of A_x for integer ages, starting at $x = 50$.
  (ii) Construct a table of values of $A_x^{(4)}$ for $x = 50, 50.25, 50.5, \ldots$ (Do not use UDD for this.)
  (iii) Hence, write down the values of A_{50}, A_{100}, $A_{50}^{(4)}$ and $A_{100}^{(4)}$.
(b) Use your values for A_{50} and A_{100} to estimate $A_{50}^{(4)}$ and $A_{100}^{(4)}$ using the UDD assumption.
(c) Compare your estimated values for the $A^{(4)}$ functions (from (b)) with your accurate values (from (a)). Comment on the differences.

Exercise 4.21 A life insurance policy issued to a life aged 50 pays $2000 at the end of the quarter year of death before age 65 and $1000 at the end of the quarter year of death after age 65. Use the Standard Ultimate Survival Model, with interest at 5% per year, in the following.

(a) Calculate the EPV of the benefit.
(b) Calculate the standard deviation of the present value of the benefit.
(c) The insurer charges a single premium of $500. Assuming that the insurer invests all funds at exactly 5% per year effective, what is the probability that the policy benefit has greater value than the accumulation of the single premium?

Exercise 4.22 The force of mortality for a survival model is given by

$$\mu_x = A + BC^x D^{x^2},$$

where

$$A = 3.5 \times 10^{-4}, \ B = 5.5 \times 10^{-4}, \ C = 1.00085, \ D = 1.0005.$$

(a) Calculate $_t p_{60}$ for $t = 0, 1/40, 2/40, \ldots, 2$.
  Hint: Use the repeated Simpson's rule.
(b) Calculate $\bar{A}^1_{60:\overline{2}|}$ using an effective rate of interest of 5% per year.
  Hint: Use the repeated Simpson's rule.

Answers to selected exercises

4.1 (a) 0.735942
   (b) 0.012656
   (c) 0.138719
   (d) 0.748974

4.2 (a) 0.00645
   (b) 0.38163
   (c) 0.05907

4.4 $33 569.47

4.7 (c) 5.07307

4.8 (a) 5 507.44
   (b) 5 507.46

4.12 0.59704

4.13 0.01

4.16 (a) 0.79267
   (b) $7519.71
   (c) 0.99825

4.19 (a) 7 186
   (b) 6 226

4.20 (a) (iii) 0.33587,   0.87508,   0.34330,   0.89647
   (b) 0.34333,   0.89453

4.21 (a) $218.83
   (b) $239.73
   (c) 0.04054

4.22 (a) Selected values are $_{1/4}p_{60} = 0.999031$, $p_{60} = 0.996049$ and $_{2}p_{60} = 0.991903$
   (b) 0.007725

5

Annuities

5.1 Summary

In this chapter we derive expressions for the valuation and analysis of life
contingent annuities. We consider benefit valuation for different payment frequencies, and we relate the valuation of annuity benefits to the valuation of the
related insurance benefits.

We consider how to calculate annuity valuation functions. If full survival
model information is available, then the calculation can be exact for benefits
payable at discrete time points, and as exact as required, using numerical integration, for benefits payable continuously. Where we are calculating benefits
payable more frequently than annual (monthly or weekly, say) using only an
integer age life table, a very common situation in practice, then some approximation is required. We derive several commonly used approximations, using
the UDD assumption and Woolhouse's formula, and explore their accuracy
numerically.

5.2 Introduction

A **life annuity** is a series of payments to (or from) an individual as long as
the individual is alive on the payment date. The payments are normally made
at regular intervals and the most common situation is that the payments are of
the same amount. The valuation of annuities is important as annuities appear
in the calculation of premiums (see Chapter 6), policy values (see Chapter 7)
and pension benefits (see Chapter 10). The present value of a life annuity is
a random variable, as it depends on the future lifetime; however, we will use
some results and notation from the valuation of annuities-certain, where there
is no uncertainty in the term, so we start with a review of these.

5.3 Review of annuities-certain

Recall that, for integer n, and for $i > 0$

$$\ddot{a}_{\overline{n}|} = 1 + v + v^2 + \cdots + v^{n-1} = \frac{1 - v^n}{d} \tag{5.1}$$

denotes the present value of an annuity-certain of 1 payable annually in advance for n years. Also

$$a_{\overline{n}|} = v + v^2 + v^3 + \cdots + v^n = \ddot{a}_{\overline{n}|} - 1 + v^n$$

denotes the present value of an annuity-certain of 1 payable annually in arrear for n years. Thirdly, for any $n > 0$,

$$\bar{a}_{\overline{n}|} = \int_0^n v^t \, dt = \frac{1 - v^n}{\delta} \tag{5.2}$$

denotes the present value of an annuity-certain payable continuously at rate 1 per year for n years.

When payments of 1 per year are made every $1/m$ years in advance for n years, in instalments of $1/m$, the present value is

$$\ddot{a}_{\overline{n}|}^{(m)} = \frac{1}{m} \left(1 + v^{\frac{1}{m}} + v^{\frac{2}{m}} + \cdots + v^{n - \frac{1}{m}} \right) = \frac{1 - v^n}{d^{(m)}}$$

and for payments made in arrears

$$a_{\overline{n}|}^{(m)} = \frac{1}{m} \left(v^{\frac{1}{m}} + v^{\frac{2}{m}} + \cdots + v^n \right) = \frac{1 - v^n}{i^{(m)}} = \ddot{a}_{\overline{n}|}^{(m)} - \frac{1}{m} \left(1 - v^n \right). \tag{5.3}$$

In these equations for $1/m$thly annuities, we assume that n is an integer multiple of $1/m$.

5.4 Annual life annuities

The annual life annuity is paid once each year, conditional on the survival of a life (the **annuitant**) to the payment date. If the annuity is to be paid throughout the annuitant's life, it is called a whole life annuity. If there is to be a specified maximum term, it is called a term or temporary annuity.

Annual annuities are quite rare. We would more commonly see annuities payable monthly or even weekly. However, the annual annuity is still important in the situation where we do not have full information about mortality between integer ages, for example because we are working with an integer age life table. Also, the development of the valuation functions for the annual annuity is a good starting point before considering more complex payment patterns.

As with the insurance functions, we are primarily interested in the EPV of a cash flow, and we also identify the present value random variables in terms of the future lifetime random variables from Chapters 2 and 4, specifically, T_x, K_x and $K_x^{(m)}$.

5.4.1 Whole life annuity-due

Consider first an annuity of 1 per year payable annually **in advance** throughout the lifetime of an individual now aged x. The life annuity with payments in advance is known as a **whole life annuity-due**. The first payment occurs immediately, the second in one year from now, provided that (x) is alive then, and payments follow at annual intervals with each payment conditional on the survival of (x) to the payment date. In Figure 5.1 we show the payments and associated probabilities and discount functions in a time-line diagram.

We note that if (x) were to die between ages $x + k$ and $x + k + 1$, for some positive integer k, then annuity payments would be made at times $0, 1, 2, \ldots, k$, for a total of $k + 1$ payments. We defined K_x such that the death of (x) occurs between $x + K_x$ and $x + K_x + 1$, so, the number of payments is $K_x + 1$, including the initial payment. This means that, for $k = 0, 1, 2, \ldots$, the present value of the annuity is $\ddot{a}_{\overline{k+1}|}$ if $K_x = k$. Thus, using equation (5.1), the present value random variable for the annuity payment series, Y, say, can be written as

$$Y = \ddot{a}_{\overline{K_x+1}|} = \frac{1 - v^{K_x+1}}{d}.$$

There are three useful ways to derive formulae for calculating the expected value of this present value random variable.

First, the mean and variance can be found from the mean and variance of v^{K_x+1}, which were derived in Section 4.4.2. For the expected value of Y, which is denoted $\ddot{a}_x$, we have

$$\ddot{a}_x = \mathrm{E}\left[\frac{1 - v^{K_x+1}}{d}\right] = \frac{1 - \mathrm{E}[v^{K_x+1}]}{d}.$$

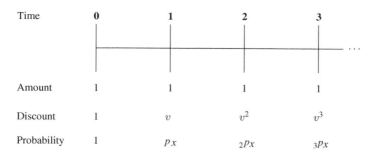

Time	0	1	2	3	
					...
Amount	1	1	1	1	
Discount	1	v	v^2	v^3	
Probability	1	p_x	$_2p_x$	$_3p_x$	

Figure 5.1 Time-line diagram for whole life annuity-due.

That is,

$$\boxed{\ddot{a}_x = \frac{1 - A_x}{d}.}$$ (5.4)

This is a useful approach, as it also immediately gives us the variance of Y as

$$V[Y] = V\left[\frac{1 - v^{K_x+1}}{d}\right] = \frac{1}{d^2}\, V[v^{K_x+1}]$$

$$= \frac{{}^2A_x - A_x^2}{d^2}.$$ (5.5)

Secondly, we may use the indicator random variable approach from Section 4.6. The condition for the payment at k, say, is that (x) is alive at age $x + k$, that is, that $T_x > k$. The present value random variable can be expressed as

$$Y = I(T_x > 0) + v\, I(T_x > 1) + v^2\, I(T_x > 2) + v^3\, I(T_x > 3) + \cdots$$ (5.6)

and the EPV of the annuity is the sum of the expected values of the individual terms. Recall that $E[I(T_x > t)] = \Pr[T_x > t] = {}_t p_x$, so that

$$\ddot{a}_x = 1 + v\, p_x + v^2\, {}_2p_x + v^3\, {}_3p_x + \cdots,$$

that is

$$\boxed{\ddot{a}_x = \sum_{k=0}^{\infty} v^k\, {}_kp_x.}$$ (5.7)

This is a very useful equation for $\ddot{a}_x$. However, this approach does not lead to useful expressions for the variance and higher moments of Y. This is because the individual terms in expression (5.6) are dependent random variables.

Finally, we can work from the probability function for K_x, that is using $\Pr[K_x = k] = {}_k|q_x$, so that

$$\ddot{a}_x = \sum_{k=0}^{\infty} \ddot{a}_{\overline{k+1}|}\, {}_k|q_x.$$ (5.8)

This is less used in practice than equations (5.4) and (5.7). The difference between the formulations for $\ddot{a}_x$ in equations (5.7) and (5.8) is that in equation (5.7) the summation is taken over the possible payment dates, and in equation (5.8) the summation is taken over the possible years of death.

Example 5.1 Show that equations (5.7) and (5.8) are equivalent – that is, show that

$$\sum_{k=0}^{\infty} \ddot{a}_{\overline{k+1}|}\, {}_k|q_x = \sum_{k=0}^{\infty} v^k\, {}_kp_x.$$

Solution 5.1 We can show this by using

$$\ddot{a}_{\overline{k+1}|} = \sum_{t=0}^{k} v^t$$

and

$$\sum_{k=t}^{\infty} {}_{k|}q_x = \sum_{k=t}^{\infty} ({}_k p_x - {}_{k+1}p_x) = {}_t p_x.$$

Then

$$\sum_{k=0}^{\infty} \ddot{a}_{\overline{k+1}|} \, {}_{k|}q_x = \sum_{k=0}^{\infty} \sum_{t=0}^{k} v^t \, {}_{k|}q_x$$

$$= q_x + (1+v) \, {}_{1|}q_x + (1+v+v^2) \, {}_{2|}q_x$$
$$+ (1+v+v^2+v^3) \, {}_{3|}q_x + \cdots .$$

Changing the order of summation on the right-hand side (that is, collecting together terms in powers of v) gives

$$\sum_{k=0}^{\infty} \sum_{t=0}^{k} v^t \, {}_{k|}q_x = \sum_{t=0}^{\infty} \sum_{k=t}^{\infty} v^t \, {}_{k|}q_x$$

$$= \sum_{t=0}^{\infty} v^t \sum_{k=t}^{\infty} {}_{k|}q_x$$

$$= \sum_{t=0}^{\infty} v^t \, {}_t p_x$$

as required. $\qquad\qquad\qquad\qquad\qquad\qquad\qquad\qquad\qquad\square$

5.4.2 Term annuity-due

Now suppose we wish to value a term annuity-due of 1 per year. We assume the annuity is payable annually to a life now aged x for a maximum of n years. Thus, payments are made at times $k = 0, 1, 2, \ldots, n-1$, provided that (x) has survived to age $x + k$. The present value of this annuity is Y, say, where

$$Y = \begin{cases} \ddot{a}_{\overline{K_x+1}|} & \text{if } K_x = 0, 1, \ldots, n-1, \\ \ddot{a}_{\overline{n}|} & \text{if } K_x \geq n, \end{cases}$$

that is

$$Y = \ddot{a}_{\overline{\min(K_x+1,n)}|} = \frac{1 - v^{\min(K_x+1,n)}}{d}.$$

The EPV of this annuity is denoted $\ddot{a}_{x:\overline{n}|}$.

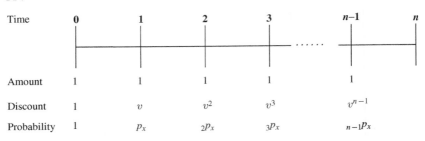

Figure 5.2 Time-line diagram for term life annuity-due.

We have seen the random variable $v^{\min(K_x+1,n)}$ before, in Section 4.4.7, where the EPV $A_{x:\overline{n}|}$ is derived. Thus, the EPV of the annuity can be determined as

$$\ddot{a}_{x:\overline{n}|} = E[Y] = \frac{1 - E[v^{\min(K_x+1,n)}]}{d}$$

that is,

$$\ddot{a}_{x:\overline{n}|} = \frac{1 - A_{x:\overline{n}|}}{d}. \qquad (5.9)$$

The time-line for the term annuity-due cash flow is shown in Figure 5.2. Notice that, because the payments are made in advance, there is no payment due at time n, the end of the annuity term.

Using Figure 5.2, and summing the EPVs of the individual payments, we have

$$\ddot{a}_{x:\overline{n}|} = 1 + v\, p_x + v^2\, {}_2p_x + v^3\, {}_3p_x + \cdots + v^{n-1}\, {}_{n-1}p_x$$

that is

$$\ddot{a}_{x:\overline{n}|} = \sum_{t=0}^{n-1} v^t\, {}_tp_x. \qquad (5.10)$$

Also, we can write the EPV as

$$\ddot{a}_{x:\overline{n}|} = \sum_{k=0}^{n-1} \ddot{a}_{\overline{k+1}|}\, {}_{k|}q_x + {}_np_x\, \ddot{a}_{\overline{n}|}$$

adapting equation (5.8) above. The second term here arises from the second term in the definition of Y – that is, if the annuitant survives for the full term, then the payments constitute an n-year annuity.

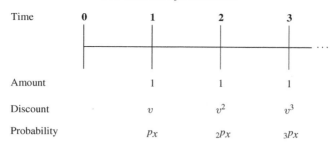

Time	0	1	2	3	

Figure 5.3 Time-line diagram for whole life immediate annuity.

5.4.3 Whole life immediate annuity

Now consider a whole life annuity of 1 per year payable in arrear, conditional on the survival of (x) to the payment dates. We use the term immediate annuity to refer to an annuity under which payments are made at the end of the time periods, rather than at the beginning. The actuarial notation for the EPV of this annuity is a_x, and the time-line for the annuity cash flow is shown in Figure 5.3.

Let Y^* denote the present value random variable for the whole life immediate annuity. Using the indicator random variable approach we have

$$Y^* = v\,\mathrm{I}(T_x > 1) + v^2\,\mathrm{I}(T_x > 2) + v^3\,\mathrm{I}(T_x > 3) + v^4\,\mathrm{I}(T_x > 4) + \cdots.$$

We can see from this expression and from the time-line, that the difference in present value between the annuity-due and the immediate annuity payable in arrear is simply the first payment under the annuity-due, which, under the annuity-due, is assumed to be paid at time $t = 0$ with certainty.

So, if Y is the random variable for the present value of the whole life annuity payable in advance, and Y^* is the random variable for the present value of the whole life annuity payable in arrear, we have $Y^* = Y - 1$, so that $E[Y^*] = E[Y] - 1$, and hence

$$a_x = \ddot{a}_x - 1. \tag{5.11}$$

Also, from equation (5.5) and the fact that $Y^* = Y - 1$, we have

$$V[Y^*] = V[Y] = \frac{{}^2A_x - A_x^2}{d^2}.$$

5.4.4 Term immediate annuity

The EPV of a term immediate annuity of 1 per year is denoted $a_{x:\overline{n}|}$. Under this annuity payments of 1 are made at times $k = 1, 2, \ldots, n$, conditional on the survival of the annuitant.

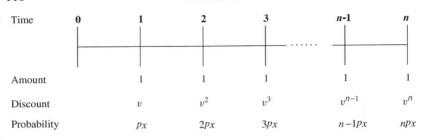

Figure 5.4 Time-line diagram for term life immediate annuity.

The random variable for the present value is

$$Y = a_{\overline{\min(K_x,n)}|},$$

and the time-line for the annuity cash flow is given in Figure 5.4.

Summing the EPVs of the individual payments, we have

$$a_{x:\overline{n}|} = v\, p_x + v^2\, {}_2p_x + v^3\, {}_3p_x + \cdots + v^n\, {}_np_x = \sum_{t=1}^{n} v^t\, {}_tp_x. \qquad (5.12)$$

The difference between the annuity-due EPV, $\ddot{a}_{x:\overline{n}|}$, and the immediate annuity EPV, $a_{x:\overline{n}|}$, is found by differencing equations (5.10) and (5.12), to give

$$\ddot{a}_{x:\overline{n}|} - a_{x:\overline{n}|} = 1 - v^n\, {}_np_x$$

so that

$$a_{x:\overline{n}|} = \ddot{a}_{x:\overline{n}|} - 1 + v^n\, {}_np_x. \qquad (5.13)$$

The difference comes from the timing of the first payment under the annuity due and the last payment under the immediate annuity.

5.5 Annuities payable continuously

5.5.1 Whole life continuous annuity

In practice annuities are payable at discrete time intervals, but if these intervals are close together, for example weekly, it is convenient to treat payments as being made continuously. Consider now the case when the annuity is payable continuously at a rate of 1 per year as long as (x) survives. If the annuity is payable weekly (and we assume 52 weeks per year), then each week, the annuity payment is $1/52$. If payments were daily, for an annuity of 1 per year, the daily payment would be $1/365$. Similarly, for an infinitesimal interval $(t, t+dt)$ the payment under the annuity is dt provided (x) is alive through the interval.

The EPV is denoted $\bar{a}_x$. The underlying random variable is Y, say, where

$$Y = \bar{a}_{\overline{T_x}|}.$$

Analogous to the annual annuity-due, we can derive formulae for the EPV of the annuity in three different ways.

The first approach is to use the annuity-certain formula

$$\bar{a}_{\overline{n}|} = \frac{1 - v^n}{\delta}$$

so that

$$Y = \frac{1 - v^{T_x}}{\delta}$$

and

$$\bar{a}_x = \mathrm{E}[Y] = \frac{1 - \mathrm{E}[v^{T_x}]}{\delta}.$$

That is,

$$\boxed{\bar{a}_x = \frac{1 - \bar{A}_x}{\delta}.} \tag{5.14}$$

Using this formulation for the random variable Y, we can also directly derive the variance for the continuous annuity present value from the variance for the continuous insurance benefit

$$\mathrm{V}[Y] = \mathrm{V}\left[\frac{1 - v^{T_x}}{\delta}\right] = \frac{^2\bar{A}_x - \bar{A}_x^2}{\delta^2}.$$

The second approach is to use the sum (here an integral) of the product of the amount paid in each infinitesimal interval $(t, t + dt)$, the discount factor for the interval and the probability that the payment is made. For each such interval, the amount is dt, the discount factor is $e^{-\delta t}$ and the probability of payment is $_t p_x$, giving

$$\boxed{\bar{a}_x = \int_0^\infty e^{-\delta t} \, _t p_x \, dt.} \tag{5.15}$$

We remark that this EPV can also be derived using indicator random variables by expressing the present value as

$$Y = \int_0^\infty e^{-\delta t} \, \mathrm{I}(T_x > t) \, dt.$$

The development of formula (5.15) is illustrated in Figure 5.5; we show the contribution to the integral from the contingent annuity payment made in an

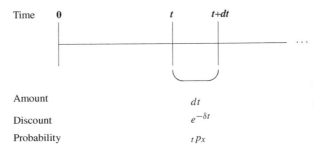

Figure 5.5 Time-line diagram for continuous whole life annuity.

infinitesimal interval of time $(t, t + dt)$. The interval is so small that payments can be treated as being made exactly at t.

Finally, we can directly write down the EPV from the distribution of T_x as

$$\bar{a}_x = \int_0^\infty \bar{a}_{\overline{t}|} {}_t p_x \, \mu_{x+t} \, dt.$$

We can evaluate this using integration by parts, noting that if we differentiate equation (5.2) we get

$$\frac{d}{dt} \bar{a}_{\overline{t}|} = v^t = e^{-\delta t}.$$

Then

$$\begin{aligned}
\bar{a}_x &= \int_0^\infty \bar{a}_{\overline{t}|} \frac{d}{dt}(-{}_t p_x) dt \\
&= -\left(\bar{a}_{\overline{t}|} \, {}_t p_x \Big|_0^\infty - \int_0^\infty {}_t p_x \, e^{-\delta t} dt \right) \\
&= \int_0^\infty e^{-\delta t} \, {}_t p_x \, dt.
\end{aligned}$$

When $\delta = 0$, we see that $\bar{a}_x$ is equal to $\overset{\circ}{e}_x$, the complete expectation of life.

5.5.2 Term continuous annuity

The term continuous life annuity present value random variable

$$\bar{a}_{\overline{\min(T_x,n)}|} = \frac{1 - v^{\min(T_x,n)}}{\delta}$$

has EPV denoted by $\bar{a}_{x:\overline{n}|}$. Analogous to the term annuity-due, we have three expressions for this EPV.

Using results for endowment insurance functions from Section 4.4.7, we have

$$\bar{a}_{x:\overline{n}|} = \frac{1 - \bar{A}_{x:\overline{n}|}}{\delta}. \tag{5.16}$$

Using the indicator random variable approach we have

$$\bar{a}_{x:\overline{n}|} = \int_0^n e^{-\delta t} \, {}_t p_x \, dt, \tag{5.17}$$

and taking the expected value of the present value random variable we obtain

$$\bar{a}_{x:\overline{n}|} = \int_0^n \bar{a}_{\overline{t}|} \, {}_t p_x \, \mu_{x+t} \, dt + \bar{a}_{\overline{n}|} \, {}_n p_x.$$

One way to understand the difference between the second and third approaches is to see that in the second approach we integrate over the possible payment dates, and in the third approach we integrate over the possible dates of death. The third approach is generally the least useful in practice.

5.6 Annuities payable 1/$m$thly

5.6.1 Introduction

For premiums, annuities and pension benefits, the annual form of the annuity would be unusual. Premiums are more commonly payable monthly, quarterly, or sometimes weekly. Pension benefits and purchased annuities are payable with similar frequency to salary benefits, which means that weekly and monthly annuities are common.

We can define the present value of an annuity payable m times per year in terms of the random variable $K_x^{(m)}$, which was introduced in Section 4.4.3. Recall that $K_x^{(m)}$ is the complete future lifetime rounded down to the lower $1/m$th of a year.

We will also use the formula for the present value of a $1/m$thly annuity-certain. For example, $\ddot{a}_{\overline{n}|}^{(m)}$ is the present value of an annuity of 1 per year, payable each year, in m instalments of $1/m$ for n years, with the first payment at time $t = 0$ and the final payment at time $n - \frac{1}{m}$. It is important to remember that $\ddot{a}_{\overline{n}|}^{(m)}$ is an **annual** factor, that is, it values a payment of 1 per year, and therefore for valuing annuities for other amounts, we need to multiply the $\ddot{a}_{\overline{n}|}^{(m)}$ factor by the **annual rate of annuity payment.**

Suppose we are interested in valuing an annuity of $12\,000$ per year, payable monthly in advance to a life aged 60. Each monthly payment is $1000. The relevant future lifetime random variable is $K_{60}^{(12)}$. If $K_{60}^{(12)} = 0$, then (60) died in the first month, there was a single payment made at $t = 0$ of \$1000, and the present value is

$$12\,000 \times \tfrac{1}{12} = 12\,000\,\ddot{a}^{(12)}_{\overline{1/12}|}.$$

If $K^{(12)}_{60} = 1/12$ then (60) died in the second month, there are two monthly annuity payments, each of \$1000, and the relevant annuity factor is

$$12\,000 \left(\tfrac{1}{12} + \tfrac{1}{12} v^{\frac{1}{12}} \right) = 12\,000\,\ddot{a}^{(12)}_{\overline{2/12}|}.$$

Continuing, we see that the present value random variable for this annuity can be written as

$$12\,000 \left(\tfrac{1}{12} + \tfrac{1}{12} v^{\frac{1}{12}} + \tfrac{1}{12} v^{\frac{2}{12}} + \cdots + \tfrac{1}{12} v^{K^{(12)}_x} \right) = 12\,000\,\ddot{a}^{(12)}_{\overline{K^{(12)}_{60}+1/12}|}.$$

5.6.2 *Whole life annuities payable* 1/*m*thly

Consider first an annuity of total amount 1 per year, payable in advance m times per year throughout the lifetime of (x), with each payment being $1/m$. Figure 5.6 shows the whole life $1/m$thly annuity time-line cash flow.

The present value random variable for this annuity is

$$\ddot{a}^{(m)}_{\overline{K^{(m)}_x+\frac{1}{m}}|} = \frac{1 - v^{K^{(m)}_x+\frac{1}{m}}}{d^{(m)}}.$$

The EPV of this annuity is denoted by $\ddot{a}^{(m)}_x$ and is given by

$$\ddot{a}^{(m)}_x = \frac{1 - \mathrm{E}[v^{K^{(m)}_x+\frac{1}{m}}]}{d^{(m)}}.$$

Figure 5.6 Time-line diagram for whole life $1/m$thly annuity-due.

giving

$$\ddot{a}_x^{(m)} = \frac{1 - A_x^{(m)}}{d^{(m)}}.$$

(5.18)

Using the indicator random variable approach we find that

$$\ddot{a}_x^{(m)} = \sum_{r=0}^{\infty} \frac{1}{m} v^{r/m} \, {}_{\frac{r}{m}}p_x.$$

(5.19)

For annuities payable $1/m$thly in arrear, we can use a comparison with the $1/m$thly annuity-due. Similar to the annual annuity case, the only difference in the whole life case is the first payment, of $\$1/m$, so that the EPV of the $1/m$thly immediate annuity is

$$a_x^{(m)} = \ddot{a}_x^{(m)} - \frac{1}{m}.$$

(5.20)

5.6.3 Term annuities payable 1/mthly

We can extend the above derivation to cover the term life annuity case, when the $1/m$thly annuity payment is limited to a maximum of n years. Consider now an annuity of total amount 1 per year, payable in advance m times per year throughout the lifetime of (x) for a maximum of n years, with each payment being $1/m$. The payments, associated probabilities and discount factors for the $1/m$thly term annuity-due are shown in the time-line diagram in Figure 5.7.

The present value random variable for this annuity is

$$\ddot{a}_{\overline{\min\left(K_x^{(m)}+\frac{1}{m},n\right)}}^{(m)} = \frac{1 - v^{\min\left(K_x^{(m)}+\frac{1}{m},n\right)}}{d^{(m)}}.$$

Figure 5.7 Time-line diagram for term life $1/m$thly annuity-due.

The EPV of this annuity is denoted by $\ddot{a}_{x:\overline{n}|}^{(m)}$ and is given by

$$\ddot{a}_{x:\overline{n}|}^{(m)} = \frac{1 - \mathrm{E}[v^{\min(K_x^{(m)} + \frac{1}{m}, n)}]}{d^{(m)}}$$

so that

$$\boxed{\ddot{a}_{x:\overline{n}|}^{(m)} = \frac{1 - A_{x:\overline{n}|}^{(m)}}{d^{(m)}}.} \qquad (5.21)$$

Using the indicator random variable approach we find that

$$\boxed{\ddot{a}_{x:\overline{n}|}^{(m)} = \sum_{r=0}^{mn-1} \frac{1}{m} v^{r/m} \, _{\frac{r}{m}}p_x.} \qquad (5.22)$$

For the $1/m$thly term immediate annuity, by comparison with the $1/m$thly annuity-due, the difference is the first payment under the annuity-due, with EPV $1/m$, and the final payment under the immediate annuity, with EPV $\frac{1}{m} v^n {}_n p_x$, so that

$$a_{x:\overline{n}|}^{(m)} = \ddot{a}_{x:\overline{n}|}^{(m)} - \frac{1}{m}\left(1 - v^n \, _n p_x\right). \qquad (5.23)$$

This is analogous to the result in equation (5.3) for the annuity-certain. Further, by setting $m = 1$ in equations (5.19) and (5.22) we obtain equations (5.7) and (5.10) for $\ddot{a}_x$ and $\ddot{a}_{x:\overline{n}|}$. Also, by letting $m \to \infty$ in equations (5.19) and (5.22) we obtain equations (5.15) and (5.17) for continuous annuities, $\bar{a}_x$ and $\bar{a}_{x:\overline{n}|}$.

We can derive expressions for the EPV of other types of annuity payable m times per year, and indeed we can also find higher moments of present values as we did for annuities payable annually.

5.7 Comparison of annuities by payment frequency

In Table 5.1 we show values for a_x, $a_x^{(4)}$, $\ddot{a}_x$, $\ddot{a}_x^{(4)}$ and $\bar{a}_x$ for $x = 20, 40, 60$ and 80, using the Standard Ultimate Survival Model from Section 4.3, with interest of 5% per year. Using equations (5.11), (5.20), (5.15), (5.19) and (5.7), we obtain the values shown in Table 5.1. We observe that each set of values decreases with age, reflecting the shorter expected life span as age increases. We also have, for each age, the ordering

$$a_x < a_x^{(4)} < \bar{a}_x < \ddot{a}_x^{(4)} < \ddot{a}_x.$$

Table 5.1 *Values of* a_x, $a_x^{(4)}$, $\bar{a}_x$, $\ddot{a}_x^{(4)}$ *and* $\ddot{a}_x$.

x	a_x	$a_x^{(4)}$	$\bar{a}_x$	$\ddot{a}_x^{(4)}$	$\ddot{a}_x$
20	18.966	19.338	19.462	19.588	19.966
40	17.458	17.829	17.954	18.079	18.458
60	13.904	14.275	14.400	14.525	14.904
80	7.548	7.917	8.042	8.167	8.548

There are two reasons for this ordering.

- While the life is alive, the payments in each year sum to 1 under each annuity, but on average, the payments under the annuity-due are paid earlier. The time value of money means that the value of an annuity with earlier payments will be higher than an annuity with later payments (for interest rates greater than zero), so the annuity values are in increasing order from the latest average payment date (a_x payments are at each year end) to the earliest ($\ddot{a}_x$ payments are at the start of each year).

- In the year that (x) dies, the different annuities pay different amounts. Under the annual annuity-due the full year's payment of $1 is paid, as the life is alive at the payment date at the start of the year. Under the annual immediate annuity, in the year of death no payment is made as the life does not survive to the payment date at the year end. For the $1/m$thly and continuous annuities, less than the full year's annuity may be paid in the year of death.

For example, suppose the life dies after seven months. Under the annual annuity-due, the full annuity payment is made for that year, at the start of the year. Under the quarterly annuity due, three payments are made, each of 1/4 of the total annual amount, at times 0, 1/4 and 1/2. The first year's final payment, due at time 3/4, is not made, as the life does not survive to that date. Under the continuous annuity, the life collects 7/12ths of the annual amount. Under the quarterly immediate annuity, the life collects payments at times 1/4, 1/2, and misses the two payments due at times 3/4 and 1. Under the annual immediate annuity, the life collects no annuity payments at all, as the due date is the year end.

This second point explains why we cannot make a simple interest adjustment to relate the annuity-due and the continuous annuity. The situation here is different from the insurance benefits; A_x and $A_x^{(4)}$, for example, both value a payment of $1 in the year of death, A_x at the end of the year, and $A_x^{(4)}$ at the end of the quarter year of death. There is no difference in the amount of the payment, only in the timing. For the annuities, the difference between $\ddot{a}_x$ and

Table 5.2 *Values of* $a_{x:\overline{10|}}$, $a^{(4)}_{x:\overline{10|}}$, $\bar{a}_{x:\overline{10|}}$, $\ddot{a}^{(4)}_{x:\overline{10|}}$ *and* $\ddot{a}_{x:\overline{10|}}$.

x	$a_{x:\overline{10|}}$	$a^{(4)}_{x:\overline{10|}}$	$\bar{a}_{x:\overline{10|}}$	$\ddot{a}^{(4)}_{x:\overline{10|}}$	$\ddot{a}_{x:\overline{10|}}$
20	7.711	7.855	7.904	7.952	8.099
40	7.696	7.841	7.889	7.938	8.086
60	7.534	7.691	7.743	7.796	7.956
80	6.128	6.373	6.456	6.539	6.789

$\ddot{a}^{(4)}_x$ arises from differences in both cashflow timing and benefit amount in the year of death.

We also note from Table 5.1 that the $\bar{a}_x$ values are close to being half way between a_x and $\ddot{a}_x$, suggesting the approximation $\bar{a}_x \approx a_x + \frac{1}{2}$. We will see in Section 5.11.3 that there is indeed a way of calculating an approximation to $\bar{a}_x$ from a_x, but it involves an extra adjustment term to a_x.

Example 5.2 Using the Standard Ultimate Survival Model, with 5% per year interest, calculate values of $a_{x:\overline{10|}}$, $a^{(4)}_{x:\overline{10|}}$, $\ddot{a}_{x:\overline{10|}}$, $\ddot{a}^{(4)}_{x:\overline{10|}}$ and $\bar{a}_{x:\overline{10|}}$ for $x = 20, 40,$ 60 and 80, and comment.

Solution 5.2 Using equations (5.10), (5.12), (5.17), (5.23) and (5.22) with $n = 10$ we obtain the values shown in Table 5.2.

We note that for a given annuity function, the values do not vary greatly with age, since the probability of death in a 10-year period is small. That means, for example, that the second term in equation (5.10) is much greater than the first term. The present value of an annuity certain provides an upper bound for each set of values. For example, for any age x, $a_{x:\overline{10|}} < a_{\overline{10|}} = 7.722$ and $\ddot{a}^{(4)}_{x:\overline{10|}} < \ddot{a}^{(4)}_{\overline{10|}} = 7.962$.

Due to the differences in timing of payments, and in amounts for lives who die during the 10-year annuity term, we have the same ordering of annuity values by payment frequency for any age x:

$$a_{x:\overline{10|}} < a^{(4)}_{x:\overline{10|}} < \bar{a}_{x:\overline{10|}} < \ddot{a}^{(4)}_{x:\overline{10|}} < \ddot{a}_{x:\overline{10|}}.$$

$\square$

5.8 Deferred annuities

A deferred annuity is an annuity under which the first payment occurs at some specified future time. Consider an annuity payable to an individual now aged x under which annual payments of 1 will commence at age $x + u$, where u is an integer, and will continue until the death of (x). This is an annuity-due deferred u years. In standard actuarial notation, the EPV of this annuity is denoted by

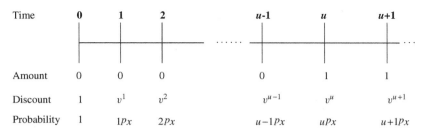

Figure 5.8 Time-line diagram for deferred annual annuity-due.

$_u|\ddot{a}_x$. Note that we have used the format $_u|...$ to indicate deferment before, both for mortality probabilities $(_u|_t q_x)$ and for insurance benefits $(_u|A_x)$. Figure 5.8 shows the time-line for a u-year deferred annuity-due.

Combining Figure 5.8 with the time-line for a u-year term annuity, see Figure 5.2, we can see that the combination of the payments under a u-year temporary annuity-due and a u-year deferred annuity-due gives the same sequence of payments as under a lifetime annuity in advance, so we obtain

$$\ddot{a}_{x:\overline{u}|} + _u|\ddot{a}_x = \ddot{a}_x, \tag{5.24}$$

or, equivalently,

$$\boxed{_u|\ddot{a}_x = \ddot{a}_x - \ddot{a}_{x:\overline{u}|}.} \tag{5.25}$$

Similarly, the EPV of an annuity payable continuously at rate 1 per year to a life now aged x, commencing at age $x + u$, is denoted by $_u|\bar{a}_x$ and given by

$$_u|\bar{a}_x = \bar{a}_x - \bar{a}_{x:\overline{u}|}.$$

Summing the EPVs of the individual payments for the deferred whole life annuity-due gives

$$_u|\ddot{a}_x = v^u \,_u p_x + v^{u+1} \,_{u+1} p_x + v^{u+2} \,_{u+2} p_x + \cdots$$
$$= v^u \,_u p_x \left(1 + v \, p_{x+u} + v^2 \,_2 p_{x+u} + \cdots \right)$$

so that

$$_u|\ddot{a}_x = v^u \,_u p_x \, \ddot{a}_{x+u} = _u E_x \, \ddot{a}_{x+u}. \tag{5.26}$$

We see again that the pure endowment function acts like a discount function. In fact, we can use the $_u E_x$ function to find the EPV of any deferred benefit. For example, for a deferred term immediate annuity,

$$_u|a_{x:\overline{n}|} = _u E_x \, a_{x+u:\overline{n}|},$$

and for an annuity-due payable $1/m$thly,

$$_u|\ddot{a}_x^{(m)} = {}_uE_x\,\ddot{a}_{x+u}^{(m)}. \tag{5.27}$$

This result can be helpful when working with tables. Suppose we have available a table of whole life annuity-due values, say $\ddot{a}_x$, along with the life table function l_x, and we need the term annuity value $\ddot{a}_{x:\overline{n}|}$. Then, using equations (5.24) and (5.26), we have

$$\ddot{a}_{x:\overline{n}|} = \ddot{a}_x - v^n\,{}_np_x\,\ddot{a}_{x+n}. \tag{5.28}$$

For $1/m$thly payments, the corresponding formula is

$$\ddot{a}_{x:\overline{n}|}^{(m)} = \ddot{a}_x^{(m)} - v^n\,{}_np_x\,\ddot{a}_{x+n}^{(m)}. \tag{5.29}$$

Example 5.3 Let Y_1, Y_2 and Y_3 denote present value random variables for a u-year deferred whole life annuity-due, a u-year term annuity-due and a whole life annuity-due, respectively. Show that $Y_3 = Y_1 + Y_2$. Assume annual payments.

Solution 5.3 The present value random variable for a u-year deferred whole life annuity-due, with annual payments is

$$
\begin{aligned}
Y_1 &= \begin{cases} 0 & \text{if } K_x \le u - 1, \\ v^u\ddot{a}_{\overline{K_x+1-u}|} & \text{if } K_x \ge u, \end{cases} \\
&= \begin{cases} 0 & \text{if } K_x \le u - 1, \\ \ddot{a}_{\overline{K_x+1}|} - \ddot{a}_{\overline{u}|} & \text{if } K_x \ge u. \end{cases}
\end{aligned} \tag{5.30}
$$

From Section 5.4.2 we have

$$
Y_2 = \begin{cases} \ddot{a}_{\overline{K_x+1}|} & \text{if } K_x \le u - 1, \\ \ddot{a}_{\overline{u}|} & \text{if } K_x \ge u. \end{cases}
$$

Hence

$$
Y_1 + Y_2 = \begin{cases} \ddot{a}_{\overline{K_x+1}|} & \text{if } K_x \le u - 1, \\ \ddot{a}_{\overline{K_x+1}|} & \text{if } K_x \ge u, \end{cases} \quad = \ddot{a}_{\overline{K_x+1}|} \quad = Y_3,
$$

as required.   □

We use deferred annuities as building blocks in later sections, noting that an n-year term annuity, with any payment frequency, can be decomposed as the sum of n deferred annuities, each with term 1 year. So, for example,

$$\bar{a}_{x:\overline{n}|} = \sum_{u=0}^{n-1} {}_u|\bar{a}_{x:\overline{1}|}. \tag{5.31}$$

5.9 Guaranteed annuities

A common feature of pension benefits is that the pension annuity is guaranteed to be paid for some period even if the life dies before the end of the period. For example, a pension benefit payable to a life aged 65, might be guaranteed for 5, 10 or even 15 years.

Suppose an annuity-due of 1 per year is paid annually to (x), and is guaranteed for a period of n years. Then the payment due at k years is paid whether or not (x) is then alive if $k = 0, 1, \ldots, n-1$, but is paid only if (x) is alive at age $x + k$ for $k = n, n+1, \ldots$. The present value random variable for this benefit is

$$
Y = \begin{cases} \ddot{a}_{\overline{n}|} & \text{if } K_x \leq n-1, \\ \ddot{a}_{\overline{K_x+1}|} & \text{if } K_x \geq n \end{cases}
$$

$$
= \begin{cases} \ddot{a}_{\overline{n}|} & \text{if } K_x \leq n-1, \\ \ddot{a}_{\overline{n}|} + \ddot{a}_{\overline{K_x+1}|} - \ddot{a}_{\overline{n}|} & \text{if } K_x \geq n \end{cases}
$$

$$
= \ddot{a}_{\overline{n}|} + \begin{cases} 0 & \text{if } K_x \leq n-1, \\ \ddot{a}_{\overline{K_x+1}|} - \ddot{a}_{\overline{n}|} & \text{if } K_x \geq n \end{cases}
$$

$$
= \ddot{a}_{\overline{n}|} + Y_1,
$$

where Y_1 denotes the present value of an n-year deferred annuity-due of 1 per year, from equation (5.30), and

$$
E[Y_1] = {}_{n|}\ddot{a}_x = {}_nE_x\, \ddot{a}_{x+n}.
$$

The expected present value of the unit n-year guaranteed annuity-due is denoted $\ddot{a}_{\overline{x:\overline{n}|}}$, so

$$
\ddot{a}_{\overline{x:\overline{n}|}} = \ddot{a}_{\overline{n}|} + {}_nE_x\, \ddot{a}_{x+n}. \tag{5.32}
$$

Figure 5.9 shows the time-line for an n-year guaranteed unit whole life annuity-due. This time-line looks like the regular whole life annuity-due time-line, except that the first n payments, from time $t = 0$ to time $t = n-1$, are certain and not life contingent.

We can derive similar results for guaranteed benefits payable $1/m$thly; for example, a monthly whole life annuity-due guaranteed for n years has EPV

$$
\ddot{a}_{\overline{x:\overline{n}|}}^{(12)} = \ddot{a}_{\overline{n}|}^{(12)} + {}_nE_x\, \ddot{a}_{x+n}^{(12)}.
$$

Example 5.4 A pension plan member is entitled to a benefit of $1000 per month, in advance, for life from age 65, with no guarantee. She can opt to take a lower benefit, with a 10-year guarantee. The revised benefit is calculated to

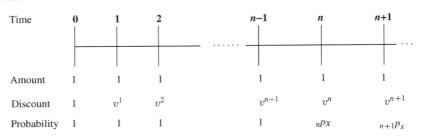

Figure 5.9 Time-line diagram for guaranteed annual annuity-due.

have equal EPV at age 65 to the original benefit. Calculate the revised benefit using the Standard Ultimate Survival Model, with interest at 5% per year.

Solution 5.4 Let B denote the revised monthly benefit. To determine B we must equate the EPV of the original benefit with that of the revised benefit. The resulting **equation of EPVs** is usually called an **equation of value**. Our equation of value is

$$12\,000\,\ddot{a}_{65}^{(12)} = 12\,B\,\ddot{a}_{\overline{65:\overline{10}|}}^{(12)}$$

where $\ddot{a}_{65}^{(12)} = 13.0870$, and

$$\ddot{a}_{\overline{65:\overline{10}|}}^{(12)} = \ddot{a}_{\overline{10}|}^{(12)} + {}_{10}p_{65}\,v^{10}\,\ddot{a}_{75}^{(12)} = 13.3791.$$

Thus, the revised monthly benefit is $B = \$978.17$. So the pension plan member can gain the security of the 10-year guarantee at a cost of a reduction of $21.83 per month in her pension.   □

5.10 Increasing annuities

In the previous sections we have considered annuities with level payments. Some of the annuities which arise in actuarial work are not level. For example, annuity payments may increase over time. For these annuities, we are generally interested in determining the EPV, and are rarely concerned with higher moments. To calculate higher moments it is generally necessary to use first principles, and a computer.

The best approach for calculating the EPV of non-level annuities is to use the indicator random variable, or time-line, approach – that is, sum over all the payment dates the product of the amount of the payment, the probability of payment (that is, the probability that the life survives to the payment date) and the appropriate discount factor.

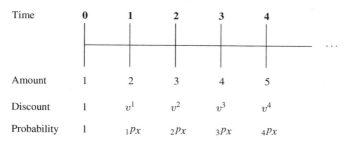

Figure 5.10 Time-line diagram for arithmetically increasing annual annuity-due.

5.10.1 Arithmetically increasing annuities

We first consider annuities under which the amount of the annuity payment increases arithmetically with time. Consider an increasing annuity-due where the amount of the annuity is $t + 1$ at times $t = 0, 1, 2, \ldots$ provided that (x) is alive at time t. The time-line is shown in Figure 5.10.

The EPV of the annuity is denoted by $(I\ddot{a})_x$ in standard actuarial notation. From the diagram we see that

$$\boxed{(I\ddot{a})_x = \sum_{t=0}^{\infty} v^t (t + 1)\, {}_t p_x.} \tag{5.33}$$

Similarly, if the annuity is payable for a maximum of n payments rather than for the whole life of (x), the EPV, denoted by $(I\ddot{a})_{x:\overline{n}|}$ in standard actuarial notation, is given by

$$\boxed{(I\ddot{a})_{x:\overline{n}|} = \sum_{t=0}^{n-1} v^t (t + 1)\, {}_t p_x.} \tag{5.34}$$

If the annuity is payable continuously, with the payments increasing by 1 at each year end, so that the rate of payment in the tth year is constant and equal to t, for $t = 1, 2, \ldots, n$, then we may consider the n-year temporary annuity as a sum of one-year deferred annuities. By analogy with formula (5.31), the EPV of this annuity, denoted in standard actuarial notation by $(I\bar{a})_{x:\overline{n}|}$, is

$$(I\bar{a})_{x:\overline{n}|} = \sum_{m=0}^{n-1} (m + 1)\, {}_m|\bar{a}_{x:\overline{1}|}.$$

We also have standard actuarial notation for the continuous annuity under which the rate of payment at time $t > 0$ is t; that is, the rate of payment is changing continuously. The notation for the EPV of this annuity is $(\bar{I}\bar{a})_x$ if it

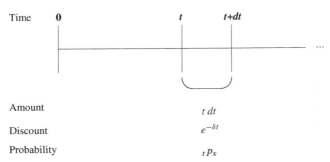

Figure 5.11 Time-line diagram for increasing continuous whole life annuity.

is a whole life annuity, and $(\bar{I}\bar{a})_{x:\overline{n}|}$ if it is a term annuity. For every infinitesimal interval, $(t, t+dt)$, the amount of annuity paid, if the life (x) is still alive, is $t \, dt$, the probability of payment is $_t p_x$ and the discount function is $e^{-\delta t} = v^t$. The time-line is shown in Figure 5.11.

To determine the EPV we integrate over all the possible intervals $(t, t + dt)$, so that

$$(\bar{I}\bar{a})_{x:\overline{n}|} = \int_0^n t \, e^{-\delta t} \, _t p_x \, dt.$$ (5.35)

5.10.2 Geometrically increasing annuities

An annuitant may be interested in purchasing an annuity that increases geometrically, to offset the effect of inflation on the purchasing power of the income. The approach is similar to the geometrically increasing insurance benefit which was considered in Examples 4.8 and 4.9.

Example 5.5 Consider an annuity-due with annual payments where the amount of the annuity is $(1 + j)^t$ at times $t = 0, 1, 2, \ldots, n - 1$ provided that (x) is alive at time t. Derive an expression for the EPV of this benefit, and simplify as far as possible.

Solution 5.5 First, consider the time-line diagram in Figure 5.12.
  By summing the product of

- the amount of the payment at time t,
- the discount factor for time t, and
- the probability that the payment is made at time t,

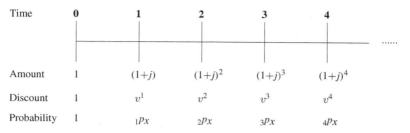

Figure 5.12 Time-line diagram for geometrically increasing annual annuity-due.

over all possible values of t, we obtain the EPV as

$$\sum_{t=0}^{n-1} (1+j)^t \, v^t \, {}_tp_x = \ddot{a}_{x:\overline{n}|i*}$$

where $\ddot{a}_{x:\overline{n}|i*}$ is the EPV of a term annuity-due evaluated at interest rate i^* where

$$i^* = \frac{1+i}{1+j} - 1 = \frac{i-j}{1+j}.$$

$\square$

5.11 Evaluating annuity functions

If we have full information about the survival function for a life, then we can use summation or numerical integration to compute the EPV of any annuity. Often, though, we have only integer age information, for example when the survival function information is derived from a life table with integer age information only. In this section we consider how to evaluate the EPV of $1/m$thly and continuous annuities given only the EPVs of annuities at integer ages. For example, we may have $\ddot{a}_x$ values for integer x. We present two methods that are commonly used, and we explore the accuracy of these methods for a fairly typical (Makeham) mortality model. First we consider recursive calculation of EPVs of annuities.

5.11.1 Recursions

In a spreadsheet, with values for ${}_tp_x$ available, we may calculate $\ddot{a}_x$ using a backward recursion. We assume that there is an integer limiting age, ω, so that $q_{\omega-1} = 1$. First, we set $\ddot{a}_{\omega-1} = 1$. The backward recursion for $x = \omega-2, \omega-3, \omega - 4, \ldots$ is

$$\boxed{\ddot{a}_x = 1 + v \, p_x \, \ddot{a}_{x+1}} \tag{5.36}$$

since

$$\ddot{a}_x = 1 + v \, p_x + v^2 \, {}_2p_x + v^3 \, {}_3p_x + \cdots$$

$$= 1 + v \, p_x \left(1 + v \, p_{x+1} + v^2 \, {}_2p_{x+1} + \cdots \right)$$

$$= 1 + v \, p_x \, \ddot{a}_{x+1}.$$

Similarly, for the $1/m$thly annuity due,

$$\ddot{a}^{(m)}_{\omega-1/m} = \frac{1}{m},$$

and the backward recursion for $x = \omega - \frac{2}{m}, \; \omega - \frac{3}{m}, \; \omega - \frac{4}{m}, \ldots$ is

$$\ddot{a}^{(m)}_x = \frac{1}{m} + v^{\frac{1}{m}} \, {}_{\frac{1}{m}}p_x \, \ddot{a}^{(m)}_{x+\frac{1}{m}}. \tag{5.37}$$

We can calculate EPVs for term annuities and deferred annuities from the whole life annuity EPVs, using, for example, equations (5.24) and (5.26).

To find the EPV of an annuity payable continuously we can use numerical integration. Note, however, that Woolhouse's formula, which is described in Section 5.11.3, gives an excellent approximation to $1/m$thly and continuous annuity EPVs.

5.11.2 Applying the UDD assumption

We consider the evaluation of $\ddot{a}^{(m)}_{x:\overline{n}|}$ under the assumption of a uniform distribution of deaths (UDD). The indication from Table 4.6 is that, in terms of EPVs for insurance benefits, UDD offers a reasonable approximation at younger ages, but may not be sufficiently accurate at older ages.

From Section 4.5.1 recall the results from equations (4.26) and (4.25) that, under the UDD assumption,

$$A^{(m)}_x = \frac{i}{i^{(m)}} A_x \qquad \text{and} \qquad \bar{A}_x = \frac{i}{\delta} A_x \, .$$

We also know, from equations (5.4), (5.18) and (5.14) in this chapter, that for any survival model

$$\ddot{a}_x = \frac{1 - A_x}{d}, \quad \ddot{a}^{(m)}_x = \frac{1 - A^{(m)}_x}{d^{(m)}} \quad \text{and} \quad \bar{a}_x = \frac{1 - \bar{A}_x}{\delta}.$$

Now, putting these equations together we have

$$\ddot{a}^{(m)}_x = \frac{1 - A^{(m)}_x}{d^{(m)}}$$

$$= \frac{1 - \frac{i}{i^{(m)}} A_x}{d^{(m)}} \qquad \text{using UDD}$$

$$= \frac{i^{(m)} - i A_x}{i^{(m)} d^{(m)}}$$

$$= \frac{i^{(m)} - i(1 - d\ddot{a}_x)}{i^{(m)} d^{(m)}} \quad \text{using (5.4)}$$

$$= \frac{id}{i^{(m)} d^{(m)}} \ddot{a}_x - \frac{i - i^{(m)}}{i^{(m)} d^{(m)}}$$

$$= \alpha(m) \ddot{a}_x - \beta(m)$$

where

$$\alpha(m) = \frac{id}{i^{(m)} d^{(m)}} \quad \text{and} \quad \beta(m) = \frac{i - i^{(m)}}{i^{(m)} d^{(m)}}. \quad (5.38)$$

For continuous annuities we can let $m \to \infty$, so that

$$\bar{a}_x = \frac{id}{\delta^2} \ddot{a}_x - \frac{i - \delta}{\delta^2}.$$

For term annuities, starting from equation (5.29) we have,

$$\ddot{a}_{x:\overline{n}|}^{(m)} = \ddot{a}_x^{(m)} - v^n {}_n p_x \ddot{a}_{x+n}^{(m)}$$

$$= \alpha(m)\ddot{a}_x - \beta(m) - v^n {}_n p_x \left(\alpha(m)\ddot{a}_{x+n} - \beta(m) \right) \quad \text{using UDD}$$

$$= \alpha(m) \left(\ddot{a}_x - v^n {}_n p_x \ddot{a}_{x+n} \right) - \beta(m) \left(1 - v^n {}_n p_x \right)$$

$$= \alpha(m) \ddot{a}_{x:\overline{n}|} - \beta(m) \left(1 - v^n {}_n p_x \right).$$

Note that the functions $\alpha(m)$ and $\beta(m)$ depend only on the frequency of the payments, not on the underlying survival model. It can be shown (see Exercise 5.15) that $\alpha(m) \approx 1$ and $\beta(m) \approx (m - 1)/2m$, leading to the approximation

$$\ddot{a}_{x:\overline{n}|}^{(m)} \approx \ddot{a}_{x:\overline{n}|} - \frac{m - 1}{2m} \left(1 - v^n {}_n p_x \right). \quad (5.39)$$

5.11.3 Woolhouse's formula

Woolhouse's formula is a method of calculating the EPV of annuities payable more frequently than annually that is not based on a fractional age assumption. It is based on the Euler–Maclaurin formula and expresses $\ddot{a}_x^{(m)}$ in terms of $\ddot{a}_x$. The Euler–Maclaurin formula is a numerical integration method. It gives a series expansion for the integral of a function, assuming that the function is differentiable a certain number of times. As discussed in Appendix B, in the case of a function $g(t)$, where $\lim_{t \to \infty} g(t) = 0$, the formula can be written in terms of a constant $h > 0$ as

$$\int_0^\infty g(t)dt = h \sum_{k=0}^\infty g(kh) - \frac{h}{2} g(0) + \frac{h^2}{12} g'(0) - \frac{h^4}{720} g'''(0) + \cdots, \quad (5.40)$$

where we have omitted terms on the right-hand side that involve higher derivatives of g.

To obtain our approximations we apply this formula twice to the function
$g(t) = v^t \, {}_t p_x$, in each case ignoring third and higher order derivatives of g,
which is reasonable as the function is usually quite smooth. Note that $g(0) = 1$,
$\lim_{t \to \infty} g(t) = 0$, and

$$
\begin{aligned}
g'(t) &= {}_t p_x \frac{d}{dt} v^t + v^t \frac{d}{dt} \, {}_t p_x \\
&= {}_t p_x \frac{d}{dt} e^{-\delta t} + v^t \frac{d}{dt} \, {}_t p_x \\
&= - {}_t p_x \, \delta \, e^{-\delta t} - v^t \, {}_t p_x \, \mu_{x+t},
\end{aligned}
$$

so $g'(0) = -(\delta + \mu_x)$.

First, let $h = 1$. As we are ignoring third and higher order derivatives, the
right-hand side of (5.40) becomes

$$
\sum_{k=0}^{\infty} g(k) - \frac{1}{2} + \frac{1}{12} g'(0) = \sum_{k=0}^{\infty} v^k \, {}_k p_x - \frac{1}{2} - \frac{1}{12} (\delta + \mu_x)
$$

$$
= \ddot{a}_x - \frac{1}{2} - \frac{1}{12} (\delta + \mu_x). \tag{5.41}
$$

Second, let $h = 1/m$. Again ignoring third and higher order derivatives, the
right-hand side of (5.40) becomes

$$
\frac{1}{m} \sum_{k=0}^{\infty} g(k/m) - \frac{1}{2m} + \frac{1}{12m^2} g'(0)
$$

$$
= \frac{1}{m} \sum_{k=0}^{\infty} v^{\frac{k}{m}} \, {}_{\frac{k}{m}} p_x - \frac{1}{2m} - \frac{1}{12m^2} (\delta + \mu_x)
$$

$$
= \ddot{a}_x^{(m)} - \frac{1}{2m} - \frac{1}{12m^2} (\delta + \mu_x). \tag{5.42}
$$

Since each of (5.41) and (5.42) approximates the same quantity, $\bar{a}_x$, we can
obtain an approximation to $\ddot{a}_x^{(m)}$ by equating them, so that

$$
\ddot{a}_x^{(m)} - \frac{1}{2m} - \frac{1}{12m^2} (\delta + \mu_x) \approx \ddot{a}_x - \frac{1}{2} - \frac{1}{12} (\delta + \mu_x).
$$

Rearranging, we obtain the important formula

$$
\boxed{\ddot{a}_x^{(m)} \approx \ddot{a}_x - \frac{m-1}{2m} - \frac{m^2 - 1}{12m^2} (\delta + \mu_x).} \tag{5.43}
$$

The right-hand side of equation (5.43) gives the first three terms of Woolhouse's formula, and this is the basis of our actuarial approximations.

For term annuities, we again start from equation (5.29),

$$\ddot{a}^{(m)}_{x:\overline{n}|} = \ddot{a}^{(m)}_x - v^n {}_n p_x \ddot{a}^{(m)}_{x+n}$$

and applying formula (5.43) gives

$$\ddot{a}^{(m)}_{x:\overline{n}|} \approx \ddot{a}_x - \frac{m-1}{2m} - \frac{m^2-1}{12m^2}(\delta + \mu_x)$$
$$- v^n {}_n p_x \left(\ddot{a}_{x+n} - \frac{m-1}{2m} - \frac{m^2-1}{12m^2}(\delta + \mu_{x+n}) \right)$$
$$= \ddot{a}_{x:\overline{n}|} - \frac{m-1}{2m}\left(1 - v^n {}_n p_x\right)$$
$$- \frac{m^2-1}{12m^2}\left(\delta + \mu_x - v^n {}_n p_x(\delta + \mu_{x+n})\right). \tag{5.44}$$

For continuous annuities, we can let $m \to \infty$ in equations (5.43) and (5.44) (or just apply equation (5.41)), so that

$$\bar{a}_x \approx \ddot{a}_x - \frac{1}{2} - \frac{1}{12}(\delta + \mu_x) \tag{5.45}$$

and

$$\bar{a}_{x:\overline{n}|} \approx \ddot{a}_{x:\overline{n}|} - \frac{1}{2}(1 - v^n {}_n p_x) - \frac{1}{12}\left(\delta + \mu_x - v^n {}_n p_x(\delta + \mu_{x+n})\right).$$

An important difference between the approximation to $\ddot{a}^{(m)}_{x:\overline{n}|}$ based on Woolhouse's formula and the UDD approximation is that we need extra information for the Woolhouse approach, specifically values for the force of mortality. In practice, the third term in equation (5.44) is often omitted (leading to the same approximation as equation (5.39)), but as we shall see in the next section, this leads to poor approximations in some cases.

If the integer age information available does not include values of μ_x, then we may still use Woolhouse's formula. As

$$_2 p_{x-1} = \exp\left\{ -\int_{x-1}^{x+1} \mu_s\, ds \right\} \approx \exp\{-2\mu_x\},$$

we can approximate μ_x as

$$\mu_x \approx -\frac{1}{2}(\log(p_{x-1}) + \log(p_x)), \tag{5.46}$$

and the results for the illustrations given in the next section are almost identical to where the exact value of the force of mortality is used.

In fact, Woolhouse's formula (with three terms) is so accurate that even if the full force of mortality curve is known, it is often a more efficient way to calculate annuity values than the more direct formulae with comparable accuracy. Also, since we have a simple relationship between annuity and insurance functions, we may use Woolhouse's formula for calculating insurance functions, for example we have

$$A_x^{(m)} = 1 - d^{(m)}\ddot{a}_x^{(m)}.$$

In Section 2.6.2 we saw an approximate relationship between the complete expectation of life and the curtate expectation of life, namely

$$\overset{\circ}{e}_x \approx e_x + \tfrac{1}{2}.$$

Setting the interest rate to 0 in equation (5.45) gives a refinement of this approximation, namely

$$\overset{\circ}{e}_x \approx e_x + \tfrac{1}{2} - \tfrac{1}{12}\mu_x.$$

5.12 Numerical illustrations

In this section we give some numerical illustrations of the different methods of computing $\ddot{a}_{x:\overline{n}|}^{(m)}$. Table 5.3 shows values of $\ddot{a}_{x:\overline{10}|}^{(12)}$ for $x = 20, 30, \ldots, 100$ when $i = 0.1$, while Table 5.4 shows values of $\ddot{a}_{x:\overline{25}|}^{(2)}$ when $i = 0.05$. The mortality basis for the calculations is the Standard Ultimate Survival Model, from Section 4.3.

The legend for each table is as follows:

Exact   denotes the true EPV, calculated from formula (5.37);

UDD   denotes the approximation to the EPV based on the uniform distribution of deaths assumption;

W2   denotes the approximation to the EPV based on Woolhouse's formula, using the first two terms only;

W3   denotes the approximation to the EPV based on Woolhouse's formula, using all three terms, including the exact force of mortality;

Table 5.3 *Values of* $\ddot{a}_{x:\overline{10}|}^{(12)}$ *for* $i = 0.1$.

x	Exact	UDD	W2	W3	W3*
20	6.4655	6.4655	6.4704	6.4655	6.4655
30	6.4630	6.4630	6.4679	6.4630	6.4630
40	6.4550	6.4550	6.4599	6.4550	6.4550
50	6.4295	6.4294	6.4344	6.4295	6.4295
60	6.3485	6.3482	6.3535	6.3485	6.3485
70	6.0991	6.0982	6.1044	6.0990	6.0990
80	5.4003	5.3989	5.4073	5.4003	5.4003
90	3.8975	3.8997	3.9117	3.8975	3.8975
100	2.0497	2.0699	2.0842	2.0497	2.0496

Table 5.4 *Values of* $\ddot{a}^{(2)}_{x:\overline{25}|}$ *for* $i = 0.05$.

x	Exact	UDD	W2	W3	W3*
20	14.5770	14.5770	14.5792	14.5770	14.5770
30	14.5506	14.5505	14.5527	14.5506	14.5506
40	14.4663	14.4662	14.4684	14.4663	14.4663
50	14.2028	14.2024	14.2048	14.2028	14.2028
60	13.4275	13.4265	13.4295	13.4275	13.4275
70	11.5117	11.5104	11.5144	11.5117	11.5117
80	8.2889	8.2889	8.2938	8.2889	8.2889
90	4.9242	4.9281	4.9335	4.9242	4.9242
100	2.4425	2.4599	2.4656	2.4424	2.4424

W3* denotes the approximation to the EPV based on Woolhouse's formula, using all three terms, but using the approximate force of mortality estimated from integer age values of p_x.

From these tables we see that approximations based on Woolhouse's formula with all three terms yield excellent approximations, even where we have approximated the force of mortality from integer age p_x values. Also, note that the inclusion of the third term is important for accuracy; the two-term Woolhouse formula is the worst approximation. We also observe that the approximation based on the UDD assumption is good at younger ages, with some deterioration for older ages. In this case approximations based on Woolhouse's formula are superior, provided the three-term version is used.

It is also worth noting that calculating the exact value of, for example, $\ddot{a}^{(12)}_{20}$ using a spreadsheet approach takes around 1200 rows, one for each month from age 20 to the limiting age ω. Using Woolhouse's formula requires only the integer age table, of 100 rows, and the accuracy all the way up to age 100 is excellent, using the exact or approximate values for μ_x. Clearly, there can be significant efficiency gains using Woolhouse's formula.

5.13 Functions for select lives

Throughout this chapter we have assumed that lives are subject to an ultimate survival model, just as we did in deriving insurance functions in Chapter 4. Just as in that chapter, all the arguments in this chapter equally apply if we have a select survival model. Thus, for example, the EPV of an n-year term annuity payable continuously at rate 1 per year to a life who is aged $x + k$ and who was select at age x is $\bar{a}_{[x]+k:\overline{n}|}$, with

$$\bar{A}_{[x]+k:\overline{n}|} = 1 - \delta \bar{a}_{[x]+k:\overline{n}|}.$$

The approximations we have developed also hold for select survival models, so that, for example

$$\ddot{a}^{(m)}_{[x]+k} \approx \ddot{a}_{[x]+k} - \frac{m-1}{2m} - \frac{m^2-1}{12m^2}(\delta + \mu_{[x]+k})$$

where

$$\ddot{a}_{[x]+k} = \sum_{t=0}^{\infty} v^t \, {}_t p_{[x]+k}$$

and

$$\ddot{a}^{(m)}_{[x]+k} = \frac{1}{m} \sum_{t=0}^{\infty} v^{t/m} \, {}_{\frac{t}{m}} p_{[x]+k}.$$

5.14 Notes and further reading

Woolhouse (1869) presented the formula which bears his name in a paper to the Institute of Actuaries in London. In this paper he also showed that his theory applied to joint-life annuities, a topic we discuss in Chapter 9. A derivation of Woolhouse's formula from the Euler–Maclaurin formula is given in Appendix B. The Euler–Maclaurin formula was derived independently (about 130 years before Woolhouse's paper) by the famous Swiss mathematician Leonhard Euler and by the Scottish mathematician Colin Maclaurin. A proof of the Euler–Maclaurin formula, and references to the original works, can be found in Graham *et al.* (1994).

5.15 Exercises

When a calculation is required in the following exercises, unless otherwise stated you should assume that mortality follows the Standard Ultimate Survival Model as specified in Section 4.3 and that interest is at 5% per year effective. This is the basis underlying the tables in Appendix D.

Exercise 5.1 Describe in words the benefits with the present values given and write down an expression in terms of actuarial functions for the expected present value.

(a) $$Y_1 = \begin{cases} \bar{a}_{\overline{T_x}|} & \text{if } T_x \le 15, \\ \bar{a}_{\overline{15}|} & \text{if } T_x > 15. \end{cases}$$

(b) $$Y_2 = \begin{cases} a_{\overline{15}|} & \text{if } 0 < K_x \le 15, \\ a_{\overline{K_x}|} & \text{if } K_x > 15. \end{cases}$$

Exercise 5.2

(a) Describe the annuity with the following present value random variable:

$$Y = \begin{cases} v^{T_x} \, \bar{a}_{\overline{n-T_x|}} & \text{if } T_x < n, \\ 0 & \text{if } T_x \geq n. \end{cases}$$

This is called a **Family Income Benefit**.

(b) Show that $E[Y] = \bar{a}_{\overline{n|}} - \bar{a}_{x:\overline{n|}}$.

(c) Explain the answer in (b) by general reasoning.

Exercise 5.3 Given $\ddot{a}_{50:\overline{10|}} = 8.2066$, $a_{50:\overline{10|}} = 7.8277$ and $_{10}p_{50} = 0.9195$, what is the effective rate of interest per year?

Exercise 5.4 Given $a_{60} = 10.996$, $a_{61} = 10.756$, $a_{62} = 10.509$ and $i = 0.06$, calculate $_2p_{60}$.

Exercise 5.5 Using the tables in Appendix D, calculate

(a) $\ddot{a}_{40:\overline{20|}}$,

(b) $\ddot{a}^{(4)}_{40:\overline{20|}}$ using Woolhouse's formula with two terms,

(c) $\bar{a}_{25:\overline{10|}}$ assuming UDD,

(d) $a^{(12)}_{50:\overline{20|}}$ using Woolhouse's formula with two terms,

(e) $_{20|}\ddot{a}^{(12)}_{45}$ assuming UDD.

Exercise 5.6 Using the tables in Appendix D, calculate the standard deviation of the present value of an annuity of \$50 000 per year payable annually in advance to a select life aged 60.

Exercise 5.7 Given $_{10|}\ddot{a}_x = 4$, $\ddot{a}_x = 10$, $_{10}E_x = 0.375$ and $v = 0.94$, calculate $A^{\,1}_{x:\overline{10|}}$.

Exercise 5.8 You are given the following extract from a select life table.

$[x]$	$l_{[x]}$	$l_{[x]+1}$	l_{x+2}	$x+2$
40	33 519	33 485	33 440	42
41	33 467	33 428	33 378	43
42	33 407	33 365	33 309	44
43	33 340	33 294	33 231	45
44	33 265	33 213	33 143	46

Calculate the following, assuming an interest rate of 6% per year:

(a) $\ddot{a}_{[40]:\overline{4}|}$,

(b) $a_{[40]+1:\overline{4}|}$,

(c) $(Ia)_{[40]:\overline{4}|}$,

(d) $(IA)_{[40]:\overline{4}|}$,

(e) the standard deviation of the present value of a four-year term annuity-due, with annual payment $1000, payable to a select life age 41, and

(f) the probability that the present value of an annuity-due of 1 per year issued to a select life aged 40 is less than 3.0.

Exercise 5.9 The force of mortality for a certain population is exactly half the sum of the forces of mortality in two standard mortality tables, denoted A and B. Thus

$$\mu_x = (\mu_x^A + \mu_x^B)/2$$

for all x. A student has suggested the approximation

$$a_x = (a_x^A + a_x^B)/2.$$

Will this approximation overstate or understate the true value of a_x?

Exercise 5.10 Consider a life aged x. Obtain the formula

$$(IA)_x = \ddot{a}_x - d(I\ddot{a})_x$$

by writing down the present value random variables for

(a) an increasing annuity-due to (x) with payments of $t+1$ at times $t = 0, 1, 2, \ldots$, and

(b) a whole life insurance benefit of amount t at time t, $t = 1, 2, 3 \ldots$, if the death of (x) occurs between ages $x + t - 1$ and $x + t$.

Hint: use the result

$$(I\ddot{a})_{\overline{n}|} = \sum_{t=1}^{n} t v^{t-1} = \frac{\ddot{a}_{\overline{n}|} - nv^n}{d}.$$

Exercise 5.11 Let $H = \min(K_x, n)$.

(a) Show that

$$V[a_{\overline{H}|}] = \frac{{}^2 A_{x:\overline{n+1}|} - \left(A_{x:\overline{n+1}|}\right)^2}{d^2}.$$

(b) An alternative form given for this variance in Bowers *et al.* (1997) is

$$\frac{(1+i)^2 \, [^2 A_{x:\overline{n}|}^{\,1} - (A_{x:\overline{n}|}^{\,1})^2] - 2(1+i) A_{x:\overline{n}|}^{\,1} \, v^n \,_n p_x + v^{2n} \,_n p_x (1 - \,_n p_x)}{i^2}.$$

Prove that this is equal to the expression in (a).

Exercise 5.12 Consider the random variables $Y = \bar{a}_{\overline{T_x}|}$ and $Z = v^{T_x}$.

(a) Derive an expression for the covariance, in terms of standard actuarial functions.
(b) Show that the covariance is negative.
(c) Explain this result in words.

Exercise 5.13 Find, and simplify where possible:

(a) $\frac{d}{dx}\ddot{a}_x$, and
(b) $\frac{d}{dx}\ddot{a}_{x:\overline{n}|}$.

Exercise 5.14 Consider the following portfolio of annuities-due currently being paid from the assets of a pension fund.

Age	Number of annuitants
60	40
70	30
80	10

Each annuity has an annual payment of $10 000 as long as the annuitant survives. The lives are assumed to be independent. Calculate

(a) the expected present value of the total outgo on annuities,
(b) the standard deviation of the present value of the total outgo on annuities, and
(c) the 95th percentile of the distribution of the present value of the total outgo on annuities using a normal approximation.

Exercise 5.15 Consider the quantities $\alpha(m)$ and $\beta(m)$ in formula (5.38). By expressing i, $i^{(m)}$, d and $d^{(m)}$ in terms of δ, show that

$$\alpha(m) \approx 1 \quad \text{and} \quad \beta(m) \approx \frac{m-1}{2m}.$$

Exercise 5.16 Using a spreadsheet, calculate the mean and variance of the present value of

(a) an arithmetically increasing term annuity-due payable to a life aged 50 for at most 10 years under which the payment at time t is $t+1$ for $t = 0, 1, \ldots, 9$, and

(b) a geometrically increasing term annuity-due payable to a life aged 50 for at most 10 years under which the payment at time t is 1.03^t for $t = 0, 1, \ldots, 9$.

Exercise 5.17 Using a spreadsheet, calculate the mean and variance of the present value of

(a) a whole life annuity-due to a life aged 65, with annual payments of 1, and

(b) a whole life annuity-due to a life aged 65, with annual payments of 1 and a guarantee period of 10 years.

Explain the ordering of the means and variances.

Exercise 5.18 Jensen's inequality states that for a function f, whose first derivative is positive and whose second derivative is negative, and a random variable X,

$$E[f(X)] \leq f(E[X]).$$

Use Jensen's inequality to show that

$$\bar{a}_x \leq \bar{a}_{\overline{E[T_x]}}.$$

Answers to selected exercises

5.3 4.0014%

5.4 0.98220

5.5 (a) 12.994

    (b) 12.756

    (c) 7.902

    (d) 12.490

    (e) 4.710

5.6 161 996

5.7 0.265

5.8 (a) 3.66643

    (b) 3.45057

    (c) 8.37502

    (d) 3.16305

    (e) 119.14

    (f) 0.00421

5.14 (a) 10 418 961
    (b) 311 534
    (c) 10 931 390
5.16 (a) 40.95,   11.057
    (b) 9.121,   0.32965
5.17 (a) 13.550,   12.497
    (b) 13.814,   8.380

6

Premium calculation

6.1 Summary

In this chapter we discuss principles of premium calculation for insurance policies and annuities. We start by reviewing what we mean by the terms 'premium', 'net premium' and 'gross premium'. We next introduce the present value of future loss random variable. We define the equivalence premium principle and we show how this premium principle can be applied to calculate premiums for different types of policy. We look at how we can use the future loss random variable to determine when a contract moves from loss to profit or vice versa. We introduce a different premium principle, the portfolio percentile premium principle, and show how, using the mean and variance of the future loss random variable, the portfolio percentile premium principle can be used to determine a premium. The chapter concludes with a discussion of how a premium can be calculated when the insured life is subject to some extra level of risk.

6.2 Preliminaries

An insurance policy is a financial agreement between the insurance company and the policyholder. The insurance company agrees to pay some benefits, for example a sum insured on the death of the policyholder within the term of a term insurance, and the policyholder agrees to pay premiums to the insurance company to secure these benefits. The premiums will also need to reimburse the insurance company for the expenses associated with the policy.

The calculation of the premium may not explicitly allow for the insurance company's expenses. In this case we refer to a **net premium** (also, sometimes, a **risk premium** or **benefit premium**). If the calculation does explicitly allow for expenses, the premium is called a **gross premium** or **office premium** or **expense-loaded premium**.

The premium may be a single payment by the policyholder – a **single premium** – or it may be a regular series of payments, possibly annually, quarterly, monthly or weekly. Monthly premiums are very common since many employed people receive their salaries monthly and it is convenient to have payments made with the same frequency as income is received.

It is common for regular premiums to be a level amount, but they do not have to be.

A key feature of any life insurance policy is that premiums are payable in advance, with the first premium payable when the policy is purchased. To see why this is necessary, suppose it were possible to purchase a whole life insurance policy with annual premiums where the first premium were payable at the end of the year in which the policy was purchased. In this case, a person could purchase the policy and then withdraw from the contract at the end of the first year before paying the premium then due. This person would have had a year of insurance cover without paying anything for it.

Regular premiums for a policy on a single life cease to be payable on the death of the policyholder. The premium paying term for a policy is the maximum length of time for which premiums are payable. The premium paying term may be the same as the term of the policy, but it could be shorter. If we consider a whole life insurance policy, it would be usual for the death benefit to be secured by regular premiums and it would be common for premium payment to cease at a certain age – perhaps at age 65 when the policyholder is assumed to retire, or at age 80 when the policyholder's real income may be diminishing.

As we discussed in Chapter 1, premiums are payable to secure annuity benefits as well as life insurance benefits. Deferred annuities may be purchased using a single premium at the start of the deferred period, or by regular premiums payable throughout the deferred period. Immediate annuities are always purchased by a single premium. For example, a person aged 45 might secure a retirement income by paying regular premiums over a 20-year period to secure annuity payments from age 65. Or, a person aged 65 might secure a monthly annuity from an insurance company by payment of a single premium.

For traditional policies, the benchmark principle for calculating both gross and net premiums is called the equivalence principle, and we discuss its application in detail in this chapter. However, there are other methods of calculating premiums and we discuss one of these, the portfolio percentile principle.

A more contemporary approach, which is commonly used for non-traditional policies, is to consider the cash flows from the contract, and to set the premium to satisfy a specified profit criterion. This approach is discussed in Chapter 12.

6.3 Assumptions

As in Chapter 4, unless otherwise stated, we use a standard set of assumptions for mortality and interest in the numerical examples in this chapter. We use the Standard Select Survival Model with a two-year select period specified in Example 3.13 with an interest rate of 5% per year effective. Recall that the survival model is specified as follows:

$$\mu_x = A + Bc^x$$

where $A = 0.00022$, $B = 2.7 \times 10^{-6}$ and $c = 1.124$, and

$$\mu_{[x]+s} = 0.9^{2-s} \mu_{x+s}$$

for $0 \leq s \leq 2$. The select and ultimate life table, at integer ages, for this model is shown in Table D.1 and values of annuity and insurance functions at an effective rate of interest of 5% per year are shown in Tables D.2 and D.3.

Example 6.1 Use the Standard Select Survival Model with interest at 5% per year, to produce a table showing values of $\ddot{a}_{[x]}$, $\ddot{a}_{[x]+1}$ and $\ddot{a}_{x+2}$ for $x = 20, 21, \ldots, 80$. Assume that $q_{131} = 1$.

Solution 6.1 The calculation of survival probabilities $p_{[x]}$, $p_{[x]+1}$ and p_x for this survival model was discussed in Example 3.13. Since we are assuming that $q_{131} = 1$, we have $\ddot{a}_{131} = 1$. Annuity values can then be calculated recursively using

$$\ddot{a}_x = 1 + v \, p_x \, \ddot{a}_{x+1},$$
$$\ddot{a}_{[x]+1} = 1 + v \, p_{[x]+1} \, \ddot{a}_{x+2},$$
$$\ddot{a}_{[x]} = 1 + v \, p_{[x]} \, \ddot{a}_{[x]+1}.$$

Values are shown in Appendix D, Table D.2.   □

6.4 The present value of future loss random variable

The cash flows for a traditional life insurance contract consist of the insurance or annuity benefit outgo (and associated expenses) and the premium income. Both are generally life contingent, that is, the income and outgo cash flows depend on the future lifetime of the policyholder, unless the contract is purchased by a single premium, in which case there is no uncertainty regarding the premium income. So we can model the future outgo less future income with the random variable that represents the present value of the future loss. When expenses are excluded we call this the **net future loss**, which we denote by L_0^n. When expenses are included, then the premiums are the gross premiums, and the random variable is referred to as the **gross future loss**, denoted L_0^g. In other words,

L_0^n = PV of benefit outgo − PV of net premium income

L_0^g = PV of benefit outgo + PV of expenses − PV of gross premium income.

In cases where the meaning is obvious from the context, we will drop the n or g superscript.

Example 6.2 An insurer issues a whole life insurance to [60], with sum insured S payable immediately on death. Premiums are payable annually in advance, ceasing at age 80 or on earlier death. The net annual premium is P.

Write down the net future loss random variable, L_0^n, for this contract in terms of lifetime random variables for [60].

Solution 6.2 From Chapter 4, we know that the present value random variable for the benefit is $Sv^{T_{[60]}}$ and from Chapter 5 we know that the present value random variable for the premium income is $P\ddot{a}_{\overline{\min(K_{[60]}+1,20)|}}$, so

$$L_0^n = Sv^{T_{[60]}} - P\ddot{a}_{\overline{\min(K_{[60]}+1,20)|}}.$$

Since both terms of the random variable depend on the future lifetime of the same life, [60], they are clearly dependent.

Note that since premiums are payable in advance, premiums *payable annually in advance, ceasing at age 80 or on earlier death* means that the last possible premium is payable on the policyholder's 79th birthday. No premium is payable on reaching age 80. □

Given an appropriate survival model together with assumptions about future interest rates and, for gross premiums, expenses, the insurer can then determine a distribution for the present value of the future loss. This distribution can be used to find a suitable premium for a given benefit, or an appropriate benefit for a specified premium. To do this, the insurer needs to use a **premium principle**. This is a method of selecting an appropriate premium using a given loss distribution. We discuss two premium principles in this chapter.

6.5 The equivalence principle

6.5.1 Net premiums

For net premiums, we take into consideration outgo on benefit payments only. Thus, expenses are not a part of net premium calculation. The benefit may be a death benefit or a survival benefit or a combination.

We start by stating the equivalence principle. Under the equivalence principle, the net premium is set such that the expected value of the future loss is zero at the start of the contract. That means that

$$E[L_0^n] = 0$$

which implies that

E[PV of benefit outgo − PV of net premium income] = 0.

That is, under the equivalence premium principle,

| **EPV of benefit outgo = EPV of net premium income.** | (6.1)

The equivalence principle is the most common premium principle in traditional life insurance, and will be our default principle – that is, if no other principle is specified, it is assumed that the equivalence principle is to be used.

Example 6.3 Consider an endowment insurance with term n years and sum insured S payable at the earlier of the end of the year of death or at maturity, issued to a select life aged x. Premiums of amount P are payable annually throughout the term of the insurance.

Derive expressions in terms of S, P and standard actuarial functions for

(a) the net future loss, L_0^n,
(b) the mean of L_0^n,
(c) the variance of L_0^n, and,
(d) the annual net premium for the contract.

Solution 6.3 (a) The future loss random variable is

$$L_0^n = S v^{\min(K_{[x]}+1,n)} - P \ddot{a}_{\overline{\min(K_{[x]}+1,n)|}}.$$

(b) The mean of L_0^n is

$$E[L_0^n] = S E \left[v^{\min(K_{[x]}+1,n)} \right] - P E \left[\ddot{a}_{\overline{\min(K_{[x]}+1,n)|}} \right]$$

$$= S A_{[x]:\overline{n}|} - P \ddot{a}_{[x]:\overline{n}|}.$$

(c) Expanding the expression above for L_0^n gives

$$L_0^n = S v^{\min(K_{[x]}+1,n)} - P \frac{1 - v^{\min(K_{[x]}+1,n)}}{d}$$

$$= \left(S + \frac{P}{d} \right) v^{\min(K_{[x]}+1,n)} - \frac{P}{d},$$

which isolates the random variable $v^{\min(K_{[x]}+1,n)}$. So the variance is

$$V\left[L_0^n\right] = \left(S + \frac{P}{d}\right)^2 V\left[v^{\min(K_{[x]}+1,n)}\right]$$

$$= \left(S + \frac{P}{d}\right)^2 \left({}^2A_{[x]:\overline{n}|} - (A_{[x]:\overline{n}|})^2\right).$$

(d) Setting the EPVs of the premiums and benefits to be equal gives the net premium as

$$P = S\frac{A_{[x]:\overline{n}|}}{\ddot{a}_{[x]:\overline{n}|}}. \tag{6.2}$$

Furthermore, using formula (6.2) and recalling that

$$\ddot{a}_{x:\overline{n}|} = \frac{1 - A_{x:\overline{n}|}}{d},$$

we see that the solution can be written as

$$P = S\left(\frac{1}{\ddot{a}_{[x]:\overline{n}|}} - d\right)$$

so that the only actuarial function needed to calculate P for a given value of S is $\ddot{a}_{[x]:\overline{n}|}$. $\square$

Example 6.4 An insurer issues a regular premium deferred annuity contract to a select life aged x. Premiums are payable monthly throughout the deferred period. The annuity benefit of X per year is payable monthly in advance from age $x + n$ for the remainder of the life of (x).

(a) Write down the net future loss random variable in terms of lifetime random variables for (x).
(b) Derive an expression for the monthly net premium.
(c) Assume now that, in addition, the contract offers a death benefit of S payable immediately on death during the deferred period. Write down the net future loss random variable for the contract, and derive an expression for the monthly net premium.

Solution 6.4 (a) Let P denote the monthly net premium, so that the total premium payable in a year is $12P$. Then

$$L_0^n = \begin{cases} 0 - 12P\ddot{a}^{(12)}_{K^{(12)}_{[x]}+\frac{1}{12}} & \text{if } T_{[x]} \leq n, \\ \\ X v^n \ddot{a}^{(12)}_{K^{(12)}_{[x]}+\frac{1}{12}-n} - 12P\ddot{a}^{(12)}_{\overline{n}|} & \text{if } T_{[x]} > n. \end{cases}$$

(b) The EPV of the annuity benefit is

$$X v^n {}_n p_{[x]} \ddot{a}^{(12)}_{[x]+n},$$

and the EPV of the premium income is

$$12 P \ddot{a}^{(12)}_{[x]:\overline{n}|}.$$

By equating these EPVs we obtain the premium equation which gives

$$P = \frac{X v^n {}_n p_{[x]} \ddot{a}^{(12)}_{[x]+n}}{12 \ddot{a}^{(12)}_{[x]:\overline{n}|}} = \frac{{}_n E_{[x]} X \ddot{a}^{(12)}_{[x]+n}}{12 \ddot{a}^{(12)}_{[x]:\overline{n}|}}.$$

(c) We now have

$$L_0^n = \begin{cases} S v^{T_{[x]}} - 12 P \ddot{a}^{(12)}_{K^{(12)}_{[x]} + \frac{1}{12}|} & \text{if } T_{[x]} \le n, \\[2em] X v^n \ddot{a}^{(12)}_{K^{(12)}_{[x]} + \frac{1}{12} - n|} - 12 P \ddot{a}^{(12)}_{\overline{n}|} & \text{if } T_{[x]} > n. \end{cases}$$

The annuity benefit has the same EPV as in part (b); the death benefit during deferral is a term insurance benefit with EPV $S \bar{A}^{1}_{[x]:\overline{n}|}$, so the premium equation now becomes

$$P = \frac{S \bar{A}^{1}_{[x]:\overline{n}|} + X v^n {}_n p_{[x]} \ddot{a}^{(12)}_{[x]+n}}{12 \ddot{a}^{(12)}_{[x]:\overline{n}|}}.$$

$\square$

Example 6.4 shows that the future loss random variable can be quite complicated to write down. Usually, the premium calculation does not require the identification of the future loss random variable. We may go directly to the equivalence principle, and equate the EPV of the benefit outgo to the EPV of the net premium income to obtain the net premium.

Example 6.5 Consider an endowment insurance with sum insured $100 000 issued to a select life aged 45 with term 20 years under which the death benefit is payable at the end of the year of death. Using the Standard Select Survival Model, with interest at 5% per year, calculate the total amount of net premium payable in a year if premiums are payable (a) annually, (b) quarterly, and (c) monthly, and comment on these values.

Solution 6.5 Let P denote the total amount of premium payable in a year. Then the EPV of premium income is $P \ddot{a}^{(m)}_{[45]:\overline{20}|}$ (where $m = 1$, 4 or 12) and the

Table 6.1 *Annuity values and premiums.*

Method	m = 4		m = 12	
	$\ddot{a}^{(4)}_{[45]:\overline{20}|}$	P	$\ddot{a}^{(12)}_{[45]:\overline{20}|}$	P
Exact	12.69859	3 022.11	12.64512	3 034.89
UDD	12.69839	3 022.16	12.64491	3 034.94
W3	12.69859	3 022.11	12.64512	3 034.89

EPV of benefit outgo is $100\,000 A_{[45]:\overline{20}|}$, giving

$$P = \frac{100\,000 A_{[45]:\overline{20}|}}{\ddot{a}^{(m)}_{[45]:\overline{20}|}}.$$

Using tables from Appendix D we have

$$\ddot{a}_{[45]:\overline{20}|} = \ddot{a}_{[45]} - \frac{l_{65}}{l_{[45]}} v^{20} \ddot{a}_{65} = 12.94092.$$

From this we get

$$A_{[45]:\overline{20}|} = 1 - d\ddot{a}_{[45]:\overline{20}|} = 0.383766.$$

Hence, for $m = 1$ the net premium is $P = \$2965.52$.

The values of $\ddot{a}^{(m)}_{[45]:\overline{20}|}$ for $m = 4$ and 12 can either be calculated exactly or from $\ddot{a}_{[45]:\overline{20}|}$ using one of the approximations in Section 5.11. Notice that the approximation labelled W3* in that section is not available since $p_{[x]-1}$ is meaningless and so we cannot estimate $\mu_{[45]}$ from the life table tabulated at integer ages. Table 6.1 shows values obtained using the UDD assumption and Woolhouse's formula with three terms. The ordering of these premiums for $m = 1, 4, 12$ reflects the ordering of EPVs of $1/m$thly annuities which we observed in Chapter 5. In this example, Woolhouse's formula provides a very good approximation, whilst the UDD assumption gives a reasonably accurate premium. □

6.6 Gross premiums

When we calculate a gross premium for an insurance policy or an annuity, we take account of the expenses the insurer incurs. There are three main types of expense associated with policies – initial expenses, renewal expenses and termination or claim expenses.

Initial expenses are incurred by the insurer when a policy is issued. When we calculate a gross premium, it is conventional to assume that the insurer incurs these expenses at exactly the same time as the first premium is payable, although in practice these expenses are usually incurred slightly ahead of this date. There are two major types of initial expenses – commission to agents for selling a policy and underwriting expenses. Commission is often paid to an agent in the form of a high percentage of the first year's premiums plus a much lower percentage of subsequent premiums, payable as the premiums are paid. Underwriting expenses may vary according to the amount of the death benefit. For example, an insurer is likely to require much more stringent medical tests on an individual wanting a $10 million death benefit compared with an individual wanting a $10 000 death benefit.

Renewal or maintenance expenses are normally incurred by the insurer each time a premium is payable, and in the case of an annuity, they are normally incurred when an annuity payment is made. These costs arise in a variety of ways. The processing of renewal and annuity payments involves staff time and investment expenses. Renewal expenses also cover the ongoing fixed costs of the insurer such as staff salaries and rent for the insurer's premises, as well as specific costs such as annual statements to policyholders about their policies.

Initial and renewal expenses may be proportional to premiums, proportional to benefits or may be 'per policy', meaning that the amount is fixed for all policies, and is not related to the size of the contract. Often, per policy renewal costs are assumed to be increasing at a compound rate over the term of the policy, to approximate the effect of inflation.

Termination or claim expenses occur when a policy expires, typically on the death of a policyholder (or annuitant) or on the maturity date of a term insurance or endowment insurance. Generally these expenses are small, and are largely associated with the paperwork required to finalize and pay a claim. In calculating gross premiums, specific allowance is often not made for termination expenses. Where allowance is made, it is usually a fixed sum or proportional to the benefit amount.

In practice, allocating the different expenses involved in running an insurance company is a complicated task, and in the examples in this chapter we simply assume that all expenses are known.

The equivalence principle applied to the gross premiums and benefits states that the EPV of the gross future loss random variable should be equal to zero. That means that

$$E[L_0^g] = 0,$$

that is

EPV of benefit outgo $+$ EPV of expenses

$-$ EPV of gross premium income $= 0$.

In other words, under the equivalence premium principle,

> **EPV of benefits + EPV of expenses = EPV of gross premium income.**

$$(6.3)$$

We conclude this section with four examples in each of which we apply the equivalence principle to calculate gross premiums.

Example 6.6 An insurer issues a 25-year annual premium endowment insurance with sum insured $100\,000$ to a select life aged 30. The insurer incurs initial expenses of $2000 plus 50% of the first premium, and renewal expenses of 2.5% of each subsequent premium. The death benefit is payable immediately on death.

(a) Write down the gross future loss random variable.
(b) Calculate the gross premium using the Standard Select Survival Model with 5% per year interest.

Solution 6.6 (a) Let $S = 100\,000$, $x = 30$, $n = 25$ and let P denote the annual gross premium. Then

$$L_0^g = S\,v^{\min(T_{[x]},n)} + 2000 + 0.475\,P + 0.025\,P\ddot{a}_{\overline{\min(K_{[x]}+1,n)}|}$$
$$- P\ddot{a}_{\overline{\min(K_{[x]}+1,n)}|}$$
$$= S\,v^{\min(T_{[x]},n)} + 2000 + 0.475\,P - 0.975\,P\ddot{a}_{\overline{\min(K_{[x]}+1,n)}|}.$$

Note that the premium related expenses, of 50% of the first premium plus 2.5% of the second and subsequent premiums, are more conveniently written as 2.5% of **all** premiums, plus an additional 47.5% of the first premium. By expressing the premium expenses this way, we can simplify the gross future loss random variable, and the subsequent premium calculation.

(b) We may look separately at the three parts of the gross premium equation of value. The EPV of premium income is

$$P\ddot{a}_{[30]:\overline{25}|} = 14.73113\,P.$$

Note that $\ddot{a}_{[30]:\overline{25}|}$ can be calculated from the tables in Appendix D.

The EPV of all expenses is

$$2000 + 0.475\,P + 0.025\,P\ddot{a}_{[30]:\overline{25}|} = 2000 + 0.475\,P + 0.025 \times 14.73113\,P$$
$$= 2000 + 0.843278\,P.$$

The EPV of the death benefit can be found using numerical integration or using Woolhouse's formula, and we obtain

$$100\,000\bar{A}_{[30]:\overline{25}|} = 100\,000 \times 0.298732 = 29\,873.2.$$

Thus, the equivalence principle gives

$$P = \frac{29\,873.2 + 2\,000}{14.73113 - 0.843278} = \$2295.04.$$

$\square$

Example 6.7 Calculate the monthly gross premium for a 10-year term insurance with sum insured \$50 000 payable immediately on death, issued to a select life aged 55, using the following basis:

Survival model: Standard Select Survival Model
                     Assume UDD for fractional ages
Interest: 5% per year
Initial expenses: \$500 +10% of each monthly premium in the first year
Renewal expenses: 1% of each monthly premium in the second and
                     subsequent policy years

Solution 6.7 Let P denote the monthly premium. Then the EPV of premium income is $12P\ddot{a}^{(12)}_{[55]:\overline{10}|}$. To find the EPV of premium related expenses, we can apply the same idea as in the previous example, noting that initial expenses apply to each premium in the first year. Thus, we can write the EPV of all expenses as

$$500 + 0.09 \times 12P\ddot{a}^{(12)}_{[55]:\overline{1}|} + 0.01 \times 12P\ddot{a}^{(12)}_{[55]:\overline{10}|}$$

where the expenses for the first year have been split as 9% plus 1%, so that we have 9% in the first year and 1% every year. The EPV of the insurance benefit is $50\,000\bar{A}^{\,1}_{[55]:\overline{10}|}$ and so the equivalence principle gives

$$12P\left(0.99\ddot{a}^{(12)}_{[55]:\overline{10}|} - 0.09\ddot{a}^{(12)}_{[55]:\overline{1}|}\right) = 500 + 50\,000\bar{A}^{\,1}_{[55]:\overline{10}|}.$$

We find that $\ddot{a}^{(12)}_{[55]:\overline{10}|} = 7.8341$, $\ddot{a}^{(12)}_{[55]:\overline{1}|} = 0.9773$ and $\bar{A}^{\,1}_{[55]:\overline{10}|} = 0.024954$, giving $P = \$18.99$ per month.

Calculating all the EPVs exactly gives the same answer for the premium to four significant figures.

$\square$

Example 6.8 A life insurance company issued a with-profits whole life policy to a select life aged 40. Under the policy, the basic sum insured of $100 000 and attaching bonuses are payable at the end of the year of death. The company declares compound reversionary bonuses at the end of each year, and these bonuses do not apply to policies which became claims during the year. Level premiums are payable annually in advance under the policy.

Calculate the annual gross premium on the following basis:

Survival model: Standard Select Survival Model
Interest: 5% per year
Bonus loading: 2.5% compound per year
Initial expenses: $200
Renewal expenses: 5% of each premium after the first

Solution 6.8 The annual gross premium, P, is calculated assuming that the death benefit increases by 2.5% each year, with the first bonus applying to deaths in the second year, so that the death benefit in the tth policy year, $t = 1, 2, 3, \ldots$, is $100\,000\,(1.025^{t-1})$.

The EPV of premiums is

$$P\,\ddot{a}_{[40]} = 18.4596\,P$$

and the EPV of expenses is

$$200 + 0.05\,P\,(\ddot{a}_{[40]} - 1) = 200 + 0.87298\,P.$$

The EPV of the death benefit is

$$100\,000 \sum_{k=0}^{\infty} (1.025^k)\,v^{k+1}\,{}_{k|}q_{[40]} = \frac{100\,000}{1.025}\,A_{[40]\,i^*} = 32\,816.71,$$

where $i^* = \frac{1.05}{1.025} - 1 = 2.439\%$. Hence $P = \$1877.38$. □

Example 6.9 Calculate the gross single premium for a deferred annuity of $80\,000 per year payable monthly in advance, issued to a select life now aged 50 with the first annuity payment on the life's 65th birthday. Allow for initial expenses of $1000, and renewal expenses on each anniversary of the issue date, provided that the policyholder is alive. Assume that the renewal expense will be $20 on the first anniversary of the issue date, and that expenses will increase with inflation from that date at the compound rate of 1% per year. Assume the Standard Select Survival Model with interest at 5% per year.

Solution 6.9 The single premium is equal to the EPV of the deferred annuity plus the EPV of expenses. The renewal expense on the tth policy anniversary is $20\left(1.01^{t-1}\right)$ for $t = 1, 2, 3, \ldots$ so that the EPV of renewal expenses is

$$20 \sum_{t=1}^{\infty} 1.01^{t-1}\, v^t\, {}_t p_{[50]} = \frac{20}{1.01} \sum_{t=1}^{\infty} 1.01^t\, v^t\, {}_t p_{[50]}$$

$$= \frac{20}{1.01} \sum_{t=1}^{\infty} v_j^t\, {}_t p_{[50]}$$

$$= \frac{20}{1.01} (\ddot{a}_{[50]\, j} - 1)$$

where the subscript j indicates that the calculation is at rate of interest j where $1.01v = 1/(1 + j)$, that is $j = 0.0396$. The EPV of the deferred annuity is $80\,000\ {}_{15|}\ddot{a}_{[50]}^{(12)}$, so the single premium is

$$1\,000 + \frac{20}{1.01} (\ddot{a}_{[50]\, j} - 1) + 80\,000\ {}_{15|}\ddot{a}_{[50]}^{(12)}.$$

As $\ddot{a}_{[50]\, j} = 19.4550$ and ${}_{15|}\ddot{a}_{[50]}^{(12)} = 6.04129$, the single premium is \$484 669. $\qquad\square$

We end this section with a comment on the premiums calculated in Examples 6.6 and 6.7. In Example 6.6, the annual premium is \$2295.04 and the expenses at time 0 are \$2000 plus 50% of the first premium, a total of \$3146.75, which exceeds the first premium. Similarly, in Example 6.7 the total premium in the first year is \$227.88 and the total expenses in the first year are \$500 plus 10% of premiums in the first year. In each case, the premium income in the first year is insufficient to cover expenses in the first year. This situation is common in practice, especially when initial commission to agents is high, and is referred to as **new business strain**. A consequence of new business strain is that an insurer needs to have funds available in order to sell policies. From time to time insurers get into financial difficulties through pursuing an aggressive growth strategy without sufficient capital to support the new business strain. Essentially, the insurer borrows from shareholder (or participating policyholder) funds in order to write new business. These early expenses are gradually paid off by the expense loadings in future premiums.

6.7 Profit

The equivalence principle does not allow explicitly for a loading for profit. Since writing business generally involves a loan from shareholder or participating policyholder funds, it is necessary for the business to be sufficiently profitable for the payment of a reasonable rate of return – in other words, to make a profit. In traditional insurance, we often load for profit implicitly, by margins in the valuation assumptions. For example, if we expect to earn an interest rate of 6% per year on assets, we might assume only 5% per year in the premium basis. The extra income from the invested premiums will contribute to profit. In participating business, much of the profit will be distributed to the policyholders in the form of cash dividends or bonuses. Some will be paid as dividends to shareholders, if the company is proprietary.

We may also use margins in the mortality assumptions. For a term insurance, we might use a slightly higher overall mortality rate than we expect. For an annuity, we might use a slightly lower rate.

More modern premium setting approaches, which use projected cash flows, are presented in Chapter 12, where more explicit allowance for profit is incorporated in the methodology.

Each individual policy sold will generate a profit or a loss. Although we calculate a premium assuming a given survival model, for each individual policy the experienced mortality rate in any year can take only the values 0 or 1. So, while the expected outcome under the equivalence principle is zero profit (assuming no margins), the actual outcome for each individual policy will either be a profit or a loss. For the actual profit from a group of policies to be reliably close to the expected profit, we need to sell a large number of contracts to individuals whose future lifetimes can be regarded as statistically independent, so that the losses and profits from individual policies are combined.

As a simple illustration of this, consider a life who purchases a one-year term insurance with sum insured $1000 payable at the end of the year of death. Let us suppose that the life is subject to a mortality of rate of 0.01 over the year, that the insurer can earn interest at 5% per year, and that there are no expenses. Then, using the equivalence principle, the premium is

$$P = 1\,000 \times 0.01/1.05 = 9.52.$$

The future loss random variable is

$$L_0^n = \begin{cases} 1\,000v - P = 942.86 & \text{if } T_x \le 1, \quad \text{with probability } 0.01, \\ -P = -9.52 & \text{if } T_x > 1, \quad \text{with probability } 0.99. \end{cases}$$

The expected loss is $0.01 \times 942.86 + 0.99 \times (-9.52) = 0$, as required by the equivalence principle, but the probability of profit is 0.99, and the probability of loss is 0.01. The balance arises because the profit, if the policyholder survives the year, is small, and the loss, if the policyholder dies, is large. Using the equivalence principle, so that the expected future loss is zero, makes sense only if the insurer issues a large number of policies, so that the overall proportion of policies becoming claims will be close to the assumed proportion of 0.01.

Now suppose the insurer were to issue 100 such policies to independent lives. The insurer would expect to make a (small) profit on 99 of them. If the outcome from this portfolio is that all lives survive for the year, then the insurer makes a profit. If one life dies, there is no profit or loss. If more than one life dies, there will be a loss on the portfolio. Let D denote the number of deaths in the portfolio, so that $D \sim B(100, 0.01)$. The probability that the profit on the whole portfolio is greater than or equal to zero is

$$\Pr[D \le 1] = 0.73576$$

compared with 99% for the individual contract. In fact, as the number of policies issued increases, the probability of profit will tend, monotonically, to 0.5. On the other hand, while the probability of loss is increasing with the portfolio size, the probability of very large aggregate losses (relative, say, to total premiums) is much smaller for a large portfolio, since there is a balancing effect from **diversification** of the risk amongst the large group of policies.

Let us now consider a whole life insurance policy with sum insured S payable at the end of the year of death, initial expenses of I, and renewal expenses of e associated with each premium payment (including the first) issued to a select life aged x by annual premiums of P. For this policy

$$L_0^g = S v^{K_{[x]}+1} + I + e\,\ddot{a}_{\overline{K_{[x]}+1}|} - P\,\ddot{a}_{\overline{K_{[x]}+1}|},$$

where $K_{[x]}$ denotes the curtate future lifetime of $[x]$.

If death occurs shortly after the policy is issued, so that only a few premiums are paid, the insurer will make a loss. Conversely, if the policyholder lives to old age, we would expect that the insurer would make a profit as the policyholder will have paid a large number of premiums, and there will have been plenty of time for the premiums to accumulate interest. We can use the future loss random variable to find the minimum future lifetime for the policyholder in order that the insurer makes a profit on this policy. The probability that the insurer makes a profit on the policy, $\Pr[L_0^g < 0]$, is given by

$$\Pr[L_0^g < 0] = \Pr\left[S v^{K_{[x]}+1} + I + e\,\ddot{a}_{\overline{K_{[x]}+1}|} - P\,\ddot{a}_{\overline{K_{[x]}+1}|} < 0 \right].$$

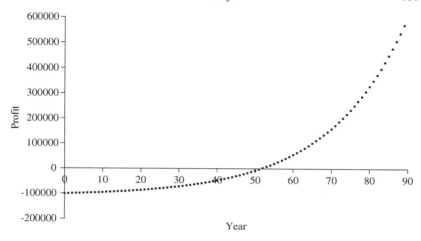

Figure 6.1 Profit at year-end if death occurs in that year for the whole life insurance described in Section 6.7.

Rearranging and replacing $\ddot{a}_{\overline{K_{[x]}+1}}$ with $(1 - v^{K_{[x]}+1})/d$, gives

$$\Pr[L_0^g < 0] = \Pr\left[v^{K_{[x]}+1} < \frac{\frac{P-e}{d} - I}{S + \frac{P-e}{d}}\right]$$

$$= \Pr\left[K_{[x]} + 1 > \frac{1}{\delta}\log\left(\frac{P - e + Sd}{P - e - Id}\right)\right]. \qquad (6.4)$$

Suppose we denote the right-hand side term of the inequality in equation (6.4) by τ, so that the contract generates a profit for the insurer if $K_{[x]} + 1 > \tau$. Generally, τ is not an integer. Thus, if $\lfloor\tau\rfloor$ denotes the integer part of τ, then the insurer makes a profit if the life survives at least $\lfloor\tau\rfloor$ years, the probability of which is $_{\lfloor\tau\rfloor}p_{[x]}$.

Let us continue this illustration by assuming that $x = 30$, $S = \$100\,000$, $I = 1000$ and $e = 50$. Then we find that $P = \$498.45$, and from equation (6.4) we find that there is a profit if $K_{[30]} + 1 > 52.57$. Thus, there is a profit if the life survives for 52 years, the probability of which is $_{52}p_{[30]} = 0.70704$.

Figure 6.1 shows the profits that arise should death occur in a given year, in terms of values at the end of that year. We see that large losses occur in the early years of the policy, and even larger profits occur if the policyholder dies at an advanced age. The probability of realizing either a large loss or profit is small. For example, if the policyholder dies in the first policy year, the loss to the insurer is $\$100\,579$, and the probability of this loss is $q_{[30]} = 0.00027$. Similarly, a profit of $\$308\,070$ arises if the death benefit is payable at time 80, and the probability of this is $_{79|}q_{[30]} = 0.00023$. It is important to appreciate that the premium has been calculated in such a way that the EPV of the profit from the policy is zero.

Example 6.10 A life insurer is about to issue a 25-year endowment insurance with a basic sum insured of \$250 000 to a select life aged exactly 30. Premiums are payable annually throughout the term of the policy. Initial expenses are \$1200 plus 40% of the first premium and renewal expenses are 1% of the second and subsequent premiums. The insurer allows for a compound reversionary bonus of 2.5% of the basic sum insured, vesting on each policy anniversary (including the last). The death benefit is payable at the end of the year of death. Assume the Standard Select Survival Model with interest at 5% per year.

(a) Derive an expression for the future loss random variable, L_0^g, for this policy.
(b) Calculate the annual premium for this policy.
(c) Let $L_0(k)$ denote the present value of the loss on the policy given that $K_{[30]} = k$ for $k \leq 24$ and let $L_0(25)$ denote the present value of the loss on the policy given that the policyholder survives to age 55. Calculate $L_0(k)$ for $k = 0, 1, \ldots, 25$.
(d) Calculate the probability that the insurer makes a profit on this policy.
(e) Calculate $V[L_0^g]$.

Solution 6.10 (a) First, we note that if the policyholder's curtate future lifetime, $K_{[30]}$, is k years where $k = 0, 1, 2, \ldots, 24$, then the number of bonus additions is k, the death benefit is payable $k+1$ years from issue, and hence the present value of the death benefit is $250\,000(1.025)^{K_{[30]}} v^{K_{[30]}+1}$. However, if the policyholder survives for 25 years, then 25 bonuses are applied. Thus, if P denotes the annual premium,

$$L_0^g = 250\,000(1.025^{\min(K_{[30]},\,25)})v^{\min(K_{[30]}+1,\,25)}$$
$$+ 1\,200 + 0.39P - 0.99P\ddot{a}_{\overline{\min(K_{[30]}+1,\,25)}}.$$

(b) The EPV of the premiums, less premium expenses, is

$$0.99P\ddot{a}_{[30]:\overline{25}|} = 14.5838P.$$

As the death benefit is \$250 000(1.025^t) if the policyholder dies in the tth policy year, the EPV of the death benefit is

$$250\,000 \sum_{t=0}^{24} v^{t+1}\,_t|q_{[30]}\,(1.025^t) = 250\,000\left(\frac{1}{1.025}A^{\;1}_{[30]:\overline{25}|\,j}\right) = 3099.37$$

where $1 + j = (1+i)/(1.025)$, so that $j = 0.02439$.

Table 6.2 *Values of the future loss*
random variable for Example 6.10.

Value of $K_{[30]}$, k	PV of loss, $L_0(k)$
0	233 437
1	218 561
$\vdots$	$\vdots$
23	1737
24	−4517
≥ 25	−1179

The EPV of the survival benefit is

$$250\,000v^{25}\ {}_{25}p_{[30]}\ 1.025^{25} = 134\,295.43,$$

and the EPV of the remaining expenses is

$$1200 + 0.39P.$$

Hence, equating the EPV of premium income with the EPV of benefits plus expenses we find that $P = \$9764.44$.

(c) Given that $K_{[30]} = k$, where $k = 0, 1, \ldots, 24$, the present value of the loss is the present value of the death benefit payable at time $k + 1$ less the present value of $k + 1$ premiums plus the present value of expenses. Hence

$$L_0(k) = 250\,000(1.025^k)\,v^{k+1} + 1200 + 0.39P - 0.99P\ddot{a}_{\overline{k+1}|}.$$

If the policyholder survives to age 55, there is one extra bonus payment, and the present value of the future loss is

$$L_0(25) = 250\,000(1.025^{25})\,v^{25} + 1200 + 0.39P - 0.99P\ddot{a}_{\overline{25}|}.$$

Some values of the present value of the future loss are shown in Table 6.2.

(d) The full set of values for the present value of the future loss shows that there is a profit if and only if the policyholder survives 24 years and pays the premium at the start of the 25th policy year. Hence the probability of a profit is ${}_{24}p_{[30]} = 0.98297$.

Note that this probability is based on the assumption that future expenses and future interest rates are known and will be as in the premium basis.

(e) From the full set of values for $L_0(k)$ we can calculate

$$\mathrm{E}[(L_0^g)^2] = \sum_{k=0}^{24}(L_0(k))^2\ {}_k|q_{[30]} + (L_0(25))^2\ {}_{25}p_{[30]} = 12\,115.55^2$$

which is equal to the variance as $\mathrm{E}[L_0^g] = 0$. $\qquad\square$

Generally speaking, for an insurance policy, the longer a life survives, the greater is the profit to the insurer, as illustrated in Figure 6.1. However, the converse is true for annuities, as the following example illustrates.

Example 6.11 An insurance company is about to issue a single premium deferred annuity to a select life aged 55. The first annuity payment will take place 10 years from issue, and payments will be annual. The first annuity payment will be $50 000, and each subsequent payment will be 3% greater than the previous payment. Ignoring expenses, and using the Standard Select Survival Model with interest at 5% per year, calculate

(a) the single premium,
(b) the probability the insurance company makes a profit from this policy, and
(c) the probability that the present value of the loss exceeds $100 000.

Solution 6.11 (a) Let P denote the single premium. Then

$$P = 50\,000 \sum_{t=10}^{\infty} v^t (1.03^{t-10}) \, {}_t p_{[55]} = \$546\,812.$$

(b) Let $L_0(k)$ denote the present value of the loss given that $K_{[55]} = k$, $k = 0, 1, \ldots$. Then

$$L_0(k) = \begin{cases} -P & \text{for } k = 0, 1, \ldots, 9, \\ -P + 50\,000 v^{10}\, \ddot{a}_{\overline{k-9}|j} & \text{for } k = 10, 11, \ldots, \end{cases} \quad (6.5)$$

where $j = 1.05/1.03 - 1 = 0.019417$.

Since $\ddot{a}_{\overline{k-9}|j}$ is an increasing function of k, formula (6.5) shows that $L_0(k)$ is an increasing function of k for $k \geq 10$. The present value of the profit will be positive if $L_0(k) < 0$. Using formula (6.5), this condition can be expressed as

$$-P + 50\,000 \, v^{10} \ddot{a}_{\overline{k-9}|j} < 0,$$

or, equivalently,

$$\ddot{a}_{\overline{k-9}|j} < (1.05)^{10} P/50\,000.$$

Writing $\ddot{a}_{\overline{k-9}|j} = (1 - v_j^{k-9})/d_j$ where $d_j = j/(1 + j)$, this condition becomes

$$v_j^{k-9} > 1 - d_j (1.05)^{10} P/50\,000,$$

and as $v_j = \exp\{-\delta_j\}$ where $\delta_j = \log(1 + j)$ this gives

$$k - 9 < -\log\left(1 - d_j (1.05)^{10} P/50\,000\right)/\delta_j.$$

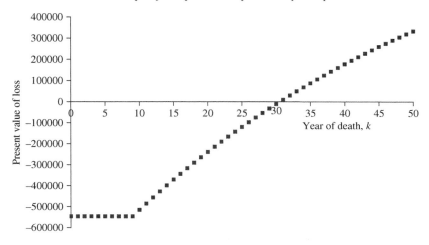

Figure 6.2 Present value of loss from Example 6.11.

Hence we find that $L_0(k) < 0$ if $k < 30.55$, and so there will be a profit if the policyholder dies before age 86. The probability of this is $1 - {}_{31}p_{[55]} = 0.41051$.

(c) The present value of the loss will exceed $100\,000$ if

$$-P + 50\,000v^{10}\ddot{a}_{\overline{k-9}\rceil j} > 100\,000,$$

and following through exactly the same arguments as in part (b) we find that $L_0(k) > 100\,000$ if $k > 35.68$.

Hence the present value of the loss will be greater than $\$100\,000$ if the policyholder survives to age 91, and the probability of this is ${}_{36}p_{[55]} = 0.38462$.

Figure 6.2 shows $L_0(k)$ for $k = 1, 2, \ldots, 50$. We can see that the loss is constant for the first 10 years at $-P$ and then increases due to annuity payments. In contrast to Figure 6.1, longevity results in large losses to the insurer. We can also clearly see from this figure that the loss is negative if k takes a value less than 31, confirming our answer to part (b). □

6.8 The portfolio percentile premium principle

The portfolio percentile premium principle is an alternative to the equivalence premium principle. We assume a large portfolio of identical and independent policies. By 'identical' we mean that the policies have the same premium, benefits, term, and so on, and that the policyholders are all subject to the same survival model. By 'independent' we mean that the policyholders are independent of each other with respect to mortality.

Suppose we know the sum insured for these policies, and wish to find an appropriate premium. As the policies are identical, each policy has the same future loss random variable. Let N denote the number of policies in the portfolio and let $L_{0,i}$ represent the future loss random variable for the ith policy in the portfolio, $i = 1, 2, 3, \ldots, N$. The total future loss in the portfolio is L, say, where

$$L = \sum_{i=1}^{N} L_{0,i}; \quad \mathrm{E}[L] = \sum_{i=1}^{N} \mathrm{E}[L_{0,i}] = N\mathrm{E}[L_{0,1}];$$

$$\mathrm{V}[L] = \sum_{i=1}^{N} \mathrm{V}[L_{0,i}] = N\mathrm{V}[L_{0,1}].$$

(Note that as $\{L_{0,i}\}_{i=1}^{N}$ are identically distributed, the mean and variance of each $L_{0,i}$ are equal to the mean and variance of $L_{0,1}$.)

The portfolio percentile premium principle sets a premium so that there is a specified probability, say α, that the total future loss is negative. That is, P is set such that

$$\mathrm{Pr}[L < 0] = \alpha.$$

Now, if N is sufficiently large (say, greater than around 30), the central limit theorem tells us that L is approximately normally distributed, with mean $\mathrm{E}[L] = N\mathrm{E}[L_{0,1}]$ and variance $\mathrm{V}[L] = N\mathrm{V}[L_{0,1}]$. In this case, the portfolio percentile principle premium can be calculated from

$$\mathrm{Pr}[L < 0] = \mathrm{Pr}\left(\frac{L - \mathrm{E}[L]}{\sqrt{\mathrm{V}[L]}} < \frac{-\mathrm{E}[L]}{\sqrt{\mathrm{V}[L]}} \right) = \Phi\left(\frac{-\mathrm{E}[L]}{\sqrt{\mathrm{V}[L]}} \right) = \alpha,$$

which implies that

$$\frac{\mathrm{E}[L]}{\sqrt{\mathrm{V}[L]}} = -\Phi^{-1}(\alpha)$$

where Φ is the cumulative distribution function of the standard normal distribution.

Our aim is to calculate P, but P does not appear explicitly in either of the last two equations. However, as illustrated in the next example, both the mean and the variance of L are functions of P.

Example 6.12 An insurer issues whole life insurance policies to select lives aged 30. The sum insured of \$100 000 is paid at the end of the month of death and level monthly premiums are payable throughout the term of the policy. Initial expenses, incurred at the issue of the policy, are 15% of the total of the first year's premiums. Renewal expenses are 4% of every premium, including those in the first year.

Assume the Standard Select Survival Model with interest at 5% per year.

(a) Calculate the monthly premium using the equivalence principle.
(b) Calculate the monthly premium using the portfolio percentile principle, such that the probability that the future loss on the portfolio is negative is 95%. Assume a portfolio of 10 000 identical, independent policies.

Solution 6.12 (a) Let P be the monthly premium. Then the EPV of premiums is

$$12P \ddot{a}_{[30]}^{(12)} = 227.065P.$$

The EPV of benefits is

$$100\,000 A_{[30]}^{(12)} = 7\,866.18,$$

and the EPV of expenses is

$$0.15 \times 12P + 0.04 \times 12P \ddot{a}_{[30]}^{(12)} = 10.8826P.$$

Equating the EPV of premiums with the EPVs of benefits and expenses gives the equivalence principle premium as \$36.39 per month.

(b) The future loss random variable for the ith policy is

$$L_{0,i} = 100\,000 v^{K_{[30]}^{(12)} + \frac{1}{12}} + 0.15 \times 12P - 0.96 \times 12P \ddot{a}_{\overline{K_{[30]}^{(12)} + \frac{1}{12}}|}^{(12)},$$

and its expected value can be calculated using the solution to part (a) as

$$E[L_{0,i}] = 7\,866.14 - 216.18P.$$

To find $V[L_{0,i}]$ we can rewrite $L_{0,i}$ as

$$L_{0,i} = \left(100\,000 + \frac{0.96 \times 12P}{d^{(12)}}\right) v^{K_{[30]}^{(12)} + \frac{1}{12}} + 0.15 \times 12P - \frac{0.96 \times 12P}{d^{(12)}}$$

so that

$$V[L_{0,i}] = \left(100\,000 + \frac{0.96 \times 12P}{d^{(12)}}\right)^2 \left(^2 A_{[30]}^{(12)} - (A_{[30]}^{(12)})^2\right)$$
$$= (100\,000 + 236.59P)^2 (0.0053515)$$

giving

$$\sqrt{V[L_{0,i}]} = (100\,000 + 236.59P)(0.073154).$$

Table 6.3 *Premiums
according to portfolio size.*

n	P
1 000	38.31
2 000	37.74
5 000	37.24
10 000	36.99
20 000	36.81

The future loss random variable for the portfolio of policies is $L = \sum_{i=1}^{10\,000} L_{0,i}$, so

$$E[L] = 10\,000(7866.18 - 216.18P)$$

and

$$V[L] = 10\,000\,(100\,000 + 236.59P)^2\,(0.0053515).$$

Using the normal approximation to the distribution of L, we set P such that

$$\Pr[L < 0] = \Phi\left(\frac{-E[L]}{\sqrt{V[L]}}\right) = \Phi\left(\frac{10\,000(216.18P - 7\,866.18)}{100\,(100\,000 + 236.59P)\,(0.073154)}\right)$$
$$= 0.95.$$

For the standard normal distribution, $\Phi(1.645) = 0.95$, so we set

$$\frac{100(216.18P - 7\,866.18)}{(100\,000 + 236.59P)\,(0.073154)} = 1.645$$

which gives $P = \$36.99$.   □

Note that the solution to part (b) above depends on the number of policies in the portfolio (10 000) and the level of probability we set for the future loss being negative (0.95). If the portfolio had n policies instead of 10 000, then the equation we would have to solve for the premium, P, is

$$\frac{\sqrt{n}(216.18P - 7\,866.18)}{(100\,000 + 236.59P)\,(0.073154)} = 1.645. \qquad (6.6)$$

Table 6.3 shows some values of P for different values of n. We note that P decreases as n increases. In fact, as $n \to \infty$, $P \to \$36.39$, which is the equivalence principle premium. The reason for this is that as $n \to \infty$ the insurer diversifies the mortality risk. We discuss diversification of risk further in Chapter 11.

6.9 Extra risks

As we discussed in Section 1.3.5, when an individual wishes to effect a life insurance policy, underwriting takes place. If underwriting determines that an individual should not be offered insurance at standard rates, the individual might still be offered insurance, but above standard rates. There are different ways in which we can model the extra mortality risk in a premium calculation.

6.9.1 Age rating

One reason why an individual might not be offered insurance at standard rates is that the individual suffers from a medical condition. In such circumstances we refer to the individual as an impaired life, and the insurer may compensate for this extra risk by treating the individual as being older. For example, an impaired life aged 40 might be asked to pay the same premium paid by a non-impaired life aged 45. This approach to modelling extra risk involves no new ideas in premium calculation – for example, we could apply the equivalence principle in our calculation, and we would simply change the policyholder's age. This is referred to as **age rating**.

6.9.2 Constant addition to μ_x

Individuals can also be deemed to be ineligible for standard rates if they regularly participate in hazardous pursuits, for example parachuting. For such individuals the extra risk is largely independent of age, and so we could model this extra risk by adding a constant to the force of mortality – just as Makeham extended Gompertz' law of mortality. The application of this approach leads to some computational shortcuts for the following reason. We are modelling the force of mortality as

$$\mu'_{[x]+s} = \mu_{[x]+s} + \phi$$

where functions with the superscript $'$ relate to the impaired life, functions without this superscript relate to a standard survival model and ϕ is the constant addition to the force of mortality. Then

$$_t p'_{[x]} = \exp\left\{-\int_0^t \mu'_{[x]+s}ds\right\} = \exp\left\{-\int_0^t \left(\mu_{[x]+s} + \phi\right)ds\right\} = e^{-\phi t} \,_t p_{[x]}.$$

This formula is useful for computing the EPV of a survival benefit since

$$e^{-\delta t} \,_t p'_{[x]} = e^{-(\delta+\phi)t} \,_t p_{[x]},$$

so that, for example,

$$\ddot{a}'_{[x]:\overline{n}|} = \sum_{t=0}^{n-1} e^{-\delta t} \,_t p'_{[x]} = \sum_{t=0}^{n-1} e^{-(\delta+\phi)t} \,_t p_{[x]} = \ddot{a}_{[x]:\overline{n}|\, j}, \qquad (6.7)$$

where j denotes calculation at interest rate $j = e^{\phi+\delta} - 1$. Note that $\ddot{a}_{[x]:\overline{n}|\, j}$ is calculated using rate of interest j and the Standard Select Survival Model.

Now suppose that the impaired life has curtate future lifetime $K'_{[x]}$. We know that

$$\ddot{a}'_{[x]:\overline{n}|} = E\left[\ddot{a}_{\overline{\min(K'_{[x]}+1,n)}|}\right] = \frac{1 - E[v^{\min(K'_{[x]}+1,n)}]}{d} = \frac{1 - A'_{[x]:\overline{n}|}}{d}.$$

So

$$A'_{[x]:\overline{n}|} = 1 - d\,\ddot{a}'_{[x]:\overline{n}|} = 1 - d\,\ddot{a}_{[x]:\overline{n}|\, j}. \qquad (6.8)$$

It is important to note here that for the insurance benefit we cannot just change the interest rate. In formula (6.8), the annuity is evaluated at rate j, but the function d uses the original rate of interest, that is $d = i/(1 + i)$. Generally, when using the constant addition to the force of mortality, it is simplest to calculate the annuity function first, using a simple adjustment of interest, then use formula (6.8) for any insurance factors. Note that the standard discount function $_n E_x = v^n \,_n p_x$ is a survival benefit value, and so can be calculated for the extra risk by an interest adjustment, so that

$$_n E'_x = v^n_j \,_n p_x.$$

Example 6.13 Calculate the annual premium for a 20-year endowment insurance with sum insured \$200 000 issued to a life aged 30 whose force of mortality at age $30+s$ is given by $\mu_{[30]+s} + 0.01$. Allow for initial expenses of \$2000 plus 40% of the first premium, and renewal expenses of 2% of the second and subsequent premiums. Use the Standard Select Survival Model with interest at 5% per year.

Solution 6.13 Let P denote the annual premium. Then by applying formula (6.7), the EPV of premium income is

$$P \sum_{t=0}^{19} v^t \,_t p'_{[30]} = P\ddot{a}_{[30]:\overline{20}|\, j}$$

where $j = 1.05e^{0.01} - 1 = 0.06055$. Similarly, the EPV of expenses is

$$2000 + 0.38P + 0.02P\ddot{a}_{[30]:\overline{20}|\, j}.$$

The EPV of the benefit is $200\,000 A'_{[30]:\overline{20}|}$, where the dash denotes extra mortality and the interest rate is $i = 0.05$. Using formula (6.8)

$$A'_{[30]:\overline{20}|} = 1 - d\,\ddot{a}_{[30]:\overline{20}|\,j}.$$

As $\ddot{a}_{[30]:\overline{20}|\,j} = 12.072$ and $d = 0.05/1.05$, we find that $A'_{[30]:\overline{20}|} = 0.425158$ and hence we find that $P = \$7600.84$. $\qquad\square$

6.9.3 Constant multiple of mortality rates

A third method of allowing for extra mortality is to assume that lives are subject to mortality rates that are higher than the standard lives' mortality rates. For example, we might set $q'_{[x]+t} = 1.1 q_{[x]+t}$ where the superscript $'$ again denotes extra mortality risk. With such an approach we can calculate the probability of surviving one year from any integer age, and hence we can calculate the probability of surviving an integer number of years. A computational disadvantage of this approach is that we have to apply approximations in calculating EPVs if payments are at other than annual intervals. Generally, this form of extra risk would be handled by recalculating the required functions in a spreadsheet.

Example 6.14 Calculate the monthly premium for a 10-year term insurance with sum insured $\$100\,000$ payable immediately on death, issued to a life aged 50. Assume that each year throughout the 10-year term the life is subject to mortality rates that are 10% higher than for a standard life of the same age. Allow for initial expenses of $\$1000$ plus 50% of the first monthly premium and renewal expenses of 3% of the second and subsequent monthly premiums. Use the UDD assumption where appropriate, and use the Standard Select Survival Model with interest at 5% per year.

Solution 6.14 Let P denote the total premium per year. Then the EPV of premium income is $P\ddot{a}^{(12)\,'}_{50:\overline{10}|}$ and, assuming UDD, we compute $\ddot{a}^{(12)\,'}_{50:\overline{10}|}$ as

$$\ddot{a}^{(12)\,'}_{50:\overline{10}|} = \alpha(12)\ddot{a}'_{50:\overline{10}|} - \beta(12)\left(1 - v^{10}\,_{10}p'_{50}\right),$$

where

$$\alpha(12) = \frac{id}{i^{(12)}d^{(12)}} = 1.0002$$

and

$$\beta(12) = \frac{i - i^{(12)}}{i^{(12)}d^{(12)}} = 0.4665.$$

As the initial expenses are 1000 plus 50% of the first premium, which is $\frac{1}{12}P$, we can write the EPV of expenses as

$$1000 + \frac{0.47P}{12} + 0.03P\ddot{a}^{(12)\,\prime}_{50:\overline{10}|}.$$

Finally, the EPV of the death benefit is $100\,000(\bar{A}^{\,1}_{50:\overline{10}|})'$ and, using UDD, we can compute this as

$$(\bar{A}^{\,1}_{50:\overline{10}|})' = \frac{i}{\delta}(A^{\,1}_{50:\overline{10}|})'$$

$$= \frac{i}{\delta}\left((A_{50:\overline{10}|})' - v^{10}\,_{10}p'_{50}\right)$$

$$= \frac{i}{\delta}\left(1 - d\ddot{a}'_{50:\overline{10}|} - v^{10}\,_{10}p'_{50}\right).$$

The formula for $\ddot{a}'_{50:\overline{10}|}$ is

$$\ddot{a}'_{50:\overline{10}|} = \sum_{t=0}^{9} v^t\,_t p'_{50}$$

where

$$_t p'_{50} = \prod_{r=0}^{t-1}(1 - 1.1q_{[50]+r}). \qquad (6.9)$$

(We have written $q_{[50]+r}$ in formula (6.9) as standard lives are subject to select mortality.) Hence $\ddot{a}'_{50:\overline{10}|} = 8.0516$, $\ddot{a}^{(12)\,\prime}_{50:\overline{10}|} = 7.8669$ and $(\bar{A}^{\,1}_{50:\overline{10}|})' = 0.01621$, which give $P = \$345.18$ and so the monthly premium is $\$28.76$.

Table 6.4 shows how we could set out a spreadsheet to perform calculations. Column (2) was created from the original mortality rates using formula (6.9), with column (3) being calculated as

$$_{t|}q'_{50} = \,_t p'_{50}\,(1 - 1.1\,q_{50+t}).$$

The total in column (6) gives $\ddot{a}'_{50:\overline{10}|}$ while the total in column (7) gives the value for $(A^{\,1}_{50:\overline{10}|})'$. Note that this must then by multiplied by i/δ to get $(\bar{A}^{\,1}_{50:\overline{10}|})'$. □

6.10 Notes and further reading

The equivalence principle is the traditional approach to premium calculation, and we apply it again in Chapter 7 when we consider the possibility that a policy may terminate for reasons other than death. However, other approaches to premium calculation are possible. We have seen one in Section 6.8, where we computed premiums by the portfolio percentile principle.

Table 6.4 *Spreadsheet calculations for Example 6.14.*

(1)	(2)	(3)	(4)	(5)	(6)	(7)
t	$_tp'_{50}$	$_t|q'_{50}$	v^t	v^{t+1}	(2) × (4)	(3) × (5)
0	1.0000	0.0011	1.0000	0.9524	1.0000	0.0011
1	0.9989	0.0014	0.9524	0.9070	0.9513	0.0013
2	0.9975	0.0016	0.9070	0.8638	0.9047	0.0014
3	0.9959	0.0018	0.8638	0.8227	0.8603	0.0015
4	0.9941	0.0020	0.8227	0.7835	0.8178	0.0015
5	0.9921	0.0022	0.7835	0.7462	0.7774	0.0016
6	0.9899	0.0024	0.7462	0.7107	0.7387	0.0017
7	0.9875	0.0027	0.7107	0.6768	0.7018	0.0018
8	0.9849	0.0030	0.6768	0.6446	0.6666	0.0019
9	0.9819	0.0033	0.6446	0.6139	0.6329	0.0020
				Total	8.0516	0.0158

A modification of the equivalence principle which builds an element of profit into a premium calculation is to select a profit target amount for each policy, Π, say, and set the premium to be the smallest possible such that $E[L_0] \leq \Pi$. Under this method of calculation we effectively set a level for the expected present value of future profit from the policy and calculate the premium by treating this amount as an additional cost at the issue date which will be met by future premium income.

Besides the premium principles discussed in this chapter, there is one further important method of calculating premiums. This is profit testing, which is the subject of Chapter 12.

The international actuarial notation for premiums may be found in Bowers *et al.* (1997). We have omitted it in this book because we find it has no particular benefit in practice.

6.11 Exercises

When a calculation is required in the following exercises, unless otherwise stated you should assume that mortality follows the Standard Select Survival Model as specified in Section 6.3, that interest is at 5% per year effective, and that the equivalence principle is used for the calculation of premiums.

Some annuity and insurance functions for the Standard Select and Ultimate Survival Models, with interest at 5% per year effective, are given in Appendix D.

Exercise 6.1 Consider a whole life insurance with annual premiums and a 20-year premium paying term issued to a select life aged 30, with sum insured $200 000 payable at the end of the year of death.

(a) Write down an expression for the net future loss random variable.
(b) Calculate the net annual premium.
(c) Calculate the probability that the contract makes a profit.

Exercise 6.2 Consider a five-year term insurance issued to a select life aged 40 by a single premium, with sum insured $1 million payable immediately on death.

(a) Write down an expression for the net future loss random variable.
(b) Calculate the net single premium, assuming UDD.
(c) Calculate the probability that the contract makes a profit.

Exercise 6.3 You are given the following extract from a select life table with a four-year select period. A select individual aged 41 purchased a three-year term insurance with a net premium of $350 payable annually. The sum insured is paid at the end of the year of death.

$[x]$	$l_{[x]}$	$l_{[x]+1}$	$l_{[x]+2}$	$l_{[x]+3}$	l_{x+4}	$x+4$
[40]	100 000	99 899	99 724	99 520	99 288	44
[41]	99 802	99 689	99 502	99 283	99 033	45
[42]	99 597	99 471	99 268	99 030	98 752	46

Use an effective rate of interest of 6% per year to calculate

(a) the sum insured, assuming the equivalence principle,
(b) the standard deviation of L_0, and
(c) $\Pr[L_0 > 0]$.

Exercise 6.4 Consider a 10-year annual premium term insurance issued to a select life aged 50, with sum insured $100 000 payable at the end of the year of death.

(a) Write down an expression for the net future loss random variable.
(b) Calculate the net annual premium.

Exercise 6.5 Consider a 20-year annual premium endowment insurance with sum insured $100 000 issued to a select life aged 35. Assume initial expenses of 3% of the basic sum insured and 20% of the first premium, and renewal expenses of 3% of the second and subsequent premiums. Assume that the death benefit is payable at the end of the year of death.

(a) Write down an expression for the gross future loss random variable.
(b) Calculate the gross annual premium.
(c) Calculate the standard deviation of the gross future loss random variable.
(d) Calculate the probability that the contract makes a profit.

Exercise 6.6 A select life aged 45 effects a 20-year endowment insurance with level annual premiums payable throughout the policy term, with sum insured $100 000 payable at the end of the year of death, or at maturity. Calculate the annual premium allowing for expenses of 10% of the first annual premium and 2% of each subsequent premium, with further initial expenses of $50 and renewal expenses (at the time of payment of the second and each subsequent premium) of $8.

Exercise 6.7 A select life aged 45 effects by a single premium a policy which provides an annuity of $40 000 per year, payable annually in advance from age 65. In the event of death before age 65, the premium is returned at the end of the year of death.

(a) Write down an expression for the net future loss random variable.
(b) Calculate the single premium.
(c) Now suppose that the annuity is guaranteed to be paid for at least 5 years if the life survives to age 65. Calculate the revised single premium.

Exercise 6.8 Consider an annual premium with-profit whole life insurance issued to a select life aged exactly 40. The basic sum insured is $200 000 payable at the end of the month of death, and the premium term is 25 years. Assume a compound reversionary bonus of 1.5% per year, vesting on each policy anniversary, initial expenses of 60% of the annual premium, renewal expenses of 2.5% of all premiums after the first, plus per policy expenses (incurred when a premium is payable) of $5 at the beginning of the first year, increasing by 6% per year compound at the beginning of each subsequent year.

Calculate the annual premium.

Exercise 6.9 A select life aged exactly 40 has purchased a deferred annuity policy. Under the terms of the policy, the annuity payments will commence 20 years from the issue date and will be payable at annual intervals thereafter. The initial annuity payment will be $50 000, and each subsequent payment will be 2% greater than the previous one. The policy has monthly premiums, payable for at most 20 years. Calculate the gross monthly premium allowing for initial expenses of 2.5% of the first annuity payment and 20% of the first premium, renewal expenses of 5% of the second and subsequent premiums, and terminal expenses, incurred at the end of the year of death, of $20 inflated from the issue date assuming an inflation rate of 3% per year.

Exercise 6.10 Find the annual premium for a 20-year term insurance with sum insured $100 000 payable at the end of the year of death, issued to a select life aged 40 with premiums payable for at most 10 years, with expenses, which are incurred at the beginning of each policy year, as follows:

	Year 1		Years 2+	
	% of premium	Constant	% of premium	Constant
Taxes	4%	0	4%	0
Sales commission	25%	0	5%	0
Policy maintenance	0%	10	0%	5

Exercise 6.11 A life insurer is about to issue a 30-year deferred annuity-due with annual payments of $20 000 to a select life aged 35. The policy has a single premium which is refunded without interest at the end of the year of death if death occurs during the deferred period.

(a) Calculate the single premium for this annuity.
(b) The insurer offers an option that if the policyholder dies before the total annuity payments exceed the single premium, then the balance will be paid as a death benefit, at the end of the year of death. Calculate the revised premium.

This is called a **Cash Refund Payout Option.**

Exercise 6.12 A whole life insurance with unit sum insured payable at the end of the year of death with a level annual premium is issued to (x). Let L_0 be the net future loss random variable with the premium determined by the equivalence principle. Let L_0^* be the net future loss random variable if the premium is determined such that $E[L_0^*] = -0.5$.

Given $V[L_0] = 0.75$, calculate $V[L_0^*]$.

Exercise 6.13 Calculate both the net and gross premiums for a whole life insurance issued to a select life aged 40. The sum insured is $100 000 on death during the first 20 years, and $20 000 thereafter, and is payable immediately on death. Premiums are payable annually in advance for a maximum of 20 years.

Use the following basis:

Survival model:
  ultimate rates   Makeham's law with $A = 0.0001$, $B = 0.00035$,
                          $c = 1.075$
  select rates   Two year select period, $q_{[x]} = 0.75q_x$, $q_{[x]+1} = 0.9q_{x+1}$
Interest: 6% per year effective
Premium expenses: 30% of the first year's premium
                          plus 3% of all premiums after the first year
Other expenses: On each premium date an additional expense
                          starting at $10 and increasing at a compound rate
                          of 3% per year

Exercise 6.14 A life insurance company issues a 10-year term insurance policy to a life aged 50, with sum insured $100 000. Level premiums are paid monthly in advance throughout the term. Calculate the gross premium allowing for initial expenses of $100 plus 20% of each premium payment in the first year, renewal expenses of 5% of all premiums after the first year, and claim expenses of $250. Assume the sum insured and claim expenses are paid one month after the date of death, and use claims acceleration.

Exercise 6.15 For a special whole life insurance on (55), you are given:

- initial annual premiums are level for 10 years; thereafter annual premiums equal one-half of initial annual premiums,
- the death benefit is $100 000 during the first 10 years of the contract, is $50 000 thereafter, and is payable at the end of the year of death, and
- expenses are 25% of the first year's premium plus 3% of all subsequent premiums.

Calculate the initial annual gross premium.

Exercise 6.16 For a whole life insurance with sum insured $150 000 paid at the end of the year of death, issued to (x), you are given:

(i) $^2A_x = 0.0143$,

(ii) $A_x = 0.0653$, and

(iii) the annual premium is determined using the equivalence principle.

Calculate the standard deviation of L_0^n.

Exercise 6.17 A life insurance company sells annuities to men aged exactly 60. Each policyholder pays a single net premium, P, and then receives an annuity of $30 000 a year in arrear (so that the first annuity payment is on the 61st birthday).

(a) Calculate P.

(b) Calculate the probability that the present value of profit on a single policy is positive.

(c) Calculate the standard deviation of the present value of profit on a single policy.

(d) Now suppose that the office sells 1000 such annuities simultaneously to independent lives. Calculate the value of P such that the probability that the present value of the profit to the insurance company is positive is 95%.

Exercise 6.18 A life is subject to extra risk that is modelled by a constant addition to the force of mortality, so that, if the extra risk functions are denoted by $'$, $\mu'_x = \mu_x + \phi$. Show that at rate of interest i,

$$\bar{A}'_x = (\bar{A}_x)_j + \phi\,(\bar{a}_x)_j,$$

where j is a rate of interest that you should specify.

Exercise 6.19 A life insurer is about to issue a 25-year annual premium endowment insurance with a basic sum insured of \$250 000 to a life aged exactly 30. Initial expenses are \$1200 plus 40% of the first premium and renewal expenses are 1% of the second and subsequent premiums. The office allows for a compound reversionary bonus of 2.5% of the basic sum insured, vesting on each policy anniversary (including the last). The death benefit is payable at the end of the year of death.

(a) Let L_0 denote the gross future loss random variable for this policy. Show that

$$L_0 = 250\,000 Z_1 + \frac{0.99 P}{d} Z_2 + 1\,200 + 0.39 P - 0.99 \frac{P}{d}$$

where P is the gross annual premium,

$$Z_1 = \begin{cases} v^{K_{[30]}+1}(1.025)^{K_{[30]}} & \text{if } K_{[30]} \le 24, \\ v^{25}(1.025)^{25} & \text{if } K_{[30]} \ge 25, \end{cases}$$

and

$$Z_2 = \begin{cases} v^{K_{[30]}+1} & \text{if } K_{[30]} \le 24, \\ v^{25} & \text{if } K_{[30]} \ge 25. \end{cases}$$

(b) Using the equivalence principle, calculate P.
(c) Calculate $E[Z_1]$, $E[Z_1^2]$, $E[Z_2]$, $E[Z_2^2]$ and $\text{Cov}[Z_1, Z_2]$. Hence calculate $V[L_0]$ using the value of P from part (b).
(d) Find the probability that the insurer makes a profit on this policy.

Hint: recall the standard results from probability theory, that for random variables X and Y and constants a, b and c, $V[X + c] = V[X]$, and

$$V[aX + bY] = a^2 V[X] + b^2 V[Y] + 2ab\,\text{Cov}[X, Y],$$

with $\text{Cov}[X, Y] = E[XY] - E[X]E[Y]$.

Exercise 6.20 An insurer issues a 20-year endowment insurance policy to (40) with a sum insured of \$250 000, payable at the end of the year of death. Premiums are payable annually in advance throughout the term of the contract.

(a) Calculate the premium using the equivalence principle.
(b) Find the mean and standard deviation of the net future loss random variable using the premium in (a).
(c) Assuming 10 000 identical, independent contracts, estimate the 99th percentile of the net future loss random variable using the premium in (a).

Answers to selected exercises

6.1 (b) $1179.73
   (c) 0.67804

6.2 (b) $2597.95
   (c) 0.99704

6.3 (a) $216 326.38
   (b) $13 731.03
   (c) 0.0052

6.4 (b) $178.57

6.5 (b) $3287.57
   (c) $4981.10
   (d) 0.98466

6.6 $3056.80

6.7 (b) $199 864.74
   (c) $200 706.50

6.8 $3262.60

6.9 $2377.75

6.10 $212.81

6.11 (a) $60 694.00
   (b) $60 774.30

6.12 1.6875

6.13 $1341.40 (net), $1431.08 (gross)

6.14 $214.38

6.15 $1131.13

6.16 $16 076.72

6.17 (a) $417 401.93
   (b) 0.36641
   (c) $97 201.23
   (d) $422 457.83

6.19 (b) $9764.44
   (c) $0.54958,   0.30251, $0.29852,   0.09020,   0.00071,
      146 786 651.
   (d) 0.98297

6.20 (a) $7333.84
   (b) 0, $14 485
   (c) $3 369 626

7

Policy values

7.1 Summary

In this chapter we introduce the concept of a policy value for a life insurance policy. Policy values are a fundamental tool in insurance risk management, as they are used to determine the economic or regulatory capital needed to remain solvent, and also to determine the profit or loss for the company over any time period.

We start by considering the case where all cash flows take place at the start or end of a year. We define the policy value as the expected value of future net cash flows for a policy in force, and distinguish gross premium policy values, which explicitly allow for expenses and for the full gross premium, from net premium policy values, where expenses are excluded from the outgoing cash flows, and only the net premium is counted as income.

We show how to calculate policy values recursively from year to year. We also show how to calculate the profit from a policy in each policy year and we introduce the asset share for a policy.

We extend the analysis to policies where the cash flows are continuous and we derive Thiele's differential equation for policy values – the continuous time equivalent of the recursions for policies with annual cash flows.

We consider how policy values can be used to evaluate policy alterations, where a policyholder chooses to withdraw, or stop paying premiums, for example.

We show how a retrospective valuation has connections both with asset shares and with the policy values determined looking at future cash flows. Finally, we consider how a simple adjustment to the net premium policy value, through modifying the net premium assumed, can be used to approximate the gross premium policy value, and we discuss why this might be useful when acquisition expenses are high.

7.2 Assumptions

In many of the examples and exercises in this chapter, we use the Standard Select Survival Model, as we did in Chapter 6, and which is described in Appendix D. We assume, generally, that lives are select at the time they purchase their policies.

The default rate of interest is 5% per year, though different rates are used in some examples. This means that the tables in Appendix D may be useful for some of the examples and exercises.

Note that the answers given in the text are calculated directly, not from tables, and may differ slightly from those derived from the tables.

7.3 Policies with annual cash flows

7.3.1 The future loss random variable

In Chapter 6 we introduced the future loss random variable, L_0. In this chapter we are concerned with the estimation of future losses at intermediate times during the term of a policy, not just at inception. We therefore extend the future loss random variable definition, in net and gross versions. Consider a policy which is still in force t years after it was issued. The present value of future net loss random variable is denoted L_t^n and the present value of gross future loss random variable is denoted L_t^g, where

$$L_t^n = \text{Present value, at time } t, \text{ of future benefits}$$
$$- \text{Present value, at time } t, \text{ of future net premiums}$$

and

$$L_t^g = \text{Present value, at time } t, \text{ of future benefits}$$
$$+ \text{Present value, at time } t, \text{ of future expenses}$$
$$- \text{Present value, at time } t, \text{ of future gross premiums.}$$

We drop the n or g superscript where it is clear from the context which is meant. Note that the future loss random variable L_t is defined only if the contract is still in force t years after issue.

The example below will help establish some ideas. The important features of this example for our present purposes are that premiums are payable annually and the sum insured is payable at the end of the year of death, so that all cash flows are at the start or end of each year.

Example 7.1 Consider a 20-year endowment policy purchased by a life aged 50. Level premiums are payable annually throughout the term of the policy and the sum insured, $500 000, is payable at the end of the year of death or at the end of the term, whichever is sooner.

The basis used by the insurance company for all calculations is the Standard Select Survival Model, 5% per year interest and no allowance for expenses.

(a) Show that the annual net premium, P, calculated using the equivalence principle, is $15 114.33.
(b) Calculate $E[L_t^n]$ for $t = 10$ and $t = 11$, in both cases just before the premium due at time t is paid.

Solution 7.1 (a) You should check that the following values are correct for this survival model at 5% per year interest:

$$\ddot{a}_{[50]:\overline{20|}} = 12.8456 \quad \text{and} \quad A_{[50]:\overline{20|}} = 0.38830.$$

The equation of value for P is

$$P\ddot{a}_{[50]:\overline{20|}} - 500\,000\,A_{[50]:\overline{20|}} = 0, \tag{7.1}$$

giving

$$P = \frac{500\,000\,A_{[50]:\overline{20|}}}{\ddot{a}_{[50]:\overline{20|}}} = \$15\,114.33.$$

(b) L_{10}^n is the present value of the future net loss 10 years after the policy was purchased, *assuming the policyholder is still alive at that time*. The policyholder will then be aged 60 and the select period for the survival model, two years, will have expired eight years ago. The present value at that time of the future benefits is $500\,000\,v^{\min(K_{60}+1,10)}$ and the present value of the future premiums is $P\,\ddot{a}_{\overline{\min(K_{60}+1,10)|}}$. Hence, the formulae for L_{10}^n and L_{11}^n are

$$L_{10}^n = 500\,000\,v^{\min(K_{60}+1,10)} - P\,\ddot{a}_{\overline{\min(K_{60}+1,10)|}}$$

and

$$L_{11}^n = 500\,000\,v^{\min(K_{61}+1,9)} - P\,\ddot{a}_{\overline{\min(K_{61}+1,9)|}}.$$

Taking expectations and using the annuity values

$$\ddot{a}_{60:\overline{10|}} = 7.9555 \quad \text{and} \quad \ddot{a}_{61:\overline{9|}} = 7.3282$$

we have

$$E[L_{10}^n] = 500\,000\,A_{60:\overline{10|}} - P\ddot{a}_{60:\overline{10|}} = \$190\,339$$

and

$$E[L_{11}^n] = 500\,000\,A_{61:\overline{9|}} - P\ddot{a}_{61:\overline{9|}} = \$214\,757.$$

$\square$

We are now going to look at Example 7.1 in a little more detail. At the time when the policy is issued, at $t = 0$, the future loss random variable, L_0^n, is given by

$$L_0^n = 500\,000\, v^{\min(K_{[50]}+1,20)} - P\ddot{a}_{\overline{\min(K_{[50]}+1,20)}|}.$$

Since the premium is calculated using the equivalence principle, we know that $E[L_0^n] = 0$, which is equivalent to equation (7.1). That is, at the time the policy is issued, the expected value of the present value of the loss on the contract is zero, so that, in expectation, the future premiums (from time 0) are exactly sufficient to provide the future benefits.

Consider the financial position of the insurer at time 10 with respect to this policy. The policyholder may have died before time 10. If so, the sum insured will have been paid and no more premiums will be received. In this case the insurer no longer has any liability with respect to this policy. Now suppose the policyholder is still alive at time 10. In this case the calculation in part (b) shows that the future loss random variable, L_{10}^n, has a positive expected value ($\$190\,339$) so that future premiums (from time 10) are **not** expected to be sufficient to provide the future benefits. For the insurer to be in a financially sound position at time 10, it should hold an amount of at least $\$190\,339$ in its assets so that, together with future premiums from time 10, it can expect to provide the future benefits.

Speaking generally, when a policy is issued the future premiums should be expected to be sufficient to pay for the future benefits and expenses. (If not, the premium should be increased!) However, it is usually the case that for a policy which is still in force t years after being issued, the future premiums (from time t) are not expected to be sufficient to pay for the future benefits and expenses. The amount needed to cover this shortfall is called the **policy value** for the policy at time t.

The insurer should be able to build up assets during the course of the policy because, with a regular level premium and an increasing level of risk, the premium in each of the early years is more than sufficient to pay the expected benefits in that year, given that the life has survived to the start of the year. For example, in the first year the premium of $\$15\,114.33$ is greater than the EPV of the benefit the insurer will pay in that year, $500\,000\, v\, q_{[50]} = \$492.04$. In fact, for the endowment insurance policy studied in Example 7.1, for each year except the last the premium exceeds the EPV of the benefits, that is

$$P > 500\,000\, v\, q_{[50]+t} \qquad \text{for } t = 0, 1, \ldots, 18.$$

The final year is different because

$$P = 15\,114.33 < 500\,000\, v = 476\,190.$$

Figure 7.1 EPV at issue of premiums minus claims for each year of a 20-year endowment insurance, sum insured \$500 000, issued to (50).

Note that if the policyholder is alive at the start of the final year, the sum insured will be paid at the end of the year whether or not the policyholder survives the year.

Figure 7.1 shows the excess of the premium over the EPV of the benefit payable at the end of the year for each year of this policy.

Figure 7.2 shows the corresponding values for a 20-year term insurance issued to (50). The sum insured is \$500 000, level annual premiums are payable throughout the term and all calculations use the same basis as in Example 7.1. The pattern is similar in that there is a positive surplus in the early years which can be used to build up the insurer's assets. These assets are needed in the later years when the premium is not sufficient to pay for the expected benefits.

The insurer will then, for a large portfolio, hold back some of the excess cash flow from the early years of the contract in order to meet the shortfall in the later years. This explains the concept of a policy value – we need to hold capital during the term of a policy to meet the liabilities in the period when outgo on benefits exceeds income from premiums. We give a formal definition of a policy value later in this section.

Before doing so, we return to Example 7.1. Suppose the insurer issues a large number, say N, of policies identical to the one in Example 7.1, to independent lives all aged 50. Suppose also that the experience of this group of policyholders is precisely as assumed in the basis used by the insurer in its calculations. In other words, interest is earned on investments at 5% every year, the mortality

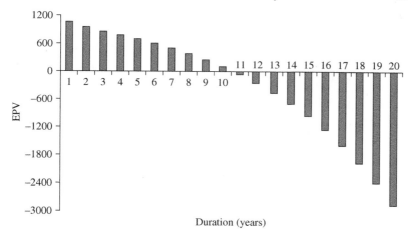

Figure 7.2 EPV at issue of premiums minus claims for each year of a 20-year term insurance, sum insured $500 000, issued to (50).

of the group of policyholders follows precisely the Standard Select Survival Model and there are no expenses.

Consider the financial situation of the insurer after these policies have been in force for 10 years. Some policyholders will have died, so that their sum insured of $500 000 will have been paid at the end of the year in which they died, and some policyholders will still be alive. With our assumptions about the experience, precisely $_{10}p_{[50]}N$ policyholders will still be alive, $q_{[50]}N$ will have died in the first year, $_1|q_{[50]}N$ will have died in the second year, and so on, until the 10th year, when $_9|q_{[50]}N$ policyholders will have died. The accumulation to time 10 at 5% interest of all premiums received (not including the premiums due at time 10) minus all sums insured which have been paid is

$$
NP\left(1.05^{10} + p_{[50]}1.05^9 + \cdots + {}_9p_{[50]}1.05\right)
$$
$$
- 500\,000N\left(q_{[50]}1.05^9 + {}_1|q_{[50]}1.05^8 + \cdots + {}_9|q_{[50]}\right)
$$
$$
= 1.05^{10}\,NP\left(1 + p_{[50]}1.05^{-1} + \cdots + {}_9p_{[50]}1.05^{-9}\right)
$$
$$
- 1.05^{10}\,500\,000N\left(q_{[50]}1.05^{-1} + {}_1|q_{[50]}1.05^{-2} + \cdots + {}_9|q_{[50]}1.05^{-10}\right)
$$
$$
= 1.05^{10}\,N\left(P\ddot{a}_{[50]:\,\overline{10|}} - 500\,000A^{\,1}_{[50]:\,\overline{10|}}\right)
$$
$$
= 186\,634N.
$$

Note that, using the values in part (a) of Example 7.1, we have

$$\ddot{a}_{[50]:\,\overline{10|}} = \ddot{a}_{[50]:\,\overline{20|}} - v^{10}\,_{10}p_{[50]}\,\ddot{a}_{60:\,\overline{10|}} = 8.0566$$

$$A^{\,1}_{[50]:\,\overline{10|}} = 1 - d\ddot{a}_{[50]:\,\overline{10|}} - v^{10}\,_{10}p_{[50]} = 0.01439.$$

So, *if* the experience over the first 10 years follows precisely the assumptions set out in Example 7.1, the insurer will have built up a fund of $186\,634N$ after 10 years. The number of policyholders still alive at that time will be $_{10}p_{[50]}N$ and so the share of this fund for each surviving policyholder is $186\,634N/(_{10}p_{[50]}N) = \$190\,339$. This is precisely the amount the insurer needs. This is not a coincidence! This happens in this example because the premium was calculated using the equivalence principle, so that the EPV of the profit was zero when the policies were issued, and we have assumed the experience up to time 10 was exactly as in the calculation of the premium. Given these assumptions, it should not be surprising that the insurer is in a 'break even' position at time 10.

We can prove that this is true in this case by manipulating the equation of value, equation (7.1), as follows:

$$P\ddot{a}_{[50]:\,\overline{20|}} = 500\,000\,A_{50:\,\overline{20|}}$$

$$\Rightarrow P\left(\ddot{a}_{[50]:\,\overline{10|}} + v^{10}\,_{10}p_{[50]}\,\ddot{a}_{60:\,\overline{10|}}\right) = 500\,000\left(A^{\,1}_{[50]:\,\overline{10|}} + v^{10}\,_{10}p_{[50]}\,A_{60:\,\overline{10|}}\right)$$

$$\Rightarrow P\ddot{a}_{[50]:\,\overline{10|}} - 500\,000\,A^{\,1}_{[50]:\,\overline{10|}} = v^{10}\,_{10}p_{[50]}\left(500\,000\,A_{60:\,\overline{10|}} - P\ddot{a}_{60:\,\overline{10|}}\right)$$

$$\Rightarrow \frac{1.05^{10}}{_{10}p_{[50]}}\left(P\ddot{a}_{[50]:\,\overline{10|}} - 500\,000\,A^{\,1}_{[50]:\,\overline{10|}}\right) = 500\,000\,A_{60:\,\overline{10|}} - P\ddot{a}_{60:\,\overline{10|}}.$$

$$(7.2)$$

The left-hand side of equation (7.2) is the share of the fund built up at time 10 for each surviving policyholder; the right-hand side is the expected value of the future net loss random variable at time 10, $E[L^n_{10}]$, and so is the amount needed by the insurer at time 10 for each policy still in force.

For this example, the proof that the total amount needed by the insurer at time 10 for all policies still in force is precisely equal to the amount of the fund built up, works because

(a) the premium was calculated using the equivalence principle,
(b) the expected value of the future loss random variable was calculated using the premium basis, and
(c) we assumed the experience followed precisely the assumptions in the premium basis.

In practice, (a) and (b) may or may not apply; assumption (c) is extremely unlikely to hold.

7.3.2 Policy values for policies with annual cash flows

In general terms, the policy value for a policy in force at duration t (≥ 0) years after it was purchased is the expected value at that time of the future loss random variable. At this stage we do not need to specify whether this is the gross or net future loss random variable – we will be more precise later in this section.

The general notation for a policy value t years after a policy was issued is $_tV$ (the V comes from 'Policy **V**alue') and we use this notation in this book. There is a standard actuarial notation associated with policy values for certain traditional contracts. This notation is not particularly useful, and so we do not use it. (Interested readers can consult the references in Section 7.10.)

Intuitively, for a policy in force at time t, the policy value at t represents the amount the insurer should have in its assets at that time, so that, in terms of expected present values at t, the policy value together with future premiums will exactly fund the future benefits and expenses. In general terms, we have the equation

$$\boxed{_tV + \text{EPV at } t \text{ of future premiums} = \text{EPV at } t \text{ of future benefits} + \text{expenses.}}$$

An important element in the financial control of an insurance company is the calculation at regular intervals, usually at least annually, of the sum of the policy values for all policies in force at that time and also the value of all the company's investments. For the company to be financially sound, the investments should have a greater value than the total policy value. This process is called a **valuation** of the company. In most countries, valuations are required annually by the insurance supervisory authority.

In the literature, the terms **reserve**, **prospective reserve** and **prospective policy value** are sometimes used in place of *policy value*. We use *policy value* to mean the expected value of the future loss random variable, and restrict *reserve* to mean the actual capital held in respect of a policy, which may be greater than or less than the policy value. We return to this topic in Chapter 12.

The precise definitions of policy value are as follows.

Definition 7.1 *The **gross premium policy value** for a policy in force at duration t (≥ 0) years after it was purchased is the expected value at that time of the gross future loss random variable on a specified basis. The premiums used in the calculation are the actual premiums payable under the contract.*

Definition 7.2 *The **net premium policy value** for a policy in force at duration t (≥ 0) years after it was purchased is the expected value at that time of the net future loss random variable on a specified basis (which makes no allowance for expenses). **The premiums used in the calculation are the net premiums calculated on the policy value basis using the equivalence principle, not the actual premiums payable.***

We make the following comments about these definitions.

(1) Throughout Section 7.3 we restrict ourselves to policies where the cash flows occur only at the start or end of a year since these policies have some simplifying features in relation to policy values. However, Definitions 7.1 and 7.2 apply to more general types of policy, as we show in later sections.

(2) The numerical value of a gross or net premium policy value depends on the assumptions – survival model, interest, expenses, future bonuses – used in its calculation. These assumptions, called the **policy value basis**, may differ from the assumptions used to calculate the premium, that is, the premium basis.

(3) A net premium policy value can be regarded as a special case of a gross premium policy value. Suppose the gross premium is calculated assuming no expenses. Then at issue, the gross and net premiums are the same. However, t years later, the gross premium policy value and the net premium policy value will be the same only if the policy value basis is the same as the original premium basis, which is unlikely to be the case. It is important to understand that the net premium policy value will use a net premium based on the policy value basis, not the original premium basis. The gross premium policy value uses the actual contract premium, with no recalculation.

(4) So, when the policy value basis changes, the net premium policy value requires the recalculation of the premium. See Example 7.2 below. This is a vestige of a time before modern computers, when easy calculation was a key issue – setting reserves based on a net premium policy value allowed the use of computational shortcuts. The net premium policy value is becoming obsolete, but is still widely used in the USA, so it is helpful to understand the concept. Where it is clear from the context whether the policy value is gross or net we refer simply to a *policy value*.

(5) If we are calculating a policy value at an integer duration, that is at the start/end of a year, there may be premiums and/or expenses and/or benefits payable at precisely that time and we need to be careful about which cash flows are included in our future loss random variable. It is the usual practice to regard a premium and any premium-related expenses due at that time as *future* payments and any insurance benefits (i.e. death or maturity

claims) and related expenses as *past* payments. Under annuity contracts, the annuity payments and related expenses may be treated either as *future* payments or as *past* payments, so we need to be particularly careful to specify which it is in such cases.

(6) If an insurance policy has a finite term, n years, for example for an endowment insurance or a term insurance, then at the maturity date there are no future cash flows due, and we say $_nV = 0$ (though, technically, it is undefined, as the policy is no longer in force). Note also that, if the premium is calculated using the equivalence principle *and* the policy value basis is the same as the premium basis, then $_0V = \mathrm{E}[L_0] = 0$.

(7) For an endowment insurance which is still in force at the maturity date, the policy value at that time must be sufficient to pay the sum insured, S, say, so in this case $_{n^-}V = S$ and $_nV = 0$, where n^- denotes the moment before time n.

(8) In the discussion following Example 7.1 in Section 7.3.1 we saw how the insurer built up the reserve for policies still in force by accumulating past premiums minus claims for a group of similar policies. Broadly speaking, this is what would happen in practice, though not with the artificial precision we saw in Section 7.3.1, where the accumulated funds were precisely the amount required by the insurer. In practice, the amount of reserve required for a policy is usually set by calculating a policy value on a specified basis; the funds for the reserve will come from accumulating past premiums, net of past benefit and expense costs. If the past experience of a portfolio of policies is better than the basis assumptions (from the insurer's perspective), for example, higher interest rates and (for death benefits) lower mortality, then the accumulated cash flows will be more than needed to fund the reserve, and some profit can be taken. When the experience is worse than the basis, then the insurer will need to find extra capital to fund the reserves required.

Example 7.2 An insurer issues a whole life insurance policy to a life aged 50. The sum insured of $\$100\,000$ is payable at the end of the year of death. Level premiums of $\$1300$ are payable annually in advance throughout the term of the contract.

(a) Calculate the gross premium policy value five years after the inception of the contract, assuming that the policy is still in force, using the following basis:

Survival model: Standard Select Survival Model
Interest: 5% per year effective
Expenses: 12.5% of each premium

(b) Calculate the net premium policy value five years after the issue of the contract, assuming that the policy is still in force, using the following basis:

Survival model: Standard Select Survival Model
Interest: 4% per year

Solution 7.2 We assume that the life is select at age 50, when the policy is purchased. At duration 5, the life is aged 55 and is no longer select since the select period for the Standard Select Survival Model is only two years. Note that a premium due at age 55 is regarded as a future premium in the calculation of a policy value.

(a) The gross future loss random variable at time 5 is

$$L_5^g = 100\,000v^{K_{55}+1} - 0.875 \times 1\,300\,\ddot{a}_{\overline{K_{55}+1}|},$$

so

$$_5V^g = E[L_5^g] = 100\,000\,A_{55} - 0.875 \times 1\,300\,\ddot{a}_{55} = \$5256.35.$$

(b) For net premium policy values we always recalculate the (hypothetical) net premium for the contract on the policy value basis.

Let P denote the net premium for the policy value. At 4% per year,

$$P = 100\,000\frac{A_{[50]}}{\ddot{a}_{[50]}} = \$1321.31.$$

So, at 4% per year,

$$L_5^n = 100\,000v^{K_{55}+1} - 1321.31\ddot{a}_{\overline{K_{55}+1}|}$$

and hence

$$_5V^n = 100\,000\,A_{55} - 1321.31\ddot{a}_{55} = \$6704.75.$$

Notice in this example that the net premium calculation ignores expenses, but uses a lower interest rate, which provides a margin, implicitly allowing for expenses and other contingencies. However, the net premium used in the policy value is greater than the gross premium of the contract. This would generally not be permitted under regulations on valuation, as it is not prudent to allow for a hypothetical net premium greater than the actual premium.   □

Example 7.3 A woman aged 60 purchases a 20-year endowment insurance with a sum insured of \$100\,000 payable at the end of the year of death or on survival to age 80, whichever occurs first. An annual premium of \$5200 is payable for at most 10 years. The insurer uses the following basis for the calculation of policy values:

Survival model: Standard Select Survival Model

Interest: 5% per year effective

Expenses: 10% of the first premium, 5% of subsequent premiums, plus $200 on payment of the sum insured

Calculate $_0V$, $_5V$, $_6V$ and $_{10}V$, that is, the gross premium policy values for this policy at times $t = 0, 5, 6$ and 10.

Solution 7.3 You should check the following values, which will be needed for the calculation of the policy values:

$$\ddot{a}_{[60]:\,\overline{10}|} = 7.9601, \quad \ddot{a}_{65:\,\overline{5}|} = 4.4889, \quad \ddot{a}_{66:\,\overline{4}|} = 3.6851,$$

$$A_{[60]:\,\overline{20}|} = 0.41004, \quad A_{65:\,\overline{15}|} = 0.51140, \quad A_{66:\,\overline{14}|} = 0.53422,$$

$$A_{70:\,\overline{10}|} = 0.63576.$$

At time 0, when the policy is issued, the future loss random variable, allowing for the expenses specified in the policy value basis, is

$$L_0 = 100\,200 v^{\min(K_{[60]}+1,20)} + 0.05\,P - 0.95\,P\,\ddot{a}_{\overline{\min(K_{[60]}+1,10)}|}$$

where $P = \$5200$. Hence

$$_0V = \mathrm{E}[L_0] = 100\,200 A_{[60]:\,\overline{20}|} - (0.95\,\ddot{a}_{[60]:\,\overline{10}|} - 0.05)P = \$2023.$$

Similarly,

$$L_5 = 100\,200 v^{\min(K_{65}+1,15)} - 0.95\,P\,\ddot{a}_{\overline{\min(K_{65}+1,5)}|}$$

$$\Rightarrow\ _5V = \mathrm{E}[L_5] = 100\,200 A_{65:\,\overline{15}|} - 0.95\,P\,\ddot{a}_{65:\,\overline{5}|} = \$29\,068,$$

$$L_6 = 100\,200 v^{\min(K_{66}+1,14)} - 0.95\,P\,\ddot{a}_{\overline{\min(K_{66}+1,4)}|}$$

$$\Rightarrow\ _6V = \mathrm{E}[L_6] = 100\,200 A_{66:\,\overline{14}|} - 0.95\,P\,\ddot{a}_{66:\,\overline{4}|} = \$35\,324.$$

Finally, as no premiums are payable after time 9,

$$L_{10} = 100\,200 v^{\min(K_{70}+1,10)}$$

$$\Rightarrow\ _{10}V = \mathrm{E}[L_{10}] = 100\,200 A_{70:\,\overline{10}|} = \$63\,703.$$

□

In Example 7.3, the initial policy value, $_0V$, is greater than zero. This means that from the outset the insurer expects to make a loss on this policy. This sounds uncomfortable but is not uncommon in practice. The explanation is that the policy value basis may be more conservative than the premium basis. For example, the insurer may assume an interest rate of 6% in the premium calculation, but, for policy value calculations, assumes investments will earn only 5%. At 6% per year interest, and with a premium of $5200, this policy generates an EPV of *profit* at issue of $2869.

Example 7.4 A man aged 50 purchases a deferred annuity policy. The annuity will be paid annually for life, with the first payment on his 60th birthday. Each annuity payment will be $10 000. Level premiums of $11 900 are payable annually for at most 10 years. On death before age 60, all premiums paid will be returned, without interest, at the end of the year of death. The insurer uses the following basis for the calculation of policy values:

Survival model: Standard Select Survival Model
Interest: 5% per year
Expenses: 10% of the first premium, 5% of subsequent premiums,
                 $25 each time an annuity payment is paid, and
                 $100 when a death claim is paid.

Calculate the gross premium policy values for this policy at the start of the policy, at the end of the fifth year, and at the end of the 15th year, just *before* and just *after* the annuity payment and expense due at that time.

Solution 7.4 We are going to need the following values, all of which you should check:

$$\ddot{a}_{[50]:\,\overline{10|}} = 8.0566, \quad \ddot{a}_{55:\,\overline{5|}} = 4.5268, \quad \ddot{a}_{60} = 14.9041, \quad \ddot{a}_{65} = 13.5498,$$

$$v^5 \, {}_5p_{55} = 0.77382, \quad v^{10} \, {}_{10}p_{[50]} = 0.60196,$$

$$A^{\,1}_{[50]:\,\overline{10|}} = 0.01439, \quad (IA)^{\,1}_{[50]:\,\overline{10|}} = 0.08639, \quad A^{\,1}_{55:\,\overline{5|}} = 0.01062,$$

$$(IA)^{\,1}_{55:\,\overline{5|}} = 0.03302.$$

Then, using the notation $_{15-}V$ and $_{15+}V$ to denote the policy values at duration 15 years just before and just after the annuity payment and expense due at that time, respectively, and noting that $P = 11\,900$, we can calculate the policy value at any time t as

EPV at t of future benefits + expenses − EPV at t of future premiums.

At the inception of the contract, the EPV of the death benefit is

$$P\,(IA)^{\,1}_{[50]:\,\overline{10|}},$$

the EPV of the death claim expenses is

$$100A^{\,1}_{[50]:\,\overline{10|}},$$

the EPV of the annuity benefit and associated expenses is

$$10\,025\,v^{10} \, {}_{10}p_{[50]}\,\ddot{a}_{60},$$

and the EPV of future premiums less associated expenses is

$$0.95 P \ddot{a}_{[50]:\,\overline{10|}} - 0.05 P,$$

so that

$$
\begin{aligned}
{}_0V &= P(IA)^{\,1}_{[50]:\,\overline{10|}} + 100 A^{\,1}_{[50]:\,\overline{10|}} + 10\,025 v^{10}\ {}_{10}p_{[50]}\,\ddot{a}_{60} \\
&\quad - (0.95\,\ddot{a}_{[50]:\,\overline{10|}} - 0.05) P \\
&= \$485.
\end{aligned}
$$

At the fifth anniversary of the inception of the contract, assuming it is still in force, the future death benefit is $6P, 7P, \ldots, 10P$ depending on whether the life dies in the 6th, 7th, ..., 10th years, respectively. We can write this benefit as a level benefit of $5P$ plus an increasing benefit of $P, 2P, \ldots, 5P$.

So at time 5, the EPV of the death benefit is

$$P\left((IA)^{\,1}_{55:\,\overline{5|}} + 5A^{\,1}_{55:\,\overline{5|}}\right),$$

the EPV of the death claim expenses is $100 A^{\,1}_{55:\,\overline{5|}}$,
the EPV of the annuity benefit and associated expenses is $10\,025\ v^5\ {}_5p_{55}\,\ddot{a}_{60}$,
and the EPV of future premiums less associated expenses is $0.95 P \ddot{a}_{55:\,\overline{10|}}$, so that

$$
\begin{aligned}
{}_5V &= P(IA)^{\,1}_{55:\,\overline{5|}} + 5\,P A^{\,1}_{55:\,\overline{5|}} + 100 A^{\,1}_{55:\,\overline{5|}} + 10\,025\, v^5\ {}_5p_{55}\,\ddot{a}_{60} - 0.95 P\,\ddot{a}_{55:\,\overline{5|}} \\
&= \$65\,470.
\end{aligned}
$$

Once the premium payment period of 10 years is completed there are no future premiums to value, so the policy value is the EPV of the future annuity payments and associated expenses. That is

$$_{15-}V = 10\,025\,\ddot{a}_{65} = \$135\,837,$$

and

$$_{15+}V = 10\,025\,a_{65} = {}_{15-}V - 10\,025 = \$125\,812.$$

$\square$

We make two comments about Example 7.4.

(1) As in Example 7.3, ${}_0V > 0$, which implies that the valuation basis is more conservative than the premium basis.
(2) In Example 7.4 we saw that $_{15+}V = {}_{15-}V - 10\,025$. This makes sense if we regard the policy value at any time as the amount of assets being held at that time in respect of a policy still in force. The policy value

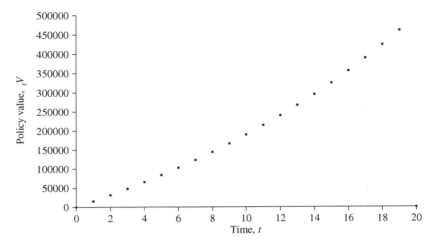

Figure 7.3 Policy values for each year of a 20-year endowment insurance, sum insured \$500 000, issued to (50).

$_{15-}V$ ($= \$135\,837$) represents the assets required at time 15 just before the payment of the annuity, \$10 000, and the associated expense, \$25. Immediately after making these payments, the insurer's required assets will have reduced by \$10 025, and the new policy value is $_{15+}V$.

We conclude this section by plotting policy values for the endowment insurance discussed in Example 7.1 and for the term insurance with the same sum insured and term. For these policies Figures 7.1 and 7.2, respectively, show the EPV at issue of premiums minus claims for each year of the policy. Figures 7.3 and 7.4, respectively, show the policy values. In Figure 7.3 we see that the policy values build up over time to provide the sum insured on maturity. By contrast, in Figure 7.4 the policy values increase then decrease. A further contrast between these figures is the level of the policy values. In Figure 7.4 the largest policy value occurs at time 13, with $_{13}V = \$9563.00$, which is a small amount compared with the sum insured of \$500 000. The reason why small policy values occur for the term insurance policy is simply that there is a small probability of the death benefit being paid.

7.3.3 Recursive formulae for policy values

In this section we show how to derive recursive formulae for policy values for policies with discrete cash flows. These formulae can be useful in the calculation of policy values in some cases – we give an example at the end of this section to illustrate this point – and they also provide an understanding of how

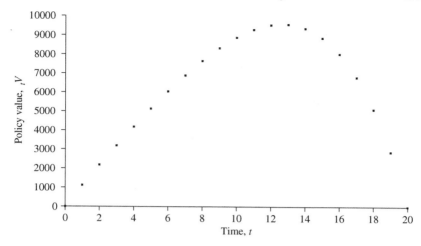

Figure 7.4 Policy values for each year of a 20-year term insurance, sum insured $500 000, issued to (50).

the policy value builds up and how profit emerges while the policy is in force. We use Examples 7.1 and 7.4 to demonstrate the principles involved.

Example 7.5 For Example 7.1 and for $t = 0, 1, \ldots, 19$, show that

$$({}_tV + P)(1 + i) = 500\,000\, q_{[50]+t} + p_{[50]+t}\, {}_{t+1}V \tag{7.3}$$

where $P = \$15\,114.33$, $i = 5\%$ and the policy value is calculated on the basis specified in Example 7.1.

Solution 7.5 From the solution to Example 7.1 we know that for $t = 0, 1, \ldots, 19$,

$$_tV = 500\,000\, A_{[50]+t:\,\overline{20-t}|} - P\, \ddot{a}_{[50]+t:\,\overline{20-t}|}.$$

Splitting off the terms for the first year for both the endowment and the annuity functions, we have

$$
\begin{aligned}
_tV &= 500\,000 \left(v q_{[50]+t} + v p_{[50]+t}\, A_{[50]+t+1:\,\overline{19-t}|} \right) \\
&\quad - P \left(1 + v p_{[50]+t}\, \ddot{a}_{[50]+t+1:\,\overline{19-t}|} \right) \\
&= v \left(500\,000 q_{[50]+t} + p_{[50]+t} \left(500\,000 A_{[50]+t+1:\,\overline{19-t}|} - P \ddot{a}_{[50]+t+1:\,\overline{19-t}|} \right) \right) \\
&\quad - P.
\end{aligned}
$$

Rearranging, multiplying both sides by $(1 + i)$ and recognizing that

$$_{t+1}V = 500\,000\,A_{[50]+t+1:\,\overline{19-t}|} - P\,\ddot{a}_{[50]+t+1:\,\overline{19-t}|}$$

gives equation (7.3). ☐

We comment on Example 7.5 after the next example.

Example 7.6 For Example 7.4 and for $t = 1, 2, \ldots, 9$ show that

$$(_tV + 0.95P)(1 + i) = ((t + 1)P + 100)\,q_{[50]+t} + p_{[50]+t}\,_{t+1}V \quad (7.4)$$

where $P = \$11\,900$, $i = 5\%$ and the policy value is calculated on the basis specified in Example 7.4.

Solution 7.6 For Example 7.4 and for $t = 1, 2, \ldots, 9$, $_tV$ has the same form as $_5V$, that is

$$_tV = P(IA)^{1}_{[50]+t:\,\overline{10-t}|} + (tP + 100)A^{1}_{[50]+t:\overline{10-t}|}$$
$$+ 10\,025v^{10-t}\,_{10-t}p_{[50]+t}\,\ddot{a}_{60} - 0.95P\ddot{a}_{[50]+t:\overline{10-t}|}.$$

Recall that recurrence relations for insurance and annuity functions can be derived by separating out the EPV of the first year's payments, so that

$$\ddot{a}_{[x]+t:\,\overline{n-t}|} = 1 + vp_{[x]+t}\,\ddot{a}_{[x]+t+1:\overline{n-t-1}|},$$
$$A^{1}_{[x]+t:\overline{n-t}|} = vq_{[x]+t} + vp_{[x]+t}\,A^{1}_{[x]+t+1:\overline{n-t-1}|}$$
$$(IA)^{1}_{[x]+t:\overline{n-t}|} = vq_{[x]+t} + vp_{[x]+t}\left((IA)^{1}_{[x]+t+1:\overline{n-t-1}|} + A^{1}_{[x]+t+1:\overline{n-t-1}|}\right).$$

Using these relations to split off the terms for the year t to $t + 1$ in the policy value equation, we have, for $t = 1, 2, \ldots, 9$,

$$_tV = P\left(vq_{[50]+t} + vp_{[50]+t}\left((IA)^{1}_{[50]+t+1:\,\overline{10-t-1}|} + A^{1}_{[50]+t+1:\,\overline{10-t-1}|}\right)\right)$$
$$+ (tP + 100)\left(vq_{[50]+t} + vp_{[50]+t}\,A^{1}_{[50]+t+1:\,\overline{10-t-1}|}\right)$$
$$+ 10\,025\,vp_{[50]+t}\left(v^{10-t-1}\,_{10-t-1}p_{[50]+t+1}\,\ddot{a}_{60}\right)$$
$$- 0.95P\left(1 + vp_{[50]+t}\,\ddot{a}_{[50]+t+1:\,\overline{10-t-1}|}\right)$$

$$\Rightarrow\,_tV = vq_{[50]+t}\,((t+1)P + 100) - 0.95P$$
$$+ vp_{[50]+t}\Bigg\{P(IA)^{1}_{[50]+t+1:\,\overline{10-t-1}|} + ((t+1)P + 100)\,A^{1}_{[50]+t+1:\,\overline{10-t+1}|}$$
$$+ 10\,025\,_{10-t-1}p_{[50]+t+1}\,v^{10-t-1}\,\ddot{a}_{60} - 0.95P\ddot{a}_{[50]+t+1:\overline{10-t-1}|}\Bigg\}.$$

Notice that the expression in curly braces, { }, is $_{t+1}V$, so, substituting and rearranging,

$$({}_tV + 0.95P)(1 + i) = ((t + 1)P + 100)\, q_{[50]+t} + p_{[50]+t}\, {}_{t+1}V, \qquad (7.5)$$

as required. □

Equations (7.3) and (7.4) are recursive formulae for policy values since they express ${}_tV$ in terms of ${}_{t+1}V$. Such formulae always exist but the precise form they take depends on the details of the policy being considered. The method we used to derive formulae (7.3) and (7.4) can be used for other policies: first write down a formula for ${}_tV$ and then break up the EPVs into EPVs of payments in the coming year, t to $t + 1$, and EPVs of payments from $t + 1$ onwards. We can demonstrate this in a more general setting as follows.

Consider a policy issued to a life (x) where cash flows – that is, premiums, expenses and claims – can occur only at the start or end of a year. Suppose this policy has been in force for t years, where t is a non-negative integer. Consider the $(t + 1)$st year, and let

P_t denote the premium payable at time t,

e_t denote the premium-related expense payable at time t,

S_{t+1} denote the sum insured payable at time $t + 1$ if the policyholder dies in the year,

E_{t+1} denote the expense of paying the sum insured at time $t + 1$,

$_tV$ denote the gross premium policy value for a policy in force at time t, and

$_{t+1}V$ denote the gross premium policy value for a policy in force at time $t + 1$.

Let $q_{[x]+t}$ denote the probability that the policyholder, alive at time t, dies in the year and let i_t denote the rate of interest assumed earned in the year. The quantities e_t, E_t, $q_{[x]+t}$ and i_t are all as assumed in the policy value basis.

Let L_t and L_{t+1} denote the gross future loss random variables at times t and $t + 1$, respectively, in both cases assuming the policyholder is alive at that time. Note that L_t involves present values at time t whereas L_{t+1} involves present values at time $t + 1$. Then, by considering what can happen in the year, we have

$$L_t = \begin{cases} (1 + i_t)^{-1}(S_{t+1} + E_{t+1}) - P_t + e_t & \text{if } K_{[x]+t} = 0, \text{ with probability } q_{[x]+t}, \\ (1 + i_t)^{-1}L_{t+1} - P_t + e_t & \text{if } K_{[x]+t} \geq 1, \text{ with probability } p_{[x]+t}. \end{cases}$$

Taking expected values, we have

$$_tV = \mathrm{E}[L_t] = q_{[x]+t}(1 + i_t)^{-1}(S_{t+1} + E_{t+1}) - (q_{[x]+t} + p_{[x]+t})(P_t - e_t)$$
$$+ p_{[x]+t}(1 + i_t)^{-1}\mathrm{E}[L_{t+1}],$$

which, after a little rearranging and recognizing that $_{t+1}V = \mathrm{E}[L_{t+1}]$, gives the important equation

$$\boxed{(_tV + P_t - e_t)(1 + i_t) = q_{[x]+t}(S_{t+1} + E_{t+1}) + p_{[x]+t}\,_{t+1}V.}$$ (7.6)

Equation (7.6) includes equations (7.3) and (7.4) as special cases and it is a little more general than either of them since it allows the premium, the sum insured, the expenses and the rate of interest all to be functions of t or of $t+1$, so that they can vary from year to year.

For policies with cash flows only at the start/end of each year, the recursive formulae always have the same general form. This form can be explained by examining equation (7.6).

◇ Assume that at time t the insurer has assets of amount $_tV$ in respect of this policy. Recall that $_tV$ is the expected value on the policy value basis of the future loss random variable, assuming the policyholder is alive at time t. Hence we can interpret $_tV$ as the value of the assets the insurer should have at time t (in respect of a policy still in force) in order to expect to break even over the future course of the policy.

◇ Now add to $_tV$ the net cash flow received by the insurer at time t as assumed in the policy value basis. In equation (7.6) this is $P_t - e_t$; in Example 7.5 this was just the premium, $P = \$15\,114.33$; in Example 7.6 this was the premium, $P = \$11\,900$, less the expense assumed in the policy value basis, $0.05P$. The new amount is the amount of the insurer's assets at time t just after these cash flows. There are no further cash flows until the end of the year.

◇ These assets are rolled up to the end of the year with interest at the rate assumed in the policy value basis, i_t ($= 5\%$ in the two examples). This gives the amount of the insurer's assets at the end of the year before any further cash flows (assuming everything is as specified in the policy value basis). This gives the left-hand sides of equations (7.6), (7.3) and (7.4).

◇ We assumed the policyholder was alive at the start of the year, time t; we do not know whether the policyholder will be alive at the end of the year. With probability $p_{[x]+t}$ the policyholder will be alive, and with probability $q_{[x]+t}$ the policyholder will die in the year (where these probabilities are calculated on the policy value basis).

◇ If the policyholder is alive at time $t+1$ the insurer needs to have assets of amount $_{t+1}V$ at that time; if the policyholder has died during the year, the insurer must pay any death benefit and related expenses. The expected amount the insurer needs for the policy being considered above is given by the right-hand side of equation (7.6) (equations (7.3) and (7.4) for Examples 7.5 and 7.6). For the general policy, and for both examples, this is precisely the amount the insurer will have (given our assumptions). This happens because the policy value is defined as the expected value of the future loss random variable *and* because we assume cash flows from t to $t + 1$ are as specified in the policy value basis. We assumed that at time t the insurer had sufficient assets to *expect (on the policy value basis)* to break even over the future course of the policy. Since we have assumed that from t to $t + 1$ all cash flows are as specified in the policy value basis, it is not surprising that at time $t + 1$ the insurer still has sufficient assets to expect to break even.

One further point needs to be made about equations (7.6), (7.3) and (7.4). We can rewrite these three formulae as follows:

$$({}_tV + P_t - e_t)(1 + i_t) = {}_{t+1}V + q_{[x]+t}(S_{t+1} + E_{t+1} - {}_{t+1}V), \qquad (7.7)$$
$$({}_tV + P)(1 + i) = {}_{t+1}V + q_{[x]+t}(500\,000 - {}_{t+1}V),$$
$$({}_tV + 0.95P)(1 + i) = {}_{t+1}V + q_{[x]+t}((t + 1)P\, q_{50+t} - {}_{t+1}V).$$

The left-hand side of each of these formulae are unchanged – they still represent the amount of assets the insurer is assumed to have at time $t + 1$ in respect of a policy which was in force at time t. The right-hand sides can now be interpreted slightly differently.

- For each policy in force at time t the insurer needs to provide the policy value, ${}_{t+1}V$, at time $t + 1$, whether the life died during the year or not.
- In addition, if the policyholder has died in the year (the probability of which is $q_{[x]+t}$), the insurer must also provide the extra amount to increase the policy value to the death benefit payable plus any related expense: $S_{t+1} + E_{t+1} - {}_{t+1}V$ for the general policy, $500\,000 - {}_{t+1}V$ in Example 7.5 and $(t + 1)P - {}_{t+1}V$ in Example 7.6.

The extra amount required to increase the policy value to the death benefit is called the **Death Strain At Risk** (DSAR), or the **Sum at Risk** or the **Net Amount at Risk**, at time $t + 1$. Generally (ignoring claim expenses) given that the death benefit payable in the tth year is S_t, then the tth year DSAR is $S_t - {}_tV$. This is an important measure of the insurer's risk if mortality exceeds the basis assumption, and is useful in determining risk management strategy, including reinsurance – which is the insurance that an insurer buys to protect itself against adverse experience.

In all the examples so far in this section it has been possible to calculate the policy value directly, as the EPV on the given basis of future benefits plus future expenses minus future premiums. In more complicated examples, in particular where the benefits are defined in terms of the policy value, this may not be possible. In these cases the recursive formula for policy values, equation (7.6), can be very useful, as the following example shows.

Example 7.7 Consider a 20-year endowment policy purchased by a life aged 50. Level premiums of \$23 500 per year are payable annually throughout the term of the policy. A sum insured of \$700 000 is payable at the end of the term if the life survives to age 70. On death before age 70 a sum insured is payable at the end of the year of death equal to the policy value at the start of the year in which the policyholder dies.

The policy value basis used by the insurance company is as follows:

Survival model: Standard Select Survival Model
Interest: 3.5% per year
Expenses: nil

Calculate $_{15}V$, the policy value for a policy in force at the start of the 16th year.

Solution 7.7 For this example, formula (7.6) becomes

$$(_tV + P) \times 1.035 = q_{[50]+t}\, S_{t+1} + p_{[50]+t}\, {}_{t+1}V \quad \text{for } t = 0, 1, \ldots, 19,$$

where $P = \$23\,500$. For the final year of this policy, the death benefit payable at the end of the year is $_{19}V$ and the survival benefit is the sum insured, \$700 000. Putting $t = 19$ in the above equation gives:

$$(_{19}V + P) \times 1.035 = q_{69}\, {}_{19}V + p_{69} \times 700\,000.$$

Tidying this up and noting that $S_{t+1} = {}_tV$, we can work backwards as follows:

$$_{19}V = (p_{69} \times 700\,000 - 1.035P)/(1.035 - q_{69}) = 652\,401,$$
$$_{18}V = (p_{68} \times {}_{19}V - 1.035P)/(1.035 - q_{68}) = 606\,471,$$
$$_{17}V = (p_{67} \times {}_{18}V - 1.035P)/(1.035 - q_{67}) = 562\,145,$$
$$_{16}V = (p_{66} \times {}_{17}V - 1.035P)/(1.035 - q_{66}) = 519\,362,$$
$$_{15}V = (p_{65} \times {}_{16}V - 1.035P)/(1.035 - q_{65}) = 478\,063.$$

Hence, the answer is \$478 063.   □

7.3.4 Annual profit by source

Consider a group of identical policies issued at the same time. The recursive formulae for policy values show that *if* all cash flows between t and $t + 1$ are as specified in the policy value basis, then the insurer will be in a break-even position at time $t + 1$, given that it was in a break-even position at time t. These cash flows depend on mortality, interest, expenses and, for participating policies, bonus rates. In practice, it is very unlikely that all the assumptions will be met in any one year. If the assumptions are not met, then the value of the insurer's assets at time $t + 1$ may be more than sufficient to pay any benefits due at that time and to provide a policy value of $_{t+1}V$ for those policies still in force. In this case, the insurer will have made a profit in the year. If the insurer's assets at time $t + 1$ are not sufficient to pay any benefits due at that time and to provide a policy value of $_{t+1}V$ for those policies still in force, the insurer will have made a loss in the year.

In general terms:

- Actual expenses less than the expenses assumed in the policy value basis will be a source of profit.
- Actual interest earned on investments less than the interest assumed in the policy value basis will be a source of loss.
- Actual mortality less than the mortality assumed in the policy value basis can be a source of either profit or loss. For whole life, term and endowment policies it will be a source of profit; for annuity policies it will be a source of loss.
- Actual bonus or dividend rates less than the rates assumed in the policy value basis will be a source of profit.

The following example demonstrates how to calculate annual profit by source from a non-participating life insurance policy.

Example 7.8 An insurer issued a large number of policies identical to the policy in Example 7.3 to women aged 60. Five years after they were issued, a total of 100 of these policies were still in force. In the following year,

- expenses of 6% of each premium paid were incurred,
- interest was earned at 6.5% on all assets,
- one policyholder died, and
- expenses of \$250 were incurred on the payment of the sum insured for the policyholder who died.

(a) Calculate the profit or loss on this group of policies for this year.
(b) Determine how much of this profit/loss is attributable to profit/loss from mortality, from interest and from expenses.

Solution 7.8 (a) At duration $t = 5$ we assume the insurer held assets for the portfolio with value exactly equal to the total of the policy values at that time for all the policies still in force. From Example 7.3 we know the value of $_5V$ and so we assume the insurer's assets at time 5, in respect of these policies, amounted to $100\ _5V$. If the insurer's assets were worth less (*resp.* more) than this, then losses (*resp.* profits) have been made in previous years. These do not concern us – we are concerned only with what happens in the 6th year.

Now consider the cash flows in the 6th year. For each of the 100 policies still in force at time 5 the insurer received a premium P (= \$5200) and paid an expense of $0.06P$ at time 5. Hence, the total assets at time 5 after receiving premiums and paying premium-related expenses were

$$100\ _5V + 100 \times 0.94\ P = \$3\,395\,551.$$

There were no further cash flows until the end of the year, so this amount grew for one year at the rate of interest actually earned, 6.5%, giving the value of the insurer's assets at time 6, before paying any death claims and expenses and setting up policy values, as

$$(100\ _5V + 100 \times 0.94\ P) \times 1.065 = \$3\,616\,262.$$

The death claim plus related expenses at the end of the year was $\$100\,250$. A policy value equal to $_6V$ (calculated in Example 7.3) is required at the end of the year for each of the 99 policies still in force. Hence, the total amount the insurer requires at the end of the year is

$$100\,250 + 99\ _6V = \$3\,597\,342.$$

Hence the insurer has made a *profit* in the sixth year of

$$(100\ _5V + 100 \times 0.94\ P) \times 1.065 - (100\,250 + 99\ _6V) = \$18\,919.$$

(b) In this example the sources of profit and loss in the sixth year are as follows.

    (i) Interest: This is a source of profit since the actual rate of interest earned, 6.5%, is higher than the rate assumed in the policy value basis.

    (ii) Expenses: These are a source of loss since the actual expenses, both premium related (6% of premiums) and claim related ($\$250$), are higher than assumed in the policy value basis (5% of premiums and $\$200$).

    (iii) Mortality: The probability of dying in the year for any of these policyholders is q_{65} ($= 0.0059$). Hence, out of 100 policyholders alive at the start of the year, the insurer expects $100\,q_{65}$ ($= 0.59$) to die. In fact, one died. Each death reduces the profit since the amount required for a death, $\$100\,250$, is greater than the amount required on survival, $_6V$ ($= \$35\,324$), and so more than the expected deaths increases the insurer's loss.

Since the overall profit is positive, (i) has had a greater effect than (ii) and (iii) combined in this year.

We can attribute the total profit to the three sources as follows.

Interest: If expenses at the start of the year had been as assumed in the policy value basis, $0.05\ P$ per policy still in force, *and* interest had been earned at 5%, the total interest received in the year would have been

$$0.05 \times (100 \; {}_5V + 100 \times 0.95 \, P) = \$170\,038.$$

The actual interest earned, before allowing for actual expenses, was

$$0.065 \times (100 \; {}_5V + 100 \times 0.95 \, P) = \$221\,049.$$

Hence, there was a profit of \$51\,011 attributable to interest.

Expenses: Now, we allow for the actual interest rate earned during the year (because the difference between actual and expected interest has already been accounted for in the interest profit above) but use the expected mortality. That is, we look at the loss arising from the expense experience given that the interest rate earned is 6.5%, but on the hypothesis that the number of deaths is $100 \, q_{65}$.

The expected expenses on this basis, valued at the year end, are

$$100 \times 0.05P \times 1.065 + 100 \, q_{65} \times 200 = \$27\,808.$$

The actual expenses, if deaths were as expected, are

$$100 \times 0.06P \times 1.065 + 100 \, q_{65} \times 250 = \$33\,376.$$

The loss from expenses, allowing for the actual interest rate earned in the year but allowing for the expected, rather than actual, mortality, was

$$33\,376 - 27\,808 = \$5568.$$

Mortality: Now, we use actual interest (6.5%) and actual expenses, and look at the difference between the expected cost from mortality and the actual cost. For each death, the cost to the insurer is the death strain at risk, in this case $100\,000 + 250 - {}_6V$, so the mortality profit is

$$(100 \, q_{65} - 1) \times (100\,000 + 250 - {}_6V) = -\$26\,524.$$

This gives a total profit of

$$51\,011 - 5568 - 26\,524 = \$18\,919$$

which is the amount calculated earlier.   □

We have calculated the profit from the three sources in the order: interest, expenses, mortality. At each step we assume that factors not yet considered are as specified in the policy value basis, whereas factors already considered are as actually occurred. This avoids 'double counting' and gives the correct total.

However, we could follow the same principle, building from expected to actual, one basis element at a time, but change the order of the calculation as follows.

Expenses: The loss from expenses, allowing for the assumed interest rate earned in the year and allowing for the expected mortality, was

$$100 \times (0.06 - 0.05)\, P \times 1.05 + 100\, q_{65} \times (250 - 200) = \$5490.$$

Interest: Allowing for the actual expenses at the start of the year, the profit from interest was

$$(0.065 - 0.05) \times (100\ _5V + 100 \times 0.94\, P) = \$50\,933.$$

Mortality: The profit from mortality, allowing for the actual expenses, was

$$(100 q_{65} - 1) \times (100\,000 + 250 - {}_6V) = -\$26\,524.$$

This gives a total profit of

$$-5490 + 50\,933 - 26\,524 = \$18\,919$$

which is the same total as before, but with (slightly) different amounts of profit attributable to interest and to expenses.

This exercise of breaking down the profit or loss into its component parts is called **analysis of surplus**, and it is an important exercise after any valuation. The analysis of surplus will indicate if any parts of the valuation basis are too conservative or too weak; it will assist in assessing the performance of the various managers involved in the business, and in determining the allocation of resources, and, for participating business it will help to determine how much surplus should be distributed.

7.3.5 Asset shares

In Section 7.3.1 we showed, using Example 7.1, that if the three conditions, (a), (b) and (c), at the end of the section were fulfilled, then the accumulation of the premiums received minus the claims paid for a group of identical policies issued simultaneously would be precisely sufficient to provide the policy value required for the surviving policyholders at each future duration. We noted that condition (c) in particular would be extremely unlikely to hold in practice; that is, it is virtually impossible for the experience of a policy or a portfolio of policies to follow exactly the assumptions in the premium basis. In practice, the invested premiums may have earned a greater or smaller rate of return than that used in the premium basis, the expenses and mortality experience will differ from the premium basis. Each policy contributes to the total assets of the insurer through the actual investment, expense and mortality experience.

It is of practical importance to calculate the share of the insurer's assets attributable to each policy in force at any given time. This amount is known as the **asset share** of the policy at that time and it is calculated by assuming the policy being considered is one of a large group of identical policies issued simultaneously. The premiums minus claims and expenses for this notional group of policies are then accumulated using values for expenses, interest, mortality and bonus rates based on the insurer's experience for similar policies over the period. At any given time, the accumulated fund divided by the (notional) number of survivors gives the asset share at that time for each surviving policyholder. If the insurer's experience is close to the assumptions in the policy value basis, then we would expect the asset share to be close to the policy value.

The policy value at duration t represents the amount the insurer *needs to have* at that time in respect of each surviving policyholder; the asset share represents (an estimate of) the amount the insurer *actually does have*.

Example 7.9 Consider a policy identical to the policy studied in Example 7.4 and suppose that this policy has now been in force for five years. Suppose that over the past five years the insurer's experience in respect of similar policies has been as follows.

- Annual interest earned on investments has been as shown in the following table.

Year	1	2	3	4	5
Interest %	4.8	5.6	5.2	4.9	4.7

- Expenses at the start of the year in which a policy was issued were 15% of the premium.
- Expenses at the start of each year after the year in which a policy was issued were 6% of the premium.
- The expense of paying a death claim was, on average, $120.
- The mortality rate, $q_{[50]+t}$, for $t = 0, 1, \ldots, 4$, has been approximately 0.0015.

Calculate the asset share for the policy at the start of each of the first six years.

Solution 7.9 We assume that the policy we are considering is one of a large number, N, of identical policies issued simultaneously. As we will see, the value of N does not affect our final answers.

Let AS_t denote the asset share per policy surviving at time $t = 0, 1, \ldots, 5$. We calculate AS_t by accumulating to time t the premiums received minus the claims and expenses paid in respect of this notional group of policies using our estimates of the insurer's actual experience over this period and then dividing by the number of surviving policies. We adopt the convention that AS_t does not include the premium and related expense due at time t. With this convention,

AS_0 is always 0 for any policy since no premiums will have been received and no claims and expenses will have been paid before time 0. Note that for our policy, using the policy value basis specified in Example 7.4, $_0V = \$490$.

The premiums minus expenses received at time 0 are

$$0.85 \times 11\,900\,N = 10\,115\,N.$$

This amount accumulates to the end of the year with interest at 4.8%, giving

$$10\,601\,N.$$

A notional $0.0015\,N$ policyholders die in the first year so that death claims plus expenses at the end of the year are

$$0.0015 \times (11\,900 + 120)\,N = 18\,N$$

which leaves

$$10\,601\,N - 18\,N = 10\,582\,N$$

at the end of the year. Since $0.9985\,N$ policyholders are still surviving at the start of the second year, AS_1, the asset share for a policy surviving at the start of the second year, is given by

$$AS_1 = 10\,582N/(0.9985\,N) = 10\,598.$$

These calculations, and the calculations for the next four years, are summarized in Table 7.1. You should check all the entries in this table. For example, the death claims and expenses in year 5 are calculated as

$$0.9985^4 \times 0.0015 \times (5 \times 11\,900 + 120)\,N = 89\,N$$

since $0.9985^4 N$ policyholders are alive at the start of the fifth year, a fraction 0.0015 of these die in the coming year, the death benefit is a return of the five premiums paid and the expense is $120.

Note that the figures in Table 7.1, except the Survivors' column, have been rounded to the nearest integer for presentation; the underlying calculations have been carried out using far greater accuracy.   □

We make the following comments about Example 7.9.

(1) As predicted, the value of N does not affect the values of the asset shares, AS_t. The only purpose of this notional group of N identical policies issued simultaneously is to simplify the presentation.
(2) The experience of the insurer over the five years has been close to the assumptions in the policy value basis specified in Example 7.4. The actual interest rate has been between 4.7% and 5.6%; the rate assumed in the policy value basis is 5%. The actual expenses, both premium-related

Table 7.1 *Asset share calculation for Example 7.9.*

Year, t	Fund at start of year	Cash flow at start of year	Fund at end of year before death claims	Death claims and expenses	Fund at end of year	Survivors	AS_t
1	0	$10\,115\,N$	$10\,601\,N$	$18\,N$	$10\,582\,N$	$0.9985\,N$	$10\,598$
2	$10\,582\,N$	$11\,169\,N$	$22\,970\,N$	$36\,N$	$22\,934\,N$	$0.9985^2\,N$	$23\,003$
3	$22\,934\,N$	$11\,152\,N$	$35\,859\,N$	$54\,N$	$35\,805\,N$	$0.9985^3\,N$	$35\,967$
4	$35\,805\,N$	$11\,136\,N$	$49\,241\,N$	$71\,N$	$49\,170\,N$	$0.9985^4\,N$	$49\,466$
5	$49\,170\,N$	$11\,119\,N$	$63\,123\,N$	$89\,N$	$63\,034\,N$	$0.9985^5\,N$	$63\,509$

(15% initially and 6% thereafter) and claim-related ($120), are a little higher than the expenses assumed in the policy value basis (10%, 5% and $100, respectively). The actual mortality rate is comparable to the rate in the policy value basis, e.g. $0.9985^5 = 0.99252$ is close to $_5p_{[50]} = 0.99283$.

As a result of this, the asset share, AS_5 (= $63\,509$), is reasonably close to the policy value, $_5V$ (= $65\,470$) in this example.

7.4 Policy values for policies with cash flows at 1/$m$thly intervals

Throughout Section 7.3 we assumed all cash flows for a policy occurred at the start or end of each year. This simplified the presentation and the calculations in the examples. In practice, this assumption does not often hold; for example, premiums are often payable monthly and death benefits are usually payable immediately following, or, more realistically, soon after, death. The definition of a policy value from Definitions 7.1 and 7.2 can be directly applied to policies with more frequent cash flows. The policy value at duration t is still the expected value of the future loss random variable, assuming the policyholder is still alive at that time – and our interpretation of a policy value is unchanged – it is still the amount the insurer needs so that, with future premiums, it can expect (on the policy value basis) to pay future benefits and expenses.

The following example illustrates these points.

Example 7.10 A life aged 50 purchases a 10-year term insurance with sum insured $500\,000$ payable at the end of the month of death. Level quarterly premiums, each of amount $P = 460$, are payable for at most five years.

Calculate the (gross premium) policy values at durations 2.75, 3 and 6.5 years using the following basis.

Survival model: Standard Select Survival Model
Interest: 5% per year
Expenses: 10% of each gross premium

Solution 7.10 To calculate $_{2.75}V$ we need the EPV of future benefits and the EPV of premiums less expenses at that time, assuming the policyholder is still alive. Note that the premium and related expense due at time $t = 2.75$ are regarded as future cash flows. Note also that from duration 2.75 years the policyholder will be subject to the ultimate part of the survival model since the select period is only two years.

Hence

$$_{2.75}V = 500\,000A^{(12)\ 1}_{52.75:\,\overline{7.25|}} - 0.9 \times 4 \times P\,\ddot{a}^{(4)}_{52.75:\,\overline{2.25|}}$$
$$= \$3091.02,$$

where

$$A^{(12)\ 1}_{52.75:\,\overline{7.25|}} = 0.01327 \quad \text{and} \quad \ddot{a}^{(4)}_{52.75:\,\overline{2.25|}} = 2.14052.$$

Similarly

$$_3V = 500\,000A^{(12)\ 1}_{53:\,\overline{7|}} - 0.9 \times 4 \times P\,\ddot{a}^{(4)}_{53:\,\overline{2|}}$$
$$= \$3357.94,$$

where

$$A^{(12)\ 1}_{53:\,\overline{7|}} = 0.013057 \quad \text{and} \quad \ddot{a}^{(4)}_{53:\,\overline{2|}} = 1.91446,$$

and

$$_{6.5}V = 500\,000A^{(12)\ 1}_{56.5:\,\overline{3.5|}}$$
$$= 500\,000 \times 0.008532 = \$4265.63. \qquad \square$$

7.4.1 Recursions

We can derive recursive formulae for policy values for policies with cash flows at discrete times other than annually. Consider $_{2.75}V$ and $_3V$ in Example 7.10. We need to be careful here because the premiums and benefits are paid with different frequency. We can use a recurrence relationship to generate the policy value at each month end, allowing for premiums only every third month. So, for example,

$$(_{2.75}V + 460 - 0.1 \times 460)\,(1.05)^{0.083}$$
$$= 500\,000\,_{0.083}q_{52.75} + _{0.083}p_{52.75}\,_{2.833}V.$$

We proceed similarly for the following two months, but adjusting because there are no premiums paid

$$_{2.833}V\,(1.05)^{0.083} = 500\,000\,_{0.083}q_{52.833} + {}_{0.083}p_{52.833}\,_{2.917}V$$

$$_{2.917}V\,(1.05)^{0.083} = 500\,000\,_{0.083}q_{52.917} + {}_{0.083}p_{52.917}\,_3V.$$

7.4.2 Valuation between premium dates

All of the calculations in the sections above considered policy values at a premium date, or after premiums have ceased. We often need to calculate policy values between premium dates; typically, we will value all policies on the same calendar date each year as part of the insurer's liability valuation process. The principle when valuing between premium dates is the same as when valuing on premium dates, that is, the policy value is the EPV of future benefits plus expenses minus premiums. The calculation may be a little more awkward. We demonstrate this in the following example, which uses the same contract as Example 7.10 above.

Example 7.11 For the contract described in Example 7.10, calculate the policy value after (a) 2 years and 10 months and (b) 2 years and 9.5 months, assuming the policy is still in force at that time in each case.

Solution 7.11 (a) The EPV of future benefits is

$$S\,A^{(12)\ 1}_{\ \ 52.833:\overline{7.167|}} = S \times 0.0132012 = 6600.58.$$

Note that the functions $A^{(m)1}_{x:\overline{n|}}$ and $\ddot{a}^{(m)}_{x:\overline{n|}}$ are defined only if n is an integer multiple of $\frac{1}{m}$, so that $A^{(12)\ 1}_{\ \ 52.833:\,\overline{7.167|}}$ is well defined, but $\ddot{a}^{(4)}_{52.833:\,\overline{7.167|}}$ is not.

The EPV of future premiums less premium expenses is

$$0.9 \times 4P\,v^{0.167}\,_{0.167}p_{52.833}\,\ddot{a}^{(4)}_{53:\overline{2|}} = 0.9 \times 4P \times 1.898466 = 3143.86.$$

So the policy value is $_{2.833}V = \$3456.72.$

(b) Now, the valuation is at neither a benefit nor a premium date. We know that the EPV of benefits minus premiums at 2 years and 10 months is $_{2.833}V$. One-half of a month earlier, we know that the life must either survive the time to the month end, in which case the EPV of future benefits less premiums is $_{2.833}V\,v^{0.042}$, or the life will die, in which case the EPV of benefits less premiums is $S\,v^{0.042}$. Allowing for the appropriate probabilities of survival or death, the policy value at time $t = 2.792$ is

$$_{2.792}V = {}_{0.042}q_{52.792}\,S\,v^{0.042} + {}_{0.042}p_{52.792}\,v^{0.042}\,_{2.833}V = \$3480.99.$$

$\square$

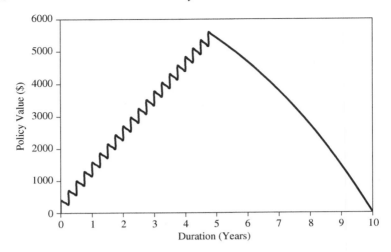

Figure 7.5 Policy values for the limited premium term insurance contract, Example 7.11.

The principle here is that we have split the EPV into the part relating to cash flows up to the next premium date, plus the EPV of the policy value at the next premium date.

It is interesting to note here that it would **not** be appropriate to apply simple interpolation to the two policy values corresponding to the premium dates before and after the valuation date, as we have, for example,

$$_{2.75}V = \$3091.02, \quad _{2.792}V = \$3480.99 \quad \text{and} \quad _{3}V = \$3357.94.$$

The reason is that the function $_tV$ is not smooth if premiums are paid at discrete intervals, since the policy value will jump immediately after each premium payment by the amount of that payment. Before the premium payment, the premium immediately due is included in the EPV of future premiums, which is deducted from the EPV of future benefits to give the policy value. Immediately after the premium payment, it is no longer included, so the policy value increases by the amount of the premium.

In Figure 7.5 we show the policy values at all durations for the policy in Examples 7.10 and 7.11. The curve jumps at each premium date, and has an increasing trend until the premiums cease. In the second half of the contract, after the premium payment term, the policy value is run down. Other types of policy will have different patterns for policy values as we have seen in Figures 7.1 and 7.2.

A reasonable approximation to the policy value between premium dates can usually be achieved by interpolating between the policy value **just after the**

previous premium and the policy value just before the next premium. That is, suppose the premium dates are k years apart, then for $s < k$, we approximate $_{t+k+s}V$ by interpolating between $_{t+k}V + P_{t+k} - E_{t+k}$ and $_{t+2k}V$; more specifically,

$$_{t+k+s}V \approx (_{t+k}V + P_{t+k} - E_{t+k})\left(1 - \frac{s}{k}\right) + _{t+2k}V\ \frac{s}{k}.$$

In the example above, this would give approximate values for $_{2.792}V$ and $_{2.833}V$ of \$3480.51 and \$3455.99, respectively, compared with the accurate values of \$3480.99 and \$3456.72, respectively.

7.5 Policy values with continuous cash flows

7.5.1 Thiele's differential equation

In the previous sections, we have defined policy values for policies with cash flows at discrete intervals and derived recursive formulae linking policy values at successive cash flow time points for these policies. These ideas extend to contracts where regular payments – premiums and/or annuities – are payable continuously and sums insured are payable immediately on death. In this case we can derive a differential equation, known as *Thiele's differential equation*. This is a continuous time version of the recursion equation, which we derived in Section 7.3.3. Recall that for discrete life insurance

$$(_tV + P_t - e_t)(1 + i_t) = _{t+1}V + q_{[x]+t}(S_{t+1} + E_{t+1} - _{t+1}V). \quad (7.7)$$

Our derivation of Thiele's differential equation is somewhat different from the derivation of equation (7.7). However, once we have completed the derivation, we explain the link with this equation.

Consider a policy issued to a select life aged x under which premiums and premium-related expenses are payable continuously and the sum insured, together with any related expenses, is payable immediately on death. Suppose this policy has been in force for t years, where $t \geq 0$. Let

P_t	denote the annual rate of premium payable at time t,
e_t	denote the annual rate of premium-related expense payable at time t,
S_t	denote the sum insured payable at time t if the policyholder dies at exact time t,
E_t	denote the expense of paying the sum insured at time t,
$\mu_{[x]+t}$	denote the force of mortality at age $[x] + t$,
δ_t	denote the force of interest per year assumed earned at time t, and,
$_tV$	denote the policy value for a policy in force at time t.

We assume that P_t, e_t, S_t, $\mu_{[x]+t}$ and δ_t are all continuous functions of t and that e_t, E_t, $\mu_{[x]+t}$ and δ_t are all as assumed in the policy value basis.

Just as we allowed the rate of interest to vary from year to year in Section 7.3.3, we are here letting the force of interest be a continuous function of time. Thus, if $v(t)$ denotes the present value of a payment of 1 at time t, we have

$$v(t) = \exp\left\{ -\int_0^t \delta_s ds \right\}. \tag{7.8}$$

Now, $_tV$ represents the difference between the EPV of benefits plus benefit-related expenses and the EPV of premiums less premium-related expenses, so we have

$$
\begin{aligned}
_tV = {}& \int_0^\infty \frac{v(t+s)}{v(t)} (S_{t+s} + E_{t+s}) \,_s p_{[x]+t} \, \mu_{[x]+t+s} \, ds \\
& - \int_0^\infty \frac{v(t+s)}{v(t)} (P_{t+s} - e_{t+s}) \,_s p_{[x]+t} \, ds.
\end{aligned}
$$

Note that we are measuring time, represented by s in the integrals, from time t, so that if, for example, the sum insured is payable at time s, the amount of the sum insured is S_{t+s} and as we are discounting back to time t, the discount factor is $v(t+s)/v(t)$. Changing the variable of integration to $r = t + s$ gives

$$
\begin{aligned}
_tV = {}& \int_t^\infty \frac{v(r)}{v(t)} (S_r + E_r) \,_{r-t} p_{[x]+t} \, \mu_{[x]+r} \, dr \\
& - \int_t^\infty \frac{v(r)}{v(t)} (P_r - e_r) \,_{r-t} p_{[x]+t} \, dr. \tag{7.9}
\end{aligned}
$$

We could use formula (7.9) to calculate $_tV$ by numerical integration. However, we are instead going to turn this identity into a differential equation. There are two main reasons why we do this:

(1) There exist numerical techniques to solve differential equations, one of which is discussed in the next section. As we will see, an advantage of such an approach over numerical integration is that we can easily calculate policy values at multiple durations.
(2) In Chapter 8 we consider more general types of insurance policy than we have so far. For such policies it is usually the case that we are unable to calculate policy values using numerical integration, and we must calculate policy values using a set of differential equations. The following development of Thiele's differential equation sets the scene for the next chapter.

In order to turn equation (7.9) into a differential equation, we note that

$$_{r-t} p_{[x]+t} = \frac{_r p_{[x]}}{_t p_{[x]}}$$

so that

$$_tV =$$

$$\frac{1}{v(t)\,_tp_{[x]}} \left(\int_t^\infty v(r)\,(S_r + E_r)\,_rp_{[x]}\,\mu_{[x]+r}\,dr - \int_t^\infty v(r)\,(P_r - e_r)\,_rp_{[x]}\,dr \right),$$

which we can write as

$$v(t)\,_tp_{[x]}\,_tV = \int_t^\infty v(r)\,(S_r + E_r)\,_rp_{[x]}\,\mu_{[x]+r}\,dr$$

$$- \int_t^\infty v(r)\,(P_r - e_r)\,_rp_{[x]}\,dr. \tag{7.10}$$

Differentiation of equation (7.10) with respect to t leads to Thiele's differential equation. First, differentiation of the right-hand side yields

$$- v(t)\,(S_t + E_t)\,_tp_{[x]}\,\mu_{[x]+t} + v(t)\,(P_t - e_t)\,_tp_{[x]}$$

$$= v(t)\,_tp_{[x]}\,(P_t - e_t - (S_t + E_t)\,\mu_{[x]+t}). \tag{7.11}$$

Differentiation of the left-hand side is most easily done in two stages, applying the product rule for differentiation at each stage. Treating $v(t)\,_tp_{[x]}$ as a single function of t we obtain

$$\frac{d}{dt}\left(v(t)\,_tp_{[x]}\,_tV\right) = v(t)\,_tp_{[x]}\,\frac{d}{dt}\,_tV + {_tV}\,\frac{d}{dt}\left(v(t)\,_tp_{[x]}\right).$$

Next,

$$\frac{d}{dt}\left(v(t)\,_tp_{[x]}\right) = v(t)\frac{d}{dt}\,_tp_{[x]} + {_tp_{[x]}}\,\frac{d}{dt}\,v(t).$$

From Chapter 2 we know that

$$\frac{d}{dt}\,_tp_{[x]} = -{_tp_{[x]}}\mu_{[x]+t}$$

and from formula (7.8)

$$\frac{d}{dt}\,v(t) = -\delta_t\,\exp\left\{-\int_0^t \delta_s ds\right\} = -\delta_t\,v(t).$$

Thus, the derivative of the left-hand side of equation (7.10) is

$$\frac{d}{dt}\left(v(t)\,_tp_{[x]}\,_tV\right) = v(t)\,_tp_{[x]}\,\frac{d}{dt}\,_tV - {_tV}\left(v(t)\,_tp_{[x]}\mu_{[x]+t} + {_tp_{[x]}}\,\delta_t\,v(t)\right)$$

$$= v(t)\,_tp_{[x]}\left(\frac{d}{dt}\,_tV - {_tV}\left(\mu_{[x]+t} + \delta_t\right)\right).$$

Equating this to (7.11) yields **Thiele's differential equation**, namely

$$\boxed{\frac{d}{dt}\,_tV = \delta_t\,_tV + P_t - e_t - (S_t + E_t - {_tV})\,\mu_{[x]+t}\,.} \tag{7.12}$$

Formula (7.12) can be interpreted as follows. The left-hand side of the formula, $d\,{}_tV/dt$, is the rate of increase in the policy value at time t. We can derive a formula for this rate of increase by considering the individual factors affecting the value of ${}_tV$:

- Interest is being earned on the current amount of the policy value. The amount of interest earned in the time interval t to $t+h$ is $\delta_t\,{}_tV\,h\,(+o(h))$, so that the rate of increase at time t is $\delta_t\,{}_tV$.
- Premium income, minus premium-related expenses, is increasing the policy value at rate $P_t - e_t$. If there were annuity payments at time t, this would decrease the policy value at the rate of the annuity payment (plus any annuity-related expenses).
- Claims, plus claim-related expenses, decrease the amount of the policy value. The expected extra amount payable in the time interval t to $t+h$ is $\mu_{[x]+t}h\,(S_t + E_t - {}_tV)$ and so the rate of decrease at time t is $\mu_{[x]+t}(S_t + E_t - {}_tV)$.

Hence the total rate of increase of the policy value at time t is

$$\delta_t\,{}_tV + P_t - e_t - \mu_{[x]+t}(S_t + E_t - {}_tV).$$

We can also relate formula (7.12) to equation (7.7) assuming that for some very small value h,

$$\frac{d}{dt}\,{}_tV \approx \frac{1}{h}\left({}_{t+h}V - {}_tV\right), \tag{7.13}$$

leading to the relationship

$$(1 + \delta_t h)\,{}_tV + (P_t - e_t)h \approx {}_{t+h}V + h\mu_{[x]+t}(S_t + E_t - {}_tV).$$

Remembering that h is very small, the interpretation of the left-hand side is that it is the accumulation from time t to time $t+h$ of the policy value at time t plus the accumulation at time $t+h$ of the premium income less premium-related expenses over the interval $(t, t+h)$. (Note that for very small h, $\bar{s}_{\overline{h}|} \approx h$.) This total accumulation must provide the policy value at time $t+h$, and, if death occurs in the interval $(t, t+h)$, it must also provide the excess $S_t + E_t - {}_tV$ over the policy value. The probability of death in the interval $(t, t+h)$ is approximately $h\mu_{[x]+t}$.

7.5.2 Numerical solution of Thiele's differential equation

In this section we show how we can evaluate policy values by solving Thiele's differential equation numerically. The key to this is to apply equation (7.13) as an identity rather than an approximation, assuming that h is very small. This leads to

$$_{t+h}V - {}_tV = h(\delta_t \, {}_tV + P_t - e_t - \mu_{[x]+t}(S_t + E_t - {}_tV)). \qquad (7.14)$$

The smaller the value of h, the better this approximation is likely to be. The values of δ_t, P_t, e_t, $\mu_{[x]+t}$, S_t and E_t are assumed to be known, so this equation allows us to calculate ${}_tV$ provided we know the value of ${}_{t+h}V$, or ${}_{t+h}V$ if we know the value of ${}_tV$. But we always know the value of ${}_tV$ as t approaches the end of the policy term since, in the limit, it is the amount that should be held in respect of a policyholder who is still alive. For an endowment policy with term n years and sum insured S, the policy value builds up so that just before the maturity date it is exactly sufficient to pay the maturity benefit, that is

$$\lim_{t \to n^-} {}_tV = S,$$

for a term insurance with term n years and sum insured S, we have

$$\lim_{t \to n^-} {}_tV = 0,$$

and for a whole life insurance with sum insured S, we have

$$\lim_{t \to \omega^-} {}_tV = S,$$

where ω is either the upper limit of the survival model, or a practical upper limit.

Using the endowment policy with term n years and sum insured S as an example, formula (7.14) with $t = n - h$ gives us

$$S - {}_{n-h}V = h \left(\delta_{n-h} \, {}_{n-h}V + P_{n-h} - e_{n-h} - \mu_{[x]+n-h} \right.$$
$$\times \left. (S_{n-h} + E_{n-h} - {}_{n-h}V) \right),$$

from which we can calculate ${}_{n-h}V$. Another application of formula (7.14) with $t = n - 2h$ gives the value of ${}_{n-2h}V$, and so on.

This method for the numerical solution of a differential equation is known as **Euler's method**. It is the continuous time version of the discrete time recursive method for calculating reserves illustrated in Example 7.7.

Example 7.12 Consider a 20-year endowment insurance issued to a life aged 30. The sum insured, $100 000, is payable immediately on death, or on survival to the end of the term, whichever occurs sooner. Premiums are payable continuously at a constant rate of $2500 per year throughout the term of the policy. The policy value basis uses a constant force of interest, δ, and makes no allowance for expenses.

(a) Evaluate ${}_{10}V$.

(b) Use Euler's method with $h = 0.05$ years to calculate ${}_{10}V$.

Perform the calculations on the following basis:

Survival model: Standard Select Survival Model
Interest: $\delta = 0.04$ per year

Solution 7.12 (a) We have

$$_{10}V = 100\,000\bar{A}_{40:\overline{10}|} - 2500\bar{a}_{40:\overline{10}|},$$

and as

$$\bar{A}_{40:\overline{10}|} = 1 - \delta\bar{a}_{40:\overline{10}|},$$

we can calculate $_{10}V$ as

$$_{10}V = 100\,000 - (100\,000\delta + 2500)\bar{a}_{40:\overline{10}|}.$$

Using numerical integration or the three-term Woolhouse formula, we get

$$\bar{a}_{40:\overline{10}|} = 8.2167,$$

and hence $_{10}V = 46\,591$.

(b) For this example, $\delta_t = 0.04$, $e_t = 0 = E_t$, $P_t = 2500$ and $\mu_{49.95} = 0.0011471$. Hence

$$100\,000 - V_{19.95} = (0.05)((0.04)V_{19.95} + 2\,500$$
$$- (0.003204)(100\,000 - V_{19.95}))$$
$$\Rightarrow V_{19.95} = 99\,676.$$

Calculating recursively $V_{19.9}$, $V_{19.85}, \dots$, we arrive at $_{10}V = 46\,635$.

We note that the answer here is close to \$46\,591, the value calculated in part (a). Using a value of $h = 0.01$ gives the closer answer of \$46\,600. $\square$

We remarked earlier that a useful feature of setting up and numerically solving a differential equation for policy values is that the numerical solution gives policy values at a variety of durations. We can see this in the above example. In part (a) we wrote down an expression for $_{10}V$ and evaluated it using numerical integration. By contrast, in part (b) with $h = 0.05$, as a by-product of our backwards recursive calculation of $_{10}V$ we also obtained values of $_{10+h}V$, $_{10+2h}V, \dots, _{20-h}V$.

Other major advantages of Thiele's equation arise from its versatility and flexibility. We can easily accommodate variable premiums, benefits and interest rates. We can also use the equation to solve numerically for the premium given the benefits, interest model and boundary values for the policy values.

7.6 Policy alterations

A life insurance policy is a contract between an individual, the policyholder, and the insurance company. This contract places obligations on both parties; for example, the policyholder agrees to pay regular premiums while he or she remains alive and the insurance company agrees to pay a sum insured, plus bonuses for a participating policy, on the death of the policyholder. So far in this book we have assumed that the terms of the contract are never broken or altered in any way. In practice, it is not uncommon, after the policy has been in force for some time, for the policyholder to request a change in the terms of the policy. Typical changes might be:

(1) The policyholder wishes to cancel the policy with immediate effect. In this case, it may be appropriate for the insurance company to pay a lump sum immediately to the policyholder. This will be the case if the policy has a significant investment component – such as an endowment insurance, or a whole life insurance. Term insurance contracts generally do not have an investment objective. A policy which is cancelled at the request of the policyholder before the end of its originally agreed term, is said to **lapse** or to be **surrendered**, and any lump sum payable by the insurance company for such a policy is called a **surrender value** or a **cash value**.

   We tend to use the term **lapse** to indicate a voluntary cessation when no surrender value is paid, and **surrender** when there is a return of assets of some amount to the policyholder, but the words may be used interchangeably.

   In the USA and some other countries, insurers are required to offer cash surrender values on certain contract types once they have been in force for one or two years. The stipulation is known as the **non-forfeiture law**. Allowing zero cash values for early surrenders reflects the need of the insurers to recover the new business strain associated with issuing the policy.

(2) The policyholder wishes to pay no more premiums but does not want to cancel the policy, so that, in the case of an endowment insurance for example, a (reduced) sum insured is still payable on death or on survival to the end of the original term, whichever occurs sooner. Any policy for which no further premiums are payable is said to be **paid-up**, and the reduced sum insured for a policy which becomes paid-up before the end of its original premium paying term is called a **paid-up sum insured**.

(3) A whole life policy may be converted to a paid-up term insurance policy for the original sum insured.

(4) Many other types of alteration can be requested: reducing or increasing premiums; changing the amount of the benefits; converting a whole life

insurance to an endowment insurance; converting a non-participating policy to a with-profit policy; and so on. The common feature of these changes is that they are requested by the policyholder and were not part of the original terms of the policy.

If the change was not part of the original terms of the policy, and if it has been requested by the policyholder, it could be argued that the insurance company is under no obligation to agree to it. However, when the insurer has issued a contract with a substantive investment objective, rather than solely offering protection against untimely death, then at least part of the funds should be considered to be the policyholder's, under the stewardship of the insurer. In the USA the non-forfeiture law states that, for investment-type policies, each of (1), (2) and (3) would generally be available on pre-specified minimum terms. In particular, fixed or minimum cash surrender values, as a percentage of the sum insured, are specified in advance in the contract terms for such policies.

For policies with pre-specified cash surrender values, let CV_t denote the cash surrender value at duration t. Where surrender values are not set in advance, the actuary would determine an appropriate value for CV_t at the time of alteration.

Starting points for the calculation of CV_t could be the policy value at t, $_tV$, if it is to be calculated in advance, or the policy's asset share, AS_t, when the surrender value is not pre-specified. Recall that AS_t represents (approximately) the cash the insurer actually has and $_tV$ represents the amount the insurer should have at time t in respect of the original policy. Recall also that if the policy value basis is close to the actual experience, then $_tV$ will be numerically close to AS_t.

Setting CV_t equal to either AS_t or $_tV$ could be regarded as over-generous to the policyholder for several reasons, including:

(1) It is the policyholder who has requested that the contract be changed. The insurer will be concerned to ensure that surrendering policyholders do not benefit at the expense of the continuing policyholders – most insurers prefer the balance to go the other way, so that policyholders who maintain their contracts through to maturity achieve greater value than those who surrender early or change the contract. Another implication of the fact that the policyholder has called for alteration is that the policyholder may be acting on knowledge that is not available to the insurer. For example, a policyholder may alter a whole life policy to a term insurance (with lower premiums or a higher sum insured) if he or she becomes aware that their health is failing. This is called **anti-selection** or **selection against the insurer**.

(2) The insurance company will incur some expenses in making the alterations to the policy, and even in calculating and informing the policyholder of the revised values, which the policyholder may not agree to accept.

(3) The alteration may, at least in principle, cause the insurance company to realize assets it would otherwise have held, especially if the alteration is a surrender. This **liquidity risk** may lead to reduced investment returns for the company. Under non-forfeiture law in the USA, the insurer has six months to pay the cash surrender value, so that it is not forced to sell assets at short notice.

For these reasons, CV_t is usually less than 100% of either AS_t or $_tV$ and may include an explicit allowance for the expense of making the alteration.

For alterations other than cash surrenders, we can apply CV_t as if it were a single premium, or an extra preliminary premium, for the future benefits. That is, we construct the equation of value for the altered benefits,

CV_t + EPV at t of future premiums, altered contract

$$= \text{EPV at } t \text{ of future benefits plus expenses, altered contract.} \quad (7.15)$$

The numerical value of the revised benefits and/or premiums calculated using equation (7.15) depends on the basis used for the calculation, that is, the assumptions concerning the survival model, interest rate, expenses and future bonuses (for a with-profits policy). This basis may be the same as the premium basis, or the same as the policy value basis, but in practice usually differs from both of them.

The rationale behind equation (7.15) is the same as that which leads to the equivalence principle for calculating premiums: together with the cash currently available (CV_t), the future premiums are expected to provide the future benefits and pay for the future expenses.

Example 7.13 Consider the policy discussed in Examples 7.4 and 7.9. You are given that the insurer's experience in the five years following the issue of this policy is as in Example 7.9. At the start of the sixth year, before paying the premium then due, the policyholder requests that the policy be altered in one of the following three ways.

(a) The policy is surrendered immediately.
(b) No more premiums are paid and a reduced annuity is payable from age 60. In this case, all premiums paid are refunded at the end of the year of death if the policyholder dies before age 60.
(c) Premiums continue to be paid, but the benefit is altered from an annuity to a lump sum (pure endowment) payable on reaching age 60. Expenses and benefits on death before age 60 follow the original policy terms. There is an expense of $100 associated with paying the sum insured at the new maturity date.

Calculate (a) the surrender value, (b) the reduced annuity and (c) the sum insured assuming the insurer uses

(i) 90% of the asset share less a charge of $200, or
(ii) 85% of the policy value less a charge of $200

together with the assumptions in the policy value basis when calculating revised benefits and premiums.

Solution 7.13 We already know from Examples 7.4 and 7.9 that

$$_5V = 65\,470 \quad \text{and} \quad AS_5 = 63\,509.$$

Hence, the amount CV_5 to be used in equation (7.15) is

(i) $0.9 \times AS_5 - 200 = 56\,958,$
(ii) $0.9 \times {_5V} - 200 = 58\,723.$

(a) The surrender values are the cash values CV_5, so we have

   (i) $56\,958,$
   (ii) $58\,723.$

(b) Let X denote the revised annuity amount. In this case, equation (7.15) gives

$$CV_5 = 5 \times 11\,900 A^{\;1}_{55:\overline{5}|} + 100 A^{\;1}_{55:\overline{5}|} + (X + 25)v^5 \, _5p_{55} \, \ddot{a}_{60}.$$

Using values calculated for the solution to Example 7.4, we can solve this equation for the two different values for CV_5 to give

   (i) $X = \$4859,$
   (ii) $X = \$5012.$

(c) Let S denote the new sum insured. Equation (7.15) now gives

$$CV_5 + 0.95 \times 11\,900 \ddot{a}_{55:\overline{5}|} = 11\,900 \left((IA)^{\;1}_{55:\overline{5}|} + 5A^{\;1}_{55:\overline{5}|} \right)$$
$$+ 100 A^{\;1}_{55:\overline{5}|} + v^5 \, _5p_{55} \, (S + 100)$$

which we solve using the two different values for CV_5 to give

   (i) $S = \$138\,314,$
   (ii) $S = \$140\,594.$ □

Example 7.14 Ten years ago a man now aged 40 purchased a with-profit whole life insurance. The basic sum insured, payable at the end of the year of death, was $200\,000. Premiums of $1500 were payable annually for life.

The policyholder now requests that the policy be changed to a with-profit endowment insurance with a remaining term of 20 years, with the same premium payable annually, but now for a maximum of 20 further years.

The insurer uses the following basis for the calculation of policy values and policy alterations.

Survival model: Standard Select Survival Model
Interest: 5% per year
Expenses: None
Bonuses: Compound reversionary bonuses at rate 1.2% per year
                  at the start of each policy year, including the first.

The insurer uses the full policy value less an expense of $1000 when calculating revised benefits. You are given that the actual bonus rate declared in each of the past 10 years has been 1.6%.

(a) Calculate the revised sum insured, to which future bonuses will be added, assuming the premium now due has not been paid and the bonus now due has not been declared.
(b) Calculate the revised sum insured, to which future bonuses will be added, assuming the premium now due has been paid and the bonus now due has been declared to be 1.6%.

Solution 7.14 (a) Before the declaration of the bonus now due, the sum insured for the original policy is

$$200\,000 \times 1.016^{10} = 234\,405.$$

Hence, the policy value for the original policy, $_{10}V$, is given by

$$_{10}V = 234\,405 A_{40\,j} - P\ddot{a}_{40}$$

where $P = 1500$ and the subscript j indicates that the rate of interest to be used is 3.75494% since

$$1.05/1.012 = 1.0375494.$$

Let S denote the revised sum insured. Then, using equation (7.15)

$$_{10}V - 1000 = S\,A_{40:\overline{20}|\,j} - P\ddot{a}_{40:\,\overline{20}|}. \qquad (7.16)$$

A point to note here is that the life was select at the time the policy was purchased, ten years ago. No further health checks are carried out at the time of a policy alteration and so the policyholder is now assumed to be subject to the ultimate part of the survival model.

You should check the following values

$$A_{40\,j} = 0.19569, \quad \ddot{a}_{40} = 18.4578,$$
$$A_{40:\overline{20}|\,j} = 0.48233, \quad \ddot{a}_{40:\,\overline{20}|} = 12.9935.$$

Hence

$$S = \$76\,039.$$

(b) Let $_{10+}V$ denote the policy value just after the premium has been paid and the bonus has been declared at time 10. The term $A_{40\,j}$ used in the calculation of $_{10}V$ assumed the bonus to be declared at time 10 would be 1.2%, so that the sum insured in the 11th year would be $234\,405 \times 1.012$, in the 12th year would be $234\,405 \times 1.012^2$, and so on. Given that the bonus declared at time 10 is 1.6%, these sums insured are now $234\,405 \times 1.016$ (this value is known) and $234\,405 \times 1.016 \times 1.012$ (this is an assumed value since it assumes the bonus declared at the start of the 12th year will be 1.2%). Hence

$$_{10+}V = (1.016/1.012) \times 234\,405 A_{40\,j} - P a_{40}$$
$$= (1.016/1.012) \times 234\,405 A_{40\,j} - P \ddot{a}_{40} + P.$$

Let S' denote the revised sum insured for the endowment policy in this case. Equation (7.15) now gives

$$_{10+}V - 1000 = (S'/1.012)\, A_{40:\overline{20}|\,j} - P a_{40:\,\overline{19}|}$$
$$= (S'/1.012)\, A_{40:\overline{20}|\,j} - P(\ddot{a}_{40:\,\overline{20}|} - 1),$$

and hence

$$S' = \$77\,331.$$

$\square$

Note that, in Example 7.14, the sum insured payable in the 11th year is $S \times 1.016 = \$149\,295$ in part (a) and $\$149\,381$ in part (b). The difference between these values is not due to rounding – the timing of the request for the alteration has made a (small) difference to the sum insured offered by the insurer for the endowment insurance. This is caused partly by the charge of $\$1000$ for making the alteration and partly by the fact that the bonus rate in the 11th year is not as assumed in the policy value basis. In Example 7.14 we would have $S' = S \times 1.012$ if there were no charge for making the alteration and the bonus rate declared in the 11th year were the same as the rate assumed in the reserve basis (and the full policy value is still used in the calculation of the revised benefit).

7.7 Retrospective policy values

7.7.1 Prospective and retrospective valuation

Our definition of a policy value is based on the future loss random variable. As noted in Section 7.3.2, what we have called a policy value is called by some authors a *prospective policy value*. Since *prospective* means looking to the future, this name has some merit. We may also define the *retrospective policy value* at duration t, which is, loosely, the accumulated value of past premiums received, less the value of the past insurance, for a large group of identical policies, assuming the experience follows precisely the assumptions in the policy value basis, divided by the expected number of survivors. This is precisely the calculation detailed in the final part of Section 7.3.1 in respect of the policy studied in Example 7.1, so that the left-hand side of formula (7.2) is a formula for the retrospective policy value (at duration 10) for this particular policy.

The main purpose of policy values is to determine the liability value for policies that are in force. That is, the policy value is used to determine the capital that the insurer needs to hold such that, together with the expected future premiums, the insurer will have sufficient assets to meet the expected future liabilities. This fund is what actuaries call the reserve at time t for the policy. Since the purpose of the policy value is to assess future needs, it is natural to take the prospective approach.

The retrospective policy value will be defined more formally below; loosely, it measures the value at time t of all the cash flows from time 0 to time t, expressed per surviving policyholder. It is connected to the asset share, which tracks the accumulated contribution of each surviving policy to the insurer's funds. The difference between the retrospective policy value and the asset share is that, by definition, the asset share at time t uses the actual experience up to time t. The asset share at time t cannot be calculated until time t. The retrospective policy value can use any basis, and can be calculated at any time. If the retrospective policy value basis exactly matches the experience, then it will be equal to the asset share.

Intuitively, we interpret the prospective policy value as a measure of the funds needed at time t, and the retrospective policy value as a measure of the funds expected to be acquired at time t. The reserve must be prospective to meet natural requirements that assets should be sufficient to meet future liabilities. At time t, also, we have an exact measure of the asset share at that time. It is not clear why the retrospective reserve is necessary, and it is not commonly used in any country which uses gross premium policy values for setting reserves.

However, there is one way in which retrospective policy values may be useful, and it arises from the fact that, under very specific conditions, the prospective and retrospective policy values are equal. That is, let $_tV^R$ denote the retrospective policy value and let $_tV^P$ denote the prospective policy value of an n-year insurance policy. There are two conditions for $_tV^P$ to be equal to $_tV^R$, in general, namely:

(1) the premiums for the contract are determined using the equivalence principle, and
(2) the same basis is used for $_tV^R$, $_tV^P$ and the equivalence principle premium.

Now, in most cases, these conditions are very unlikely to be satisfied. Policies are very long term, and the basis used to determine the premiums will be updated regularly to reflect more up-to-date information about interest rates, expenses and mortality. The valuation assumptions might be quite different from the premium basis, as the former are likely to be more regulated to manage solvency risk.

However, there is one circumstance when the conditions may be satisfied, and the equality of the prospective and retrospective policy values may be useful. This is the case when the insurer uses the net premium policy value for determination of the reserves. Recall from Definition 7.2 that under the net premium policy value calculation, the premium used is *always* calculated using the valuation basis (regardless of the true or original premium). If, as is customary, the premium is calculated using the equivalence principle, then the retrospective and prospective net premium policy values will be the same. This can be useful if the premium or benefit structure is complicated, so that it may be simpler to take the accumulated value of past premiums less accumulated value of benefits, per surviving policyholder (the retrospective policy value), than to use the prospective policy value. It is worth noting that many policies in the USA are still valued using net premium policy values, often using a retrospective formula. In all other major developed insurance markets, regulators require some form of gross premium policy value calculation, and in these countries the retrospective approach would be inappropriate.

7.7.2 Defining the retrospective net premium policy value

Consider an insurance sold to (x) at time $t = 0$ with term n (which may be ∞ for a whole life contract). For a policy in force at time t, let L_t denote the present value at time t of all the future benefits less net premiums, under the terms of the contract. The prospective policy value, $_tV^P$, was defined for policies in force at time $t < n$ as

$$_tV^P = E[L_t].$$

If (x) does not survive to time t then L_t is undefined.

The value at issue of all future benefits less premiums payable from time $t < n$ onwards is the random variable

$$I(T_x > t)\,v^t\,L_t$$

where I is the indicator function.

Further, we define $L_{0,t}$, for $t \leq n$, as

$L_{0,t}$ = Present value, at issue, of future benefits payable up to time t
   − Present value, at issue, of future net premiums payable up to time t.

If premiums and benefits are paid at discrete intervals, and t is a premium or benefit payment date, then the convention is that $L_{0,t}$ would include benefits payable at time t, but not premiums. At issue (time 0) the future net loss random variable L_0 comprises the value of benefits less premiums up to time t, $L_{0,t}$, plus the value of benefits less premiums payable after time t, that is

$$L_0 = L_{0,t} + I(T_x > t)v^t L_t.$$

We now define the retrospective net premium policy value as

$$_tV^R = \frac{-E[L_{0,t}](1+i)^t}{_tp_x} = \frac{-E[L_{0,t}]}{_tE_x}$$

and this formula corresponds to the calculation in Section 7.2 for the policy from Example 7.1. The term $-E[L_{0,t}](1+i)^t$ is the expected value of premiums less benefits in the first t years, accumulated to time t. Dividing by $_tp_x$ expresses the expected accumulation per expected surviving policyholder.

Recall the conditions listed for equality of the retrospective and prospective values:

(1) the premium is calculated using the equivalence principle, and
(2) the same basis is used for prospective policy values, retrospective policy values and the equivalence principle premium.

By the equivalence principle,

$$E[L_0] = E\left[L_{0,t} + I(T_x > t)\, v^t\, L_t\right] = 0,$$
$$\Rightarrow -E[L_{0,t}] = E\left[I(T_x > t)\, v^t\, L_t\right]$$
$$\Rightarrow -E[L_{0,t}] = {}_tp_x\, v^t\, {}_tV^P$$
$$\Rightarrow {}_tV^R = {}_tV^P.$$

The same result could easily be derived for gross premium policy values, but the assumptions listed are very unlikely to hold when expenses and gross premiums are taken into consideration.

Example 7.15 An insurer issues a whole life insurance policy to a life aged 40. The death benefit in the first five years of the contract is $5000. In subsequent years, the death benefit is $100 000. The death benefit is payable at the end of the year of death. Premiums are paid annually for a maximum of 20 years. Premiums are level for the first five years, then increase by 50%.

(a) Write down the equation of value for calculating the net premium, using standard actuarial functions.
(b) Write down equations for the net premium policy value at time $t = 4$ using (i) the retrospective policy value approach, and (ii) the prospective policy value approach.
(c) Write down equations for the net premium policy value at time $t = 20$ using (i) the retrospective policy value approach, and (ii) the prospective policy value approach.

Solution 7.15 For convenience, we work in units of $1000.

(a) The equivalence principle premium is P for the first 5 years, and $1.5\,P$ thereafter, where

$$P = \frac{5\,A^{\,1}_{40:\overline{5}|} + 100\,{}_5E_{40}\,A_{45}}{\ddot{a}_{40:\,\overline{5}|} + 1.5\,{}_5E_{40}\,\ddot{a}_{45:\,\overline{15}|}}. \tag{7.17}$$

(b) The retrospective and prospective policy value equations at time $t = 4$ are

$$_4V^R = \frac{P\,\ddot{a}_{40:\,\overline{4}|} - 5A^{\,1}_{40:\overline{4}|}}{{}_4E_{40}} \tag{7.18}$$

and

$$_4V^P = 5\,A^{\,1}_{44:\,\overline{1}|} + 100\,{}_1E_{44}\,A_{45} - P\left(\ddot{a}_{44:\,\overline{1}|} + 1.5\,{}_1E_{44}\,\ddot{a}_{45:\,\overline{15}|}\right). \tag{7.19}$$

(c) The retrospective and prospective policy value equations at time $t = 20$ are

$$_{20}V^R = \frac{P\left(\ddot{a}_{40:\,\overline{5}|} + 1.5\,{}_5E_{40}\,\ddot{a}_{45:\,\overline{15}|}\right) - 5\,A^{\,1}_{40:\overline{5}|} - 100\,{}_5E_{40}\,A_{45:\,\overline{15}|}}{{}_{20}E_{40}}$$

and

$$_{20}V^P = 100\,A_{60}.$$

□

From these equations, we see that for this contract, the retrospective policy value offers an efficient calculation method at the start of the contract, when the premium and benefit changes are ahead, and the prospective approach is more efficient at later durations, when the changes are in the past.

Example 7.16 For Example 7.15 above, show that the prospective and retrospective policy values at time $t = 4$, given in equations (7.18) and (7.19), are equal under the standard assumptions (premium and policy values all use the same basis, and the equivalence principle premium).

Solution 7.16 Note that, assuming all calculations use the same basis,

$$A_{40:\overline{5}|}^{1} = A_{40:\overline{4}|}^{1} + {}_4E_{40}\, A_{44:\overline{1}|}^{1},$$

$$\ddot{a}_{40:\overline{5}|} = \ddot{a}_{40:\overline{4}|} + {}_4E_{40}\, \ddot{a}_{44:\overline{1}|}$$

$$_5E_{40} = {}_4E_{40}\ {}_1E_{44}.$$

Now we use these to rewrite the equivalence principle premium equation (7.17),

$$P\left(\ddot{a}_{40:\overline{5}|} + 1.5\,{}_5E_{40}\,\ddot{a}_{45:\overline{15}|}\right) = 5A_{40:\overline{5}|}^{1} + 100\,{}_5E_{40}\,A_{45}$$

$$\Rightarrow P\left(\ddot{a}_{40:\overline{4}|} + {}_4E_{40}\,\ddot{a}_{44:\overline{1}|} + 1.5\,{}_4E_{40}\,{}_1E_{44}\,\ddot{a}_{45:\overline{15}|}\right)$$

$$= 5\left(A_{40:\overline{4}|}^{1} + {}_4E_{40}\,A_{44:\overline{1}|}^{1}\right) + 100\,{}_4E_{40}\,{}_1E_{44}\,A_{45}.$$

Rearranging gives

$$P\ddot{a}_{40:\overline{4}|} - 5A_{40:\overline{4}|}^{1} = {}_4E_{40}\left(5\,A_{44:\overline{1}|}^{1} + 100\,{}_1E_{44}\,A_{45}\right.$$

$$\left. - P\left(\ddot{a}_{44:\overline{1}|} + 1.5\,{}_1E_{44}\,\ddot{a}_{45:\overline{15}|}\right)\right).$$

Dividing both sides by ${}_4E_{40}$ gives ${}_4V^R = {}_4V^P$ as required. □

7.8 Negative policy values

In all our examples in this chapter, the policy value was either zero or positive. It can happen that a policy value is negative. In fact, negative gross premium policy values are not unusual in the first few months of a contract, after the initial expenses have been incurred, and before sufficient premium is collected to defray these expenses. However, it would be unusual for policy values to be negative after the early period of the contract. If we consider the policy value equation

$$_tV = \text{EPV at } t \text{ of future benefits} + \text{Expenses} - \text{EPV at } t \text{ of future premiums},$$

then we can see that, since the future benefits and premiums must both have non-negative EPVs, the only way for a negative policy value to arise is if the future benefits are worth less than the future premiums.

In practice, negative policy values would generally be set to zero when carrying out a valuation of the insurance company. Allowing them to be entered as assets (negative liabilities) ignores the policyholder's option to lapse the contract, in which case the excess premium will not be received.

Negative policy values arise when a contract is poorly designed, so that the value of benefits in early years exceeds the value of premiums, followed by a period when the order is reversed. If the policyholder lapses then the policyholder will have benefitted from the higher benefits in the early years without waiting around to pay for the benefit in the later years. In fact, the policyholder may be able to achieve the same benefit at a cheaper price by lapsing and buying a new policy – called the lapse and re-entry option.

7.9 Deferred acquisition expenses and modified premium reserves

The principles of reserve calculation, such as whether to use a gross or net premium policy value, and how to determine the appropriate basis, are established by insurance regulators. While most jurisdictions use a gross premium policy value approach, as mentioned above, the net premium policy value is still used in the USA.

The use of the net premium approach can offer some advantages, in computation, and perhaps in smoothing results, but it can be quite a severe standard when there are large initial expenses (called acquisition expenses) incurred by the insurer. To reduce the impact, the reserve is not calculated directly as the net premium policy value, but can be modified, to approximate a gross premium policy value approach, whilst maintaining the advantages of the net premium approach. In this section we explain why this approach is used, by considering the impact of acquisition expenses on the policy value calculations.

Let $_t V^n$ denote the net premium policy value for a contract which is in force t years after issue, and let $_t V^g$ denote the gross premium policy value for the same contract, using the equivalence premium principle and using the original premium interest and mortality basis. Then we have

$$_t V^n = \text{EPV future benefits} - \text{EPV future net premiums}$$
$$_t V^g = \text{EPV future benefits} + \text{EPV future expenses}$$
$$- \text{EPV future gross premiums}$$
$$_0 V^n = {_0 V^g} = 0.$$

So we have

$$_t V^g = \text{EPV future benefits} + \text{EPV future expenses}$$
$$- (\text{EPV future net premiums} + \text{EPV future expense loadings})$$
$$= {_t V^n} + \text{EPV future expenses} - \text{EPV future expense loadings}.$$

That is $_tV^g = {}_tV^n + {}_tV^e$, say, where $_tV^e$ is the expense policy value,

$$_tV^e = \text{EPV future expenses} - \text{EPV future expense loadings.}$$

What is important about this relationship is that, generally, $_tV^e$ is negative, meaning that, for $t > 0$, the net premium policy value is greater than the gross premium policy value, assuming the same interest and mortality assumptions for both. This may appear counterintuitive – the reserve which takes expenses into consideration is smaller than the reserve which does not – but remember that the gross premium approach offsets the higher future outgo with higher future premiums. If expenses were incurred as a level annual amount, and assuming premiums are level and payable throughout the policy term, then the net premium and gross premium policy values would be the same, as the extra expenses valued in the gross premium case would be exactly offset by the extra premium. In practice though, expenses are not incurred at a flat rate. The acquisition expenses (commission, underwriting and administrative) are large relative to the renewal and claims expenses. This results in negative values for $_tV^e$, in general.

Suppose the gross premium for a level premium contract is P^g, and the net premium is P^n. The difference, P^e, say, is the **expense loading** (or expense premium) for the contract. This is the level annual amount paid by the policy-holder to cover the policy expenses. If expenses were incurred as a level sum at each premium date, then P^e would equal those incurred expenses (assuming premiums are paid throughout the policy term). If expenses are weighted to the start of the contract, as is normally the case, then P^e will be greater than the renewal expense as it must fund both the renewal and initial expenses. We illustrate these ideas with an example.

Example 7.17 An insurer issues a whole life insurance policy to a life aged 50. The sum insured of $100 000 is payable at the end of the year of death. Level premiums are payable annually in advance throughout the term of the contract. All premiums and policy values are calculated using the Standard Select Survival Model, and an interest rate of 4% per year effective. Initial expenses are 50% of the gross premium plus $250. Renewal expenses are 3% of the gross premium plus $25 at each premium date after the first.

Calculate

(a) the expense loading, P^e, and

(b) $_{10}V^e$, $_{10}V^n$ and $_{10}V^g$.

Solution 7.17 (a) The expense loading, P^e, depends on the gross premium, P^g, which we calculate first as

$$P^g = \frac{100\,000\, A_{[50]} + 25\, \ddot{a}_{[50]} + 225}{0.97\, \ddot{a}_{[50]} - 0.47} = \$1435.89.$$

Now P^e can be calculated by finding the EPV of future expenses, and calculating the level premium to fund those expenses – that is

$$P^e\, \ddot{a}_{[50]} = 25\, \ddot{a}_{[50]} + 225 + 0.03 P^g\, \ddot{a}_{[50]} + 0.47\, P^g.$$

Alternatively, we can calculate the net premium, $P^n = 100\,000 A_{[50]}/\ddot{a}_{[50]}$ $= 1321.31$, and use $P^e = P^g - P^n$. Either method gives $P^e = \$114.58$.

Compare the expense premium with the incurred expenses. The annual renewal expenses, payable at each premium date after the first, are \$68.08. The rest of the expense loading, \$46.50 at each premium date, reimburses the acquisition expenses, which total \$967.94 at inception. Thus, at any premium date after the first, the value of the future expenses will be smaller than the value of the future expense loadings.

(b) The expense reserve at time $t = 10$ for an in-force contract is

$$_{10}V^e = 25\, \ddot{a}_{60} + 0.03 P^g\, \ddot{a}_{60} - P^e\, \ddot{a}_{60} = -46.50\, \ddot{a}_{60} = -770.14,$$

the net premium policy value is

$$_{10}V^n = 100\,000\, A_{60} - P^n\, \ddot{a}_{60} = 14\,416.12,$$

and the gross premium policy value is

$$_{10}V^g = 100\,000\, A_{60} + 25\, \ddot{a}_{60} - 0.97 P^g\, \ddot{a}_{60} = 13\,645.98.$$

We note that, as expected, the expense reserve is negative, and that

$$_{10}V^g = {_{10}V^n} + {_{10}V^e}.$$

$\square$

The negative expense reserve is referred to as the **deferred acquisition cost**, or DAC. The use of the net premium reserve can be viewed as being overly conservative, as it does not allow for the DAC reimbursement. The idea is that an insurer should not be required to hold the full net premium policy value as a reserve, when the true future liability value is smaller because of the DAC. One solution would be to use a gross premium reserve, but to do so would lose some of the numerical advantage offered by the net premium approach, including simple formulae for standard contracts, and including the ability to use either a retrospective or prospective formula to perform the valuation. An alternative method, which maintains most of the numerical simplicity of the net premium approach, is to modify the net premium method to allow for the DAC, in a way that is at least approximately correct. Modified premium reserves use a net premium policy value approach to reserve calculation, but instead of assuming a level annual premium, we assume a lower initial premium to allow implicitly for the DAC.

The most common method of adjusting the net premium policy value is the **Full Preliminary Term** (FPT) approach. We describe this approach for a simple contract, to illustrate the principles, but the method can be quite easily generalized to more complex products.

Consider a whole life insurance with level annual premiums payable throughout the term. Let $P_{[x]+s}$ denote the net premium for a contract issued to a life aged $[x] + s$, who was select at age x. Let $_1P_{[x]}$ denote the single premium to fund the benefits payable during the first year of the contract (this is called the first year Cost of Insurance). Then the FPT reserve for a contract issued to a select life aged x is the net premium policy value assuming that the net premium in the first year is $_1P_{[x]}$ and in all subsequent years is $P_{[x]+1}$. This is equivalent to considering the policy as two policies, a one-year term insurance, and a separate contract issued to the same life one year later, if the life survives.

Example 7.18 (a) Calculate the premiums $_1P_{[50]}$ and $P_{[50]+1}$ for the policy in Example 7.17.

(b) Compare the net premium policy value, the gross premium policy value and the FPT reserve for the policy in Example 7.17 at durations 0, 1, 2 and 10.

Solution 7.18 (a) The modified net premium assumed at time $t = 0$ is

$$_1P_{[50]} = 100\,000\,A^{\,1}_{[50]:\,\overline{1}|} = 100\,000\,v\,q_{[50]} = 99.36.$$

The modified net premium assumed paid at all subsequent premium dates is

$$P_{[50]+1} = \frac{100\,000\,A_{[50]+1}}{\ddot{a}_{[50]+1}} = 1387.89.$$

(b) Let P^g denote the gross premium for the policy. This is the gross premium calculated in Example 7.17, payable annually throughout the term. At time 0,

$$_0 V^n = 100\,000\, A_{[50]} - P_{[50]}\, \ddot{a}_{[50]} = 0,$$

$$_0 V^g = 100\,000\, A_{[50]} + 225 + 25\, \ddot{a}_{[50]} + 0.47 P^g - 0.97 P^g\, \ddot{a}_{[50]} = 0,$$

$$_0 V^{FPT} = 100\,000\, A_{[50]} - {_1 P_{[50]}} - P_{[50]+1}\, v\, p_{[50]}\, \ddot{a}_{[50]+1}$$

$$= 100\,000 \left(A^{\,1}_{[50]:\,\overline{1}|} + v\, p_{[50]}\, A_{[50]+1} \right) - 100\,000 A^{\,1}_{[50]:\,\overline{1}|}$$

$$- \left(\frac{100\,000 A_{[50]+1}}{\ddot{a}_{[50]+1}} \right) v\, p_{[50]}\, \ddot{a}_{[50]+1}$$

$$= 0.$$

At time 1,

$$_1 V^n = 100\,000\, A_{[50]+1} - P_{[50]}\, \ddot{a}_{[50]+1} = 1272.15,$$

$$_1 V^g = 100\,000\, A_{[50]+1} + 25\, \ddot{a}_{[50]+1} - 0.97 P^g\, \ddot{a}_{[50]+1} = 383.73,$$

$$_1 V^{FPT} = 100\,000\, A_{[50]+1} - P_{[50]+1}\, \ddot{a}_{[50]+1} = 0.$$

At time 2,

$$_2 V^n = 100\,000\, A_{52} - P_{[50]}\, \ddot{a}_{52} = 2574.01,$$

$$_2 V^g = 100\,000\, A_{52} + 25\, \ddot{a}_{52} - 0.97 P^g\, \ddot{a}_{52} = 1697.30,$$

$$_2 V^{FPT} = 100\,000\, A_{52} - P_{[50]+1}\, \ddot{a}_{52} = 1318.63.$$

At time 10, we know from Example 7.17 that

$$_{10} V^n = 14\,416.12 \qquad \text{and} \qquad _{10} V^g = 13\,645.98,$$

and we have

$$_{10} V^{FPT} = 100\,000\, A_{60} - P_{[50]+1}\, \ddot{a}_{60} = 13\,313.34.$$

The FPT reserve is intended to approximate the gross premium policy value, particularly in the first few years of the contract. We see in this example that the insurer would benefit significantly in the first year from using the FPT approach rather than the net premium policy value. As the policy matures, all the policy values converge (though perhaps not until extremely advanced ages).

The FPT method implicitly assumes that the whole first year premium is spent on the cost of insurance and the acquisition expenses. In this case, that assumption overstates the acquisition expenses slightly, with the result that the FPT reserve is actually a little lower than the gross premium policy value. Modifications of the method (partial preliminary term) would allow for a net premium after the first year that lies somewhere between the FPT premium and the level net premium.

□

For more complicated policies, the FPT approach may still be applicable. For example, if the premium term is limited, say, to a maximum of k years, then the FPT modified policy value would assume that the first year's premium covers the cost of insurance (as above), and that subsequent premiums would be the net premium payable for a policy issued one year later, with a premium term of $k - 1$ years, that is, one year less.

7.10 Notes and further reading

Thiele's differential equation is named after the Danish actuary Thorvald N. Thiele (1838–1910). For information about Thiele, see Hoem (1983).

Euler's method for the numerical solution of a differential equation has the advantages that it is relatively simple to implement and it relates to the recursive formulae for policy values for policies with annual cash flows. In practice, there are better methods for solving such equations, for example the Runge–Kutta method. See Burden and Faires (2010).

Texts such as Neill (1977) and Bowers *et al.* (1997) contain standard actuarial notation for policy values.

7.11 Exercises

When a calculation is required in the following exercises, unless otherwise stated you should assume that mortality follows the Standard Select Survival Model, as specified in Appendix D, and that the equivalence principle is used for the calculation of premiums.

Exercise 7.1 You are given the following extract from a select life table with four-year select period. A select individual aged 41 purchased a three-year term insurance with a sum insured of $200 000, with premiums payable annually throughout the term.

$[x]$	$l_{[x]}$	$l_{[x]+1}$	$l_{[x]+2}$	$l_{[x]+3}$	l_{x+4}	
[40]	100 000	99 899	99 724	99 520	99 288	44
[41]	99 802	99 689	99 502	99 283	99 033	45
[42]	99 597	99 471	99 268	99 030	98 752	46

The basis for all calculations is an effective rate of interest of 6% per year, and no expenses.

(a) Show that the premium for the term insurance is $P = \$323.59$.
(b) Calculate the mean and standard deviation of the present value of future loss random variable, L_1, for the term insurance.

(c) Calculate the sum insured for a three-year endowment insurance for a select life age 41, with the same premium as for the term insurance, $P = \$323.59$.

(d) Calculate the mean and standard deviation of the present value of future loss random variable, L_1, for the endowment insurance.

(e) Comment on the differences between the values for the term insurance and the endowment insurance.

Exercise 7.2 For a whole life insurance issued to (40), you are given:

(i) The death benefit, which is payable at the end of the year of death, is $\$50\,000$ in the first 20 years, and $\$100\,000$ thereafter.

(ii) Level annual premiums are payable for 20 years or until earlier death.

(iii) The mortality basis for policy values is the Standard Ultimate Survival Model.

(iv) The interest basis for policy values is 5% per year.

Calculate the net premium policy value, $_{10}V$.
(Based on SOA, Fall 2012.)

Exercise 7.3 A whole life insurance with sum insured $\$100\,000$ is issued to a select life aged 35. Premiums are paid annually in advance and the death benefit is paid at the end of the year of death.

The premium is calculated using the Standard Select Survival Model, and assuming

Interest:	6% per year effective
Initial Expenses:	40% of the gross premium plus $125
Renewal expenses:	5% of gross premiums plus $40, due at the start of each policy year from the second onwards

(a) Calculate the gross premium.

(b) Calculate the net premium policy value at $t = 1$ using the premium basis.

(c) Calculate the gross premium policy value at $t = 1$ using the premium basis.

(d) Explain why the gross premium policy value is less than the net premium policy value.

(e) Calculate the gross premium policy value at $t = 1$ assuming interest of 5.5% per year. All other assumptions follow the premium basis.

(f) Calculate the asset share per policy at the end of the first year of the contract if experience exactly follows the premium basis.

(g) Calculate the asset share per policy at the end of the first year of the contract if the experienced mortality rate is given by $q_{[35]} = 0.0012$, the interest rate earned on assets was 10%, and expenses followed the premium basis, except that there was an additional initial expense of $25 per policy.

(h) Calculate the surplus at the end of the first year per policy issued given that the experience follows (g) and assuming the policy value used is as calculated in (c) above.

(i) Analyse the surplus in (h) into components for interest, mortality and expenses.

Exercise 7.4 A whole life insurance with reduced early sum insured is issued to a life age 50. The sum insured payable at the end of the year of death in the first two years is equal to $1000 plus the end year policy value in the year of death (that is, the policy value that would have been required if the life had survived).

The benefit payable at the end of the year of death in any subsequent year is $20 000. The annual premium P is calculated using the equivalence principle. The insurer calculates premiums and policy values using the standard select survival model, with interest at 6% per year and no expenses.

(a) (i) Write down the equations for the recursive relationship between successive policy values for the policy values in the first two years of the contract, and simplify as far as possible.

(ii) Write down an expression for the policy value at time 2, $_2V$, in terms of the premium P and standard actuarial functions.

(iii) Using (i) and (ii) above, or otherwise, calculate the annual premium and $_2V$.

(b) Calculate $_{2.25}V$, the policy value for the contract after $2\frac{1}{4}$ years.

Exercise 7.5 A special deferred annuity issued to (30) provides the following benefits:

A whole life annuity of $10 000 per year, deferred for 30 years, payable monthly in advance.

The return of all premiums paid, without interest, at the moment of death, in the event of death within the first 30 years.

Premiums are payable continuously for a maximum of 10 years.

(a) Write down expressions for

(i) the present value random variable for the benefits, and

(ii) L_0, the future loss random variable for the contract.

(b) Write down an expression in terms of annuity and insurance functions for the net annual premium rate, P, for this contract.

(c) Write down an expression for L_5, the net present value of future loss random variable for a policy in force at duration 5.

(d) Write down an expression for $_5V$, the net premium policy value at time 5 for the contract, in terms of annuity and insurance functions, and the net annual premium rate, P.

Exercise 7.6 An insurer issues a 20-year term insurance policy to (35). The sum insured of $100\,000$ is payable at the end of the year of death, and premiums are paid annually throughout the term of the contract. The basis for calculating premiums and policy values is:

Survival model: Standard Select Survival Model
Interest: 5% per year effective
Expenses: Initial: $200 plus 15% of the first premium
                 Renewal: 4% of each premium after the first

(a) Show that the premium is $91.37 per year.

(b) Show that the policy value immediately after the first premium payment is

$$_{0+}V = -\$122.33.$$

(c) Explain briefly why the policy value in (b) is negative.

(d) Calculate the policy values at each year end for the contract, just before and just after the premium and related expenses incurred at that time, and plot them on a graph. At what duration does the policy value first become strictly positive?

(e) Suppose now that the insurer issues a large number, N say, of identical contracts to independent lives, all aged 35 and all with sum insured $100\,000$. Show that if the experience exactly matches the premium/policy value basis, then the accumulated value at (integer) time k of all premiums less claims and expenses paid out up to time k, expressed per surviving policyholder, is exactly equal to the policy value at time k.

Exercise 7.7 Recalculate the analysis of surplus in Example 7.8 in the order: mortality, interest, expenses. Check that the total profit is as before and note the small differences from each source.

Exercise 7.8 Consider a 20-year endowment policy issued to (40), with premiums, P per year payable continuously, and sum insured of $200\,000$ payable immediately on death. Premiums and policy values are calculated assuming:

Survival model: Standard Select Survival Model
Interest: 5% per year effective
Expenses: None

(a) Show that the premium, P, is $6020.40 per year.
(b) Show that the policy value at duration $t = 4$, $_4V$, is $26 131.42.
(c) Assume that the insurer decides to change the valuation basis at $t = 4$ to Makeham's mortality with $A = 0.0004$, with $B = 2.7 \times 10^{-6}$ and $c = 1.124$ as before. Calculate the revised policy value at $t = 4$ (using the premium calculated in part (a)).
(d) Explain why the policy value does not change very much.
(e) Now assume again that $A = 0.00022$ but that the interest assumption changes from 5% per year to 4% per year. Calculate the revised value of $_4V$.
(f) Explain why the policy value has changed considerably.
(g) A colleague has proposed that policyholders wishing to alter their contracts to paid-up status should be offered a sum insured reduced in proportion to the number of premiums paid. That is, the paid-up sum insured after k years of premiums have been paid, out of the original total of 20 years, should be $S \times k/20$, where S is the original sum insured. This is called the **proportionate paid-up sum insured.**

Calculate the EPV of the proportionate paid-up sum insured at each year end, and compare these graphically with the policy values at each year end, assuming the original basis above is used for each. Explain briefly whether you would recommend the proportionate paid-up sum insured for this contract.

Exercise 7.9 Consider a whole life insurance policy issued to a select life aged x. Premiums of P per year are payable continuously throughout the policy term, and the sum insured of S is paid immediately on death.

(a) Show that

$$V[L_t^n] = \left(S + \frac{P}{\delta} \right)^2 \left({}^2\bar{A}_{[x]+t} - \left(\bar{A}_{[x]+t} \right)^2 \right).$$

(b) Assume the life is aged 55 at issue, and that premiums are $1200 per year. Show that the sum insured on the basis below is $77 566.44.

Mortality: Standard Select Survival Model
Interest: 5% per year effective
Expenses: None

(c) Calculate the standard deviation of L_0^n, L_5^n and L_{10}^n. Comment briefly on the results.

Exercise 7.10 For an n-year endowment policy, level monthly premiums are payable throughout the term of the contract, and the sum insured is payable at the end of the month of death.

Derive the following formula for the net premium policy value at time t years, where t is a premium date:

$$_tV = S\left(1 - \frac{\ddot{a}^{(12)}_{[x]+t:\overline{n-t}|}}{\ddot{a}^{(12)}_{[x]:\overline{n}|}}\right).$$

Exercise 7.11 A life aged 50 buys a participating whole life insurance policy with sum insured $10 000. The sum insured is payable at the end of the year of death. The premium is payable annually in advance. Profits are distributed through cash dividends paid at each year end to policies in force at that time.

The premium basis is:

Initial expenses: 22% of the annual gross premium plus $100
Renewal expenses: 5% of the gross premium plus $10
Interest: 4.5%
Survival model: Standard Select Survival Model

(a) Show that the annual premium, calculated with no allowance for future bonuses, is $144.63 per year.
(b) Calculate the policy value at each year end for this contract using the premium basis.
(c) Assume the insurer earns interest of 5.5% each year. Calculate the dividend payable each year assuming
  (i) the policy is still in force at the end of the year,
  (ii) experience other than interest exactly follows the premium basis, and
  (iii) that 90% of the profit is distributed as cash dividends to policyholders.
(d) Calculate the expected present value of the profit to the insurer per policy issued, using the same assumptions as in (c).
(e) What would be a reasonable surrender benefit for lives surrendering their contracts at the end of the first year?

Exercise 7.12 A 10-year endowment insurance is issued to a life aged 40. The sum insured is payable at the end of the year of death or on survival to the maturity date. The sum insured is $20 000 on death, $10 000 on survival to age 50. Premiums are paid annually in advance.

(a) The premium basis is:

Expenses: 5% of each gross premium including the first
Interest: 5%
Survival model: Standard Select Survival Model
Show that the gross premium is $807.71.

(b) Calculate the policy value on the premium basis just before the fifth premium is due.

(c) Just before the fifth premium is due the policyholder requests that all future premiums, including the fifth, be reduced to one-half their original amount. The insurer calculates the revised sum insured – the maturity benefit still being half of the death benefit – using the policy value in part (b) with no extra charge for making the change.

Calculate the revised death benefit.

Exercise 7.13 An insurer issues a whole life insurance policy to a life aged 40. The death benefit in the first three years of the contract is $1000. In subsequent years the death benefit is $50 000. The death benefit is payable at the end of the year of death and level premiums are payable annually throughout the term of the contract.

Basis for premiums and policy values:

Survival model: Standard Select Survival Model
Interest: 6% per year effective
Expenses: None

(a) Calculate the premium for the contract.
(b) Write down the policy value formula for any integer duration $t \geq 3$.
(c) Calculate the policy value at $t = 3$.
(d) Use the recurrence relation to determine the policy value after two years.
(e) The insurer issued 1000 of these contracts to identical, independent lives aged 40. After two years there are 985 still in force. In the following year there were four further deaths in the cohort, and the rate of interest earned on assets was 5.5%. Calculate the profit or loss from mortality and interest in the year.

Exercise 7.14 A 20-year endowment insurance issued to a life aged 40 has level premiums payable continuously throughout the term. The sum insured on survival is $60 000. The sum insured payable immediately on death within the term is $20 000 if death occurs within the first 10 years and $_t V$ if death occurs after t years, $10 \leq t < 20$, where $_t V$ is the policy value calculated on the premium basis.

Premium basis:

Survival model: Standard Select Survival Model
Interest: $\delta_t = 0.06 - 0.001t$ per year
Expenses: None

(a) Write down Thiele's differential equation for $_tV$, separately for $0 < t < 10$ and $10 < t < 20$, and give any relevant boundary conditions.
(b) Determine the premium rate P by solving Thiele's differential equation using Euler's method, with a time step $h = 0.05$.
(c) Plot the graph of $_tV$ for $0 < t < 20$.

Exercise 7.15 On 1 June 2008 an insurer issued a 20-year level term insurance to a life then aged exactly 60. The single premium was paid on 1 June 2008. The benefit is $1.

Let $_tV$ denote the policy value after t years.

(a) Suppose the death benefit is paid at the year end. Write down and explain a recurrence relation between $_tV$ and $_{t+1}V$ for $t = 0, 1, \ldots, 19$.
(b) Suppose the benefit is payable at the end of every h years, where $h < 1$. Write down a recurrence relation between $_tV$ and $_{t+h}V$ for

$$t = 0, h, 2h, \ldots, 20 - h.$$

(c) By considering the limit as $h \to 0$, show that Thiele's differential equation for the policy value for a benefit payable continuously is

$$\frac{d\,_tV}{dt} = (\mu_{[60]+t} + \delta)_t V - \mu_{[60]+t} \quad \text{for } 0 < t < 20$$

where δ is the force of interest, and state any boundary conditions.
(d) Show that

$$_tV = \bar{A}^{\ 1}_{[60]+t:\overline{20-t}|}$$

is the solution to the differential equation in (c).

Exercise 7.16 An insurer issues identical deferred annuity policies to 100 independent lives aged 60 at issue. The deferred period is 10 years, after which the annuity of $10 000 per year is paid annually in advance. Level premiums are payable annually throughout the deferred period. The death benefit during deferment is $50 000, payable at the end of the year of death.

The basis for premiums and policy values is:

Survival model: Standard Select Survival Model
Interest: 6% per year
Expenses: None

(a) Calculate the premium for each contract.

(b) Write down the recursive relationship for the policy values, during and after the deferred period.

(c) Calculate the death strain at risk in the third year of the contract, for each contract still in force at the start of the third year.

(d) Calculate the death strain at risk in the 13th year of the contract, per contract in force at the start of the year.

(e) Two years after the issue date, 97 policies remain in force. In the third year, three lives die. Calculate the total mortality profit in the third year, assuming all other experience follows the assumptions in the premium basis.

(f) Twelve years after the issue date 80 lives survive; in the 13th year there are four deaths. Calculate the total mortality profit in the 13th year.

Exercise 7.17 Consider Example 7.1. Calculate the policy values at intervals of $h = 0.1$ years from $t = 0$ to $t = 2$.

Exercise 7.18 An insurer issues a deferred annuity with a single premium to (x). The annuity is payable continuously at a level rate of $50\,000$ per year after the 20-year deferred period, if the policyholder survives. On death during the deferred period, the single premium is returned at the time of death with interest at rate i per year effective.

(a) Write down an equation for the prospective net premium policy value (i) during the deferred period and (ii) after the deferred period, using standard actuarial functions. Assume an interest rate of i per year effective, the same as the accumulation rate for the return of premium benefit.

(b) Repeat (a) for the retrospective net premium policy value.

(c) Show that the retrospective and prospective policy values are equal.

Exercise 7.19 An insurer issues a 20-year term insurance benefit to (40). The sum insured is $600\,000$ for the first five years, and $300\,000$ for the remainder of the term. The gross premium is level for five years, and then reduces to 50% of the original value for the remainder of the term. Premiums are paid annually in advance and death benefits are paid at the end of the year of death.

The insurer calculates premiums and policy values using the following basis for mortality and expenses:

Initial expenses: 50% of the first premium plus $200
Renewal expenses:10% of all premiums after the first
Mortality: Standard Select Mortality Model

Gross premiums are calculated using an interest rate of 5% per year.
   All policy values are calculated using an interest rate of 4.5% per year.

(a) Calculate the gross premium in the first year.
(b) Calculate the gross premium, net premium and Full Preliminary Term, (FPT) policy values at times $t = 0, 1, 2$.
(c) Explain briefly the rationale for the FPT approach. Does this example support the use of the FPT policy value? Justify your answer.

Exercise 7.20 Repeat Example 7.18, assuming now that the premium term is limited to a maximum of 20 years.

Answers to selected exercises

7.1 (a) $323.59
    (b) $116.68, $11 663.78
    (c) $1090.26
    (d) $342.15, $15.73
7.2 $11 149.02
7.3 (a) $469.81
    (b) $381.39
    (c) $132.91
    (e) $1125.54
    (f) $132.91
    (g) $25.10
    (h) −$107.67
    (i) $6.28,   −$86.45,   −$27.50
7.4 (a) (iii) $185.08, $401.78
    (b) $588.91
7.6 (a) $91.37
    (b) −$122.33
    (d) Selected values: $_4V = -\$32.53$, $_{4+}V = \$55.18$,
        $_{13}V = \$238.95$, $_{13+}V = \$326.67$
        The policy value first becomes positive at duration 3+.
7.7 −$26 504.04, $51 011.26,   −$5588.00
7.8 (a) $6020.40
    (b) $26 131.42
    (c) $26 348.41
    (e) $36 575.95
    (g) $t = 10$: $61 678.46, $76 070.54
7.9 (c) $14 540.32, $16 240.72, $17 619.98
7.11 (b) Selected values: $_5V = \$509.93$, $_{10}V = \$1241.77$
    (c) Selected values: Bonus at $t = 5$: $4.55
        Bonus at $t = 10$: $10.96

(d) $263.37/9 = $29.26

(e) $0

7.12 (b) $3429.68

(c) $14 565.95

7.13 (a) $256.07

(c) $863.45

(d) $558.58

(e) −$4476.57

7.14 (b) $1810.73

(c) Selected values: $_5V = \$10\,400.92,$ $_{10}V = \$23\,821.21,$
$_{15}V = \$40\,387.35$

7.16 (a) $7909.25

(c) $23 671.76

(d) −$102 752.83

(e) −$61 294.26

(f) $303 485.21

7.17 Selected values: $_{0.5}V = \$15\,255.56,$ $_1V = \$15\,369.28,$
$_{1.5}V = \$30\,962.03,$ $_2V = \$31\,415.28$

7.19 (a) $710.33

(b) Gross: $96.93, −$6.95, $338.85;   Net: $0, $353.08, $670.50;
FPT $0, $0, $345.25

7.20 (a) $99.36, $1980.39

(b) Gross: $0, $685.01, $2595.64, $20 338.41;   Net: $0, $1817.02,
$3686.39, $21 037.88;   FPT: $0, $0, $1935.61, $19 915.15

8

Multiple state models

8.1 Summary

In this chapter we reformulate the survival model introduced in Chapter 2 as an example of a multiple state model. We then introduce several other multiple state models which are useful for different types of life insurance policies, for example when benefits depend on the policyholder's health as well as survival, or when extra benefits are payable where death is accidental.

A general definition of a multiple state model, together with assumptions and notation, is given in Section 8.3. In Section 8.4 we discuss the derivation of formulae for probabilities and in Section 8.5 the numerical evaluation of these probabilities. This is extended in Section 8.6 to premium calculation and in Section 8.7 to the numerical evaluation of policy values. In Section 8.9 we describe multiple decrement models and tables, and in Section 8.12 we demonstrate how the results can be adapted when one of the underlying assumptions is relaxed.

The general results in this chapter are derived for continuous-time transitions, for example, from healthy to disabled. In Section 8.13 we consider the discrete time model, where the states are observed at discrete intervals.

8.2 Examples of multiple state models

Multiple state models are one of the most exciting developments in actuarial science in recent years. They are a natural tool for many important areas of practical interest to actuaries. They are intuitive, and easy to work with using some straightforward but powerful numerical techniques. They also simplify and provide a sound foundation for pricing and valuing some complex insurance contracts. In this section we illustrate some of the uses of multiple state models using a number of examples which are common in current actuarial practice.

Figure 8.1 The alive–dead model.

8.2.1 The alive–dead model

So far, we have modelled the uncertainty over the duration of an individual's future lifetime by regarding the future lifetime as a random variable, T_x, for an individual currently aged x, with a given cumulative distribution function, $F_x(t)$ $(= \Pr[T_x \leq t])$, and survival function, $S_x(t) = 1 - F_x(t)$. This is a **probabilistic model** in the sense that for an individual aged x we have a single random variable, T_x, whose distribution, and hence all associated probabilities, is assumed to be known.

We can represent this model diagrammatically as shown in Figure 8.1. Our individual is, at any time, in one of two **states**, 'Alive' and 'Dead'. For convenience we label these states '0' and '1', respectively. Transition from state 0 to state 1 is allowed, as indicated by the direction of the arrow, but transitions in the opposite direction cannot occur. This is an example of a **multiple state model** with two states.

We can use this multiple state model to reformulate our survival model as follows. Suppose we have a life aged $x \geq 0$ at time $t = 0$. For each $t \geq 0$ we define a random variable $Y(t)$ which takes one of the two values 0 and 1. The event '$Y(t) = 0$' means that our individual is alive at age $x + t$, and '$Y(t) = 1$' means that our individual died before age $x + t$. The set of random variables $\{Y(t)\}_{t \geq 0}$ is an example of a **continuous time stochastic process**. A continuous time stochastic process is a collection of random variables indexed by a continuous time variable. For all t, $Y(t)$ is either 0 or 1, and T_x is connected to this model as the time at which $Y(t)$ jumps from 0 to 1, that is

$$T_x = \max\{t : Y(t) = 0\}.$$

The alive–dead model represented by Figure 8.1 captures all the life contingent information that is necessary for calculating insurance premiums and policy values for policies where payments (premiums, benefits and expenses) depend only on whether the individual is alive or dead at any given age. We have seen examples of these contracts, such as term insurance or deferred annuities, in previous chapters. But there are more complicated forms of insurance which require more sophisticated models. We introduce more examples of such

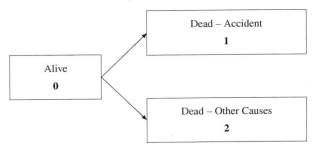

Figure 8.2 The accidental death model.

models in the remainder of this section, before giving a formal definition of a multiple state model in Section 8.3. All these models consist of a finite set of states with arrows indicating possible movements between some, but not necessarily all, pairs of states. Each state represents the status of an individual or a set of individuals. Loosely speaking, each model is appropriate for a given insurance policy, in the sense that the condition for a payment relating to the policy, for example a premium, an annuity or a sum insured, is either that the individual is in a specified state at that time or that the individual makes an instantaneous transfer between a specified pair of states at that time.

8.2.2 Term insurance with increased benefit on accidental death

Suppose we are interested in a term insurance policy under which the death benefit is $100 000 if death is due to an accident during the policy term and $50 000 if it is due to any other cause. The alive–dead model in Figure 8.1 is not sufficient for this policy since, when the individual dies – that is, transfers from state 0 to state 1 – we do not know whether death was due to an accident, and so we do not know the amount of the death benefit to be paid.

An appropriate model for this policy is shown in Figure 8.2. This model has three states, and we can define a continuous time stochastic process, $\{Y(t)\}_{t \geq 0}$, where each random variable $Y(t)$ takes one of the values 0, 1 and 2. Hence, for example, the event '$Y(t) = 1$' indicates that the individual, who is aged x at time $t = 0$, has died from an accident before age $x + t$.

The model in Figure 8.2 is an extension of the model in Figure 8.1. In both cases an individual starts by being alive, that is, starts in state 0, and, at some future time, dies. The difference is that we now distinguish between deaths due to accident and deaths due to other causes. Notice that it is the benefits provided by the insurance policy which determine the nature of the model. Because the

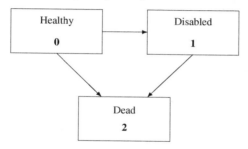

Figure 8.3 The permanent disability model.

benefit is contingent on the cause of death, the model must specify the cause of death appropriately.

8.2.3 The permanent disability model

Figure 8.3 shows a model appropriate for a policy which provides some or all of the following benefits:

(i) an annuity while permanently disabled,
(ii) a lump sum on becoming permanently disabled, and,
(iii) a lump sum on death,

with premiums payable while healthy. An important feature of this model is that disablement is permanent – there is no arrow from state 1 back to state 0.

8.2.4 The disability income insurance model

Disability income insurance pays a benefit during periods of sickness; the benefit ceases on recovery. Figure 8.4 shows a model suitable for a policy which provides an annuity while the person is sick, with premiums payable while the person is healthy. It could also be used for valuing lump sum payments contingent on becoming sick or on dying. The model represented by Figure 8.4 differs from that in Figure 8.3 in only one respect: it is possible to transfer from state 1 to state 0, that is, to recover from an illness.

This model illustrates an important general feature of multiple state models which was not present for the models in Figures 8.1, 8.2 and 8.3. This feature is the possibility of entering one or more states many times. In terms of our interpretation of the model, this means that several periods of sickness could occur before death, with healthy (premium paying) periods in between.

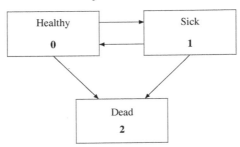

Figure 8.4 The disability income insurance model.

8.3 Assumptions and notation

The multiple state models introduced above are all extremely useful in an insurance context. We study several of these models in detail later in this chapter. Before doing so, we need to introduce some assumptions and some notation.

In this section we consider a general multiple state model. We have a finite set of $n + 1$ states labelled $0, 1, \ldots, n$, with instantaneous transitions being possible between selected pairs of states. These states represent different conditions for an individual. For each $t \geq 0$, the random variable $Y(t)$ takes one of the values $0, 1, \ldots, n$, and we interpret the event $Y(t) = i$ to mean that the individual is in state i at age $x + t$. The set of random variables $\{Y(t)\}_{t \geq 0}$ is then a continuous time stochastic process.

The multiple state model will be an appropriate model for an insurance policy if the payment of benefits or premiums is dependent on the life being in a given state or moving between a given pair of states at a given time, as illustrated in the examples in the previous section. Note that in these examples there is a natural starting state for the policy, which we always label state 0. This is the case for all examples based on multiple state models. For example, a policy providing an annuity during periods of sickness in return for premiums payable while healthy, as described in Section 8.2.4 and illustrated in Figure 8.4, would be issued only to a person who was healthy at that time.

Assumption 8.1 *We assume that for any states i and j and any times t and $t + s$, where $s \geq 0$, the conditional probability $\Pr[Y(t + s) = j \mid Y(t) = i]$ is well defined in the sense that its value does not depend on any information about the process before time t.*

Intuitively, this means that the probabilities of future events for the process are completely determined by knowing the current state of the process. In particular, these probabilities do not depend on how the process arrived at the current state or how long it has been in the current state. This property, that probabilities of future events depend on the present but not on the past, is known as the **Markov property**. Using the language of probability theory, we are assuming that $\{Y(t)\}_{t \geq 0}$ is a Markov process.

Assumption 8.1 was not made explicitly for the models represented by Figures 8.1 and 8.2 since it was unnecessary, given our interpretation of these models. In each of these two cases, if we know that the process is in state 0 at time x (so that the individual is alive at age x) then we know the past of the process (the individual was alive at all ages before x). Assumption 8.1 is more interesting in relation to the models in Figures 8.3 and 8.4. Suppose, for example, in the disability income insurance model (Figure 8.4) we know that $Y(t) = 1$, which means that the individual is sick at time t. Then Assumption 8.1 says that the probability of any future move after time t, either recovery or death, does not depend on any further information, such as how long the life has been sick up to time t, or how many different periods of sickness the life has experienced up to time t. In practice, we might believe that the probability of recovery in, say, the next week would depend on how long the current sickness has already lasted. If the current sickness has already lasted for, say, six months then it is likely to be a very serious illness and recovery within the next week is possible but not likely; if the current sickness has lasted only one day so far, then it may well be a trivial illness and recovery within a week could be very likely. It is important to understand the limitations of any model and also to bear in mind that no model is a perfect representation of reality. Assumption 8.1 can be relaxed to allow for some dependency on the process history, but these more general (non-Markov) models are beyond the scope of this book.

Assumption 8.2 *We assume that for any positive interval of time h,*

Pr[*Two or more transitions within a time period of length h*] $= o(h)$.

Recall that any function of h, say $g(h)$, is said to be $o(h)$ if

$$\lim_{h \to 0} \frac{g(h)}{h} = 0.$$

Intuitively, a function is $o(h)$ if, as h converges to 0, the function converges to zero faster than h.

Assumption 8.2 tells us that for a small time interval of length h, the probability of two or more transitions in that interval is so small that it can be ignored. This assumption is unnecessary for the models in Figures 8.1 and 8.2 since in both cases only one transition can ever take place. However, it is an assumption we need to make for technical reasons for the models in Figures 8.3 and 8.4.

In these cases, given our interpretation of the models, it is not an unreasonable assumption.

In Chapter 2 we introduced the standard actuarial notation for what we are now calling the alive–dead model, as shown in Figure 8.1; specifically, $_tp_x$, $_tq_x$ and μ_x. For multiple state models with more than two states, or more than one possible transition, we need a more flexible notation. We introduce the following notation for a general multiple state model to be used throughout this chapter and in later chapters.

Notation For states i and j in a multiple state model and for $x, t \geq 0$, we define

$$_tp_x^{ij} = \Pr[Y(x+t) = j \mid Y(x) = i], \tag{8.1}$$

$$_tp_x^{\overline{ii}} = \Pr[\,Y(x+s) = i \text{ for all } s \in [0,t] \mid Y(x) = i\,], \tag{8.2}$$

so that $_tp_x^{ij}$ is the probability that a life aged x in state i is in state j at age $x+t$, where j may be equal to i, while $_tp_x^{\overline{ii}}$ is the probability that a life aged x in state i stays in state i throughout the period from age x to age $x+t$.

For $i \neq j$ we define

$$\mu_x^{ij} = \lim_{h \to 0^+} \frac{_hp_x^{ij}}{h} \quad \text{for } i \neq j. \tag{8.3}$$

Assumption 8.3 *For all states i and j and all ages $x \geq 0$, we assume that $_tp_x^{ij}$ is a differentiable function of t.*

Assumption 8.3 is a technical assumption needed to ensure that the mathematics proceeds smoothly. Consequences of this assumption are that the limit in the definition of μ_x^{ij} always exists and that the probability of a transition taking place in a time interval of length t converges to 0 as t converges to 0. We also assume that μ_x^{ij} is a bounded and integrable function of x. These assumptions are not too restrictive in practice. However, there are some circumstances where we need to put aside Assumption 8.3 and these are discussed in Section 8.12.

In terms of the alive–dead model represented by Figure 8.1, we can make the following observations:

$_tp_x^{00}$ is the same as $_tp_x$ in the notation of Chapter 2, and $_tp_x^{01}$ is the same as $_tq_x$.

$_tp_x^{10} = 0$ since backward transitions, 'Dead' to 'Alive', are not permitted in this model.

$_0p_x^{ij}$ equals 1 if $i = j$ and zero otherwise.

μ_x^{01} is the same as μ_x, the force of mortality at age x.

In the general case, with states $0, 1, 2, \ldots, n$, we refer to μ_x^{ij} as the **force of transition** or **transition intensity** between states i and j at age x.

Another way of expressing formula (8.3) is to write for $h > 0$

$$_h p_x^{ij} = h \, \mu_x^{ij} + o(h). \tag{8.4}$$

From this formulation we can say that for small positive values of h

$$_h p_x^{ij} \approx h \, \mu_x^{ij}. \tag{8.5}$$

This is equivalent to formula (2.8) in Chapter 2 for the alive–dead model and will be very useful to us.

Example 8.1 Explain why, for a general multiple state model, $_t p_x^{\overline{ii}}$ is not equivalent to $_t p_x^{ii}$. Write down an inequality linking these two probabilities and explain why

$$_t p_x^{ii} = {}_t p_x^{\overline{ii}} + o(t). \tag{8.6}$$

Solution 8.1 From formulae (8.1) and (8.2) we can see that $_t p_x^{\overline{ii}}$ is the probability that the process/individual does not leave state i between ages x and $x + t$, whereas $_t p_x^{ii}$ is the probability that the process/individual is in state i at age $x + t$, in both cases given that the process was in state i at age x. The important distinction is that $_t p_x^{ii}$ includes the possibility that the process leaves state i between ages x and $x + t$, provided it is back in state i at age $x + t$. For any individual state which either (a) can never be left or (b) can never be re-entered once it has been left, these two probabilities *are* equivalent. This applies to all the states in the models illustrated in Figures 8.1, 8.2, 8.3 and 8.4 *except* states 0 and 1 in Figure 8.4.

The following inequality is always true since the left-hand side is the probability of a set of events which is included in the set of events whose probability is on the right-hand side

$$_t p_x^{\overline{ii}} \leq {}_t p_x^{ii}.$$

The difference between these two probabilities is the probability of those paths where the process makes two or more transitions between ages x and $x + t$ so that it is back in state i at age $x + t$. From Assumption 8.2 we know that this probability is $o(t)$. This gives us formula (8.6). □

Example 8.2 Show that, for a general multiple state model and for $h > 0$,

$$_h p_x^{\overline{ii}} = 1 - h \sum_{j=0, j \neq i}^{n} \mu_x^{ij} + o(h). \tag{8.7}$$

Solution 8.2 First note that $1 - {_h}p_x^{\overline{ii}}$ is the probability that the process *does* leave state i at some time between ages x and $x + h$, possibly returning to state i before age $x + h$. If the process leaves state i between ages x and $x + h$ then at age $x + h$ it must be in some state j ($\neq i$) or be in state i having made at least two transitions in the time interval of length h. Using formula (8.4) and Assumption 8.2, the sum of these probabilities is

$$h \sum_{j=0, j \neq i}^{n} \mu_x^{ij} + o(h),$$

which proves (8.7). $\square$

8.4 Formulae for probabilities

In this section we show how to derive formulae for all probabilities in terms of the transition intensities, which we assume to be known. This is the same approach as we adopted in Chapter 2, where we assumed the force of mortality, μ_x, was known and derived formula (2.19) for ${_t}p_x$ in terms of μ_{x+t}.

The fact that all probabilities can be expressed in terms of the transition intensities is important. It tells us that the transition intensities $\{\mu_x^{ij}; x \geq 0; i, j = 0, \ldots, n, i \neq j\}$ are fundamental quantities which determine everything we need to know about a multiple state model.

The first result generalizes formula (2.19) from Chapter 2, and is valid for any multiple state model. It gives a formula for ${_t}p_x^{\overline{ii}}$ in terms of all the transition intensities out of state i, μ_x^{ij}.

For any state i in a multiple state model with $n+1$ states, satisfying Assumptions 8.1–8.3,

$$\boxed{{_t}p_x^{\overline{ii}} = \exp\left\{ -\int_0^t \sum_{j=0;\, j \neq i}^{n} \mu_{x+s}^{ij}\, ds \right\}.}$$
$$(8.8)$$

We can derive this as follows. For any $h > 0$, consider the probability ${_{t+h}}p_x^{\overline{ii}}$. This is the probability that the process (or individual) stays in state i throughout the time period $[0, t + h]$, given that the process was in state i at age x. We can split this event into two sub-events:

- the process stays in state i from age x until (at least) age $x + t$, given that it was in state i at age x, and then
- the process stays in state i from age $x + t$ until (at least) age $x + t + h$, given that it was in state i at age $x + t$ (note the different conditioning).

The probabilities of these two sub-events are $_tp_x^{\overline{ii}}$ and $_hp_{x+t}^{\overline{ii}}$, respectively, and, using the rules for conditional probabilities, we have

$$_{t+h}p_x^{\overline{ii}} = {}_tp_x^{\overline{ii}} \, {}_hp_{x+t}^{\overline{ii}}.$$

Using the result in Example 8.2, this can be rewritten as

$$_{t+h}p_x^{\overline{ii}} = {}_tp_x^{\overline{ii}} \left(1 - h \sum_{j=0,\, j\neq i}^{n} \mu_{x+t}^{ij} + o(h)\right).$$

Rearranging this equation, we get

$$\frac{_{t+h}p_x^{\overline{ii}} - {}_tp_x^{\overline{ii}}}{h} = -\,{}_tp_x^{\overline{ii}} \sum_{j=0,\, j\neq i}^{n} \mu_{x+t}^{ij} + \frac{o(h)}{h},$$

and letting $h \to 0$ we have

$$\frac{d}{dt}\,{}_tp_x^{\overline{ii}} = -\,{}_tp_x^{\overline{ii}} \sum_{j=0,\, j\neq i}^{n} \mu_{x+t}^{ij},$$

so that

$$\frac{d}{dt} \log\left({}_tp_x^{\overline{ii}}\right) = -\sum_{j=0,\, j\neq i}^{n} \mu_{x+t}^{ij}.$$

Integration over $(0, t)$ gives

$$\log\left({}_tp_x^{\overline{ii}}\right) - \log\left({}_0p_x^{\overline{ii}}\right) = -\int_0^t \sum_{j=0,\, j\neq i}^{n} \mu_{x+r}^{ij}\,dr.$$

So, by exponentiating both sides, we see that the solution to the differential equation is

$$_tp_x^{\overline{ii}} = {}_0p_x^{\overline{ii}} \exp\left(-\int_0^t \sum_{j=0,\, j\neq i}^{n} \mu_{x+s}^{ij}\,ds\right).$$

Since $_0p_x^{\overline{ii}} = 1$, this proves (8.8).

We comment on this result after the next example.

Example 8.3 Consider the model for permanent disability illustrated in Figure 8.3. Explain why, for $x \geq 0$ and $t, h > 0$,

$$_{t+h}p_x^{01} = {}_tp_x^{01} \, {}_hp_{x+t}^{\overline{11}} + {}_tp_x^{00} \, h\,\mu_{x+t}^{01} + o(h). \tag{8.9}$$

Hence show that

$$\frac{d}{dt}\left({}_tp_x^{01} \exp\left\{\int_0^t \mu_{x+s}^{12}\,ds\right\}\right) = {}_tp_x^{\overline{00}} \mu_{x+t}^{01} \exp\left\{\int_0^t \mu_{x+s}^{12}\,ds\right\}, \tag{8.10}$$

and hence that for $u > 0$

$$_u p_x^{01} = \int_0^u {}_t p_x^{\overline{00}} \, \mu_{x+t}^{01} \, {}_{u-t} p_{x+t}^{\overline{11}} \, dt. \tag{8.11}$$

Give a direct intuitive derivation of formula (8.11).

Solution 8.3 To derive (8.9), consider a life who is healthy at age x. The left-hand side of (8.9) is the probability that this life is alive and disabled at age $x + t + h$. We can write down a formula for this probability by conditioning on which state the life was in at age $x + t$. Either:

- the life was disabled at age $x + t$ (probability ${}_t p_x^{01}$) and remained disabled between ages $x + t$ and $x + t + h$ (probability ${}_h p_{x+t}^{\overline{11}}$), or,

- the life was healthy at age $x + t$ (probability ${}_t p_x^{\overline{00}}$) and then became disabled between ages $x + t$ and $x + t + h$ (probability $h \, \mu_{x+t}^{01} + o(h)$).

Combining the probabilities of these events gives (8.9). (Note that the probability of the life being healthy at age $x + t$, becoming disabled before age $x + t + h$ and then dying before age $x + t + h$ is $o(h)$ since this involves two transitions in a time interval of length h.)

Using Example 8.2, formula (8.9) can be rewritten as

$$_{t+h} p_x^{01} = {}_t p_x^{01} (1 - h \, \mu_{x+t}^{12}) + {}_t p_x^{\overline{00}} h \, \mu_{x+t}^{01} + o(h). \tag{8.12}$$

Rearranging, dividing by h and letting $h \to 0$ gives

$$\frac{d}{dt} {}_t p_x^{01} + {}_t p_x^{01} \, \mu_{x+t}^{12} = {}_t p_x^{\overline{00}} \, \mu_{x+t}^{01}.$$

Multiplying all terms in this equation by $\exp\left\{ \int_0^t \mu_{x+s}^{12} \, ds \right\}$, we have

$$\frac{d}{dt} \left({}_t p_x^{01} \exp\left\{ \int_0^t \mu_{x+s}^{12} \, ds \right\} \right) = {}_t p_x^{\overline{00}} \, \mu_{x+t}^{01} \exp\left\{ \int_0^t \mu_{x+s}^{12} \, ds \right\}.$$

Integrating both sides of this equation from $t = 0$ to $t = u$, and noting that ${}_0 p_x^{01} = 0$, we have

$$_u p_x^{01} \exp\left\{ \int_0^u \mu_{x+s}^{12} \, ds \right\} = \int_0^u {}_t p_x^{\overline{00}} \mu_{x+t}^{01} \exp\left\{ \int_0^t \mu_{x+s}^{12} \, ds \right\} dt.$$

Finally, dividing both sides by $\exp\left\{ \int_0^u \mu_{x+s}^{12} \, ds \right\}$ and noting that, using formula (8.8),

$$_{u-t} p_{x+t}^{\overline{11}} = \exp\left\{ -\int_t^u \mu_{x+s}^{12} \, ds \right\},$$

we have formula (8.11).

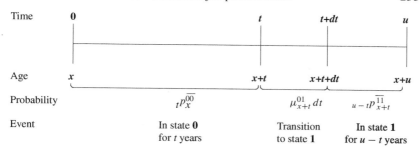

Figure 8.5 Time-line diagram for formula (8.11).

The intuitive derivation of (8.11) is as follows: for the life to move from state 0 to state 1 between ages x and $x + u$, the life must stay in state 0 until some age $x + t$, transfer to state 1 between ages $x + t$ and $x + t + dt$, where dt is small, and then stay in state 1 from age $x + t + dt$ to age $x + u$. We illustrate this event sequence using the time-line in Figure 8.5.

The infinitesimal probability of this path is

$$_t p_x^{\overline{00}} \; \mu_{x+t}^{01} \; _{u-t} p_{x+t}^{\overline{11}} dt$$

where we have written $_{u-t} p_{x+t}^{\overline{11}}$ instead of $_{u-t-dt} p_{x+t}^{\overline{11}}$ since the two are approximately equal if dt is small. Since the age at transfer, $x + t$, can be anywhere between x and $x + u$, the total probability, $_u p_x^{01}$, is the 'sum' (i.e. integral) of these probabilities from $t = 0$ to $t = u$. □

We can make the following comments about formula (8.8) and Example 8.3.

(1) As we have already noted, formula (8.8) is an extension of formula (2.19) in Chapter 2 for $_t p_x$.

(2) Throughout Example 8.3 we could have replaced $_t p_x^{\overline{ii}}$ by $_t p_x^{ii}$ for $i = 0, 1$, since, for the disability insurance model, neither state 0 nor state 1 can be re-entered once it has been left. See the solution to Example 8.1.

(3) Perhaps the most important point to note about formula (8.8) and Example 8.3 is how similar the derivations are in their basic approach. In particular, in both cases we wrote down an expression for the probability of being in the required state at age $x + t + h$ by conditioning on the state occupied at age $x + t$. This led to a formula for the derivative of the required probability which we were then able to solve. An obvious question for us is, 'Can this method be applied to a general multiple state model to derive formulae for probabilities?' The answer is, 'Yes'. This is demonstrated in Section 8.4.1.

8.4.1 Kolmogorov's forward equations

Let i and j be any two, not necessarily distinct, states in a multiple state model which has a total of $n + 1$ states. For $x, t, h \geq 0$, we derive the formula

$$_{t+h}p_x^{ij} = {}_tp_x^{ij} - h \sum_{k=0,k\neq j}^{n} \left({}_tp_x^{ij} \mu_{x+t}^{jk} - {}_tp_x^{ik} \mu_{x+t}^{kj} \right) + o(h), \qquad (8.13)$$

and hence show the main result, that

$$\boxed{\frac{d}{dt} {}_tp_x^{ij} = \sum_{k=0,k\neq j}^{n} \left({}_tp_x^{ik} \mu_{x+t}^{kj} - {}_tp_x^{ij} \mu_{x+t}^{jk} \right).} \qquad (8.14)$$

Formula (8.14) gives a set of equations for a Markov process known as Kolmogorov's forward equations.

To derive Kolmogorov's forward equations, we proceed as we did in formula (8.8) and in Example 8.3. We consider the probability of being in the required state, j, at age $x + t + h$, and condition on the state of the process at age $x + t$: either it is already in state j, or it is in some other state, say k, and a transition to j is required before age $x + t + h$. Thus, we have

$$_{t+h}p_x^{ij} = {}_tp_x^{ij} {}_hp_{x+t}^{jj} + \sum_{k=0,k\neq j}^{n} {}_tp_x^{ik} {}_hp_{x+t}^{kj}.$$

Using formulae (8.6), (8.7) and (8.4), this can be rewritten as

$$_{t+h}p_x^{ij} = {}_tp_x^{ij} \left(1 - h \sum_{k=0,k\neq j}^{n} \mu_{x+t}^{jk} - o(h) \right) + h \sum_{k=0,k\neq j}^{n} {}_tp_x^{ik} \mu_{x+t}^{kj} + o(h).$$

Rearranging the right-hand side of this expression gives (8.13). Further rearranging, dividing by h and letting $h \to 0$ gives (8.14).

In the following section we give several examples of the application of the Kolmogorov forward equations as we use them to calculate probabilities for some of the models described in Section 8.2.

8.5 Numerical evaluation of probabilities

In this section we discuss methods for the numerical evaluation of probabilities for a multiple state model given that all the transition intensities are known. In some cases, the probabilities can be calculated directly from formulae in terms of integrals, as the following example shows.

Example 8.4 Consider the permanent disability model illustrated in Figure 8.3.

(a) Suppose the transition intensities for this model are all constants, as follows

$$\mu_x^{01} = 0.0279, \quad \mu_x^{02} = 0.0229, \quad \mu_x^{12} = \mu_x^{02}.$$

Calculate $_{10}p_{60}^{00}$ and $_{10}p_{60}^{01}$.

(b) Now suppose the transition intensities for this model are as follows

$$\mu_x^{01} = a_1 + b_1 \exp\{c_1 x\},$$
$$\mu_x^{02} = a_2 + b_2 \exp\{c_2 x\},$$
$$\mu_x^{12} = \mu_x^{02},$$

where

$$a_1 = 4 \times 10^{-4}, \quad b_1 = 3.4674 \times 10^{-6}, \quad c_1 = 0.138155,$$
$$a_2 = 5 \times 10^{-4}, \quad b_2 = 7.5858 \times 10^{-5}, \quad c_2 = 0.087498.$$

Calculate $_{10}p_{60}^{00}$ and $_{10}p_{60}^{01}$.

Solution 8.4 For this model, neither state 0 nor state 1 can be re-entered once it has been left, so that

$$_tp_x^{ii} \equiv _tp_x^{\overline{ii}}$$

for $i = 0, 1$ and any $x, t \geq 0$. See the solution to Example 8.1.

(a) Using formula (8.8) we have

$$_tp_{60}^{00} \equiv _tp_{60}^{\overline{00}} = \exp\left\{-\int_0^t (0.0279 + 0.0229)\, ds\right\} = \exp\{-0.0508t\},$$

$$(8.15)$$

giving

$$_{10}p_{60}^{00} = \exp\{-0.508\} = 0.60170.$$

Similarly

$$_{10-t}p_{60+t}^{11} = \exp\{-0.0229(10-t)\},$$

and we can calculate $_{10}p_{60}^{01}$ using formula (8.11) as

$$_{10}p_{60}^{01} = \int_0^{10} {}_tp_{60}^{00}\, \mu_{60+t}^{01}\, {}_{10-t}p_{60+t}^{11}\, dt$$

$$= \int_0^{10} \exp\{-0.0508t\} \times 0.0279 \times \exp\{-0.0229(10-t)\}\, dt$$

$$= 0.19363.$$

(b) In this case

$$
{}_tp_{60}^{00} = \exp\left\{-\int_0^t (\mu_{60+r}^{01} + \mu_{60+r}^{02})\,dr\right\}
$$

$$
= \exp\left\{-\left((a_1 + a_2)t + \frac{b_1}{c_1}e^{60\,c_1}(e^{c_1\,t} - 1) + \frac{b_2}{c_2}e^{60\,c_2}(e^{c_2\,t} - 1)\right)\right\}
$$

and

$$
{}_tp_{60}^{11} = \exp\left\{-\int_0^t \mu_{60+r}^{12}\,dr\right\}
$$

$$
= \exp\left\{-\left(a_2\,t + \frac{b_2}{c_2}e^{60\,c_2}(e^{c_2\,t} - 1)\right)\right\}.
$$

Hence

$$
{}_{10}p_{60}^{00} = 0.58395.
$$

Substituting the expressions for ${}_tp_{60}^{00}$ and ${}_{10-t}p_{60+t}^{11}$ and the formula for μ_{60+t}^{01} into formula (8.11) and integrating numerically, we obtain

$$
{}_{10}p_{60}^{01} = 0.20577.
$$

□

Probabilities of the form ${}_tp_x^{\overline{ii}}$ can be evaluated analytically provided the sum of the relevant intensities can be integrated analytically. In other cases numerical integration can be used. However, the approach used in Example 8.4 part (b) to calculate a more complicated probability, ${}_{10}p_{60}^{01}$ – deriving an integral formula for the probability which can then be integrated numerically – is not tractable except in the simplest cases. Broadly speaking, this approach works if the model has relatively few states and if none of these states can be re-entered once it has been left. These conditions are met by the permanent disability model, illustrated in Figure 8.3 and used in Example 8.4, but are not met, for example, by the disability income insurance model illustrated in Figure 8.4 since states 0 and 1 can both be re-entered. This means, for example, that ${}_tp_x^{01}$ is the sum of the probabilities of exactly one transition (0 to 1), plus three transitions (0 to 1, then 1 to 0, then 0 to 1 again), plus five transitions, and so on. A probability involving k transitions involves multiple integration with k nested integrals.

Euler's method, introduced in Chapter 7, can be used to evaluate probabilities for all models in which we are interested. The key to using this method is formula (8.13) and we illustrate it by applying it in the following example.

Example 8.5 Consider the disability income insurance model illustrated in Figure 8.4. Suppose the transition intensities for this model are as follows

$$\mu_x^{01} = a_1 + b_1 \exp\{c_1 x\},$$
$$\mu_x^{10} = 0.1 \, \mu_x^{01},$$
$$\mu_x^{02} = a_2 + b_2 \exp\{c_2 x\},$$
$$\mu_x^{12} = \mu_x^{02},$$

where a_1, b_1, c_1, a_2, b_2 and c_2 are as in Example 8.4, part (b) (though this is a different model).

Calculate $_{10}p_{60}^{00}$ and $_{10}p_{60}^{01}$ using formula (8.13) with a step size of $h = 1/12$ years (we use a monthly time step, because this generates values of $_tp_{60}^{00}$ and $_tp_{60}^{01}$ for $t = 0, 1, 2, \ldots, 120$ months, which we use in Example 8.6).

Solution 8.5 For this particular model, formula (8.13) gives us the two formulae

$$_{t+h}p_{60}^{00} = {_t}p_{60}^{00} - h \, {_t}p_{60}^{00} \left(\mu_{60+t}^{01} + \mu_{60+t}^{02} \right) + h \, {_t}p_{60}^{01} \, \mu_{60+t}^{10} + o(h)$$

and

$$_{t+h}p_{60}^{01} = {_t}p_{60}^{01} - h \, {_t}p_{60}^{01} \left(\mu_{60+t}^{12} + \mu_{60+t}^{10} \right) + h \, {_t}p_{60}^{00} \, \mu_{60+t}^{01} + o(h).$$

As in Chapter 6, we choose a small step size h, ignore the $o(h)$ terms and regard the resulting approximations as exact formulae. This procedure changes the above formulae into

$$_{t+h}p_{60}^{00} = {_t}p_{60}^{00} - h \, {_t}p_{60}^{00} \left(\mu_{60+t}^{01} + \mu_{60+t}^{02} \right) + h \, {_t}p_{60}^{01} \, \mu_{60+t}^{10}$$

and

$$_{t+h}p_{60}^{01} = {_t}p_{60}^{01} - h \, {_t}p_{60}^{01} \left(\mu_{60+t}^{12} + \mu_{60+t}^{10} \right) + h \, {_t}p_{60}^{00} \, \mu_{60+t}^{01}.$$

By choosing successively $t = 0, h, 2h, \ldots, 10 - h$, we can use these formulae, together with the initial values $_0p_{60}^{00} = 1$ and $_0p_{60}^{01} = 0$, to calculate $_hp_{60}^{00}$, $_hp_{60}^{01}$, $_{2h}p_{60}^{00}$, $_{2h}p_{60}^{01}$, and so on until we have a value for $_{10}p_{60}^{00}$, as required. These calculations are very well suited to a spreadsheet. For a step size of $h = 1/12$ years, selected values are shown in Table 8.1. Note that the calculations have been carried out using more significant figures than are shown in this table. $\square$

The implementation of Euler's method in this example differs in two respects from the implementation in Example 7.10:

Table 8.1 *Calculation of* $_{10}p_{60}^{00}$ *and* $_{10}p_{60}^{01}$ *using a step size* $h = 1/12$ *years.*

t	μ_{60+t}^{01}	μ_{60+t}^{02}	μ_{60+t}^{10}	μ_{60+t}^{12}	$_t p_{60}^{00}$	$_t p_{60}^{01}$
0	0.01420	0.01495	0.00142	0.01495	1.00000	0.00000
$\frac{1}{12}$	0.01436	0.01506	0.00144	0.01506	0.99757	0.00118
$\frac{2}{12}$	0.01453	0.01517	0.00145	0.01517	0.99512	0.00238
$\frac{3}{12}$	0.01469	0.01527	0.00147	0.01527	0.99266	0.00358
$\vdots$	$\vdots$	$\vdots$	$\vdots$	$\vdots$	$\vdots$	$\vdots$
1	0.01625	0.01628	0.00162	0.01628	0.96977	0.01479
$\vdots$	$\vdots$	$\vdots$	$\vdots$	$\vdots$	$\vdots$	$\vdots$
$9\frac{11}{12}$	0.05473	0.03492	0.00547	0.03492	0.59189	0.20061
10	0.05535	0.03517	0.00554	0.03517	0.58756	0.20263

(1) We work forward recursively from initial values for the probabilities rather than backwards from the final value of the policy value. This is determined by the boundary conditions for the differential equations.

(2) We have two equations to solve simultaneously rather than a single equation. This is a typical feature of applying Euler's method to the calculation of probabilities for multiple state models. In general, the number of equations increases with the number of states in the model.

8.6 Premiums

So far in this chapter we have shown that multiple state models are a natural way of modelling cash flows for insurance policies and we have also shown how to evaluate probabilities for such models given only the transition intensities between pairs of states. The next stage in our study of multiple state models is to calculate premiums and policy values for a policy represented by such a model and to show how we can evaluate them.

To do this we can generalize our definitions of insurance and annuity functions to a multiple state framework. We implicitly use the indicator function approach, which leads directly to intuitive formulae for the expected present values, but does not give higher moments. There is no standard notation for annuity and insurance functions in the multiple state model framework. The notation used in this chapter generalizes the notation introduced in Chapters 4 and 5.

Suppose we have a life aged x currently in state i of a multiple state model. We wish to value an annuity of 1 per year payable continuously while the life is in some state j (which may be equal to i).

The EPV of the annuity, at force of interest δ per year, is

$$
\begin{aligned}
\bar{a}_x^{ij} &= \mathrm{E}\left[\int_0^\infty e^{-\delta t} I(Y(t) = j | Y(0) = i) dt\right] \\
&= \int_0^\infty e^{-\delta t} \mathrm{E}\left[I(Y(t) = j | Y(0) = i)\right] dt \\
&= \int_0^\infty e^{-\delta t}\; {}_t p_x^{ij}\, dt,
\end{aligned}
$$

where I is the indicator function.

Similarly, if the annuity is payable at the start of each year, from the current time, conditional on the life being in state j, given that the life is currently in state i, the EPV is

$$
\ddot{a}_x^{ij} = \sum_{k=0}^\infty v^k\; {}_k p_x^{ij}.
$$

Annuity benefits payable more frequently can be valued similarly.

For insurance benefits, the payment is usually conditional on making a transition. A death benefit is payable on transition into the dead state; a critical illness insurance policy might pay a sum insured on death or earlier diagnosis of one of a specified group of illnesses.

Suppose a unit benefit is payable immediately on each future transfer into state k, given that the life is currently in state i (which may be equal to k). Then the EPV of the benefit is

$$
\bar{A}_x^{ik} = \int_0^\infty \sum_{j \neq k} e^{-\delta t}\; {}_t p_x^{ij}\, \mu_{x+t}^{jk} dt. \tag{8.16}
$$

To derive this, we consider payment in the interval $(t, t + dt)$;

- the amount of the payment is 1,
- the discount factor (for sufficiently small dt) is $e^{-\delta t}$, and
- the probability that the benefit is paid is the probability that the life transfers into state k in $(t, t + dt)$, given that the life is in state i at time 0. In order to transfer into state k in $(t, t + dt)$, the life must be in some state j that is not k immediately before (the probability of two transitions in infinitesimal time being negligible), with probability ${}_t p_x^{ij}$, then transfer from j to k during the interval $(t, t + dt)$, with probability (loosely) $\mu_{x+t}^{jk}\, dt$.

Summing (that is, integrating) over all the possible time intervals gives equation (8.16).

Other benefits and annuity designs are feasible; for example, a lump sum benefit might be paid on the first transition from healthy to sick, or premiums may be paid only during the first sojourn in state 0. Most practical cases can be managed from first principles using the indicator function approach.

In general, premiums are calculated using the equivalence principle and we assume that lives are in state 0 at the policy inception date.

Example 8.6 An insurer issues a 10-year disability income insurance policy to a healthy life aged 60. Calculate the premiums for the following two policy designs using the model and parameters from Example 8.5. Assume an interest rate of 5% per year effective, and that there are no expenses.

(a) Premiums are payable continuously while in the healthy state. A benefit of $20 000 per year is payable continuously while in the disabled state. A death benefit of $50 000 is payable immediately on death.
(b) Premiums are payable monthly in advance conditional on the life being in the healthy state at the premium date. The sickness benefit of $20 000 per year is payable monthly in arrear, if the life is in the sick state at the payment date. A death benefit of $50 000 is payable immediately on death.

Solution 8.6 (a) We equate the EPV of the premiums with the EPV of the benefits.

The computation of the EPV of the benefits requires numerical integration. All values below have been calculated using the repeated Simpson's rule, with $h = 1/12$ (where h is as in Section B.1.2 in Appendix B), using Table 8.1.

Let P denote the annual rate of premium. Then the EPV of the premium income is

$$P\bar{a}^{00}_{60:\overline{10|}} = P \int_0^{10} e^{-\delta t} \, {}_tp^{00}_{60} \, dt$$

and numerical integration gives $\bar{a}^{00}_{60:\overline{10|}} = 6.5714$.

Next, the EPV of the sickness benefit is

$$20\,000\, \bar{a}^{01}_{60:\overline{10|}} = 20\,000 \int_0^{10} e^{-\delta t} \, {}_tp^{01}_{60} \, dt,$$

and numerical integration gives $\bar{a}^{01}_{60:\overline{10|}} = 0.66359$.

Last, the EPV of the death benefit is

$$50\,000\, \bar{A}^{02}_{60:\overline{10|}} = 50\,000 \int_0^{10} e^{-\delta t} \left({}_tp^{00}_{60} \, \mu^{02}_{60+t} + {}_tp^{01}_{60} \, \mu^{12}_{60+t} \right) dt.$$

Using numerical integration, we find $\bar{A}^{02}_{60:\overline{10|}} = 0.16231$.

Hence, the annual premium rate is

$$P = \frac{20\,000\,\bar{a}^{01}_{60:\overline{10|}} + 50\,000\,\bar{A}^{02}_{60:\overline{10|}}}{\bar{a}^{00}_{60:\overline{10|}}} = \$3254.65.$$

(b) We now need to find the EPV of annuities payable monthly, and we can calculate these from Table 8.1. First, to find the EPV of premium income we calculate

$$\ddot{a}^{(12)\,00}_{60:\overline{10|}} = \frac{1}{12}\left(1 + {}_{\frac{1}{12}}p^{00}_{60}\,v^{\frac{1}{12}} + {}_{\frac{2}{12}}p^{00}_{60}\,v^{\frac{2}{12}} + {}_{\frac{3}{12}}p^{00}_{60}\,v^{\frac{3}{12}} + \cdots + {}_{9\frac{11}{12}}p^{00}_{60}\,v^{9\frac{11}{12}}\right)$$

$$= 6.5980,$$

and to find the EPV of the sickness benefit we require

$$a^{(12)\,01}_{60:\overline{10|}} = \frac{1}{12}\left({}_{\frac{1}{12}}p^{01}_{60}\,v^{\frac{1}{12}} + {}_{\frac{2}{12}}p^{01}_{60}\,v^{\frac{2}{12}} + {}_{\frac{3}{12}}p^{01}_{60}\,v^{\frac{3}{12}} + \cdots + {}_{10}p^{01}_{60}\,v^{10}\right)$$

$$= 0.66877.$$

Note that the premiums are payable in advance, so that the final premium payment date is at time $9\frac{11}{12}$. However, the disability benefit is payable in arrear so that a payment will be made at time 10 if the policyholder is disabled at that time.

The death benefit is unchanged from part (a), so the premium is \$3257.20 per year, or \$271.43 per month. $\square$

8.7 Policy values and Thiele's differential equation

The definition of the time t policy value for a policy modelled using a multiple state model is exactly as in Chapter 7 – it is the expected value at that time of the future loss random variable – with one additional requirement. For a policy described by a multiple state model, the future loss random variable, and hence the policy value at duration t years may depend on which state the policyholder is in at that time. We can express this formally as follows: a policy value is the expected value at that time of the future loss random variable conditional on the policy being in a given state at that time. We use the following notation for policy values.

Notation ${}_tV^{(i)}$ denotes the policy value at duration t for a policy which is in state i at that time.

This additional feature was not necessary in Chapter 7 since all policies discussed in that, and earlier, chapters were based on the 'alive–dead' model illustrated in Figure 8.1, and for that model the policyholder was either dead at time t, in which case no policy value was required, or was in state 0.

As in Chapter 7, a policy value depends numerically on the basis used in its calculation, that is

(a) the transition intensities between pairs of states, as functions of the individual's age,
(b) the force of interest,
(c) the assumed expenses.

The key to calculating policy values is Thiele's differential equation, which can be solved numerically using Euler's method, or more sophisticated techniques. To establish some ideas we start by considering a particular example represented by the disability income insurance model, Figure 8.4. We then consider the general case.

8.7.1 *The disability income insurance model*

Consider a policy with a term of n years issued to a life aged x. Premiums are payable continuously throughout the term at rate P per year while the life is healthy, an annuity benefit is payable continuously at rate B per year while the life is sick, and a lump sum, S, is payable immediately on death within the term. Recovery from sick to healthy is possible and the disability income insurance model, Figure 8.4, is appropriate.

We are interested in calculating policy values for this policy and also in calculating the premium using the equivalence principle. For simplicity we ignore expenses in this section, but these could be included as extra 'benefits' or negative 'premiums' provided only that they are payable continuously at a constant rate while the life is in a given state and/or are payable as lump sums immediately on transition between pairs of states. Also for simplicity, we assume that the premium, the benefits and the force of interest, δ per year, are constants rather than functions of time.

Example 8.7 (a) Show that, for $0 < t < n$,

$$_tV^{(0)} = B\bar{a}^{01}_{x+t:\overline{n-t}|} + S\bar{A}^{02}_{x+t:\overline{n-t}|} - P\bar{a}^{00}_{x+t:\overline{n-t}|} \tag{8.17}$$

and derive a similar expression for $_tV^{(1)}$.

(b) Show that, for $0 < t < n$,

$$\frac{d}{dt}\,_tV^{(0)} = \delta\,_tV^{(0)} + P - \mu^{01}_{x+t}\left(_tV^{(1)} - _tV^{(0)}\right) - \mu^{02}_{x+t}\left(S - _tV^{(0)}\right) \tag{8.18}$$

and

$$\frac{d}{dt}\,_tV^{(1)} = \delta\,_tV^{(1)} - B - \mu^{10}_{x+t}\left(\,_tV^{(0)} - \,_tV^{(1)}\right) - \mu^{12}_{x+t}\left(S - \,_tV^{(1)}\right).$$

(8.19)

(c) Suppose that

$$x = 40, \ n = 20, \ \delta = 0.04, \ B = \$100\,000, \ S = \$500\,000$$

and

$$\mu^{01}_x = a_1 + b_1\exp\{c_1 x\},$$
$$\mu^{10}_x = 0.1\,\mu^{01}_x,$$
$$\mu^{02}_x = a_2 + b_2\exp\{c_2 x\},$$
$$\mu^{12}_x = \mu^{02}_x,$$

where a_1, b_1, c_1, a_2, b_2 and c_2 are as in Example 8.4.

(i) Calculate $_{10}V^{(0)}$, $_{10}V^{(1)}$ and $_0V^{(0)}$ for $n = 20$ using Euler's method with a step size of 1/12 years given that
   (1) $P = \$5500$, and
   (2) $P = \$6000$.

(ii) Calculate P using the equivalence principle.

Solution 8.7 (a) The policy value $_tV^{(0)}$ equals

> EPV of future benefits − EPV of future premiums
>> conditional on being in state 0 at time t
>>> = EPV of future disability income benefit + EPV of future death benefit
>>> − EPV of future premiums
>> conditional on being in state 0 at time t.

This leads directly to formula (8.17).

The policy value for a life in state 1 is similar, but conditioning on being in state 1 at time t, so that

$$_tV^{(1)} = B\bar{a}^{11}_{x+t:\overline{n-t}|} + S\bar{A}^{12}_{x+t:\overline{n-t}|} - P\bar{a}^{10}_{x+t:\overline{n-t}|}$$

(8.20)

where the annuity and insurance functions are defined as in Section 8.6.

(b) It is helpful to think of $_tV^{(0)}$ as the amount of cash the insurer is holding at time t, given that the policyholder is in state 0 and that, in terms of expected values, the accumulation of this amount and future premiums is exactly sufficient to provide for future losses.

Let h be such that $t < t + h < n$ and let h be small. Consider what happens between times t and $t + h$. Premiums received and interest earned will increase the insurer's cash to

$$_t V^{(0)} e^{\delta h} + P \bar{s}_{\overline{h}|}.$$

Recall that $e^{\delta h} = 1 + \delta h + o(h)$ and $\bar{s}_{\overline{h}|} = (e^{\delta h} - 1)/\delta = h + o(h)$, so that

$$_t V^{(0)} e^{\delta h} + P \bar{s}_{\overline{h}|} = {}_t V^{(0)}(1 + \delta h) + Ph + o(h).$$

This amount must be sufficient to provide the amount the insurer expects to need at time $t + h$. This amount is a policy value of $_{t+h} V^{(0)}$ and possible extra amounts of

(i) $S - {}_{t+h} V^{(0)}$ if the policyholder dies, the probability of which is $h \, \mu_{x+t}^{02} + o(h)$, and

(ii) $_{t+h} V^{(1)} - {}_{t+h} V^{(0)}$ if the policyholder falls sick, the probability of which is $h \, \mu_{x+t}^{01} + o(h)$.

Hence

$$_t V^{(0)}(1 + \delta h) + Ph = {}_{t+h} V^{(0)} + h \left\{ \mu_{x+t}^{02} \left(S - {}_{t+h} V^{(0)} \right) \right.$$
$$\left. + \mu_{x+t}^{01} \left({}_{t+h} V^{(1)} - {}_{t+h} V^{(0)} \right) \right\} + o(h).$$

Rearranging, dividing by h and letting $h \to 0$ gives formula (8.18).

Formula (8.19) is derived similarly.

(c) (i) Euler's method for the numerical evaluation of $_t V^{(0)}$ and $_t V^{(1)}$ is based on replacing the differentials on the left-hand sides of formulae (8.18) and (8.19) by discrete time approximations based on a step size h, which are correct up to $o(h)$. We could write, for example,

$$\frac{d}{dt} {}_t V^{(0)} = ({}_{t+h} V^{(0)} - {}_t V^{(0)})/h + o(h)/h.$$

Putting this into formula (8.18) would give a formula for $_{t+h} V^{(0)}$ in terms of $_t V^{(0)}$ and $_t V^{(1)}$. This is not ideal since the starting values for using Euler's method are $_n V^{(0)} = 0 = {}_n V^{(1)}$ and so we will be working backwards, calculating successively policy values at durations $n - h, n - 2h, \ldots, h, 0$. For this reason, it is more convenient to have formulae for $_{t-h} V^{(0)}$ and $_{t-h} V^{(1)}$ in terms of $_t V^{(0)}$ and $_t V^{(1)}$. We can achieve this by writing

$$\frac{d}{dt} {}_t V^{(0)} = ({}_t V^{(0)} - {}_{t-h} V^{(0)})/h + o(h)/h$$

and

$$\frac{d}{dt}\, {}_tV^{(1)} = ({}_tV^{(1)} - {}_{t-h}V^{(1)})/h + o(h)/h.$$

Putting these expressions into formulae (8.18) and (8.19), multiplying through by h, rearranging and ignoring terms which are $o(h)$, gives the following two (approximate) equations

$$\begin{aligned}
{}_{t-h}V^{(0)} &= {}_tV^{(0)}(1 - \delta h) - Ph + h\mu_{x+t}^{01}({}_tV^{(1)} - {}_tV^{(0)}) \\
&\quad + h\mu_{x+t}^{02}(S - {}_tV^{(0)})
\end{aligned} \tag{8.21}$$

and

$$\begin{aligned}
{}_{t-h}V^{(1)} &= {}_tV^{(1)}(1 - \delta h) + Bh + h\mu_{x+t}^{10}({}_tV^{(0)} - {}_tV^{(1)}) \\
&\quad + h\mu_{x+t}^{12}(S - {}_tV^{(1)}).
\end{aligned} \tag{8.22}$$

These equations, together with the starting values at time n and given values of the step size, h, and premium rate, P, can be used to calculate successively

$$\begin{aligned}
&{}_{n-h}V^{(0)},\ {}_{n-h}V^{(1)},\ {}_{n-2h}V^{(0)},\ {}_{n-2h}V^{(1)},\dots,\ {}_{10}V^{(0)}, \\
&{}_{10}V^{(1)},\dots,\ {}_0V^{(0)}.
\end{aligned}$$

(1) For $n = 20$, $h = 1/12$ and $P = \$5500$, we get

$${}_{10}V^{(0)} = \$18\,084, \quad {}_{10}V^{(1)} = \$829\,731, \quad {}_0V^{(0)} = \$3815.$$

(2) For $n = 20$, $h = 1/12$ and $P = \$6000$, we get

$${}_{10}V^{(0)} = \$14\,226, \quad {}_{10}V^{(1)} = \$829\,721, \quad {}_0V^{(0)} = -\$2617.$$

(ii) Let P^* be the premium calculated using the equivalence principle. Then, for this premium we have (by definition) ${}_0V^{(0)} = 0$. Using the results in part (i) and assuming ${}_0V^{(0)}$ is (approximately) a linear function of P, we have

$$\frac{P^* - 5500}{6000 - 5500} \approx \frac{0 - 3815}{-2617 - 3815}$$

so that $P^* \approx \$5797$.

Using Solver in Excel, setting ${}_0V^{(0)}$ to be equal to zero, by varying P gives the equivalence principle premium $P = \$5796.59$.

Using the techniques of Example 8.6 gives

$$\bar{a}_{40:\overline{20|}}^{00} = 12.8535, \quad \bar{a}_{40:\overline{20|}}^{01} = 0.31593, \quad \bar{A}_{40:\overline{20|}}^{02} = 0.08521,$$

and hence an equivalence principle premium of $\$5772.56$. The difference arises because we are using two different approximation methods. $\qquad\square$

The above example illustrates why the policy value at duration t depends on the state the individual is in at that time. If, in this example, the individual is in state 0 at time 10, then it is quite likely that no benefits will ever be paid and so only a modest policy value is required. On the other hand, if the individual is in state 1, it is very likely that benefits at the rate of $100\,000$ per year will be paid for the next 10 years and no future premiums will be received. In this case, a substantial policy value is required. The difference between the values of $V_{10}^{(0)}$ and $V_{10}^{(1)}$ in part (c), and the fact that the latter are not much affected by the value of the premium, demonstrate this point.

8.7.2 Thiele's differential equation – the general case

Consider an insurance policy issued at age x and with term n years described by a multiple state model with $n+1$ states, labelled $0, 1, 2, \ldots, n$. Let

μ_y^{ij} denote the transition intensity between states i and j at age y,

δ_t denote the force of interest per year at time t,

$B_t^{(i)}$ denote the rate of payment of benefit at time t while the policyholder is in state i, and

$S_t^{(ij)}$ denote the lump sum benefit payable instantaneously at time t on transition from state i to state j.

We assume that δ_t, $B_t^{(i)}$ and $S_t^{(ij)}$ are continuous functions of t. Note that premiums are included within this model as negative benefits and expenses can be included as additions to the benefits.

For this very general model, **Thiele's differential equation** is as follows. For $i = 0, 1, \ldots, n$ and $0 < t < n$,

$$\frac{d}{dt} {}_t V^{(i)} = \delta_t\, {}_t V^{(i)} - B_t^{(i)} - \sum_{j=0,\ j \neq i}^{n} \mu_{x+t}^{ij} \left(S_t^{(ij)} + {}_t V^{(j)} - {}_t V^{(i)} \right).$$

(8.23)

Formula (8.23) can be interpreted in exactly the same way as formula (7.12). At time t the policy value for a policy in state i, ${}_t V^{(i)}$, is changing as a result of

◇ interest being earned at rate $\delta_t\, {}_t V^{(i)}$, and
◇ benefits being paid at rate $B_t^{(i)}$.

The policy value will also change if the policyholder jumps from state i to any other state j at this time. The intensity of such a jump is μ_{x+t}^{ij} and the effect on the policy value will be

◇ a decrease of $S_t^{(ij)}$ as the insurer has to pay any lump sum benefit contingent on jumping from state i to state j,

◇ a decrease of $_tV^{(j)}$ as the insurer has to set up the appropriate policy value in the new state, and

◇ an increase of $_tV^{(i)}$ as this amount is no longer needed.

Formula (8.23) can be derived more formally by writing down an integral equation for $_tV^{(i)}$ and differentiating it. See Exercise 8.8.

We can use formula (8.23) to calculate policy values exactly as we did in Example 8.7. We choose a small step size h and replace the left-hand side by

$$(_tV^{(i)} - {}_{t-h}V^{(i)} + o(h))/h.$$

Multiplying through by h, rearranging and ignoring terms which are $o(h)$, we have a formula for $V_{t-h}^{(i)}$, $i = 0, \ldots, n$, in terms of the policy values at duration t. We can then use Euler's method, starting with $V_n^{(i)} = 0$, to calculate the policy values at durations $n - h$, $n - 2h, \ldots, h,\ 0$.

8.8 Multiple decrement models

Multiple decrement models are special types of multiple state models which occur frequently in actuarial applications. A multiple decrement model is characterized by having a single starting state and several exit states with a possible transition from the starting state to any of the exit states, but no further transitions. Figure 8.6 illustrates a general multiple decrement model. The accidental death model, illustrated in Figure 8.2, is an example of a multiple decrement model with two exit states.

Calculating probabilities for a multiple decrement model is relatively easy since only one transition can ever take place. For such a model we have for $i = 1, 2, \ldots, n$ and $j = 0, 1, \ldots, n (j \neq i)$,

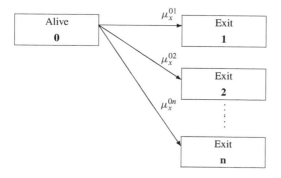

Figure 8.6 A general multiple decrement model.

$$_tp_x^{00} \equiv _tp_x^{\overline{00}} = \exp\left\{-\int_0^t \sum_{i=1}^n \mu_{x+s}^{0i}\, ds\right\},$$

$$_tp_x^{0i} = \int_0^t {_sp_x^{00}}\, \mu_{x+s}^{0i}\, ds,$$

$$_0p_x^{ii} = 1,$$

$$_0p_x^{ij} = 0.$$

Assuming we know the transition intensities as functions of x, we can calculate $_tp_x^{00}$ and $_tp_x^{0i}$ using numerical or, in some cases, analytic integration.

The following example illustrates a feature which commonly occurs when a multiple decrement model is used. We discuss the general point after completing the example.

Example 8.8 A 10-year term insurance policy is issued to a life aged 50. The sum insured, payable immediately on death, is \$200 000 and premiums are payable continuously at a constant rate throughout the term. No benefit is payable if the policyholder lapses, that is, cancels the policy during the term.

Calculate the annual premium rate using the following two sets of assumptions.

(a) The force of interest is 2.5% per year.
   The force of mortality is given by $\mu_x = 0.002 + 0.0005(x - 50)$.
   No allowance is made for lapses.
   No allowance is made for expenses.
(b) The force of interest is 2.5% per year.
   The force of mortality is given by $\mu_x = 0.002 + 0.0005(x - 50)$.
   The transition intensity for lapses is a constant equal to 0.05.
   No allowance is made for expenses.

Solution 8.8 (a) Since lapses are being ignored, an appropriate model for this policy is the 'alive–dead' model shown in Figure 8.1.

The annual premium rate, P, calculated using the equivalence principle, is given by

$$P = 200\,000 \frac{\bar{A}_{50:\overline{10|}}^{01}}{\bar{a}_{50:\overline{10|}}^{00}}$$

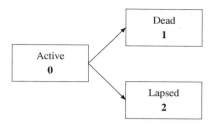

Figure 8.7 The insurance-with-lapses model.

where

$$\bar{A}^{01}_{50:\overline{10}|} = \int_0^{10} e^{-\delta t} \, {}_t p^{00}_{50} \, \mu^{01}_{50+t} \, dt,$$

$$\bar{a}^{00}_{50:\overline{10}|} = \int_0^{10} e^{-\delta t} \, {}_t p^{00}_{50} \, dt$$

and

$${}_t p^{00}_{50} = \exp\{-0.002t - 0.00025t^2\}.$$

Using numerical integration to calculate the integrals, we find

$$P = 200\,000 \times 0.03807/8.6961 = \$875.49.$$

(b) To allow for lapses, the model should be as in Figure 8.7. Note that this has the same structure as the accidental death model illustrated in Figure 8.2 – a single starting state and two exit states – but with different labels for the states. Using this model, the formula for the premium, P, is, again,

$$P = 200\,000 \frac{\bar{A}^{01}_{50:\overline{10}|}}{\bar{a}^{00}_{50:\overline{10}|}}$$

but now

$${}_t p^{00}_{50} = \exp\{-0.052t - 0.00025t^2\},$$

which gives

$$P = 200\,000 \times 0.02890/6.9269 = \$834.54. \qquad \Box$$

We make the following observations about Example 8.8.

(1) The premium allowing for lapses is a little lower than the premium which does not allow for lapses. This was to be expected. The insurer will make a

profit from any lapses in this example because, without allowing for lapses, the policy value at any duration is positive and a lapse (with no benefit payable) releases this amount as profit to the insurer. If the insurer allows for lapses, these profits can be used to reduce the premium.

(2) In practice, the insurer may prefer not to allow for lapses when pricing policies if, as in this example, this leads to a higher premium. The decision to lapse is totally at the discretion of the policyholder and depends on many factors, both personal and economic, beyond the control of the insurer. When lapses are used to reduce the premium, the business is called **lapse supported**. Because lapses are unpredictable, lapse supported pricing is considered somewhat risky and has proved to be a controversial technique.

(3) Note that two different models were used in the example to calculate a premium for the policy. The choice of model depends on the terms of the policy and on the assumptions made by the insurer.

(4) The two models used in this example are clearly different, but they are connected. The difference is that the model in Figure 8.7 has more exit states; the connections between the models are that the single exit state in Figure 8.1, 'Dead', is one of the exit states in Figure 8.7 *and* the transition intensity into this state, μ_x^{01}, is the same in the two models.

(5) The probability that the policyholder, starting at age 50, 'dies', that is enters state 1, before age $50 + t$ is different for the two models. For the model in Figure 8.1 this is

$$\int_0^t \exp\{-0.002r - 0.00025r^2\}(0.002 + 0.0005r)dr,$$

whereas for the model in Figure 8.7 it is

$$\int_0^t \exp\{-0.052r - 0.00025r^2\}(0.002 + 0.0005r)dr.$$

The explanation for this is that for the model in Figure 8.7, we interpret 'dies' as dying before lapsing. The probability of this is affected by the intensity of lapsing. If we increase this intensity, the probability of dying (before lapsing) decreases, as more lives lapse before they die.

Points (4) and (5) illustrate common features in the application of multiple decrement models. When working with a multiple decrement model we are often interested in a simpler model with only one of the exit states and with the same transition intensity into this state. For exit state j, the reduced model, represented in Figure 8.8, is called **the associated single decrement model for decrement** j.

Figure 8.8 Independent single decrement model, exit j.

For the multiple decrement model in Figure 8.6, starting in state 0 at age x, the probability of being in state $j \neq 0$ at age $x + t$ is

$$
{}_tp_x^{0j} = \int_0^t \exp\left\{ -\int_0^s \sum_{i=1}^n \mu_{x+u}^{0i}\, du \right\} \mu_{x+s}^{0j}\, ds
$$

and

$$
{}_tp_x^{00} = \exp\left\{ -\int_0^t \sum_{i=1}^n \mu_{x+u}^{0i}\, du \right\}.
$$

For the related (reduced) single decrement model in Figure 8.8, where we have only two states (0 and j), we use the methods and results of Chapter 2 to derive survival and transition probabilities, denoted by ${}_tp_x^{*(j)}$ and ${}_tq_x^{*(j)}$, respectively, of

$$
{}_tp_x^{*(j)} = \exp\left\{ -\int_0^t \mu_{x+u}^{0j}\, du \right\}
$$

and

$$
{}_tq_x^{*(j)} = \int_0^t {}_sp_x^{*(j)} \mu_{x+s}^{0j}\, ds
$$

for $j \neq 0$.

The probabilities ${}_tp_x^{00}$ and ${}_tp_x^{0j}$ are called the **dependent** probabilities of survival or exit by decrement j, because the values depend on the values of the other transition intensities, μ_{x+s}^{0k} for $0 \leq s \leq t$ and $k \neq j$; the probabilities from the reduced, two-state model, ${}_tp_x^{*(j)}$ and ${}_tq_x^{*(j)}$, are called the **independent** probabilities of surviving and exiting for decrement j, because the values are independent of the effect of other transitions. The purpose of identifying the independent probabilities is usually associated with changing assumptions, which we explore in Section 8.10 below.

8.9 Multiple decrement tables

It is sometimes convenient to express a multiple decrement model in tabular form, similar to the use of the life table functions l_x and d_x for the alive-dead model. The multiple dcrement table can be used to calculate survival

Table 8.2 *Excerpt from a critical illness multiple decrement table.*

x	l_x	$d_x^{(1)}$	$d_x^{(2)}$	$d_x^{(3)}$
40	100 000	51	4 784	44
41	95 121	52	4 526	47
42	90 496	53	4 268	50
43	86 125	54	4 010	53
44	82 008	55	3 753	56
45	78 144	56	3 496	59
46	74 533	57	3 239	62
47	71 175	57	2 983	65
48	68 070	58	2 729	67
49	65 216	58	2 476	69
50	62 613	58	2 226	70

probabilities and exit probabilities, by mode of exit, for integer ages and durations. With a fractional age assumption for decrements between integer ages, the multiple decrement table can be used to estimate all survival and exit probabilities for ages within the range of the table. We expand the life table notation of Section 3.2 as follows.

Let l_{x_0} be the radix of the table (an arbitrary positive number) at the initial age x_0. Define

$$l_{x+t} = l_{x_0} \, {}_t p_{x_0}^{00}$$

and for $j = 1, 2, \ldots, n$, and $x \geq x_0$,

$$d_x^{(j)} = l_x \times p_x^{0j}.$$

Given integer age values for l_x and for $d_x^{(j)}$, all integer age and duration probabilities can be calculated. We may interpret $l_x, x > x_0$, as the expected number of survivors in the starting state 0 at age x out of l_{x_0} in state 0 at age $x_0 \leq x$, although as l_{x_0} is an arbitrary starting value, it does not need to be an integer. Similarly, $d_x^{(j)}$ may be interpreted as the expected number of lives exiting by mode of decrement j in the year of age x to $x+1$, out of l_{x_0} lives in the starting state at age x_0.

Example 8.9 Table 8.2 is an excerpt from a multiple decrement table for an insurance policy offering benefits on death or diagnosis of critical illness. The insurance expires on the earliest event of death ($j = 1$), surrender ($j = 2$) and critical illness diagnosis ($j = 3$).

(a) Calculate (i) $_3p_{45}^{00}$ (ii) p_{40}^{01} (iii) $_5p_{41}^{03}$.

(b) Calculate the probability that a policy issued to a life aged 45 generates a claim for death or critical illness before age 47.

(c) Calculate the probability that a policy issued to a life aged 40 is surrendered between ages 45 and 47.

Solution 8.9 (a) (i) $_3p_{45}^{00} = l_{48}/l_{45} = 0.87108$.

(ii) $p_{40}^{01} = d_{40}^{(1)}/l_{40} = 0.00051$.

(iii) $_5p_{41}^{03} = \left(d_{41}^{(3)} + d_{42}^{(3)} + \cdots + d_{45}^{(3)}\right)/l_{41} = 0.00279$.

(b) $_2p_{45}^{01} + _2p_{45}^{03} = \left(d_{45}^{(1)} + d_{46}^{(1)} + d_{45}^{(3)} + d_{46}^{(3)}\right)/l_{45} = 0.00299$.

(c) $_5p_{40}^{00} {}_2p_{45}^{02} = \left(d_{45}^{(2)} + d_{46}^{(2)}\right)/l_{40} = 0.06735$.

□

8.9.1 Fractional age assumptions for decrements

Suppose the only information that we have about a multiple decrement model are the integer age values of l_x and $d_x^{(j)}$. To calculate non-integer age or duration probabilities, we need to make an assumption about the decrement probabilities or forces between integer ages.

UDD in the multiple decrement table

Here UDD stands for uniform distribution of decrements. For $0 \leq t \leq 1$, and integer x, and for each exit mode j, assume that

$$_tp_x^{0j} = tp_x^{0j}. \tag{8.24}$$

The assumption of UDD in the multiple decrement model can be interpreted as assuming that, for each decrement, the exits from the starting state are uniformly spread over each year.

Constant transition forces

For $0 \leq t < 1$, and integer x, assume that for each exit mode j, μ_{x+t}^{0j} is a constant for each age x, equal to $\mu^{0j}(x)$, say. Let

$$\mu^{0\bullet}(x) = \sum_{k=1}^{n} \mu^{0k}(x)$$

so that $\mu^{0\bullet}(x)$ represents the total force of transition out of state 0 at age $x+t$ for $0 \leq t < 1$. It is convenient also to denote the total exit probability from state 0 for the year of age x to $x+1$ as $p_x^{0\bullet}$. That is

$$p_x^{0\bullet} = 1 - p_x^{00} = \sum_{k=1}^{n} p_x^{0k} = 1 - e^{-\mu^{0\bullet}(x)},$$

so that $p_x^{00} = e^{-\mu^{0\bullet}(x)}$. Assuming constant transition forces between integer ages for all decrements,

$$_t p_x^{0j} = \frac{p_x^{0j}}{p_x^{0\bullet}} \left(1 - \left(p_x^{00} \right)^t \right). \tag{8.25}$$

We prove this as follows:

$$_t p_x^{0j} = \int_0^t {_r p_x^{00}} \, \mu_{x+r}^{0j} dr \tag{8.26}$$

$$= \int_0^t e^{-r \mu^{0\bullet}(x)} \mu^{0j}(x) dr \qquad \text{by the constant force assumption}$$

$$= \frac{\mu^{0j}(x)}{\mu^{0\bullet}(x)} \left(1 - e^{-t \mu^{0\bullet}(x)} \right)$$

$$= \frac{\mu^{0j}(x)}{\mu^{0\bullet}(x)} \left(1 - \left(p_x^{00} \right)^t \right). \tag{8.27}$$

Now let $t \to 1$, and rearrange, giving

$$\frac{\mu^{0j}(x)}{\mu^{0\bullet}(x)} = \frac{p_x^{0j}}{p_x^{0\bullet}} \tag{8.28}$$

where the left-hand side is the ratio of the mode j force of exit to the total force of exit, and the right-hand side is the ratio of the mode j probability of exit to the total probability of exit. Substitute from equation (8.28) back into (8.27) to complete the proof.

The intuition here is that the term $1 - \left(p_x^{00} \right)^t$ represents the total probability of exit under the constant transition force assumption, and the term $p_x^{0j}/p_x^{0\bullet}$ divides this exit probability into the different decrements in proportion to the full one-year exit probabilities.

Example 8.10 Calculate $_{0.2} p_{50}^{0j}$ for $j = 1, 2, 3$ using the model summarized in Table 8.2, and assuming (a) UDD in all the decrements between integer ages, and (b) constant transition forces in all decrements between integer ages.

Solution 8.10 (a) $_{0.2} p_{50}^{0j} = 0.2 \, p_{50}^{0j}$ which gives

$$_{0.2} p_{50}^{01} = 0.000185, \qquad _{0.2} p_{50}^{02} = 0.007110, \qquad _{0.2} p_{50}^{03} = 0.000224.$$

(b)

$$_{0.2} p_{50}^{0j} = \frac{p_{50}^{0j}}{p_{50}^{0\bullet}} \left(1 - (p_{50}^{00})^{0.2} \right)$$

which gives

$$_{0.2} p_{50}^{01} = 0.000188, \qquad _{0.2} p_{50}^{02} = 0.007220, \qquad _{0.2} p_{50}^{03} = 0.000227. \quad \square$$

8.10 Constructing a multiple decrement table

The multiple decrement table may be constructed from underlying transition intensities, but when the underlying transition rates are not known, tables may be constructed by combining independent decrement rates to construct a table of dependent rates.

For example, suppose an insurer is using a double decrement table for deaths and lapses to model the liabilities for a lapse-supported product. When a new mortality table is issued, the insurer may want to adjust the dependent rates to allow for the more up-to-date mortality probabilities. However, the mortality table is an independent table – the probabilities are the pure mortality probabilities. In the double decrement table, what we are interested in is the probability that death occurs from the 'in-force' state – so deaths after lapsation do not count here.

The relationship between dependent and independent rates depends on exit patterns between integer ages, for each decrement in the model. For example, suppose we have dependent rates of mortality and withdrawal for some age x in a double decrement table, of $p_x^{01} = 0.01$ and $p_x^{02} = 0.10$, respectively. This means that, given 100 lives in force at age x, we expect one to die, before withdrawing, and 10 to withdraw. Suppose we know that withdrawals all happen right at the end of the year. Then from 100 lives in force, we expect one person to die from 100 lives observed for one year, which gives an independent mortality rate $q_x^{*(1)} = 1/100$. We expect 10 lives to withdraw, from 99 expected to survive to the year end, so the independent withdrawal rate would be $q_x^{*(2)} = 10/99$. If, instead, all the withdrawals occur right at the beginning of the year, then we have one expected death from 90 lives observed for one year, so the independent mortality rate is $q_x^{*(1)} = 1/90$, and the independent withdrawal rate is $q_x^{*(2)} = 10/100$.

If we do not have such specific information, we use the fractional age assumptions of the previous section to derive the relationships between the dependent and independent probabilities.

8.10.1 Deriving independent rates from dependent rates

1. UDD in the multiple decrement table

Assume that each decrement is uniformly distributed in the multiple decrement model. Then we know that for integer x, and for $0 \le t < 1$,

$$_t p_x^{0k} = t \, p_x^{0k}, \qquad _t p_x^{00} = 1 - t \, p_x^{0\bullet} \quad \text{and} \quad _t p_x^{00} \, \mu_{x+t}^{0j} = p_x^{0j} \qquad (8.29)$$

where the last equation is derived exactly analogously to equation (3.9). Notice that the right-hand side of the last equation does not depend on t. Then from (8.29) above

$$\mu_{x+t}^{0j} = \frac{p_x^{0j}}{1 - t\, p_x^{0\bullet}}$$

and integrating both sides gives

$$\int_0^1 \mu_{x+t}^{0j}\, dt = \frac{p_x^{0j}}{p_x^{0\bullet}} \left(-\log(1 - p_x^{0\bullet}) \right) = \frac{p_x^{0j}}{p_x^{0\bullet}} \left(-\log p_x^{00} \right).$$

Note that the decrement j independent survival probability is

$$p_x^{*(j)} = e^{-\int_0^1 \mu_{x+t}^{0j} dt}$$

and substituting for the exponent, we have

$$p_x^{*(j)} = \left(p_x^{00} \right)^{\left(p_x^{0j}/p_x^{0\bullet} \right)}. \tag{8.30}$$

So, given the table of dependent rates of exit, p_x^{0j}, we can use equation (8.30) to calculate the associated independent rates, under the assumption of UDD in the multiple decrement table.

2. Constant forces of transition in the multiple decrement table

Interestingly, the relationship between dependent and independent rates under the constant force fractional age assumption is exactly that in equation (8.30). From equation (8.28) we have

$$\mu^{0j}(x) = \mu^{0\bullet}(x)\, \frac{p_x^{0j}}{p_x^{0\bullet}},$$

so

$$p_x^{*(j)} = e^{-\mu^{0j}(x)} = \left(e^{-\mu^{0\bullet}(x)} \right)^{\left(p_x^{0j}/p_x^{0\bullet} \right)} = \left(p_x^{00} \right)^{\left(p_x^{0j}/p_x^{0\bullet} \right)}.$$

Example 8.11 Calculate the independent one-year exit probabilities for each decrement for ages 40 to 50, using Table 8.2 above. Assume a uniform distribution of decrements in the multiple decrement model.

Solution 8.11 The results are given in Table 8.3.   □

You might notice in this example that the independent rates are greater than the dependent rates. This will always be true, as the effect of exposure to multiple forces of decrement must reduce the probability of exit by each individual mode, compared with the probability when only a single force of exit is present.

Now suppose we know the independent rates, and wish to construct the table of dependent rates. We consider this next.

Table 8.3 *Independent rates of exit for the multiple decrement model, Table 8.2, assuming UDD in the multiple decrement table.*

x	$q_x^{*(1)}$	$q_x^{*(2)}$	$q_x^{*(3)}$
40	0.000523	0.047863	0.000451
41	0.000560	0.047607	0.000506
42	0.000600	0.047190	0.000566
43	0.000642	0.046590	0.000630
44	0.000687	0.045795	0.000699
45	0.000733	0.044771	0.000773
46	0.000782	0.043493	0.000851
47	0.000819	0.041947	0.000933
48	0.000870	0.040128	0.001005
49	0.000907	0.038004	0.001079
50	0.000944	0.035589	0.001139

8.10.2 Deriving dependent rates from independent rates

1. UDD in the multiple decrement table or constant forces of transition
We can rearrange equation (8.30), which applies to both fractional age assumptions, to give

$$p_x^{0j} = \frac{\log p_x^{*(j)}}{\log p_x^{00}} \, p_x^{0\bullet}. \tag{8.31}$$

In order to apply this, we use the fact that the product of the independent survival probabilities gives the dependent survival probability as

$$\prod_{j=1}^{n} {}_tp_x^{*(j)} = \prod_{j=1}^{n} \exp\left(-\int_0^t \mu_{x+r}^{0j} dr\right) = \exp\left(-\int_0^t \sum_{j=1}^{n} \mu_{x+r}^{0j} dr\right) = {}_tp_x^{00}.$$

2. UDD in the independent models
If we assume a uniform distribution of decrements in each of the independent models, the result will be slightly different from the assumption of UDD in the multiple decrement table. That is, if we assume UDD in the independent models, then the transitions in the multiple decrement model will not be UDD.

The UDD assumption in the independent models means that for each decrement j, and for integer x, $0 \le t < 1$,

$$ {}_tq_x^{*(j)} = t \, q_x^{*(j)} \Rightarrow {}_tp_x^{*(j)} \, \mu_{x+t}^{0j} = q_x^{*(j)}.$$

Then

$$p_x^{0j} = \int_0^1 {}_tp_x^{00} \mu_{x+t}^{0j} dt = \int_0^1 {}_tp_x^{*(1)} \, {}_tp_x^{*(2)} \cdots {}_tp_x^{*(n)} \mu_{x+t}^{0j} \, dt.$$

Extract $_tp_x^{*(j)}\,\mu_{x+t}^{0j} = q_x^{*(j)}$ to give

$$p_x^{0j} = q_x^{*(j)} \int_0^1 \prod_{k=1,k\neq j}^n {}_tp_x^{*(j)}\,dt$$

$$= q_x^{*(j)} \int_0^1 \prod_{k=1,k\neq j}^n \left(1 - t\,q_x^{*(k)}\right)\,dt.$$

The integrand here is just a polynomial in t, so for example, if there are two decrements, we have

$$p_x^{01} = q_x^{*(1)} \int_0^1 \left(1 - t\,q_x^{*(2)}\right)\,dt$$

$$= q_x^{*(1)} \left(1 - \frac{1}{2}q_x^{*(2)}\right)$$

and similarly for p_x^{02}.

It is simple to show that, with three decrements, under the assumption of UDD in each of the single decrement models, we have

$$p_x^{01} = q_x^{*(1)} \left(1 - \frac{1}{2}\left(q_x^{*(2)} + q_x^{*(3)}\right) + \frac{1}{3}q_x^{*(2)}\,q_x^{*(3)}\right),$$

and similarly for p_x^{02} and p_x^{03}. The proof is left as an exercise.

Generally it will make little difference whether the assumption used is UDD in the multiple decrement model or UDD in the single decrement models. The differences may be noticeable though when the transition forces are changing rapidly between integer ages.

Example 8.12 The insurer using Table 8.2 wishes to revise the underlying assumptions. The independent annual surrender probabilities are to be decreased by 10% and the independent annual critical illness diagnosis probabilities are to be increased by 30%. The independent mortality probabilities are unchanged.

Construct the revised multiple decrement table for ages 40 to 50 assuming UDD in the multiple decrement model and comment on the impact of the changes on the dependent mortality probabilities.

Solution 8.12 This is a straightforward application of equation (8.31). The results are given in Table 8.4. We note the increase in the mortality ($j = 1$) probabilities, even though the underlying (independent) mortality rates were not changed. This arises because fewer lives are withdrawing, so more lives are expected to die before withdrawal. □

Table 8.4 *Revised multiple decrement table for Example 8.12.*

x	l_x	$d_x^{(1)}$	$d_x^{(2)}$	$d_x^{(3)}$
40	100 000.00	51.12	4 305.31	57.34
41	95 586.22	52.38	4 093.01	61.55
42	91 379.28	53.64	3 878.36	65.80
43	87 381.48	54.92	3 661.31	70.07
44	83 595.18	56.19	3 442.71	74.39
45	80 021.90	57.47	3 221.64	78.73
46	76 664.06	58.75	2 998.07	83.09
47	73 524.15	59.00	2 772.92	87.48
48	70 604.74	60.28	2 547.17	90.53
49	67 906.76	60.50	2 319.97	93.58
50	65 432.71	60.71	2 093.26	95.27

8.11 Comments on multiple decrement notation

Multiple decrement models have been used by actuaries for many years, but the associated notation is not in the set of standardized international actuarial notation. We have retained the more general multiple state notation for multiple decrement (dependent) probabilities, although it is unnecessarily unwieldy, perhaps, since every probability will be in the form p_x^{0j}.

The introduction of the reduced single decrement, or independent, models associated with the multiple decrement model is not easily incorporated into our multiple state model notation, which is why we have fallen back on the p and q notation from the alive–dead model.

In the table below we have summarized the multiple decrement notation that has evolved in North America and in the UK and Australia. In the first column we show the equivalent probabilities in the multiple state notation, which is mainly what we use in this text. We will also use the North American notation where it is more convenient (in particular, in double decrement death and surrender models).

8.12 Transitions at exact ages

A feature of all the multiple state models considered so far in this chapter is that transitions take place in continuous time, and the probability of a transition taking place in a time interval of length h converges to 0 as h converges to 0. This follows from Assumption 8.3 in Section 8.3. In practice, there are situations where this assumption is not realistic. One common example arises in pension plans, when there is a minimum retirement age, leading to a mass

	AMLCR	US and Canada	UK and Australia
Dependent survival probability	$_tp_x^{00}$	$_tp_x^{(\tau)}$	$_t(ap)_x$
Dependent transition probability	$_tp_x^{0j}$	$_tq_x^{(j)}$	$_t(aq)_x^j$
Dependent total transition probability	$_tp_x^{0\bullet}$	$_tq_x^{(\tau)}$	$_t(aq)_x$
Independent transition probability	$_tq_x^{*(j)}$	$_tq_x^{\prime(j)}$	$_tq_x^j$
Independent survival probability	$_tp_x^{*(j)}$	$_tp_x^{\prime(j)}$	$_tp_x^j$
Forces of transition	μ_{x+t}^{0j}	$\mu_x^{(j)}(t)$	μ_{x+t}^j
Total force of transition	$\mu_{x+t}^{0\bullet}$	$\mu_x^{(\tau)}(t)$	$(a\mu)_{x+t}$

of retirements at that age. For example, if employees can retire with an immediate pension at any age above 60, there may be a significant probability that an individual retires at exact age 60, breaching Assumption 8.3, which requires (loosely) that the probability of exit at any specified instant must be infinitesimal. The situation also arises in relation to surrenders in life insurance, where policyholders might surrender immediately before a premium payment date.

Exact age or duration transitions can be managed by separating the analysis into periods of continuous transition, where Assumption 8.3 applies, and periods of discrete transition, where there are bulk exits from the starting state.

In this section, we demonstrate this with an example, in the context of a pension plan.

Example 8.13 Exits from employment are modelled using a three decrement model, as shown in Figure 8.9. You are given the following information on exits between integer ages:

$$\mu_x^{01} = \begin{cases} 0.05 & x < 60, \\ 0.00 & x \geq 60, \end{cases}$$

$$\mu_x^{02} = \begin{cases} 0.00 & x < 60, \\ 0.10 & 60 < x < 62, \end{cases}$$

$$\mu_x^{03} = \begin{cases} 0.003 & 59 \leq x < 60, \\ 0.004 & 60 \leq x < 61, \\ 0.005 & 61 \leq x < 62. \end{cases}$$

In addition to the continuous time exits modelled using the transition intensities above, there are retirements at exact age 60, when 20% of all employees still working retire immediately, and at exact age 62, when all remaining employees retire immediately.

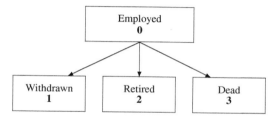

Figure 8.9 Multiple decrement model for Example 8.13.

(a) Construct the multiple decrement table for this model, for integer ages from 59 to 62, using a radix of $l_{59} = 100\,000$.

(b) Calculate the probability that an employee aged 59 will retire before age 62.

(c) Calculate the EPV of a death in service benefit of $100\,000, paid immediately on death, for an employee aged 59. Assume an interest rate of 4% per year, and use (i) exact calculation and (ii) the multiple decrement table from (a), with claims acceleration – that is, assume all payments between integer durations occur exactly half-way through the year.

(d) Calculate the EPV of a lump sum benefit of $100\,000, paid immediately on retirement, for an employee aged 59. Assume an interest rate of 4% per year, and use claims acceleration as in part (c).

Solution 8.13 (a) We will calculate the transition probabilities and build up the multiple decrement table, starting from age 59. The probability of survival to age $59 + t$, for $0 < t < 1$, is

$$_t p_{59}^{00} = e^{-\int_0^t 0.053\,dt} = e^{-0.053t}.$$

So the probabilities of exit for the year are

$$p_{59}^{01} = \int_0^1 {}_t p_{59}^{00}\, \mu_{59+t}^{01}\, dt$$

$$= \int_0^1 e^{-0.053t}\, 0.05\, dt = \frac{1 - e^{-0.053}}{0.053}\, 0.05 = 0.04870,$$

$$p_{59}^{02} = 0,$$

$$p_{59}^{03} = \int_0^1 e^{-0.053t}\, 0.003\, dt = 0.00292,$$

which give the first row of the multiple decrement table:

Age	l_x	$d_x^{(1)}$	$d_x^{(2)}$	$d_x^{(3)}$
59	100 000	4 869.8	0	292.2

So, from $l_{59} = 100\,000$ employees aged 59, we expect $4869.1 + 292.2$ to exit before age 60, leaving 94 838 in employment at exact age 60. Of these, 20% are expected to retire immediately, leaving the remainder to continue working beyond age 60. We will identify the exact age exits with a special row in the multiple decrement table. Exits between ages 60 and 61, after the exact age transitions, will be denoted as applying to age 60$^+$. The table becomes:

Age	l_x	$d_x^{(1)}$	$d_x^{(2)}$	$d_x^{(3)}$
59	100 000.0	4 869.8	0.0	292.2
60 exact	94 838.0	0.0	18 967.6	0.0
60$^+$	75 870.4			

Once the exact age transitions are accounted for, transitions between ages 60$^+$ and 61 follow using the standard multiple state model formulae. We have $_tp_{60^+}^{00} = e^{-0.104t}$ for $0 \leq t \leq 1$, and

$$p_{60^+}^{01} = 0,$$

$$p_{60^+}^{02} = \int_0^1 e^{-0.104t}\, 0.1\, dt = 0.09498,$$

$$p_{60^+}^{03} = \int_0^1 e^{-0.104t}\, 0.004\, dt = 0.00380,$$

and multiplying these by l_{60^+} gives the $d_{60^+}^{(j)}$ values required:

Age	l_x	$d_x^{(1)}$	$d_x^{(2)}$	$d_x^{(3)}$
59	100 000.0	4 869.8	0.0	292.2
60 exact	94 838.0	0.0	18 967.6	0.0
60$^+$	75 870.4	0.0	7205.8	288.2
61	68 376.3			

We then repeat the process for age 61:

$$p_{61}^{01} = 0,$$

$$p_{61}^{02} = \int_0^1 e^{-0.105t} \, 0.1 \, dt = 0.09493,$$

$$p_{61}^{03} = \int_0^1 e^{-0.105t} \, 0.005 \, dt = 0.00475,$$

which give the full table up to exact age 62, when all remaining employees are assumed to retire immediately:

Age	l_x	$d_x^{(1)}$	$d_x^{(2)}$	$d_x^{(3)}$
59	100 000.0	4 869.8	0.0	292.2
60 exact	94 838.0	0.0	18 967.6	0.0
60$^+$	75 870.4	0.0	7 205.8	288.2
61	68 376.3	0.0	6 490.9	324.5
62 exact	61 560.9	0.0	61 560.9	0.0

(b) To distinguish between probabilities before exact age exits and after exact age exits, we use superscripts t^- and t^+, for the age or term, as appropriate. So, using the table, the probability that an employee aged 59 retires before age 62^- is

$$_{3^-}p_{59}^{02} = \frac{18\,967.6 + 7\,205.8 + 6\,490.9}{100\,000} = 0.32664.$$

(c) (i) The death in service benefit may be valued in three parts, corresponding to the three possible years of service. We then have the EPV as $100\,000 \bar{A}_{59:\overline{3}|}^{03}$ where $\delta = \log 1.04$ and

$$\bar{A}_{59:\overline{3}|}^{03} = \int_0^1 e^{-0.053t} \, 0.003 \, e^{-\delta t} dt$$

$$+ \,_{1^+}p_{59}^{00} e^{-\delta} \int_0^1 e^{-0.104t} \, 0.004 \, e^{-\delta t} dt$$

$$+ \,_{2}p_{59}^{00} e^{-2\delta} \int_0^1 e^{-0.105t} \, 0.005 \, e^{-\delta t} dt$$

$$= 0.0085281$$

giving the EPV for the death in service benefit as \$852.81.

(ii) With the claims acceleration approach (which is very common in pension calculations), we can use the table to determine the probability of death in service over each year, and assume that the benefits are paid, on average, midway through the year of age, giving the EPV as

$$100\,000\,\frac{292.2v^{0.5} + 288.2v^{1.5} + 324.5v^{2.5}}{100\,000} = \$852.51.$$

We notice that the claims acceleration approach is simpler to calculate and quite accurate, compared with the exact calculation, in this case.

(d) The continuous time retirement benefits are discounted from the mid-year of payment, and the exact age retirements at ages 60 and 62 are discounted from the exact dates, giving the EPV of the retirement lump sum as

$$100\,000 \left(\frac{18\,967.6\,v + 7\,205.8\,v^{1.5} + 6\,490.9\,v^{2.5} + 61\,560.9\,v^3}{100\,000} \right)$$

$$= \$85\,644.28.$$

□

8.13 Markov multiple state models in discrete time

In the multiple decrement table, we summarize information about probabilities of transition for integer ages and integer terms. For some analysis, that is sufficient information, and, as we saw in Example 8.13, even when cash flows do not correspond to the integer ages and durations, the discrete time model can be quite efficient in calculation in the multiple decrement case.

For a more general multiple state model, it is not common to use tables of l_x and $d_x^{(j)}$ values, as the possibility of multiple transitions makes such a table unwieldy even in quite simple cases. However, we do sometimes work with discrete time models, rather than continuous time transitions. In this section, we derive some methods for working with more general multiple state models in discrete time. Markov models in discrete time are called **Markov chains**. To be more precise, given a set of states labelled (say) $\{0, 1, \ldots, n\}$, a discrete time stochastic process $\{Y(t),\ t = 0, 1, 2, \ldots\}$ is a Markov chain if for any non-negative integers t and k, and for any state s,

$$\Pr[Y(t + k) = s | Y(0), Y(1), \ldots, Y(t)] = \Pr[Y(t + k) = s | Y(t)].$$

This means that (as in the continuous time case), the probability that the process is in any given state at some future date depends only on the current state, not on the history of the process before the current date.

We now illustrate the principles with an example.

Example 8.14 An insurer uses the disability income model, illustrated in Figure 8.4, to evaluate policies with sickness and death contingent benefits. In this example we refer to state 0 as 'healthy', state 1 as 'sick' and state 2 as 'dead'.

The insurer has calculated a table of annual probabilities for the model. An excerpt is given in Table 8.5.

Table 8.5 *Annual probabilities for the three state model, Example 8.14.*

x	p_x^{00}	p_x^{01}	p_x^{02}	p_x^{10}	p_x^{11}	p_x^{12}
50	0.981176	0.012036	0.006788	0.038658	0.951752	0.009590
51	0.978813	0.013822	0.007365	0.038593	0.950916	0.010491
52	0.976009	0.015996	0.007995	0.038517	0.950003	0.011480
53	0.972673	0.018643	0.008684	0.038429	0.949005	0.012566
54	0.968702	0.021862	0.009436	0.038325	0.947915	0.013760
55	0.963966	0.025773	0.010261	0.038204	0.946726	0.015070

(a) Calculate the probability that a healthy life aged 50 is healthy at age 52.
(b) Calculate the probability that a healthy life aged 50 is sick at age 52.
(c) Calculate the probability that a healthy life aged 50 is healthy at age 53.
(d) A healthy life aged 50 purchases a policy with premiums of $10 000 payable annually in advance for up to five years. The insurer waives premiums for policyholders who are sick at the premium payment date. Calculate the reduction in the EPV of the premium income resulting from the waiver, compared with a policy where payments are contingent only on the policyholder being alive. Assume an interest rate of 4% per year effective.
(e) At the end of the fifth year, the policyholder receives a level life annuity if she survives, payable annually in advance. There is a benefit of $50 000 payable at the end of the year of death if the policyholder dies before age 55. The premium is $10 000 per year, payable in advance for five years, and is waived on sickness (as in part (d)). You are given that, at 4% per year, the EPV at age 55 of a life annuity of 1 per year for a life who is healthy at that time is 13.285, and the EPV at age 55 of an annuity of 1 per year to a life who is sick at that time is 12.350.

Calculate the level annual benefit payable under the deferred annuity. Ignore expenses.

Solution 8.14 (a) The probability is $_2p_{50}^{00}$. We calculate this by considering the two possible states at age 51, that could lead to the event that (50) is healthy at age 52, given that she is healthy at age 50. Either (i) she is healthy at age 51, and healthy at age 52, or (ii) she is sick at age 51, and healthy at age 52. So, the states at ages 50, 51 and 52 are either $0 \rightarrow 0 \rightarrow 0$ or $0 \rightarrow 1 \rightarrow 0$.

Constructing the probabilities for these events, we have

$$_2p_{50}^{00} = p_{50}^{00}\, p_{51}^{00} + p_{50}^{01}\, p_{51}^{10} = 0.960852.$$

It is worth noting here that we have no information from the one-year p_x^{00} probabilities about whether the life transitioned out and back into state 0 between integer dates. The table tells us only probabilities associated with end-year states, and should not be interpreted as offering any information about paths between states within each year.

(b) Similarly to (a), given that the life is healthy at age 50, to be sick at age 52 the life must, subsequently, either be healthy at age 51, and transition to sick by age 52, or must be sick at age 51, and sick also at age 52. The probabilities combine for the two year transition probability

$$_2p_{50}^{01} = p_{50}^{00}\, p_{51}^{01} + p_{50}^{01}\, p_{51}^{11} = 0.025007.$$

(c) The probability required is $_3p_{50}^{00}$. We can follow the argument from (a), and work out all the possible states for the life at ages 51 and 52. It is convenient to work backwards from age 53; if she is to be healthy at age 53, at age 52, she could be either healthy or sick. So, we can break down the three-year probability as

$$_3p_{50}^{00} = {_2p_{50}^{00}}\, p_{52}^{00} + {_2p_{50}^{01}}\, p_{52}^{10}$$

and since we calculated the two-year probabilities in parts (a) and (b), we have

$$_3p_{50}^{00} = 0.960852 \times 0.976009 + 0.025007 \times 0.038517 = 0.938764.$$

(d) The EPV of premiums with no sickness waiver is

$$1000\left(1 + \left(p_{50}^{00} + p_{50}^{01}\right) v + \left(_2p_{50}^{00} + {_2p_{50}^{01}}\right) v^2 + \left(_3p_{50}^{00} + {_3p_{50}^{01}}\right) v^3\right.$$
$$\left. + \left(_4p_{50}^{00} + {_4p_{50}^{01}}\right) v^4\right),$$

and with sickness waiver is

$$1000\left(1 + p_{50}^{00} v + {_2p_{50}^{00}} v^2 + {_3p_{50}^{00}} v^3 + {_4p_{50}^{00}} v^4\right).$$

Generalizing the approach in part (c), we see that the values for $_tp_{50}^{00}$, $_tp_{50}^{01}$ and $_tp_{50}^{02}$, can be calculated recursively as

$$_{t+1}p_{50}^{00} = {_tp_{50}^{00}}\, p_{50+t}^{00} + {_tp_{50}^{01}}\, p_{50+t}^{10},$$
$$_{t+1}p_{50}^{01} = {_tp_{50}^{00}}\, p_{50+t}^{01} + {_tp_{50}^{01}}\, p_{50+t}^{11},$$
$$_{t+1}p_{50}^{02} = {_tp_{50}^{00}}\, p_{50+t}^{02} + {_tp_{50}^{01}}\, p_{50+t}^{12} + {_tp_{50}^{02}}$$
$$= 1 - {_{t+1}p_{50}^{00}} - {_{t+1}p_{50}^{01}}$$

which give the values shown in Table 8.6.

Table 8.6 *Probabilities for Example 8.14.*

t	${}_tp_{50}^{00}$	${}_tp_{50}^{01}$	${}_tp_{50}^{02}$
0	1.000000	0.000000	0.000000
1	0.981176	0.012036	0.006788
2	0.960852	0.025007	0.014141
3	0.938764	0.039127	0.022110
4	0.914614	0.054633	0.030754
5	0.888082	0.071782	0.040136

Note that these recursions are specific to this model. The intuition for the ${}_{t+1}p_{50}^{0j}$ recursion, for $j = 0, 1, 2$, is that we consider all the possible states for (50) at age $50 + t$, and then consider what transition is required for (50) to be in state j at age $50 + t + 1$. So for the first recursion above, where $j = 0$, (50) must either be in state 0 at age $50 + t$ (with probability ${}_tp_{50}^{00}$) and then go from state 0 to 0 in the final year (with probability p_{50+t}^{00}), or be in state 1 at age $50 + t$ (with probability ${}_tp_{50}^{01}$) and then go from state 1 to 0 in the final year (with probability p_{50+t}^{10}). Combining these two possible routes gives the first recursion.

Similarly, for ${}_{t+1}p_{50}^{01}$, (50) must either be in state 0 at age $50 + t$ (with probability ${}_tp_{50}^{00}$) and then go from state 0 to 1 in the final year (with probability p_{50+t}^{01}) or be in state 1 at age $50 + t$ (with probability ${}_tp_{50}^{01}$) and then go from state 1 to 1 in the final year (with probability p_{50+t}^{11}). Combining these two possible routes gives the second recursion.

For ${}_{t+1}p_{50}^{02}$, there are three possibilities for (50) at age $50 + t$; she could already be in state 2 (with probability ${}_tp_{50}^{02}$) or she could be in state 0 at age $50 + t$ (with probability ${}_tp_{50}^{00}$) and then go from state 0 to 2 in the final year (with probability p_{50+t}^{02}), or be in state 1 at age $50+t$ (with probability ${}_tp_{50}^{01}$) and then go from state 1 to 2 in the final year (with probability p_{50+t}^{12}). Combining these three possible routes gives the third recursion.

Using the probabilities in Table 8.6, we find that the EPV of the annual premium of $1000 is $4564.35 without the waiver of premiums on sickness, and $4448.17 with the waiver, so the EPV of the waiver is $116.18.

(e) The probability ${}_{t+1}p_{50}^{02}$ is the probability that 50 dies before age $50+t+1$, given that she is healthy at age 50. To value the death benefit, we need the probability that the life dies in the year t to $t + 1$, which can be written as

$$ {}_{t+1}p_{50}^{02} - {}_tp_{50}^{02} $$

Multiple state models

or

$$_tp_{50}^{00}\, p_{50+t}^{02} + {}_tp_{50}^{01}\, p_{50+t}^{12}.$$

In the first expression, we take the probability of death by age $50 + t$ away from the probability of death by age $50 + t + 1$, and what remains is the probability of death in the year t to $t + 1$. In the second expression, we consider the two possible ways that the life can transition to state 2 in the year t to $t + 1$; at the start of the year, the life must either be in state 0 or in state 1, and then transition in the final year to state 2.

Using the first version, and the probabilities from part (d), we calculate the EPV of the death benefit as

$$50\,000 \left(p_{50}^{02}\, v + \left(_2p_{50}^{02} - p_{50}^{02}\right) v^2 + \cdots + \left(_5p_{50}^{02} - {}_4p_{50}^{02}\right) v^5 \right) = 1775.48.$$

The EPV at age 50 of an annuity of X per year, payable from age 55 whilst alive (healthy or sick) can be broken down into

(i) the EPV of an annuity that is payable if healthy at age 55, multiplied by the probability that (50) is healthy at age 55, discounted for interest, plus

(ii) the EPV of an annuity that is payable if sick at age 55, multiplied by the probability that (50) is sick at age 55, discounted for interest.

That is, the EPV at age 50 in state 0 of a lifetime annuity-due of X per year payable from age 55 is

$$X \left(_5p_{50}^{00}\, v^5 \left(\ddot{a}_{55}^{00} + \ddot{a}_{55}^{01} \right) + {}_5p_{50}^{01}\, v^5 \left(\ddot{a}_{55}^{10} + \ddot{a}_{55}^{11} \right) \right).$$

Note that the question tells us that

$$\ddot{a}_{55}^{00} + \ddot{a}_{55}^{01} = 13.285 \quad \text{and} \quad \ddot{a}_{55}^{10} + \ddot{a}_{55}^{11} = 12.350,$$

so we have EPV for the annuity of $10.42588\, X$.

Using the equivalence principle, we have

$$4481.74 = 1775.48 + 10.42588\, X \Rightarrow X = \$256.35.$$

$\square$

8.13.1 The Chapman–Kolmogorov equations

In the example above, we used recursions developed from the specific Markov chain of the question to calculate transition probabilities for the process. In this section we generalize the recursions for application to any Markov chain process. The results are known as the Chapman–Kolmogorov equations for the Markov chain.

Consider a general Markov chain with $n + 1$ states, that is, with state space $S = \{0, 1, \ldots, n\}$. For any non-negative integers t and r, and for any states $i, j \in S$ (i, j could be the same state), we have

$$_{t+r}p_x^{ij} = \sum_{k=0}^{n} {_t}p_x^{ik} \, {_r}p_{x+t}^{kj}. \tag{8.32}$$

The intuition for these equations is exactly as explained in part (c) of the example above. Any transition probability over $t + r$ years (and we use the term transition probability even when the starting and end state are the same) can be broken down into the probability for the first t years, followed by the remaining r years. That is, if $Y(t)$ denotes the state that (x) is in at time t, then the event

$$Y(t + r) = j \,|\, Y(0) = i$$

can be broken down into the $n+1$ mutually exclusive and exhaustive sub-events

$$[Y(t) = 0|Y(0) = i] \cap [Y(t+r) = j|Y(t) = 0]$$
$$[Y(t) = 1|Y(0) = i] \cap [Y(t+r) = j|Y(t) = 1]$$
$$\cdots$$
$$[Y(t) = n|Y(0) = i] \cap [Y(t+r) = j|Y(t) = n]$$

which means that the event probability

$$_{t+r}p_x^{ij} = \Pr[Y(t + r) = j|Y(0) = i]$$

can be similarly broken down as

$$_t p_x^{i0} \, {_r}p_{x+t}^{0j} + {_t}p_x^{i1} \, {_r}p_{x+t}^{1j} + \cdots + {_t}p_x^{in} \, {_r}p_{x+t}^{nj}.$$

In most examples of Markov chains in life contingent applications, many of the transitions will not be possible, so that the transition probabilities will be zero. Examples would include $_r p_{x+t}^{20}$ in Example 8.14.

8.13.2 Transition matrices

It is often convenient to express the transition probabilities $_t p_x^{ij}$, for integer $t \geq 1$ and for a given age x, in matrix form. Consider a multiple state model with $n+1$ states. The one-year transition matrix P_x, say, is an $(n+1) \times (n+1)$ matrix

$$P_x = \begin{pmatrix} p_x^{00} & p_x^{01} & \cdots & p_x^{0n} \\ \vdots & & \ddots & \vdots \\ p_x^{n0} & p_x^{n1} & \cdots & p_x^{nn} \end{pmatrix}.$$

This is a stochastic matrix, meaning that all entries are non-negative, and the sum of entries in each row is 1.

In the three-state model of Example 8.14, the transition matrix of one-year probabilities for (x) (noting, again, that there are no transitions out of state 2) is

$$P_x = \begin{pmatrix} p_x^{00} & p_x^{01} & p_x^{02} \\ p_x^{10} & p_x^{11} & p_x^{12} \\ 0 & 0 & 1 \end{pmatrix}.$$

The reason that this is a useful representation comes from the fact that multiplying matrices generates Chapman–Kolmogorov equations for the system. For example, consider the three-state model from Example 8.14. We have

$$P_x \times P_{x+1} =$$

$$\begin{pmatrix} p_x^{00} p_{x+1}^{00} + p_x^{01} p_{x+1}^{10} & p_x^{00} p_{x+1}^{01} + p_x^{01} p_{x+1}^{11} & p_x^{00} p_{x+1}^{02} + p_x^{01} p_{x+1}^{12} + p_x^{02} \\ p_x^{10} p_{x+1}^{00} + p_x^{11} p_{x+1}^{10} & p_x^{10} p_{x+1}^{01} + p_x^{11} p_{x+1}^{11} & p_x^{10} p_{x+1}^{02} + p_x^{11} p_{x+1}^{12} + p_x^{12} \\ 0 & 0 & 1 \end{pmatrix}.$$

Comparing the individual terms with the Chapman–Kolmogorov equations, with $t = r = 1$, we see that each element in the matrix product is a two-year transition probability. That is, the product of one-year transition matrices at successive ages is a two-year transition matrix:

$$P_x \, P_{x+1} = {}_2P_x = \begin{pmatrix} {}_2p_x^{00} & {}_2p_x^{01} & {}_2p_x^{02} \\ {}_2p_x^{10} & {}_2p_x^{11} & {}_2p_x^{12} \\ {}_2p_x^{20} & {}_2p_x^{21} & {}_2p_x^{22} \end{pmatrix}.$$

Continuing the matrix multiplication through subsequent ages, we can determine the t-year transition matrix for any integer t, and this can be used for projecting expected numbers of claims or for valuing state contingent benefits.

A special case of the transition matrices and Chapman–Kolmogorov equations arises when probabilities for each successive time period are the same. In most examples for life insurance this will not be the case, as probabilities depend on age, which changes each time unit. There are cases, however, where the overall time-scale is sufficiently short that it may be possible to simplify the process such that probabilities do not depend on age. In this case, the transition matrix does not change over successive time units, and the process is said to be *time-homogeneous*.

Example 8.15 Employees in Company OHB transition at the end of every six months between the three states

State 0 – junior management
State 1 – senior management
State 2 – terminated

The probability of moving from junior to senior management is 0.1; the probability of being terminated from junior management is 0.04.

No senior managers are demoted to junior management. The probability of termination for senior managers is 0.08 every six months.

At 1 January 2013 Olivia is a senior manager and Harriet is a junior manager. Calculate the probability that both are terminated by the end of 2014. Assume transitions are independent, and ignore mortality or any other mode of exit.

Solution 8.15 We work in time units of six-months, which means that there are four time periods between 1 January 2013 and 31 December 2014.

The transition matrix for each time unit is

$$P = \begin{pmatrix} 0.86 & 0.10 & 0.04 \\ 0.00 & 0.92 & 0.08 \\ 0.00 & 0.00 & 1.00 \end{pmatrix}.$$

As this process is time-homogeneous, the four-period transition matrix is

$$P^4 = \begin{pmatrix} 0.5470 & 0.2823 & 0.1707 \\ 0.0000 & 0.7164 & 0.2836 \\ 0.0000 & 0.0000 & 1.0000 \end{pmatrix}.$$

The probability that Olivia is terminated within two years is $_4p^{12} = 0.2836$. The probability that Harriet is terminated within two years is $_4p^{02} = 0.1707$. So, the probability that both are terminated (given independence) is $0.2836 \times 0.1707 = 0.0484$. □

8.14 Notes and further reading

The general, continuous time multiple state models of this chapter are known to probabilists as Markov processes with discrete states in continuous time. The processes of interest to actuaries are usually time-inhomogeneous since the transition intensities are functions of time/age. Good references for such processes are Cox and Miller (1965) and Ross (1995). Rolski *et al.* (1999) provide a brief treatment of such models within an insurance context.

Andrei Andreyevich Markov (1865–1922) was a Russian mathematician best known for his work in probability theory. Andrei Nikolaevich Kolmogorov (1903–1987) was also a Russian mathematician, who made many fundamental contributions to probability theory and is generally credited with putting probability theory on a sound mathematical basis.

The application of multiple state models to problems in actuarial science goes back at least to Sverdrup (1965). Hoem (1988) provides a very comprehensive treatment of the mathematics of such models. Multiple state models are not only a natural framework for modelling conventional life and health insurance policies, they are also a valuable research tool in actuarial science. See, for example, Macdonald *et al.* (2003a, b).

Norberg (1995) shows how to calculate the kth moment, $k = 1, 2, 3, \ldots$, for the present value of future cash flows from a very general multiple state model. He also reports that the transition intensities used in part (b) of Example 8.4, and subsequent examples, are those used at that time by Danish insurance companies.

In Section 8.4 we remarked that the transition intensities are fundamental quantities which determine everything we need to know about a multiple state model. They are also in many insurance-related contexts the natural quantities to estimate from data. See, for example, Sverdrup (1965) or Waters (1984).

We can extend multiple state models in various ways. One way is to allow the transition intensities out of a state to depend not only on the individual's current age but also on how long they have been in the current state. This breaks the Markov assumption and the new process is known as a **semi-Markov process**. This could be appropriate for the disability income insurance process (Figure 8.4) where the intensities of recovery and death from the sick state could be assumed to depend on how long the individual had been sick, as well as on current age. Precisely this model has been applied to UK insured lives data. See CMI (1991).

As noted at the end of Chapter 7, there are more sophisticated ways of solving systems of differential equations than Euler's method. Waters and Wilkie (1988) present a method specifically designed for use with multiple state models. For a discussion on how to use mathematical software to tackle the problems discussed in this chapter see Dickson (2006).

8.15 Exercises

Exercise 8.1 An insurer prices disability income insurance using the model in Figure 8.4. A certain policy provides an income while disabled, a death benefit of $100 000 immediately on death (from either live state), and includes a 'bonus' of $10 000 at the end of the policy term should the policyholder not make any claim during the policy term. For a policy with a 10-year term issued to a life aged 50, write down expressions involving transition intensities and probabilities for the EPV at force of interest δ per year of the death and bonus benefits.

Exercise 8.2 An insurer calculates premiums for permanent disability insurance using the model in Figure 8.3. A life aged 60 purchases a policy with a five-year term which provides a benefit of $100 000 on exit from the healthy state.

(a) Write down an expression in terms of transition intensities, probabilities and δ for the EPV of this benefit at force of interest δ per year.
(b) Calculate the EPV of the benefit when $\mu_x^{01} = 0.01$ and $\mu_x^{02} = 0.015$ for $60 \leq x \leq 65$ and $\delta = 0.05$.

Exercise 8.3 An insurer prices disability income insurance using the model in Figure 8.4. The following probabilities apply at age 50:

$$_t p_{50}^{00} = \frac{2}{3} e^{-0.015t} + \frac{1}{3} e^{-0.01t},$$
$$_t p_{50}^{02} = 1 - e^{-0.01t}.$$

Policyholders pay premiums continuously throughout the policy term while they are healthy, and receive benefits while they are disabled. Policyholders are assumed to be healthy at the issue date. Using a force of interest of 5% per year, calculate the total premium per year for a policy with term two years for a life aged 50 that provides a disability benefit at the rate of $60 000 per year.

Exercise 8.4 An insurer issues a whole life disability income insurance policy to a healthy life aged 50. The policy provides a disability income of $50 000 per year payable continuously while the life is disabled. In addition the policy pays a death benefit of $200 000 at the moment of death. The policyholder pays premiums continuously, at a rate of P per year, while in the healthy state. The insurer calculates premiums using the model in Figure 8.4.

(a) Assuming no expenses and a constant force of interest δ per year, write down Thiele's differential equation for the policy value in state 1 at time t.
(b) Use the table below to determine the premium for the policy issued to (50). Assume interest of 5% per year effective, and ignore expenses.
(c) Ten years after the policy was issued, the policyholder is in the disabled state. Calculate the policy value, using the factors from the table below and interest at 5% per year effective.

x	$\bar{a}_x^{00}$	$\bar{a}_x^{01}$	$\bar{a}_x^{11}$	$\bar{a}_x^{10}$	$\bar{A}_x^{02}$	$\bar{A}_x^{12}$
50	11.9520	1.3292	8.9808	3.2382	0.34980	0.39971
⋮	⋮	⋮	⋮	⋮	⋮	⋮
60	8.6097	1.7424	7.1596	1.7922	0.49511	0.56316

Exercise 8.5 A disability income insurance policy pays B per year, continuously, while the policyholder is sick, and pays a lump sum death benefit of S. The policyholder pays a premium of P per year, continuously, when in the healthy state. The policy is issued to a healthy life aged 40, and ceases at age 60. The insurer prices policies using the model in Figure 8.4.

(a) Write down the Kolmogorov forward equations for $_tp_x^{00}$, $_tp_x^{01}$ and $_tp_x^{02}$.
(b) Explain, in words, the meaning of $\bar{a}_{x:\overline{n}|}^{01}$ and $\bar{A}_{x:\overline{n}|}^{02}$, and write down the integral formulae to calculate them.
(c) Write down a formula in terms of $\bar{a}_{x:\overline{n}|}^{ij}$ and $\bar{A}_{x:\overline{n}|}^{ij}$ functions for the net premium policy value for this disability income insurance policy at duration $t < 20$, given that the life is sick at that time.
(d) You are given the following transition intensities for this model.

t	μ_{40+t}^{01}	μ_{40+t}^{02}	μ_{40+t}^{10}	μ_{40+t}^{12}
0	0.01074	0.00328	0.09012	0.00712
0.1	0.01094	0.00330	0.09003	0.00719
0.2	0.01116	0.00333	0.08994	0.00726
$\vdots$	$\vdots$	$\vdots$	$\vdots$	$\vdots$
19.8	0.54261	0.01700	0.07663	0.05813
19.9	0.55356	0.01714	0.07658	0.05876
20.0	0.56474	0.01730	0.07653	0.05941

(i) Using a time step of $h = 0.1$, estimate $_{0.2}p_{40}^{00}$ and $_{0.2}p_{40}^{01}$.
(ii) Write down Thiele's differential equations for $_tV^{(0)}$ and $_tV^{(1)}$, $0 < t < 20$, for this policy.
(iii) You are given that $B = 20\,000$, $S = 100\,000$, $P = 6\,000$ and $\delta = 0.05$. Use the table above to estimate $_{19.9}V^{(1)}$ and $_{19.9}V^{(0)}$.

Exercise 8.6 Consider the accidental death model illustrated in Figure 8.2. Let

$$\mu_x^{01} = 10^{-5} \quad \text{and} \quad \mu_x^{02} = A + Bc^x \quad \text{for all } x$$

and assume $A = 5 \times 10^{-4}$, $B = 7.6 \times 10^{-5}$ and $c = 1.09$.

(a) Calculate

  (i) $_{10}p_{30}^{00}$,
  (ii) $_{10}p_{30}^{01}$, and
  (iii) $_{10}p_{30}^{02}$.

(b) An insurance company uses the model to calculate premiums for a special 10-year term life insurance policy. The basic sum insured is \$100 000, but the death benefit doubles to \$200 000 if death occurs as a result of an accident. The death benefit is payable immediately on death. Premiums are payable continuously throughout the term. Using an effective rate of interest of 5% per year and ignoring expenses, for a policy issued to a life aged 30

  (i) calculate the annual premium for this policy, and
  (ii) calculate the policy value at time 5.

Exercise 8.7 Consider the following model for an insurance policy combining disability income insurance benefits and critical illness benefits.

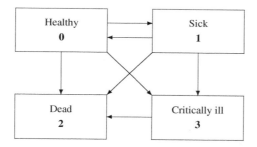

The transition intensities are as follows:

$$\mu_x^{01} = a_1 + b_1 \exp\{c_1 x\}, \qquad \mu_x^{02} = a_2 + b_2 \exp\{c_2 x\},$$
$$\mu_x^{12} = \mu_x^{02}, \qquad \mu_x^{32} = 1.2\mu_x^{02},$$
$$\mu_x^{10} = 0.1\mu_x^{01}, \qquad \mu_x^{03} = 0.05\mu_x^{01}, \qquad \mu_x^{13} = \mu_x^{03}$$

where

$$a_1 = 4 \times 10^{-4}, \quad b_1 = 3.5 \times 10^{-6}, \quad c_1 = 0.14,$$
$$a_2 = 5 \times 10^{-4}, \quad b_2 = 7.6 \times 10^{-5}, \quad c_2 = 0.09.$$

(a) Using Euler's method with a step size of $\frac{1}{12}$, calculate values of $_t p_{30}^{00}$ for $t = 0, \frac{1}{12}, \frac{2}{12}, \ldots, 35$.
(b) An insurance company issues a policy with term 35 years to a life aged 30 which provides a death benefit, a disability income benefit, and a critical illness benefit as follows:

 • a lump sum payment of \$100 000 is payable immediately on the life becoming critically ill,

- a lump sum payment of $100 000 is payable immediately on death, provided that the life has not already been paid a critical illness benefit,
- a disability income annuity of $75 000 per year payable whilst the life is disabled payable continuously.

Premiums are payable monthly in advance provided that the policyholder is healthy.

(i) Calculate the monthly premium for this policy on the following basis:

Transition intensities:	As in (a)
Interest:	5% per year effective
Expenses:	Nil

Use the repeated Simpson's rule with $h = \frac{1}{12}$.

(ii) Suppose that the premium is payable continuously rather than monthly. Use Thiele's differential equation to solve for the total premium per year, using Euler's method with a step size of $h = \frac{1}{12}$.

(iii) Using your answer to part (ii), find the policy value at time 10 for a healthy life.

Exercise 8.8 In Section 8.7.2 Thiele's differential equation for a general multiple state model was stated as

$$\frac{d}{dt} {}_tV^{(i)} = \delta_t \, {}_tV^{(i)} - B_t^{(i)} - \sum_{j=0, \, j\neq i}^{n} \mu_{x+t}^{ij} \left(S_t^{(ij)} + {}_tV^{(j)} - {}_tV^{(i)} \right).$$

(a) Let $v(t) = \exp\{-\int_0^t \delta_s ds\}$. Explain why

$$
\begin{aligned}
{}_tV^{(i)} = & \sum_{j=0, \, j\neq i}^{n} \int_0^\infty \frac{v(t+s)}{v(t)} \left(S_{t+s}^{(ij)} + {}_{t+s}V^{(j)} \right) {}_sp_{x+t}^{\overline{ii}} \, \mu_{x+t+s}^{ij} \, ds \\
& + \int_0^\infty \frac{v(t+s)}{v(t)} B_{t+s}^{(i)} \, {}_sp_{x+t}^{\overline{ii}} \, ds.
\end{aligned}
$$

(b) Using the techniques introduced in Section 7.5.1, differentiate the above expression to obtain Thiele's differential equation.

Exercise 8.9 Consider the permanent disability model in Figure 8.3, and suppose that $\mu_x^{02} = \mu_x^{12}$ for all x.

(a) Deduce that

$${}_tp_x^{00} \, {}_{n-t}p_{x+t}^{11} = \exp\left\{ -\int_0^t \mu_{x+s}^{01} \, ds \right\} \exp\left\{ -\int_0^n \mu_{x+s}^{02} \, ds \right\}.$$

(b) Hence show that

$$ {}_n p_x^{01} = \exp\left\{-\int_0^n \mu_{x+s}^{02}\, ds\right\}\left(1 - \exp\left\{-\int_0^n \mu_{x+s}^{01}\, ds\right\}\right). $$

Exercise 8.10 Consider the insurance-with-lapses model illustrated in Figure 8.7. Suppose that this model is adjusted to include death after withdrawal, i.e. the transition intensity μ_x^{21} is introduced into the model.

(a) Show that if withdrawal does not affect the transition intensity to state 1 (i.e. that $\mu_x^{21} = \mu_x^{01}$), then the probability that an individual aged x is dead by age $x + t$ is the same as that under the 'alive–dead' model with the transition intensity μ_x^{01}.

(b) Why is this intuitively obvious?

Exercise 8.11 An insurer prices critical illness insurance policies on the basis of a double decrement model, in which there are two modes of decrement – death (state 1) and becoming critically ill (state 2). For all $x \geq 0$, $\mu_x^{01} = A + Bc^x$ where $A = 0.0001$, $B = 0.00035$ and $c = 1.075$, and $\mu_x^{02} = 0.05\mu_x^{01}$. On the basis of interest at 4% per year effective, calculate the monthly premium, payable for at most 20 years, for a life aged exactly 30 at the issue date of a policy which provides \$50 000 immediately on death, provided that the critical illness benefit has not already been paid, and \$75 000 immediately on becoming critically ill, should either event occur within 20 years of the policy's issue date. Ignore expenses.

Exercise 8.12 In a certain country, members of its regular armed forces can leave active service (state 0) by transfer (state 1), by resignation (state 2) or by death (state 3). The transition intensities are

$$ \mu_x^{01} = 0.001x, $$
$$ \mu_x^{02} = 0.01, $$
$$ \mu_x^{03} = A + Bc^x, $$

where $A = 0.001$, $B = 0.0004$ and $c = 1.07$. New recruits join only at exact age 25.

(a) Calculate the probability that a new recruit
  (i) is transferred before age 27,
  (ii) dies aged 27 last birthday, and
  (iii) is in active service at age 28.

(b) New recruits who are transferred within three years of joining receive a lump sum payment of \$10 000 immediately on transfer. This sum is provided by a levy on all recruits in active service on the first and second anniversary of joining. On the basis of interest at 6% per year effective, calculate the levy payable by a new recruit.

(c) Those who are transferred enter an elite force. Members of this elite force are subject to a force of mortality at age x equal to $1.5\mu_x^{03}$, but are subject to no other decrements. Calculate the probability that a new recruit into the regular armed forces dies before age 28 as a member of the elite force.

Exercise 8.13 A university offers a four-year degree course. Semesters are half a year in length and the probability that a student progresses from one semester of study to the next is 0.85 in the first year of study, 0.9 in the second year, 0.95 in the third, and 0.98 in the fourth. All students entering the final semester obtain a degree. Students who fail in any semester may not continue in the degree.

Students pay tuition fees at the start of each semester. For the first semester the tuition fee is $10 000. Allowing for an increase in fees of 2% each semester, and assuming interest at 5% per year effective, calculate the EPV of fee income to the university for a new student aged 19. Assume that the student is subject to a constant force of mortality between integer ages x and $x + 1$ of $5x \times 10^{-5}$ for $x = 19, 20, 21$ and 22, and that there are no means of leaving the course other than by death or failure.

Exercise 8.14 An insurance company sells 10-year term insurance policies with sum insured $100 000 payable immediately on death to lives aged 50. Calculate the monthly premium for this policy on the following basis.

Survival:	Makeham's law, with $A = 0.0001$, $B = 0.0004$ and $c = 1.075$
Lapses:	2% of policyholders lapse their policy on each of the first two policy anniversaries
Interest:	5% per year effective
Initial expenses:	$200
Renewal expenses:	2.5% of each premium (including the first)

Value the death benefit using the UDD assumption.

Exercise 8.15 You are given the following three-decrement service table for modelling employment.

x	l_x	$d_x^{(1)}$	$d_x^{(2)}$	$d_x^{(3)}$
60	10 000	350	150	25
61	9 475	360	125	45
62	8 945	380	110	70

(a) Calculate $_3p_{60}^{01}$.

(b) Calculate $_2p_{61}^{00}$.

(c) Calculate the EPV of a benefit of $\$10\,000$ payable at the end of the year of exit, if a life aged 60 leaves by decrement 3 before age 63. Use an effective rate of interest of 5% per year.

(d) Calculate the EPV of an annuity of $\$1000$ per year payable at the start of each of the next three years if a life currently aged 60 remains in service. Use an effective rate of interest of 5% per year.

(e) Show that $q_{62}^{*(1)} = 0.04292$, assuming a constant force of decrement for each decrement.

(f) Calculate the revised service table for age 62 if $q_{62}^{*(1)}$ is increased to 0.1, with the other independent rates remaining unchanged. Use (i) the constant force assumption, and (ii) the UDD in the single decrement models assumption.

Exercise 8.16 Employees of a certain company enter service at exact age 20, and, after a period in Canada, may be transferred to an overseas office. While in Canada, the only causes of decrement, apart from transfer to the overseas office, are death and resignation from the company.

(a) Using a radix of $100\,000$ at exact age 39, construct a multiple decrement table covering service in Canada for ages 39, 40 and 41 last birthday, given the following information about (independent) probabilities:

Mortality $(j = 1)$:   Standard Ultimate Survival Model

Transfer $(j = 2)$: $q_{39}^{*(2)} = 0.09$, $q_{40}^{*(2)} = 0.10$, $q_{41}^{*(2)} = 0.11$

Resignation $(j = 3)$:   20% of those reaching age 40 resign on their 40th birthday. No other resignations take place.

Assume a uniform distribution of deaths and transfers between integer ages in the single decrement models.

(b) Calculate the probability that an employee in service in Canada at exact age 39 will still be in service in Canada at exact age 42.

(c) Calculate the probability that an employee in service in Canada at exact age 39 will transfer to the overseas office between exact ages 41 and 42.

(d) The company has decided to set up a scheme to give each employee transferring to the overseas office between exact ages 39 and 42 a grant of $\$10\,000$ at the date of transfer. To pay for these grants the company will deposit a fixed sum in a special account on the 39th, 40th and 41st birthday of each employee still working in Canada (excluding resignations on the 40th birthday). The special account is invested to produce interest of 8% per year.

Calculate the annual deposit required.

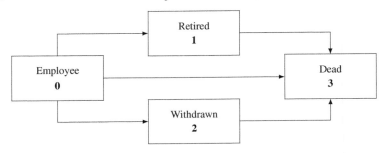

Figure 8.10 A withdrawal/retirement model.

Exercise 8.17 The following table is an extract from a multiple decrement table modelling withdrawals from life insurance contracts. Decrement (1) represents withdrawal, and decrement (2) represents death.

x	l_x	$d_x^{(1)}$	$d_x^{(2)}$
40	15 490	2 400	51
41	13 039	2 102	58
42	10 879	1 507	60

(a) Stating clearly any assumptions, calculate $q_{40}^{*(2)}$.
(b) What difference would it make to your calculation in part (a) if you were given the additional information that all withdrawals occurred on the policyholders' birthdays?

Exercise 8.18 The employees of a large corporation can leave the corporation in three ways: they can withdraw from the corporation, they can retire or they can die while they are still employees. Figure 8.10 illustrates this model.

You are given:

• The force of mortality depends on the individual's age but not on whether the individual is an employee, has withdrawn or is retired, so that for all ages x
$$\mu_x^{03} \equiv \mu_x^{13} \equiv \mu_x^{23} = \mu_x, \text{ say.}$$

• Withdrawal can take place at any age up to age 60 and the intensity of withdrawal is a constant denoted μ^{02}. Hence
$$\mu_x^{02} = \begin{cases} \mu^{02} & \text{for } x < 60, \\ 0 & \text{for } x \geq 60. \end{cases}$$

• Retirement can take place only on an employee's 60th, 61st, 62nd, 63rd, 64th or 65th birthday. It is assumed that 40% of employees reaching exact age 60, 61, 62, 63 and 64 retire at that age and 100% of employees who reach age 65 retire immediately.

The corporation offers the following benefits to the employees:

- For those employees who die while still employed, a lump sum of $200 000 is payable immediately on death.
- For those employees who retire, a lump sum of $150 000 is payable immediately on death after retirement.

Show that the EPVs of these benefits to an employee currently aged 40 can be written as follows, where $\bar{A}_{65}$ and $_{25}E_{40}$ are standard single life functions based on the force of mortality μ_x, and assuming a constant force of interest δ per year.

Death in service benefit

$$200\,000\left(\bar{A}^{1}_{40:\overline{20}|} + {}_{20}E_{40}\,e^{-20\mu^{02}}\left(\sum_{k=1}^{5}0.6^{k}\,{}_{k-1}|\bar{A}^{1}_{60:\overline{1}|}\right)\right).$$

Death after retirement benefit

$$150\,000\,{}_{20}E_{40}\,e^{-20\mu^{02}}\left(0.4\sum_{k=0}^{4}0.6^{k}\,{}_{k}|\bar{A}_{60} + 0.6^{5}\,{}_{5}|\bar{A}_{60}\right).$$

Exercise 8.19 Consider the previous exercise, and suppose that

$$\mu_x = A + Bc^x \quad \text{and} \quad \mu^{02} = 0.02,$$

where $A = 0.0001$, $B = 0.0004$ and $c = 1.07$.

A corporation contributes $10 000 to a pension fund when an employee joins the corporation and on each anniversary of that person joining the corporation, provided the person is still an employee. On the basis of interest at 5% per year effective, calculate the EPV of contributions to the pension fund in respect of a new employee aged 30.

Exercise 8.20 Consider the permanent disability model illustrated in Figure 8.3. An insurer uses this model to price an insurance policy with term two years issued to a life aged 58. The policy provides a benefit of $100 000 if death occurs from the healthy state, $75 000 if the policyholder becomes permanently disabled, and $25 000 if death occurs after permanent disability. Benefits are payable at the end of the year in which a transition takes place, and premiums are payable at the start of each policy year.

Annual transition probabilities are as follows:

x	p_x^{00}	p_x^{01}	p_x^{02}	p_x^{11}	p_x^{12}
58	0.995	0.002	0.003	0.992	0.008
59	0.993	0.003	0.004	0.990	0.010

Calculate the annual premium assuming an effective rate of interest of 5% per year.

Answers to selected exercises

8.2 (b) $10 423.69

8.3 $195.99

8.4 (b) $11 413.99

  (c) $450 155.85

8.5 (d) (i) 0.99719,   0.00216

    (ii) −$427, $2594

8.6 (a) (i) 0.979122

    (ii) 0.020779

    (iii) 0.000099

  (b) (i) $206.28

    (ii) $167.15

8.7 (a) $35 p_{30}^{00} = 0.581884$

  (b) (i) $206.56

    (ii) $2498.07

    (iii) $16 925.88

8.11 $28.01

8.12 (a) (i) 0.050002

    (ii) 0.003234

    (iii) 0.887168

  (b) $397.24

  (c) 0.000586

8.13 $53 285.18

8.14 $225.95

8.15 (a) 0.109

  (b) 0.8850

  (c) $125.09

  (d) $2738.74

  (f) (i) 885.4, 106.7, 67.9

    (ii) 885.3, 106.8, 68.0

8.16 (a) 0.58220

  (b) 0.07198

  (c) $943.11

8.17 (a) 0.00367 (UDD)

      0.00358 (Constant force)

8.19 $125 489.33

8.20 $509.90

9

Joint life and last survivor benefits

9.1 Summary

Insurance benefits which are dependent on the joint mortality of two lives, typically a married couple, form an important part of the insurance portfolio. In this chapter we develop the concepts and models from previous chapters to examine *joint life* insurance policies. There are also important applications in pension design and valuation, as spousal benefits are a common part of a pension benefit package.

In Section 9.2 we describe the typical benefits offered by such policies and introduce standard notation used for probabilities and expected present value functions for annuity and insurance benefits. In Section 9.4 we develop an approach for pricing and valuing these policies, based on the future lifetime random variables, and making the strong assumption that the two lives are independent with respect to mortality.

In Section 9.5 we show how joint life mortality can be analysed using multiple state models. This creates a flexible framework to introduce dependence between lives, and we can apply the methods of Chapter 8 to calculate probabilities and value benefits.

9.2 Joint life and last survivor benefits

All the development up to and including Chapter 7, and all the applications of multiple state models in Chapter 8, relate to a life insurance policy on a single insured life. In practice, policies based on two lives are common. The two lives are typically a couple who are jointly organizing their financial security, but other situations are also feasible, for example, annuities dependent on the lives of a parent and their child, or insurance on the lives of business partners. Policies based on more than two lives are also available, but are less common.

In this chapter we consider policies based on two lives, whom we label, for convenience, (x) and (y). Throughout, we assume that at some inception time

$t = 0$, (x) and (y) are alive, are aged x and y, respectively, at $t = 0$, and are partners in some joint life contingent benefit context.

The most common types of benefit which are contingent on two lives are described briefly below.

A **joint life annuity** is an annuity payable until the first death of (x) and (y).

A **last survivor annuity** is an annuity payable until the second death of (x) and (y).

A common benefit design is an annuity payable at a higher rate while both partners are alive and at a lower rate following the first death. The annuity ceases on the second death. This could be viewed as a last survivor annuity for the lower amount, plus a joint life annuity for the difference.

A **reversionary annuity** is a life annuity that starts payment on the death of a specified life, say (x), if (y) is alive at that time, and continues through the lifetime of (y). A pension plan may offer a reversionary annuity benefit as part of the pension package, where (x) would be the pension plan member, and (y) would be a partner eligible for spousal benefits.

A **joint life insurance** pays a death benefit on the first death of (x) and (y).

A **last survivor insurance** pays a death benefit on the second death of (x) and (y).

A **contingent insurance** pays a death benefit contingent on multiple events. The most common is a benefit paid on the death of (x), say, but only if (y) is still living at that time.

9.3 Joint life notation

Following the same approach as in Chapters 4 and 5, we express the present values of the joint life benefits in terms of random variables, so that we can value them as the expected value of the present value.

Throughout this chapter, we assume that at the inception point for a contract, the lives (x) and (y) are alive. From Chapter 2, we recall that the future life-times of (x) and (y) are represented by T_x and T_y. At this stage we make no assumption about the independence, or otherwise, of these two random variables.

Given T_x and T_y, we define two more random variables, representing the times until the first and second to die of (x) and (y).

Time to first death $T_{xy} = \min(T_x, T_y)$.
Time to last death $T_{\overline{xy}} = \max(T_x, T_y)$.

We refer to the subscript, xy or $\overline{xy}$, as a **status**; xy (also written as $\{xy\}$) is the **joint life status** and $\overline{xy}$ is the **last survivor status**. Hence, T_{xy} and $T_{\overline{xy}}$ are random variables representing the time until the failure of the joint life status and the last survivor status, respectively. It is implicit throughout that the definitions of joint life and last survivor random variables for the couple (x) and (y) are conditional on both lives being alive, and a couple (at least, in the sense of being connected for the purpose of the insurance contract) at some starting point.

It is very useful to observe that, with only two lives involved, either

(1) (x) dies first so that the realized values of T_x and T_{xy} are the same, and consequently the realized values of T_y and $T_{\overline{xy}}$ are the same, or
(2) (y) dies first so that the realized values of T_y and T_{xy} are the same, and consequently the realized values of T_x and $T_{\overline{xy}}$ are the same.

Thus, regardless of the order of deaths, the realized value of T_x matches one of T_{xy} and $T_{\overline{xy}}$, and the realized value of T_y matches the other.

Important consequences of these observations include the following relationships:

$$T_x + T_y = T_{xy} + T_{\overline{xy}}; \tag{9.1}$$
$$v^{T_x} + v^{T_y} = v^{T_{xy}} + v^{T_{\overline{xy}}}; \tag{9.2}$$
$$\bar{a}_{\overline{T_x}|} + \bar{a}_{\overline{T_y}|} = \bar{a}_{\overline{T_{xy}}|} + \bar{a}_{\overline{T_{\overline{xy}}}|}. \tag{9.3}$$

Policies on multiple lives have their own standard notation for probabilities and for annuity and insurance functions. The notation is an extension of the notation introduced in Chapters 2, 4 and 5. The list below shows the new notation for probabilities, in each case followed by the definition in words, and in terms of the T_{xy} or $T_{\overline{xy}}$ random variables.

$_t p_{xy} = \Pr[(x) \text{ and } (y) \text{ are both alive in } t \text{ years}] = \Pr[T_{xy} > t].$

$_t q_{xy} = \Pr[(x) \text{ and } (y) \text{ are not both alive in } t \text{ years}] = \Pr[T_{xy} \le t].$

$_{u|t} q_{xy} = \Pr[(x) \text{ and } (y) \text{ are both alive in } u \text{ years, but not in } u + t \text{ years}]$
$\qquad = \Pr[u < T_{xy} \le u + t].$

$_t q^1_{xy} = \Pr[(x) \text{ dies before } (y) \text{ and within } t \text{ years}] = \Pr[T_x \le t \text{ and } T_x < T_y].$

$_t q^2_{xy} = \Pr[(x) \text{ dies after } (y) \text{ and within } t \text{ years}] = \Pr[T_y < T_x \le t].$

$_t p_{\overline{xy}} = \Pr[\text{at least one of } (x) \text{ and } (y) \text{ is alive in } t \text{ years}] = \Pr[T_{\overline{xy}} > t].$

$_t q_{\overline{xy}} = \Pr[(x) \text{ and } (y) \text{ are both dead in } t \text{ years}] = \Pr[T_{\overline{xy}} \le t].$

The '1' over x in $_t q^1_{xy}$ indicates that we are interested in the probability of (x) dying *first*. We have already used this notation, in $A^1_{x:\overline{n}|}$, where the benefit is paid only if x dies first, before the term, n years, expires.

In cases where it makes the notation clearer, we put a colon between the ages in the right subscript. For example, we write $_t p_{\overline{30:40}}$ rather than $_t p_{\overline{30\,40}}$.

For each of the standard joint life benefits, we list here the notation for the EPV, as a function of the joint life random variables T_{xy} or $T_{\overline{xy}}$. We assume a constant force of interest δ per year.

$\bar{a}_{xy}$ **Joint life annuity:** a continuous payment at unit rate per year while both (x) and (y) are still alive:

$$\bar{a}_{xy} = \mathrm{E}\left[\bar{a}_{\overline{T_{xy}}}\right].$$

If there is a maximum period, n years, for the annuity, then we refer to a 'temporary' or 'term' joint life annuity. The notation for the EPV is $\bar{a}_{xy:\overline{n}|}$ and the formula for this is

$$\bar{a}_{xy:\overline{n}|} = \mathrm{E}\left[\bar{a}_{\overline{\min(T_{xy},n)}|}\right].$$

$\bar{A}_{xy}$ **Joint life insurance:** a unit payment immediately on the death of the first to die of (x) and (y):

$$\bar{A}_{xy} = \mathrm{E}\left[v^{T_{xy}}\right].$$

$\bar{a}_{\overline{xy}}$ **Last survivor annuity:** a continuous payment at unit rate per year while at least one of (x) and (y) is still alive:

$$\bar{a}_{\overline{xy}} = \mathrm{E}\left[\bar{a}_{\overline{T_{\overline{xy}}}|}\right].$$

$\bar{A}_{\overline{xy}}$ **Last survivor insurance:** a unit payment immediately on the death of the second to die of (x) and (y):

$$\bar{A}_{\overline{xy}} = \mathrm{E}\left[v^{T_{\overline{xy}}}\right].$$

$\bar{a}_{x|y}$ **Reversionary annuity:** a continuous payment at unit rate per year, starting on the death of (x) if (y) is still alive then, and continuing until the death of (y):

$$\bar{a}_{x|y} = \mathrm{E}\left[\left(v^{T_x}\bar{a}_{\overline{T_y-T_x}|}\right)I(T_x < T_y)\right].$$

$\bar{A}^1_{xy}$ **Contingent insurance:** a unit payment immediately on the death of (x) provided (x) dies before (y):

$$\bar{A}^1_{xy} = \mathrm{E}\left[v^{T_x}I(T_x < T_y)\right],$$

where I is the indicator function.

If there is a time limit on this payment, say n years, then it is called a 'temporary' or 'term' contingent insurance. The notation for the EPV is $\bar{A}^1_{x:y:\overline{n}|}$ and the formula is

$$\bar{A}^1_{x:y:\overline{n}|} = \mathrm{E}\left[v^{T_x}I(T_x < T_y)I(T_x < n)\right].$$

Although we have defined these functions in terms of continuous benefits, the annuity and insurance functions can easily be adapted for payments made at discrete points in time. For example, the EPV of a monthly joint life annuity-due would be denoted $\ddot{a}_{xy}^{(12)}$, and would represent the EPV of an annuity of $1/12 per month payable contingent on both (x) and (y) surviving to the payment date.

We can write down the following important relationships:

$$\bar{a}_{\overline{xy}} = \bar{a}_x + \bar{a}_y - \bar{a}_{xy}, \tag{9.4}$$

$$\bar{A}_{\overline{xy}} = \bar{A}_x + \bar{A}_y - \bar{A}_{xy}, \tag{9.5}$$

$$\bar{a}_{x|y} = \bar{a}_y - \bar{a}_{xy}. \tag{9.6}$$

Formula (9.4) follows by taking expectations in formula (9.3), and formula (9.5) follows by taking expectations in formula (9.2).

Formula (9.6) is most easily derived by noting that $\bar{a}_{xy} + \bar{a}_{x|y}$ is the EPV of an annuity of 1 per year payable continuously to (y) while (x) is alive, and after (x) has died. So

$$\bar{a}_y = \bar{a}_{xy} + \bar{a}_{x|y}.$$

The notation for the EPV of the reversionary annuity uses the status $x|y$; the vertical line indicates deferral in standard actuarial notation. In this case, the status is deferred until the death of x, and then continues as long as (y) is alive.

Equations (9.4), (9.5) and (9.6) can be derived, alternatively, by considering the cash flows involved. This is a useful trick for verifying joint life EPV formulae more generally. For example, in formula (9.6) for the reversionary annuity, the right-hand side values an annuity of 1 per year payable continuously while (y) is alive, minus an annuity of 1 per year payable continuously while both (x) and (y) are alive. What remains is an annuity of 1 per year payable continuously after the death of (x) while (y) is alive.

Similarly, in formula (9.5) for the last survivor insurance, the right-hand side values a payment of 1 when (x) dies, plus 1 when (y) dies, minus 1 on the first death; what remains is 1 paid on the second death, which is the last survivor insurance benefit.

Recall formula (5.14), linking whole life annuity and insurance functions for a single life:

$$\bar{a}_x = \frac{1 - \bar{A}_x}{\delta}.$$

The following corresponding relationships are derived in exactly the same way:

$$\bar{a}_{xy} = \frac{1 - \bar{A}_{xy}}{\delta} \quad \text{and} \quad \bar{a}_{\overline{xy}} = \frac{1 - \bar{A}_{\overline{xy}}}{\delta}.$$

All the expressions and relationships in this section are true for *any* model of dependence between T_x and T_y. Our objective now is to specify appropriate joint models for the future lifetimes of (x) and (y) and derive expressions for EPVs of future payments. We can then calculate premium rates and policy values for benefits and premiums which are dependent on two lives, analogously to the premiums and policy values derived for single lives in Chapters 6 and 7. In the remainder of this chapter we introduce and discuss different ways of modelling the future lifetimes of two possibly dependent lives.

9.4 Independent future lifetimes

Our first approach to modelling the survival of two lives assumes that the future lifetime for each individual is not affected in any way by the other life. This is a very strong assumption, and in later sections we relax it somewhat. However, it is a simple assumption which gives practical formulae that are easily implemented. It is still commonly used in practice, though models incorporating dependence are also becoming popular, especially if the dependence could have a material impact on the valuation.

To be precise, throughout this section, including all the examples, we make the following very important assumption.

Independence Assumption 1. The random variables T_x and T_y are independent.

We also assume throughout this section that we know all about the survival models for these two random variables, so that we know the survival functions, $_tp_x$ and $_tp_y$, and the forces of mortality μ_{x+t} and μ_{y+t}. Note that we do not assume that these survival functions come from the same survival model. If the two lives are indeed husband and wife, then, since mortality rates for females are generally lower than those for males, the survival models are likely to be different.

From our assumption of independence, we can write for $t \geq 0$

$$_tp_{xy} = \Pr[T_x > t \text{ and } T_y > t] = \ _tp_x \ _tp_y, \tag{9.7}$$

and

$$_tp_{\overline{xy}} = \Pr[T_x > t \text{ or } T_y > t] = 1 - \ _tq_x \ _tq_y$$
$$= \ _tp_x + \ _tp_y - \ _tp_x \ _tp_y. \tag{9.8}$$

The probability on the left-hand side of formula (9.7) relates to the survival model for the joint lives, whereas the probabilities on the right-hand side relate to two, possibly different, survival models for the individual lives. When we use labels, such as x and y, for the lives, we assume the context makes it clear what we mean by $_tp_x$ and $_tp_y$. We often have notational confusion though if we use numbers for x and y; for example, if (x) is a male aged 40, and (y) is a female aged 40, then we have two probabilities on the right-hand side, both labelled $_tp_{40}$, but which are actually based on different survival models. When we need to be more specific about the probabilities we might write the joint probability relationship more carefully as $_tp_{x:y}^{m\ f} = {_tp_x^m}\ {_tp_y^f}$, so, for example, $_tp_{45:40}^{m\ f} = {_tp_{45}^m}\ {_tp_{40}^f}$, which indicates that the two single life survival probabilities are from different distributions.

Using the joint life and last survivor probabilities, we can develop annuity and insurance functions for the EPV of benefits contingent on two lives, by summing over all the possible payment dates the EPVs of the individual payments. For example,

$$\ddot{a}_{xy:\overline{n}|} = \sum_{k=0}^{n-1} v^k\ {_kp_{xy}},$$

$$\ddot{a}_{\overline{xy}} = \sum_{k=0}^{\infty} v^k\ {_kp_{\overline{xy}}} = \ddot{a}_x + \ddot{a}_y - \ddot{a}_{xy},$$

$$A_{xy} = \sum_{k=0}^{\infty} v^{k+1}\ {_k|q_{xy}},$$

where $_k|q_{xy} = {_kp_{xy}}(1 - p_{x+k:\,y+k}) = {_kp_{xy}} - {_{k+1}p_{xy}}$, and

$$A_{\overline{xy}} = \sum_{k=0}^{\infty} v^{k+1}\ {_k|q_{\overline{xy}}} = A_x + A_y - A_{xy}.$$

Example 9.1 The table below shows extracts from two life tables appropriate for a husband and wife, who are assumed independent with respect to mortality.

	Husband		Wife
x	l_x	y	l_y
65	43 302	60	47 260
66	42 854	61	47 040
67	42 081	62	46 755
68	41 351	63	46 500
69	40 050	64	46 227

(a) Calculate $_3p_{xy}$ for a husband aged $x = 66$ and a wife aged $y = 60$.
(b) Calculate $_2p_{\overline{xy}}$ for a husband aged $x = 65$ and a wife aged $y = 62$.
(c) Calculate the probability that a husband, currently aged 65, dies within two years and that his wife, currently aged 61, survives at least two years.
(d) Explain the meaning of the symbol $\ddot{a}_{xy:\overline{n}|}$.
(e) Explain the meaning of the symbol $\ddot{a}_{\overline{xy}:\overline{n}|}$.
(f) Calculate $\ddot{a}_{xy:\overline{5}|}$ and $\ddot{a}_{\overline{xy}:\overline{5}|}$ for a husband aged $x = 65$ and a wife aged $y = 60$ at a rate of interest 5% per year.

Solution 9.1 (a) Using formula (9.7)

$$_3p_{xy} = {}_3p_x\,{}_3p_y = \frac{40\,050}{42\,854} \times \frac{46\,500}{47\,260} = 0.9195.$$

(b) Using formula (9.8)

$$_2p_{\overline{xy}} = \frac{42\,081}{43\,302} + \frac{46\,227}{46\,755} - \frac{42\,081}{43\,302} \times \frac{46\,227}{46\,755} = 0.9997.$$

(c) Since the two lives are assumed to be independent with respect to mortality, the required probability is

$$\left(1 - \frac{42\,081}{43\,302}\right) \times \frac{46\,500}{47\,040} = 0.0279.$$

(d) The symbol $\ddot{a}_{xy:\overline{n}|}$ represents the EPV, at a given constant rate of interest, of a series of at most n annual payments, each of unit amount with the first payment due now, with each payment being made only if the lives (x) and (y) are both alive at the time the payment is due.

(e) The symbol $\ddot{a}_{\overline{xy}:\overline{n}|}$ represents the EPV, at a given constant rate of interest, of a series of at most n annual payments, each of unit amount with the first payment due now, with each payment being made only if at least one of (x) and (y) is alive at the time the payment is due.

(f) From the definitions in parts (d) and (e), we can write down the following formulae

$$\ddot{a}_{xy:\overline{5}|} = \sum_{t=0}^{4} v^t\,{}_tp_{xy},$$

$$\ddot{a}_{\overline{xy}:\overline{5}|} = \sum_{t=0}^{4} v^t\,{}_tp_{\overline{xy}},$$

where $v = 1/1.05$, $x = 65$ and $y = 60$. These are derived in exactly the same way as formula (5.10). The numerical values of the annuities are

$$\ddot{a}_{xy:\overline{5}|} = 4.3661 \quad \text{and} \quad \ddot{a}_{\overline{xy}:\overline{5}|} = 4.5437.$$

Note that $\ddot{a}_{xy:\overline{5}|} \le \ddot{a}_{\overline{xy}:\overline{5}|}$ since $T_{xy} \le T_{\overline{xy}}$. $\qquad\qquad\Box$

For the following example, we use the $1/m$thly joint life and last survivor annuities

$$\ddot{a}_{xy}^{(m)} = \frac{1}{m}\left(1 + \tfrac{1}{m}p_{xy}\,v^{\frac{1}{m}} + \tfrac{2}{m}p_{xy}\,v^{\frac{2}{m}} + \cdots\right)$$

and

$$\ddot{a}_{\overline{xy}}^{(m)} = \ddot{a}_x^{(m)} + \ddot{a}_y^{(m)} - \ddot{a}_{xy}^{(m)},$$

and the joint life term insurance

$$A_{\overset{\frown}{xy}:\overline{n}|}^{\,1} = \sum_{k=0}^{n-1} v^{k+1}\,_{k|}q_{xy}.$$

Note that we use $\overset{\frown}{x\,y}$ here to denote that it is the failure of the *joint life* status, before n years, that triggers the death benefit payment. Without the $\frown$, the symbol could be confused with the EPV of a contingent term insurance payable on the death of (x) before (y), and before n years.

Example 9.2 A husband, currently aged 55, and his wife, currently aged 50, have just purchased a deferred annuity policy. Level premiums are payable monthly for at most 10 years but only if both are alive. If either dies within 10 years, a sum insured of \$200 000 is payable at the end of the year of death. If both lives survive 10 years, an annuity of \$50 000 per year is payable monthly in advance while both are alive, reducing to \$30 000 per year, still payable monthly, while only one is alive. The annuity ceases on the death of the last survivor.

Calculate the monthly premium on the following basis:

Survival model: Standard Select Survival Model for both lives
                  (55) and (50) are independent with respect to mortality
                  (55) and (50) are select at the time the policy is purchased
Interest: 5% per year effective
Expenses: None

Solution 9.2 Since the two lives are independent with respect to mortality, we can write the probability that they both survive t years as

$$_tp_{[55]}\,_tp_{[50]}$$

where each single life probability is calculated using the Standard Select Survival Model.

Let P denote the annual amount of the premium. Then the EPV of the premiums is

$$P\,\ddot{a}_{[55]:[50]:\overline{10}|}^{(12)} = 7.7786\,P.$$

The EPV of the death benefit is

$$200\,000\, A_{\underbrace{\phantom{[55]:[50]:\overline{10|}}}_{[55]:[50]:\,\overline{10|}}}^{\;\;1} = 7660.$$

To find the EPV of the annuities we note that if both lives are alive at time 10 years, the EPV of the payments is

$$30\,000\, \ddot{a}^{(12)}_{65:60} + 20\,000\, \ddot{a}^{(12)}_{65:60}$$

$$= 30\,000\, \ddot{a}^{(12)}_{65} + 30\,000\, \ddot{a}^{(12)}_{60} - 10\,000\, \ddot{a}^{(12)}_{65:60}. \qquad (9.9)$$

For the EPV at issue, we discount for survival for the 10-year deferred period, and for interest, giving the EPV as

$$v^{10}\, {}_{10}p_{[55]}\, {}_{10}p_{[50]}\left(30\,000\, \ddot{a}^{(12)}_{65} + 30\,000\, \ddot{a}^{(12)}_{60} - 10\,000\, \ddot{a}^{(12)}_{65:60}\right) = 411\,396.$$

Hence the monthly premium, $P/12$, is given by

$$P/12 = (7\,660 + 411\,396)/(12 \times 7.7786) = \$4489.41.$$

$\square$

   In this solution we calculated the monthly premium values exactly, by summing the monthly terms. However, we have noted in earlier chapters that it is sometimes the case in practice that the only information available to us to calculate the EPV of an annuity payable more frequently than annually is a life table specified at integer ages only. In Section 5.11 we illustrated methods of approximating the EPV of an annuity payable m times per year, and these methods can also be applied to joint life annuities. To illustrate, consider the annuity EPVs in equation (9.9). These can be approximated from the corresponding annual values using UDD as

$$\ddot{a}^{(12)}_{65} \approx \alpha(12)\, \ddot{a}_{65} - \beta(12)$$
$$= 1.000197 \times 13.5498 - 0.466508$$
$$= 13.0860,$$

$$\ddot{a}^{(12)}_{60} \approx \alpha(12)\, \ddot{a}_{60} - \beta(12)$$
$$= 1.000197 \times 14.9041 - 0.466508$$
$$= 14.4405,$$

$$\ddot{a}^{(12)}_{65:60} \approx \alpha(12)\, \ddot{a}_{65:60} - \beta(12)$$
$$= 1.000197 \times 12.3738 - 0.466508$$
$$= 11.9097,$$

and

$$\ddot{a}^{(12)}_{[55]:[50]:\overline{10|}} \approx \alpha(12)\,\ddot{a}_{[55]:[50]:\overline{10|}} - \beta(12)(1 - {}_{10}p_{[55]}\,{}_{10}p_{[50]}\,v^{10})$$

$$= 1.000197 \times 7.9716 - 0.466508 \times 0.41790$$

$$= 7.7782.$$

The approximate value of the monthly premium is then

$$P/12 \approx \frac{32\,715 + 0.54923 \times (30\,000(13.0860 + 14.4405) - 10\,000 \times 11.9097)}{12 \times 7.7782}$$

$$= \$4489.33.$$

An important point to appreciate here is that, under UDD for individual lives, we have

$$\ddot{a}^{(m)}_x = \alpha(m)\ddot{a}_x - \beta(m)$$

but for a joint life status, under the assumption of UDD for each life, we do not get a simple exact relationship between, for example $\ddot{a}^{(m)}_{xy}$ and $\ddot{a}_{xy}$. It is, however, true that

$$\ddot{a}^{(m)}_{xy} \approx \alpha(m)\ddot{a}_{xy} - \beta(m). \tag{9.10}$$

Our calculations above illustrate the general point that this approximation is usually very accurate. See Exercise 9.12. In Exercise 9.13 we illustrate how Woolhouse's formula can be applied to find the EPV of a joint life annuity payable m times per year.

Example 9.3 Derive integral expressions in terms of survival probabilities and a constant force of interest δ for $\bar{a}_{xy}$ and $\bar{a}_{\overline{xy}}$.

Solution 9.3 Integral expressions are as follows:

$$\bar{a}_{xy} = \int_0^\infty e^{-\delta t}\,{}_t p_{xy}\,dt, \tag{9.11}$$

$$\bar{a}_{\overline{xy}} = \int_0^\infty e^{-\delta t}\,{}_t p_{\overline{xy}}\,dt. \tag{9.12}$$

These expressions can be derived in the same way that Figure 5.5 was used to derive formula (5.15) for a single life annuity. Consider formula (9.11): the amount paid between times t and $t + dt$ is dt, provided both lives survive to that time, and its present value now is $e^{-\delta t}\,dt$; the probability of this amount being paid is ${}_t p_{xy}$; hence the EPV of this possible payment is $e^{-\delta t}\,{}_t p_{xy}\,dt$ and the total EPV is the sum (integral) of this expression over all values of t. $\quad\square$

We can derive integral expressions for insurance functions using arguments similar to those used in Section 4.4.1 for a single life based on Figure 4.1. For example, $\bar{A}^1_{x\,y}$ can be written

$$\bar{A}^1_{x\,y} = \int_0^\infty e^{-\delta t}\,{}_t p_{xy}\,\mu_{x+t}\,dt \tag{9.13}$$

and this can be justified as follows. Consider the possible payment between times t and $t + dt$, where dt is small. This has unit amount and present value $e^{-\delta t}$. For this payment to be made, both lives must be alive at time t (probability ${}_t p_{xy}$) and x must die before time $t + dt$ (probability $\mu_{x+t}\,dt$) – the probability that both die before time $t + dt$ is negligible if dt is small. Hence the EPV of this payment is $e^{-\delta t}\,{}_t p_{xy}\,\mu_{x+t}\,dt$ and the total EPV is the integral over all possible values of t. The following integral expressions can be justified in similar ways:

$$\bar{A}_{xy} = \int_0^\infty e^{-\delta t}\,{}_t p_{xy}(\mu_{x+t} + \mu_{y+t})\,dt,$$

$$\bar{A}_{\overline{xy}} = \int_0^\infty e^{-\delta t}\,({}_t p_x\,\mu_{x+t}(1 - {}_t p_y) + {}_t p_y\,\mu_{y+t}(1 - {}_t p_x))\,dt.$$

Similar arguments can be used to construct integral expressions for many annuity and insurance functions based on two lives, but the approach has drawbacks. When benefits are complex, it is easy to mis-state probabilities. In the following section we present another approach to deriving these equations, using a multiple state model, that gives the insurance and annuity EPV formulae more directly, and that also proves fruitful in terms of generalizing the model to incorporate dependence.

9.5 A multiple state model for independent future lifetimes

In Section 8.2, we described how the single life future lifetime random variable, T_x, is related to a two-state multiple state model, which we called the 'alive–dead' model. Loosely, for a life aged x, T_x is the time to the transition from state 0 ('alive') to state 1 ('dead').

In our joint life case, we can, similarly, create a multiple state model that provides a different perspective on the future lifetime random variables, T_x and T_y, as well as the joint life and last survivor random variables, T_{xy} and $T_{\overline{xy}}$.

We use the multiple state model shown in Figure 9.1. For illustration, we assume (x) is male and (y) is female, and that the male and female transition intensities are labelled m and f, respectively. The process starts in state 0 with both (x) and (y) alive. It moves to state 1 on the death of (y) if she dies before (x), or to state 2 if (x) dies first. The process moves to state 3 on the death of the

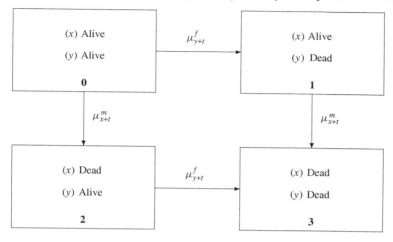

Figure 9.1 The independent joint life and last survivor model.

surviving partner. The model is specified in terms of the transition intensities between the states. We assume these are known.

In this and the following sections, we use the multiple state probability notation from Chapter 8, but with a right subscript that references both (x) and (y), for probabilities involving state 0, where both are alive. For transitions from state 1 and state 2, we use the subscript appropriate to the surviving life. So, for example,

$$_tp^{00}_{xy} = \Pr[(x) \text{ and } (y) \text{ both alive at time } t \mid \text{both alive at time } 0],$$

$$_tp^{01}_{xy} = \Pr[(x) \text{ alive and } (y) \text{ dead at time } t \mid \text{both alive at time } 0],$$

and for $0 < s < t$,

$$_tp^{22}_{y+s} = \Pr[(y) \text{ alive at time } t + s \mid (y) \text{ alive and } (x) \text{ dead at time } s].$$

Our model, in this form, incorporates the following important assumption. We will show that this assumption is equivalent to assuming independence of T_x and T_y.

Independence Assumption 2. The transition intensities from state 0 to state 1, and from state 2 to state 3, are identical and depend on (y)'s age, but not on (x)'s age or survival. Similarly, the transition intensities from state 0 to state 2 and from state 1 to state 3, representing the death of (x), are identical functions of (x)'s age, with no dependence on (y)'s age or survival.

Under this assumption, the force of mortality for (x) at age $x + t$ is μ^m_{x+t}, whether (y) is then alive or not. Hence, T_x has a distribution determined by

$\{\mu^m_{x+t}\}_{t\geq 0}$. Similarly, T_y has a distribution determined by $\{\mu^f_{y+t}\}_{t\geq 0}$. Since there is no connection between the mortality of (x) and (y), it is not surprising that the future lifetimes of (x) and (y) are independent random variables, and, hence, that the multiple state model in this section is equivalent to the model studied in Section 9.4. We show this more formally in Example 9.4.

Example 9.4 Show that, under the multiple state model in Figure 9.1, with the assumption labelled 'Independence Assumption 2', the future lifetimes of (x) and (y), both currently in state 0, are independent.

Solution 9.4 Let s and t be any positive numbers. It is sufficient to show that

$$\Pr[T_x > s \text{ and } T_y > t] = \Pr[T_x > s]\Pr[T_y > t], \tag{9.14}$$

and we can assume, without loss of generality, that $s \leq t$. Let

$$_s p_x = \exp\left\{-\int_0^s \mu^m_{x+u}\, du\right\} \quad \text{and} \quad _t p_y = \exp\left\{-\int_0^t \mu^f_{y+u}\, du\right\}.$$

We know that these are the survival probabilities in the single life models. We need to show that they are also survival probabilities in the multiple state model in Figure 9.1. We have

$$\Pr[T_y > t] = {}_t p^{00}_{xy} + {}_t p^{02}_{xy}.$$

Now

$${}_t p^{00}_{xy} = {}_t p_{xy} = \exp\left\{-\int_0^t (\mu^m_{x+u} + \mu^f_{y+u})\, du\right\} = {}_t p_x\, {}_t p_y \tag{9.15}$$

and

$$\begin{aligned}
{}_t p^{02}_{xy} &= \int_0^t {}_r p^{00}_{xy}\, \mu^m_{x+r}\, {}_{t-r} p^{22}_{y+r}\, dr \\
&= \int_0^t {}_r p_x\, {}_r p_y\, \mu^m_{x+r}\, {}_{t-r} p_{y+r}\, dr \\
&= {}_t p_y \int_0^t {}_r p_x\, \mu^m_{x+r}\, dr \\
&= {}_t p_y\, (1 - {}_t p_x).
\end{aligned} \tag{9.16}$$

So

$$\Pr[T_y > t] = {}_t p_y\, ({}_t p_x + 1 - {}_t p_x) = {}_t p_y$$

and, similarly, $\Pr[T_x > s] = {}_s p_x$.

Now consider $\Pr[T_x > s \text{ and } T_y > t]$; this requires either (i) both (x) and (y) survive to time t, or (ii) (x) and (y) both survive to time $s < t$, and, subsequently, (x) dies and (y) survives in the interval from time s to time t. This gives the joint survival probability

$$\Pr[T_x > s \text{ and } T_y > t] = {}_tp^{00}_{xy} + {}_sp^{00}_{xy}\,{}_{t-s}p^{02}_{x+s:y+s},$$

where we have used the Markov property to write the probability for case (ii). Using (9.15) and (9.16), we have

$$_tp^{00}_{xy} = {}_tp_x\,{}_tp_y \quad \text{and} \quad {}_{t-s}p^{02}_{x+s:\,y+s} = {}_{t-s}p_{y+s}\left(1 - {}_{t-s}p_{x+s}\right).$$

Hence

$$
\begin{aligned}
\Pr[T_x > s \text{ and } T_y > t] &= {}_tp_x\,{}_tp_y + {}_sp_x\,{}_sp_y\left({}_{t-s}p_{y+s}\left(1 - {}_{t-s}p_{x+s}\right)\right)\\
&= {}_tp_x\,{}_tp_y + {}_tp_y\left({}_sp_x - {}_tp_x\right)\\
&= {}_sp_x\,{}_tp_y\\
&= \Pr[T_x > s]\,\Pr[T_y > t],
\end{aligned}
$$

which completes the proof. □

We emphasize here that throughout this proof we have used the assumption that forces of mortality for (x) and (y) are unaffected by the model state. More generally, this assumption will not be true, and the breakdown of the joint life probabilities into single life probabilities will no longer be valid.

Example 9.5 Using the multiple state model, with the independence assumption, shown in Figure 9.1, write down integral equations for each of the following, and describe the benefit being valued.

(a) $\bar{A}^{01}_{xy}$,
(b) $\bar{A}^{01}_{xy} + \bar{A}^{02}_{xy}$,
(c) $\bar{a}^{01}_{xy}$.

Solution 9.5 (a)

$$\bar{A}^{01}_{xy} = \int_0^\infty e^{-\delta t}\,{}_tp^{00}_{xy}\,\mu^f_{y+t}\,dt = \bar{A}^{1}_{x:y}$$

noting that $\mu^{01}_{x+t:y+t} = \mu^f_{y+t}$.

This is the EPV of a unit benefit paid on the death of (y) provided (x) is still alive at that time.

(b)

$$\bar{A}^{01}_{xy} + \bar{A}^{02}_{xy} = \int_0^\infty e^{-\delta t}\,{}_tp^{00}_{xy}\left(\mu^f_{y+t} + \mu^m_{x+t}\right)dt = \bar{A}_{xy}.$$

This is the EPV of a unit benefit paid on the first death of (x) and (y).

(c)

$$\bar{a}_{xy}^{01} = \int_0^\infty e^{-\delta t} \, _tp_{xy}^{01} \, dt = \int_0^\infty e^{-\delta t} \, _tp_x(1 - \, _tp_y) \, dt = \bar{a}_x - \bar{a}_{xy} = \bar{a}_{y|x}.$$

This is the EPV of a unit reversionary annuity payable to (x) after the death of (y). $\qquad\square$

Note here that, as expected, the independent multiple state model generates results consistent with the model of Section 9.4.

Example 9.6 Use the independent multiple state model to write down equations for the EPVs of the following benefits, and simplify as far as possible. Assume that at time 0 the lives (x) and (y) are in state 0.

(a) An insurance of 1 payable on the death of (y), conditional on (x) dying first.
(b) A joint life annuity of 1 per year, payable continuously, guaranteed for n years.
(c) A last survivor annuity of 1 per year, payable continuously, deferred for n years.

Solution 9.6 (a) The EPV is

$$\bar{A}_{x:y}^{\;\;2} = \int_0^\infty e^{-\delta t} \, _tp_{xy}^{02} \, \mu_{y+t}^f \, dt = \int_0^\infty e^{-\delta t} \, _tp_y(1 - \, _tp_x) \, \mu_{y+t}^f \, dt$$
$$= \bar{A}_y - \bar{A}_{x:y}^{\;\;1}.$$

(b) For guaranteed annuities, we separate the value of the first n years payments, which are certain, and the value of the annuity after n years, which depends on which state the process is in at that time. In this example, after n years, the annuity continues if the process is then in state 0, and ceases otherwise. Hence

$$\bar{a}_{\overline{xy:n}|} = \bar{a}_{\overline{n}|} + e^{-\delta n} \, _np_{xy}^{00} \, \bar{a}_{x+n:y+n}^{00}.$$

(c) This follows similarly to (b), but we must now also take into consideration the possibility that exactly one life survives the guarantee period. We have

$$_n|\bar{a}_{\overline{xy}} = e^{-\delta n} \, _np_{xy}^{00} \, \bar{a}_{\overline{x+n:y+n}} + e^{-\delta n} \, _np_{xy}^{01} \, \bar{a}_{x+n} + e^{-\delta n} \, _np_{xy}^{02} \, \bar{a}_{y+n}$$
$$= \, _n|\bar{a}_x + \, _n|\bar{a}_y - \, _n|\bar{a}_{xy}.$$

$\qquad\square$

9.6 A model with dependent future lifetimes

The disadvantage of the approach in Sections 9.4 and 9.5 is that the assumption of independence may not be appropriate for couples who purchase joint life insurance or annuity products. The following three factors are often cited as sources of dependence between married partners.

- The death of the first to die could adversely affect the mortality of the survivor. This is sometimes called the 'broken heart syndrome'.
- The two lives could die together in an accident. This is called the 'common shock' risk.
- The two lives are likely to share a common lifestyle. For example, mortality is related to wealth and levels of education. Married couples tend to have similar levels of wealth and similar levels of education. They may also share interests, for example, related to health and fitness.

In this section, we relax the assumption of independence, introducing dependence in a relatively intuitive way, allowing us to apply the methods and results of Chapter 8 to cash flows contingent on two dependent lives.

The modification is illustrated in Figure 9.2; we now allow for the force of mortality of (x) to depend on whether (y) is still alive, and what age (y) is, and *vice versa*.

More formally, we incorporate the following assumption.

State Dependent Mortality Assumption. The force of mortality for each life depends on whether the other partner is still alive. If the partner is alive, the intensity may depend on the exact age of the partner, as well as the age of the

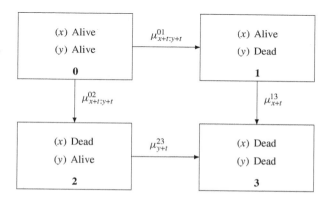

Figure 9.2 A joint life and last survivor model.

life being considered. If one partner has died, the transition intensity for the survivor depends only on the survivor's age and state.

Our notation is adjusted appropriately for this assumption. For example, $\mu^{01}_{x+t:y+t}$ is the intensity of mortality for (y) at age $y+t$ given that (x) is still alive and aged $x+t$. However, if one partner, say (x), has died, the intensity of mortality for (y) depends on her then current age, and the fact that (x) has died, but not on how long he has been dead. Since the age at death of (x) is assumed not to affect the transition intensity from state 2 to state 3, this intensity is denoted μ^{23}_{y+t}, where $y+t$ is the current age of (y).

This model allows for some dependence between the lives; the death of, say, (x) affects the transition intensity of (y). It does not allow for both lives dying simultaneously; we discuss a way of incorporating this in the next section.

Since none of the states in the model can be re-entered once it has been left, we have

$$_t p^{ii}_{xy} \equiv {}_t p^{\overline{ii}}_{xy} \quad \text{for } i = 0, 1, 2, 3$$

so that using formula (8.8)

$$_t p^{00}_{xy} = \exp \left\{ -\int_0^t (\mu^{01}_{x+s:y+s} + \mu^{02}_{x+s:y+s}) \, ds \right\}, \qquad (9.17)$$

$$_t p^{11}_{x} = \exp \left\{ -\int_0^t \mu^{13}_{x+s} \, ds \right\},$$

$$_t p^{22}_{y} = \exp \left\{ -\int_0^t \mu^{23}_{y+s} \, ds \right\},$$

and, for example,

$$_t p^{01}_{xy} = \int_0^t {}_s p^{00}_{xy} \, \mu^{01}_{x+s:y+s} \, {}_{t-s} p^{11}_{x+s} \, ds. \qquad (9.18)$$

Assuming as usual that we know the transition intensities, probabilities for the model can be evaluated either by starting with Kolmogorov's forward equations, (8.14), and then using Euler's, or some more sophisticated, method, or, alternatively, by starting with formulae corresponding to (9.17) and (9.18) and integrating, probably numerically.

The probabilities listed in Section 9.2 do not all correspond to $_t p^{ij}$ type probabilities. We examine two in more detail, in the context of the model discussed in this section, in the following example.

Example 9.7 (a) Explain why $_t q^1_{xy}$ is not the same as $_t p^{02}_{xy}$, and write down an integral equation for $_t q^1_{xy}$.

(b) Write down an integral equation for $_t q^2_{xy}$.

Solution 9.7 (a) The probability ${}_tq^1_{xy}$ is the probability that (x) dies within t years, and that (y) is alive at the time of (x)'s death.

The probability ${}_tp^{02}_{xy}$ is the probability that (x) dies within t years, and that (y) is alive at time t years. So the first probability allows for the possibility that (y) dies after (x), within t years, and the second does not.

The probability that (x) dies within t years, and that (y) is alive at the time of the death of (x) can be constructed by summing (integrating) over all the infinitesimal intervals in which (x) could die, conditioning on the survival of both (x) and (y) up to that time, so that

$$_tq^1_{xy} = \int_0^t {}_rp^{00}_{xy}\, \mu^{02}_{x+r:y+r}\, dr.$$

(b) The probability ${}_tq^2_{xy}$ is the probability that (x) dies within t years and that (y) is already dead when (x) dies, conditional on (x) and (y) both being alive at time 0. In terms of the model in Figure 9.2, the process must move into state 1 and then into state 3 within t years, given that it starts in state 0 at time 0. Summing all the probabilities of such a move over infinitesimal intervals, we have

$$_tq^2_{xy} = \int_0^t {}_rp^{01}_{xy}\, \mu^{13}_{x+r}\, dr.$$

□

Example 9.8 Derive the following expression for the probability that (x) has died before reaching age $x + t$, given that (x) is married to (y) at time 0:

$$\int_0^t {}_sp^{00}_{xy}\, \mu^{02}_{x+s:y+s}\, ds + \int_0^t \int_0^s {}_up^{00}_{xy}\, \mu^{01}_{x+u:y+u}\, {}_{s-u}p^{11}_{x+u}\, du\, \mu^{13}_{x+s}\, ds.$$

Solution 9.8 For (x) to die before time t we require the process either to

(1) enter state 2 from state 0 at some time s ($0 < s \le t$), or
(2) enter state 1 ((y) dies while (x) is alive) at some time u ($0 < u \le t$) and then enter state 3 at some time s ($u < s \le t$).

The total probability of these events, integrating over the time of death of (x), is

$$\int_0^t {}_sp^{00}_{xy}\, \mu^{02}_{x+s:y+s}\, ds + \int_0^t {}_sp^{01}_{xy}\, \mu^{13}_{x+s}\, ds$$

where

$$_sp^{00}_{xy} = \exp\left\{ -\int_0^s (\mu^{01}_{x+u:y+u} + \mu^{02}_{x+u:y+u})du \right\},$$

$$_sp^{01}_{xy} = \int_0^s {}_up^{00}_{xy}\, \mu^{01}_{x+u:y+u}\, {}_{s-u}p^{11}_{x+u}\, du,$$

and

$$_{s-u}p^{11}_{x+u} = \exp\left\{-\int_0^{s-u} \mu^{13}_{x+u+r}\,dr\right\}.$$

This gives the required formula.   □

We can write down formulae for the EPVs of annuities and insurances in terms of probabilities, the transition intensities and the interest rate. For annuities we have the following formulae, given (x) and (y) are alive at time $t = 0$:

$$\bar{a}_y = \int_0^\infty e^{-\delta t}\,({}_tp^{00}_{xy} + {}_tp^{02}_{xy})\,dt,$$

$$\bar{a}_x = \int_0^\infty e^{-\delta t}\,({}_tp^{00}_{xy} + {}_tp^{01}_{xy})\,dt,$$

$$\bar{a}_{xy} = \int_0^\infty e^{-\delta t}\,{}_tp^{00}_{xy}\,dt,$$

$$\bar{a}_{\overline{xy}} = \int_0^\infty e^{-\delta t}\,({}_tp^{00}_{xy} + {}_tp^{01}_{xy} + {}_tp^{02}_{xy})\,dt,$$

$$\bar{a}_{x|y} = \int_0^\infty e^{-\delta t}\,{}_tp^{02}_{xy}\,dt.$$

For the EPVs of the lump sum payments we have the following formulae:

$$\bar{A}_y = \int_0^\infty e^{-\delta t}\,({}_tp^{00}_{xy}\,\mu^{01}_{x+t:y+t} + {}_tp^{02}_{xy}\,\mu^{23}_{y+t})\,dt,$$

which values a unit benefit paid on transition from state 0 to state 1, or from state 2 to state 3;

$$\bar{A}_{xy} = \int_0^\infty e^{-\delta t}\,{}_tp^{00}_{xy}\,(\mu^{01}_{x+t:y+t} + \mu^{02}_{x+t:y+t})\,dt,$$

which values a unit benefit paid on transition out of state 0, with EPV $A^{01}_{xy} + A^{02}_{xy}$;

$$\bar{A}_{\overline{xy}} = \int_0^\infty e^{-\delta t}\,({}_tp^{01}_{xy}\,\mu^{13}_{x+t} + {}_tp^{02}_{xy}\,\mu^{23}_{y+t})\,dt,$$

which values a benefit paid on transition from state 1 to state 3, or from state 2 to state 3;

$$\bar{A}^1_{xy} = \int_0^\infty e^{-\delta t}\,{}_tp^{00}_{xy}\,\mu^{02}_{x+t:y+t}\,dt,$$

which values a benefit paid on transition from state 0 to state 2, that is A^{02}_{xy}; and

$$\bar{A}^1_{xy:\overline{n}|} = \int_0^n e^{-\delta t}\,{}_tp^{00}_{xy}\,\mu^{02}_{x+t:y+t}\,dt,$$

which values a benefit paid on transition from state 0 to state 2, provided it occurs within n years.

Example 9.9 For the model illustrated in Figure 9.2, you are given the following information.

$$\mu^{01}_{x+t:y+t} = B_f \, c_f^{y+t},$$
$$\mu^{02}_{x+t:y+t} = B_m \, c_m^{x+t},$$
$$\mu^{13}_{x+t} = C_m \, d_m^{x+t},$$
$$\mu^{23}_{y+t} = C_f \, d_f^{y+t}$$

where

$$B_f = 9.741 \times 10^{-7} \qquad c_f = 1.1331,$$
$$B_m = 2.622 \times 10^{-5} \qquad c_m = 1.0989,$$
$$C_m = 3.899 \times 10^{-4} \qquad d_m = 1.0725,$$
$$C_f = 2.638 \times 10^{-5} \qquad d_f = 1.1020.$$

For a husband and wife currently aged $x = 65$ and $y = 62$, respectively, calculate the probability that

(a) both are alive in 15 years,
(b) (x) is alive in 15 years,
(c) (y) is alive in 15 years,
(d) at least one is alive in 15 years.

Solution 9.9 Note first that each of the four forces of mortality has a Gompertz formula, so that each can be integrated analytically. Also, we see that the force of mortality for each partner depends on whether the spouse is still alive, though not on the age of the spouse. If (x) survives (y), his force of mortality increases from μ^{02}_{x+t} to μ^{13}_{x+t}. Similarly, (y)'s mortality increases if she is widowed. Thus, the two lives are not independent with respect to mortality.

(a) The probability that both are alive in 15 years is

$$_{15}p^{00}_{65:62} = \exp\left\{-\int_0^{15} (\mu^{01}_{65+t:62+t} + \mu^{02}_{65+t:62+t})\, dt\right\}$$
$$= g_f^{c_f^{62}(c_f^{15}-1)} \times g_m^{c_m^{65}(c_m^{15}-1)}$$
$$= 0.905223 \times 0.671701 = 0.608039$$

where

$$g_f = \exp\left\{-\frac{B_f}{\log c_f}\right\} \quad \text{and} \quad g_m = \exp\left\{-\frac{B_m}{\log c_m}\right\}.$$

(b) The probability that (x) is alive in 15 years is $_{15}p^{00}_{65:62} + {_{15}}p^{01}_{65:62}$. We already know from part (a) that $_{15}p^{00}_{65:62} = 0.608039$. By considering the time, t, at which (y) dies, we can write

$$_{15}p^{01}_{65:62} = \int_0^{15} {_t}p^{00}_{65:62}\, \mu^{01}_{65+t:62+t}\, {_{15-t}}p^{11}_{65+t}\, dt, \qquad (9.19)$$

where, following the steps in part (a),

$$_t p^{00}_{65:62} = g_f^{c_f^{62}(c_f^t - 1)} \times g_m^{c_m^{65}(c_m^t - 1)}$$

and

$$\begin{aligned}
_{15-t}p^{11}_{65+t} &= \exp\left\{ -\int_0^{15-t} \mu^{13}_{65+t+s}\, ds \right\} \\
&= h_m^{d_m^{65+t}(d_m^{15-t} - 1)}
\end{aligned}$$

where $h_m = \exp\{-C_m / \log d_m\}$.

The integral in formula (9.19) can now be evaluated numerically, giving

$$_{15}p^{01}_{65:62} = 0.050402$$

so that

$$_{15}p^{00}_{65:62} + {_{15}}p^{01}_{65:62} = 0.658442.$$

(c) The probability that (y) is alive in 15 years is $_{15}p^{00}_{65:62} + {_{15}}p^{02}_{65:62}$, where

$$_{15}p^{02}_{65:62} = \int_0^{15} {_t}p^{00}_{65:62}\, \mu^{02}_{65+t:62+t}\, {_{15-t}}p^{22}_{62+t}\, dt \qquad (9.20)$$

and

$$\begin{aligned}
_{15-t}p^{22}_{62+t} &= \exp\left\{ \int_0^{15-t} \mu^{23}_{62+t+s}\, ds \right\} \\
&= h_f^{d_f^{62+t}(d_f^{15-t} - 1)}
\end{aligned}$$

where $h_f = \exp\{-C_f / \log d_f\}$.

We can evaluate numerically the integral in formula (9.20), giving

$$_{15}p^{02}_{65:62} = 0.258823$$

so that

$$_{15}p^{00}_{65:62} + {_{15}}p^{02}_{65:62} = 0.866862.$$

(d) The probability that at least one is alive in 15 years is

$$\begin{aligned}
_{15}p^{00}_{65:62} + {_{15}}p^{01}_{65:62} + {_{15}}p^{02}_{65:62} &= 0.608039 + 0.050402 + 0.258823 \\
&= 0.917265.
\end{aligned}$$

□

9.7 The common shock model

The model illustrated in Figure 9.2 incorporates dependence between (x) and (y) by allowing the transition intensity of each to depend on whether the other is still alive. We can extend this dependence by allowing for (x) and (y) to die at the same time, for example as the result of a car accident. This is illustrated in Figure 9.3, the so-called **common shock model**.

Example 9.10 In the context of the common shock model, calculate $_{10}p_{70:65}^{00}$, $_{10}p_{70:65}^{01}$ and $_{10}p_{70:65}^{02}$ using the following transition intensities:

$$\mu_{x+t:y+t}^{01} = B_f \, c_f^{y+t},$$
$$\mu_{x+t:y+t}^{02} = B_m \, c_m^{x+t},$$
$$\mu_{x+t}^{13} = C_m \, d_m^{x+t},$$
$$\mu_{y+t}^{23} = C_f \, d_f^{y+t},$$
$$\mu_{x+t:y+t}^{03} = \lambda$$

where

$$
\begin{aligned}
B_f &= 9.741 \times 10^{-7} & c_f &= 1.1331, \\
B_m &= 2.622 \times 10^{-5} & c_m &= 1.0989, \\
C_m &= 3.899 \times 10^{-4} & d_m &= 1.0725, \\
C_f &= 2.638 \times 10^{-5} & d_f &= 1.1020, \\
\lambda &= 1.407 \times 10^{-3}.
\end{aligned}
$$

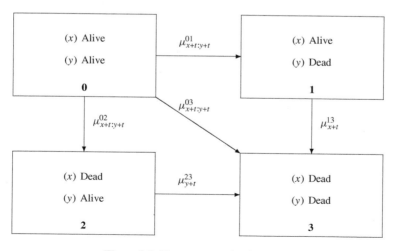

Figure 9.3 The common shock model.

Note that the transition intensities in this example are the same as the previous example, except that in this case we have added the common shock transition, which is assumed to be constant.

Solution 9.10 Let $x = 70$ and $y = 65$. We can evaluate ${}_{10}p_{xy}^{00}$ directly from the formula

$$
{}_{10}p_{70:65}^{00} = \exp\left\{-\int_0^{10} (\mu_{x+u:y+u}^{01} + \mu_{x+u:y+u}^{02} + \mu_{x+u:y+u}^{03})\, du\right\}
$$
$$
= g_f^{c_f^{65}(c_f^{10}-1)} \times g_m^{c_m^{70}(c_m^{10}-1)} \times e^{-10\lambda}
$$
$$
= 0.670051
$$

where g_m and g_f are as defined in the solution to Example 9.9.
For the probabilities of transition to state 1 or state 2, we have

$$
{}_{10}p_{70:65}^{01} = \int_0^{10} {}_t p_{70:65}^{00}\, \mu_{70+t:65+t}^{01}\, {}_{10-t}p_{70+t}^{11}\, dt \tag{9.21}
$$

$$
{}_{10}p_{70:65}^{02} = \int_0^{10} {}_t p_{70:65}^{00}\, \mu_{70+t:65+t}^{02}\, {}_{10-t}p_{65+t}^{22}\, dt \tag{9.22}
$$

and

$$
{}_s p_{x:y}^{00} = g_f^{c_f^{y}(c_f^{s}-1)}\, g_m^{c_m^{x}(c_m^{s}-1)}\, e^{-s\lambda}
$$
$$
{}_s p_x^{11} = h_m^{d_m^{x}(d_m^{s}-1)}
$$
$$
{}_s p_y^{22} = h_f^{d_f^{y}(d_f^{s}-1)}
$$

where h_m and h_f are as defined in the solution to Example 9.9.
Numerical integration gives

$$
{}_{10}p_{70:65}^{01} = 0.03771 \quad \text{and} \quad {}_{10}p_{70:65}^{02} = 0.23255.
$$

$\square$

Note the similarity between formulae (9.21) and (9.22) and formulae (9.19) and (9.20). The difference is that the ${}_t p_{xy}^{00}$ values are calculated differently, with the extra term $e^{-\lambda t}$ allowing for the common shock risk.

Example 9.11 A husband and wife, aged 63 and 61, respectively, have just purchased a joint life 15-year term insurance with sum insured $200\,000 payable immediately on the death of the first to die, or on their simultaneous deaths, within 15 years. Level premiums are payable monthly for at most 15 years while both are still alive.

Calculate

(a) the monthly premium, and
(b) the gross premium policy value after 10 years, assuming both husband and wife are still alive.

Use the common shock model with the following basis.

Interest:	4% per year
Survival model:	As in Example 9.10.
Expenses:	Initial expenses of $500
	Renewal expenses of 10% of all premiums
	$200 on payment of the sum insured

Solution 9.11 (a) The EPV of a unit sum insured is

$$\int_0^{15} v^t \, {}_t p_{63:61}^{00} \, (\mu_{63+t:61+t}^{01} + \mu_{63+t:61+t}^{02} + \mu_{63+t:61+t}^{03}) \, dt$$

and the EPV of a unit premium per month is

$$12 \, \ddot{a}_{63:61:\overline{15|}}^{(12)} = \sum_{t=0}^{179} v^{t/12} \, {}_{t/12} p_{63:61}^{00} .$$

Let $\mu_{x+t:y+t}^{00} = \sum_{R=1}^{3} \mu_{x+t:y+t}^{0k}$. Then the formula for the monthly premium, P, is

$$12 P \, \ddot{a}_{63:61:\overline{15|}}^{(12)} = 200\,200 \int_0^{15} v^t \, {}_t p_{63:61}^{00} \, \mu_{63+t:61+t}^{00} \, dt$$

$$+ \, 500 + 0.1 \times 12 P \, \ddot{a}_{63:61:\overline{15|}}^{(12)}$$

giving

$$P = (200\,200 \times 0.25574 + 500)/(0.9 \times 12 \times 9.87144)$$
$$= \$484.94.$$

(b) The gross premium policy value at duration 10 years, just before the premium then due is paid, is

$$_{10}V = 200\,200 \int_0^{5} v^t \, {}_t p_{73:71}^{00} \, (\mu_{73+t:71+t}^{01} + \mu_{73+t:71+t}^{02} + \mu_{73+t:71+t}^{03}) \, dt$$

$$- 0.9 \, P \sum_{t=0}^{59} v^{t/12} \, {}_{t/12} p_{73:71}^{00}$$

$$= 200\,200 \times 0.17776 - 0.9 \times 484.94 \times 12 \times 4.14277$$
$$= \$13\,890.$$

□

9.8 Notes and further reading

The multiple state model approach is very flexible, allowing us to introduce dependence in various ways. In Section 9.6 we modelled 'broken heart syndrome' by allowing the mortality of each partner to depend on whether the other was still alive and in Section 9.7 we extended this by allowing for the possibility that the two lives die simultaneously. A more realistic model for broken heart syndrome would allow for the mortality of the surviving partner to depend not only on their current age and the fact that their spouse had died, but also on the time since the spouse died. This would make the model semi-Markov, rather than Markov, and is beyond the scope of this book.

The paper by Ji *et al.* (2011) discuss Markov, semi-Markov and other models for multiple life statuses. They use data from a large Canadian insurance company from 1988–93 to parameterize the common shock model in Section 9.7. Their parameterization is used in Example 9.10. Note that their definition of 'simultaneous death' is death within five days, though they do investigate the effects of altering this definition.

9.9 Exercises

Exercise 9.1 Two lives aged 60 and 70 are independent with respect to mortality. Given that $_{10}p_{60} = 0.94$ and $_{10}p_{70} = 0.83$, calculate the probability that

(a) both lives are alive 10 years from now,
(b) at least one life is alive 10 years from now,
(c) exactly one of the lives is alive 10 years from now,
(d) the joint life status fails within the next 10 years, and
(e) the last survivor status fails within the next 10 years.

Exercise 9.2 Two lives aged 30 and 40 are independent with respect to mortality, and each is subject to Makeham's law of mortality with $A = 0.0001$, $B = 0.0003$ and $c = 1.075$. Calculate

(a) $_{10}p_{30:40}$,
(b) $_{10}q^1_{30:40}$,
(c) $_{10}q^2_{30:40}$, and
(d) $_{10}p_{\overline{30:40}}$.

Exercise 9.3 Smith and Jones are both aged exactly 30. Smith is subject to Gompertz' law of mortality with $B = 0.0003$ and $c = 1.07$, and Jones is subject to a force of mortality at all ages x of $Bc^x + 0.039221$. Calculate the probability that Jones dies before reaching age 50 and before Smith dies. Assume that Smith and Jones are independent with respect to mortality.

Exercise 9.4 Two lives aged 25 and 30 are independent with respect to mortality, and each is subject to Makeham's law of mortality with $A = 0.0001$, $B = 0.0003$ and $c = 1.075$. Using an effective rate of interest of 5% per year, calculate

(a) $\ddot{a}_{25:30}$,

(b) $\ddot{a}_{\overline{25:30}}$,

(c) $\ddot{a}_{25|30}$,

(d) $\bar{A}_{25:30}$,

(e) $\bar{A}^{\,1}_{25:30:\,\overline{10|}}$, and

(f) $\bar{A}^{\,2}_{25:30}$.

Exercise 9.5 Two lives aged 60 and 70 are independent with respect to mortality, and the Standard Ultimate Survival Model is applicable for each. On the basis of an effective rate of interest of 5% per year, calculate the EPV of

(a) an annuity of $20 000 a year, payable in arrear as long as least one of the lives is alive,

(b) an annuity of $30 000 a year, payable annually in advance for at most 10 years, provided that both lives are alive, and

(c) a reversionary annuity of $25 000 a year, payable annually to (60) following the death of (70).

Exercise 9.6 Two independent lives, (x) and (y), experience mortality according to Gompertz' law, that is, $\mu_x = Bc^x$.

(a) Show that $_tp_{xy} = {_tp_w}$ for $w = \log(c^x + c^y)/\log c$.

(b) Show that

$$A^1_{x:y} = \frac{c^x}{c^w}\,A_w.$$

Exercise 9.7 By considering the cases $T_y > T_x$ and $T_y \le T_x$, show that the present value random variable for a reversionary annuity payable continuously at rate 1 per year to (y) following the death of (x) is

$$\bar{a}_{\overline{T_y|}} - \bar{a}_{\overline{T_{xy}|}}.$$

Exercise 9.8 Assume that T_x and T_y are independent.

(a) Show that the probability density function of T_{xy} is

$$f_{T_{xy}}(t) = {_tp_{xy}}(\mu_{x+t} + \mu_{y+t}).$$

(b) What is the joint probability density function of (T_x, T_y)? Use this joint probability density function to obtain formulae (9.13) for $\bar{A}^1_{xy}$.

(c) $\bar{A}^2_{xy}$ is the EPV of a benefit of 1 payable on the death of (x) provided that the death of (x) occurs after the death of (y). Using the same approach as in part (b), show that

$$\bar{A}^2_{xy} = \bar{A}_x - \bar{A}^1_{xy}.$$

Explain this result.

Exercise 9.9 Bob and Mike are independent lives, both aged 25. They effect an insurance policy which provides $100 000, payable at the end of the year of Bob's death, provided Bob dies after Mike. Annual premiums are payable in advance throughout Bob's lifetime. Calculate

(a) the net annual premium, and
(b) the net premium policy value after 10 years (before the premium then due is payable) if
    (i) only Bob is then alive, and
    (ii) both lives are then alive.

Basis:

Survival model: Gompertz' law, with $B = 0.0003$ and $c = 1.075$ for both lives

Interest: 5% per year effective
Expenses: None

Exercise 9.10 Ryan is entitled to an annuity of $100 000 per year at retirement, paid monthly in advance, and the normal retirement age is 65. Ryan's wife, Lindsay, is two years younger than Ryan.

(a) Calculate the EPV of the annuity at Ryan's retirement date.
(b) Calculate the revised annual amount of the annuity (payable in the first year) if Ryan chooses to take a benefit which provides Lindsay with a monthly annuity following Ryan's death equal to 60% of the amount payable whilst both Ryan and Lindsay are alive.
(c) Calculate the revised annual amount of the annuity (payable in the first year) if Ryan chooses the benefit in part (b), with a 'pop-up' – that is, the annuity reverts to the full $100 000 on the death of Lindsay if Ryan is still alive. (Note that under a 'pop-up', the benefit reverts to the amount to which Ryan was originally entitled.)

Basis:

• Male mortality before and after widowerhood: Makeham's law, $A = 0.0001$, $B = 0.0004$ and $c = 1.075$
• Female survival before widowhood: Makeham's law, $A = 0.0001$, $B = 0.00025$ and $c = 1.07$

- Female survival after widowhood: Makeham's law, $A = 0.0001$, $B = 0.0003$ and $c = 1.072$
- Interest: 5% per year effective

Exercise 9.11 A man and his wife are aged 28 and 24, respectively. They are about to effect an insurance policy that pays $100\,000$ immediately on the first death. Calculate the premium for this policy, payable monthly in advance as long as both are alive and limited to 25 years, on the following basis:

- Male survival: Makeham's law, with $A = 0.0001$, $B = 0.0004$ and $c = 1.075$
- Female survival: Makeham's law, with $A = 0.0001$, $B = 0.0003$ and $c = 1.07$
- Interest: 5% per year effective
- Initial expenses: $250
- Renewal expenses: 3% of each premium

Assume that this couple are independent with respect to mortality.

Exercise 9.12 Let A_{xy} denote the EPV of a benefit of 1 payable at the end of the year in which the first death of (x) and (y) occurs, and let $A_{xy}^{(m)}$ denote the EPV of a benefit of 1 payable at the end of the $\frac{1}{m}$th of a year in which the first death of (x) and (y) occurs.

(a) As an EPV, what does the following expression represent?

$$\sum_{t=1}^{m} v^{\frac{t}{m}} \left({}_{\frac{t-1}{m}} p_{xy} - {}_{\frac{t}{m}} p_{xy} \right).$$

(b) Write down an expression for $A_{xy}^{(m)}$ in summation form by considering the insurance benefit as comprising a series of deferred one-year term insurances with the benefit payable at the end of the $\frac{1}{m}$th of a year in which the first death of (x) and (y) occurs.

(c) Assume that two lives (x) and (y) are independent with respect to mortality. Show that under the UDD assumption,

$$_{\frac{t-1}{m}} p_{xy} - {}_{\frac{t}{m}} p_{xy} = \frac{1}{m}(1 - p_{xy}) + \frac{m - 2t + 1}{m^2} q_x\, q_y$$

and that

$$v^{\frac{t}{m}} \left({}_{\frac{t-1}{m}} p_{xy} - {}_{\frac{t}{m}} p_{xy} \right) = (1 - p_{xy})\frac{i\,v}{i^{(m)}} + q_x\, q_y \sum_{t=1}^{m} v^{t/m} \frac{m - 2t + 1}{m^2}.$$

(d) Deduce that under the assumptions in part (c),

$$A_{xy}^{(m)} \approx \frac{i}{i^{(m)}} A_{xy}.$$

Exercise 9.13 (a) Show that for independent lives (x) and (y)

$$\frac{d}{dt} v^t\, _tp_x\, _tp_y = -\delta\, v^t\, _tp_x\, _tp_y - v^t\, _tp_x\, _tp_y\mu_{x+t:y+t},$$

where (in the general case) $\mu_{x+t:y+t}$ is the total transition intensity out of state 0 for the joint life process.

(b) Use Woolhouse's formula to show that

$$\ddot{a}_{xy}^{(m)} \approx \ddot{a}_{xy} - \frac{m-1}{2m} - \frac{m^2-1}{12m^2}\left(\delta + \mu_{x:y}\right).$$

Exercise 9.14 For independent lives (x) and (y), show that

$$Cov\left(v^{T_{\overline{xy}}}, v^{T_{xy}}\right) = \left(\bar{A}_x - \bar{A}_{xy}\right)\left(\bar{A}_y - \bar{A}_{xy}\right).$$

Exercise 9.15 An insurance company issues a joint life insurance policy to a married couple. The husband is aged 28 and his wife is aged 27. The policy provides a benefit of $500\,000$ immediately on the death of (x) provided that he dies first. The policy terms stipulate that if the couple die at the same time, the elder life is deemed to have died first. Premiums are payable annually in advance while both lives are alive for at most 30 years.

Use the common shock model illustrated in Figure 9.3 to calculate the annual net premium using an effective rate of interest of 5% per year and transition intensities of

$$\mu_{xy}^{01} = A + Bc^y, \quad \mu_{xy}^{02} = A + Dc^x, \quad \mu_{xy}^{03} = 5 \times 10^{-5},$$

where $A = 0.0001$, $B = 0.0003$, $c = 1.075$ and $D = 0.00035$.

Exercise 9.16 A husband and wife, aged 65 and 60, respectively, purchase an insurance policy, under which the benefits payable on first death are a lump sum of $10\,000$, payable immediately on death, plus an annuity of 5000 per year payable continuously throughout the lifetime of the surviving spouse. A benefit of 1000 is paid immediately on the second death. Premiums are payable continuously until the first death.

You are given that $\bar{A}_{60} = 0.353789$, $\bar{A}_{65} = 0.473229$ and that $\bar{A}_{60:65} = 0.512589$ at 4% per year effective rate of interest. The lives are assumed to be independent.

(a) Calculate the EPV of the lump sum death benefits, at 4% per year interest.
(b) Calculate the EPV of the reversionary annuity benefit, at 4% per year interest.
(c) Calculate the annual rate of premium, at 4% per year interest.
(d) Ten years after the contract is issued the insurer is calculating the policy value.

(i) Write down an expression for the policy value at that time assuming that both lives are still surviving.

(ii) Write down an expression for the policy value assuming that (x) has died but (y) is still alive.

(iii) Write down Thiele's differential equation for the policy value assuming (1) both lives are still alive, and (2) only (y) is alive.

Answers to selected exercises

9.1 (a) 0.7802
    (b) 0.9898
    (c) 0.2096
    (d) 0.2198
    (e) 0.0102

9.2 (a) 0.886962
    (b) 0.037257
    (c) 0.001505
    (d) 0.997005

9.3 0.567376

9.4 (a) 15.8901
    (b) 18.9670
    (c) 1.2013
    (d) 0.2493
    (e) 0.0208
    (f) 0.0440

9.5 (a) $293 808.37
    (b) $225 329.46
    (c) $92 052.87

9.9 (a) $243.16
    (b) (i) $18 269.42
        (ii) $2817.95

9.10 (a) $802 639
    (b) $76 846
    (c) $73 942

9.11 $161.78

9.15 $4948.24

9.16 (a) $5440.32
    (b) $25 262.16
    (c) $2470.55

10

Pension mathematics

10.1 Summary

In this chapter we introduce some of the notation and concepts of pension plan valuation and funding. We discuss the difference between defined benefit (DB) and defined contribution (DC) pension plans. We introduce the salary scale function, and show how to calculate an appropriate contribution rate in a DC plan to meet a target level of pension income.

We then define the service table, which is a summary of the multiple state model appropriate for a pension plan. Using the service table and the salary scale, we can value the benefits and contributions of a pension plan, using the same principles as we have used for valuing benefits under an insurance policy.

10.2 Introduction

The pension plans we discuss in this chapter are typically employer sponsored plans, designed to provide employees with retirement income. Employers sponsor plans for a number of reasons, including

- competition for new employees;
- to facilitate turnover of older employees by ensuring that they can afford to retire;
- to provide incentive for employees to stay with the employer;
- pressure from trade unions;
- to provide a tax efficient method of remunerating employees;
- responsibility to employees who have contributed to the success of the company.

The plan design will depend on which of these motivations is most important to the sponsor. If competition for new employees is the most important factor, for example, then the employer's plan will closely resemble other employer sponsored plans within the same industry. Ensuring turnover of older employees, or rewarding longer service might lead to a different benefit design.

The two major categories of employer sponsored pension plans are **defined contribution** (DC) and **defined benefit** (DB).

The defined contribution pension plan specifies how much the employer will contribute, as a percentage of salary, into a plan. The employee may also contribute, and the employer's contribution may be related to the employee's contribution (for example, the employer may agree to match the employee's contribution up to some maximum). The contributions are accumulated in a notional account, which is available to the employee when he or she leaves the company. The contributions may be set to meet a target benefit level, but the actual retirement income may be well below or above the target, depending on the investment experience.

The defined benefit plan specifies a level of benefit, usually in relation to salary near retirement (final salary plans), or to salary throughout employment (career average salary plans). The contributions, from the employer and, possibly, employee are accumulated to meet the benefit. If the investment or demographic experience is adverse, the contributions can be increased; if experience is favourable, the contributions may be reduced. The pension plan actuary monitors the plan funding on a regular basis to assess whether the contributions need to be changed.

The benefit under a DB plan, and the target under a DC plan, are set by consideration of an appropriate **replacement ratio**. The pension plan replacement ratio is defined as

$$R = \frac{\text{pension income in the year after retirement}}{\text{salary in the year before retirement}}$$

where we assume the plan member survives the year following retirement. The target for the plan replacement ratio depends on other post-retirement income, such as government benefits. A total replacement ratio, including government benefits and personal savings, of around 70% is often assumed to allow retirees to maintain their pre-retirement lifestyle. Employer sponsored plans often target 50–70% as the replacement ratio for an employee with a full career in the company.

10.3 The salary scale function

The contributions and the benefits for most employer sponsored pension plans are related to salaries, so we need to model the progression of salaries through an individual's employment. We use a deterministic model even though future changes in salary cannot usually be predicted with the certainty a deterministic model implies. However, this model is almost universally used in practice and a more realistic model would complicate the presentation in this chapter.

We start by defining the **rate of salary function**, $\{\bar{s}_y\}_{y \geq x_0}$, where x_0 is some suitable initial age. The value of $\bar{s}_{x_0}$ can be set arbitrarily as any positive number. For $y > x \geq x_0$ the value of $\bar{s}_y/\bar{s}_x$ is defined to be the ratio of the annual rate of salary at age y to the annual rate of salary at age x, where we assume the individual is employed from age x to age y.

Example 10.1 Consider an employee aged 30 whose current annual salary rate is \$30 000 and assume she will still be employed at exact age 41.

(a) Suppose the employee's rate of salary function $\{\bar{s}_y\}_{y \geq 20}$ is given by

$$\bar{s}_y = 1.04^{y-20}.$$

    (i) Calculate her annual rate of salary at exact age 30.5.

    (ii) Calculate her salary for the year of age 30 to 31.

    (iii) Calculate her annual rate of salary at exact age 40.5.

    (iv) Calculate her salary for the year of age 40 to 41.

(b) Now suppose that each year the rate of salary increases by 4%, three months after an employee's birthday and then remains constant for a year. Repeat parts (i)–(iv) of (a) above.

Solution 10.1 (a)   (i) From the definition of the rate of salary function, her annual rate of salary at age 30.5 will be

$$30\,000 \times 1.04^{0.5} = \$30\,594.$$

    (ii) Consider a small interval of age $30 + t$ to $30 + t + dt$, where $0 \leq t < t + dt \leq 1$. The rate of salary in this age interval will be $30\,000\,\bar{s}_{30+t}/\bar{s}_{30}$ and the amount received by the employee will be $30\,000\,(\bar{s}_{30+t}/\bar{s}_{30})\,dt$. Hence, her total income for the year of age 30 to 31 will be

$$\int_0^1 30\,000\,(\bar{s}_{30+t}/\bar{s}_{30})\,dt = \int_0^1 30\,000 \times 1.04^t\,dt$$
$$= 30\,000\,(1.04 - 1)/\log 1.04$$
$$= \$30\,596.$$

    (iii) Her salary rate at exact age 40.5 will be $30\,000 \times 1.04^{10.5} = \$45\,287.$

(iv) Using the same argument as in part (ii), her income for the year of age 40 to 41 will be

$$30\,000 \int_{10}^{11} 1.04^t \, dt = 30\,000\,(1.04^{11} - 1.04^{10})/\log 1.04$$

$$= \$45\,290.$$

(b) (i) She will receive a salary increase of 4% at age 30.25 and her rate of salary will then remain constant until she reaches age 31.25, so her rate of salary at age 30.5 will be

$$30\,000 \times 1.04 = \$31\,200.$$

(ii) The income for the three months following her 30th birthday will be $30\,000 \times 0.25 = \$7500$ and her income for the following nine months will be $30\,000 \times 1.04 \times 0.75 = \$23\,400$. Hence, her income for the year of age 30 to 31 will be

$$7\,500 + 23\,400 = \$30\,900.$$

(iii) Her rate of salary income at age 40.5 will be

$$30\,000 \times 1.04^{10} = \$44\,407.$$

(iv) Her income for the year of age 40 to 41 will be

$$30\,000 \times (0.25 \times 1.04^9 + 0.75 \times 1.04^{10}) = \$43\,980.$$

$\square$

In practice it is very common to model the progression of salaries using a **salary scale**, $\{s_y\}_{y \geq x_0}$, rather than a rate of salary function. The salary scale can be derived from the rate of salary function as follows. The value of s_{x_0} can be set arbitrarily as any positive number. For $y > x \geq x_0$ we define

$$\frac{s_y}{s_x} = \frac{\int_0^1 \bar{s}_{y+t} \, dt}{\int_0^1 \bar{s}_{x+t} \, dt}$$

so that, using the same argument as in Example 10.1 parts (ii) and (iv),

$$\frac{s_y}{s_x} = \frac{\text{salary received in year of age } y \text{ to } y + 1}{\text{salary received in year of age } x \text{ to } x + 1}$$

where we assume the individual remains in employment throughout the period from age x to $y + 1$.

Salaries usually increase as a result of promotional increases and inflation adjustments. We assume in general that the salary scale allows for both forces, but it is straightforward to manage these separately.

Table 10.1 *Salary scale for Example 10.2.*

x	s_x	x	s_x	x	s_x	x	s_x
30	1.000	40	2.005	50	2.970	60	3.484
31	1.082	41	2.115	51	3.035	61	3.536
32	1.169	42	2.225	52	3.091	62	3.589
33	1.260	43	2.333	53	3.139	63	3.643
34	1.359	44	2.438	54	3.186	64	3.698
35	1.461	45	2.539	55	3.234		
36	1.566	46	2.637	56	3.282		
37	1.674	47	2.730	57	3.332		
38	1.783	48	2.816	58	3.382		
39	1.894	49	2.897	59	3.432		

Example 10.2 The final average salary for the pension benefit provided by a pension plan is defined as the average salary in the three years before retirement. Members' salaries are increased each year, six months before the valuation date.

(a) A member aged exactly 35 at the valuation date received $75 000 in salary in the year to the valuation date. Calculate his predicted final average salary assuming retirement at age 65.

(b) A member aged exactly 55 at the valuation date was paid salary at a rate of $100 000 per year at that time. Calculate her predicted final average salary assuming retirement at age 65.

Assume

(i) a salary scale where $s_y = 1.04^y$, and

(ii) the integer age salary scale in Table 10.1.

Solution 10.2 (a) The member is aged 35 at the valuation date, so that the salary in the previous year is the salary from age 34 to age 35. The predicted final average salary in the three years to age 65 is then

$$75\,000 \frac{s_{62} + s_{63} + s_{64}}{3\,s_{34}}$$

which gives $234 019 under assumption (i) and $201 067 under assumption (ii).

(b) The current annual salary rate is $100 000, so the final average salary is

$$100\,000 \frac{s_{62} + s_{63} + s_{64}}{3\,\bar{s}_{55}} \approx 100\,000 \frac{s_{62} + s_{63} + s_{64}}{3\,s_{54.5}}.$$

Under assumption (i) this is $139 639. Under assumption (ii) we need to estimate $s_{54.5}$, which we would normally do using linear interpolation,

so that

$$s_{54.5} = (s_{54} + s_{55})/2 = 3.210,$$

giving a final average salary of $113 499. □

Example 10.3 The current annual salary rate of an employee aged exactly 40 is $50 000. Salaries are revised continuously. Using the salary scale $\{s_y\}$, where $s_y = 1.03^y$, estimate

(a) the employee's salary between ages 50 and 51, and
(b) the employee's annual rate of salary at age 51.

In both cases, you should assume the employee remains in employment until at least age 51.

Solution 10.3 (a) The estimated earnings between ages 50 and 51 are given by

$$50\,000\,\frac{\bar{s}_{50}}{\bar{s}_{40}} \approx 50\,000\,\frac{s_{50}}{s_{39.5}} = 50\,000 \times 1.03^{10.5} = \$68\,196.$$

(b) The estimated salary rate at age 51 is given by

$$50\,000\,\frac{\bar{s}_{51}}{\bar{s}_{40}} \approx 50\,000\,\frac{s_{50.5}}{s_{39.5}} = 50\,000 \times 1.03^{11} = \$69\,212.$$

□

10.4 Setting the DC contribution

To set the contribution rate for a DC plan to aim to meet a target replacement ratio for a 'model' employee, we need

- the target replacement ratio and retirement age,
- assumptions on the rate of return on investments, interest rates at retirement, a salary scale and a model for post-retirement mortality, and
- the form the benefits should take.

With this information we can set a contribution rate that will be adequate if experience follows all the assumptions. We might also want to explore sensitivity to the assumptions, to assess a possible range of outcomes for the plan member's retirement income. The following example illustrates these points.

Example 10.4 An employer establishes a DC pension plan. On withdrawal from the plan before retirement age, 65, for any reason, the proceeds of the invested contributions are paid to the employee or the employee's survivors.

The contribution rate is set using the following assumptions.

- The employee will use the proceeds at retirement to purchase a pension for his lifetime, plus a reversionary annuity for his wife at 60% of the employee's pension.
- At age 65, the employee is married, and the age of his wife is 61.
- The target replacement ratio is 65%.
- The salary rate function is given by $s_y = 1.04^y$ and salaries are assumed to increase continuously.
- Contributions are payable monthly in arrear at a fixed percentage of the salary rate at that time.
- Contributions are assumed to earn investment returns of 10% per year.
- Annuities purchased at retirement are priced assuming an interest rate of 5.5% per year.
- Male survival: Makeham's law, with $A = 0.0004$, $B = 4 \times 10^{-6}$, $c = 1.13$.
- Female survival: Makeham's law, with $A = 0.0002$, $B = 10^{-6}$, $c = 1.135$.
- Members and their spouses are independent with respect to mortality.

Consider a male new entrant aged 25.

(a) Calculate the contribution rate required to meet the target replacement ratio for this member.

(b) Assume now that the contribution rate will be 5.5% of salary, and that over the member's career, his salary will actually increase by 5% per year, investment returns will be only 8% per year and the interest rate for calculating annuity values at retirement will be 4.5% per year. Calculate the actual replacement ratio for the member.

Solution 10.4 (a) First, we calculate the accumulated DC fund at retirement. Mortality is not relevant here, as in the event of the member's death, the fund is paid out anyway; the DC fund is more like a bank account than an insurance policy.

We then equate the accumulated fund with the expected present value at retirement of the pension benefits.

Suppose the initial salary rate is $\$S$. As everything is described in proportion to salary, the value assumed for S does not matter. The annual salary rate at age $x > 25$ is $S(1.04)^{x-25}$, which means that the contribution at time t, where $t = 1/12, 2/12, \ldots, 40$, is

$$\frac{c}{12} S(1.04^t)$$

where c is the contribution rate per year. Hence, the accumulated amount
of contributions at retirement is

$$\frac{cS}{12}\sum_{k=1}^{480} 1.04^{\frac{k}{12}}\, 1.1^{40-\frac{k}{12}} = cS\left(\frac{1.1^{40} - 1.04^{40}}{12\left(\left(\frac{1.1}{1.04}\right)^{\frac{1}{12}} - 1\right)}\right) = 719.6316cS.$$

The salary received in the year prior to retirement, under the assumptions, is

$$\frac{S_{64}}{S_{24.5}}\, S = 1.04^{39.5}\, S = 4.7078S.$$

Since the target replacement ratio is 65%, the target pension benefit per
year is $0.65 \times 4.7078S = 3.0601S$.

The EPV at retirement of a benefit of $3.0601S$ per year to the member,
plus a reversionary benefit of $0.6 \times 3.0601S$ per year to his wife, is

$$3.0601S\left(\ddot{a}^{(12)}_{\underset{65}{m}} + 0.6\,\ddot{a}^{(12)}_{\underset{65|61}{m\,f}}\right)$$

where the m and f scripts indicate male and female mortality, respectively.

Using the given survival models and an interest rate of 5.5% per year,
we have

$$\ddot{a}^{(12)}_{\underset{65}{m}} = 10.5222,$$

$$\ddot{a}^{(12)}_{\underset{65|61}{m\,f}} = \ddot{a}^{(12)}_{\underset{61}{f}} - \ddot{a}^{(12)}_{\underset{65:61}{m\,f}},$$

$$\ddot{a}^{(12)}_{\underset{61}{f}} = 13.9194,$$

$$\ddot{a}^{(12)}_{\underset{65:61}{m\,f}} = \sum_{k=0}^{\infty} \frac{1}{12}\, v^{\frac{k}{12}} \,_{\frac{k}{12}}p^{\underset{65+k}{m}}\,_{\frac{k}{12}}p^{\underset{61+k}{f}}$$

$$= 10.0066, \tag{10.1}$$

giving

$$\ddot{a}^{(12)}_{\underset{65|61}{m\,f}} = 3.9128.$$

Note that we can write the joint life survival probability in formula (10.1)
as the product of the single life survival probabilities using the independence assumption, as in Section 9.5.

Hence, the value of the benefit at retirement is

$$3.0601S\,(10.5222 + 0.6 \times 3.9128) = 39.3826S.$$

Equating the accumulation of contributions to age 65 with the EPV of the benefits at age 65 gives

$$c = 5.4726\% \text{ per year.}$$

(b) We now repeat the calculation, using the actual experience rather than estimates. We use an annual contribution rate of 5.5%, and solve for the amount of benefit funded by the accumulated contributions, as a proportion of the final year's salary.

The accumulated contributions at age 65 are now $28.6360S$, and the annuity values at 4.5% per year interest are

$$\ddot{a}^{(12)}_{m \atop 65} = 11.3576, \qquad \ddot{a}^{(12)}_{f \atop 61} = 15.4730, \qquad \ddot{a}^{(12)}_{m \ f \atop 65:61} = 10.7579.$$

Thus, the EPV of a benefit of X per year to the member and of $0.6X$ reversionary benefit to his spouse is $14.1867X$. Equating the accumulation of contributions to age 65 with the EPV of benefits at age 65 gives $X = 2.0185S$.

The final year salary, with 5% per year increases, is $6.8703S$. Hence, the replacement ratio is

$$R = \frac{2.0185S}{6.8703S} = 29.38\%.$$

□

We note that apparently quite small differences between the assumptions used to set the contribution and the experience can make a significant difference to the level of benefit, in terms of the pre-retirement income. This is true for both DC and DB benefits. In the DC case, the risk is taken by the member, who takes a lower benefit, relative to salary, than the target. In the DB case, the risk is usually taken by the employer, whose contributions are usually adjusted when the difference becomes apparent. If the differences are in the opposite direction, then the member benefits in the DC case, and the employer contributions may be reduced in the DB case.

10.5 The service table

The demographic elements of the basis for pension plan calculations include assumptions about survival models for members and their spouses, and about the exit patterns from employment. There are several reasons why a member might exit the plan. At early ages, the employee might withdraw to take another job with a different employer. At later ages, employees may be offered a range of ages at which they may retire with the pension that they have accumulated.

A small proportion of employees will die while in employment, and another group may leave early through disability retirement.

In a DC plan the benefit on exit is the same, regardless of the reason for the exit, so there is no need to model the member employment patterns.

In a DB plan different benefits may be payable on the different forms of exit. In the UK it is common on the death in service of a member for the pension plan to offer both a lump sum and a pension benefit for the member's surviving spouse. In North America, any lump sum benefit is more commonly funded through separate group life insurance, and so the liability does not fall on the plan. There may be a contingent spouse's benefit.

The extent to which the DB plan actuary needs to model the different exits depends on how different the values of benefits are from the values of benefits for people who do not leave until the normal retirement age.

For example, if an employer offers a generous benefit on disability (or ill health) retirement, that is worth substantially more than the benefit that the employee would have been entitled to if they had remained in good health, then it is necessary to model that exit and to value that benefit explicitly. Otherwise, the liability will be understated. On the other hand, if there is no benefit on death in service (for example, because of a separate group life arrangement), then to ignore mortality before retirement would overstate the liabilities within the pension plan.

If all the exit benefits have roughly the same value as the normal age retirement benefit, the actuary may assume that all employees survive to retirement. It is not a realistic assumption, but it simplifies the calculation and is appropriate if it does not significantly overestimate or underestimate the liabilities.

It is relatively common to ignore withdrawals in the basis, even if a large proportion of employees do withdraw, especially at younger ages. It is reasonable to ignore withdrawals if the effect on the valuation of benefits is small, compared with allowing explicitly for withdrawals. By ignoring withdrawals, we are valuing age retirement benefits for lives who withdraw, instead of valuing the withdrawal benefits. This is a reasonable shortcut if the age retirement benefits have similar value to the withdrawal benefits, which is often the case. For example, in a final salary plan, if withdrawal benefits are increased in line with inflation, the value of withdrawal and age benefits will be similar. Even if the difference is relatively large, withdrawals may be ignored. This creates an implicit margin in the valuation if withdrawal benefits are less valuable than retirement benefits, which is often the case. An additional consideration is that withdrawals are notoriously unpredictable, as they are strongly affected by economic and social factors, so that historical trends may not provide a good indicator of future exit patterns.

Figure 10.1 A multiple decrement model for a pension plan.

When the actuary does model the exits from a plan, an appropriate multiple decrement model could be similar to the one shown in Figure 10.1. All the model assumptions of Chapter 8 apply to this model, except that some age retirements will be exact age retirements, as discussed in Section 8.12.

Example 10.5 A pension plan member is entitled to a lump sum benefit on death in service of four times the salary paid in the year up to death.

Assume the appropriate multiple decrement model is as in Figure 10.1, with

$$\mu_x^{01} \equiv \mu_x^w = \begin{cases} 0.1 & \text{for } x < 35, \\ 0.05 & \text{for } 35 \leq x < 45, \\ 0.02 & \text{for } 45 \leq x < 60, \\ 0 & \text{for } x \geq 60, \end{cases}$$

$$\mu_x^{02} \equiv \mu_x^i = 0.001,$$

$$\mu_x^{03} \equiv \mu_x^r = \begin{cases} 0 & \text{for } x < 60, \\ 0.1 & \text{for } 60 < x < 65. \end{cases}$$

In addition, 30% of the members surviving in employment to age 60 retire at that time, and 100% of the lives surviving in employment to age 65 retire at that time. For transitions to state 4,

$$\mu_x^{04} \equiv \mu_x^d = A + Bc^x; \text{ with } A = 0.00022, \ B = 2.7 \times 10^{-6}, \ c = 1.124.$$

(This is the Standard Ultimate Survival Model.)

(a) For a member aged 35, calculate the probability of retiring at age 65.
(b) For each mode of exit, calculate the probability that a member currently aged 35 exits employment by that mode.

Solution 10.5 (a) Since all surviving members retire at age 65, the probability can be written $_{30}p_{35}^{00}$. To calculate this, we need to consider separately the periods before and after the jump in the withdrawal transition intensity, and before and after the exact age retirements at age 60.

For $0 < t < 10$,

$$_t p_{35}^{00} = \exp\left\{-\int_0^t \left(\mu_{35+s}^w + \mu_{35+s}^i + \mu_{35+s}^d\right) ds\right\}$$

$$= \exp\left\{-\left((A + 0.05 + 0.001)t + \frac{B}{\log c}c^{35}(c^t - 1)\right)\right\},$$

giving

$$_{10} p_{35}^{00} = 0.597342.$$

For $10 \le t < 25$,

$$_t p_{35}^{00} = {}_{10} p_{35}^{00} \exp\left\{-\int_0^{t-10} \left(\mu_{45+s}^w + \mu_{45+s}^i + \mu_{45+s}^d\right) ds\right\}$$

$$= {}_{10} p_{35}^{00} \exp\left\{-\left((A + 0.02 + 0.001)(t - 10)\right.\right.$$

$$\left.\left. + \frac{B}{\log c}c^{45}(c^{t-10} - 1)\right)\right\}$$

giving

$$_{25^-} p_{35}^{00} = 0.597342 \times 0.712105 = 0.425370.$$

At $t = 25$, 30% of the survivors retire, so at $t = 25^+$ we have

$$_{25^+} p_{35}^{00} = 0.7 \, _{25^-} p_{35}^{00} = 0.297759.$$

For $25 < t < 30$,

$$_t p_{35}^{00} = {}_{25^+} p_{35}^{00} \exp\left\{-\int_0^{t-25} \left(\mu_{60+s}^r + \mu_{60+s}^i + \mu_{60+s}^d\right) ds\right\}$$

$$= 0.297759 \exp\left\{-\left((A + 0.1 + 0.001)(t - 25)\right.\right.$$

$$\left.\left. + \frac{B}{\log c}c^{60}(c^{t-25} - 1)\right)\right\}$$

giving

$$_{30^-} p_{35}^{00} = 0.297759 \times 0.590675 = 0.175879.$$

The probability of retirement at exact age 65 is then 0.1759.

(b) We know that all members leave employment by or at age 65.

All withdrawals occur by age 60. To compute the probability of withdrawal, we split the period into before and after the change in the withdrawal force at age 45.

The probability of withdrawal by age 45 is

$$_{10}p_{35}^{01} = \int_0^{10} {}_t p_{35}^{00}\, \mu_{35+t}^w\, dt = 0.05 \int_0^{10} {}_t p_{35}^{00}\, dt$$

which we can calculate using numerical integration to give

$$_{10}p_{35}^{01} = 0.05 \times 7.8168 = 0.3908.$$

The probability of withdrawal between ages 45 and 60 is

$$_{10}p_{35}^{00}\, {}_{15}p_{45}^{01} = 0.597342 \int_0^{15} {}_t p_{45}^{00}\, \mu_{45+t}^w\, dt$$

$$= 0.597342 \times 0.02 \int_0^{15} {}_t p_{45}^{00}\, dt$$

which, again using numerical integration, gives

$$_{10}p_{35}^{00}\, {}_{15}p_{45}^{01} = 0.597342 \times 0.02 \times 12.7560 = 0.1524.$$

So, the total probability of withdrawal is 0.5432.

We calculate the probability of disability retirement similarly. The probability of disability retirement by age 45 is

$$_{10}p_{35}^{02} = \int_0^{10} {}_t p_{35}^{00}\, \mu_{35+t}^i\, dt = 0.001 \int_0^{10} {}_t p_{35}^{00}\, dt$$

$$= 0.001 \times 7.8168 = 0.0078,$$

and the probability of disability retirement between ages 45 and 60 is

$$_{10}p_{35}^{00}\, {}_{15}p_{45}^{02} = 0.597342 \int_0^{15} {}_t p_{45}^{00}\, \mu_{45+t}^i\, dt$$

$$= 0.597342 \times 0.001 \int_0^{15} {}_t p_{45}^{00}\, dt$$

$$= 0.597342 \times 0.001 \times 12.7560 = 0.0076.$$

The probability of disability retirement in the final five years is

$$_{25+}p_{35}^{00}\, {}_5 p_{60}^{02} = 0.297759 \int_0^5 {}_t p_{60}^{00}\, \mu_{60+t}^i\, dt$$

$$= 0.297759 \times 0.001 \times 3.8911$$

$$= 0.0012.$$

So, the total probability of disability retirement is $0.0078 + 0.0076 + 0.0012 = 0.0166$.

The probability of age retirement is the sum of the probabilities of exact age retirements and retirements between ages 60 and 65.

The probability of exact age 60 retirement is

$$0.3 \,{}_{25^-}p_{35} = 0.1276,$$

and the probability of exact age 65 retirement is

$${}_{30^-}p_{35} = 0.1759.$$

The probability of retirement between exact ages 60 and 65 is

$$
\begin{aligned}
{}_{25^+}p_{35}^{00} \,{}_5p_{60}^{03} = 0.297759 \int_0^5 {}_tp_{60}^{00} \, \mu_{60+t}^r \, dt \\
= 0.297759 \times 0.1 \times 3.8911 \\
= 0.1159.
\end{aligned}
$$

So, the total age retirement probability is 0.4194.

We could infer the death in service probability, by the law of total probability, but we instead calculate it directly as a check on the other results. We use numerical integration for all these calculations.

The probability of death in the first 10 years is

$${}_{10}p_{35}^{04} = \int_0^{10} {}_tp_{35}^{00} \, \mu_{35+t}^d \, dt = 0.0040,$$

and the probability of death in the next 15 years is

$${}_{10}p_{35}^{00} \,{}_{15}p_{45}^{04} = 0.59734 \int_0^{15} {}_tp_{45}^{00} \, \mu_{45+t}^d \, dt = 0.0120.$$

The probability of death in the final five years is

$$
\begin{aligned}
{}_{25^+}p_{35}^{00} \,{}_5p_{60}^{04} = 0.297759 \int_0^5 {}_tp_{60}^{00} \, \mu_{60+t}^r \, dt \\
= 0.297759 \times 0.016323 \\
= 0.0049.
\end{aligned}
$$

So the total death in service probability is 0.0208.

We can check our calculations by summing the probabilities of exiting by each mode. This gives a total of 1 (= 0.5432 + 0.0166 + 0.4194 + 0.0208), as it should. □

Often the multiple decrement model is summarized in tabular form at integer ages, in the same way that a life table summarizes a survival model. Such a summary is called a pension plan **service table**. We start at some minimum integer entry age, x_0, by defining an arbitrary radix, for example, $l_{x_0} = 1\,000\,000$. Using the model of Figure 10.1, we then define for integer ages $x_0 + k$ $(k = 0, 1, \ldots)$

$$w_{x_0+k} = l_{x_0}\, {}_k p_{x_0}^{00}\, p_{x_0+k}^{01},$$

$$i_{x_0+k} = l_{x_0}\, {}_k p_{x_0}^{00}\, p_{x_0+k}^{02},$$

$$r_{x_0+k} = l_{x_0}\, {}_k p_{x_0}^{00}\, p_{x_0+k}^{03},$$

$$d_{x_0+k} = l_{x_0}\, {}_k p_{x_0}^{00}\, p_{x_0+k}^{04},$$

$$l_{x_0+k} = l_{x_0}\, {}_k p_{x_0}^{00}.$$

Since the probability that a member aged x_0 withdraws between ages $x_0 + k$ and $x_0 + k + 1$ is ${}_k p_{x_0}^{00}\, p_{x_0+k}^{01}$, we can interpret w_{x_0+k} as the number of members expected to withdraw between ages $x_0 + k$ and $x_0 + k + 1$ out of l_{x_0} members aged exactly x_0; i_{x_0+k}, r_{x_0+k} and d_{x_0+k} can be interpreted similarly. We can interpret l_{x_0+k} as the expected number of lives who are still plan members at age $x_0 + k$ out of l_{x_0} members aged exactly x_0. We can extend these interpretations to say that for any integer ages x and y $(>x)$, w_y is the number of members expected to withdraw between ages y and $y + 1$ out of l_x members aged exactly x and l_y is the expected number of members at age y out of l_x members aged exactly x. These interpretations are precisely in line with those for a life table – see Section 3.2.

Note that, using the law of total probability, we have the following identity for any integer age $x > x_0$

$$l_x = l_{x-1} - w_{x-1} - i_{x-1} - r_{x-1} - d_{x-1}. \tag{10.2}$$

A service table summarizing the model in Example 10.5 is shown in Table 10.2 from age 20 with the radix $l_{20} = 1\,000\,000$. This service table has been constructed by calculating, for each integer age x (>20), w_x, i_x, r_x and d_x as described above. The value of l_x shown in the table is then calculated recursively from age 20. The table is internally consistent in the sense that identity (10.2) holds for each row of the table. However, this does not appear to be the case in Table 10.2 because all values have been rounded to the nearer integer. The exact age exits at ages 60 and 65 are shown in the rows labelled 60^- and 65^-. In all subsequent calculations based on Table 10.2, we use the exact values rather than the rounded ones.

We use the model underlying this service table for several examples and exercises. For convenience, the service table is also available in Appendix D, as Table D.4.

Having constructed a service table, the calculation of the probability of any event between integer ages can be performed relatively simply. To see this,

Table 10.2 *Pension plan service table.*

x	l_x	w_x	i_x	r_x	d_x	x	l_x	w_x	i_x	r_x	d_x
20	1 000 000	95 104	951	0	237	44	137 656	6 708	134	0	95
21	903 707	85 946	859	0	218	45	130 719	2 586	129	0	100
22	816 684	77 670	777	0	200	46	127 904	2 530	127	0	106
23	738 038	70 190	702	0	184	47	125 140	2 476	124	0	113
24	666 962	63 430	634	0	170	48	122 428	2 422	121	0	121
25	602 728	57 321	573	0	157	49	119 763	2 369	118	0	130
26	544 677	51 800	518	0	145	50	117 145	2 317	116	0	140
27	492 213	46 811	468	0	134	51	114 572	2 266	113	0	151
28	444 800	42 301	423	0	125	52	112 042	2 216	111	0	163
29	401 951	38 226	382	0	117	53	109 553	2 166	108	0	176
30	363 226	34 543	345	0	109	54	107 102	2 118	106	0	190
31	328 228	31 215	312	0	102	55	104 688	2 070	103	0	206
32	296 599	28 207	282	0	96	56	102 308	2 023	101	0	224
33	268 014	25 488	255	0	91	57	99 960	1 976	99	0	243
34	242 181	23 031	230	0	86	58	97 642	1 930	96	0	264
35	218 834	10 665	213	0	83	59	95 351	1 884	94	0	288
36	207 872	10 131	203	0	84	60^-	93 085	0	0	27 926	0
37	197 455	9 623	192	0	84	60^+	65 160	0	62	6 188	210
38	187 555	9 141	183	0	85	61	58 700	0	56	5 573	212
39	178 147	8 682	174	0	86	62	52 860	0	50	5 018	213
40	169 206	8 246	165	0	87	63	47 579	0	45	4 515	214
41	160 708	7 832	157	0	89	64	42 805	0	41	4 061	215
42	152 631	7 438	149	0	90	65^-	38 488	0	0	38 488	0
43	144 954	7 064	141	0	93						

consider the calculations required for Example 10.5. For part (a), the probability that a member aged 35 survives in service to age 65, calculated using Table 10.2, is

$$\frac{l_{65}}{l_{35}} = \frac{38\,488}{218\,834} = 0.1759.$$

For part (b), the probability that a member aged 35 withdraws is

$$(w_{35} + w_{36} + \cdots + w_{59})/l_{35}$$
$$= \frac{10\,665 + 10\,131 + \cdots + 1\,930 + 1\,884}{218\,834} = 0.5432.$$

The probability that the member retires in ill health is

$$(i_{35} + i_{36} + \cdots + i_{64})/l_{35} = \frac{213 + 203 + \cdots + 45 + 41}{218\,834} = 0.0166.$$

The probability that the member retires on age grounds is

$$(r_{35} + r_{36} + \cdots + r_{65})/l_{35}$$
$$= \frac{27\,926 + 6\,188 + 5\,573 + 5\,018 + 4\,515 + 4\,061 + 38\,488}{218\,834} = 0.4194.$$

The probability that the member dies in service is

$$(d_{35} + d_{36} + \cdots + d_{64})/l_{35} = \frac{83 + 84 + \cdots + 214 + 215}{218\,834} = 0.0208.$$

Example 10.6 Employees in a pension plan pay contributions of 6% of their previous month's salary at each month end. Calculate the EPV at entry of contributions for a new entrant aged 35, with a starting salary rate of $100\,000$, using

(a) exact calculation using the multiple decrement model specified in Example 10.5, and
(b) the values in Table 10.2, adjusting the EPV of an annuity payable annually in the same way as under the UDD assumption in Chapter 5.

Other assumptions:

- Salary rate function: Salaries increase at 4% per year continuously;
- Interest: 6% per year effective.

Solution 10.6 (a) The EPV is

$$\frac{0.06 \times 100\,000}{12} \left(\sum_{k=1}^{299} {}_{\frac{k}{12}} p_{35}^{00} (1.04)^{\frac{k}{12}} v^{\frac{k}{12}} + {}_{25^-} p_{35}^{00} (1.04)^{25} v^{25} \right.$$

$$\left. + \sum_{k=301}^{360} {}_{\frac{k}{12}} p_{35}^{00} (1.04)^{\frac{k}{12}} v^{\frac{k}{12}} \right)$$

$$= \frac{0.06 \times 100\,000}{12} \left(\sum_{k=1}^{299} {}_{\frac{k}{12}} p_{35}^{00} v_j^{\frac{k}{12}} + {}_{25^-} p_{35}^{00} v_j^{25} + \sum_{k=301}^{360} {}_{\frac{k}{12}} p_{35}^{00} v_j^{\frac{k}{12}} \right)$$

$$= 6\,000 \times 13.3529 = \$80\,117$$

where $j = 0.02/1.04 = 0.01923$ and where we have separated out the term relating to age 60 to emphasize the point that contributions would be paid by all employees reaching ages 60 and 65, even those who retire at those ages.

(b) Recall from Chapter 5 that the UDD approximation to the EPV of a term annuity payable monthly in arrear $a_{x:\overline{n}|}^{(12)}$, in terms of the corresponding value for annual payments in advance, $\ddot{a}_{x:\overline{n}|}$, is

$$a_{x:\overline{n}|}^{(12)} \approx \alpha(12)\, \ddot{a}_{x:\overline{n}|} - \left(\beta(12) + \frac{1}{12} \right)(1 - v^n\, {}_n p_x).$$

This approximation will work for the monthly multiple decrement annuity, which we will denote $a_{x:\overline{n}|}^{00(12)}$, provided that the decrements, in total, are approximately UDD. This is **not** the case for our service table, because between ages 60^- and 61, the vast majority of decrements occur at exact age 60. We can take account of this by splitting the annuity into two parts, up to age 60^- and from age 60^+, and applying a UDD-style adjustment to each part as follows:

$$a^{00(12)}_{35:\overline{30|}} = a^{00(12)}_{35:\overline{25|}} + \frac{l_{60^+}}{l_{35}} v_j^{25} a^{00(12)}_{60^+:\overline{5|}}$$

$$\approx \alpha(12)\, \ddot{a}^{00}_{35:\overline{25|}} - \left(\beta(12) + \frac{1}{12}\right)\left(1 - \frac{l_{60^-}}{l_{35}} v_j^{25}\right)$$

$$+ \frac{l_{60^+}}{l_{35}} v_j^{25}\left(\alpha(12)\, \ddot{a}^{00}_{60^+:\overline{5|}} - \left(\beta(12) + \frac{1}{12}\right)\left(1 - \frac{l_{65^-}}{l_{60^+}} v_j^5\right)\right).$$

As $\ddot{a}^{00}_{35:\overline{25|}} = 13.0693$ and $\ddot{a}^{00}_{60^+:\overline{5|}} = 3.9631$ we find that

$$6\,000\, a^{00(12)}_{35:\overline{30|}} \approx \$80\,131.$$

$\square$

Using the service table and the UDD-based approximation has resulted in a relative error of the order of 0.03% in this example. This demonstrates again that the service table summarizes the underlying multiple decrement model sufficiently accurately for practical purposes.

In applying the UDD adjustment we are effectively saying that the arguments we applied to deaths in Chapter 5 can be applied to total decrements. However, just as in Section 8.9, if we were to assume a uniform distribution of decrements in each of the related single decrement models, we would find that there is not a uniform distribution of the overall decrements. Nevertheless, the assumption of a uniform distribution of total decrements provides a useful, and relatively accurate, means of calculating the EPV of an annuity payable m times a year from a service table.

It is very common in pension plan valuation to use approximations, primarily because of the long-term nature of the liabilities and the huge uncertainty in the parameters of the models used. To calculate values with great accuracy when there is so much uncertainty involved would be spurious. While this argument is valid, one needs to ensure that the approximation methods do not introduce potentially significant biases in the final results, for example, by systematically underestimating the value of liabilities.

10.6 Valuation of benefits

10.6.1 Final salary plans

In a DB final salary pension plan, the basic annual age retirement pension benefit is equal to

$$n\, S_{\text{Fin}}\, \alpha$$

where

n is the total number of years of service,

S_{Fin} is the average salary in a specified period before retirement; for example, in the three years preceding exit, and

α is the **accrual rate**, typically between 0.01 and 0.02. For an employee who has been a member of the plan all her working life, say $n = 40$ years, this typically gives a replacement ratio in the range 40–80%.

We interpret this benefit formula to mean that the employee earns a pension of $100\alpha\%$ of final average salary for each year of employment.

Consider a member who is currently aged y, who joined the pension plan at age x ($\leq y$) and for whom the normal retirement age is 60. Our estimate of her annual pension at retirement is

$$(60 - x)\, \hat{S}_{\text{Fin}}\, \alpha$$

where $\hat{S}_{\text{Fin}}$ is the current estimate of S_{Fin}. This estimate is calculated using her current salary and an appropriate salary scale. We can split this annual amount into two parts

$$(60 - x)\, \hat{S}_{\text{Fin}}\, \alpha = (y - x)\, \hat{S}_{\text{Fin}}\, \alpha + (60 - y)\, \hat{S}_{\text{Fin}}\, \alpha.$$

The first part is related to her past service, and is called the **accrued benefit**. The second part is related to future service. Note that both parts use an estimate of the final average salary at retirement, $\hat{S}_{\text{Fin}}$.

The employer who sponsors the pension plan retains the right to stop offering pension benefits in the future. If this were to happen, the final benefit would be based on the member's past service at the wind-up of the pension plan; in this sense, the accrued benefits (also known as the past service benefits) are already secured. The future service benefits are more of a statement of intent, but do not have the contractual nature of the accrued benefits.

In valuing the plan liabilities then, modern valuation approaches often consider only the accrued benefits, even when the plan is valued as a going concern.

Example 10.7 The pension plan in Example 10.5 offers an age retirement pension of 1.5% of final average salary for each year of service, where final average salary is defined as the earnings in the three years before retirement.

Use Table 10.2 to estimate the EPV of the accrued age retirement pension for a member aged 55 with 20 years of service, whose salary in the year prior to the valuation date was $50 000.

The pension benefit is paid monthly in advance for life, with no spouse's benefit.

Other assumptions:

- Salary scale: From Table 10.1;
- Post-retirement survival: Standard Ultimate Survival Model, Appendix D;
- Interest: 5% per year effective.

Solution 10.7 Age retirement can take place at exact age 60, at exact age 65, or at any age in between. We assume that mid-year age retirements (the retirements that do not occur at exact age 60 or 65) that are assumed to occur between ages x and $x + 1$ ($x = 60, 61, \ldots, 64$) take place at age $x + 0.5$ exact. This is a common assumption in pensions calculation and is a similar approach to the claims acceleration approach for continuous benefits in Section 4.5. The assumption considerably simplifies calculations for complex benefits, as it converts a continuous model for exits into a discrete model, more suitable for efficient spreadsheet calculation, and the inaccuracy introduced is generally small.

Suppose retirement takes place at age y. Then the projected final average salary is

$$\hat{S}_{\text{fin}} = 50\,000 \, \frac{z_y}{s_{54}}$$

where

$$z_y = (s_{y-3} + s_{y-2} + s_{y-1})/3$$

and where we use the values in Table 10.1 and linear interpolation to calculate, for example, $s_{58.5}$. The function z_y is the averaging function for the salary scale to give the final average salary, so that if we multiply the salary in the year of age x to $x + 1$ by z_y/s_x we get the final average salary on exit at exact age y.

If the member retires at exact age 60, the accrued benefit, based on 20 years' past service and an accrual rate of 1.5%, is a pension payable monthly in advance from age 60 of annual amount

$$50\,000 \, \frac{z_{60}}{s_{54}} \times 20 \times 0.015 = \$15\,922.79.$$

To value this we need to use life annuity values from the age at exit. The annuity values used below have been calculated accurately, but interpolating values from Table D.3 with a UDD adjustment gives similar results.

The EPV of the accrued age retirement pension is then

$$
50\,000 \times 0.015 \times 20 \left(\frac{r_{60^-}}{l_{55}} \frac{z_{60}}{s_{54}} v^5 \ddot{a}_{60}^{(12)} + \frac{r_{60^+}}{l_{55}} \frac{z_{60.5}}{s_{54}} v^{5.5} \ddot{a}_{60.5}^{(12)} \right.
$$

$$
\left. + \frac{r_{61}}{l_{55}} \frac{z_{61.5}}{s_{54}} v^{6.5} \ddot{a}_{61.5}^{(12)} + \cdots + \frac{r_{64}}{l_{55}} \frac{z_{64.5}}{s_{54}} v^{9.5} \ddot{a}_{64.5}^{(12)} + \frac{r_{65^-}}{l_{55}} \frac{z_{65}}{s_{54}} v^{10} \ddot{a}_{65}^{(12)} \right)
$$

$$
= \$137\,508.
$$

This type of repetitive calculation is ideally suited to spreadsheet software.
□

Withdrawal pension

When an employee leaves employment before being eligible to take an immediate pension, the usual benefit (subject to some minimum period of employment) in a DB plan is a deferred pension. The benefit would be based on the same formula as the retirement pension, that is, Accrual Rate × Service × Final Average Salary, but would not be paid until the member attains the normal retirement age. Note that Final Average Salary here is based on earnings in the years immediately preceding withdrawal.

The deferred period could be very long, perhaps 35 years for an employee who changes jobs at age 30. If the deferred benefit is not increased during the deferred period, then inflation, even at relatively low levels, will have a significant effect on the purchasing power of the pension. In some plans the withdrawal benefit is adjusted through the deferred period to make some, possibly partial, allowance for inflation. Such adjustments are called **cost of living adjustments**, or COLAs. In the UK, some inflation adjustment is mandatory. Some plans outside the UK do not guarantee any COLA but apply increases on a discretionary basis.

Example 10.8 A final salary pension plan offers an accrual rate of 2%, and the normal retirement age is 65. Final average salary is the average salary in the three years before retirement or withdrawal. Pensions are paid monthly in advance for life from age 65, with no spouse's benefit, and are guaranteed for five years.

(a) Estimate the EPV of the accrued withdrawal pension for a life now aged 35 with 10 years of service whose salary in the past year was $100\,000

  (i) with no COLA, and
  (ii) with a COLA in deferment of 3% per year.

(b) On death during deferment, a lump sum benefit of five times the accrued annual pension, with a COLA of 3% per year, is paid immediately. Estimate the EPV of this benefit.

Basis:

- Service table: From Table D.4
- Salary scale: From Table 10.1
- Post-withdrawal survival: Standard Ultimate Survival Model
- Interest: 5% per year effective.

Solution 10.8 According to our service table assumptions, the member can withdraw at any age up to 60. There are no 'exact age' withdrawals, unlike age retirements, so if the member withdraws between ages x and $x + 1$ ($x = 35, 36, \ldots, 59$) we assume that withdrawal takes place at age $x + 0.5$.

Since the deferred pension is based on final average salary, which is defined as the average annual salary in the three years before withdrawal, we define

$$z_y = (s_{y-3} + s_{y-2} + s_{y-1})/3$$

as we did in Example 10.7.

(a) The guaranteed annuity EPV factor at age 65 is $\ddot{a}^{(12)}_{\overline{65:5|}}$, which can be evaluated as follows

$$\ddot{a}^{(12)}_{\overline{65:5|}} = \ddot{a}^{(12)}_{\overline{5|}} + {}_5p_{65}\, v^5\, \ddot{a}^{(12)}_{70}$$
$$= 4.4459 + 0.75455 \times 11.5451$$
$$= 13.1573$$

where the annuity function and the survival probability are calculated using the Standard Ultimate Survival Model, from Appendix D.

(i) If the member withdraws between integer ages $35 + t$ and $35 + t + 1$, the accrued withdrawal pension, with no COLA, payable from age 65, is estimated to be

$$100\,000 \times \frac{z_{35+t+0.5}}{s_{34}} \times 10 \times 0.02.$$

The EPV of this at age 65 is

$$100\,000 \times \frac{z_{35+t+0.5}}{s_{34}} \times 10 \times 0.02 \times \ddot{a}^{(12)}_{\overline{65:5|}}$$

and the EPV at age $35 + t + 0.5$ is

$$100\,000 \times \frac{z_{35+t+0.5}}{s_{34}} \times 10 \times 0.02\, \ddot{a}^{(12)}_{\overline{65:5|}}\, ({}_{29.5-t}p_{35+t+0.5})\, v^{29.5-t}$$

where the ${}_tp_x$ factor is for survival only, not for the multiple decrement, as we are applying it to a life who has just withdrawn.

The probability that the member withdraws between integer ages $35 + t$ and $35 + t + 1$ is w_{35+t}/l_{35}. Applying this probability and the discount factor $v^{t+0.5}$ we obtain the EPV at age 35 of the accrued withdrawal benefit as

$$\frac{100\,000 \times 10 \times 0.02}{l_{35}\,s_{34}} \sum_{t=0}^{24} w_{35+t}\, z_{35+t+0.5}\, \ddot{a}_{\overline{65:5}}^{(12)}\, (29.5-t\,p_{35+t+0.5})\, v^{30}$$

which is \$48 246.

(ii) To allow for a COLA at 3% per year during deferment, the above formula for the EPV of the accrued withdrawal benefit must be adjusted by including a term $1.03^{29.5-t}$, so that it becomes

$$\frac{100\,000 \times 10 \times 0.02}{l_{35}\,s_{34}} \sum_{t=0}^{24} w_{35+t}\, z_{35+t+0.5}\, 1.03^{29.5-t}\, \ddot{a}_{\overline{65:5}}^{(12)}$$

$$\times\, (29.5-t\,p_{35+t+0.5})\, v^{30}$$

which is \$88 853.

(b) Suppose the member withdraws between integer ages $35+t$ and $35+t+1$; the probability that this happens is w_{35+t}/l_{35}. The estimated initial annual accrued pension is

$$0.02 \times 10 \times 100\,000\, \frac{z_{35+t+0.5}}{s_{34}}$$

and the sum insured on death before age 65 is five times this annual amount increased by the COLA. Hence the EPV of the benefit on death after withdrawal is

$$\sum_{t=0}^{24} 5 \times 0.02 \times 10 \times 100\,000\, v^{t+0.5}\, \frac{z_{35+t+0.5}}{s_{34}}\, \frac{w_{35+t}}{l_{35}}$$

$$\times\, \bar{A}^{\,1}_{35+t+0.5:\,\overline{65-(35+t+0.5)}\,|\,j}$$

$$= 5 \times 0.02 \times 10 \times 100\,000 \times 0.01813$$

$$= \$1813$$

where the subscript j indicates that the rate of interest used to calculate the term insurances is $j = 0.02/1.03$. $\square$

Throughout this section, we have assumed that the accrued benefit allows fully for future salary increases. However, as for the future service benefit, future salary increases are not guaranteed and there is a case for omitting them from the accrued liabilities. When a salary increase is actually declared, then it would be brought into the liability valuation.

The approach which uses salaries projected to the exit date is called the **projected unit** method. Valuing the accrued benefits with no allowance for future salary increases is the **traditional unit** or **current unit** approach. Each has its adherents.

To adapt the methodology above to the current unit approach, the z_{x+t}/s_x factors would be replaced by z_x/s_x in the valuation formulae, or by the actual average pensionable earnings at valuation. That is, if the pension calculation uses the average of three year earnings to retirement, the current unit valuation could use the average of the three year earnings to the valuation date. This would need to be adjusted for a member with less than three years' service. For simplicity, the valuation in a current unit approach may use the current salary at valuation.

10.6.2 Career average earnings plans

Under a career average earnings (CAE) defined benefit pension plan, the benefit formula is based on the average salary during the period of pension plan membership, rather than the final average salary. Suppose a plan member retires at age xr with n years of service and total pensionable earnings during their service of $(\text{TPE})_{xr}$. Then their career average earnings are $(\text{TPE})_{xr}/n$. So a CAE plan with an accrual rate of α would provide a pension benefit on retirement at age xr, for a member with n years of service, of

$$\alpha\, n\, \frac{(\text{TPE})_{xr}}{n} = \alpha\,(\text{TPE})_{xr}.$$

Under a career average earnings plan, the accrued, or past service, benefit that we value at age x is $\alpha\,(\text{TPE})_x$, where $(\text{TPE})_x$ denotes the total pensionable earnings up to age x. The methods available for valuing such benefits are the same as for a final salary benefit.

A popular variation of the career average earnings plan is the career average revalued earnings plan, in which an inflation adjustment of the salary is made before averaging. The accrual principle is the same. The accrued benefit is based on the total past earnings after the revaluation calculation.

Example 10.9 A pension plan offers a retirement benefit of 4% of career average earnings for each year of service. The pension benefit is paid monthly in advance for life, guaranteed for five years, with no spousal benefit. On withdrawal, a deferred pension is payable from age 65. The multiple decrement model in Example 10.5 is appropriate for this pension plan, including the assumption that members can retire at exact age 60 and at exact age 65.

Consider a member now aged 35 who has 10 years of service, with total past earnings of \$525 000.

(a) Write down an integral formula for an accurate calculation of the EPV of his accrued age and withdrawal benefits.

(b) Use Table 10.2 to estimate the EPV of his accrued age and withdrawal benefits.

Other assumptions:

Post-retirement/withdrawal survival: Standard Ultimate Survival Model;
Interest: 5% per year effective.

Solution 10.9 (a) The EPV of the accrued age retirement benefit is

$$0.04 \, (TPE)_{35} \left(\int_0^{25^-} {}_t p_{35}^{00} \, \mu_{35+t}^{03} \, v^t \, \ddot{a}_{\overline{35+t:5|}}^{(12)} \, dt + 0.3 \, {}_{25} p_{35}^{00} v^{25} \ddot{a}_{\overline{60:5|}}^{(12)} \right.$$

$$\left. + \int_{25^+}^{30^-} {}_t p_{35}^{00} \, \mu_{35+t}^{03} \, v^t \, \ddot{a}_{\overline{35+t:5|}}^{(12)} \, dt + {}_{30} p_{35}^{00} v^{30} \ddot{a}_{\overline{65:5|}}^{(12)} \right)$$

where the second and fourth terms allow for the exact age retirements.
The EPV of the accrued withdrawal benefit is

$$0.04 \, (TPE)_{35} \, v^{30} \, \ddot{a}_{\overline{65:5|}}^{(12)} \int_0^{30} {}_t p_{35}^{00} \, \mu_{35+t}^{01} \, {}_{30-t} p_{35+t} \, dt$$

where the survival probability ${}_{30-t} p_{35+t}$ is calculated using a mortality assumption appropriate for members who have withdrawn.

(b) The EPV of the accrued age retirement benefit is estimated as

$$\frac{0.04 \, (TPE)_{35}}{l_{35}} \left(r_{60^-} \, v^{25} \, \ddot{a}_{\overline{60:5|}}^{(12)} + r_{60^+} \, v^{25.5} \, \ddot{a}_{\overline{60.5:5|}}^{(12)} + r_{61} \, v^{26.5} \, \ddot{a}_{\overline{61.5:5|}}^{(12)} + \cdots \right.$$

$$\left. + r_{64} \, v^{29.5} \, \ddot{a}_{\overline{65.5:5|}}^{(12)} + r_{65} \, v^{30} \, \ddot{a}_{\overline{65:5|}}^{(12)} \right)$$

$$= \$31\,666.$$

Note the exact age retirement terms for ages 60 and 65.
The EPV of the accrued withdrawal benefit is

$$\frac{0.04 \, (TPE)_{35} \, v^{30} \, \ddot{a}_{\overline{65:5|}}^{(12)}}{l_{35}} \left(w_{35}(_{29.5}p_{35.5}) + w_{36}(_{28.5}p_{36.5}) + \cdots \right.$$

$$\left. + w_{59}(_{5.5}p_{59.5}) \right)$$

$$= \$33\,173.$$

□

10.7 Funding the benefits

In a typical DB pension plan the employee pays a fixed contribution, and the balance of the cost of the employee benefits is funded by the employer. The employer's contribution is set at the regular actuarial valuations, and is expressed as a percentage of salary.

With an insurance policy, the policyholder pays for a contract typically through a level, regular premium or a single premium. The nature of the pension plan is that there is no need for the funding to be constant, as contributions can be adjusted from time to time. The level of contribution from the employer is not usually a part of the contract, the way that the premium is specified in the insurance contract. Nevertheless, because the employer will have an interest in smoothing its contributions, there is some incentive for the funding to be reasonably smooth and predictable.

We assume that the benefit valuation approach from the previous section is used to establish a **reserve** level at the start of the year. The reserve refers to the assets set aside to meet the accrued liabilities as they fall due in the future. So, the reserve at time t, say, is the sum of the EPVs of all the accrued benefits at that time, taking into consideration all the appropriate benefits. We denote this reserve $_t V$. It is also called the **actuarial liability**.

We then set the funding level for the year to be the amount required to be paid such that, together with the fund value at the start of the year, the assets are exactly sufficient to pay the expected cost of any benefits due during the year, and to pay the expected cost of establishing the new actuarial liability at the year end.

We assume that (i) all employer contributions are paid at the start of the year, (ii) there are no employee contributions, and (iii) any benefits payable during the year are paid exactly half-way through the year. These are simplifying assumptions that make the development of the principles and formulae clearer, but they can be relaxed quite easily. With these assumptions, the **normal contribution** due at the start of the year t to $t + 1$ for a member aged x at time t, denoted C_t, is found from

$$_t V + C_t = \text{EPV of benefits for mid-year exits} + v \, _1 p_x^{00} \, _{t+1}V, \qquad (10.3)$$

that is

$$C_t = v \, _1 p_x^{00} \, _{t+1} V + \text{EPV of benefits for mid-year exits} - _t V.$$

By *EPV of benefits for mid-year exits* we mean the EPV at the start of the year of benefits that would be payable given that the life exits during the year, multiplied by the probability of exit during the year.

The funding equation (10.3) is interpreted as follows: the start of year actuarial liability plus normal contributions must be sufficient, on average, to pay for the benefits if the member exits during the following year, or to fund the value of the actuarial liability at the year end if the member remains in employment. The ideas, which are similar to those developed when we discussed policy values in Section 7.3.3, are demonstrated in the following example.

Example 10.10 A member aged 50 has 20 years past service. His salary in the year to valuation was $50 000. Calculate the value of his accrued pension benefit and the normal contribution due at the start of the year assuming (a) projected unit credit (PUC) funding, and (b) traditional unit credit (TUC) funding, assuming valuation uses 'final pensionable earnings' at the valuation date

You are given the pension plan information and valuation assumptions below.

- Accrual rate: 1.5%
- Final salary plan
- Pension based on earnings in the year before age retirement
- Normal retirement age 65
- The pension benefit is a life annuity payable monthly in advance
- There is no benefit due on death in service.

Assumptions:

- No exits other than by death before normal retirement age;
- Interest rate: 5% per year effective;
- Salaries increase at 4% per year (projected unit credit);
- Mortality before and after retirement follows the Standard Ultimate Survival Model.

Solution 10.10 (a) Using the projected unit credit approach, the funding and valuation are based on projected final average earnings, so

$$S_{\text{Fin}} = 50\,000 s_{64}/s_{49} = 50\,000(1.04)^{15} = 90\,047.$$

The actuarial liability is the value at the start of the year of the accrued benefits, which is

$$_0V = 0.015 \times 20 \times S_{\text{Fin}} \times {}_{15}p_{50} \times v^{15} \times \ddot{a}_{65}^{(12)} = 163\,161.$$

(Note that $\ddot{a}_{65}^{(12)} = 13.0870$.)

The value at the start of the following year of the accrued benefits, assuming the member is still alive, is

$$_1V = 0.015 \times 21 \times S_{\text{Fin}} \times {}_{14}p_{51} \times v^{14} \times \ddot{a}_{65}^{(12)}$$

and we take the value at time 0 of this liability,

$$v\,p_{50}\,{}_1V = 0.015 \times 21 \times S_{\text{Fin}} \times {}_{15}p_{50} \times v^{15} \times \ddot{a}_{65}^{(12)} = \frac{21}{20}\,{}_0V.$$

In this example there are no benefits payable on mid-year exit, so the funding equation is

$$_0V + C = \frac{21}{20}\,{}_0V$$

which gives

$$C = \frac{{}_0V}{20} = 8158$$

or 16.3% of salary in the previous year.

This contribution formula can be explained intuitively: the normal contribution in the year of age x to $x + 1$ must be sufficient to fund one extra year of accrual, on average.

(b) Using the traditional unit credit approach, the valuation at time t is based on the final average earnings at time t. At the start of the year, the salary for valuation is $50\,000$; at the year end the projected salary is $50\,000 \times 1.04 = \$52\,000$. Let S_x denote the salary earned (or projected) in the year of age x to $x + 1$. Then

$$_0V = 0.015 \times 20 \times S_{49} \times {}_{15}p_{50} \times v^{15} \times \ddot{a}_{65}^{(12)}$$

and

$$_1V = 0.015 \times 21 \times S_{50} \times {}_{14}p_{51} \times v^{14} \times \ddot{a}_{65}^{(12)}.$$

So

$$v\, p_{50}\, {}_1V = 0.015 \times 21 \times S_{50} \times {}_{15}p_{50} \times v^{15} \times \ddot{a}_{65}^{(12)} = {}_0V \frac{21\, S_{50}}{20\, S_{49}}.$$

Hence

$$C = {}_0V \left(\frac{21\, S_{50}}{20\, S_{49}} - 1 \right) = 8\,335$$

or 16.7% of the previous year's salary.

We can decompose the normal contribution here as

$$C = {}_0V \left(\frac{S_{50}}{S_{49}} - 1 \right) + {}_0V \frac{S_{50}}{S_{49}} \frac{1}{20}.$$

The first term represents the contribution required to adjust the previous valuation for the increase in salary over the year, and the second term represents the contribution required for the extra year's accrual. The first term is required here because the TUC valuation does not allow for future salary increases, so they must be funded year by year, through the contributions, as the salaries increase each year. □

Note that in this example the normal contributions are similar, though the valuation liability under the TUC approach is rather less than that under the

PUC approach. In fact, under both funding approaches the contribution rate tends to increase as the member acquires more service, and gets closer to retirement. The TUC contribution starts rather smaller than the PUC contribution, and rises more steeply, ending at considerably more than the PUC contribution. Ultimately, if all the assumptions in the basis are realized, both methods generate exactly the same amount at the normal retirement age for surviving members, specifically $0.015 \times 35 \times S_{\text{Fin}} \times \ddot{a}_{65}^{(12)}$, which is exactly enough to fund the retirement benefit at that time.

In the example above, we showed how the PUC and TUC funding plans allow for the normal contribution to fund the extra year of accrual (and the salary increase, in the TUC case). The situation is slightly more complicated when there are benefits payable on exit during the year, as discussed in the next example. However, if the employee leaves before the year end, then the normal contribution only has to fund the additional accrual up to exit. We typically assume that mid-year exits occur, on average, half-way through the valuation year, in which case the members leaving accrue an extra half-year of benefits. We explore this in the following example.

Example 10.11 A pension plan offers a pension benefit of $1000 for each year of service, with fractional years counting pro rata. A member aged 61 has 35 years past service. Value the accrued age retirement benefit and determine the normal contribution rate payable in respect of age retirement benefits using the following plan information and valuation assumptions.

- Age retirements are permitted at any age between 60 and 65.
- The pension is paid monthly in advance for life.
- Contributions are paid annually at the start of each year.
- The unit credit funding method is used. We do not need to specify whether we use projected or traditional unit credit as this is not a final salary plan.

Assumptions:

- Exits follow the service table given in Table D.4
- Interest rate: 6% per year effective
- All lives taking age retirement exit exactly half-way through the year of age (except at age 65)
- Survival after retirement follows the Standard Ultimate Survival Model.

Solution 10.11 Apart from the pension benefit, this example differs from the previous one because we need to allow for mid-year exits. We noted above that the contribution under a unit credit approach pays for the extra one year of accrued benefit for the lives who stay, and pays for an extra half-year's accrued benefit (on average) for the lives who leave. We have

$$
{}_0V = 1000 \times 35 \times \left(\frac{r_{61}}{l_{61}} v^{0.5} \ddot{a}^{(12)}_{61.5} + \frac{r_{62}}{l_{61}} v^{1.5} \ddot{a}^{(12)}_{62.5} + \frac{r_{63}}{l_{61}} v^{2.5} \ddot{a}^{(12)}_{63.5} \right.
$$
$$
\left. + \frac{r_{64}}{l_{61}} v^{3.5} \ddot{a}^{(12)}_{64.5} + \frac{r_{65^-}}{l_{61}} v^4 \ddot{a}^{(12)}_{65} \right)
$$

$$
= 345\,307
$$

and

$$
v\, p^{00}_{61}\, {}_1V = 1000 \times 36 \times \left(\frac{r_{62}}{l_{61}} v^{1.5} \ddot{a}^{(12)}_{62.5} + \frac{r_{63}}{l_{61}} v^{2.5} \ddot{a}^{(12)}_{63.5} \right.
$$
$$
\left. + \frac{r_{64}}{l_{61}} v^{3.5} \ddot{a}^{(12)}_{64.5} + \frac{r_{65^-}}{l_{61}} v^4 \ddot{a}^{(12)}_{65} \right)
$$

$$
= 312\,863.
$$

Note the exact age retirement terms for age 65.

The EPV of the benefits for lives exiting by age retirement in the middle of the valuation year is

$$
1000 \times 35.5 \times \frac{r_{61}}{l_{61}} v^{0.5} \ddot{a}^{(12)}_{61.5} = 41\,723.
$$

Hence, the normal contribution required at the start of the year is C where

$$
{}_0V + C = \text{EPV benefits to mid-year exits} + p^{00}_{61} v\, {}_1V
$$

giving

$$
C = 41\,723 + 312\,863 - 345\,307 = 9278.
$$

$\square$

10.8 Notes and further reading

In this chapter we have introduced some of the language and concepts of pension plan funding and valuation. The presentation has been relatively simplified to bring out some of the major concepts, in particular, accruals funding principles. In North America, what we have called the normal contribution is called the **normal cost**. The difference between the normal contribution and the actual contribution paid represents a paying down of surplus or deficit. Such practical considerations are beyond the scope of this book – we are considering pensions here in the specific context of the application of life contingent mathematics. For more information on pension plan design and related issues, texts such as McGill *et al.* (2010) and Blake (2006) are useful.

10.9 Exercises

Where an exercise uses the service table summarized in Table 10.2, the calculations are based on the exact values underlying the table. Using the integer-rounded values presented in the table may result in very slight differences from the numerical answers printed at the end of this chapter.

The service table is reproduced in Appendix D, as Table D.4. The Standard Ultimate Survival Model is also described and summarized in Appendix D, with annuity values given in Tables D.3.

Exercise 10.1 In order to value the benefits in a final salary pension scheme as at 1 January 2008, a salary scale, s_x, has been defined so that s_{x+t}/s_x is the ratio of a member's total earnings between ages $x + t$ and $x + t + 1$ to the member's total earnings between ages x and $x + 1$.

One member, whose date of birth is 1 April 1961, has an annual salary rate of \$75 000 on the valuation date. Using the salary scale in Table 10.1, estimate the member's expected earnings during 2008.

Exercise 10.2 Assume the salary scale given in Table 10.1 and a valuation date of 1 January.

(a) A plan member aged 35 at valuation received \$75 000 in salary in the year to the valuation date. Given that final average salary is defined as the average salary in the four years before retirement, calculate the member's expected final average salary assuming retirement at age 60.

(b) A plan member aged 55 at valuation was paid salary at a rate of \$100 000 per year at the valuation date. Calculate the expected average salary earned in the two years before retirement at age 65.

Exercise 10.3 A pension plan member is aged 55. One of the plan benefits is a death in service benefit payable on death before age 60.

(a) Calculate the probability that the employee dies in service before age 60.

(b) Assuming that the death in service benefit is \$200 000, and assuming that the death benefit is paid immediately on death, calculate the EPV at age 55 of the death in service benefit.

(c) Now assume that the death in service benefit is twice the annual salary rate at death. At age 55 the member's salary rate is \$85 000 per year. Assuming that deaths occur evenly throughout the year, estimate the EPV of the death in service benefit.

Basis:

- Service table from Table D.4
- Interest rate 6% per year effective;
- Salary scale follows Table 10.1.

Exercise 10.4 A new member aged 35 exact, expecting to earn $40 000 in the next 12 months, has just joined a pension plan. The plan provides a pension on age retirement of 1/60th of final pensionable salary for each year of service, with fractions counting proportionately, payable monthly in advance for life. There are no spousal benefits.

Final pensionable salary is defined as the average salary over the three years prior to retirement. Members contribute a percentage of salary, the rate depending on age. Those under age 50 contribute 4% and those aged 50 and over contribute 5%.

The employer contributes a constant multiple of members' contributions to meet exactly the expected cost of pension benefits. Calculate the multiple needed to meet this new member's age retirement benefits. Assume all contributions are paid exactly half-way through the year of age in which they are paid.

Basis:

- Service table: from Table D.4
- Survival after retirement: Standard Ultimate Survival Model;
- Interest: 4% per year effective.

Exercise 10.5 (a) A new employee aged 25 joins a DC pension plan. Her starting salary is $40 000 per year. Her salary is assumed to increase continuously at a rate of 7% per year for the first 20 years of her career and 4% per year for the following 15 years.

At retirement she is to receive a pension payable monthly in advance, guaranteed for 10 years. She plans to retire at age 60, and she wishes to achieve a replacement ratio of 70% through the pension plan. Using the assumptions below, calculate the level annual contribution rate c (% of salary) that would be required to achieve this replacement ratio.

Assumptions:

- Interest rate 7% per year effective before retirement, 5% per year effective after retirement.
- Survival after retirement follows the Standard Ultimate Survival Model.

(b) Now assume that this contribution rate is paid, but her salary increases at a rate of 5% throughout her career, and interest is earned at 6% on her contributions, rather than 7%. In addition, at retirement, interest rates have fallen to 4.5% per year. Calculate the replacement ratio achieved using the same mortality assumptions.

Exercise 10.6 A pension plan member aged 61 has 35 years of past service at the funding valuation date. His salary in the year to the valuation date was $50 000.

The death in service benefit is 10% of salary at death for each year of service. Calculate the value of the accrued death in service benefit and the normal contribution rate for the death in service benefit.

Basis:

- Service table from Table D.4
- Interest rate 6% per year effective;
- Salary scale follows Table 10.1; all salary increases take place on the valuation date;
- Projected unit credit funding method.

Exercise 10.7 A new company employee is 25 years old. Her company offers a choice of a defined benefit or a defined contribution pension plan. All contributions are paid by the employer, none by the employee.

Her starting salary is \$50 000 per year. Salaries are assumed to increase at a rate of 5% per year, increasing at each year end.

Under the defined benefit plan her final pension is based on the salary received in the year to retirement, using an accrual rate of 1.6% for each year of service. The normal retirement age is 65. The pension is payable monthly in advance for life.

Under the defined contribution plan, contributions are deposited into the member's account at a rate of 12% of salary per year. The total accumulated contribution is applied at the normal retirement age to purchase a monthly life annuity-due.

(a) Assuming the employee chooses the defined benefit plan and that she stays in employment through to age 65, calculate her projected annual rate of pension.

(b) Calculate the contribution, as a percentage of her starting salary, for the retirement pension benefit for this life, for the year of age 25–26, using the projected unit credit method. Assume no exits except mortality, and that the survival probability is $_{40}p_{25} = 0.8$. The valuation interest rate is 6% per year effective. The annuity factor $\ddot{a}_{65}^{(12)}$ is expected to be 11.0.

(c) Now assume that the employee joins the defined contribution plan. Contributions are expected to earn a rate of return of 8% per year. The annuity factor $\ddot{a}_{65}^{(12)}$ is expected to be 11.0. Assuming the employee stays in employment through to age 65, calculate (i) the projected fund at retirement and (ii) her projected annual rate of pension, payable from age 65.

(d) Explain briefly why the employee might choose the defined benefit plan even though the projected pension is smaller.

(e) Explain briefly why the employer might prefer the defined contribution plan even though the contribution rate is higher.

Exercise 10.8 In a pension plan, a member who retires before age 65 has their pension reduced by an actuarial reduction factor. The factor is expressed as a rate per month, k, say, and is then applied to reduce the member's pension to $(1 - t \times k) B$, where B is the accrued benefit, based on service and final average salary at the date of early retirement, and t is the time in months from the actual retirement age to age 65.

The plan sponsor wishes to calculate k such that the EPV at early retirement of the reduced pension benefit is the same as the EPV of the accrued benefit payable at age 65, assuming no exits from mortality or any other decrement before age 65, and ignoring pay increases up to age 65. The pension is assumed to be paid monthly in advance for the member's lifetime.

Calculate k for a person who entered the plan at age 25 and who wishes to retire at age (i) 55 and (ii) 60, using the following further assumptions:

- Survival after retirement: Standard Ultimate Survival Model
- Interest rate: 6% per year effective

Exercise 10.9 A pension plan has only one member, who is aged 35 at the valuation date, with five years past service. The plan benefit is $350 per year pension for each year of service, payable monthly in advance. There is no actuarial reduction for early retirement.

Calculate the actuarial liability and the normal contribution for the age retirement benefit for the member. Use the service table from Table D.4. Post-retirement mortality follows the Standard Ultimate Survival Model. Assume 6% per year interest and use the unit credit funding method.

Exercise 10.10 An employer offers a career average pension scheme, with accrual rate 2.5%. A plan member is aged 35 with five years past service, and total past salary $175 000. His salary in the year following valuation is projected to be $40 000.

Using the service table from Table D.4, calculate the actuarial liability and the normal contribution for the age retirement benefit for the member. There is no actuarial reduction for early retirement. Post-retirement mortality follows the Standard Ultimate Survival Model. Assume 6% per year interest and use the unit credit funding method.

Exercise 10.11 Allison is a member of a pension plan. At the valuation date, 31 December 2008, she is exactly 45, and her salary in the year before valuation is $100 000. Final average salary is defined as the average salary in the two years before exit, and salaries are revised annually on 1 July each year in line with the salary scale in Table 10.1.

The pension plan provides a benefit of 1.5% of final average salary for each year of service. The benefits are valued using the Standard Ultimate Survival

Model, using an interest rate of 5% per year effective. Allison has 15 years service at the valuation date. She is contemplating three possible retirement dates.

- She could retire at 60.5, with an actuarial reduction applied to her pension of 0.5% per month up to age 62. That is, if her accrued benefit at retirement, based on her salary in the two years prior to retirement is B, her reduced pension would be $(1 - 18 \times 0.005) B$, where B would be the usual final salary benefit, calculated as $B = n \, S_{\text{Fin}} \, \alpha$, where n is the years of service from entry to exit at age 60.5.
- She could retire at age 62 with no actuarial reduction.
- She could retire at age 65 with no actuarial reduction.

(a) Calculate the replacement ratio provided by the pension for each of the retirement dates.
(b) Calculate the EPV of Allison's retirement pension for each of the possible retirement dates, assuming mortality is the only decrement. The basic pension benefit is a single life annuity, paid monthly in advance.
(c) Now assume Allison leaves the company and withdraws from active membership of the pension plan immediately after the valuation. Her total salary in the two years before exit is $186\,000$. She is entitled to a deferred pension of 1.5% of her final average earnings in the two years before withdrawal for each year of service, payable at age 62. There is no COLA for the benefit. Calculate the EPV of the withdrawal benefit using the valuation assumptions.

Exercise 10.12 Using the unit credit method, calculate the actuarial liability and the normal contribution for the following pension plan.

- Benefit: $300 per year pension for each year of service
- Normal retirement age: 60
- Survival model: Standard Ultimate Survival Model
- Interest: 6% per year effective
- Pension: payable weekly, guaranteed for five years
- Pre-retirement exits: mortality only.

Active membership data at valuation

Age of employee	Service	Number of employees
25	0	3
35	10	3
45	15	1
55	25	1

Age	Service	Number of employees
35	7	1 (deferred pensioner)
75	25	1 (pension in payment)

Exercise 10.13 A defined benefit pension plan offers an annual pension of 2% of the final year's salary for each year of service payable monthly in advance. You are given the following information.

- Interest rate: 4% per year effective
- Salary growth rate: salary scale follows Table 10.1; all increases occur on 31 December each year
- Retirement age: 65
- Pre-retirement exits: None
- Retirement survival: Standard Ultimate Survival Model.

Membership

Name	Age at entry	Age at 1 January 2009	Salary at 1 January 2008	Salary at 1 January 2009
Giles	30	35	38 000	40 000
Faith	30	60	47 000	50 000

(a) (i) Calculate the actuarial liability at 1 January 2009 using the projected unit credit method.

  (ii) Calculate the normal contribution rate in 2009 separately for Giles and Faith, as a proportion of their 2009 salary, using the projected unit credit funding method.

(b) (i) Calculate the actuarial liability at 1 January 2009 using the traditional unit credit method.

  (ii) Calculate the normal contribution rate in 2009 separately for Giles and Faith, as a proportion of their 2009 salary, using the traditional unit credit funding method.

(c) Comment on your answers.

Answers to selected exercises

10.1 $76 311

10.2 (a) $185 265
     (b) $114 346

10.3 (a) 0.01171
     (b) $2011.21
     (c) $1776.02

10.4 2.15

10.5 (a) 20.3%

     (b) 56.1%

10.6 Accrued death benefit value: $2351.48

     Normal contribution: $58.31

10.7 (a) $214 552

     (b) 9.18%

     (c) (i) $3 052 123,   (ii) $277 466

10.8 0.43%, 0.53%

10.9 Actuarial liability: $1842.26

     Normal contribution: $368.45

10.10 Actuarial liability: $4605.65

      Normal contribution: $1052.72

10.11 (a) 41.3%,   47.6%,   52.1%

      (b) $383 700, $406 686, $372 321

      (c) $123 143

10.12 Total actuarial liability: $197 691

      Total normal contribution: $8619

10.13 (a) (i) $422 201

          (ii) Giles: 22.5%,   Faith: 25.1%

      (b) (i) $350 945

          (ii) Giles: 11.1%,   Faith: 66.3%

11

Yield curves and non-diversifiable risk

11.1 Summary

In this chapter we consider the effect on annuity and insurance valuation of interest rates varying with the duration of investment, as summarized by a yield curve, and of uncertainty over future interest rates, which we will model using stochastic interest rates. We introduce the concepts of diversifiable and non-diversifiable risk and give conditions under which mortality risk can be considered to be diversifiable. In the final section we demonstrate the use of Monte Carlo methods to explore distributions of uncertain cash flows and loss random variables through simulation of both future lifetimes and future interest rates.

11.2 The yield curve

In practice, at any given time interest rates vary with the duration of the investment; that is, a sum invested for a period of, say, five years, would typically earn a different rate of interest than a sum invested for a period of 15 years or a sum invested for a period of six months.

Let $v(t)$ denote the current market price of a t-year zero-coupon bond; that is, the current market price of an investment which pays a unit amount with certainty t years from now. Note that, at least in principle, there is no uncertainty over the value of $v(t)$ although this value can change at any time as a result of trading in the market. The t-year **spot rate of interest**, denoted y_t, is the yield per year on this zero-coupon bond, so that

$$v(t)(1 + y_t)^t = 1 \iff v(t) = (1 + y_t)^{-t}. \tag{11.1}$$

The **term structure** of interest rates describes the relationship between the term of the investment and the interest rate on the investment, and it is expressed graphically by the **yield curve**, which is a plot of $\{y_t\}_{t>0}$ against t. Figures 11.1–11.4 show different yield curves, derived using government

371

Figure 11.1 Canadian government bond yield curve (spot rates), May 2007.

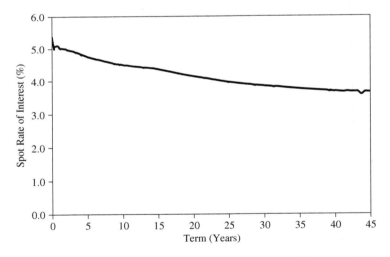

Figure 11.2 UK government bond yield curve (spot rates), November 2006.

issued bonds from the UK, the US and Canada, at various dates from relatively recent history. The UK issues longer term bonds than most other countries, so the UK yield curve is longer.

These figures illustrate some of the shapes a yield curve can have. Figure 11.1 shows a relatively flat curve, so that interest rates vary little with

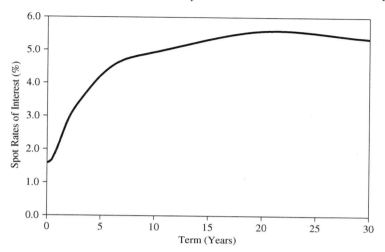

Figure 11.3 US government bond yield curve (spot rates), January 2002.

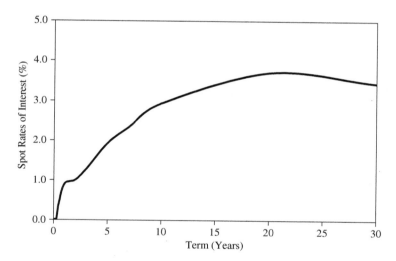

Figure 11.4 US government bond yield curve (spot rates), November 2008.

the term of the investment. Figure 11.2 shows a falling curve. Both of these shapes are relatively uncommon; the most common shape is that shown in Figures 11.3 and 11.4, a rising yield curve, flattening out after 10–15 years, with spot rates increasing at a decreasing rate.

Previously in this book we have assumed a flat term structure. This assumption has allowed us to use v^t or $e^{-\delta t}$ as discount functions for any term t, with v and δ as constants. When we relax this assumption, and allow interest rates to vary by term, the v^t discount function is no longer appropriate. Figure 11.3 shows that the rate of interest on a one-year US government bond in January 2002 was 1.6% per year and on a 20-year bond was 5.6%. The difference of 4% may have a significant effect on the valuation of an annuity or insurance benefit. The present value of a 20-year annuity-due of $1 per year payable in advance, valued at 1.6%, is $17.27; valued at 5.6% it is $12.51. The value of the annuity should be the amount required to be invested now to produce payments of 1 at the start of each of the next 20 years – this is how we have been implicitly valuing annuities when we discount at the rate of interest on assets. When we have a term structure this means we should discount each future payment using the spot interest rate appropriate to the term until that payment is due. This is a replication argument: the present value of any cash flow is the cost of purchasing a portfolio which exactly replicates the cash flow.

Since an investment now of amount $v(t)$ in a t-year zero-coupon bond will accumulate to 1 in t years, $v(t)$ can be interpreted as a discount function which generalizes v^t.

The price of the 20-year annuity-due with this discount function is $\sum_{t=0}^{19} v(t)$ which means that the price of the annuity-due is the cost of purchasing 20 zero-coupon bonds, each with $1 face value, with maturity dates corresponding to the annuity payment dates. The spot rates underlying the yield curve in Figure 11.3 give a value of $13.63 for the 20-year annuity-due, closer to, but significantly higher than the cost using the long-term rate of 5.6%.

At any given time the market will determine the price of zero-coupon bonds and this will determine the yield curve. These prices also determine **forward rates of interest** at that time. Let $f(t, t + k)$ denote the forward rate, contracted at time zero, effective from time t to $t + k$, expressed as an effective annual rate. This represents the interest rate contracted at time 0 earned on an investment made at t, maturing at $t + k$. To determine forward rates in terms of spot rates of interest, consider two different ways of investing 1 for $t + k$ years. Investing for the whole period, the $t + k$-year spot rate, y_{t+k}, gives the accumulation of this investment as $(1 + y_{t+k})^{t+k}$. On the other hand, if the unit sum is invested first for t years at the t year spot rate, then reinvested for k years at the k year forward rate starting at time t, the accumulation will be $(1 + y_t)^t (1 + f(t, t + k))^k$. Since there is no uncertainty involved in either of these schemes – note that y_{t+k}, y_t and $f(t, t + k)$ are all known now – the accumulation at $t + k$ under these two schemes must be the same. That is

$$(1 + f(t, t + k))^k = \frac{(1 + y_{t+k})^{t+k}}{(1 + y_t)^t} = \frac{v(t)}{v(t + k)}.$$

This is (implicitly) a *no-arbitrage argument*, which, essentially, says in this situation that we should not be able to make money from nothing in risk-free bonds by disinvesting and then reinvesting. The no-arbitrage assumption is discussed further in Chapter 15.

11.3 Valuation of insurances and life annuities

The present value random variable for a life annuity-due with annual payments, issued to a life aged x, given a yield curve $\{y_t\}$, is

$$Y = \sum_{k=0}^{K_x} v(k) \tag{11.2}$$

where $v(k) = (1 + y_k)^{-k}$. The EPV of the annuity, denoted $\ddot{a}(x)_y$, can be found using the payment-by-payment (or indicator function) approach, so that

$$\ddot{a}(x)_y = \sum_{k=0}^{\infty} {}_k p_x v(k). \tag{11.3}$$

Similarly, the present value random variable for a whole life insurance for (x), payable immediately on death, is

$$Z = v(T_x) \tag{11.4}$$

and the EPV is

$$\bar{A}(x)_y = \int_0^{\infty} v(t)\, {}_t p_x \, \mu_{x+t} \, dt. \tag{11.5}$$

Note that we have to depart from International Actuarial Notation here as it is defined in terms of interest rates that do not vary by term, though we retain the spirit of the notation.

By allowing for a non-flat yield curve we lose many of the relationships that we have developed for flat interest rates, such as the equation linking $\ddot{a}_x$ and A_x.

Example 11.1 You are given the following spot rates of interest per year.

y_1	y_2	y_3	y_4	y_5	y_6	y_7	y_8	y_9	y_{10}
0.032	0.035	0.038	0.041	0.043	0.045	0.046	0.047	0.048	0.048

(a) Calculate the discount function $v(t)$ for $t = 1, 2, \ldots, 10$.
(b) A survival model follows Makeham's law with $A = 0.0001$, $B = 0.00035$ and $c = 1.075$. Calculate the net level annual premium for a 10-year term

Table 11.1 *Calculations for Example 11.1.*

t	$v(t)$	p_{80+t}	$_tp_{80}$
0	1.0000	0.88845	1.00000
1	0.9690	0.88061	0.88845
2	0.9335	0.87226	0.78237
3	0.8941	0.86337	0.68243
4	0.8515	0.85391	0.58919
5	0.8102	0.84387	0.50312
6	0.7679	0.83320	0.42456
7	0.7299	0.82188	0.35374
8	0.6925	0.80988	0.29073
9	0.6558	0.79718	0.23546
10	0.6257	0.78374	0.18770

insurance policy, with sum insured $100\,000$ payable at the end of the year of death, issued to a life aged 80:

(i) using the spot rates of interest in the table above, and,

(ii) using a level interest rate of 4.8% per year effective.

Solution 11.1 (a) Use equations (11.1) for the discount function values and (2.26) for the Makeham survival probabilities. Table 11.1 summarizes some of the calculations.

(b) (i) The expected present value for the 10-year life annuity-due is

$$\ddot{a}(80 : \overline{10|}) = \sum_{k=0}^{9} v(k)\,_kp_{80} = 5.0507.$$

The EPV of the term insurance benefit is

$$100\,000\,A^{1}(80 : \overline{10|}) = \sum_{k=0}^{9} {}_kp_{80}(1 - p_{80+k})v(k+1) = 66\,739.$$

So the annual premium is $13\,213.72$.

(ii) Assuming a 4.8% per year flat yield curve gives a premium of $13\,181.48$.   □

In general, life insurance contracts are relatively long term. The influence of the yield curve on long-term contracts may not be very great since the yield curve tends to flatten out after around 15 years. It is common actuarial practice to use the long-term rate in traditional actuarial calculations, and in many cases, as in the example above, the answer will be close. However, using the long-term rate may overstate the interest income when the yield curve is rising, which is the most common shape. Overstating the interest results in a premium that is lower than the true premium. An insurer that systematically charges premiums less than the true price, even if each is only a little less, may face solvency problems in time. With a rising yield curve, if a level interest rate is assumed, it should be a little less than the long-term rate.

11.3.1 Replicating the cash flows of a traditional non-participating product

In this section we continue Example 11.1. Recall that the forward rate is contracted at the inception of the contract. This means that, assuming an equivalence principle premium, if we take the premium and any surplus cash flow brought forward each year and invest them at the forward rate, then there will be exactly enough to fund the sums insured, provided that the mortality and survival experience exactly follows the premium assumptions. That is, if the premiums and benefit cash flows are completely predictable, and are invested in the forward rates each year, the resulting cash flows exactly match the claims outgo, without risk.

This may be illustrated using the policy value recursion from Chapter 7, adjusted now to allow for the yield curve. Suppose we have a regular premium policy with term n years, issued to (x), with annual premium and benefit cash flows. Let P denote the premium and S denote the sum insured. We ignore expenses to keep things simple. As usual, the policy value at integer duration $t \geq 0$ is the EPV of the future loss random variable at time t, for a policy in force at that time. The recursive relationship between policy values can be written as

$$(_t V + P)(1 + f(t, t+1)) = S\, q_{x+t} + {}_{t+1}V\, p_{x+t}.$$

The recursion shows that if we have N identical, independent policies at time t, and exactly $p_{x+t}\, N$ lives survive to time $t + 1$, and exactly $q_{x+t}\, N$ lives do not, then the forward rate of interest is exactly enough to balance income and outgo, with no residual interest rate risk.

What this means is that if the cash flows are certain, and if the policy term is not so long that it extends beyond the scope of risk-free investments, then there is no need for the policy to involve interest rate uncertainty. At the inception of the contract, we can lock in forward rates that will exactly replicate the required cash flows.

This raises two interesting questions.

First, we know that mortality is uncertain, so that the mortality related cash flows are not certain. To what extent does this invalidate the replication argument? The answer is that, if the portfolio of life insurance policies is sufficiently large, and, crucially, if mortality can be treated as **diversifiable**, then it is reasonable to treat the life contingent cash flows as if they were certain.

In Section 11.4.1 we discuss in detail what we mean by diversifiability, and under what conditions it might be a reasonable assumption for mortality.

The second question is, what risks are incurred by an insurer if it chooses not to replicate, or is unable to replicate for lack of appropriate risk-free investments? If the insurer does not replicate the cash flows, then interest rate risk is introduced, and must be modelled and managed. Interest rate risk is inherently non-diversifiable, as we shall discuss in Section 11.4.2.

11.4 Diversifiable and non-diversifiable risk

Consider a portfolio consisting of N life insurance policies. We can model as a random variable, X_i, $i = 1, \ldots, N$, many quantities of interest for the ith policy in this portfolio. For example, X_i could take the value 1 if the policyholder is still alive, say, 10 years after the policy was issued and the value zero otherwise. In this case, $\sum_{i=1}^{N} X_i$ represents the number of survivors after 10 years. Alternatively, X_i could represent the present value of the loss on the ith policy so that $\sum_{i=1}^{N} X_i$ represents the present value of the loss on the whole portfolio. Suppose for convenience that the X_is are identically distributed with common mean μ and standard deviation σ. Let ρ denote the correlation coefficient for any pair X_i and X_j ($i \neq j$). Then

$$E\left[\sum_{i=1}^{N} X_i\right] = N\mu \quad \text{and} \quad V\left[\sum_{i=1}^{N} X_i\right] = N\sigma^2 + N(N-1)\rho\sigma^2.$$

Suppose now that the X_is are independent, so that ρ is zero. Then

$$V\left[\sum_{i=1}^{N} X_i\right] = N\sigma^2$$

and the central limit theorem (which is described in Appendix A) tells us that, provided N is reasonably large,

$$\sum_{i=1}^{N} X_i \sim N(N\mu, N\sigma^2) \Rightarrow \frac{\left(\sum_{i=1}^{N} X_i\right) - N\mu}{\sqrt{N}\sigma} \sim N(0, 1).$$

In this case, the probability that $\sum_{i=1}^{N} X_i/N$ deviates from its expected value decreases to zero as N increases. More precisely, for any $k > 0$

$$\Pr\left[\left|\sum_{i=1}^{N} X_i/N - \mu\right| \geq k\right] = \Pr\left[\left|\sum_{i=1}^{N} X_i - N\mu\right| \geq kN\right]$$

$$= \Pr\left[\left|\frac{\sum_{i=1}^{N} X_i - N\mu}{\sqrt{N}\sigma}\right| \geq \frac{k\sqrt{N}}{\sigma}\right].$$

If we now let $N \rightarrow \infty$, so that we can assume from the central limit theorem that $(\sum_{i=1}^{N} X_i - N\mu)/(\sqrt{N}\sigma)$ is normally distributed, then the probability can be written as

$$\lim_{N\to\infty} \Pr\left[|Z| \geq \frac{k\sqrt{N}}{\sigma} \right] = \lim_{N\to\infty} 2\Phi\left(-\frac{k\sqrt{N}}{\sigma} \right) = 0,$$

where $Z \sim N(0, 1)$.

So, as N increases, the variation of the mean of the X_i from their expected value will tend to zero, if $V[\sum_{i=1}^{N} X_i]$ is linear in N. In this case we can reduce the risk measured by X_i relative to its mean value, by increasing the size of the portfolio. This result relies on the fact that we have assumed that the X_is are independent; it is not generally true if ρ is not equal to zero, as in that case $V[\sum_{i=1}^{N} X_i]$ is of order N^2, which means that increasing the number of policies increases the risk relative to the mean value.

So, we say that the risk within our portfolio, as measured by the random variable X_i, is said to be **diversifiable** if the following condition holds

$$\lim_{N\to\infty} \frac{\sqrt{V\left[\sum_{i=1}^{N} X_i \right]}}{N} = 0.$$

A risk is **non-diversifiable** if this condition does not hold. In simple terms, a risk is diversifiable if we can eliminate it (relative to its expectation) by increasing the number of policies in the portfolio. An important aspect of financial risk management is to identify those risks which can be regarded as diversifiable and those which cannot. Diversifiable risks are generally easier to deal with than those which are not.

11.4.1 Diversifiable mortality risk

In Section 11.2 we employed the no-arbitrage principle to argue that the value of a deterministic payment stream should be the same as the price of the zero-coupon bonds that replicate that payment stream. In Section 11.3.1 we explored the replication idea further. To do this we need to assume that the mortality risk associated with a portfolio is diversifiable and we discuss conditions for this to be a reasonable assumption.

Consider a group of N lives all now aged x who have just purchased identical insurance or annuity policies. We will make the following two assumptions throughout the remainder of this chapter, except where otherwise stated.

(i) The N lives are independent with respect to their future mortality.
(ii) The survival model for each of the N lives is known.

We also assume, for convenience, that each of the N lives has the same survival model.

The cash flow at any future time t for this group of policyholders will depend on how many are still alive at time t and on the times of death for those not still alive. These quantities are uncertain. However, with the two assumptions above the mortality risk is diversifiable. This means that, provided N is large, the variability of, say, the number of survivors at any time relative to the expected number is small so that we can regard mortality, and hence the cash flows for the portfolio, as deterministic. This is demonstrated in the following example.

Example 11.2 For $0 \leq t \leq t+s$, let $N_{t,s}$ denote the number of deaths between ages $x + t$ and $x + t + s$ from N lives aged x. Show that

$$\lim_{N \to \infty} \frac{\sqrt{V[N_{t,s}]}}{N} = 0.$$

Solution 11.2 The random variable $N_{t,s}$ has a binomial distribution with parameters N and $_tp_x\,(1 - {_sp_{x+t}})$. Hence

$$V[N_{t,s}] = N\,{_tp_x}\,(1 - {_sp_{x+t}})\,(1 - {_tp_x}\,(1 - {_sp_{x+t}}))$$

$$\Rightarrow \frac{\sqrt{V[N_{t,s}]}}{N} = \sqrt{\frac{{_tp_x}(1 - {_sp_{x+t}})(1 - {_tp_x}(1 - {_sp_{x+t}}))}{N}}$$

$$\Rightarrow \lim_{N \to \infty} \frac{\sqrt{V[N_{t,s}]}}{N} = 0.$$

$\square$

In practice most insurers sell so many contracts over all their life insurance or annuity portfolios that mortality risk can be treated in many situations as fully diversified away. There are exceptions; for example, for very old age mortality, where the number of policyholders tends to be small, or where an insurance has a very high sum at risk, in which case the outcome of that particular contract may have a significant effect on the portfolio as a whole, or where the survival model for the policyholders cannot be predicted with confidence.

If mortality risk can be treated as fully diversified then we can assume that the mortality experience is deterministic – that is, we may assume that the number of claims each year is equal to the expected number. In the following section we use this deterministic assumption for mortality to look at the replication of the term insurance cash flows in Example 11.1 above.

11.4.2 Non-diversifiable risk

In practice, many insurers do not replicate with forward rates or zero-coupon bonds either because they choose not to or because there are practical difficulties in trying to do so. By locking into forward rates at the start of a contract, the insurer can remove (much of) the investment risk, as noted in Section 11.3.1. However, while this removes the risk of losses, it also removes the possibility of profits. Also there may be practical constraints. For example, in some countries it may not be possible to find risk-free investments for terms longer than around 20 years, which is often not long enough. A whole life insurance contract issued to a life aged 40 may not expire for 50 years. The rate of interest that would be appropriate for an investment to be made over 20 years ahead could be very difficult to predict.

If an insurer does not lock into the forward rates at inception, there is a risk that interest rates will move, resulting in premiums that are either too low or too high. The risk that interest rates are lower than those expected in the premium calculation is an example of non-diversifiable risk. Suppose an insurer has a large portfolio of whole life insurance policies issued to lives aged 40, with level premiums payable throughout the term of the contract, and that mortality risk can be considered diversified away. The insurer decides to invest all premiums in 10-year bonds, reinvesting when the bonds mature. The price of 10-year bonds at each of the future premium dates is unknown now. If the insurer determines the premium assuming a fixed interest rate of 6% per year, and the actual interest rate earned is 5% per year, then the portfolio will make a substantial loss, and in fact each individual contract is expected to make a loss. Writing more contracts will only increase the loss, because each policy experiences the same interest rates. The key point here is that the policies are not independent of each other with respect to the interest rate risk.

Previous chapters in this book have focused on the mortality risk in insurance, which, under the conditions discussed in Section 11.4.1 can be considered to be diversifiable. However, non-diversifiable risk is, arguably, even more important. Most life insurance company failures occur because of problems with non-diversifiable risk related to assets. Note also that not all mortality risk is diversifiable. In Example 11.4 below, we look at a situation where the mortality risk is not fully diversifiable. First, in Example 11.3 we look at an example of non-diversifiable interest rate risk.

Example 11.3 An insurer issues a whole life insurance policy to (40), with level premiums payable continuously throughout the term of the policy, and with sum insured $50 000 payable immediately on death. The insurer assumes that an appropriate survival model is given by Makeham's law with parameters $A = 0.0001$, $B = 0.00035$ and $c = 1.075$.

(a) Suppose the insurer prices the policy assuming an interest rate of 5% per year effective. Show that the annual premium rate is $P = \$1010.36$.

(b) Now suppose that the effective annual interest rate is modelled stochastically, denoted **i**, with the following distribution.

$$i = \begin{cases} 4\% \text{ with probability } 0.25, \\ 5\% \text{ with probability } 0.5, \\ 6\% \text{ with probability } 0.25. \end{cases}$$

Calculate the expected value and the standard deviation of the present value of the future loss on the contract. Assume that the future lifetime is independent of the interest rate.

Solution 11.3 (a) At 5% we have

$$\bar{a}_{40} = 14.49329 \qquad \text{and} \qquad \bar{A}_{40} = 0.29287$$

giving a premium of

$$P = 50\,000 \frac{\bar{A}_{40}}{\bar{a}_{40}} = \$1010.36.$$

(b) Let $S = 50\,000$, $P = 1\,010.36$ and $T = T_{40}$. The present value of the future loss on the policy, L_0, is given by

$$L_0 = S\,v_i^T - P\bar{a}_{\overline{T}|i}.$$

To calculate the moments of L_0 we condition on the value of **i** and then use iterated expectation (see Appendix A for a review of conditional expectation). As

$$L_0|\mathbf{i} = S\,v_i^T - P\bar{a}_{\overline{T}|i}, \tag{11.6}$$

$$E[L_0|\mathbf{i}] = (S\bar{A}_{40} - P\bar{a}_{40})|\mathbf{i}$$

$$= \begin{cases} 1\,587.43 & \text{with probability } 0.25 \ (\mathbf{i} = 4\%), \\ 0 & \text{with probability } 0.50 \ (\mathbf{i} = 5\%), \\ -1\,071.49 & \text{with probability } 0.25 \ (\mathbf{i} = 6\%), \end{cases} \tag{11.7}$$

so

$$E[L_0] = E\,[E[L_0|\mathbf{i}]] = 0.25\,(1\,587.43) + 0.5\,(0) + 0.25\,(-1\,071.49)$$

$$= \$128.99. \tag{11.8}$$

For the standard deviation, we use

$$V[L_0] = E[V[L_0|\mathbf{i}]] + V[E[L_0|\mathbf{i}]]. \tag{11.9}$$

We can interpret the first term as the risk due to uncertainty over the future lifetime and the second term as the risk due to the uncertain interest rate.

Now

$$L_0|i = S\,v_i^T - P\bar{a}_{\overline{T}|i} = \left(S + \frac{P}{\delta_i}\right)v_i^T - \frac{P}{\delta_i}$$

so

$$V[L_0|i] = \left(S + \frac{P}{\delta_i}\right)^2 \left({}^2\bar{A}_{40} - \bar{A}_{40}^2\right)_i$$

$$= \begin{cases} 14\,675^2 & \text{with probability } 0.25 & (i = 4\%) \\ 14\,014^2 & \text{with probability } 0.5 & (i = 5\%) \\ 13\,316^2 & \text{with probability } 0.25 & (i = 6\%). \end{cases}$$

Hence

$$E[V[L_0|i]] = \$196\,364\,762.$$

Also, from equation (11.7),

$$\begin{aligned} V[E[L_0|i]] &= ((1\,587.43^2)\,0.25 + (0^2)\,0.5 \\ &\quad + (-1\,071.49^2)\,0.25) - 128.99^2 \\ &= 900\,371 \\ &= \$948.88^2. \end{aligned}$$

So

$$V[L_0] = 196\,364\,762 + 900\,371 = 197\,265\,133 = \$14\,045^2. \quad (11.10)$$

□

Comments

This example illustrates some important points.

(1) The fixed interest assumption, 5% in this example, is what is often called the 'best estimate' assumption – it is the expected value, as well as the most likely value, of the future interest rate. It is tempting to calculate the premium using the best estimate assumption, but this example illustrates that doing so may lead to systematic losses. In this example, using a 5% per year interest assumption to price the policy leads to an expected loss of $128.99 on every policy issued.

(2) Breaking the variance down into two terms separates the diversifiable risk from the non-diversifiable risk. Consider a portfolio of, say, N contracts. Let $L_{0,j}$ denote the present value of the loss at inception on the jth policy and let

$$L = \sum_{j=1}^{N} L_{0,j}$$

so that L denotes the total future loss random variable.

Following formula (11.9), and noting that, given our assumptions at the start of this section, the random variables $\{L_{0,j}|\mathbf{i}\}_{j=1}^{N}$ are independent and identically distributed, we can write

$$V[L] = E[V[L|\mathbf{i}]] + V[E[L|\mathbf{i}]]$$

$$= E\left[V\left[\sum_{j=1}^{N} L_{0,j}|\mathbf{i}\right]\right] + V\left[E\left[\sum_{j=1}^{N} L_{0,j}|\mathbf{i}\right]\right]$$

$$= E[N\,V[L_0|\mathbf{i}]] + V[N\,E[L_0|\mathbf{i}]]$$

$$= 196\,364\,762\,N + 900\,371\,N^2.$$

Now consider separately each component of the variance of L. The first term represents diversifiable risk since it is a multiple of N and the second term represents non-diversifiable risk since it is a multiple of N^2. We can see that, for an individual policy ($N = 1$), the future lifetime uncertainty is very much more influential than the interest rate uncertainty, as the first term is much greater than the second term. But, for a large portfolio, the contribution of the interest uncertainty to the total standard deviation is far more important than the future lifetime uncertainty.

The conclusion above, that for large portfolios, interest rate uncertainty is more important than mortality uncertainty, relies on the assumption that the future survival model is known and that the separate lives are independent with respect to mortality. The following example shows that if these conditions do not hold, mortality risk can be non-diversifiable.

Example 11.4 A portfolio consists of N identical one-year term insurance policies issued simultaneously. Each policy was issued to a life aged 70, has a sum insured of $50\,000$ payable at the end of the year of death and was purchased with a single premium of 1300. The insurer uses an effective interest rate of 5% for all calculations but is unsure about the mortality of this group of policyholders over the term of the policies. The probability of dying within the year, regarded as a random variable $\mathbf{q}_{70}$, is assumed to have the following distribution

$$\mathbf{q}_{70} = \begin{cases} 0.022 & \text{with probability } 0.25, \\ 0.025 & \text{with probability } 0.5, \\ 0.028 & \text{with probability } 0.25. \end{cases}$$

The value of $\mathbf{q}_{70}$ is the same for all policies in the portfolio and, given this value, the policies are independent with respect to mortality.

(a) Let $D(N)$ denote the number of deaths during the one-year term. Show that

$$\lim_{N \to \infty} \frac{\sqrt{V[D(N)]}}{N} \neq 0.$$

(b) Let $L(N)$ denote the present value of the loss from the whole portfolio. Show that

$$\lim_{N \to \infty} \frac{\sqrt{V[L(N)]}}{N} \neq 0.$$

Solution 11.4 (a) We have

$$V[D(N)] = V[E[D(N)|\mathbf{q_{70}}]] + E[V[D(N)|\mathbf{q_{70}}]].$$

Now

$$\begin{aligned}
V[E[D(N)|\mathbf{q_{70}}]] &= 0.25((0.022 - 0.025)N)^2 + 0 \\
&\quad + 0.25((0.028 - 0.025)N)^2 \\
&= 4.5 \times 10^{-6} N^2
\end{aligned}$$

and

$$\begin{aligned}
E[V[D(N)|\mathbf{q_{70}}]] &= 0.25 \times 0.022(1 - 0.022)N \\
&\quad + 0.5 \times 0.025(1 - 0.025)N \\
&\quad + 0.25 \times 0.028(1 - 0.028)N \\
&= 0.0243705 N.
\end{aligned}$$

Hence

$$V[D(N)] = 4.5 \times 10^{-6} N^2 + 0.0243705 N$$

and so

$$\lim_{N \to \infty} \frac{\sqrt{V[D(N)]}}{N} = 0.002121.$$

(b) The arguments are as in part (a). We have

$$V[L(N)] = E[V[L(N)|\mathbf{q_{70}}]] + V[E[L(N)|\mathbf{q_{70}}]].$$

As

$$L(N) = 50\,000 v D(N) - 1\,300 N,$$

we have

$$\begin{aligned}
V[L(N)|\mathbf{q_{70}}] &= (50\,000 v)^2 V[D(N)|\mathbf{q_{70}}] \\
&= (50\,000 v)^2 N \mathbf{q_{70}} (1 - \mathbf{q_{70}})
\end{aligned}$$

and

$$E[L(N)|\mathbf{q_{70}}] = 50\,000v N\mathbf{q_{70}} - 1\,300N.$$

Thus

$$E[V[L(N)|\mathbf{q_{70}}]] = (50\,000v)^2 N(E[\mathbf{q_{70}}] - E[\mathbf{q_{70}}^2])$$
$$= (50\,000v)^2 N(0.025 - 0.0006295)$$

and

$$V[E[L(N)|\mathbf{q_{70}}]] = (50\,000v)^2 N^2 V[\mathbf{q_{70}}]$$
$$= (50\,000v)^2 N^2 \times 4.5 \times 10^{-6}.$$

Hence

$$\lim_{N\to\infty} \frac{\sqrt{V[L(N)]}}{N} = 50\,000v\sqrt{V[\mathbf{q_{70}}]} = 101.02.$$

□

11.5 Monte Carlo simulation

Suppose we wish to explore a more complex example of interest rate variation than in Example 11.3. If the problem is too complicated, for example if we want to consider both lifetime variation and the interest rate uncertainty, then the numerical methods used in previous chapters may be too unwieldy. An alternative is Monte Carlo, or stochastic, simulation. Using Monte Carlo techniques allows us to explore the distributions of present values for highly complicated problems, by generating a random sample from the distribution. If the sample is large enough, we can get good estimates of the moments of the distribution, and, even more interesting, the full picture of a loss distribution. Appendix C gives a brief review of Monte Carlo simulation.

In this section we demonstrate the use of Monte Carlo methods to simulate future lifetimes and future rates of interest, using a series of examples based on the following deferred annuity policy issued to a life aged 50.

- Policy terms:
  - An annuity of \$10 000 per year is payable continuously from age 65 contingent on the survival of the policyholder.
  - Level premiums of amount $P = \$4447$ per year are payable continuously throughout the period of deferment.
  - If the policyholder dies during the deferred period, a death benefit equal to the total premiums paid (without interest) is due immediately on death.

- Basis for all calculations:
  - The survival model follows Gompertz' law with parameters $B = 0.0004$ and $c = 1.07$.
  - The force of interest during deferment is $\delta = 5\%$ per year.
  - The force of interest applying at age 65 is denoted **r**.

In the next three examples we will assume that **r** is fixed and known. In the final example we will assume that **r** has a fixed but unknown value.

Example 11.5 Assume the force of interest from age 65 is 6% per year, so that $\mathbf{r} = 0.06$.

(a) Calculate the EPV of the loss on the contract.

(b) Calculate the probability that the present value of the loss on the policy will be positive.

Solution 11.5 (a) The expected present value of the loss on this contract is

$$10\,000\,{}_{15}E_{50}\,\bar{a}^*_{65} + P\,(\bar{I}\bar{A})^{\,1}_{50:\,\overline{15|}} - P\,\bar{a}_{50:\,\overline{15|}}$$

where * denotes calculation using a force of interest 6% per year and all other functions are calculated using a force of interest 5% per year. This gives the expected present value of the loss as

$$10\,000 \times 0.34773 \times 8.51058 + 4\,447 \times 1.32405 - 4\,447 \times 9.49338$$
$$= -\$6735.38.$$

(b) The present value of the loss, L, can be written in terms of the expected future lifetime, T_{50}, as follows

$$L = \begin{cases} P\,T_{50}\,v^{T_{50}} - P\,\bar{a}_{\overline{T_{50}|}} & \text{if } T_{50} \le 15, \\ 10\,000\,\bar{a}^*_{\overline{T_{50}-15|}}\,v^{15} - P\,\bar{a}_{\overline{15|}} & \text{if } T_{50} > 15. \end{cases}$$

By looking at the relationship between L and T_{50} we can see that the policy generates a profit if the life dies in the deferred period, or in the early years of the annuity payment period, and that

$$\Pr[L > 0] = \Pr\left[10\,000\,e^{-15\delta}\,\bar{a}_{\overline{T_{50}-15|}6\%} - P\bar{a}_{\overline{15|}5\%} > 0\right]$$
$$= \Pr\left[T_{50} > 15 - \frac{1}{0.06}\log\left(1 - \frac{P}{10^4}e^{15(0.05)}\bar{a}_{\overline{15|}5\%}(0.06)\right)\right]$$
$$= \Pr[T_{50} > 30.109] = {}_{30.109}p_{50} = 0.3131.$$

□

Example 11.6 Use the three $U(0, 1)$ random variates below to simulate values for T_{50} and hence values for the present value of future loss, L_0, for the deferred annuity contract. Assume that the force of interest from age 65 is 6% per year:

$$u_1 = 0.16025, \qquad u_2 = 0.51720, \qquad u_3 = 0.99855.$$

Solution 11.6 Let F_T be the distribution function of T_{50}. Each simulated u_j generates a simulated future lifetime t_j through the inverse transform method, where

$$u_j = F_T(t_j).$$

See Appendix C. Hence

$$
\begin{aligned}
u &= F_T(t) \\
&= 1 - e^{-(B/\log(c))c^{50}(c^t - 1)} \\
\Rightarrow t = F_T^{-1}(u) \\
&= \frac{1}{\log(c)} \left(\log \left(1 - \frac{\log(c)(\log(1-u))}{B\, c^{50}} \right) \right).
\end{aligned}
\tag{11.11}
$$

So

$$
\begin{aligned}
t_1 &= F_T^{-1}(0.16025) = 10.266, \\
t_2 &= F_T^{-1}(0.5172) = 24.314, \\
t_3 &= F_T^{-1}(0.9985) = 53.969.
\end{aligned}
$$

These simulated lifetimes can be checked by noting in each case that $t_j q_{50} = u_j$.

We can convert the sample lifetimes to the corresponding sample of the present value of future loss random variable, L_0, as follows. If (50) dies after exactly 10.266 years, then death occurs during the deferred period, the death benefit is $10.266P$, the present value of the premiums paid is $P\bar{a}_{\overline{10.266}|}$, and so the present value of the future loss is

$$L_0 = 10.266\, P\, e^{-10.266\,\delta} - P\bar{a}_{\overline{10.266}|\delta} = -\$8383.80.$$

Similarly, the other two simulated future lifetimes give the following losses

$$
\begin{aligned}
L_0 &= 10\,000 e^{-15\delta}\, \bar{a}_{\overline{9.314}|_{r=6\%}} - P\bar{a}_{\overline{15}|\delta} = -\$13\,223.09, \\
L_0 &= 10\,000 e^{-15\delta}\, \bar{a}_{\overline{38.969}|_{r=6\%}} - P\bar{a}_{\overline{15}|\delta} = \$24\,202.36.
\end{aligned}
$$

The first two simulations generate a profit, and the third generates a loss. $\qquad \square$

Example 11.7 Repeat Example 11.6, generating 5000 values of the present value of future loss random variable. Use the simulation output to:

(a) Estimate the expected value and the standard deviation of the present value of the future loss from a single policy.
(b) Calculate a 95% confidence interval for the expected value of the present value of the loss.
(c) Estimate the probability that the contract generates a loss.
(d) Calculate a 95% confidence interval for the probability that the contract generates a loss.

Solution 11.7 Use an appropriate random number generator to produce a sequence of 5000 $U(0, 1)$ random numbers, $\{u_j\}$. Use equation (11.11) to generate corresponding values of the future lifetime, $\{t_j\}$, and the present value of the future loss for a life with future lifetime t_j, say $\{L_{0,j}\}$, as in Example 11.6.

The result is a sample of 5000 independent values of the future loss random variable. Let $\bar{l}$ and s_l represent the mean and standard deviation of the sample.

(a) The precise answers will depend on the random number generator (and seed value) used. Our calculations gave

$$\bar{l} = -\$6592.74; \qquad s_l = \$15\,733.98.$$

(b) Let μ and σ denote the (true) mean and standard deviation of the present value of the future loss on a single policy. Using the central limit theorem, we can write

$$\frac{1}{5000} \sum_{j=1}^{5000} L_{0,j} \sim N(\mu, \sigma^2/5000).$$

Hence

$$\Pr\left[\mu - 1.96 \frac{\sigma}{\sqrt{5000}} \leq \frac{1}{5000} \sum_{j=1}^{5000} L_{0,j} \leq \mu + 1.96 \frac{\sigma}{\sqrt{5000}}\right] = 0.95.$$

Since $\bar{l}$ and s_l are estimates of μ and σ, respectively, a 95% confidence interval for the mean loss is

$$\left(\bar{l} - 1.96 \frac{s_l}{\sqrt{5000}}, \quad \bar{l} + 1.96 \frac{s_l}{\sqrt{5000}}\right).$$

Using the values of $\bar{l}$ and s_l from part (a) gives $(-7028.86, -6156.61)$ as a 95% confidence interval for μ.

(c) Let L^- denote the number of simulations which produce a loss, that is, the number for which $L_{0,i}$ is positive. Let p denote the (true) probability that the present value of the loss on a single policy is positive. Then

$$L^- \sim B(5000, \ p)$$

and our estimate of p, denoted $\hat{p}$, is given by

$$\hat{p} = \frac{l^-}{5000}$$

where l^- is the simulated realization of L^-, that is, the number of losses which are positive out of the full set of 5000 simulated losses. Using a normal approximation, we have

$$\frac{L^-}{5000} \sim N\left(p, \ \frac{p(1-p)}{5000}\right)$$

and so an approximate 95% confidence interval for p is

$$\left(\hat{p} - 1.96\sqrt{\frac{\hat{p}(1-\hat{p})}{5000}}, \ \ \hat{p} + 1.96\sqrt{\frac{\hat{p}(1-\hat{p})}{5000}}\right)$$

where we have replaced p by its estimate $\hat{p}$. Our calculations gave a total of 1563 simulations with a positive value for the expected present value of the future loss. Hence

$$\hat{p} = 0.3126$$

and an approximate 95% confidence interval for this probability is

$$(0.2998, \ 0.3254).$$

Different sets of random numbers would result in different values for each of these quantities.   □

In fact it was not necessary to use simulation to calculate μ or p in this example. As we have seen in Example 11.5, the values of μ and p can be calculated as $-\$6735.38$ and 0.3131, respectively. The 95% confidence intervals calculated in Example 11.7 parts (b) and (d) comfortably span these true values. We used simulation in this example to illustrate the method and to show how accurate we can be with 5000 simulations.

An advantage of Monte Carlo simulation is that we can easily adapt the simulation to model the effect of a random force of interest from age 65, which would be less tractable analytically. The next example demonstrates this in the case where the force of interest from age 65 is fixed but unknown.

Example 11.8 Repeat Example 11.7, but now assuming that $\mathbf{r}$ is a random variable with a $N(0.06, 0.015^2)$ distribution. Assume the random variables T_{50} and $\mathbf{r}$ are independent.

Solution 11.8 For each of the 5000 simulations generate both a value for T_{50}, as in the previous example, and also, independently, a value of $\mathbf{r}$ from the $N(0.06, 0.015^2)$ distribution. Let t_j and r_j denoted the simulated values of T_{50} and $\mathbf{r}$, respectively, for the jth simulation. The simulated value of the present value of the loss for this simulation, $L_{0,j}$, is

$$
L_{0,j} = \begin{cases} P\, t_i\, v^{t_j} - P\, \ddot{a}_{\overline{t_j}|} & \text{if } t_j \leq 15, \\ 10\,000\, \ddot{a}^*_{\overline{t_j-15}|} v^{15} - P\, \ddot{a}_{\overline{15}|} & \text{if } t_j > 15, \end{cases}
$$

where $*$ now denotes calculation at the simulated force of interest r_j. The remaining steps in the solution are as in Example 11.7.

Our simulation gave the following results.

$$
\bar{l} = -\$6220.5; \quad s_l = \$16\,903.1; \quad L^- = 1502.
$$

Hence, an approximate 95% confidence interval for the mean loss is

$$
(-6689, -5752).
$$

An estimated probability that a policy generates a loss is

$$
\hat{p} = 0.3004,
$$

with an approximate 95% confidence interval for this probability of

$$
(0.2877, 0.3131).
$$

Note that allowing for the future interest variability has reduced the expected profit and increased the standard deviation. The probability of loss is not significantly different from the fixed interest case. □

11.6 Notes and further reading

The simple interest rate models we have used in this chapter are useful for illustrating the possible impact of interest rate uncertainty, but developing more realistic interest rate models is a major topic in its own right, beyond the scope of this text. Some models are presented in McDonald (2009) and a comprehensive presentation of the topic is available in Cairns (2004).

We have shown in this chapter that uncertainty in the mortality experience is a source of non-diversifiable risk. This is important because improving mortality has been a feature in many countries and the rate of improvement has been difficult to predict. See, for example, Willets *et al.* (2004). In these circumstances, the assumptions about the survival model in Section 11.4.1 may not be reasonable and so a significant aspect of mortality risk is non-diversifiable. Note that in Examples 11.6–11.8 we simulated the future lifetime random variable T_{50} assuming the survival model and its parameters were known. Monte Carlo methods could be used to model uncertainty about the survival model; for example, by assuming that the two parameters in the Gompertz formula were unknown but could be modelled as random variables with specified distributions.

Monte Carlo simulation is a key tool in modern risk management. A general introduction is presented in, e.g. Ross (2006), and Glasserman (2004) offers a text more focused on financial modelling. Algorithms for writing your own generators are given in the *Numerical Recipes* reference texts, such as Press *et al.* (2007).

11.7 Exercises

Exercise 11.1 You are given the following zero-coupon bond prices:

Term, t(years)	$P(t)$ as % of face value
1	94.35
2	89.20
3	84.45
4	79.95
5	75.79

(a) Calculate the annual effective spot rates for $t = 1, 2, 3, 4, 5$.
(b) Calculate the one-year forward rates, at $t = 0, 1, 2, 3, 4$.
(c) Calculate the EPV of a five-year term life annuity-due of $1000 per year, assuming that the probability of survival each year is 0.99.

Exercise 11.2 Consider an endowment insurance with sum insured $100 000 issued to a life aged 45 with term 15 years under which the death benefit is payable at the end of the year of death. Premiums, which are payable annually in advance, are calculated using the Standard Ultimate Survival Model, assuming a yield curve of effective annual spot rates given by

$$y_t = 0.035 + \frac{\sqrt{t}}{200}.$$

(a) Show that the net premium for the contract is $4207.77.
(b) Calculate the net premium determined using a flat yield curve with effective rate of interest $i = y_{15}$ and comment on the result.
(c) Calculate the net policy value for a policy still in force three years after issue, using the rates implied by the original yield curve, using the premium basis.

Exercise 11.3 An insurer issues a portfolio of identical five-year term insurance policies to independent lives aged 75. One-half of all the policies have a sum insured of $10 000, and the other half have a sum insured of $100 000. The sum insured is payable immediately on death.

The insurer wishes to measure the uncertainty in the total present value of claims in the portfolio. The insurer uses the Standard Ultimate Survival Model, and assumes an interest rate of 6% per year effective.

(a) Calculate the standard deviation of the present value of the benefit for an individual policy, chosen at random.
(b) Calculate the standard deviation of the total present value of claims for the portfolio assuming that 100 contracts are issued.
(c) By comparing the portfolio of 100 policies with a portfolio of 100 000 policies, demonstrate that the mortality risk is diversifiable.

Exercise 11.4 (a) The coefficient of variation for a random variable X is defined as the ratio of the standard deviation of X to the mean of X. Let X denote the aggregate loss on a portfolio, so that $X = \sum_{j=1}^{N} X_j$. Assume that, for each j, $X_j > 0$ and X_j has finite mean and variance.

Show that, if the portfolio risk is diversifiable, then the limiting value of the coefficient of variation of aggregate loss X, as $N \to \infty$, is zero.
(b) An insurer issues a portfolio of identical 15-year term insurance policies to independent lives aged 65. The sum insured for each policy is $100 000, payable at the end of the year of death.

The mortality for the portfolio is assumed to follow Makeham's law with $A = 0.00022$ and $B = 2.7 \times 10^{-6}$. The insurer is uncertain whether the parameter c for Makeham's mortality law is 1.124, as in the Standard Ultimate Survival Model, or 1.114. The insurer models this uncertainty assuming that there is a 75% probability that $c = 1.124$ and a 25% probability that $c = 1.114$. Assume the same mortality applies to each life in the portfolio. The effective rate of interest is assumed to be 6% per year.

(i) Calculate the coefficient of variation of the present value of the benefit for an individual policy.

(ii) Calculate the coefficient of variation of the total present value of benefits for the portfolio assuming that 10 000 policies are issued.
(iii) Demonstrate that the mortality risk is not fully diversifiable, and find the limiting value of the coefficient of variation.

Exercise 11.5 An insurer issues a 25-year endowment insurance policy to (40), with level premiums payable continuously throughout the term of the policy, and with sum insured $100 000 payable immediately on death or at the end of the term. The insurer calculates the premium assuming an interest rate of 7% per year effective, and using the Standard Ultimate Survival Model.

(a) Calculate the annual net premium payable.
(b) Suppose that the effective annual interest rate is a random variable, i, with the following distribution:

$$i = \begin{cases} 5\% \text{ with probability } 0.5, \\ 7\% \text{ with probability } 0.25, \\ 11\% \text{ with probability } 0.25. \end{cases}$$

Write down the EPV of the net future loss on the policy using the mean interest rate, and the premium calculated in part (a).
(c) Calculate the EPV of the net future loss on the policy using the modal interest rate, and the premium calculated in part (a).
(d) Calculate the EPV and the standard deviation of the present value of the net future loss on the policy. Use the premium from (a) and assume that the future lifetime is independent of the interest rate.
(e) Comment on the results.

Exercise 11.6 An insurer issues 15-year term insurance policies to lives aged 50. The sum insured of $200 000 is payable immediately on death. Level premiums of $550 per year are payable continuously throughout the term of the policy. The insurer assumes the lives are subject to Gompertz' law of mortality with $B = 3 \times 10^{-6}$ and $c = 1.125$, and that interest rates are constant at 5% per year.

(a) Generate 1000 simulations of the future loss.
(b) Using your simulations from (a), estimate the mean and variance of the future loss random variable.
(c) Calculate a 90% confidence interval for the mean future loss.

(d) Calculate the true value of the mean future loss. Does it lie in your confidence interval in (c)?

(e) Repeat the 1000 simulations 20 times. How often does the confidence interval calculated from your simulations not contain the true mean future loss?

(f) If you calculated a 90% confidence interval for the mean future loss a large number of times from 1000 simulations, how often (as a percentage) would you expect the confidence interval not to contain the true mean?

(g) Now assume interest rates are unknown. The insurer models the interest rate on all policies, I, as a lognormal random variable, such that

$$1 + I \sim LN(0.0485, 0.0241^2).$$

Re-estimate the 90% confidence interval for the mean of the future loss random variable, using Monte Carlo simulation. Comment on the effect of interest rate uncertainty.

Exercise 11.7 An actuary is concerned about the possible effect of pandemic risk on the term insurance portfolio of her insurer. She assesses that in any year there is a 1% probability that mortality rates at all ages will increase by 25%, for that year only.

(a) State, with explanation, whether pandemic risk is diversifiable or non-diversifiable.

(b) Describe how the actuary might quantify the possible impact of pandemic risk on her portfolio.

Answers to selected exercises

11.1 (a) (0.05988, 0.05881, 0.05795, 0.05754, 0.05701)
     (b) (0.05988, 0.05774, 0.05625, 0.05629, 0.05489)
     (c) $4395.73

11.2 (b) $4319.50
     (c) $13 548

11.3 (a) $19 784
     (b) $193 054

11.4 (b) (i) 2.2337
          (ii) 0.2204
          (iii) 0.2192

11.5 (a) $1608.13
     (b) $0

 (c) $7325.40

 (d) $2129.80, $8489.16

11.6 (d) −$184.07

 (f) 10% of sets of simulated values should generate a 90% confidence interval that does not contain the true mean.

 (g) Term insurance is not very sensitive to interest rate uncertainty, as the standard deviation of outcomes with interest rate uncertainty is very similar to that without interest rate uncertainty.

12

Emerging costs for traditional life insurance

12.1 Summary

In this chapter we introduce emerging costs, or cash flow analysis for traditional life insurance contracts. This is often called *profit testing* when applied to life insurance.

We introduce profit testing in two stages. First we consider only those cash flows generated by the policy, then we introduce reserves to complete the cash flow analysis.

We define several measures of the profitability of a contract: internal rate of return, expected present value of future profit (net present value), profit margin and discounted payback period. We show how cash flow analysis can be used to set premiums to meet a given measure of profit.

We restrict our attention in this chapter to deterministic profit tests, ignoring uncertainty. We introduce stochastic profit tests in Chapter 14.

12.2 Introduction

Traditionally, actuarial analysis has focused on determining the EPV of a cash flow series, usually under a constant interest rate assumption. This emphasis on the EPV was important in an era of manual computation, but with powerful computers available we can do better. In this chapter, we look at techniques for projecting the cash flows emerging from an individual contract in each time period, using some specified assumptions about the interest and demographic experience. The use of cash flow projections offers much more flexibility in the input assumptions than the EPV approach – for example, it is easy to incorporate yield curves, or more sophisticated models of policyholder behaviour – and provides actuaries with a better understanding of the liabilities under their management and the relationship between the liabilities and the corresponding assets. For modern contracts, with variable premiums and complex financial guarantees, traditional valuation techniques are not very useful. Profit testing techniques offer the flexibility to explore risk and return for a wide range of modern and traditional contracts.

The purpose of a profit test is to identify the profit which the insurer can expect from a contract at the end of each time period. There are many reasons why this might be valuable. Some of the ways in which profit tests are applied in practice are described here.

1. **To set premiums**

   The traditional approach to premium calculation in Chapter 6 does not explicitly allow for profit, nor for yield curves. Even when a profit loading is explicitly introduced, the methods of Chapter 6 do not give a picture of how the profit might emerge over time, and do not allow the insurer to determine return on capital from the contract. Profit testing allows premiums to be set to meet specified profit measures, and allows the insurer to stress test the assumptions to consider how sensitive the emerging profit would be to different assumptions.

2. **To set reserves**

   We use the term 'reserve' to indicate the capital that the insurer holds (or is projected to hold in the future), to meet the future net liabilities of a contract. As we discussed in Chapter 7, the term 'reserve' has often been used interchangeably with 'policy value', which was defined, for a policy in force at time t, say, as the expected value at t of the present value of the future loss random variable, L_t.

   The traditional approach to the reserve calculation has been to use a policy value, following the methods in Chapter 7. However, it is not necessary to do so. Reserves can be determined arbitrarily, or by determining the capital required to support the liabilities under specified assumptions. Profit test analysis allows reserves to be determined and tested under a range of more complex assumptions for interest rates and policyholder behaviour than is feasible using the traditional calculations of Chapter 7.

3. **To measure profitability**

   The insurer will be interested in projecting emerging cash flows to assess liquidity needs. For example, new business strain for new contracts creates a need for available capital, which may be available from surplus emerging from more mature business. Developing cash flow models allows the insurer to manage portfolios taking different maturities and cash flow patterns into account. The insurer may use cash flow emergence and profitability measures to determine strategies for marketing and product development.

4. **To stress test profitability**

   The assumptions used to project future cash flows can be adjusted to explore the impact of adverse experience. Usually, the insurer would profit test contracts using a range of assumptions to get a feel for the sensitivity of the cash flows to different adverse scenarios.

5. **To determine distributable surplus**

When insurance portfolios generate surplus, it may be distributed in the form of dividends to shareholders, or retained in the equity of the company. For some forms of insurance, profit is shared with the policyholders. Policyholders of participating or with-profit contracts will be entitled to a share of the profits generated within a specified fund. Universal Life policyholders will share the investment profits generated by the funds supporting their contracts. The form in which such profit-share should be distributed, especially for participating (or 'par') business, is a matter of current interest. It is apparent that in order to anticipate surplus distribution, it would be helpful to have an idea of how the surplus will emerge, and we may also use profit testing to explore risks associated with different methods for distributing surplus.

In this chapter, we look at how profit tests can be used for premium setting, reserve calculations and for measuring profitability, all in the context of non-participating insurance. In Chapters 13 and 14 we consider applications to participating and non-traditional insurance.

12.3 Profit testing a term insurance policy

We introduce profit testing by studying in some detail a 10-year term insurance issued to a life aged 60. The details of the policy are as follows. The sum insured, denoted S, is \$100 000, payable at the end of the year of death. Level annual premiums, denoted P, of amount \$1500 are payable throughout the term.

12.3.1 Time step

We will project the cash flows from this policy at discrete intervals throughout its term. It would be very common to choose one month as the interval since premiums are often paid monthly, and the profit test would be regularly updated through the term of the contract. However, to illustrate more clearly the mechanics of profit testing, we use a time interval of one year for this example, taking time 0 to be the moment when the policy is issued.

12.3.2 Profit test basis

To estimate the future cash flows, the insurer needs to make assumptions about the expenses which will be incurred, the survival model for the policyholder, the rate of interest to be earned on cash flows within each time period before the profit is released and possibly other items such as an assessment of the probability that the policyholder surrenders the policy. For ease of presentation, we ignore the possibility of surrender in this example.

The set of assumptions used in the profit test is called the **profit test basis**.

Survival probabilities

We project cash flows using expected values for mortality costs. For example, the expected cost of a death benefit of S paid at the end of the first year, for a life aged 60 at the start of the year, is $q_{60}\,S$.

In this example, we assume a survival model for the profit test following

$$q_{60+t} = 0.01 + 0.001\,t \text{ for } t = 0, 1, \ldots, 9.$$

The survival model used in a profit test may be different from the premium basis. For example, the insurer may incorporate margins in the premium basis – meaning, adopt more conservative assumptions – to allow for adverse experience. In the profit test, the insurer may be interested in a 'best estimate' picture of the emerging profits, in which case the survival model would not incorporate any margins.

Expenses

In Chapter 6 we discussed how expenses are incorporated into the calculation of the premium for a policy. Typically, the acquisition expenses, incurred at the start of the contract, are high, and the later expenses, associated with record maintenance and premium collection, tend to be smaller.

In profit testing, it is necessary to be more specific about the acquisition expenses. As we project cash flows, we assume that some expenses arise even before the first premium is collected. These expenses are treated as being incurred at the start of the contract, at time $t = 0$. This differs from the treatment of expenses allocated to subsequent time periods, where expenses are combined with all the other sources of income and outgo for the period, and values accumulated to the year end.

The reason for treating the acquisition expenses differently is that prudent capital management requires us to recognize losses as early as possible; surplus may be carried forward, but losses should be accounted for as soon as they are incurred. In this example we are projecting cash flows to the year end before analyzing the surplus emerging. It would not generally be prudent to combine the high acquisition costs with the other first year income and outgo, as that would delay recognition of those expenses, and lessen their impact.

In our examples we will identify, specifically, the initial expenses which should be allocated to time 0, as distinct from the expenses which arise at inception, but may be accounted for with the other first year cash flows. The time 0 expenses will be identified as *pre-contract expenses*; other expenses that arise during the first policy year are intended to be included in the first year cash flows. If no distinction is made, it should be assumed that all initial expenses should be allocated to the time 0 cash flows. This is a common approach, because it gives the most conservative result.

For this example, we use the following expense assumptions basis.

Pre-contract expenses: $400 plus 20% of the first premium.
Renewal expenses: 3.5% of premiums, including the first.

Interest on insurer assets

In each year that the policy is still in force, the expected cash flows contributing to the surplus emerging at the end of that year are the premiums, less any premium-related expenses, plus interest earned on the invested assets, less the expected cost of a claim at the end of the year. We therefore require an assumption about the interest rate earned on insurer assets during the projection year. Often, this will be a best estimate, which will differ from assumptions for premiums and reserves which will typically incorporate margins for adverse experience, or for implicit profit loading.

The step-by-step process for profit testing makes it very simple to allow for different interest rates in different projection periods, so that a yield curve could easily be accommodated. In this example though, we will assume a constant interest rate of 5.5% per year.

Emerging surplus for the term insurance example, without reserves

The calculations of the emerging surplus, called the **net cash flows** for the policy, are summarized in Table 12.1.

Table 12.1 *Net cash flows for the 10-year term insurance in Section 12.3.*

Time t	Premium at $t-1$	Expenses E_t	Interest I_t	Claims EDB_t	Surplus emerging at t
0		700.00			−700.00
1	1500	52.50	82.50	1000	527.11
2	1500	52.50	79.61	1100	427.11
3	1500	52.50	79.61	1200	327.11
4	1500	52.50	79.61	1300	227.11
5	1500	52.50	79.61	1400	127.11
6	1500	52.50	79.61	1500	27.11
7	1500	52.50	79.61	1600	−72.89
8	1500	52.50	79.61	1700	−172.89
9	1500	52.50	79.61	1800	−272.89
10	1500	52.50	79.61	1900	−372.89

For time $t = 0$ the only entry is the acquisition expense for the policy, $\$(400 + 0.2\,P)$. This expense is assumed to occur and to be paid at time 0, so no interest accrues. In all our profit test tables throughout this and subsequent chapters, the first row will account for costs (not income) at $t = 0$, and will not be accumulated. In the table, and in the examples following in this and subsequent chapters, we let E_0 denote the pre-contract, acquisition expenses, assumed incurred at time 0, and we let E_t denote the tth year expenses, incurred at the start of the year from $t - 1$ to t, for $t = 1, 2, \ldots, 10$.

After the time 0 row for pre-contract costs, each subsequent row shows the income and outgo cash flows for the specified policy year.

The second row refers to cash flows in the first policy year, which we label as $t = 1$, and which runs from time 0 (after the acquisition expenses already accounted for in the time 0 row) to time 1.

There is a premium payable at time 0; there are premium expenses of $3.5\%\,P$ that are incurred at the start of the year, and are not included in the time 0 acquisition expenses. Interest is earned at 5.5% through the year. At the year end, the expected cost of death benefits is

$$EDB_1 = q_{60}\,S = 0.01 \times 100\,000 = 1000.$$

Hence the emerging surplus, or net cash flow, at time 1 is

$$1500 + 82.5 - 1000 = 582.5.$$

For subsequent policy years, we will adopt the convention that the net cash flows are calculated *assuming the policy is still in force at the start of the year*. This means that we are starting each time step with a new assumption. For example, considering the second year of the policy, we project all cash flows assuming the policy is in force at the start of the year, at $t = 1$, but by the end of the year, the policy may be in force (with probability p_{x+1}), or the policyholder may have died (with probability q_{x+1}). When we move to the third policy year, we assume the policy is in force at the start of the year. We discuss this convention in more detail after we work through the examples.

Using this convention, consider, for example, the seventh year of the projection. We assume the policy is in force at the start of the year, and the insurer receives the premium then due, of $P = 1500$; at the same time, the insurer incurs expenses of 3.5% of the premium, $E_7 = 52.5$. The balance is invested for the year at the assumed interest rate of 5.5%, generating $I_7 = 0.055(P - E_7) = 79.61$. At the year end, the expected cost of death benefits is $EDB_7 = q_{66}\,S = 1600$. Hence, the expected value at time 7 of the net cash flows received during the seventh year, for a policy in force at the start of the year, is

$$P - E_7 + I_7 - EDB_7 = -72.89.$$

12.3.3 Incorporating reserves

Table 12.1 reveals a typical feature of net cash flows, in that several of the net cash flows in later years are negative. This occurs because the level premium is more than sufficient to pay the expected death claims and expenses in the early years, but, with an increasing probability of death, the premium is not sufficient in the later years. The expected cash flow values in the final column of Table 12.1 show the same general features as the values illustrated in Figures 6.1 and 6.2.

In Chapter 7 we explained why the insurer needed to set aside assets to cover negative expected future cash flows. The policy values that we calculated in that chapter represented the amount that would, in expectation, be sufficient with the future premiums to meet future benefits. In modelling cash flows, we use reserves rather than policy values. The reserve is the actual amount of money held by the insurer to meet future liabilities. The reserve may be equal to a policy value, but does not need to be. For traditional insurance such as the term policy in this example, it is common to use a policy value calculation to set reserves, perhaps using conservative assumptions, or using a net premium approach with a different (hypothetical) premium to the actual gross premium for the contract.

Note that the negative cash flow at time 0 in Table 12.1 does not require a reserve since it will have been paid as soon as the policy was issued.

Suppose that at the start of each year the insurer sets reserves for this policy equal to the net premium policy values on the following (reserve) basis.

Interest:	4% per year effective on all cash flows.
Survival model:	$q_{60+t} = 0.011 + 0.001\,t$ for $t = 0, 1, \ldots, 9$.

Then the reserve required at the start of the $(t+1)$th year, i.e. at time t, is

$$100\,000\,A^{\,1}_{60+t:\overline{10-t}|} - P^n\,\ddot{a}_{60+t:\overline{10-t}|}$$

where the net premium, P^n, is calculated as

$$P^n = 100\,000\,\frac{A^{\,1}_{60:\overline{10}|}}{\ddot{a}_{60:\overline{10}|}} = \$1447.63,$$

Table 12.2 *Reserves for the 10-year
term insurance in Section 12.3.*

t	$_tV$	t	$_tV$
0	0.00	5	1219.94
1	410.05	6	1193.37
2	740.88	7	1064.74
3	988.90	8	827.76
4	1150.10	9	475.45

and all functions are calculated using the reserve basis. The values for the reserves are shown in Table 12.2. We now include in our profit test the cost of capital arising from the need to allocate the reserves to the policies in force. We do this by following (loosely) the accounting approach, where reserves brought forward are treated as income at the start of each year, and reserves carried forward are treated as a cost at the end of each year.

To illustrate this, consider, for example, the reserve required at time 1, $_1V = 410.05$. This amount is required for every policy *still in force at time 1*. The cost to the insurer of setting up this reserve is assigned to the previous time period and this cost is

$$_1V \, p_{60} = 410.05 \times (1 - 0.01) = 405.95.$$

The cost includes the factor p_{60} since all costs relating to the previous time period are per policy in force *at the start of that time period*, that is, at time 0. The expected proportion of policyholders surviving to the start of the following time period, i.e. to age 61, is p_{60}. Note that p_{60} is calculated on the profit test basis, not the reserve basis which is used solely for determining the $_tV$ values. In general, the cost at the end of the year from $t - 1$ to t of setting up a reserve of amount $_tV$ at time t for each policy still in force at time t is $_tV \, p_{60+t-1}$.

The profit test calculations, including reserves, are set out in Table 12.3, and the individual calculations are described in more detail here.

Column (1) labels the rows. The first row, labelled $t = 0$, is for the the cash flows required immediately before the inception of the contract. For subsequent rows, the cash flows in the tth year are those from $t - 1$ to t. In each row, we assume the contract is in force at the start of the year.

Column (2) shows the reserve brought forward at the start of each year, at time $t - 1$, assuming the contract is in force at that time. The reserve brought forward is treated as an item of income in the cash flows for the tth year.

Column (3) shows the premium paid at the start of the year, assuming the policy is in force at that time, $P = 1500$.

Table 12.3 *Emerging surplus, per policy in force at the start of each year, for the 10-year term insurance in Section 12.3.*

t (0)	$_{t-1}V$ (2)	P (3)	E_t (4)	I_t (5)	EDB_t (6)	E_tV (7)	Pr_t (8)
0			700.00				−700.00
1	0.00	1500	52.50	82.50	1000	405.95	121.17
2	410.05	1500	52.50	102.17	1100	732.73	126.99
3	740.88	1500	52.50	120.36	1200	977.04	131.70
4	988.90	1500	52.50	134.00	1300	1135.15	135.26
5	1150.10	1500	52.50	142.87	1400	1202.86	137.61
6	1219.94	1500	52.50	146.71	1500	1175.47	138.68
7	1193.37	1500	52.50	145.25	1600	1047.70	138.41
8	1064.74	1500	52.50	138.17	1700	813.69	136.72
9	827.76	1500	52.50	125.14	1800	466.89	133.52
10	475.45	1500	52.50	105.76	1900	0.00	128.71

Column (4) shows the expenses. E_0 denotes the initial expenses incurred at time 0 and for $t = 1, 2, \ldots, 10$, E_t denotes the renewal expenses incurred at the start of the year from $t − 1$ to t.

Column (5) shows I_t, which denotes the interest earned in the year from $t − 1$ to t on the assets invested at the start of the year. In this case, for $t = 1, 2, \ldots, 10$, with an assumed interest rate of 5.5%, we have

$$I_t = 0.055 \, (_{t-1}V + P − E_t).$$

Column (6) shows the expected cost of death benefits in the tth year, EDB_t, assuming the policy is in force at time $t − 1$. So, with a sum insured of $S = 100\,000$, the expected death benefit at time t for a contract in force at time $t − 1$ is

$$EDB_t = S \, q_{60+t-1}.$$

Column (7) shows E_tV, which denotes the expected cost of the reserve carried forward at time t, for a policy in force at time $t − 1$, that is

$$E_tV = p_{60+t-1} \, _tV.$$

Note that, if the reserve basis generated a value for $_0V > 0$, then $_0V$ would be included in the first row, $t = 0$, in column (7), and would be treated as an acquisition cost. Then, in the second row, $_0V$ would be in column (2) as an item of income for the year from 0 to 1.

Column (8) shows the expected profit emerging at time t given that the policy is in force at time $t − 1$, except for the first row, where Pr_0 represents the acquisition costs. That is

$$Pr_0 = −E_0 − {_0V} = −700$$

and for $t = 1, 2, \ldots, 10$,

$$\mathrm{Pr}_t = {}_{t-1}V + P - E_t + I_t - EDB_t - E_tV. \tag{12.1}$$

Equation (12.1) is sometimes expressed slightly differently, as

$$\mathrm{Pr}_t = (P - E_t)(1 + i) + \Delta_t V - EDB_t,$$

where $\Delta_t V$ is called the **change in reserve** in year t and is defined as

$$\Delta_t V = (1 + i)\,{}_{t-1}V - {}_tV\, p_{60+t-1}.$$

This alternative version reflects the difference between the reserves and the other cash flows. The incoming and outgoing reserves each year are not real income and outgo in the same way as premiums, claims and expenses; they are accounting transfers. It also allows for the use of a different return on assets underlying reserves than on other cash flows.

12.3.4 Profit signature

We have used an important convention in the construction of Tables 12.1 and 12.3, that is worth emphasizing. The entries in each row are calculated *assuming the policy is in force at the start of the year*. We use this convention because it is very convenient; it makes the profit test more flexible, and (once you are used to it) easier to construct. However, it also means that we cannot simply gather together all the Pr_t entries from the table to analyse the future profits on a contract, since each entry is based on a different assumption about the probability that the policy is still in force.

The vector $\mathrm{Pr} = (\mathrm{Pr}_0, \ldots, \mathrm{Pr}_{10})'$ is called the **profit vector** for the contract. So, the elements of Pr denote the expected profit emerging at the end of each year, given that the policy is in force at the start of the year. For an overall, unconditional projection of the emerging surpluses from a newly issued contract, we need to adjust the Pr_t values to remove the conditioning.

Let Π_t represent the expected profit emerging at time t from the cash flows in the year $t - 1$ to t, given that the contract is in force at time $t = 0$ (i.e. unconditionally). The relationship between Π_t and Pr_t for $t = 1, 2, \ldots, 10$, is

$$\Pi_t = \mathrm{Pr}_t \times \mathrm{Pr}\,[\text{in force at time } t - 1 \,|\, \text{in force at time } 0]\,.$$

The vector Π is called the **profit signature** for the contract. We have, for the current example,

$$\Pi_0 = \mathrm{Pr}_0; \qquad \Pi_t = {}_{t-1}p_{60}\,\mathrm{Pr}_t \quad \text{for } t = 1, 2, \ldots, 10. \tag{12.2}$$

Table 12.4 *Profit vector and profit signature for the 10-year term insurance.*

t	Pr_t	Π_t	t	Pr_t	Π_t
0	−700.00	−700.00	6	138.68	130.56
1	121.17	121.17	7	138.41	128.35
2	126.99	125.72	8	136.72	124.75
3	131.70	128.95	9	133.52	119.76
4	135.26	130.84	10	128.71	113.37
5	137.61	131.39			

The profit signature is the key to assessing the profitability of a new contract. The profit signature for the 10-year term example is given alongside the profit vector Pr in Table 12.4. We show them together to emphasize the difference between the two vectors, which is important in applying and interpreting the profit test. The profit vector, Pr_t, represents the profit emerging at time t from the cash flows in the year $t - 1$ to t, given that the contract is in force at time $t - 1$, for $t = 1, 2, \ldots, 10$.

12.4 Profit testing principles

12.4.1 Assumptions

In this section we generalize the process described in the example of the previous section. In this description we label the emerging profit assuming annual time steps, but the method can be very easily adapted to other frequencies.

We assume a contract with a term of n years, issued to (x), with cash flows dependent on whether the policyholder dies, surrenders or continues in force through to the end of the policy year.

We assume that a policyholder whose policy is in force at time $t - 1$, dies in the year $t - 1$ to t with probability p_{x+t-1}^{0d}, withdraws or surrenders the contract with probability p_{x+t-1}^{0w} and remains in force at time t with probability $p_{x+t-1}^{00} = 1 - p_{x+t-1}^{0d} - p_{x+t-1}^{0w}$.

12.4.2 The profit vector

The profit vector is

$$\mathrm{Pr} = (\mathrm{Pr}_0, \mathrm{Pr}_1, \ldots, \mathrm{Pr}_n)'.$$

The profit vector elements Pr_t, for $t \geq 1$, represent the expected surplus emerging at each year end for a contract in force at time $t - 1$, i.e. at the start of the year. The first element of the vector, Pr_0, has a slightly different interpretation.

It represents the value at time $t = 0$ of the pre-contract cash flows, including the acquisition expenses, E_0, and the cost of setting up initial reserves, $_0V$, where required. So

$$\mathrm{Pr}_0 = -E_0 - {}_0V$$

and for $t = 1, 2, \ldots, n$,

$$\mathrm{Pr}_t = {}_{t-1}V + P_t - E_t + I_t - EDB_t - ESB_t - EEB_t - E_tV$$

where

$_tV$ is the reserve required at time t for a policy in force at that time;

P_t is the tth premium, paid at time $t - 1$, for a policy in force at time $t - 1$;

E_t is the premium expense incurred at time $t - 1$ for a policy in force at time $t - 1$.

I_t is the investment income earned on the insurer's funds over $t - 1$ to t for a policy in force at time $t - 1$. That is, $I_t = i_t \, ({}_{t-1}V + P_t - E_t)$ where i_t is the yield on investments from time $t - 1$ to t.

EDB_t is the expected cost of death benefits at time t for a policy in force at time $t - 1$. That is, $EDB_t = p^{0d}_{x+t-1} S_t$, where S_t is the sum insured.

ESB_t is the expected cost of surrender benefits at time t for a policy in force at time $t - 1$. That is, $ESB_t = p^{0w}_{x+t-1} CV_t$ where CV_t is the cash or surrender value payable for surrenders at time t.

EEB_t is the expected cost of endowment or survivor benefits at time t for a policy in force at time $t - 1$. This would be applicable for a maturity benefit under an endowment policy, or for end-year annuity benefits.

E_tV is the expected cost of setting the reserve at time t for a policy in force at time $t - 1$. That is, $E_tV = p^{00}_{x+t-1} \, {}_tV$.

12.4.3 The profit signature

The profit signature is

$$\Pi = (\Pi_0, \Pi_1, \ldots, \Pi_n)'.$$

The profit signature elements Π_t, for $t \geq 1$, represent the expected surplus emerging at the tth year-end **for a contract in force at the issue date, i.e at time $t = 0$**. The first term of the vector, Π_0, represents the value at time $t = 0$ of the pre-contract cash flows. So

$$\Pi_0 = \mathrm{Pr}_0$$

and for $t = 1, 2, \ldots, n$, we multiply Pr_t, which is the expected surplus conditional on the contract being in force at time $t - 1$, by the probability of being in force at time $t - 1$, to get the unconditional expected surplus at time t for a new contract, so

$$\Pi_t = t - 1\, P_x^{00}\, \text{Pr}_t.$$

12.4.4 The net present value

Having developed the projected expected year-end emerging surplus for a new contract, it is often convenient to express the values in a single metric. The **net present value (NPV)** of the contract is the present value of the projected emerging surplus values. To determine the present values, we discount at an appropriate rate of interest, which is normally higher than the assumed yield on assets which is specified in the profit testing basis. The interest rate for discounting surplus represents the return on capital required by the shareholders, since the emerging surplus can be considered as the return to shareholders on capital supplied to support the contract liability. The rate is sometimes called the **risk discount rate** or **hurdle rate**.

Assuming a risk discount rate of r per year effective, the net present value of a policy is

$$\text{NPV} = \sum_{t=0}^{n} \Pi_t\, v_r^t.$$

12.4.5 Notes on the profit testing method

1. For a large portfolio of similar policies, the profit signature describes the expected surplus emerging at each year end for each contract issued. This is clearly useful information, and begs the question: why take the intermediate step of calculating the profit vector, for which each term is conditional on the contract being in force at successive policy anniversaries? The answer is that the profit vector is also useful, particularly for a portfolio of in-force contracts at different durations.

   Suppose an insurer has a portfolio of 10-year term insurance policies, all issued to lives aged 60 at different times in the previous 10 years, and all represented by the policy terms and assumptions used for the example in Section 12.3. The profit vector can be used to analyse expected emerging surplus from each cohort. For example, for each contract still in force after $k \geq 1$ complete years (at age $60+k$), the profit signature from future surplus can be calculated as

$$\left(\text{Pr}_{k+1}, \quad {}_1p_{60+k}^{00}\, \text{Pr}_{k+2}, \quad {}_2p_{60+k}^{00}\, \text{Pr}_{k+3}, \quad \ldots, {}_{9-k}p_{60+k}^{00}\, \text{Pr}_{10} \right)'$$

and the NPV of the future surplus is

$$\sum_{u=1}^{10-k} {}_{u-1}p^{00}_{60+k}\, \mathrm{Pr}_{k+u}\; v_r^u.$$

2. We have been rather loose about random variables and expectation in this chapter. In practice, profit testing would be carried out on large portfolios, rather than on individual contracts. Aggregating makes the individual cash flows relatively more predictable, and it may be reasonable to assume that death benefits and reserve costs will be quite close to the expected values. The approach used here is described as deterministic, which is loosely used to mean that we project cash flows without allowing for random variation.

3. The process described in this section can be used with traditional style contracts, allowing for multiple decrements or multiple states, but assumes that the contract is in force in only one state. When there are two or more states representing the in-force contracts, the process requires some extra steps which we describe in Section 12.8 below.

12.5 Profit measures

Once we have projected the cash flows, we need to assess whether the emerging profit is adequate. There are a number of ways to measure profit, all based on the profit signature.

The net present value is a commonly used measure of profit for project appraisals in all fields. For the example in Section 12.3, if the insurer uses a risk discount rate of 10% per year, then the NPV of the contract is $74.13. We define also the **partial net present value**. For $t \le n$, NPV(t) is the net present value of all cash flows up to and including time t, so that

$$\mathrm{NPV}(t) = \sum_{k=0}^{t} \Pi_k\, v_r^k.$$

Often the partial NPV is negative in the early years of a contract, reflecting the acquisition costs, and has a single sign change at some point of the contract, assuming the NPV of the contact is positive. The partial NPV values for $t = 0, 1, \ldots, 10$ for the 10-year term insurance example are given in Table 12.5, showing this typical pattern for emerging profit. The NPV for the contract is the final value in the partial NPV vector.

The NPV is closely related to the **internal rate of return (IRR)**, which is the interest rate j such that the net present value is zero. That is, given a profit

Table 12.5 *Partial NPVs for Section 12.3
example, 10% risk discount rate.*

t	NPV(t)	t	NPV(t)
0	−700.00	6	−144.43
1	−589.85	7	−78.56
2	−485.95	8	−20.37
3	−389.07	9	30.42
4	−299.70	10	74.13
5	−218.12		

signature $(\Pi_0, \Pi_1, \ldots, \Pi_n)'$ for an n-year contract, the internal rate of return is j where

$$\sum_{t=0}^{n} \Pi_t \, v_j^t = 0. \tag{12.3}$$

The IRR is commonly used as a metric for assessing profitability, with insurers setting minimum values for the IRR of the hurdle rate. One problem with the internal rate of return is that there may be no real solution to equation (12.3), or there may be many. However, a quick check on the IRR can be determined by using the hurdle rate to calculate the NPV. If the NPV is greater than zero, and if the partial NPV has a single sign change, then there is a single solution to the IRR equation, and the IRR is greater than the hurdle rate. If the NPV is negative, then the IRR, if it exists, is less than the hurdle rate.

For the policy in Section 12.3, we know that the IRR is greater than 10%, as, at 10% risk discount rate, the NPV is greater than zero, and the partial NPV has a single sign change. In fact, the internal rate of return in this case is $j = 12.4\%$.

The partial NPV is useful for another profit measure, the **discounted payback period (DPP)**, also known as the break-even period. This is defined as the first time at which the partial NPV is greater than zero, using the risk discount rate. In other words, the DPP is m where

$$m = \min\{t : \text{NPV}(t) \geq 0\}.$$

The DPP represents the time until the insurer starts to make a profit on the contract. For the example in Section 12.3, the DPP is nine years.

The **profit margin** is the NPV expressed as a proportion of the EPV of the premiums, evaluated at the risk discount rate. For a contract with level premiums of P per year payable annually throughout an n year contract issued to a life aged x, the profit margin is

$$\text{Profit margin} = \frac{\sum_{t=0}^{n} \Pi_t \, v_r^t}{P \sum_{t=0}^{n-1} {}_tp_x^{00} \, v_r^t} \qquad (12.4)$$

using the risk discount rate for all calculations.

For the example in Section 12.3, the profit margin using a risk discount rate of 10% is

$$\frac{\text{NPV}}{P\ddot{a}_{60:\overline{10}|}} = \frac{74.13}{9\,684.5} = 0.77\%.$$

Another profit measure is the NPV as a proportion of the acquisition costs. For the example in Section 12.3, the acquisition costs are $700, so the NPV is 10.6% of the total acquisition costs.

None of these measures of profit explicitly takes into consideration the risk associated with the contract. Most of the inputs we have used in the emerging surplus calculation are, in practice, uncertain. If the experience is adverse, the profit will be smaller, or there could be significant losses.

12.6 Using the profit test to calculate the premium

Setting a premium using the profit test can be achieved by finding the minimum premium that satisfies the insurer's required profit measure.

For example, suppose the insurer requires a profit margin of 5% for the 10-year term insurance from Section 12.3, using the same 10% per year risk discount rate, and the same basis for the profit test and reserves as before. With the premium tested, $P = 1500$, the profit margin is only 0.77%. Increasing the premium to $1575.21 gives an NPV of $508.50 at the 10% per year risk discount rate, and an EPV of premiums of $10\,170.03, which gives the profit margin required.

The revised profit signature is

$$(-715.0, 197.7, 201.5, 203.9, 204.9, 204.5, 202.6, 199.4, 194.6, 188.4, 180.8)'$$

which gives a DPP of 5 years, at 10% risk discount rate, and an IRR of 25.0% per year.

In this example, we can solve the equation for the unknown premium, given a profit margin, because the equation is a linear function of the premium. This will not always be the case, but numerical methods, or appropriate software such as Solver in Excel, usually work well.

12.7 Using the profit test to calculate reserves

In the first part of the example in Section 12.3, we saw that if the insurer holds no reserves, negative surplus emerges in later years of the contract, which is unacceptable under risk management or accounting principles. In the second part of the example, it was assumed that the insurer held net premium reserves, which resulted in positive emerging surplus in each year after the initial outgo from acquisition expenses. This result is acceptable, but using capital to support the liabilities is expensive. The NPV of the emerging profit for the 10-year term insurance example is $270.39 without reserves, compared with $74.13 with the net premium reserves from Table 12.2. This means that, even though term insurance is not very demanding on capital (as reserves are relatively small), the NPV without reserves is more than three times the NPV when reserves are taken into account.

Because holding capital reduces profitability, the insurer will not want to hold more than necessary. The objective of the capital is to avoid negative surpluses in later contract years. We can use the profit test to determine the minimum reserve that would be required at each year end to eliminate negative surpluses emerging in any year, after the initial outgo.

We now demonstrate this process using the 10-year term insurance example. We work backwards from the final contract year; for each year, we calculate the reserve required at the start of the year to match exactly the expected outgo in that year with no excess surplus emerging.

Consider the final year of the term insurance contract, $t = 10$. At the start of the year the insurer receives $1500 premium, of which 3.5% is immediately spent on renewal expenses, leaving $1447.50. This sum, together with the reserve, and with interest earned on the premium plus reserve less expenses (at 5.5% according to the profit test basis), must be exactly enough to meet the expected year end outgo of $1900.

Suppose the reserve at the start of the year (i.e. at time $t = 9$) which exactly eliminates a negative emerging cash flow in the final year is denoted $_9V^Z$. Then we have

$$1.055 \left(_9V^Z + 1447.5 \right) = q_{69} S = 1900 \quad \Rightarrow \quad _9V^Z = 353.45.$$

In other words, putting $_9V = 353.45$ into the profit test, in place of the net premium policy value of $475.45, generates a value of $\text{Pr}_{10} = 0$. Now, this is smaller than the value in Table 12.2, so it might look as if this is not going to help, but what is actually happening is that surplus will emerge sooner, which should increase the profitability.

We then move back to the ninth policy year. Now the reserve at the start of the year, together with the premium, net of expenses, and with the interest

Table 12.6 *Zeroized reserves.*

t	$_tV^Z$
6	732.63
5	658.32
4	494.78
3	247.62
2	−78.17

income, must be sufficient to meet the expected cost of death benefit for a contract in force at the start of the year ($EDB_9 = 1800$) and also to support the cost of carrying forward the final year reserve ($_9V^Z = \$353.45$). Hence, the reserve equation for the minimum reserve at time $t = 8$ is

$$1.055 \left(_8V^Z + 0.965P \right) = q_{68}\, S + p_{68}\, _9V^Z$$
$$\Rightarrow {}_8V^Z = (1800 + 0.982 \times 353.45)\,/1.055 - 0.965P = 587.65.$$

Continuing back, at time $t = 7$, we need a reserve of $_7V^Z$ where

$$1.055 \left(_7V^Z + 0.965P \right) = q_{67}\, S + p_{67}\, _8V^Z$$
$$\Rightarrow {}_7V^Z = (1700 + 0.983 \times 587.65)\,/1.055 - 0.965P = 711.42.$$

Continuing in this way we obtain the values in Table 12.6.

We see that $_2V^Z$ is negative, but reserves cannot be negative. Policy values can be negative, as expected values, but the capital held for future liabilities cannot be negative. See Section 7.8 for more discussion of this. Rather than allow a negative reserve, we set $_2V^Z = 0$. Repeating the process for $t = 1$ and $t = 0$ generates negative values in both cases, so we set both $_0V^Z$ and $_1V^Z$ equal to 0.

Now we re-do the profit test to see the impact of using these minimum reserves on the profit signature and the NPV. The results are shown in Table 12.7, using a 10% per year risk discount rate for the partial NPVs.

We have set the reserve to be exactly sufficient, together with the premium and interest income, to meet the projected outgo, leaving emerging surplus of zero, for the years from $t = 4$ onwards. This process for determining reserves is called **zeroization**, and the resulting reserves are called **zeroized** reserves. By comparing the partial NPVs using the higher reserves (from Table 12.5) with the zeroized reserves, we have a higher ultimate NPV using the zeroized reserves – increased from \$74.13 per policy to \$189.31. We also see a faster emergence of surplus, with a DPP of two years, down from nine years with the higher reserves.

Table 12.7 *Emerging profit after zeroization*

t	Pr_t	Π_t	$\mathrm{NPV}(t)$
0	−700.00	−700.00	−700.00
1	527.11	527.11	−220.81
2	427.11	422.84	128.65
3	82.47	80.74	189.31
4	0.00	0.00	189.31
5	0.00	0.00	189.31
6	0.00	0.00	189.31
7	0.00	0.00	189.31
8	0.00	0.00	189.31
9	0.00	0.00	189.31
10	0.00	0.00	189.31

Holding less capital increases the NPV here, because, as is typical, the interest assumed to be earned on the capital, at 5.5% per year, is less than the risk discount rate, at 10% per year. The risk discount rate indicates the return required on the equity invested. Within the profit test, assets are earning only 5.5% per year, but the high risk discount rate means that (loosely) the capital required for the contract needs to earn 10% per year. If less capital is required, the cost of that capital is lower, allowing more profit in the form of NPV.

We may generalize the algorithm in the example, to develop an expression for the zeroized reserves in principle. Using the assumptions and notation of Section 12.4 above, and given the zeroized reserve at t, $_tV^Z$, then the zeroized reserve at time $t - 1 \geq 0$ is

$$_{t-1}V^Z = \max\left(\left(EDB_t + ESB_t + EEB_t + E_tV^Z\right)/(1 + i_t) - (P_t - E_t), 0\right).$$

So, given that at the maturity of the contract, we can assume $_nV^Z = 0$, it is possible to work backwards through the cash flows to determine the schedule of zeroized reserves for any policy.

12.8 Profit testing for multiple state models

The term insurance example used throughout the previous sections was useful for introducing profit testing concepts, as the policy is relatively uncomplicated. We need to adapt the profit testing algorithm for more complex examples, and a particular case worth considering in more detail arises where there are multiple in-force states.

Policies with two or more in-force states would include any policy with disability benefits, such as a waiver of premium on sickness. For example, under the model in Figure 8.4, policyholders in both the 'Healthy' and 'Sick' states would be in the in-force portfolio, but the cash flows expected from each state would be quite different. Similarly, for a joint life contract, the projected cash flows while both partners are alive could be quite different from the cash flows projected after one partner has died.

In this section we present an example of a partially accelerated critical illness (CI) and term insurance policy. The term 'partially accelerated' refers to the fact that some of the sum insured under the contract will be paid on diagnosis of a critical illness, with the remainder paid if and when the policyholder subsequently dies. If the policyholder dies without a CI diagnosis, the full sum insured is payable on death. The policy is in force in the healthy state and also after CI diagnosis, provided the policyholder has not lapsed or died. In Section 8.7, we showed that in a multiple state insurance model, policy values (and, consequently, reserves) are dependent on the state that the policy is in at valuation, and the multiple state version of Thiele's equation for the disability income insurance model required two simultaneous differential equations for the two in-force states.

Profit testing similarly requires separate consideration of the in-force states. When the contract has different in-force states, we must calculate different, state dependent profit vectors. We can, subsequently, combine the profit vectors with state dependent probabilities to determine a profit signature for a contract. We demonstrate this in the following example.

Example 12.1 A 10-year partially accelerated CI and term insurance policy is issued to (x). The multiple state model used to analyse the policy is shown in Figure 12.1.

The benefits payable under the contract are

- $50 000 at the end of the year if (x) is diagnosed with a CI during the year, and survives to the year end.

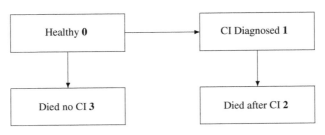

Figure 12.1 Multiple state model for Example 12.1.

Table 12.8 *Reserves for Example 12.1.*

t	$_tV^{(0)}$	$_tV^{(1)}$	t	$_tV^{(0)}$	$_tV^{(1)}$
0	0	0	5	2000	40 000
1	700	43 000	6	1600	38 000
2	1200	43 000	7	1200	34 000
3	1600	42 000	8	1000	27 000
4	2000	42 000	9	500	17 000

- $100\,000$ at the end of the year if (x) dies during the year, having been healthy at the start of the year.
- $50\,000$ at the end of the year if (x) dies during the year, having been diagnosed with a CI before the start of the year.

Premiums of $2500 are payable annually in advance, whilst in the healthy state.
Reserves at each year end are conditional on whether the policyholder is in state 0 or state 1, and are given in Table 12.8.

One-year transition probabilities for the model are, for $t = 0, 1, 2, \ldots, 9$,

$$p_{x+t}^{01} = 0.01, \qquad\qquad p_{x+t}^{02} = 0.005 + 0.001t,$$

$$p_{x+t}^{03} = 0.002 + 0.001t, \quad p_{x+t}^{12} = 0.35.$$

Other profit test assumptions:

Acquisition expenses:	$250
Premium expenses:	5% of each premium
Renewal expenses in state 1:	$25
Interest on investments:	6% per year
Risk discount rate:	12% per year

(a) Calculate the profit vector conditional on being in state 0 at the start of the policy year, $\Pr^{(0)}$, and the profit vector conditional on being in state 1 at the start of the policy year, $\Pr^{(1)}$.

(b) Comment on the two profit vectors. Do you see any problem with the conditional emerging cash flows?

(c) Calculate the profit signature and partial net present value vector for a new policy. Does the policy meet a requirement that the IRR exceeds 12%?

(d) Calculate the profit margin for the policy.

Solution 12.1 (a) The profit test table for $\Pr^{(0)}$ is given in Table 12.9, where numbers (other than the elements of $\Pr^{(0)}$) are rounded for presentation. We give a general description of principles here, followed by a more detailed derivation of each column in the description below.

Table 12.9 *Example 12.1 profit vector calculation conditional on the policy being in state 0 at the start of each year.*

t (1)	$_{t-1}V^{(0)}$ (2)	$P_t - E_t$ (3)	I_t (4)	EB_t^{01} (5)	EB_t^{02} (6)	EB_t^{03} (7)	$E_t V^{01}$ (8)	$E_t V^{00}$ (9)	$\Pr^{(0)}$ (10)
0	0	−250	0					0	−250.00
1	0	2375	143	500	500	200	430	688	199.40
2	700	2375	185	500	600	300	430	1177	252.30
3	1200	2375	215	500	700	400	420	1566	203.10
4	1600	2375	239	500	800	500	420	1954	39.50
5	2000	2375	263	500	900	600	400	1950	287.50
6	2000	2375	263	500	1000	700	380	1557	500.70
7	1600	2375	239	500	1100	800	340	1165	308.30
8	1200	2375	215	500	1200	900	270	969	−49.50
9	1000	2375	203	500	1300	1000	170	483	124.00
10	500	2375	173	500	1400	1100	0	0	47.50

In this table, each row is calculated assuming that the policy is in state 0 at the start of the year. The policy could move to state 1 by the year end, in which case there will be a cash flow corresponding to the CI diagnosis benefit, and it will also be necessary to carry forward a reserve to the following year, which is appropriate for a policy in state 1 at that time. The policy could move to state 2 by the year end, resulting in a benefit payment of $100 000, and no further cash flows. The policy could move to state 3 by the year end, with the same outcome as for state 2, and the policy could be still in state 0 at the year end, in which case there must be a reserve carried forward for the following year, appropriate for a policy in state 0.

Column (1) shows the time at the year end, except for $t = 0$ which represents the timing of pre-contract cash flows.

Column (2) shows the reserve brought forward at the start of the tth year, for a policy in state 0 at that time. These numbers are taken from Table 12.8.

Column (3) shows the premiums minus expenses at the start of each year, and shows the acquisition expenses at $t = 0$.

Column (4) shows the interest earned on reserves and premiums net of expenses in each year, with interest at 6% per year. That is, for $t = 1, 2, \ldots, 10$,

$$I_t = 0.06(_{t-1}V^{(0)} + P_t - E_t).$$

Column (5) Shows the expected cost of paying the benefit for a life who moves from state 0 to state 1 in the time period from $t - 1$ to t, and remains in state 1 at the year end. The benefit is \$50 000 and the transition probability is $p^{01}_{x+t-1} = 0.01$, so

$$EB^{01}_t = 50\,000\, p^{01}_{x+t-1} = 500.$$

Column (6) shows the expected cost of paying the benefit for a life who moves from state 0 to state 2 in the time period from $t-1$ to t. The benefit is \$100 000 and the transition probability is $p^{02}_{x+t-1} = 0.005 + 0.001(t-1)$, so

$$EB^{02}_t = 100\,000\, p^{02}_{x+t-1}.$$

Column (7) shows the expected cost of paying the benefit for a life who moves from state 0 to state 3 in the time period from $t-1$ to t. The benefit is \$100 000 and the transition probability is $p^{03}_{x+t-1} = 0.002 + 0.001(t-1)$, so

$$EB^{03}_t = 100\,000\, p^{03}_{x+t-1}.$$

Column (8) shows the expected cost of the reserve carried forward at the end of the tth year, for a life who is in state 1 at time t, given that the life was in state 0 at time $t-1$, for $t = 1, 2, \ldots, 9$. That is

$$E_t V^{01} = {}_t V^{(1)}\, p^{01}_{x+t-1}.$$

Column (9) shows the expected cost of the reserve carried forward from t to $t+1$ for a life who is in state 0 at time t, given that the life was in state 0 at time $t-1$, for $t = 1, 2, \ldots, 9$. That is

$$E_t V^{00} = {}_t V^{(0)}\, p^{00}_{x+t-1}.$$

Column (10) shows $\mathrm{Pr}^{(0)}_t$, which is the emerging profit at time t for a policy which is in state 0 at time $t-1$. So, for $t = 1, 2, \ldots, 10$,

$$\mathrm{Pr}^{(0)}_t = {}_{t-1} V^{(0)} + P_t - E_t + I_t - EB^{01}_t - EB^{02}_t$$
$$- EB^{03}_t - E_t V^{01} - E_t V^{00}.$$

The calculations for $\mathrm{Pr}^{(1)}$, which is the profit vector for policies in state 1 at the start of each year, are given in Table 12.10, and a more detailed explanation is given below.

Column (1) shows the policy year. Note that there are no policies in state 1 at the start of the first year, so the profit vector calculation starts in the second policy year.

Table 12.10 *Example 12.1 profit vector calculation conditional on the policy being in state 1 at the start of each year.*

t (1)	$_{t-1}V^{(1)}$ (2)	E_t (3)	I_t (4)	EB_t^{12} (5)	E_tV^{11} (6)	$\Pr^{(1)}$ (7)
2	43 000	25	2578.5	17 500	27 950	103.5
3	43 000	25	2578.5	17 500	27 300	753.5
4	42 000	25	2518.5	17 500	27 300	−306.5
5	42 000	25	2518.5	17 500	26 000	993.5
6	40 000	25	2398.5	17 500	24 700	173.5
7	38 000	25	2278.5	17 500	22 100	653.5
8	34 000	25	2038.5	17 500	17 550	963.5
9	27 000	25	1618.5	17 500	11 050	43.5
10	17 000	25	1018.5	17 500	0	493.5

Column (2) shows the reserve (from Table 12.8) brought forward for a contract in state 1 at time $t - 1$, i.e. $_{t-1}V^{(1)}$. This is the same amount whether the policy holder was in state 0 or state 1 in the previous year.

Column (3) shows the renewal expenses for the tth year for a policy in state 1.

Column (4) shows the interest income, for a policy in state 1 at time $t - 1$,

$$I_t = 0.06\left(_{t-1}V^{(1)} - E_t\right).$$

Column (5) shows the expected cost of benefits paid on death during the year $t - 1$ to t, for a policy in state 1 at time $t - 1$. The benefit payable is $50 000$, and the probability of payment is p_{x+t-1}^{12}, so

$$EB_t^{12} = 50\,000\, p_{x+t-1}^{12} = 17\,500.$$

Column (6) shows the expected cost of the reserve carried forward at the year end, for those policies still in state 1 at time t, so

$$E_tV^{11} = {_tV^{(1)}}\, p_{x+t-1}^{11}.$$

Column (7) shows the profit emerging at time t for a policy in state 1 at time $t - 1$, so

$$\Pr_t^{(1)} = {_{t-1}V^{(1)}} - E_t + I_t - EB_t^{12} - E_tV^{11}.$$

(b) We note that there are some negative expected emerging cash flows, both for the state 1 conditional emerging profit and for the state 0 conditional

Table 12.11 *Profit signature and NPV function for Example 12.1.*

t (1)	$_tp_x^{00}$ (2)	$_tp_x^{01}$ (3)	$\mathrm{Pr}^{(0)}$ (4)	$\mathrm{Pr}^{(1)}$ (5)	Π (6)	NPV (7)
0	1.00000	0.00000	−250.00	0.00	−250.00	−250.00
1	0.98300	0.01000	199.40	0.00	199.40	−71.96
2	0.96432	0.01633	252.30	103.50	249.05	126.57
3	0.94407	0.02026	203.10	753.50	208.16	274.74
4	0.92236	0.02261	39.50	−306.50	31.08	294.49
5	0.89930	0.02392	287.50	993.50	287.64	457.70
6	0.87502	0.02454	500.70	173.50	454.43	687.93
7	0.84964	0.02470	308.30	653.50	285.81	817.22
8	0.82330	0.02455	−49.50	963.50	−18.26	809.84
9	0.79614	0.02419	124.00	43.50	103.16	847.04
10	0.76827	0.02369	47.50	493.50	49.76	863.06

emerging profit. For each policy in state 1 at time $t = 3$, the expected surplus emerging at the year end is −$306.50. Similarly, for each policy in state 0 at the start of the eighth year, the expected surplus emerging at the year end is −$49.50. A negative emerging profit indicates that inadequate capital is allocated to meet the outgo in those years. Thus, the reserves should be adjusted to avoid the negative values arising.

(c) In Table 12.11 we show the calculation of the profit signature and the partial NPV function. More detailed explanations of each column follow.

Column (1) shows the time at the year end, except for $t = 0$ which represents the timing of pre-contract cash flows.

Column (2) shows the state 0 survival probability. Since there are no return transitions to state 0 in this model, we have $_0p_x^{00} = 1$, and we can calculate subsequent probabilities recursively as

$$_tp_x^{00} = {}_{t-1}p_x^{00}\ p_{x+t-1}^{00}.$$

Column (3) shows the probability that a policy which is in state 0 at age x is in state 1 at age $x + t$. We have $_0p_x^{01} = 0$, and we can use the Chapman–Kolmogorov equations to calculate $_tp_x^{01}$ recursively, as

$$_tp_x^{01} = {}_{t-1}p_x^{00}\ p_{x+t-1}^{01} + {}_{t-1}p_x^{01}\ p_{x+t-1}^{11}.$$

Columns (4) and (5) show the conditional profit vectors from part (a).

Column (6) is the profit signature vector. Π_t represents the expected profit emerging at time t for a policy issued (and therefore in state 0) at time 0.

Recall that $\mathrm{Pr}_t^{(0)}$ is the emerging profit at time t conditional on being in state 0 at time $t − 1$, and $\mathrm{Pr}_t^{(1)}$ is the emerging profit at time

t conditional on being in state 1 at time $t - 1$, so the profit signature is

$$\Pi_t = {}_{t-1}p_x^{00}\,\Pr_t^{(0)} + {}_{t-1}p_x^{01}\,\Pr_t^{(1)}.$$

Column (7) is the partial NPV function, at a risk discount rate of $r = 12\%$. So

$$\mathrm{NPV}(t) = \sum_{k=0}^{t} \Pi_k\, v_r^k.$$

We note that the final NPV, at 12%, is \$863.06, which is greater than 0, and also that there is only one sign change in the partial NPV function, so the IRR is uniquely determined, and is greater than 12%.

(d) The profit margin is the NPV divided by the EPV of premiums. As premiums are payable only if the life is in state 0, the EPV of premiums is

$$2500 \sum_{t=0}^{9} {}_{t}p_x^{00}\, v_r^t = 14\,655.31$$

which gives a profit margin of 5.89%.   □

12.9 Notes

For each of the policies considered in this chapter, benefits are payable at the end of a time period. However, in practice, benefits are usually payable on, or shortly after, the occurrence of a specified event. For example, for the term insurance policy considered in Section 12.3, the death benefit is payable at the end of the year of death. If, instead, the death benefit had been payable immediately on death, then we could allow for this in our profit test by assuming all deaths occurred in the middle of the year. Taking this approach, the expected death claims in Table 12.1 would all be adjusted by multiplying by a factor of $1.055^{1/2}$.

In practice, as we have mentioned, it would be normal to use monthly steps in a profit test, and the assumption that benefits are paid at the end of the month of claim is less artificial than the assumption of payment at the end of the year of death.

Throughout this chapter we have used deterministic assumptions for all the factors. By doing this we gain no insight into the effect of uncertainty on the results. In Chapter 14 we describe how we might use stochastic scenarios for emerging cost analysis for equity-linked contracts. Stochastic scenarios can also be used for traditional insurance.

12.10 Exercises

Exercise 12.1 A profit test of a 20-year term insurance issued to (40) is to be carried out on the following basis:

Survival model:	$q_{40+t} = 0.001 + 0.0001t$
Interest:	6% effective per year
Pre-contract expenses:	25% of the first premium
Renewal expenses:	1.5% of each premium after the first
Claim expenses:	$60.

The annual premium is $270 and the sum insured, payable at the end of the year of death, is $150 000. Calculate the emerging surplus at the end of the tenth policy year, per policy in force at the start of that year, given that the insurer holds reserves of $300 per policy in force at the start of each year.

Exercise 12.2 A profit test of a 20-year endowment insurance issued to (45) is to be carried out on the following basis:

Survival model:	$q_{45+t} = 0.0015 + 0.0001t$
Interest:	5% effective per year
Pre-contract expenses:	20% of the first premium
Renewal expenses:	2.5% of each premium after the first
Claim expenses:	$40.

The annual premium is $8400 and the sum insured, payable at the end of the year of death, or at maturity, is $250 000. Calculate the emerging surplus for the following two cases:

(a) at the end of the tenth policy year, per policy in force at the start of that year, and
(b) at the end of the 20th policy year, per policy in force at the start of that year,

given that $_9V = 88\,129$, $_{10}V = 100\,001$ and $_{19}V = 232\,012$.

Exercise 12.3 A profit test of a deferred annuity issued to (45) is to be carried out on the following basis:

Survival model:	Standard Ultimate Survival Model
Interest:	5% effective per year
Pre-contract expenses:	20% of the first premium
Renewal expenses:	$25 on each policy anniversary
Annuity payment expenses:	$15 each time an annuity payment is made.

The annuity is payable annually from age 65; the first annuity payment is $50 000, and payments increase by 2% each year. The annual premium, payable throughout the deferred period, is $26 100.

(a) Calculate the emerging surplus at the end of years 1 and 2, per policy in force at the start of each year, and hence calculate NPV(2) using a risk discount rate of 10% per year.
(b) Calculate the emerging surplus in the 30th policy year, per policy in force at the start of that year. Assume the annuity is paid at the start of each policy year.

You are given that $_1V = 26\,845$, $_2V = 54\,924$, $_{29}V = 768\,919$ and $_{30}V = 753\,464$.

Exercise 12.4 A five-year policy with annual cash flows issued to a life (x) produces the profit vector

$$\mathrm{Pr} = (-360.98, 149.66, 14.75, 273.19, 388.04, 403.00)',$$

where Pr_0 is the profit at time 0 and Pr_t $(t = 1, 2, \ldots, 5)$ is the profit at time t per policy in force at time $t - 1$.

The survival model used in the profit test is given by

$$q_{x+t} = 0.0085 + 0.0005t.$$

(a) Calculate the profit signature for this policy.
(b) Calculate the NPV for this policy using a risk discount rate of 10% per year.
(c) Calculate the NPV for this policy using a risk discount rate of 15% per year.
(d) Comment briefly on the difference between your answers to parts (b) and (c).
(e) Calculate the IRR for this policy.

Exercise 12.5 A 10-year term insurance issued to a life aged 55 has sum insured $200 000 payable immediately on death, and monthly premiums of $100 payable throughout the term.

Initial, pre-contract expenses are $500 plus 50% of the first monthly premium; renewal expenses are 5% of each monthly premium after the first. The insurer earns interest at 6% per year on all cash flows and assumes the policyholder is subject to the Standard Ultimate Survival Model.

Calculate the profit vector at monthly intervals for this policy, assuming deaths occur at the mid-point of each month.

Exercise 12.6 An insurer issues a four-year term insurance contract to a life aged 60. The sum insured, $100 000, is payable at the end of the year of death.

The gross premium for the contract is $1100 per year. The reserve at each year end is 30% of the gross premium.

The company uses the following assumptions to assess the profitability of the contract:

Survival model:	$q_{60} = 0.008$, $q_{61} = 0.009$, $q_{62} = 0.010$, $q_{63} = 0.012$
Interest:	8% effective per year
Pre-contract expense:	30% of the first gross premium
Renewal expenses:	2% of each gross premium after the first
Claim expenses:	$60
Lapses:	None.

(a) Calculate the profit vector for the contract.
(b) Calculate the profit signature for the contract.
(c) Calculate the net present value of the contract using a risk discount rate of 12% per year.
(d) Calculate the profit margin for the contract using a risk discount rate of 12% per year.
(e) Calculate the discounted payback period using a risk discount rate of 12% per year.
(f) Determine whether the internal rate of return for the contract exceeds 50% per year.
(g) If the insurer has a hurdle rate of 15% per year, is this contract satisfactory?

Exercise 12.7 A life insurer issues a 20-year endowment insurance policy to a life aged 55. The sum insured is $100 000, payable at the end of the year of death or on survival to age 75. Premiums are payable annually in advance for at most 10 years. The insurer assumes that initial expenses will be $300, and renewal expenses, which are incurred at the beginning of the second and subsequent years in which a premium is payable, will be 2.5% of the gross premium. The funds invested for the policy are expected to earn interest at 7.5% per year. The insurer holds net premium reserves, using an interest rate of 6% per year. The Standard Ultimate Survival Model is used for the premium and the net premium reserve calculations.

The insurer sets premiums so that the profit margin on the contract is 15%, using a risk discount rate of 12% per year.

Calculate the gross annual premium.

Exercise 12.8 Repeat Exercise 12.7 assuming that the sum insured is paid immediately on death, premiums are payable monthly for at most 10 years and expenses are $300 initially and then 2.5% of each monthly premium after the first.

Exercise 12.9 A life insurance company issues a special 10-year term insurance policy to two lives aged 50 at the issue date, in return for the payment of a single premium. The following benefits are payable under the contract.

- In the event of either of the lives dying within 10 years, a sum insured of $100 000 is payable at the year end.
- In the event of the second death within 10 years, a further sum insured of $200 000 is payable at the year end. (If both lives die within 10 years and in the same year, a total of $300 000 is paid at the end of the year of death.)

The basis for the calculation of the premium and the reserves is as follows.

Survival model:	Assume the two lives are independent with respect to survival and the model for each follows the Standard Ultimate Survival Model.
Interest:	4% per year.
Expenses:	3% of the single premium at the start of each year that the contract is in force.

(a) Calculate the single premium using the equivalence principle.
(b) Calculate the reserves on the premium basis assuming that
   (i) only one life is alive, and
   (ii) both lives are still alive.
(c) Using the premium and reserves calculated, determine the profit signature for the contract assuming:

Survival model:	As for the premium basis
Interest:	8% per year
Expenses:	1.5% of the premium at issue, increasing at 4% per year.

Exercise 12.10 A five-year term insurance policy with annual cash flows issued to a life (x) produces the profit vector

$$\text{Pr} = (-310, 436, 229, 94, -55, -217)',$$

where Pr_0 is the profit at time 0 and Pr_t $(t = 1, 2, \ldots, 5)$ is the profit at time t per policy in force at time $t - 1$. This profit vector has been calculated without allowance for reserves.

The survival model used in the profit test is given by $p_{x+t} = 0.987 - 0.001t$, and the interest rate is 5% per year.

The insurer determines reserves by zeroization. Calculate the revised profit vector after allowance for reserves.

Exercise 12.11 A life insurance company issues a reversionary annuity policy to a husband and wife, both of whom are aged exactly 60. The annuity commences at the end of the year of death of the wife and is payable subsequently while the husband is alive, for a maximum period of 20 years after the commencement date of the policy. The annuity is payable annually at $10 000 per year. The premium for the policy is payable annually while the wife and husband are both alive and for a maximum of five years.

The basis for calculating the premium and reserves is as follows.

Survival model: Assume the two lives are independent with respect to survival and the model for each follows the Standard Ultimate Survival Model.

Interest: 4% per year.

Expenses: Initial expense of $300 and an expense of 2% of each annuity payment whenever an annuity payment is made.

(a) Calculate the annual premium.
(b) Calculate the NPV for the policy assuming:

a risk discount rate of 15% per year,

expenses and the survival model are as in the premium basis, and

interest is earned at 6% per year on cash flows.

Exercise 12.12 A life aged 60 purchases a deferred life annuity, with a five-year deferred period. At age 65 the annuity vests, with payments of $20 000 per year at each year end, so that the first payment is on the 66th birthday. All payments are contingent on survival. The policy is purchased with a single premium.

If the policyholder dies before the first annuity payment, the insurer returns her gross premium, with interest of 5% per year, at the end of the year of her death.

(a) Calculate the single premium using the following premium basis:

Survival model: $\mu_x = 0.9(0.00022 + 2.7 \times 10^{-6} \times 1.124^x)$ for all x
Interest: 6% per year before vesting; 5% per year thereafter
Expenses: $275 at issue plus $20 with each annuity payment.

(b) Gross premium reserves are calculated using the premium basis. Calculate the year end reserves (**after** the annuity payment) for each year of the contract.

(c) The insurer conducts a profit test of the contract assuming the following basis:

Survival model: Standard Ultimate Survival Model
Interest: 8% per year before vesting; 6% per year thereafter
Expenses: $275 at issue plus $20 with each annuity payment.

   (i) Calculate the profit signature for the contract.
   (ii) Calculate the profit margin for the contract using a risk discount rate of 10% per year.

Exercise 12.13 A special 10-year endowment insurance is issued to a healthy life aged 55. The benefits under the policy are

- $50 000 if at the end of a month the life is disabled, having been healthy at the start of the month,
- $100 000 if at the end of a month the life is dead, having been healthy at the start of the month,
- $50 000 if at the end of a month the life is dead, having been disabled at the start of the month,
- $50 000 if the life survives as healthy to the end of the term.

On withdrawal at any time, a surrender value equal to 80% of the net premium policy value is paid, and level monthly premiums are payable throughout the term while the life is healthy.

The survival model used for profit testing is shown in Figure 12.2. The transition intensities μ_x^{01}, μ_x^{02}, μ_x^{03} and μ_x^{12} are constant for all ages x with values per year as follows:

$$\mu_x^{01} = 0.01, \quad \mu_x^{02} = 0.015, \quad \mu_x^{03} = 0.01, \quad \mu_x^{12} = 0.03.$$

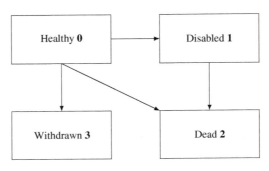

Figure 12.2 Multiple state model for Exercise 12.13.

Other elements of the profit testing basis are as follows.

- Interest: 7% per year.
- Expenses: 5% of each gross premium, including the first, together with an additional initial expense of $1000.
- The benefit on withdrawal is payable at the end of the month of withdrawal and is equal to 80% of the sum of the reserve held at the start of the month and the premium paid at the start of the month.
- Reserves are set equal to the net premium policy values.
- The gross premium and net premium policy values are calculated using the same survival model as for profit testing except that withdrawals are ignored, so that $\mu_x^{03} = 0$ for all x.
- The net premium policy values are calculated using an interest rate of 5% per year.

The monthly gross premium is calculated using the equivalence principle on the following basis:

- Interest: 5.25% per year.
- Expenses: 5% of each premium, including the first, together with an additional initial expense of $1000.

(a) Calculate the monthly premium on the net premium policy value basis.
(b) Calculate the reserves at the start of each month for both healthy lives and for disabled lives.
(c) Calculate the monthly gross premium.
(d) Project the emerging surplus using the profit testing basis.
(e) Calculate the internal rate of return.
(f) Calculate
    (i) the NPV,
    (ii) the profit margin (using the EPV of gross premiums),
    (iii) the NPV as a percentage of the acquisition costs, and
    (iv) the discounted payback period for the contract,
    in all cases using a risk discount rate of 15% per year.

Answers to selected exercises

12.1 $15.36
12.2 (a) $773.86,
    (b) $2172.10
12.3 (a) $580.70, $688.11,   −$4067.02
    (b) $3503.74

12.4 (a) $(-360.98,\ 149.66,\ 14.62,\ 268.43,\ 377.66,\ 388.29)'$
 (b) \$487.88
 (c) \$365.69
 (e) 42.7%
12.5 Selected values are $Pr_{30} = 54.53$ and $Pr_{84} = 28.75$, measuring time in months
12.6 (a) $(-330.00,\ 60.16,\ 293.07,\ 193.34,\ 319.92)'$
 (b) $(-330.00,\ 60.16,\ 290.73,\ 190.07,\ 311.36)'$
 (c) \$288.64
 (d) 7.8%
 (e) 3 years
 (f) No (The IRR is 42%.)
 (g) Yes
12.7 \$4553.75
12.8 \$394.27 (per month)
12.9 (a) \$4180.35
 (b) Selected values are (i) $_4V = \$3126.04$, and (ii) $_4V = \$3146.06$
 (c) Selected values are $\Pi_0 = -\$62.71$, $\Pi_5 = \$177.03$ and $\Pi_{10} = \$62.52$
12.10 $(-310,\ 436,\ 89.68,\ 0,\ 0,\ 0)'$
12.11 (a) \$1832.79
 (b) \$779.26
12.12 (a) \$192 805.84
 (b) Selected values are $_4V = \$243\,148.51$ and $_{10}V = \$226\,245.94$
 (c) (i) Selected values are $\Pi_4 = \$4538.90$ and $\Pi_{10} = \$2429.55$
 (ii) 14.8%
12.13 (a) \$452.00
 (b) Selected values are $_4V^{(0)} = 15\,613.44$ and $_4V^{(1)} = 7157.17$, and $_8V^{(0)} = 36\,761.39$ and $_8V^{(1)} = 2769.93$ (time in years)
 (c) \$484.27
 (d) Selected values are \$35.48 and \$11.43 at time 4 years, and \$72.27 and \$4.54 at time 8 years, for states 0 and 1 respectively.
 (e) 32.7%
 (f) (i) \$992.29
 (ii) 3.84%
 (iii) 97%
 (iv) 5 years and 5 months

13

Participating and Universal Life insurance

13.1 Summary

In this chapter we introduce two forms of variable insurance. Participating, or with-profit life insurance introduces variability in the cash flows of whole life or endowment insurance through a profit sharing arrangement. Universal Life insurance is a form of whole life (or endowment) insurance, with some profit sharing incorporated in the design, and which also has more flexible payment schedules than traditional insurance.

We demonstrate how to use the profit testing techniques from Chapter 12 to analyse a participating whole life insurance contract, and we consider the impact of different methods of paying the policyholder's share of profits.

We then introduce the language, notation and policy terms for Universal Life insurance, and demonstrate how these policies may also be analysed using profit testing.

Finally, we discuss how a Universal Life policy can mimic the payoffs of a traditional whole life or endowment policy.

13.2 Introduction

Life insurance and annuity products serve a range of purposes for customers. Term insurance, offering death benefit cover, for limited periods, to younger lives in good health, is usually intended to provide protection against financial hardship arising from the death of the policyholder. Most term insurance policies expire without any payment to the policyholder. There are no cash values on surrender. Individuals do not buy term insurance for the investment benefits; they buy term insurance to indemnify their families against the financial consequences of the death of the insured life.

The purpose of whole life insurance (also known as permanent insurance) or endowment insurance is different. For these policies, a benefit payment, on death or surrender or, for endowment insurance, on survival to maturity, is

431

almost inevitable. The exception would be a surrender during the early years of a contract, when no payment would be made, allowing the insurer to recover any outstanding acquisition costs. There are some special whole life policies issued without surrender benefits, but the more traditional whole life insurance should offer significant surrender values at longer durations. The purpose of the whole life insurance policy is to provide an efficient, secure investment, either for enhancing the policyholder's bequest to their heirs, or for the policyholder themselves to enjoy, where the benefit is paid before their death. Because endowment insurance is relatively rare in most developed markets, we focus on whole life insurance in this chapter, but if we assume that the policy is surrendered by policyholders reaching a very advanced age, with appropriate cash value on surrender, the analysis of whole life and endowment policies is very similar.

So, whole life policies combine insurance and investment objectives, and this creates risk for both the insurer and the policyholder, especially for the traditional contract design with fixed premiums and benefits. A life who is in middle age at the inception of a policy may have an expected contract term of over 40 years, much longer than the term of almost all available fixed interest investments. Suppose the insurer is pricing a whole life policy at a time when long-term interest rates of 7% per year are available, for a 25-year investment. The insurer may calculate the premium assuming 6% per year interest, allowing the difference of 1% (the **interest spread**) to cover profit and allow a margin for adverse experience. The risk to the insurer is that, on reinvestment, interest rates may fall below 6% per year, in which case they would not be sufficient to support the benefits. On the other hand, if the insurer is more cautious, perhaps assuming only 4% per year interest, the investment part of the policy will look quite unattractive for the customer, compared with the 7% per year available from direct investment.

One solution to this problem is to make benefits or premiums more flexible, in particular to be more responsive to the investment experience of the underlying assets. Introducing flexibility removes the need for the insurer to be so cautious in its pricing assumptions. It also allows the insurer more investment freedom, with the potential for better returns than those achieved by locking in fixed rates, and the investment profits would then be shared with the policyholders. This is the principle behind the development of *participating* insurance, where 'participating' means participating in the distribution of profits. Participating insurance is also called 'par' insurance for short, and is more commonly called '*with-profit*' outside North America.

A traditional participating policy would have level premiums and benefits, similar to a non-participating (non-par or without-profit) contract. The premium would be set on a fairly conservative basis, meaning that it is designed to be more than adequate to pay the fixed benefits. As surpluses emerge, a portion is returned to the policyholders, and the rest is retained by the company. The policyholders' share of profits can be distributed in different ways, including cash payments, or through increasing the sum insured. We discuss the range of distribution methods more fully in Section 13.3.3.

Participating insurance was very popular for many years, as profit sharing proved to be a very creative way to solve the problems arising from the need to set premiums and benefits for very long-term contracts. However, the traditional form has drawbacks that led to a decline in popularity. Policyholders sign up for decades of premiums; when circumstances change, a policyholder may not be able to continue paying the premiums. A policyholder can surrender the contract, for a cash value, but the cash value could be quite poor. Insurers prefer policyholders not to surrender their whole life policies, so they may offer low cash values to create disincentives for policyholders to surrender, and to generate surpluses from those who do. Even when profits can be used to offset premiums, there still may not be sufficient flexibility for policyholders who find themselves unable to continue to pay the premiums for the policy. Insurers found participating insurance sales declining as middle-income households found more opportunities to invest more directly in capital markets, through pooled investment arrangements such as mutual funds. More recently, however, insurers in North America have found customers increasingly interested in the traditional par products, perhaps in response to increased concerns over market volatility. Participating insurance therefore remains an important product in North America and in some emerging markets.

To create insurance policies that could compete with the flexibility and upside potential of mutual fund type investments, insurers devised a range of new style, variable contracts, with greater flexibility, greater transparency, and with profit sharing integrated in the policy design. These modern contracts can be placed in two broad categories. The first, which we might call flexible insurance, is developed from the traditional insurance model, with added flexibility in premiums and benefits, and increased emphasis on the investment returns, compared with traditional with-profits insurance. The second category, which we call equity-linked insurance, or separate account insurance, uses the mutual fund investment as a starting point, and adds in elements of insurance, such as additional life insurance benefits, and guaranteed minimum payments. We discuss equity-linked insurance in subsequent chapters. In this chapter we first discuss the traditional participating insurance design, using the profit test to analyse the impact of the participation. We then introduce the form of flexible insurance known as **Universal Life** insurance, which is a very popular product in North America. We then use the profit testing framework to compare Universal Life and participating insurance.

13.3 Participating insurance

13.3.1 Introduction

A standard participating policy is issued with a schedule of level premiums and a fixed sum insured. The premiums are priced conservatively, perhaps by using a significant margin in the interest rate assumption – that is, by assuming a low interest rate in the premium calculation, compared with the rates expected to be earned. As funds from premiums and reserves are invested, higher returns will generate surplus. There may also be profits from other loadings and margins, and from favourable experience, for example with respect to mortality, expenses or lapses.

The profits from non-participating policies belong to the insurer. The profits from a portfolio of participating policies are shared between the policyholders and the insurer, usually in pre-specified proportions. The payments of share of profits to policyholders are called **dividends** in North America, and **bonuses** elsewhere. In this chapter we use the term 'dividend' when the profit share is distributed in the form of cash (or cash equivalent, such as a reduction in premium), and 'bonus' when the profit share is distributed in the form of additional insurance. In fact, the form of distribution is an important design feature for participating insurance, with different jurisdictions favouring different distribution methods, with the following being the most common.

Cash refunds may be distributed at regular (e.g. annual) intervals, based on the profit emerging in the preceding year.

Premium reductions work very similarly to cash refunds. The profit allocated to the policyholder for the year may be used to reduce the premiums due in the period to the subsequent allocation date.

Increased death benefits are determined by applying the emerging profit to purchase additional death benefit cover; this also affects cash values.

Additional benefits may be purchased, such as extra term insurance.

There are many variants of these methods. It is common in North America for policyholders to be given some choice about the distribution – for example, offering a premium reduction as a standard benefit, but with options to convert to additional whole life or term insurance. If there are no premiums due – for example, for single or limited premium contracts – the policyholder may receive the cash dividend, may convert it to additional benefit, or may leave it with the insurer until the policy is surrendered or matures.

In the UK, profits are invariably distributed in the form of benefit increases. Bonuses are awarded in two stages. **Reversionary bonuses** are applied to contracts in force, increasing the benefits by a specified percentage. There are three variations:

- *simple reversionary bonus* means the bonus rate is applied to the original sum insured only;
- *compound reversionary bonus* means the bonus rate is applied to the total of the sum insured and previous reversionary bonuses;
- *super-compound reversionary bonus* is a method with two bonus rates each year, the first applying to the original sum insured, and the second applying to the total of previous bonus declarations.

Terminal bonuses are used to top up the sum insured when the benefit is finally paid. Separating the profit share into reversionary and terminal bonuses allows insurers to take a more cautious attitude to distributing unrealized capital gains.

It is important to note that for all traditional participating insurance, dividends and bonuses are never negative. Only profits are shared, not losses.

13.3.2 Examples

Example 13.1 A life aged 60 purchases a participating whole life contract. The sum insured is $100 000, payable at the end of the year of death. Premiums of $2300 are payable annually in advance.

Reserves are calculated using net premium policy values, modified using the full preliminary term approach, assuming an interest rate of 5% per year.

Cash values are $0 for the first four years, 10% of the year end reserve for surrenders in the fifth year, 20% in the sixth year, 30% in the seventh year, and continue increasing at the same rate to 90% of the year end reserve in the 13th year. All policies surrendering after the 13th year receive a surrender benefit of 90% of the year end reserve. In addition, all surrendering policyholders receive the cash dividend due for their final contract year.

Construct the profit test and determine the NPV and the profit margin of this contract to the insurer, using the following assumptions.

- The survival model is the Standard Ultimate Survival Model.
- For the first nine years, 5% of the surviving in-force policyholders are assumed to surrender their contracts at each year end; from the 10th to the 29th years, 7.5% of survivors surrender at each year end. All surviving policyholders are assumed to surrender at the end of the 30th year.
- Premiums and reserves earn an investment return of 6% per year.
- 90% of surplus emerging each year from the second policy anniversary onwards is distributed to the policyholders as a cash dividend. No dividend is payable in the first policy year. No dividend is declared if the surplus emerging is negative.
- Initial, pre-contract expenses are $1800, assumed incurred at time $t = 0$.

Table 13.1 *Profit vector calculation for the participating whole life policy, with cash dividends; Example 13.1.*

t (1)	$_{t-1}V$ (2)	$P - E_t$ (3)	I_t (4)	EDB_t (5)	ECV_t (6)	$E_t V$ (7)	Pr_{t-} (8)	Div_t (9)	Pr_t (10)
0	—	−1 800	—	—	—	—	−1 800	0	−1 800
1	0	2 200	132	340	0	0	1 992	0	1 992
2	0	2 200	132	379	0	1 699	254	228	25
3	1 795	2 200	240	423	0	3 448	364	327	36
4	3 645	2 200	351	473	0	5 246	477	429	48
5	5 548	2 200	465	529	37	7 091	556	500	56
6	7 504	2 200	582	591	95	8 983	618	556	62
⋮	⋮	⋮	⋮	⋮	⋮	⋮	⋮	⋮	⋮
28	58 149	2 200	3 621	7 224	3 780	51 800	1 166	1 049	120
29	60 361	2 200	3 754	8 080	3 879	53 157	1 199	1 079	120
30	62 518	2 200	3 883	9 033	52 901	0	6 667	6 001	667

- Premium expenses of $100 are incurred with each premium payment, including the first.
- The risk discount rate for determining the NPV is 10% per year.

Solution 13.1 We show the first and last few rows of the profit test in Table 13.1. Details of the column calculations are given below. Some numbers in the table are rounded for presentation.

(1) t denotes the tth policy year, from time $t - 1$ to time t, except that $t = 0$ denotes time 0 when pre-contract expenses are incurred.

(2) gives the reserve brought forward each year. The full preliminary term policy value has $_0V = {_1V} = 0$, and for $t = 2, 3, \ldots$ is calculated as the net premium policy value for a contract issued one year later (in this case to a life aged 61). Thus, the full preliminary term policy value can be calculated as follows, where $S = 100\,000$ denotes the sum insured:

$$_tV = S\, A_{60+t} - P^*\ddot{a}_{60+t} \quad \text{where } P^* = \frac{S\, A_{61}}{\ddot{a}_{61}} = 2\,064.47$$

$$= S\left(1 - \frac{\ddot{a}_{60+t}}{\ddot{a}_{61}}\right).$$

All annuity and insurance factors are calculated at 5% per year, using the Standard Ultimate Survival Model. Hence, for example,

$$_4V = S\left(1 - \frac{\ddot{a}_{64}}{\ddot{a}_{61}}\right) = S\left(1 - \frac{13.8363}{14.6491}\right) = 5\,548.$$

Alternatively

$$_4V = SA_{64} - P^*\ddot{a}_{64} = 0.34113\,S - 13.8363\,P^* = 5\,548.$$

(3) shows $P - E_t$, the premium received less expenses incurred at the start of the year.

(4) shows I_t, the interest on funds invested in the tth year. The assumed return is 6% per year, so, for example,

$$I_4 = 0.06\,(_3V + P - E_4) = 0.06\,(3\,644.88 + 2\,300 - 100) = 350.69.$$

(5) shows the expected death benefit at time t, denoted EDB_t, for a policy in force at the start of the year, i.e. at time $t - 1$. We have

$$EDB_t = S \times p^{0d}_{60+t-1}$$

where p^{0d}_{x+t-1} is the probability of a death benefit claim in the tth year, given that the policy is in force at the start of the year. In this case, this is equal to the mortality rate q_{x+t-1} under the Standard Ultimate Survival Model, as all withdrawals are assumed to take place at the year end. Note that the expected death benefit does not include the dividend paid in the tth year.

(6) shows the expected cash value payment at time t, denoted ECV_t, for a policy in force at the start of the year. The probability of surrender is

$$p^{0w}_{x+t-1} = (1 - p^{0d}_{x+t-1})\,q^{*w}_t$$

where p^{0d}_{x+t-1} is as above, and q^{*w}_t is the probability of surrender for a policy that is in force at the end of the tth year – that is, $q^{*w}_t = 0.05$ for $t = 1, 2, \ldots, 9$, $q^{*w}_t = 0.075$ for $t = 10, 11, \ldots, 29$ and $q^{*w}_{30} = 1$.

The cash value is, say, $h_t\,_tV$ for surrenders at time t, where

$$h_t = 0 \text{ for } t = 1, 2, 3, 4;\ \ h_5 = 0.1,\ h_6 = 0.2, \ldots, h_{12} = 0.8$$
$$\text{and } h_t = 0.9 \text{ for } t \geq 13.$$

The expected cash value is the product of the probability of surrender and the cash value paid on surrender under the profit test assumptions, so, for example,

$$ECV_5 = p^{0w}_{64} \times 0.1 \times {_5V} = (0.99471 \times 0.05) \times 0.1 \times 7504.02 = 37.32$$

and

$$ECV_{30} = p^{0w}_{89} \times 0.9 \times {_{30}V} = 0.90967 \times 0.9 \times 64\,615 = 52\,901.$$

Note that policyholders who surrender at the year end will be eligible for a share of the profit emerging during the year. The expected cash value calculated in this column is the cash value arising without taking the year end share of profit into consideration.

(7) shows the expected cost of the reserve carried forward, denoted $E_t V$, for policies remaining in force at the year end, given the policy was in force at the start of the year. For example, the probability that a policy is in force at time 5 given that it is in force at time 4 is

$$p_{64}^{00} = 1 - p_{64}^{0d} - p_{64}^{0w} = 0.94498$$

so that

$$E_5 V = p_{64}^{00} \, {}_5 V = 0.94498 \times 7504.02 = 7091.12.$$

(8) shows Pr_{t-}, the profit emerging at time t for a policy in force at time $t - 1$, before sharing the profits between the insurer and the policyholder. Hence, for example,

$$\mathrm{Pr}_{5-} = {}_4 V + P - E_5 + I_5 - EDB_5 - ECV_5 - E_5 V = 555.68.$$

(9) shows Div_t, the share of profits (or dividend) distributed to policyholders, per policy in force at time $t - 1$, which is 90% of the pre-dividend profit, or 0 if greater. Hence, for example,

$$Div_5 = 0.90 \times 555.68 = 500.11.$$

(10) shows Pr_t, the insurer's surplus emerging at time t per policy in force at time $t - 1$, which is the balance of surplus after the policyholder's dividend. Hence, for example,

$$\mathrm{Pr}_5 = \mathrm{Pr}_{5-} - Div_5 = 55.57.$$

We calculate the NPV and profit margin from the profit vector, Pr, following the usual procedure from Chapter 12, giving a NPV of \$303.79, and a profit margin of 1.96%. □

Example 13.2 Repeat Example 13.1 above, but assume now that for policies remaining in force at each year end, the dividend is converted to an addition to the sum insured as a reversionary bonus. If the policyholder exits by death or surrender, they are paid the full cash dividend at the year end, in addition to any benefits based on the bonuses declared in the previous years. For example, death claims in the tth year are based on the bonuses up to the end of the $(t - 1)$th year, and then are supplemented with the tth year cash dividend as part of the distribution of profit.

Table 13.2 *Profit vector calculation for the participating whole life policy, with reversionary bonuses; Example 13.2.*

t (1)	$_{t-1}V$ (2)	$P - E_t$ (3)	I_t (4)	EDB_{t-} (5)	ECV_{t-} (6)	$E_t \cdot V$ (7)	Pr_{t-} (8)	Div_t (9)	Pr_t (10)
0	—	−1 800	—	—	—	—	−1 800		−1 800
1	0	2 200	132	340	0	0	1 992	0	1 992
2	0	2 200	132	379	0	1 699	254	228	25
3	2 024	2 200	253	426	0	3 673	378	340	38
4	4 223	2 200	385	481	0	5 814	513	461	51
5	6 610	2 200	529	545	43	8 135	616	554	62
6	9 163	2 200	682	619	112	10 611	703	632	70
⋮	⋮	⋮	⋮	⋮	⋮	⋮	⋮	⋮	⋮
28	89 167	2 200	5 482	10 388	5 765	78 999	1 697	1 527	170
29	93 581	2 200	5 747	11 790	5 983	81 990	1 765	1 588	176
30	98 018	2 200	6 013	13 374	82 541	0	10 316	9 284	1 032

The additional sum insured is calculated using the Standard Ultimate Survival Model and an interest rate of 5% per year, following the reserve assumptions.

(a) Determine the profit vector, NPV and profit margin.
(b) Determine the cash value for policyholders surrendering after 30 years.
(c) Determine the reversionary bonus rates applying each year, assuming (i) simple reversionary bonus rates, (ii) compound reversionary bonus rates, and (iii) super-compound reversionary bonus rates, with a maximum rate of 1.4% of the sum insured, and the remainder of the bonus (if any) expressed as a percentage of the total bonus previously declared.

Solution 13.2 (a) Table 13.2 summarizes the profit test calculations for this example and has the same format as Table 13.1, but note that the headings for columns (5), (6) and (7) now have the subscript $t-$ rather than t to indicate that they show the expected costs of the death benefit, cash value and reserve for the next year *before* the distribution of surplus at the end of the year. The only difference between this example and Example 13.1 is in the distribution of the surplus. Since no dividend is payable in the first policy year, the entries for $t = 0$ and 1 are the same as the corresponding entries in Table 13.1.

Now consider the entries for $t = 2$ in Table 13.2. For columns (2) to (7) these are the same as in Table 13.1 since they are calculated before the distribution of surplus at the end of the year. Hence, the profit to the insurer at the end of the year before the distribution of surplus, Pr_{2-} in column (8), is the same as the corresponding entry in Table 13.1. This profit, $254, is the expected profit to the insurer for each policy in force at the start of the second policy year. Under the terms of the policy, 90% of this profit, $228, is given to the policyholder. Policies in force at the start of the year can, at the end of the year, be divided into three groups:

(i) those where the policyholder has died in the year,

(ii) those where the policyholder surrenders the policy at the end of the year, and,

(iii) those still in force at the start of the third year.

Group (i) receive their dividend as an addition to their death benefit and group (ii) receive theirs as an increase to their surrender value. These payments do not affect the insurer's profit. Nor does the dividend paid to group (iii), but this needs to be considered more carefully.

Let B_t denote the bonus declared at the end of year t and RB_t denote the total bonus declared up to and including year t, so that $RB_t = RB_{t-1} + B_t$. The dividend at the end of year 2 for group (iii), $228, is used to increase their sum insured by an amount B_2, where

$$B_2 = 228/A_{62} = \$725.$$

Before the payment of the dividend, the sum insured was $100 000 and the cost of setting up a reserve for this at the end of year 2 was $1699 *per policy in force at the start of the year*; this is shown as $E_2\text{-}V$ in Table 13.2. The reserve required at the start of year 3 for each policy then in force is $2024 = 1795 + 228$ (allowing for rounding), where $1795 is the reserve for the sum insured of $100 000 (see Table 13.1) and $228 is the cost of the extra reserve required for the bonus. Note that this extra cost is equal to the dividend because the bonus is calculated using the reserve basis. It is important to note that there is no additional cost to the insurer at the end of year 2 of setting up this extra reserve; the insurer just retains the dividend of $228 allocated to each continuing policyholder. Consequently, the insurer's profit at the end of year 2, after allowing for the distribution of dividends, Pr_2, is 10% of $Pr_2\text{-}$, and is the same as Pr_2 in Table 13.1. However, from year 3 onwards the entries in Tables 13.1 and 13.2 differ because the increased reserves in the latter affect the profit calculation.

Consider the entries for $t = 3$ in Table 13.2. The insurer's profit, before the distribution of dividends, is

$$Pr_{3\text{-}} = {}_2V + P - E_3 + I_3 - EDB_{3\text{-}} - ECV_{3\text{-}} - E_3\text{-}V = \$378.$$

Hence, the dividend for each policy in force at the start of the year, Div_3, is $0.9 \times 378 = 340$ and the insurer's remaining profit is $Pr_3 = \$38$. For policies continuing into year 4, the dividend of $340 is converted to a bonus

Table 13.3 *Bonuses and bonus rates (%) – simple, compound and super-Compound – for Example 13.2.*

	Bonuses		Bonus rates			
					Super Compound	
t	B_t $\$$	RB_t $\$$	Simple %	Compound %	Sum Insured %	Bonus %
1	0	0	0.00	0.00	0.00	0.00
2	725	725	0.73	0.73	0.73	0.00
3	1037	1762	1.04	1.03	1.04	0.00
4	1352	3115	1.35	1.33	1.35	0.00
5	1562	4677	1.56	1.51	1.40	5.20
6	1715	6392	1.72	1.64	1.40	6.74
$\vdots$	$\vdots$	$\vdots$	$\vdots$	$\vdots$	$\vdots$	$\vdots$
28	2110	45 918	2.11	1.47	1.40	1.62
29	2151	48 068	2.15	1.47	1.40	1.64
30	12 327	60 395	–	–	–	–

of amount $B_4 = \$1037$ so that the total bonus for each of these policies, RB_3, is \$1762. The extra reserve required to cover this increase in the sum insured for continuing policyholders is equal to the amount of the dividend, \$340. This dividend is retained by the insurer, so, as at the end of year 2, there is no additional cost to the insurer in setting up this extra reserve.

The profit signature for the contract is determined by applying the time $t - 1$ survival probabilities to the profit vector entries, after distribution of surplus, so

$$\Pi_t = {}_{t-1}p_{60}^{00} \, \text{Pr}_t.$$

The NPV of the policy is \$354.47 and the profit margin is 2.28%. The use of reversionary bonus results in a higher profit for the insurer, compared with the cash bonus in Example 13.1, because more funds are retained under the insurer's management, which increases the projected profit from the interest spread – that is, the difference between the valuation interest assumption (5% per year) and the projected earned rate (6% per year).

(b) The cash value at time $t = 30$ is 90% of the reserve at the end of year 30 (before bonus), plus the cash dividend (which is 90% of Pr_{30-}), so

$$CV_{30} = 0.9\left((S + RB_{29})A_{90} - P^*\ddot{a}_{90}\right) + 0.9 \times 10\,316$$
$$= 90\,737 + 9284$$
$$= \$100\,021.$$

(c) The bonus rates are shown in Table 13.3. To calculate these rates, let S_t denote the sum insured in the tth year, with $S_1 = S$. As the difference between the sums insured in years t and $t + 1$ is the bonus declared at the end of the tth year, $S_{t+1} - S_t = B_t$.

- Let b_t denote the rate of simple reversionary bonus declared at the end of the tth year. Then, as bonus applies only to the initial sum insured of S,

$$S_{t+1} = S_t + b_t S$$

gives $b_t = B_t/S$.

- Next, let b_t denote the rate of compound reversionary bonus declared at the end of the tth year. Then, as bonus applies to the initial sum insured and all previously declared bonuses,

$$S_{t+1} = (1 + b_t) S_t$$

gives $b_t = B_t/S_t$.

- Let α_t denote the rate of bonus that applies to the initial sum insured of S at the end of the tth year, and let β_t denote the rate that applies to the previously declared bonuses. Then

$$S_{t+1} = S_t + \alpha_t S + \beta_t RB_{t-1}.$$

Recall that the maximum rate of bonus on S is 1.4%. Thus, if $S_{t+1} \geq S_t + 0.014S$, we have $\alpha_t = 0.014$. If $S_{t+1} < S_t + 0.014S$, then

$$S_{t+1} = S_t + \alpha_t S,$$

giving $\alpha_t = B_t/S$, and hence $\beta_t = 0$. If $\alpha_t = 0.014$, then

$$S_{t+1} = S_t + 0.014S + \beta_t RB_{t-1},$$

giving $\beta_t = (B_t - 0.014S)/RB_{t-1}$. In summary,

$$\alpha_t = \min(B_t/S, 0.014),$$
$$\beta_t = \max((B_t - 0.014S)/RB_{t-1}, 0).$$

The discontinuities appearing around times $t = 5$, $t = 10$ and $t = 30$ arise because of the shift in the assumed withdrawal rates and cash values for surrendering policyholders at those dates. The bonus on bonus rates under the super-compound system appear very volatile in the early years, but that is not too significant financially, as the amounts of accumulated bonus (the denominator for the bonus-on-bonus rates) are small.

   In practice, the insurer would announce the same bonus rates for all policies, so a bonus system that creates reasonably constant rates for policies of different durations is preferred.   □

Some points to note about Example 13.2 are:

(1) It may not always be the case that the full dividend emerging is awarded on death or surrender. The insurer may, for example, award no dividend to surrendering policyholders, in which case the calculation of bonus would change.

(2) The method of distributing cash dividends to exiting policyholders in this example is not necessarily realistic. In Exercise 13.5 a different system for determining bonuses is proposed, where the bonus rate is determined first, and the payments for deaths and surrenders are based on the updated total reversionary bonus, rather than the previous total plus cash dividend, as in this example.

(3) In the year from time $t - 1$ to time t, for $t = 3, 4, \ldots, 30$, the reserve brought forward is

$$_{t-1}V = (S + RB_{t-1}) A_{60+t-1} - P^* \ddot{a}_{60+t-1}$$

where $P^* = \$2064.47$ is the net premium based on the original sum insured, which we found in Example 13.1. Note that the net premium used, P^*, is not affected by the bonus declarations. This means that the formula for policy values that uses $(1 - \ddot{a}_{60+t}/\ddot{a}_{61})$ per \$1 of death benefit no longer works, as the bonus changes the death benefit without changing the net premium.

13.3.3 Notes on profit distribution methods

Distribution methods for participating insurance have an important impact on the management of risk, and on the techniques for pricing and marketing of policies. We note some of the more important considerations here, but a more in-depth analysis is beyond the scope of this text.

- Cash dividends are attractive to policyholders; they are easy to understand, and offer flexibility. If a policyholder is in financial difficulty, the cash may enable the policyholder to maintain the policy longer, as it can be used to offset premiums.
- If the policyholder prefers extra death cover to cash, the cash bonus can be used to buy more insurance – but at greater cost, probably, than the reversionary bonus, if the new insurance means there is a new set of acquisition expenses.
- Cash dividends may be taxable, and if the policyholder has no need for the cash, it is not likely to be a tax-efficient asset.

- Reversionary bonuses are more complex for policyholders to understand, but do offer a tax efficient distribution that is consistent with the purpose of the policy – to provide mortality benefit over long terms.
- Insurers may offer limited participation for policies that are surrendered, leading to potential issues of loss of trust and policyholder dissatisfaction.
- Cash dividends require the insurer to liquidate assets, which may not be in the best interests of maximizing return. Reversionary bonus remains under the insurer's management, and so reduces the liquidity risk, and also provides more potential for profit (and loss) for the insurer.
- Generally, insurers prefer to offer smooth bonuses and dividends, that is, with little variation from year to year. This is generally easier with reversionary and terminal bonus, as the actual payment is delayed until the policy matures.
- Cash dividends are expensive to operate, if every policyholder is issued a cheque each year.

In the UK, with-profit insurance was often issued with a target reversionary bonus rate specifically assumed in the premium. The actual bonus rate declared could be higher or lower than the target. Insurers used the flexibility from the with-profit design to invest much more heavily in more variable investments, such as stocks and shares. Non-participating business is more likely to be supported predominantly by fixed interest investments. The with-profit contract is still an important part of the in-force insurance business in the UK, but little new business is sold. In North America the distributed profits tend to be smaller, as a proportion of the original benefits, compared with the UK policies. The margins for profit are smaller, which offers stronger guarantees for policyholders, but less investment flexibility for insurers.

13.4 Universal Life insurance

13.4.1 Introduction

Universal Life (UL) insurance is a very important product, particularly in North America. It is generally issued as a whole life contract, but with transparent cash values allowing policyholders the flexibility to use it more as an endowment insurance. The policyholder may vary the amount and timing of premiums, within some constraints. The premium is deposited into a notional account, which is used to determine the death and survival benefits. The account is notional because assets are not actually segregated from the insurer's general funds (unlike equity-linked insurance, which we discuss in Chapter 14).

The insurer shares the profits through the **credited interest rate** which is declared and applied by the insurer at regular intervals (typically monthly).

The policy contract specifies a minimum value for the credited interest rate, regardless of the investment performance of the insurer's assets. The notional account, made up of the premiums and credited interest, is subject to monthly deductions (also notional); there is a charge for the cost of life insurance cover, and a separate charge to cover expenses. The **account balance** or **account value** is the balance of funds in the notional account. Note that the cost of insurance and expense charge deductions are set by the insurer, and need not be the best estimate of the anticipated expenses or insurance costs. In the profit test examples that follow in this section, the best estimate assumptions for incurred expenses and for the cost of death benefits are quite different from the charges set by the insurer for expenses and the cost of insurance. The account value represents the insurer's liability, analogous to the reserve under a traditional contract. The account value also represents the cash value for a surrendering policyholder, after an initial period (typically 7–10 years) when surrender charges are applied to ensure recovery of the acquisition costs.

In this section we consider the basic UL policy, which may be viewed as a variation of the traditional participating contract. We have simplified the terms of a standard UL policy to demonstrate the key principles. The most obvious simplification is that we have assumed annual cash flows where monthly would be more common. We have also assumed a fixed term for the UL contracts in the examples, even though UL contracts are generally whole life policies. However, it would be common for policyholders to use the contracts for fixed horizon planning, and the policy design assumes that most policies will be surrendered as the policyholder moves into retirement.

13.4.2 Key design features

Death benefit On the policyholder's death the total benefit paid is the account value of the policy, plus an **additional death benefit** (ADB).

The ADB is required to be a significant proportion of the total death benefit, except at very advanced ages, to justify the policy being considered an insurance contract. The proportions are set through the **corridor factor requirement** which sets the minimum value for the ratio of the total death benefit (i.e. account value + ADB) to the account value at death. In the US the corridor factor is around 2.5 up to age 40, decreasing to 1.05 at age 90, and to 1.0 at age 95 and above.

There are two types of death benefit, Type A and Type B.

Type A offers a level total death benefit, which comprises the account value plus the additional death benefit. As the account value increases, the ADB decreases. However the ADB cannot decline to zero, except at very old ages, because of the corridor factor requirement. For a Type A UL policy, the level death benefit is the **face amount** of the policy.

Type B offers a level ADB. The amount paid on death would be the account value plus the level ADB selected by the policyholder, provided this satisfies the corridor factor requirement.

Premiums may be subject to some minimum level and payment term, but otherwise are highly flexible.

Expense charges are expressed as a percent of account value, or of premiums, and may also include a flat fee. It may be referred to as the **MER**, for Management Expense Rate, a term used more widely for mutual fund investment. The expense charge is deducted from the account value, at rates which are variable at the insurer's discretion, subject to a maximum which is specified in the original contract.

Credited interest is usually determined at the insurer's discretion, but may be based on published rates, such as yields on government bonds. A minimum guaranteed annual credited interest rate is specified in the policy document.

Cost of insurance (CoI) is the charge deducted from the policyholder's funds to cover the cost of the death benefit cover. Usually, the CoI is calculated using an estimate (perhaps conservative) of the mortality rate for that period, which is known as the **CoI rate**. As the policyholder ages, the mortality charge (per $1 of ADB) increases, so the CoI can be interpreted as the single premium for a one-year term insurance with sum insured equal to the ADB, assuming mortality equal to the CoI rate discounted to the start of the period of insurance. The rate of interest used to determine the COI may differ from the credited rate.

Not all UL has increasing CoI. 'Level CoI' policies treat the death benefit cover as traditional term or whole life insurance, with a level risk premium through the term of the contract deducted from the account value.

Surrender charge If the policyholder chooses to surrender the policy, the surrender value paid will be the policyholder's account balance reduced by a surrender charge. The main purpose of the surrender charge is to ensure that the insurer receives enough to pay its acquisition expenses. The total sum available to the policyholder on surrender is the account value minus the surrender charge (or zero if greater), and is referred to as the **cash value** of the contract at each duration.

No-lapse guarantee An additional feature of some policies is the no-lapse guarantee, under which the death benefit cover continues even if the account value declines to zero, provided that the policyholder pays a pre-specified minimum premium at each premium date. This guarantee could apply if expense and mortality charges increase sufficiently to exceed the minimum premium. The policyholder's account value would support the balance until it is exhausted, at which time the no-lapse guarantee would come into effect.

13.4.3 Projecting account values

The insurer must determine appropriate schedules for expense charges and cost of insurance charges to create a contract that is marketable and profitable. An important objective of the UL policy is transparency; the policyholder can see her account value growing, can identify the expense and cost of insurance deductions. She will see the credited interest rate and will therefore have some measure of the success of the contract as an investment.

We will illustrate how account values accumulate with the simplifying assumption of annual cash flows. First, we introduce some notation.

AV_t denotes the policyholder's account value at time t.

EC_t denotes the expense charge deducted from the account value at the beginning of the tth year.

CoI_t denotes the cost of insurance deducted from the account value at the beginning of the tth year.

i_t^c denotes the credited interest rate applied to investments during the tth year.

P_t denotes the premium paid at the start of the tth year.

DB_t denotes the death benefit cover in the tth year.

CV_t denotes the cash value paid on surrender at the end of the tth year.

Then the fundamental equation of a UL policy is the following recursion:

$$(AV_{t-1} + P_t - EC_t - CoI_t)(1 + i_t^c) = AV_t. \qquad (13.1)$$

It is interesting to consider the insurer's perspective here. The account value represents a reserve for the policy – it is a measure of the capital the insurer needs to hold in respect of the policy liabilities. The expense charge, CoI and credited interest rate are factors used in the development of the account value, but otherwise do not represent real cash flows. That is, it would make no difference to any of the contract cash flows if the insurer charged $50 less in expense charges and $50 more in CoI. In fact, EC_t, CoI_t and i_t^c can be changed, jointly, in innumerable ways, but if they generate the same account values it would make no difference to any of the cash flows of the policy. The only important numbers in the contract cash flows are the premiums, the account values, the death benefits and the cash surrender values. The only purpose of specifying EC_t, CoI_t and i_t^c is to derive the account values.

An analogy with traditional insurance is that we may assume a premium basis to determine premiums and a policy value basis to determine the reserves. Once the premiums and reserves are calculated, the assumptions in these two bases do not impact the policy cash flows. In fact, when we profit test a traditional product, we generally use different assumptions for mortality, expenses, surrender rates and interest than we use in either the premium basis or the reserve basis. Similarly, here, the expense charges, CoI and credited interest impact the cash flows only through the account values. They do not represent actual cash flows into or out of the insurer's funds.

13.4.4 Profit testing Universal Life policies

Universal Life policies are best analysed using profit testing. The process is similar to profit testing traditional insurance, even though the contracts appear different.

For the first step, before the profit test, we project the annual account values of the policy **assuming the policy remains in force to the final projection date**, just as, for traditional insurance, we have to calculate reserves before we can profit test the policy.

To project the account values, we need an assumed schedule of premiums, P_t, a specification of the expense charges, EC_t, and we need to calculate the cost of insurance charges, CoI_t.

The additional death benefit in the tth year is the total death benefit minus the year end account value (similar to the sum at risk for a traditional policy), that is

$$ADB_t = DB_t - AV_t.$$

The CoI charge is a single premium for a one-year term insurance for a death benefit of ADB_t. The CoI basis will be specified. Let q^*_{x+t} denote the CoI mortality rate and i_q denote the CoI interest rate. Expenses are ignored. Then

$$CoI_t = q^*_{x+t-1} \, v_q \, ADB_t. \tag{13.2}$$

The CoI pays for the additional death benefit; it is not based on the full death benefit. This is because the account value is available to fund the balance, $DB_t - ADB_t = AV_t$.

For Type B policies the ADB is fixed. For Type A policies, the total death benefit is fixed (except for corridor factor adjustments), which means the ADB is a function of the account value, which makes the CoI calculation a little more complicated.

Once the AV_t values are determined through the account value projection, the profit test proceeds, very similarly to a traditional policy, except that AV_t

takes the role of the reserve, and the sum insured (DB_t) is variable, depending on the account values.

In the following sections we demonstrate profit testing for some UL policies. The first is a Type B policy, which is the simpler case. The second is a Type A policy, which is the more common contract design in practice.

13.4.5 Universal Life Type B

Example 13.3 (Step 1: account value projection)

A UL policy is sold to a 45 year old man. The initial premium is $2250 and the ADB is $100 000. The policy charges are:

Cost of insurance: 120% of the mortality of the Standard Select Mortality Model, $i_q = 5\%$ per year interest.

Expense charges: $48+1% of premium at the start of each year.

Surrender penalties at each year end are the lesser of the full account value and the following surrender penalty schedule:

Year of surrender	1	2	3–4	5–7	8–10	> 10
Penalty	$4500	$4100	$3500	$2500	$1200	$0

Assume

(i) the policy remains in force for 20 years,
(ii) interest is credited to the account at 5% per year,
(iii) all cash flows occur at policy anniversaries, and
(iv) there is no corridor factor requirement for the policy.

Project the account value and the cash value at each year end for the 20-year projected term, given that the policyholder pays the full premium of $2250 for six years, and then pays no further premiums.

Solution 13.3 The key formulae for UL account values are (13.1) and (13.2), that is

$$(AV_{t-1} + P_t - EC_t - CoI_t)(1 + i_t^c) = AV_t$$

and

$$CoI_t = q_{x+t-1}^* \, v_q \, ADB_t.$$

Applying these formulae gives the projected account values in Table 13.4. Specifically, the columns in Table 13.4 are calculated as follows:

Table 13.4 *Projected account values for the Type B UL policy in Example 13.3, assuming level premiums for six years.*

t^{th} year t (1)	P_t (2)	EC_t (3)	CoI_t (4)	Credited interest (5)	AV_t (6)	CV_t (7)
1	2250	70.50	75.34	105.21	2 209.37	0.00
2	2250	70.50	91.13	214.89	4 512.63	412.63
3	2250	70.50	104.71	329.37	6 916.79	3 416.79
4	2250	70.50	114.57	449.09	9 430.80	5 930.80
5	2250	70.50	125.66	574.23	12 058.87	9 558.87
6	2250	70.50	138.12	705.01	14 805.27	12 305.27
7	0	48.00	152.12	730.26	15 335.41	12 835.41
⋮	⋮	⋮	⋮	⋮	⋮	⋮
19	0	48.00	540.59	1 034.47	21 723.82	21 723.82
20	0	48.00	604.34	1 053.57	22 125.05	22 125.05

(1) denotes the term at the end of the policy year.

(2) is the tth premium, P_t, assumed paid at time $t - 1$.

(3) is the tth year expense charge deduction, $EC_t = 48 + 0.01\, P_t$.

(4) is the CoI for the year from time $t - 1$ to time t, assumed to be deducted at the start of the year. The mortality rate (or CoI rate) assumed is

$$q^{*}_{[45]+t-1} = 1.2\, q^{d}_{[45]+t-1}$$

where $q^{d}_{[x]+t}$ is taken from the Standard Select Survival Model. Multiply by the ADB, and discount from the year end payment date, to get the CoI as

$$CoI_t = 100\,000\, q^{*}_{[45]+t-1}\, v_{5\%}.$$

Note that the interest rate is specified in the CoI pricing assumptions – in this case it is the same as the crediting rate, but it may be different.

(5) is the credited interest at time t, assuming a 5% level crediting rate applied to the account value from the previous year, plus the premium, minus the expense loading and CoI.

(6) is the year end account value, from recursion formula (13.1) for AV_t.

(7) is the year end cash value, which is the account value minus the applicable surrender penalty, with a minimum value of $0.

In more detail, the first two rows are calculated as follows:

First year

AV_0:	0
P_1:	2250
EC_1:	$48 + 0.01 \times 2250 = 70.50$
CoI rate:	$q^*_{[45]} = 1.2 \times 0.000659$
CoI_1:	$100\,000 \times q^*_{[45]} \times v_{5\%} = 75.34$
Credited interest:	$0.05\,(2250 - 70.50 - 75.34) = 105.21$
AV_1:	$2250 - 70.50 - 75.34 + 105.21 = 2209.37$
CV_1:	$\max(2209.37 - 4500, 0) = 0$

Second year

AV_1:	2209.37
P_2:	2250
EC_2:	$48 + 0.01 \times 2250 = 70.50$
CoI rate:	$q^*_{[45]+1} = 1.2 \times 0.000797$
CoI_1:	$100\,000 \times q^*_{[45]+1} \times v_{5\%} = 91.13$
Credited interest:	$0.05\,(2209.37 + 2250 - 70.50 - 91.13) = 214.89$
AV_2:	$2209.37 + 2250 - 70.50 - 91.13 + 214.89 = 4512.63$
CV_2:	$4512.63 - 4100 = 412.63$

☐

Example 13.4 (Step 2: the profit test) For the scenario described below, calculate the profit signature, the discounted payback period and the net present value, using a hurdle interest rate of 10% per year effective, for the UL policy described in Example 13.3.

Assume

- Policies remain in force for a maximum of 20 years.
- Premiums of $2250 are paid for six years, and no premiums are paid thereafter.
- The insurer does not change the CoI rates or expense charges from the values given in Example 13.3.
- Interest is credited to the policyholder's account value in the tth year using a 2% interest spread, with a minimum credited interest rate of 2%. In other words, if the insurer earns more than 4%, the credited interest will be the earned interest rate less 2%. If the insurer earns less than 4%, the credited interest rate will be 2%.
- The ADB remains at $100\,000 throughout.
- Interest earned on all insurer's funds at 7% per year.

- Mortality experience is 100% of the Standard Select Survival Model.
- Incurred expenses are $2000 at inception, $45 plus 1% of premium at renewal, $50 on surrender (even if no cash value is paid), $100 on death.
- Surrenders occur at year ends. The surrender rate given in the following table is the proportion of in-force policyholders surrendering at each year end.

Duration at year end	Surrender rate q^w_{45+t-1}
1	5%
2–5	2%
6–10	3%
11	10%
12–19	15%
20	100%

- The insurer holds the full account value as reserve for this contract.

Solution 13.4 We use the account values from Example 13.3, as the credited interest rate of 5% used there corresponds to the profit test assumption for the credited rate (7% earned rate, minus the 2% spread, with a 2% minimum).

Note that the expense charge, CoI and credited interest rate used in the AV calculation are not needed in the profit test. The expenses, mortality and earned interest rate assumptions for the profit test are different from the expense charge, CoI mortality, and credited interest rate used in the AV projection, much as the profit test assumptions for a traditional contract usually differ from the premium basis.

The cash flows for the profit test in the tth year, $t \geq 1$, assuming the policy is in force at the start of the year, are

AV_{t-1} the account value (reserve) brought forward.

P_t the premium paid at the start of the tth year.

E_t the incurred expenses at the start of the tth year.

I_t the interest earned through the year on the invested funds,

EDB_t the expected cost of death benefits paid at the end of the tth year. If $p^{0d}_{[45]+t-1}$ is the profit test mortality rate assumed, and DB_t is the total death benefit payable, then

$$DB_t = AV_t + ADB \quad \text{and} \quad EDB_t = p^{0d}_{[45]+t-1}(DB_t + 100)$$

where $ADB = 100\,000$ is the fixed additional death benefit, and the $100 allows for claims expenses.

Table 13.5 *UL Type B policy from Example 13.4: calculating the profit vector.*

Year t	AV_{t-1}	P_t	E_t	I_t	EDB_t	ESB_t	EAV_t	Pr_t
0	0	0	2 000					−2 000
1	0	2 250	0	158	67	2	2 098	240
2	2 209	2 250	68	307	83	9	4 419	188
3	4 513	2 250	68	469	98	69	6 772	224
4	6 917	2 250	68	637	110	119	9 233	274
5	9 431	2 250	68	813	123	192	11 805	306
6	12 059	2 250	68	997	139	370	14 344	385
7	14 805	0	45	1 033	154	386	14 856	398
⋮	⋮	⋮	⋮	⋮	⋮	⋮	⋮	⋮
18	20 797	0	45	1 453	514	3 186	18 010	495
19	21 278	0	45	1 486	576	3 251	18 378	514
20	21 724	0	45	1 518	646	22 058	–	492

ESB_t the expected cost of surrender benefits at time t:

$$ESB_t = p^{0w}_{[45]+t-1} (CV_t + 50),$$

where $p^{0w}_{[45]+t-1} = (1 - p^{0d}_{[45]+t-1}) q^{w}_{45+t-1}$ is the probability that the life survives the year, and then withdraws at the year end; CV_t is the cash value in the tth year, which is AV_t minus the surrender penalty at time t, and 50 is the associated expense.

EAV_t the expected cost of the account value carried forward at the year end for policies that continue in force. The probability that a policy which is in force at time $t - 1$ remains in force at time t is

$$p^{00}_{[45]+t-1} = 1 - p^{0d}_{[45]+t-1} - p^{0w}_{[45]+t-1}.$$

So

$$EAV_t = p^{00}_{[45]+t-1} AV_t.$$

The net income at the end of each year, assuming the policy is in force at the start of the year, is the profit vector entry

$$Pr_t = AV_{t-1} + P_t - E_t + I_t - EDB_t - ESB_t - EAV_t.$$

The profit test table is presented (partially) in Table 13.5. As usual, the first row represents the pre-contract outgo, given in the example as $2000. The following rows are determined using the formulae described above.

In Table 13.6 we show the profit signature and partial NPV calculations, exactly following the methodology of Chapter 12. To help understand the

Table 13.6 *UL Type B policy from Example 13.4: profit signature, NPV and DPP at 10% per year risk discount rate.*

t	Pr[in force at start of year]	Pr_t	Π_t	$NPV(t)$
0	1.00000	−2000.00	−2000.00	−2000.00
1	1.00000	240.04	240.04	−1781.78
2	0.94937	187.79	178.28	−1634.44
⋮	⋮	⋮	⋮	⋮
16	0.34500	457.56	157.86	−6.29
17	0.29225	475.98	139.11	21.23
18	0.24747	494.96	122.49	43.26
19	0.20946	514.47	107.76	60.88
20	0.17720	492.22	87.22	73.84

derivation of these tables, we show here the detailed calculations for the first two years' cash flows.

At time $t = 0$

Initial expenses, E_0:   2000
Profit vector, Pr_0:   −2000
Profit signature, Π_0: −2000
Partial NPV, $NPV(0)$: −2000

First year

AV_0	0
P_1:	2250
E_1:	0 (all accounted for in Pr_0)
I_1:	$0.07 \times 2250 = 157.50$
EDB_1	$0.000659 \times (100\,000 + 2209.37 + 100) = 67.44$
ESB_1:	$0.999341 \times 0.05 \times (0 + 50) = 2.50$
EAV_1:	$0.999341 \times 0.95 \times 2209.37 = 2097.52$
Pr_1:	$2250 + 157.50 - 67.44 - 2.50 - 2097.52 = 240.04$
Π_1:	240.04
$NPV(1)$:	$-2000 + 240.04\, v_{10\%} = -1781.78$

Second year

AV_1:	2209.37
P_2:	2250
E_2:	$45 + 0.01 \times 2250 = 67.50$
I_2:	$0.07 \times (2209.37 + 2250 - 67.50) = 307.43$
EDB_2:	$0.000797 \times (100\,000 + 4512.63 + 100) = 83.41$
ESB_2:	$0.999203 \times 0.02 \times (412.63 + 50) = 9.25$

EAV_2: $0.999203 \times 0.98 \times 4512.63 = 4418.85$

Pr$_2$: $2209.37 + 2250 - 67.50 + 307.43 - 83.41 - 9.25 - 4418.85 =$
              187.79

Π_2: $0.999341 \times 0.95 \times 187.79 = 178.28$

NPV(2): $-1781.78 + 178.28\, v^2_{10\%} = -1634.44$

From the final column of Table 13.6, we see that the NPV of the emerging profit, using the 10% per year risk discount rate, is $73.84. The table also shows that the discounted payback period is 17 years.

13.4.6 Universal Life Type A

The Type A contract is a little more complicated than Type B. The total death benefit is set at the face amount (FA), so the ADB is the excess of the face amount over the account value (AV); however, there is also, generally, a corridor factor requirement. The corridor factor is a guaranteed minimum ratio of the total death benefit to the account value. Given a corridor factor of γ, say, the total death benefit is the greater of FA and $\gamma\, AV$. The ADB is the difference between the total death benefit and the account value.

We illustrate first with a simple example. Suppose a Type A UL contract, issued some time ago to a life now aged 50, has face amount $FA = \$100\,000$. The assumed AV growth rate for the CoI calculation is 5%, the CoI (mortality) rate for the year is $q^*_{50} = 0.004$, and the CoI interest rate is 0%. The account value at the start of the year is $AV_{t-1} = \$50\,000$. The corridor factor for the year is $\gamma_t = 2.2$. There is no premium paid and no expense deduction from the account value in the year.

The ADB for the year depends on whether the corridor factor applies. Let ADB^f denote the additional death benefit based on the excess of the face amount over the account value, that is

$$ADB^f_t = FA - AV_t,$$

and let $ADB_t{}^c$ denote the additional death benefit based on the corridor factor, so that

$$ADB^c_t = \gamma_t\, AV_t - AV_t = (\gamma_t - 1)\, AV_t.$$

Then $ADB_t = \max(ADB^f_t, ADB^c_t)$.

The cost of insurance at time $t - 1$ is $0.004\, ADB_t$. This calculation depends on AV_t which depends on the credited interest and on the cost of insurance. We use the assumed credited interest rate to project AV_t as a function of the CoI, and then solve for the CoI.

We note that in this example, the CoI is calculated assuming a 5% per year credited interest rate, and discounting at 0%. We have the following results, where we use the superscript ^{f} to refer to the CoI based on ADB^f, and the superscript ^{c} for the CoI based on ADB^c. The final CoI value is the maximum of these two values. We have

$$AV_t = 1.05\,(AV_{t-1} - CoI_t).$$

So, for the face amount CoI,

$$ADB^f_t = FA - AV_t = 100\,000 - 1.05\,(50\,000 - CoI^f_t)$$

$$CoI^f_t = 0.004\,ADB^f_t = 0.004\left(100\,000 - 1.05 \times 50\,000 + 1.05\,CoI^f_t\right)$$

$$\Rightarrow CoI^f_t = \frac{0.004\,(100\,000 - 1.05 \times 50\,000)}{1 - 0.004 \times 1.05} = 190.80,$$

and for the corridor factor CoI,

$$ADB^c_t = (2.2 - 1) \times 1.05 \times (50\,000 - CoI^c_t)$$

$$CoI^c_t = 0.004\left(1.2 \times 1.05\left(50\,000 - CoI^c_t\right)\right)$$

$$\Rightarrow CoI^c_t = \frac{0.004 \times 1.2 \times 1.05 \times 50\,000}{1 + 0.004 \times 1.2 \times 1.05} = 250.74.$$

This means that ADB^f_t is \$47\,700 and ADB^c_t is \$62\,684. As ADB^c is greater, the corridor factor has come into effect, and we use ADB^c in the profit test calculations.

We now develop the CoI for a Type A UL policy more generally. First we define or review the notation.

FA:	face amount
AV_t:	account value at time t, before premium and deductions
γ_t:	corridor factor applying in the tth year
P_t:	premium in the tth year, paid at time $t - 1$
EC_t:	expense charge in the tth year, deducted from the account value at time $t - 1$
q^*_{x+t-1}:	mortality rate for calculating the CoI in the tth year
v_q:	discount factor for calculating the CoI
i^c_t:	assumed credited interest rate in the tth year
ADB^f_t:	$FA - AV_t$
ADB^c_t:	$(\gamma_t - 1) \times AV_t$
CoI^f_t:	$q^*_{x+t-1} \times v_q \times ADB^f_t$
CoI^c_t:	$q^*_{x+t-1} \times v_q \times ADB^c_t$
CoI_t:	$\max(CoI^f_t,\ CoI^c_t)$
ADB_t:	$\max(ADB^f_t,\ ADB^c_t)$

Then we have, for the tth year (from time $t-1$ to time t),

$$AV_t = (AV_{t-1} + P_t - EC_t - CoI_t) \times (1 + i_t^c)$$

and

$$ADB_t^f = FA - AV_t = FA - (AV_{t-1} + P_t - EC_t)(1 + i_t^c) + CoI_t^f (1 + i_t^c)$$
$$CoI_t^f = q_{x+t-1}^* v_q ADB_t^f$$
$$= q_{x+t-1}^* v_q \left(FA - (AV_{t-1} + P_t - EC_t)(1 + i_t^c) + CoI_t^f (1 + i_t^c) \right)$$
$$\Rightarrow CoI_t^f = \frac{q_{x+t-1}^* v_q \left(FA - (AV_{t-1} + P_t - EC_t)(1 + i_t^c) \right)}{1 - q_{x+t-1}^* v_q (1 + i_t^c)}.$$

Similarly,

$$ADB_t^c = (\gamma_t - 1) AV_t$$
$$= (\gamma_t - 1) \left((AV_{t-1} + P_t - EC_t)(1 + i_t^c) - CoI_t^c (1 + i_t^c) \right)$$
$$CoI_t^c = q_{x+t-1}^* v_q ADB_t^c$$
$$= q_{x+t-1}^* v_q (1 + i_t^c)(\gamma_t - 1) \left((AV_{t-1} + P_t - EC_t) - CoI_t^c \right)$$
$$\Rightarrow CoI_t^c = \frac{q_{x+t-1}^* v_q (1 + i_t^c)(\gamma_t - 1)(AV_{t-1} + P_t - EC_t)}{1 + q_{x+t-1}^* v_q (1 + i_t^c)(\gamma_t - 1)}.$$

Finally

$$CoI_t = \max \left(CoI_t^f, CoI_t^c \right) \quad \text{and} \quad ADB_t = \max \left(ADB_t^f, ADB_t^c \right).$$

Although we have derived these formulae, the resulting formulae are not the main point here. Minor changes to the standard UL premium and benefit conditions will result in different formulae. The important message here is how the formulae are derived – assuming either the face amount total death benefit, or the corridor factor total death benefit, solving the AV_t equation for the CoI in both cases, and selecting whichever is greater.

Example 13.5 (Type A UL profit test)
Consider the following UL policy issued to a life aged 45:

- Face amount $100 000.
- Type A death benefit with corridor factors (γ_t) applying to benefits paid in respect of deaths in the tth year, as follows:

t	1	2	3	4	5	6	7	8	9	10
γ_t	2.15	2.09	2.03	1.97	1.91	1.85	1.78	1.71	1.64	1.57

t	11	12	13	14	15	16	17	18	19	20
γ_t	1.50	1.46	1.42	1.38	1.34	1.30	1.28	1.26	1.24	1.24

- CoI based on: 120% of mortality rates from the Standard Select Mortality Model, and 4% interest; the CoI is calculated assuming the fund earns 4% interest during the year.
- Expense charges: 20% of the first premium + $200, 3% of subsequent premiums.
- Initial premium: $3500.
- Surrender penalties:

Year of surrender	1	2	3–4	5–7	≥ 8
Penalty	$2500	$2100	$1200	$600	$0

(a) Project the account and cash values for this policy assuming level premiums of $3500 are paid annually in advance, that the policyholder surrenders the contract after 20 years, and that the credited interest rate is 4% per year.

(b) Profit test the contract using the basis below. Use annual steps, and determine the NPV and DPP using a risk discount rate of 10% per year.

  Assume

- Level premiums of $3500 paid annually in advance.
- Insurer's funds earn 6% per year.
- Policyholders' accounts are credited at 4% per year.
- Surrender rates are as in Example 13.4 above. All surviving policyholders surrender after 20 years.
- Mortality follows the Standard Select Survival Model.
- Incurred expenses are:
  - Pre-contract expenses of 60% of the premium due immediately before the issue date,
  - Maintenance expenses of 2% of premium at each premium date including the first,
  - $50 on surrender,
  - $100 on death.
- The insurer holds reserves equal to the policyholder's account value.

Solution 13.5 (a) Following the same methodology as for the Type B policy, we first project the AV_t and CV_t values, assuming that the policy stays in force throughout the term. The results are shown in Table 13.7.

  We describe the calculations for the first two years in more detail to clarify the table.

Table 13.7 *Type A UL account value and cash value projection for Example 13.5.*

t	AV_{t-1}	P_t	EC_t	CoI_t	AV_t	CV_t
1	0	3500	900	74.07	2626.97	126.97
2	2626.97	3500	105	86.32	6173.08	4073.08
3	6173.08	3500	105	95.30	9851.68	8651.68
4	9851.68	3500	105	99.86	13 672.70	12 472.70
$\vdots$	$\vdots$	$\vdots$	$\vdots$	$\vdots$	$\vdots$	$\vdots$
19	86 055.68	3500	105	121.69	92 902.15	92 902.15
20	92 902.15	3500	105	146.43	99 996.75	99 996.75

First year

P_1:   3 500

EC_1: $200 + 20\% \times 3\,500 = 900$

CoI assuming the death benefit is $FA - AV$:

$$CoI^f = v_{4\%} \times 1.2 \times q_{[45]} \left(100\,000 - (1.04) \left(3500 - 900 - CoI^f \right) \right)$$
$$= \frac{(100\,000\, v_{4\%} - 2600) \times 1.2 \times 0.0006592}{1 - 1.2 \times 0.0006592} = 74.07.$$

CoI assuming the death benefit is based on the corridor factor:

$$CoI^c = v_{4\%} \times q_{[45]} \times (\gamma_1 - 1) \times 1.04\,(3500 - 900 - CoI^c)$$
$$= \frac{1.2 \times 0.0006592 \times 1.15 \times 2600}{1 + 1.2 \times 0.0006592 \times 1.15} = 2.36.$$

CoI_1: $\max(CoI^f, CoI^c) = 74.07$

AV_1: $(3500 - 900 - 74.07) \times 1.04 = 2626.97$

CV_1: $\max(2626.97 - 2500, 0) = 126.97$

Second year

P_2:   3 500

EC_2: $3\% \times 3\,500 = 105$

CoI assuming the death benefit is $FA - AV$:

$$CoI^f = v_{4\%} \times 1.2$$
$$\times q_{[45]+1} \times \left(100\,000 - 1.04 \left(2626.97 + 3500 - 105 - CoI^f \right) \right)$$
$$= \frac{(100\,000\, v_{4\%} - 6021.97) \times 1.2 \times 0.0007974}{1 - 1.2 \times 0.0007974} = 86.32.$$

Table 13.8 *Emerging profit for Type A UL policy in Example 13.5.*

t	AV_{t-1}	P_t	E_t	I_t	EDB_t	ESB_t	EAV_t	Pr_t
0			2100					−2100
1	0	3500	70	206	66	9	2494	1067
2	2627	3500	70	363	80	82	6045	213
3	6173	3500	70	576	92	174	9646	268
4	9852	3500	70	797	100	250	13386	342
⋮	⋮	⋮	⋮	⋮	⋮	⋮	⋮	⋮
19	86056	3500	70	5369	545	13877	78593	1839
20	92902	3500	70	5780	656	99518	−	1938

Table 13.9 *Profit signature and emerging NPV at 10% per year risk discount rate for Type A UL policy in Example 13.5.*

t	Π_t	NPV_t
0	−2100.00	−2100.00
1	1066.99	−1130.01
2	202.59	−962.58
3	249.02	−775.49
4	311.49	−562.73
⋮	⋮	⋮
19	385.26	2159.49
20	343.44	2210.54

CoI assuming the death benefit is based on the corridor factor:

$$CoI^c = v_{4\%} \times q_{[45]+1} \times (\gamma_2 - 1) \times 1.04\,(2626.97 + 3500 - 105 - CoI^c)$$
$$= \frac{1.2 \times 0.0007974 \times 1.09 \times 6091.27}{1 + 1.2 \times 0.0007974 \times 1.09} = 6.27.$$

CoI_2: $\max(CoI^f, CoI^c) = 86.32$
AV_2: $(2626.97 + 3500 - 105 - 86.32) \times 1.04 = 6173.08$
CV_2: $\max(6173.08 - 2100, 0) = 4073.08.$

(b) The profit test results are presented in Tables 13.8 and 13.9. In Table 13.8, we derive the profit vector, and in Table 13.9 we show the profit signature and the emerging NPV using the 10% per year risk discount rate.

Given the Standard Select Survival Model mortality rate $q_{[45]+t-1}$, and q_t^w, the probability that a life aged $45 + t$ surrenders at the end of the tth year, given that the policy is still in force at that time, the probabilities for mortality, surrender and surviving in force in the tth year are

Mortality: $p_{[45]+t-1}^{0d} = q_{[45]+t-1}$

Surrender: $p_{[45]+t-1}^{0w} = (1 - q_{[45]+t-1})\, q_t^w$

Surviving: $p_{[45]+t-1}^{00} = 1 - p_{[45]+t-1}^{0d} - p_{[45]+t-1}^{0w}.$

The profit vector is, as in the previous example,

$$\mathrm{Pr}_t = AV_{t-1} + P_t - E_t + I_t - EDB_t - ESB_t - EAV_t$$

where

$$EDB_t = p_{[45]+t-1}^{0d}(AV_t + ADB_t + 100),$$
$$ESB_t = p_{[45]+t-1}^{0w}(CV_t + 50),$$
$$EAV_t = p_{[45]+t-1}^{00}\, AV_t.$$

Notes:

(1) The total death benefit, $AV_t + ADB_t$, will be equal to the face amount, unless the corridor factor applies, in which case it will be $\gamma_t\, AV_t$.
(2) In the final year, the year end account value is zero, as we assume all policyholders have surrendered.

For a more detailed explanation, we show here the calculations for the cash flows in the final two years, represented by the final two rows in Table 13.8. Values for AV_t and CV_t are taken from Table 13.7. Values in Table 13.8 have been rounded to the nearer dollar for presentation only.

19th year

AV_{18}:   86 055.68 (from Table 13.7)

P_{19}:   3500

E_{19}: $0.02 \times 3500 = 70.$

I_{19}: $0.06 \times (86\,056 + 3500 - 70) = 5\,369.14$

EDB_{19}: $p_{63}^{0d} \times (\max(100\,000, \gamma_{19}\, AV_{19}) + 100)$
         $= 0.004730 \times (\max(100\,000, 115\,199) + 100) = 545.38$

ESB_{19}: $p_{63}^{0w} \times (CV_{19} + 50)$
         $= 0.995270 \times 0.15 \times 92\,952.15 = 13\,876.87.$

EAV_{19}: $0.995270 \times 0.85 \times 92\,902.15 = 78\,593.30$

Pr_{19}: $86\,055.68 + 3\,500 - 70 + 5\,369.14$
         $-545.38 - 13\,876.87 - 78\,593.30 = 1\,839.27.$

20th year

AV_{19}:   92 902.15 (from Table 13.7)

P_{20}:   3500

E_{20}: $0.02 \times 3500 = 70.$

I_{20}: $0.06 \times (92\,902 + 3500 - 70) = 5\,779.93$

EDB_{20}: $p_{64}^{0d} \times (\max(100, 000, \gamma_{20}\, AV_{20}) + 100)$
              $= 0.005288 \times (\max(100\,000, 123\,996) + 100) = 656.22$

ESB_{20}: $p_{64}^{0w} \times (CV_{20} + 50)$
              $= 0.994712 \times 1 \times 100\,046.75 = 99\,517.70$

EAV_{20}:   0

Pr_{20}: $92\,902.15 + 3\,500 - 70 + 5\,779.93$
              $-656.22 - 99\,517.70 = 1\,938.16.$

From Table 13.9, we see that the NPV of the contract is \$2210 and the DPP is seven years. $\square$

13.4.7 No-lapse guarantees

UL policies are often offered with 'secondary guarantees', a term that refers to a range of benefits additional to the basic contract terms, sometimes offered as optional riders. The most common secondary guarantee for a UL policy is the no-lapse guarantee. With this benefit, once a specified number of premiums have been paid in full, the death benefit cover remains in place even if no further premiums are paid, and even if the account value is insufficient to support the CoI in any future year.

For a Type A policy, ignoring corridor factors, the value of the no-lapse guarantee can be considered by analogy with a traditional paid-up whole life insurance, which we discussed in Chapter 7.

Suppose the UL policy has been issued to (x), and has been in force for t years. The policyholder has the right to cease premiums and maintain their death benefit insurance. Suppose that the face value is S and the account value is AV_t. Assuming annual cash flows, the EPV of the death benefit is $S\,A_{x+t}$. If this is less than the account value, then the assets of the policy are sufficient to support the no-lapse guarantee. If $S\,A_{x+t}$ is greater than the account value, then the insurer must set aside additional reserves to cover the additional costs.

It follows that the reserve for the no-lapse guarantee at time t can be set as

$$_tV^{nlg} = \max(S\,A_{x+t} - AV_t, 0).$$

Note that the expense charges and CoI are not needed for this calculation.

The no-lapse guarantee may have an expiry date – that is, the death benefit continues up to a specified age, say $x + n$, without further premiums. In this case the reserve would be calculated using a term insurance factor

$$_t V^{nlg} = \max(S\, A^{\,1}_{x+t:\overline{n-t}|} - AV_t,\, 0).$$

In the UL profit tests above we have assumed that the insurer holds the full account value of the policy, but does not hold any additional reserve. The account value takes the role of the reserve in the profit test, with the account value brought forward entering the profit test as an item of income at the start of each time step, and the expected cost of the account value carried forward as an item of outgo at the end of each time step. When there are potential costs in excess of the account value, then there will be additional reserves brought forward and carried forward.

13.4.8 Comments on UL profit testing

As discussed in the previous section, we assume that UL reserves are the account values, together, if necessary, with additional reserves for no-lapse guarantees or other ancillary benefits. Additional reserves will be required if the cost of insurance is set at a level amount.

If there are no secondary guarantees, it might be possible to hold a reserve less than the full account value, to allow for the reduced payouts on surrender, and perhaps to take advantage of future profits from the interest spread.

From a risk management perspective, allowing for the surrender penalty in advance by holding less than the account value is not ideal; surrenders are notoriously difficult to predict. History does not always provide a good model, as economic circumstances and variations in policy conditions have a significant impact on policyholder behaviour. In addition, surrenders are not as diversifiable as deaths; that is, the impact of the general economy on surrenders is a systematic risk, impacting the whole portfolio at the same time.

The worked examples in this chapter are simplified to provide a better illustration of the key features of a UL contract. In particular, we have not addressed the fact that the expense charge, CoI and credited interest are changeable at the discretion of the insurer. However, there will be maximum, guaranteed rates set out at issue for expense and CoI charges, and a minimum guaranteed credited interest rate. The profit test would be conducted using several assumptions for these charges, including the guaranteed rates. However, it may be unwise to set the reserves assuming the future charges and credited interest are at the guaranteed level. Although the insurer has the right to move charges up and interest down, it may be difficult, commercially, to do so unless other insurers are moving in the same direction. When there is so much discretion, both for the policyholder and the insurer, it would be usual to conduct a large number of profit tests with different scenarios to assess the full range of potential profits and losses.

13.5 Comparison of UL and whole life insurance policies

The UL contract appears quite different from the traditional life insurance contract, but it can be used to generate very similar benefits to a par or non-par whole life or endowment policy. In Example 13.5, the UL policy is projected to pay a benefit of close to $100 000 on survival for 20 years, and also pays (subject to corridor factor adjustment) a death benefit of $100 000 on death within 20 years. See Table 13.7 where the projected final cash value is $99 997 for a Type A policy with face value $100 000. This appears very similar to a traditional, non-participating endowment insurance policy, with a sum insured of $100 000. The differences are significant though – in particular, the cash value at time $t = 20$ is not guaranteed under the UL policy, but is guaranteed for a 20-year endowment insurance. Also, the endowment insurance premiums would be required and fixed for the whole term. For the UL policy, the policyholder may take premium holidays, or pay additional premiums, in both cases impacting the ultimate cash value of the contract.

A more appropriate comparison might be to compare the UL policy with a traditional, participating whole life policy with reversionary bonus. In both cases, the benefits are increased at intervals, as insurer profits are shared with policyholders, through bonus distribution for participating insurance, or through the credited interest rate for UL. UL policies generally offer better surrender benefits, as well as offering greater flexibility in premiums and partial withdrawals. The par-WL policy with reversionary bonus may offer better death benefits, particularly if investment returns are strong.

13.6 Notes and further reading

We have assumed annual time steps for the examples in this chapter. As in Chapter 12, this is a simplification, applied to make the examples easier to follow. Typically, UL expense and CoI charges would be deducted monthly. Participating policies would also, typically, involve monthly payments, although the distribution of profits might be determined annually.

For both participating whole life (par-WL) and UL insurance, the insurer has significant discretion about the dividends or bonus declared (for par-WL) and the crediting rate (for UL). It is common for the insurer to apply some smoothing, so that changes in dividends or crediting rates are not sudden or dramatic. The methods and impact of smoothing are beyond the scope of this text, but some information is available, for example, in Atkinson and Dallas (2000).

For participating insurance with reversionary bonuses, the insurer may incorporate a bonus assumption into the pricing. However, the actual bonuses declared may be greater or less than the pricing assumption, and will depend on the emerging surplus.

13.7 Exercises

Note: Several questions are adapted from exam questions used by the Society of Actuaries (SOA) for their MLC examination. These questions are copyrighted to the Society of Actuaries, and are reproduced with permission.

The convention for the SOA questions is that the 'CoI rate' refers to the mortality rate used in the CoI calculation, and that the rate of interest for the CoI calculation is the same as the credited rate unless otherwise indicated.

Exercise 13.1 You are calculating asset shares for a portfolio of Universal Life insurance policies with a death benefit of $1000 on (x), payable at the end of the year of death.

You are given, for an individual policy in force throughout the fifth year:

- The account value at the end of year 4 is $30.
- The asset share at the end of year 4 is $20.
- During the fifth year:
  - A premium of $20 is paid at the start of the year.
  - Annual cost of insurance charges of $2 and annual expense charges of $7 are deducted from the account value at the start of the year.
  - The insurer incurs expenses of $2 at the start of the year.
  - The mortality rate for the Universal Life portfolio was 0.1%.
  - The withdrawal rate for the portfolio was 5%.
  - The credited interest rate was 6%.
  - The investment return experienced by the insurer was 8%.
- All withdrawals occur at the end of the policy year; the withdrawal benefit is the account value less a surrender charge of $20.

Calculate the asset share at the end of year 5.
(SOA, Fall 2012)

Exercise 13.2 For a Universal Life insurance policy with a death benefit of $50 000 plus the account value, you are given the following information.

(i)

Policy year	Monthly premium	% Premium charge	CoI rate per month	Monthly expense charge	Surrender charge
1	300	W%	0.2%	10	500
2	300	15%	0.3%	10	125

(ii) The credited interest rate is $i^{(12)} = 0.054$.

(iii) The cash surrender value at the end of month 11 is $1200.00.

(iv) The cash surrender value at the end of month 13 is $1802.94.

Calculate W%, the percent of premium charge in policy year 1.
(SOA, Fall 2012)

Exercise 13.3 You are given the following about a Universal Life insurance policy on (60).

(i) The death benefit equals the account value plus $200 000.

(ii)

Age x	Annual premium	Annual CoI rate per 1000	Annual expense charges
60	5000	5.40	100
61	5000	6.00	100

(iii) Interest is credited at 6% per year.

(iv) Surrender value equals 93% of account value during the first two years. Surrenders occur at the end of the policy year.

(v) Surrenders are 6% per year of those who survive.

(vi) Mortality rates are $q_{60} = 0.00340$ and $q_{61} = 0.00380$.

(vii) $i = 7\%$.

Calculate the present value at issue of the insurer's expected surrender benefits paid in the second year.
(SOA, Fall 2012)

Exercise 13.4 A life aged 40 holds a participating, paid-up whole life insurance contract. The sum insured is $100 000, paid at the end of the year of death. The insurer distributes a cash dividend to holders of policies which are in force at the year end (after surrender and death exits). The cash dividend is determined using 80% of the emerging surplus at each year end, if the surplus is positive.

(a) Calculate the cash dividend projected for this policy at the end of the current policy year, assuming the policy is in force at the year end, and using the following additional assumptions and information.

 (i) The mortality probability for the year is 0.0004, and 8% of surviving policyholders surrender their policies at the year end.
 (ii) Reserves are held equal to the policy value calculated assuming mortality rates from the Standard Ultimate Survival Model, and an interest rate of 4%, ignoring expenses.
 (iii) Surrender values are held equal to the policy value calculated assuming mortality rates from the Standard Ultimate Survival Model, and an interest rate of 5%, ignoring expenses.
 (iv) Interest at 6% per year is earned on the insurer's assets.
 (v) Expenses of $20 are incurred at the start of each year.

(b) Your colleague suggests that policyholders should not participate in profits arising from surrenders. Calculate the revised dividend ignoring surrender profits, and critique this approach.

Exercise 13.5 Suppose that the insurer in Example 13.2 calculates the bonus **before** allowing for deaths and surrenders, rather than after. That is, the insurer declares a bonus (additional sum insured) of $\widetilde{B}_t$ in the tth year. Policies with a death benefit due at time t have the benefit increased by $\$\widetilde{B}_t$, the total reversionary benefit at time t is $\widetilde{RB}_t$, the year end reserve for policies in force is

$$_{t+}V = (S + \widetilde{RB}_t)A_{60+t} - P^*\ddot{a}_{60+t},$$

and cash values for surrendering policies are $h_t\,_{t+}V$.

(a) Calculate the bonuses declared in the first four years.
(b) Comment on the difference between this method of distribution and the method in Example 13.2.

Exercise 13.6 An insurer issues a Type B UL policy with a death benefit of $50 000 plus the account value, to (50). Premiums of $300 per month are paid at the start of each month.

Expense charges in the first year are 20% of premium plus $20 each month. In the second year, the charges are reduced to 15% of premium plus $10 each month.

The CoI is calculated assuming a mortality rate of $\frac{1}{12}q_x = 0.002$ for $50 \le x \le 50\frac{11}{12}$, and $\frac{1}{12}q_x = 0.003$ for $51 \le x \le 51\frac{11}{12}$, and interest of 4% per year effective.

The cash value is determined by deducting a surrender charge from the account value, with a minimum cash value of $0. The surrender charge is $500 for surrenders during the first year, and $125 for surrenders in the second year.

You are given that the credited interest rate is 0.45% per month throughout the first two years, and that the cash value is $860 at the end of the 11th month. Calculate the cash value for the policy at the end of the 13th month.

Exercise 13.7 A life insurance company issues a with-profit whole life insurance policy to a life aged 55. The sum insured is $75 000 together with any attaching bonuses and is payable immediately on death. Level premiums are payable annually in advance, ceasing on the policyholder's death. Simple annual bonuses are added at the end of each policy year. The company calculates the premium on the following basis:

- Survival model: Standard Select Survival Model.
- Interest: 4% per year.
- Initial expenses (before the first premium): $160.
- Maintenance expenses: $65 at the start of each policy year, including the first.
- Claim expenses: $200 on payment of death benefit.
- Commission
  - Initial: 75% of the first year's premium (paid immediately before receipt of first premium);
  - Renewal: 2.5% of all premiums, including the first.

(a) (i) Calculate the annual premium with no allowance for bonus.
    (ii) Calculate the annual premium assuming a simple bonus of 2% per year, each year including the first.
(b) Project the bonuses emerging each year for the policy from the second to the tenth years, assuming
    - Reserves are held equal to the maximum of the gross premium policy values on the premium basis and zero, using the premium from (a)(ii), and without allowance for future bonuses. Allow full recognition of past bonus.
    - No bonus distribution in the first policy year.
    - 100% of emerging surplus (if positive) is converted into reversionary bonus in the second and subsequent years.
    - All other assumptions follow the premium basis.

    Express the bonus emerging as a simple reversionary bonus rate, and comment on the results.
(c) Repeat (b), but now assuming net premium policy values are held as reserves, and that no bonus is declared in the first policy year.
(d) Which reserving method generates more appropriate bonuses? Why?

Exercise 13.8 A Type A UL policy was issued $t - 1$ years ago to (x). The face amount of the policy is $100 000. In the tth year, the corridor factor is 1.95, the CoI mortality rate is 0.005, the interest rate for the CoI is 4%, and the crediting rate is 5%. Expense charges of $25 +0.4% of the account value are deducted from the account value at the start of each year. The account value at the start of the year is $49 500. No premium is paid.

Calculate the cost of insurance charge, the additional death benefit and the year end account value in the tth year.

Exercise 13.9 For a Universal Life insurance policy with death benefit of $100 000 issued to (40), you are given:

- The account value at the end of year 5 is $2029.
- A premium of $200 is paid at the start of year 6.
- Expense charges in renewal years are $40 per year plus 10% of premium.
- The cost of insurance charge for year 6 is $400.
- Expense and cost of insurance charges are payable at the start of the year.
- Under a no-lapse guarantee, after the premium at the start of year 6 is paid, the insurance is guaranteed to continue until the insured reaches age 65.
- If the expected present value of the guaranteed insurance coverage is greater than the account value, the company holds a reserve for the no-lapse guarantee equal to the difference. The expected present value is based on the Standard Ultimate Survival Model at 5% interest and no expenses.

Calculate the reserve for the no-lapse guarantee, immediately after the premium and charges have been accounted for at the start of year 6.

(SOA, Fall 2012)

Exercise 13.10 A life insurance company issues a four-year universal life policy to (65). The main features of the contract are as follows.

Premiums: $3000 per year, payable yearly in advance.

Expense charges: 4% of premium is deducted at the start of the first year; $100 plus 0.4% of the account value (before premium) is deducted at the start of each subsequent policy year.

CoI: $25 is deducted from the account value at the start of each year.

Death benefit: greater of $12 000 or 1.5 times the account value at the year end.

Maturity benefit: 100% of the account value.

The company uses the following assumptions in carrying out a profit test of this contract.

Interest rate: 4.5% per year in year 1, 5.5% per year in year 2, and 6.5% per year in years 3 and 4.

Credited interest: Earned rate minus 1%, with a 4% minimum.

Survival model: Standard Ultimate Survival Model.

Withdrawals: None.

Initial expenses: $200 pre-contract expenses.

Renewal expenses: payable annually at each premium date, initial cost (with first premium) $50, increasing with inflation of 2% per year.

Risk discount rate: 8% per year.

There are no reserves held other than the account value.

(a) Calculate the profit signature and NPV of a newly issued contract.

(b) Calculate the profit signature and NPV for the policy given that the policyholder dies in the first year of the contract.

(c) Calculate the profit signature and NPV for the policy given that the policyholder survives to the contract end.

(d) Calculate the profit signature and NPV for the policy given that the policyholder surrenders at the end of the second year, assuming (i) that the cash value is 100% of the year end account value, and then (ii) that the cash value is 90% of the year end account value.

(e) Calculate the surrender penalty at time 2, as a proportion of AV_2, which gives the same profit margin for surrendering policyholders as for policyholders who remain in force throughout.

(f) Comment on your results.

Exercise 13.11 A with-profit whole life insurance policy was sold to a life aged 70. The sum insured is $100 000 payable at the end of year of death and premiums are payable annually in advance throughout life. The premium is determined assuming that compound reversionary bonuses will be applied to the policy at 2.5% per year.

Assume that bonuses are declared at the end of each policy year, and do not apply to death benefits payable at the year end, but are included in the year-end reserve for continuing policies.

(a) Calculate the annual premium.

(b) Use a profit test to determine the profit margin for the policy, assuming the bonus rates are paid according to the premium basis.

(c) Determine the profit margin for the policy, and the compound bonus rates declared, assuming

- No bonus in the first policy year
- Bonuses are determined by distributing all available emerging surplus for the second and subsequent policy years.

(d) Comment on your results. In particular, explain why the emerging profit before bonus is constant in (c) from the second policy year, derive an expression for its value, and interpret the expression in words.

Basis for premiums

Survival model:	Standard Ultimate Survival Model
Interest rate:	5% per year
Initial expenses:	$200 before the first premium
	$50 + 60% of the first premium, on payment of the first premium
Renewal expenses:	$50 plus 2% of all premiums after the first

Basis for reserves

Survival model:	Standard Ultimate Survival Model
Method:	Net premium policy values
	Declared bonus included, no allowance for future bonuses
Interest:	5% per year interest

Basis for profit tests

Survival model:	Standard Ultimate Survival Model
Withdrawals:	None
Interest:	5% per year
Risk discount rate:	10% per year

Answers to selected exercises

13.1 $40.96

13.2 25%

13.3 $380.01

13.4 (a) $700.32

  (b) $299.56

13.5 (a) $0, $756.50, $1083.47, $1413.82

13.6 $1464.60

13.7 (a) (i) $1438.94

  (ii) $2197.87

  (b) Selected values are $B_2 = \$6087$, $B_4 = \$5452$, $B_6 = \$0$

  (c) Selected values are $B_2 = \$2559$, $B_4 = \$2387$, $B_6 = \$2230$

13.8 CoI is $235.19,   ADB is $48 919.20,   AV is $51 493.90

13.9 $622.29

13.10 (a) $(-200.00, 60.14, 109.19, 156.20, 182.16)'$, $207.19

   (b) $(-200, -8 917.25, 0, 0, 0)'$, $-$8456.71

   (c) $(-200, 113.55, 148.92, 193.14, 239.57)'$, $362.23

   (d) (i) $(-200, 113.55, 148.92, 0, 0)'$, $32.82

      (ii) $(-200, 113.55, 758.40, 0, 0)'$, $555.35

   (e) 3.1%

13.11 (a) $5693.79

   (b) 0.49%

   (c) -3.0%; selected bonus rates are 4.54% in year 2, 2.50% in year 40

14

Emerging costs for equity-linked insurance

14.1 Summary

In this chapter we introduce equity-linked insurance contracts. We explore deterministic emerging cost techniques with examples, and demonstrate that deterministic profit testing cannot adequately model these contracts.

We introduce stochastic cash flow analysis, which gives a fuller picture of the characteristics of the equity-linked cash flows, particularly when guarantees are present, and we demonstrate how stochastic cash flow analysis can be used to determine better contract design.

Finally we discuss the use of quantile and conditional tail expectation reserves for equity-linked insurance.

14.2 Equity-linked insurance

In Chapter 1 we described some modern insurance contracts where the main purpose of the contract is investment. These contracts generally include some death benefit, predominantly as a way of distinguishing them from pure investment products, but they are designed to emphasize the investment opportunity, with a view to competing with pure investment products sold by banks and other financial institutions. Equity-linked insurance can be viewed as a natural development from the traditional participating insurance and Universal Life (UL) products, which offer both insurance and investment benefits.

The equity-linked insurance which we explore in this chapter differs from UL and participating insurance, in that the assets of the policyholders are kept separate from the insurer's main funds. In contrast, UL premiums are combined with the general assets of the insurer, and there is no identifiable 'policyholder account'. Essentially, for equity-linked contracts, policyholders may select the funds in which they invest, making the policies look very similar to the collective investment products such as mutual funds in North America, and unit trusts in the UK, Australia and elsewhere.

473

The contracts we consider are called **unit-linked policies** in the UK and parts of Europe, **variable annuities** in the USA (though there is often no actual annuity component) and **segregated fund policies** in Canada. All fall under the generic title of equity-linked insurance. The basic premise of these contracts is that a policyholder pays a single or regular premium which, after deducting expenses, is invested on the policyholder's behalf in specified collective investment funds. These form the **policyholder's fund**. The value of the policyholder's fund moves up or down each month, just like a mutual fund investment. Regular **management charges** are deducted from the fund by the insurer and paid into the **insurer's fund** to cover expenses and insurance charges.

On survival to the end of the contract term the benefit may be just the policyholder's fund and no more, or there may be a **guaranteed minimum maturity benefit** (GMMB).

On death during the term of the policy, the policyholder's estate would receive the policyholder's fund, possibly with an extra amount – for example, a death benefit of 110% of the policyholder's fund means an additional death benefit of 10% of the policyholder's fund at the time of death. There may also be a **guaranteed minimum death benefit** (GMDB).

Some conventions and jargon have developed around these contracts, particularly in the UK where the policyholder is deemed to buy units in an underlying asset fund (hence 'unit-linked'). One example is the **bid-offer spread**. If a contract is sold with a bid-offer spread of, say, 5%, only 95% of the premium paid is actually invested in the policyholder's fund; the remainder goes to the insurer's fund. There may also be an **allocation percentage**; if 101% of the premium is allocated to units at the offer price, and there is a 5% bid-offer spread, then 101% of 95% of the premium (that is 95.95%) goes to the policyholder's fund and the rest goes to the insurer's fund. The bid-offer spread mirrors the practice in unitized investment funds that are major competitors for policyholders' investments.

Because the policyholder's funds are not mixed with the general assets of the company, but are held separately, another general term for this type of contract is **separate account insurance**. The fact that the policyholder's assets are held separately from the insurer's assets makes a difference to our analysis of these policies; the policyholder's funds do not directly contribute to the insurer's profit or loss; investment gains and losses are all passed straight to the policyholder. However, the policyholder's fund contributes indirectly. The insurer receives income from the regular management charges that depend on the policyholder's fund value; the additional death benefit cover will be a function of the fund value, and the cost of any guarantees offered will also depend on the fund value.

14.3 Deterministic profit testing for equity-linked insurance

Equity-linked insurance policies are usually analysed using emerging surplus techniques. The process is similar to the UL profit test, except that we separate the cash flows into those that are in the policyholder's fund and those that are income or outgo for the insurer. It is the insurer's cash flows that are important in pricing, reserving and profit projections, but since the insurer's income and outgo depend on how much is in the policyholder's fund, we must first project the cash flows for the policyholder's fund and use these to project the cash flows for the insurer's fund. The projected cash flows for the insurer's fund can then be used to calculate the profitability of the contract using the profit vector, profit signature, and perhaps the NPV, IRR, profit margin and discounted payback period, in the same way as in Chapters 12 and 13. We show two examples in this section. The first assumes annual cash flows, to make the calculations easier to follow. The second uses monthly time steps, which is more realistic.

Before we present the examples, we introduce some notation and key relationships. For annual time steps, the t subscript refers to the cash flows in the tth policy year. In order to project the emerging profit from the insurer's cash flows, we first need to project the policyholder's fund through the term of the contract, as the insurer's cash flows depend on the fund values. The relevant cash flows, with notation, are described here.

Policyholder's fund: F_t is the amount in the policyholder's separate account at time t.

Premium: P_t is the total premium paid by the policyholder at time $t - 1$; the insurer will make some deductions for expenses and contingencies. The remainder is invested in the policyholder's fund.

Allocated premium: AP_t is the part of the tth premium that is invested in the policyholder's fund.

Interest on policyholder's assets: i_t^f is the assumed rate of interest earned on the policyholder's fund in the tth year. It will depend on the type of assets available, and in practice is highly variable. In this section we adopt simple deterministic assumptions for i_t^f, but in Section 14.4 we explore a stochastic approach.

Management charge: MC_t is the management charge deducted from the policyholder's fund during the tth year. The management charge may be deducted at the start or the end of the year; we generally assume the year end in our examples. This passes to the insurer's assets.

So, assuming that the management charge is deducted from the policyholder's fund at the year end, we have

$$F_t = (F_{t-1} + AP_t)(1 + i_t^f) - MC_t. \qquad (14.1)$$

The first step in a profit test of an equity-linked policy is the projection of the policyholder's fund, *assuming that the policyholder stays in force throughout the contract.* This is exactly the process we used for Universal Life profit testing in Chapter 13. We are not directly interested in the policyholder's fund. We project the fund values because the insurer cash flows in, say, the tth policy year depend on the fund values in respect of policies in force during the tth year.

Following the conventions of profit testing, we first calculate the profit vector by projecting the insurer's cash flows each year, assuming that the policy is in force at the start of the year. We use the following notation for the insurer's cash flows and profit. Some of these terms have been introduced in previous chapters, and are repeated here for convenience.

Reserve $_{t-1}V$: Often the policyholder's funds are sufficient for the policyholder's benefits, as maturity or surrender values. The insurer's reserve, which is additional to the separate account holding the policyholder's funds, is only required if there are potential additional future liabilities that need advance reserves. If required, $_{t-1}V$ is the reserve brought forward to the tth year in respect of a policy in force at the start of the tth year.

Unallocated premium, UAP_t: This is $P_t - AP_t$, which is the difference between the full premium paid and the allocated premium paid into the policyholder's fund. The unallocated premium is paid into the insurer's funds.

Expenses, E_t: this refers to the projected incurred expenses. Pre-contract expenses will be allocated to time 0, as usual. Other expenses are assumed to be incurred at the start of each policy year (i.e. at time $t - 1$).

Interest, I_t: this is the interest income on the insurer's assets invested through the tth year.

Expected cost of death benefit, EDB_t: this covers any additional death benefit not covered by the policyholder's fund. That is, if the benefit paid at the end of the year of death is DB_t, the policyholder's fund will cover F_t, and the additional death benefit is $DB_t - F_t$. If the mortality probability for the tth year is p_{x+t-1}^{0d}, then

$$EDB_t = p_{x+t-1}^{0d}(DB_t - F_t).$$

Expected cost of surrender or maturity cash values, ECV_t: this covers any additional cash value not covered by the policyholder's fund. If there is a surrender penalty, so that the surrendering policyholder receives less than their fund value, then ECV_t will be negative, i.e. an item of income not outgo. In the final year of the contract, there may be a sum payable at maturity, additional to the policyholder's fund – for example, if a guaranteed minimum maturity benefit applies. If the probability of surrender in the tth year is p^{0w}_{x+t-1}, then

$$ECV_t = p^{0w}_{x+t-1} (CV_t - F_t),$$

where, in the final year, CV_t refers to the payment at maturity.

Expected cost of year end reserve, $E_t V$: as used throughout Chapters 12 and 13, if p^{00}_{x+t-1} is the probability that a policy in force at the start of the tth year is still in force at the start of the $(t + 1)$th year, then

$$E_t V = p^{00}_{x+t-1} {}_t V.$$

Assuming that the management charge is paid from the policyholder's fund to the insurer at each year end, for a policy in force at the start of the year, we have the profit vector calculation, that is, profit emerging at time t for a policy in force at time $t - 1$,

$$\Pr_t = {}_{t-1}V + UAP_t - E_t + I_t + MC_t - EDB_t - ECV_t - E_t V. \tag{14.2}$$

In practice, not all of these terms may be needed. Some policies will not carry reserves, and it would be common for the cash value to be equal to the policyholder's fund, which would mean that the cost to the insurer (ECV_t) would be zero. Also, formula (14.2) may need some adjustment, for example, if management charges are deducted at the start of the year rather than the end.

Once the profit vector has been calculated, the profit signature, NPV and profit margin can all be determined using the techniques from Chapter 12.

The following two examples illustrate the calculations.

Example 14.1 A 10-year equity-linked contract is issued to a life aged 55 with the following terms.

The policyholder pays an annual premium of $5000. The insurer deducts a 5% expense allowance from the first premium and a 1% allowance from subsequent premiums. The remainder is invested into the policyholder's fund.

At the end of each year a management charge of 0.75% of the policyholder's fund is transferred from the policyholder's fund to the insurer's fund.

If the policyholder dies during the contract term, a benefit of 110% of the value of the policyholder's year end fund (after management charge deductions) is paid at the end of the year of death.

If the policyholder surrenders the contract, he receives the value of the policyholder's fund at the year end, after management charge deductions.

If the policyholder holds the contract to the maturity date, he receives the greater of the value of the policyholder's fund and the total of the premiums paid.

(a) Assume the policyholder's fund earns interest at 9% per year. Project the year end fund values for a contract that remains in force for 10 years.
(b) Calculate the profit vector for the contract using the following basis.

   Survival model: The probability of dying in any year is 0.005.

   Lapses: 10% of lives in force at year end surrender in the first year of the contract, 5% in the second year and none in subsequent years. All surrenders occur at the end of a year immediately after the management charge deduction.

   Initial expenses: 10% of the first premium plus $150, incurred before the first premium payment.

   Renewal expenses: 0.5% of the second and subsequent premiums.

   Interest: The insurer's funds earn interest at 6% per year.

   Reserves: The insurer holds no reserves for the contract.
(c) Calculate the profit signature for the contract.
(d) Calculate the NPV using a risk discount rate of 15% per year effective.

Solution 14.1 (a) The first step in a profit test is the projection of F_t, assuming the policy is in force for the full 10-year contract. We extract from all the information above the parts that relate to the policyholder's fund.

   We are given that the annual premium is $5000; 5% is deducted from the first premium, giving an allocated premium of $AP_1 = 4750$. In subsequent years, the allocated premium is 99% of the premium, so that for $t = 2, 3, \ldots, 10, AP_t = 4950$.

   We are also given the assumption that $i_t^f = 0.09$.

   The management charge in the tth year is

$$MC_t = 0.0075 \times ((F_{t-1} + AP_t) \times 1.09),$$

and, following equation (14.1), for $t = 1, 2, 3, \ldots, 10$, we have

$$F_t = (F_{t-1} + AP_t) \times 1.09 - MC_t = (F_{t-1} + AP_t) \times 1.09 \times 0.9925.$$

The projection of the policyholder's fund is shown in Table 14.1. The key to the columns of Table 14.1 is as follows.

(1) The entries for t are the years of the contract, from time $t-1$ to time t.
(2) This shows the allocated premium, AP_t, invested in the policyholder's fund at time $t-1$.
(3) This shows the fund brought forward from the previous year end.
(4) This shows the amount in the policyholder's fund at the year end, just before the annual management charge is deducted.
(5) This shows the management charge, at 0.75% of the previous column.
(6) This shows the remaining fund, which is carried forward to the next year.

Table 14.1 *Projection of policyholder's fund for Example 14.1.*

t (1)	AP_t (2)	F_{t-1} (3)	F_{t-} (4)	MC_t (5)	F_t (6)
1	4750	0.00	5177.50	38.83	5138.67
2	4950	5138.67	10 996.65	82.47	10 914.17
3	4950	10 914.17	17 291.95	129.69	17 162.26
4	4950	17 162.26	24 102.36	180.77	23 921.60
5	4950	23 921.60	31 470.04	236.03	31 234.01
6	4750	31 234.01	39 440.58	295.80	39 144.77
7	4950	39 144.77	48 063.30	360.47	47 702.83
8	4950	47 702.83	57 391.58	430.44	56 961.14
9	4950	56 961.14	67 483.15	506.12	66 977.02
10	4950	66 977.02	78 400.45	588.00	77 812.45

(b) The sources of income and outgo for the insurer's funds, for a contract in force at the start of the year, are:

Unallocated premium: $UAP_t = 5\,000 - AP_t$. This is the amount the insurer takes when the premiums are paid. The rest goes into the policyholder's fund.

Expenses, E_t:

Initial expenses (pre-contract) of $E_0 = 0.1 \times 5000 + 150 = 650$.

First year expenses of $E_1 = 0$ (all included in E_0).

For $t = 2, 3, \ldots, 10$, $E_t = 0.005 \times 5000 = 25$.

Interest, I_t: earned at 6% per year, so for $t = 1, 2, \ldots, 10$,

$$I_t = 0.06\,(UAP_t - E_t).$$

Note that there are no reserves required for this policy.

Management charge: MC_t is assumed to be received at the year end. The values are taken from Table 14.1.

Expected cost of deaths: the death benefit is greater than the policyholder's fund value, which means there is a cost to the insurer if the policyholder dies. The death benefit is 110% of F_t, so the insurer's liability if the policyholder dies in the tth year is 10% of F_t (the rest is paid from the policyholder's fund). The mortality probability is given as 0.005, so the expected cost of the additional death benefit is

$$EDB_t = 0.005 \times (1.1F_t - F_t) = 0.005 \times 0.1F_t.$$

Expected cost of cash values: There is no cost to the insurer if the policyholder surrenders the contract early, but there is a potential cost from the GMMB at maturity. The fund value at maturity is F_{10} which is projected to

Table 14.2 *Emerging surplus for Example 14.1.*

t	Unallocated premium UAP_t	Expenses E_t	Interest I_t	Management charge MC_t	Expected death benefit EDB_t	Pr_t
0	0.00	650.00	0.00	0.00	0.00	−650.00
1	250.00	0.00	15.00	38.83	2.57	301.26
2	50.00	25.00	1.50	82.47	5.46	103.52
3	50.00	25.00	1.50	129.69	8.58	147.61
4	50.00	25.00	1.50	180.77	11.96	195.31
5	50.00	25.00	1.50	236.03	15.62	246.91
6	50.00	25.00	1.50	295.80	19.57	302.73
7	50.00	25.00	1.50	360.47	23.85	363.12
8	50.00	25.00	1.50	430.44	28.48	428.46
9	50.00	25.00	1.50	506.12	33.49	499.14
10	50.00	25.00	1.50	588.00	38.91	575.60

Table 14.3 *Calculation of the profit signature for Example 14.1.*

t	Probability in force	Π_t	t	Probability in force	Π_t
0	1.00000	−650.00	6	0.83384	252.43
1	1.00000	301.26	7	0.82967	301.27
2	0.89550	92.70	8	0.82552	353.70
3	0.84647	124.95	9	0.82139	409.99
4	0.84224	164.50	10	0.81729	470.43
5	0.83803	206.92			

be \$77 812.45. The GMMB requires a final payment of at least 10×5000. Since this is smaller than F_{10}, there is no projected cost from the GMMB.

Following equation (14.2), we have

$$Pr_t = UAP_t - E_t + I_t + MC_t - EDB_t.$$

The emerging surplus is shown in Table 14.2.

(c) For the profit signature we multiply the tth element of the profit vector, Pr_t, by the probability that the contract is still in force at the start of the year for $t = 1, 2, \ldots, 10$. (For $t = 0$, the required probability is 1.) The values are shown in Table 14.3.

(d) The NPV is calculated by discounting the profit signature at the risk discount rate of interest, $r = 15\%$, so that

$$\text{NPV} = \sum_{t=0}^{10} \Pi_t \, (1+r)^{-t} = \$531.98.$$

□

Example 14.2 The terms of a five-year equity-linked insurance policy issued to a life aged 60 are as follows.

The policyholder pays a single premium of $10 000. The insurer deducts 3% of the premium for expenses. The remainder is invested in the policyholder's fund.

At the start of the second and subsequent months, a management charge of 0.06% of the policyholder's fund is transferred to the insurer's fund.

If the policyholder dies during the term, the policy pays out 101% of all the money in her fund. In addition, the insurer guarantees a minimum benefit. The guaranteed minimum death benefit in the tth year is $10 000 (1.05)^{t-1}$, where $t = 1, 2, \ldots, 5$.

If the policyholder surrenders the contract during the first year, she receives 90% of the money in the policyholder's fund. In the second year a surrendered contract pays 95% of the policyholder's fund. If the policyholder surrenders the contract after the second policy anniversary, she receives 100% of the policyholder's fund.

If the policyholder holds the contract to the maturity date, she receives the money in the policyholder's fund with a guarantee that the payout will not be less than $10 000.

The insurer assesses the profitability of the contract by projecting cash flows on a monthly basis using the following assumptions.

Survival model: The force of mortality is constant for all ages and equal to 0.006 per year.

Death benefit: This is paid at the end of the month in which death occurs.

Lapses: Policies are surrendered only at the end of a month. The probability of surrendering at the end of any particular month is 0.004 in the first year, 0.002 in the second year and 0.001 in each subsequent year.

Interest: The policyholder's fund earns interest at 8% per year effective. The insurer's fund earns interest at 5% per year effective.

Initial expenses: 1% of the single premium plus $150.

Renewal expenses: 0.008% of the single premium plus 0.01% of the policyholder's funds at the end of the previous month. Renewal expenses are payable at the start of each month after the first.

(a) Calculate the probabilities that a policy in force at the start of a month is still in force at the start of the next month.

(b) Construct a table showing the projected policyholder's fund assuming the policy remains in force throughout the term.

(c) Construct a table showing the projected insurer's fund.

(d) Calculate the NPV for the contract using a risk discount rate of 12% per year.

Solution 14.2 (a) The probability of not dying in any month is

$$\exp\{-0.006/12\} = 0.9995.$$

Hence, allowing for lapses, the probability that a policy in force at the start of a month, at time t, say, is still in force at the start of the following month is as follows, where $h = \frac{1}{12}$ is the time step for this example:

$$_h p^{00}_{x+t-h} = (1 - 0.004) \exp\{-0.006/12\} = 0.9955 \qquad \text{in the first year,}$$

$$_h p^{00}_{x+t-h} = (1 - 0.002) \exp\{-0.006/12\} = 0.9975 \qquad \text{in the second year,}$$

$$_h p^{00}_{x+t-h} = (1 - 0.001) \exp\{-0.006/12\} = 0.9985 \qquad \text{in subsequent years.}$$

(b) Table 14.4 shows the projected policyholder's fund at selected durations assuming the policy remains in force throughout the five years. Note that in this example the management charge is deducted at the start of the month rather than the end. The guaranteed minimum death benefit is also given in this table – in the first year this is the full premium and it increases by 5% at the start of each year.

(c) The projected cash flows for the insurer's fund are shown in Table 14.5.

UAP_t: the unallocated premium is $300 in the first month, and $0 thereafter, as this is a single premium policy.

MC_t: the management charge is taken from Table 14.4. In this example, it is assumed to be paid at the start of each month.

E_t: the expenses are described in the example; the pre-contract expenses are allocated to time 0.

I_t is calculated as $(1.05^{1/12} - 1)(UAP_t + MC_t - E_t)$.

EDB_t is the expected cost of additional death benefits. The death benefit at time t is $DB_t = \max(1.01 \times F_t, GMDB_t)$, where $GMDB_t$ is the guaranteed minimum death benefit shown in Table 14.4. Hence, the additional death benefit is

Table 14.4 *Deterministic projection of the policyholder's fund for Example 14.2.*

t	AP_t	F_{t-1}	MC_t	F_t	$GMDB_t$
$\frac{1}{12}$	9 700	0.00	0.00	9 762.41	10 000.00
$\frac{2}{12}$	0	9 762.41	5.86	9 819.33	10 000.00
$\frac{3}{12}$	0	9 819.33	5.89	9 876.57	10 000.00
$\frac{4}{12}$	0	9 876.57	5.93	9 934.16	10 000.00
$\frac{5}{12}$	0	9 934.16	5.96	9 992.07	10 000.00
$\frac{6}{12}$	0	9 992.07	6.00	10 050.33	10 000.00
$\vdots$	$\vdots$	$\vdots$	$\vdots$	$\vdots$	$\vdots$
1	0	10 346.74	6.21	10 407.07	10 000.00
$1\frac{1}{12}$	0	10 407.07	6.24	10 467.74	10 500.00
$\vdots$	$\vdots$	$\vdots$	$\vdots$	$\vdots$	$\vdots$
2	0	11 094.29	6.66	11 158.97	10 500.00
$2\frac{1}{12}$	0	11 158.97	6.70	11 224.03	11 025.00
$\vdots$	$\vdots$	$\vdots$	$\vdots$	$\vdots$	$\vdots$
3	0	11 895.85	7.14	11 965.20	11 025.00
$3\frac{1}{12}$	0	11 965.20	7.18	12 034.96	11 576.25
$\vdots$	$\vdots$	$\vdots$	$\vdots$	$\vdots$	$\vdots$
4	0	12 755.32	7.65	12 829.68	11 576.25
$4\frac{1}{12}$	0	12 829.68	7.70	12 904.48	12 155.06
$\vdots$	$\vdots$	$\vdots$	$\vdots$	$\vdots$	$\vdots$
5	0	13 676.89	8.21	13 756.62	12 155.06

$$ADB_t = DB_t - F_t = \max(0.01 \times F_t, GMDB_t - F_t),$$

and the expected cost of the additional death benefit in the month from time $t - h$ to time t is

$$EDB_t = {}_hp^{0d}_{60+t-h} \max(0.01 \times F_t, GMDB_t - F_t)$$

where ${}_hp^{0d}_{60+t-h} = 1 - e^{-0.006/12}$ is the probability of death in the month.

ECV_t is the expected cost of surrender and maturity payments. In this case, expected profits on surrenders in the first two years are a source of income for the insurer's fund since, on surrendering her policy, the policyholder receives less than the full amount of the policyholder's

Table 14.5 *Deterministic projection of the insurer's fund for Example 14.2.*

t	UAP_t	MC_t	E_t	I_t	EDB_t	ECV_t	Pr_t
0	0	0.00	250.00	0.00	0.00	0.00	−250.00
$\frac{1}{12}$	300	0.00	0.80	1.22	0.12	−3.90	304.20
$\frac{2}{12}$	0	5.86	1.78	0.02	0.09	−3.93	7.93
$\frac{3}{12}$	0	5.89	1.78	0.02	0.06	−3.95	8.01
$\frac{4}{12}$	0	5.93	1.79	0.02	0.05	−3.97	8.08
$\frac{5}{12}$	0	5.96	1.79	0.02	0.05	−3.99	8.13
$\frac{6}{12}$	0	6.00	1.80	0.02	0.05	−4.02	8.18
$\vdots$	$\vdots$	$\vdots$	$\vdots$	$\vdots$	$\vdots$	$\vdots$	$\vdots$
1	0	6.21	1.83	0.02	0.05	−4.16	8.50
$1\frac{1}{12}$	0	6.24	1.84	0.02	0.05	−1.05	5.42
$\vdots$	$\vdots$	$\vdots$	$\vdots$	$\vdots$	$\vdots$	$\vdots$	$\vdots$
2	0	6.66	1.91	0.02	0.06	−1.12	5.83
$2\frac{1}{12}$	0	6.70	1.92	0.02	0.06	0.00	4.74
$\vdots$	$\vdots$	$\vdots$	$\vdots$	$\vdots$	$\vdots$	$\vdots$	$\vdots$
3	0	7.14	1.99	0.02	0.06	0.00	5.11
$3\frac{1}{12}$	0	7.18	2.00	0.02	0.06	0.00	5.14
$\vdots$	$\vdots$	$\vdots$	$\vdots$	$\vdots$	$\vdots$	$\vdots$	$\vdots$
4	0	7.65	2.08	0.02	0.06	0.00	5.54
$4\frac{1}{12}$	0	7.70	2.08	0.02	0.06	0.00	5.57
$\vdots$	$\vdots$	$\vdots$	$\vdots$	$\vdots$	$\vdots$	$\vdots$	$\vdots$
5	0	8.21	2.17	0.02	0.00	0.00	5.99

fund. Let $_hp^{0w}_{60+t-h}$ denote the lapse probability for the month, and let CV_t denote the total cash value paid on surrender at time t. Then

$$ECV_t = {}_hp^{0w}_{60+t-h}(CV_t - F_t).$$

In the first year (i.e. for $t = \frac{1}{12}, \frac{2}{12}, \ldots, 1$), $CV_t = 0.9\,F_t$, and in the second year $CV_t = 0.95\,F_t$. For $t = 2\frac{1}{12}, 2\frac{2}{12}, \ldots,$ $CV_t = F_t$. For example, for $t = \frac{3}{12}$, $_hp^{0w}_{60+t-h} = 0.004 \times e^{-0.006/12}$, so

$$ECV_t = 0.004 \times e^{-0.006/12} \times (-0.10\,F_t).$$

There is no projected maturity benefit other than the policyholder's fund.

Table 14.6 *Calculation of the profit signature for Example 14.2.*

t	Pr_t	Probability in force	Π_t
0	−250.00	1.0000	−250.00
$\frac{1}{12}$	304.20	1.0000	304.20
$\frac{2}{12}$	7.93	0.9955	7.90
$\frac{3}{12}$	8.01	0.9910	7.94
$\frac{4}{12}$	8.08	0.9866	7.97
$\frac{5}{12}$	8.13	0.9821	7.98
$\frac{6}{12}$	8.18	0.9777	8.00
$\vdots$	$\vdots$	$\vdots$	$\vdots$
1	8.50	0.9516	8.09
$1\frac{1}{12}$	5.42	0.9492	5.14
$\vdots$	$\vdots$	$\vdots$	$\vdots$
2	5.83	0.9235	5.38
$2\frac{1}{12}$	4.74	0.9221	4.37
$\vdots$	$\vdots$	$\vdots$	$\vdots$
3	5.11	0.9070	4.63
$3\frac{1}{12}$	5.14	0.9056	4.66
$\vdots$	$\vdots$	$\vdots$	$\vdots$
4	5.54	0.8908	4.93
$4\frac{1}{12}$	5.57	0.8895	4.96
$\vdots$	$\vdots$	$\vdots$	$\vdots$
5	5.99	0.8749	5.24

Pr_t: the expected profit at the end of the month per policy in force at the
start of the month is calculated, following equation (14.2), as

$$\mathrm{Pr}_t = UAP_t - E_t + MC_t + I_t - EDB_t - ECV_t.$$

(d) Table 14.6 shows, for selected durations, the expected profit at the end of
the month per policy in force at the start of the tth month, Pr_t, the probability that the policy is in force at the start of the month (given only that it
was in force at time 0) and the profit signature, Π_t, which is the product of
these two elements.

The net present value for this policy is calculated by summing the elements of the profit signature discounted to time 0 at the risk discount
rate, r. Hence

$$\text{NPV} = \sum_{k=0}^{60} \Pi_{\frac{k}{12}} (1+r)^{-\frac{k}{12}} = \$302.42.$$

$\square$

In both the examples in this section, the benefit involved a guarantee. In the first example the guarantee had no effect at all on the calculations, and in the second the effect was negligible. This does not mean that the guarantees are cost-free. In practice, even though the policyholder's fund may earn on average a return of 9% or more, the return could be very volatile. A few years of poor returns could generate a significant cost for the guarantee. We can explore the sensitivity of the emerging profit to adverse scenarios by using stress testing.

In Example 14.1 there is a GMMB – the final payout is guaranteed to be at least the total amount invested, \$50 000. Assume as an adverse scenario that the return on the policyholder's fund is only 5% rather than 9%. The result is that the GMMB still has no effect, and the NPV changes from \$531.98 to \$417.45. We must reduce the return assumption to 1% or lower for the guarantee to have any cost. However, under the deterministic model there is no way to turn this analysis into a price for the guarantee.

Furthermore, the deterministic approach does not reflect the potentially huge uncertainty involved in the income and outgo for equity-linked insurance. The insurer's cash flows depend on the policyholder's fund, and the policyholder's fund depends on market conditions.

The deterministic profit tests described in this section can be quite misleading. The investment risks in equity-linked insurance cannot be treated deterministically. It is crucial that the uncertainty is properly taken into consideration for adequate pricing, reserving and risk management. In the next section we develop the methodology introduced in this section to allow appropriately for uncertainty.

14.4 Stochastic profit testing

For traditional insurance policies we often assume that the demographic uncertainty dominates the investment uncertainty – which may be a reasonable assumption if the underlying assets are invested in low-risk fixed interest securities of appropriate duration. The uncertainty involved in equity-linked insurance is very different. The mortality element is assumed diversifiable and is not usually the major factor. The uncertainty in the investment performance is a far more important element, and it is not diversifiable. Selling 1000 equity-linked contracts with GMMBs to identical lives is almost the same as issuing one big contract; when one policyholder's fund dips in value, then all dip, increasing the chance that the GMMB will cost the insurer money for every contract.

Using a deterministic profit test does not reflect the reality of the situation adequately in most cases. The EPV of future profit – expected in terms of demographic uncertainty only – does not contain any information about the uncertainty from investment returns. The profit measure for an equity-linked contract is modelled more appropriately as a random variable rather than a single number. This is achieved by stochastic profit testing.

The good news is that we have done much of the work for stochastic profit testing in the deterministic profit testing of the previous section. The difference is that in the earlier section we assumed deterministic interest and demographic scenarios. In this section we replace the deterministic investment scenarios with stochastic scenarios. The most common practical way to do this is with Monte Carlo simulation, which we introduced in Section 11.5, and used already for this purpose with interest rates in Chapter 11.

Using Monte Carlo simulation, we generate a large number of outcomes for the investment return on the policyholder's fund. The simulated returns are used in place of the constant investment return assumption in the deterministic case. The profit test proceeds exactly as described in the deterministic approach, except that we repeat the test for each simulated investment return outcome, so we generate a random sample of outcomes for the contract, which we can use to determine the probability distribution for each profit measure for a contract.

Typically, the policyholder's fund may be invested in a mixed fund of equities or equities and bonds. The policyholder may have a choice of funds available, involving greater or lesser amounts of uncertainty.

A very common assumption for returns on equity portfolios is the independent lognormal assumption. This assumption, which is very important in financial modelling, can be expressed as follows. Let $R_1, R_2, \ldots$ be a sequence of random variables, where R_t represents the accumulation at time t of a unit amount invested in an equity fund at time $t - 1$, so that $R_t - 1$ is the rate of interest earned in the year. These random variables are assumed to be mutually independent, and each R_t is assumed to have a lognormal distribution (see Appendix A). Note that if R_t has a lognormal distribution with parameters μ_t and σ_t^2, then

$$\log R_t \sim N(\mu_t, \sigma_t^2).$$

Hence, values for R_t can be simulated by simulating values for $\log R_t$ and exponentiating.

We demonstrate stochastic profit testing for equity-linked insurance by considering further the 10-year policy discussed in Example 14.1. In the discus-

Table 14.7 *A single simulation of the profit test.*

t (1)	Simulated z_t (2)	Simulated r_t (3)	Management charge (4)	Fund c/f (5)	Pr_t (6)	Π_t (7)
0					−650.00	−650.00
1	0.95518	1.24384	44.31	5 863.94	306.38	306.38
2	−2.45007	0.74633	60.53	8 010.27	83.03	74.35
3	−1.23376	0.89571	87.07	11 521.61	107.80	90.80
4	0.55824	1.17194	144.78	19 159.03	161.70	135.51
5	−0.62022	0.98206	177.57	23 498.89	192.32	160.37
6	0.01353	1.08000	230.44	30 494.26	241.69	200.52
7	−1.22754	0.89655	238.33	31 539.16	249.06	205.61
8	0.07758	1.09042	298.41	39 490.18	305.17	250.66
9	−0.61893	0.98225	327.38	43 323.89	332.22	271.52
10	−0.25283	1.03770	375.70	49 717.95	96.71	78.64

sion of Example 14.1 in Section 14.3 we assumed a rate of return of 9% per year on the policyholder's fund. This resulted in a zero cost for the GMMB. We now assume that the accumulation factor for the policyholder's fund over the tth policy year is R_t, where the sequence $\{R_t\}_{t=1}^{10}$ satisfies the independent lognormal assumption. To simplify our presentation we further assume that these random variables are identically distributed, with $R_t \sim LN(\mu, \sigma^2)$, where $\mu = 0.074928$ and $\sigma^2 = 0.15^2$. Note that the expected accumulation factor each year is

$$E[R_t] = e^{\mu + \sigma^2/2} = 1.09,$$

which is the same as under the deterministic assumption in Section 14.3.

Table 14.7 shows the results of a single simulation of the investment returns on the policyholder's fund for the policy in Example 14.1.

The values in column (2), labelled $z_1, \ldots, z_{10}$, are simulated values from a $N(0, 1)$ distribution. These values are converted to simulated values from the specified lognormal distribution using $r_t = \exp\{0.074928 + 0.15z_t\}$, giving the annual accumulation factors shown in column (3). The values $\{r_t\}_{t=1}^{10}$ are a single simulation of the random variables $\{R_t\}_{t=1}^{10}$. These simulated annual accumulation factors should be compared with the value 1.09 used in the calculation of Table 14.1. The values in columns (4) and (5) are calculated in the same way as those in columns (5) and (6) in Table 14.1, using the annual interest rate $r_t - 1$ in place of 0.09. Note that in some years, for example the second policy year, the accumulation factor for the policyholder's fund is less than one. The values in column (6) are calculated in the same way as those in the final column of Table 14.2 except that there is an extra deduction in the calculation of Pr_{10} of amount

$$p_{54}^{00} \max(50\,000 - F_{10}, 0)$$

where F_{10} denotes the final fund value. This deduction was not needed in our calculations in Section 14.3 since, with the deterministic interest assumption, the final fund value, \$77 812.45, was greater than the GMMB. For this simulation, F_{10} is less than the GMMB so there is a deduction of amount

$$0.995 \times (50\,000 - 49\,717.95) = \$280.64.$$

The values for Π_t are calculated by multiplying the corresponding value of $\Pr_t$ by the probability of the policy being in force, as shown in Table 14.3. The values for $\Pr_t$ and Π_t shown in Table 14.7 should be compared with the corresponding values in Tables 14.2 and 14.3, respectively. Using a risk discount rate of 15% per year, the NPV using this single simulation of the investment returns on the policyholder's fund is \$232.09.

To measure the effect of the uncertainty in rates of return, we generate a large number, N, of sets of rates of return and for each set carry out a profit test as above. Let NPV_i denote the net present value calculated from the ith simulation, for $i = 1, 2, \ldots, N$. Then the net present value for the policy, NPV, is being modelled as a random variable and $\{NPV_i\}_{i=1}^{N}$ is a set of N independent values sampled from the distribution of NPV. From this sample we can estimate the mean, standard deviation and percentiles of this distribution. We can also count the number of simulations for which NPV_i is negative, denoted N^-, and the number of simulations, denoted N^*, for which the final fund value is greater than \$50 000, so that there is no liability for the GMMB.

Let m and s be the estimates of the mean and standard deviation of NPV. Since N is large, we can appeal to the central limit theorem to say that a 95% confidence interval (CI) for $E[NPV]$ is given by

$$\left(m - 1.96 \, \frac{s}{\sqrt{N}}, \; m + 1.96 \, \frac{s}{\sqrt{N}} \right).$$

It is important whenever reporting summary results from a stochastic simulation to give some measure of the variability of the results, such as a standard deviation or a confidence interval.

Calculations by the authors using $N = 1000$ gave the results shown in Table 14.8. To calculate the median and the percentiles we arrange the simulated values of NPV in ascending or descending order. Let $\{NPV_{(i)}\}_{i=1}^{1\,000}$ denote the simulated values for NPV arranged in ascending order. Then the median is estimated as $(NPV_{(500)} + NPV_{(501)})/2$, so that 50% of the observations lie above the estimated median, and 50% lie above. This would be true for any value lying between $NPV_{(500)}$ and $NPV_{(501)}$, and taking the mid-point is a conventional approach. Similarly the fifth percentile value is estimated as

Table 14.8 *Results from 1000
simulations of the net present value.*

E[NPV]	380.91
SD[NPV]	600.61
95% CI for E[NPV]	(343.28, 417.74)
5th percentile	−859.82
Median of NPV	498.07
95th percentile	831.51
N^-	87
N^*	897

$(\text{NPV}_{(50)} + \text{NPV}_{(51)})/2$ and the 95th percentile is estimated as $(\text{NPV}_{(950)} + \text{NPV}_{(951)})/2$.

The results in Table 14.8 put a very different light on the profitability of the contract. Under the deterministic analysis, the profit test showed no liability for the guaranteed minimum maturity benefit, and the contract appeared to be profitable overall – the net present value was \$531.98. Under the stochastic analysis, the GMMB plays a very important role. The value of N^* shows that in most cases the GMMB liability is zero and so it does not affect the median. However, it does have a significant effect on the mean, which is considerably lower than the median. From the fifth percentile figure, we see that very large losses are possible; from the 95th percentile we see that there is somewhat less upside potential with this policy. Note also that an estimate of the probability that the net present value is negative, calculated using a risk discount rate of 15% per year, is

$$N^-/N = 0.087,$$

indicating a probability of around 9% that this apparently profitable contract actually makes a loss.

This profit test reveals what we are really doing with the deterministic test, which is, approximately at least, projecting the median result. Notice how close the median value of NPV is to the deterministic value.

14.5 Stochastic pricing

Recall from Chapter 6 that the equivalence principle premium is defined such that the expected value of the present value of the future loss at the issue of the policy is zero. In fact, the expectation is usually taken over the future lifetime uncertainty (given fixed values for the mortality rates), not the uncertainty in investment returns or non-diversifiable mortality risk. This is an example of an expected value premium principle, where premiums are set considering

Table 14.9 *Results from changing the structure of the policy in Example 14.1.*

	Change			
	Increase P (1)	Increase MC (2)	Increase UAP (3)	Decrease $GMMB$ (4)
E[NPV]	433.56	939.60	594.68	460.33
SD[NPV]	660.67	725.97	619.75	384.96
95% CI	(392.61, 474.51)	(894.60, 984.60)	(556.27, 633.09)	(436.47, 484.19)
5%-ile	−930.81	−617.22	−724.40	145.29
Median of NPV	562.87	1 065.66	721.74	500.00
95%-ile	929.66	1 625.44	1 051.78	831.51
N^-	86	78	80	46
N^*	897	882	894	939

only the expected value of future loss, not any other characteristics of the loss distribution.

The example studied in Section 14.4 above demonstrates that incorporating a guarantee may add significant risk to a contract and that this only becomes clear when modelled stochastically. The risk cannot be quantified deterministically. Using the mean of the stochastic output is generally not adequate as it fails to protect the insurer against significant non-diversifiable risk of loss.

For this reason it is not advisable to use the equivalence premium principle when there is significant non-diversifiable risk. Instead we can use stochastic simulation with different premium principles.

The quantile premium principle is similar to the portfolio percentile premium principle in Section 6.8. This principle is based on the requirement that the policy should generate a profit with a given probability. We can extend this principle to the pricing of equity-linked policies. For example, we might be willing to write a contract if, using a given risk discount rate, the lower fifth percentile point of the net present value is positive and the expected net present value is at least 65% of the acquisition costs.

The example studied throughout Section 14.4 meets neither of these requirements; the lower fifth percentile point is −$859.82 and the expected net present value, $380.91, is 58.6% of the acquisition costs, $650.

We cannot determine a premium analytically for this contract which would meet these requirements. However, we can investigate the effects of changing the structure of the policy. For the example studied in Section 14.4, Table 14.9 shows results in the same format as in Table 14.8 for four changes to the policy structure. These changes are as follows.

(1) Increasing the premium from $5000 to $5500, and hence increasing the GMMB to $55 000 and the acquisition costs to $700.

(2) Increasing the annual management charge from 0.75% to 1.25%.
(3) Increasing the expense deductions from the premiums from 5% to 6% in the first year and from 1% to 2% in subsequent years.
(4) Decreasing the GMMB from 100% to 90% of premiums paid.

In each of the four cases, the remaining features of the policy are as described in Example 14.1.

Increasing the premium, change (1), makes little difference in terms of our chosen profit criterion. The lower fifth percentile point is still negative – the increase in the GMMB means that even larger losses can occur – and the expected net profit is still less than 65% of the increased acquisition costs. The premium for an equity-linked contract is not like a premium for a traditional contract, since most of it is unavailable to the insurer. The role of the premium in a traditional policy – to compensate the insurer for the risk coverage offered – is taken in equity-linked insurance by the management charge on the policyholder's funds and any loading taken from the premium before it is invested.

Increasing the management charge, change (2), or the expense loadings, change (3), does increase the expected net present value to the required level but the probability of a loss is still greater than 5%.

The one change that meets both parts of our profit criterion is change (4), reducing the level of the maturity guarantee. This is a demonstration of the important principle that risk management begins with the design of the benefits.

An alternative, and in many ways more attractive, method of setting a premium for such a contract is to use modern financial mathematics to both price the contract and reduce the risk of making a loss. We return to this topic in Chapter 16.

14.6 Stochastic reserving

14.6.1 Reserving for policies with non-diversifiable risk

In Chapter 7 we defined a policy value as the EPV of the future loss from the policy (using a deterministic interest rate assumption). This, like the use of the equivalence principle to calculate a premium, is an example of the application of the expected value principle. When the risk is almost entirely diversifiable, the expected value principle works adequately. When the risk is non-diversifiable, which is usually the case for equity-linked insurance, the expected value principle is inadequate both for pricing, as discussed in Section 14.5, and for calculating appropriate reserves.

Consider the further discussion of Example 14.1 in Section 14.4. On the basis of the assumptions in that section, there is a 5% chance that the insurer will make a loss in excess of \$859.82, in present value terms calculated using the risk discount rate of 15% per year, on each policy issued. If the insurer has issued a large number of these policies, such losses could have a disastrous effect on its solvency, unless the insurer has anticipated the risk by reserving for it, by hedging it in the financial markets (which we explain in Chapter 16) or by reinsuring it (which means passing the risk on by taking out insurance with another insurer).

Calculating reserves for policies with significant non-diversifiable risk requires a methodology that takes account of more than just the expected value of the loss distribution. Such methodologies are called **risk measures**. A risk measure is a functional that is applied to a random loss to give a reserve value that reflects the riskiness of the loss.

There are two common risk measures used to calculate reserves for non-diversifiable risks: the quantile reserve and the conditional tail expectation reserve.

14.6.2 Quantile reserving

A quantile reserve (also known as **Value-at-Risk**, or VaR) is defined in terms of a parameter α, where $0 \leq \alpha \leq 1$. Suppose we have a random loss L. The quantile reserve with parameter α represents the amount which, with probability α, will not be exceeded by the loss.

If L has a continuous distribution function, F_L, the α-quantile reserve is Q_α, where

$$\Pr[L \leq Q_\alpha] = \alpha, \tag{14.3}$$

so that

$$Q_\alpha = F_L^{-1}(\alpha).$$

If F_L is not continuous, so that L has a discrete or a mixed distribution, Q_α needs to be defined more carefully. In the example below (which continues in the next section) we assume that F_L is continuous.

To see how to apply this in practice, consider again Example 14.1 as discussed in Section 14.4. Suppose that immediately after issuing the policy, and paying the acquisition costs of \$650, the insurer wishes to set up a 95% quantile reserve, denoted $_0V$. In other words, after paying the acquisition costs the insurer wishes to set aside an amount of money, $_0V$, so that, with probability 0.95, it will be able to pay its liabilities.

We need some notation. Let j denote the rate of interest per year assumed to be earned on reserves. In practice, j will be a conservative rate of interest, probably much lower than the risk discount rate. Let $_tp_{55}^{00}$ denote the probability that a policy is still in force at duration t. This is consistent with our notation from Chapter 8 since our underlying model for the policy contains three states: in force (which we denote by 0), lapsed and dead.

The reserve, $_0V$, is calculated by simulating N sets of future accumulation factors for the policyholder's fund, exactly as in Section 14.4, and for each of these we calculate $\text{Pr}_{t,i}$, the profit emerging at time t, $t = 1, 2, \ldots, 10$ for simulation i, per policy in force at duration $t - 1$. For simulation i we calculate the EPV of the future loss, say L_i, as

$$L_i = -\sum_{t=1}^{10} \frac{{}_{t-1}p_{55}^{00}\,\text{Pr}_{t,i}}{(1+j)^t}. \tag{14.4}$$

Note that in the definition of L_i we are considering *future* profits at times $t = 1, 2, \ldots, 10$, and we have not included $\text{Pr}_{0,i}$ in the definition.

Then $_0V$ is set equal to the upper 95th percentile point of the empirical distribution of L obtained from our simulations, provided that the upper 95th percentile is positive, so that the reserve is positive. If the upper 95th percentile point is negative, $_0V$ is set equal to zero.

Calculations by the authors, with $N = 1000$ and $j = 0.06$, gave a value for $_0V$ of \$1259.56. Hence, if, after paying the acquisition costs, the insurer sets aside a reserve of \$1259.56 for each policy issued, it will be able to meet its future liabilities with probability 0.95 **provided** all the assumptions underlying this calculation are realized. These assumptions relate to

- expenses,
- lapse rates,
- the survival model, and, in particular, the diversification of the mortality risk,
- the interest rate earned on the insurer's fund,
- the interest rate earned on the reserve,
- the interest rate model for the policyholder's fund,
- the accuracy of our estimate of the upper 95th percentile point of the loss distribution.

The reasoning underlying this calculation assumes that no adjustment to this reserve will be made during the course of the policy. In practice, the insurer will review its reserves at regular intervals, possibly annually, during the term of the policy and adjust the reserve if necessary. For example, if after one year the rate of return on the policyholder's fund has been low and future expenses are now expected to be higher than originally estimated, the insurer may need to increase the reserve. On the other hand, if the experience in the first year has been favourable, the insurer may be able to reduce the reserve. The new reserve would be calculated by simulating the present value of the future loss from time $t = 1$, using the information available at that time, and setting the reserve equal to the greater of zero and the upper 95th percentile of the simulated loss distribution.

In our example, the initial reserve, $_0V = \$1259.56$, is around 25% of the annual premium, \$5000. This amount is expected to earn interest at a rate, 6%, considerably less than the insurer's risk discount rate, 15%. Setting aside substantial reserves, which may not be needed when the policy matures, will have a serious effect on the profitability of the policy.

14.6.3 CTE reserving

The quantile reserve assesses the 'worst case' loss, where worst case is defined as the event with a $1 - \alpha$ probability. One problem with the quantile approach is that it does not take into consideration what the loss will be if that $1 - \alpha$ worst case event actually occurs. In other words, the loss distribution above the quantile does not affect the reserve calculation. The conditional tail expectation (or CTE) was developed to address some of the problems associated with the quantile risk measure. It was proposed more or less simultaneously by several research groups, so it has a number of names, including tail value at risk (or Tail-VaR), tail conditional expectation (or TCE) and expected shortfall.

As for the quantile reserve, the CTE is defined using some confidence level α, where $0 \leq \alpha \leq 1$, which is typically 90%, 95% or 99% for reserving.

In words, CTE_α is the expected loss given that the loss falls in the worst $1 - \alpha$ part of the loss distribution for L. The worst $1 - \alpha$ part of the loss distribution is the part above the α-quantile, Q_α. If Q_α falls in a continuous part of the loss distribution, that is, not in a probability mass, then we can define the CTE at confidence level α as

$$\mathrm{CTE}_\alpha = \mathrm{E}\,[L|L > Q_\alpha].\tag{14.5}$$

If L has a discrete or a mixed distribution, then more care needs to be taken with the definition. If Q_α falls in a probability mass, that is, if there is some $\epsilon > 0$ such that $Q_{\alpha+\epsilon} = Q_\alpha$, then, if we consider only losses strictly greater than Q_α, we are using less than the worst $1 - \alpha$ of the distribution; if we consider losses greater than or equal to Q_α, we may be using more than the worst $1 - \alpha$ of the distribution. We therefore adapt the formula of equation (14.5) as follows. Define $\beta' = \max\{\beta : Q_\alpha = Q_\beta\}$. Then

$$\mathrm{CTE}_\alpha = \frac{(\beta' - \alpha)Q_\alpha + (1 - \beta')\,E[L|L > Q_\alpha]}{1 - \alpha}.\tag{14.6}$$

It is worth noting that, given that the CTE_α is the mean loss given that the loss lies above the VaR at level α (at least when the VaR does not lie in a probability mass) then CTE_α is always greater than or equal to Q_α, and usually strictly greater. Hence, for a given value of α, the CTE_α reserve is generally considerably more conservative than the Q_α quantile reserve.

Suppose the insurer wishes to set a $\text{CTE}_{0.95}$ reserve, just after paying the acquisition costs, for the policy studied in Example 14.1 and throughout Sections 14.4, 14.5 and 14.6.2. We proceed by simulating a large number of times the present value of the future loss using formula (14.4), with the rate of interest j per year we expect to earn on reserves, exactly as in Section 14.6.2. From our calculations in Section 14.6.2 with $N = 1000$ and $j = 0.06$, the 50 worst losses, that is, the 50 highest values of L_i, ranged in value from \$1260.76 to \$7512.41, and the average of these 50 values is \$3603.11. Hence we set the $\text{CTE}_{0.95}$ reserve at the start of the first year equal to \$3603.11.

The same remarks that were made about quantile reserves apply equally to CTE reserves.

(1) The CTE reserve in our example has been estimated using simulations based only on information available at the start of the policy.

(2) In practice, the CTE reserve would be updated regularly, perhaps yearly, as more information becomes available, particularly about the rate of return earned on the policyholder's fund. If the returns are good in the early years of the contract, then it is possible that the probability that the guarantee will cost anything reduces, and part of the reserves can be released back to the insurer before the end of the term.

(3) Holding a large CTE reserve, which earns interest at a rate lower than the insurer's risk discount rate, and which may not be needed when the policy matures, will have an adverse effect on the profitability of the policy.

14.6.4 Comments on reserving

The examples in this chapter illustrate an important general point. Financial guarantees are risky and can be expensive. Several major life insurance companies have found their solvency at risk through issuing guarantees that were not adequately understood at the policy design stage, and were not adequately reserved for thereafter. The method of covering that risk by holding a large quantile or CTE reserve reduces the risk, but at great cost in terms of tying up amounts of capital that are huge in terms of the contract overall. This is a passive approach to managing the risk and is usually not the best way to manage solvency or profitability.

Using modern financial theory we can take an active approach to financial guarantees that for most equity-linked insurance policies offers less risk, and, since the active approach requires less capital, it generally improves profitability when the required risk discount rate is large enough to make carrying capital very expensive.

The active approach to risk mitigation and management comes from option pricing theory. We utilize the fact that the guarantees in equity-linked insurance are financial options embedded in insurance contracts. There is an extensive literature available on the active risk management of financial options. In Chapter 15 we review the science of option risk management, at an introductory level, and in Chapter 16 we apply the science to equity-linked insurance.

14.7 Notes and further reading

A practical feature of equity-linked contracts in the UK which complicates the analysis a little is **capital** and **accumulation units**. The premiums paid at the start of the contract, which are notionally invested in capital units, are subject to a significantly higher annual management charge than later premiums, which are invested in accumulation units. This contract design has been developed to defray the insurer's acquisition costs at an early stage.

Stochastic profit testing can also be used for traditional insurance. We would generally simulate values for the interest earned on assets, and we might also simulate expenses and withdrawal rates. Exercise 14.2 demonstrates this.

For shorter term insurance, the sensitivity of the profit to the investment assumptions may not be very great. The major risk for such insurance is mis-estimation of the underlying mortality rates. This is also non-diversifiable risk, as underestimating the mortality rates affects the whole portfolio. It is therefore useful with term insurance to treat the force of mortality as a stochastic input.

The CTE has become a very important risk measure in actuarial practice. It is intuitive, easy to understand and to apply with simulation output. As a mean, it is more robust with respect to sampling error than a quantile. The CTE is used for stochastic reserving and solvency testing for Canadian and US equity-linked life insurance.

Hardy (2003) discusses risk measures, quantile reserves and CTE reserves in the context of equity-linked life insurance. In particular, she gives full definitions of quantile and CTE reserves, and shows how to simulate the emerging costs and calculate profit measures when stochastic reserving is used.

14.8 Exercises

Exercise 14.1 An insurer sells a one-year variable annuity contract. The policyholder deposits $100, and the insurer deducts 3% for expenses and profit. The expenses incurred at the start of the year are 2.5% of the premium.

The remainder of the premium is invested in an investment fund. At the end of one year the policyholder receives the fund proceeds; if the proceeds are less than the initial $100 investment the insurer pays the difference.

Assume that a unit investment in the fund accumulates to R after 1 year, where $R \sim LN(0.09, 0.18^2)$.

Let F_1 denote the fund value at the year end. Let L_0 denote the present value of future outgo minus the margin offset income random variable, assuming a force of interest of 5% per year, i.e.

$$L_0 = \max(100 - 97\,R, 0)\,e^{-0.05} - (3 - 2.5).$$

(a) Calculate $\Pr[F_1 < 100]$.
(b) Calculate $E[F_1]$.
(c) Show that the fifth percentile of the distribution of R is 0.81377.
(d) Hence, or otherwise, calculate $Q_{0.95}(L_0)$.
(e) Let f be the probability density function of a lognormal random variable with parameters μ and σ^2. Use the result (which is derived in Appendix A)

$$\int_0^A x\,f(x)dx = e^{\mu + \sigma^2/2}\,\Phi\left(\frac{\log A - \mu - \sigma^2}{\sigma}\right),$$

where Φ is the standard normal distribution function, to calculate
  (i) $E[L_0]$, and
  (ii) $\text{CTE}_{0.95}(L_0)$.
(f) Now simulate the year end fund, using 100 projections. Compare the results of your simulations with the accurate values calculated in (a)–(e).

Exercise 14.2 A life insurer issues a special five-year endowment insurance policy to a life aged 50. The death benefit is \$10 000 and is payable at the end of the year of death, if death occurs during the five-year term. The maturity benefit on survival to age 55 is \$20 000. Level annual premiums are payable in advance.

Reserves are required at integer durations for each policy in force, are independent of the premium, and are as follows:

$$_0V = 0, \quad _1V = 3\,000, \quad _2V = 6\,500, \quad _3V = 10\,500, \quad _4V = 15\,000, \quad _5V = 0.$$

The company determines the premium by projecting the emerging cash flows according to the projection basis given below. The profit objective is that the EPV of future profit must be 1/3 of the gross annual premium, using a risk discount rate of 10% per year.

Projection basis

Initial expenses:	10% of the gross premium plus \$100
Renewal expenses:	6% of the second and subsequent gross premiums
Survival model:	Standard Ultimate Survival Model
Interest on all funds:	8% per year effective

(a) Calculate the annual premium.
(b) Generate 500 different scenarios for the cash flow projection, assuming a premium of $3740, and assuming interest earned follows a lognormal distribution, such that if I_t denotes the return in the tth year,

$$(1 + I_t) \sim LN(0.07, 0.13^2).$$

  (i) Estimate the probability that the policy will make a loss in the final year, and calculate a 95% confidence interval for this probability.
 (ii) Calculate the exact probability that the policy will make a loss in the final year, assuming mortality exactly follows the projection basis, so that the interest rate uncertainty is the only source of uncertainty. Compare this with the 95% confidence interval for the probability determined from your simulations.
(iii) Estimate the probability that the policy will achieve the profit objective, and calculate a 95% confidence interval for this probability.

Exercise 14.3 An insurer issues an annual premium unit-linked contract with a five-year term. The policyholder is aged 60 and pays an annual premium of $100. A management charge of 3% per year of the policyholder's fund is deducted annually in advance.

The death benefit is the greater of $500 and the amount of the fund, payable at the end of the year of death. The maturity benefit is the greater of $500 and the amount of the fund, paid on survival to the end of the five-year term.

Mortality rates assumed are: $q_{60} = 0.0020$, $q_{61} = 0.0028$, $q_{62} = 0.0032$, $q_{63} = 0.0037$ and $q_{64} = 0.0044$. There are no lapses.

(a) Assuming that interest of 8% per year is earned on the policyholder's fund, project the policyholder's fund values for the term of the contract and hence calculate the insurer's management charge income.
(b) Assume that the insurer's fund earns interest of 6% per year. Expenses of 2% of the policyholder's funds are incurred by the insurer at the start of each year. Calculate the profit signature for the contract assuming that no reserves are held.
(c) Explain why reserves may be established for the contract even though no negative cash flows appear after the first year in the profit test.
(d) Explain how you would estimate the 99% quantile reserve and the 99% CTE reserve for this contract.
(e) The contract is entering the final year. Immediately before the final premium payment the policyholder's fund is $485.

   Assume that the accumulation factor for the policyholder's fund each year is lognormally distributed with parameters $\mu = 0.09$ and $\sigma^2 = 0.18^2$.

Table 14.10 *Largest 100 values from 1000 simulations.*

6.255	6.321	6.399	6.460	6.473	6.556	6.578	6.597	6.761	6.840
6.865	6.918	6.949	7.042	7.106	7.152	7.337	7.379	7.413	7.430
7.585	7.614	7.717	7.723	7.847	7.983	8.051	8.279	8.370	8.382
8.416	8.508	8.583	8.739	8.895	8.920	8.981	9.183	9.335	9.455
9.477	9.555	9.651	9.675	9.872	9.972	10.010	10.199	10.216	10.268
10.284	10.814	10.998	11.170	11.287	11.314	11.392	11.546	11.558	11.647
11.840	11.867	11.966	12.586	12.662	12.792	13.397	13.822	13.844	14.303
14.322	14.327	14.404	14.415	14.625	14.733	14.925	15.076	15.091	15.343
15.490	15.544	15.617	15.856	16.369	16.458	17.125	17.164	17.222	17.248
17.357	17.774	18.998	19.200	21.944	21.957	22.309	24.226	24.709	26.140

Let L_4 represent the present value of future loss random variable at time 4, using an effective rate of interest of 6% per year.

(i) Calculate the probability of a payment under either of the guarantees.
(ii) Calculate $Q_{99\%}(L_4)$ assuming that insurer's funds earn 6% per year as before.

Exercise 14.4 An insurer used 1000 simulations to estimate the present value of future loss distribution for a segregated fund contract. Table 14.10 shows the largest 100 simulated values of L_0.

(a) Estimate $\Pr[L_0 > 10]$.
(b) Calculate an approximate 99% confidence interval for $\Pr[L_0 > 10]$.
(c) Estimate $Q_{0.99}(L_0)$.
(d) Estimate $CTE_{0.99}(L_0)$.

Exercise 14.5 A life insurance company issues a five-year unit-linked endowment policy to a life aged 50 under which level premiums of $750 are payable yearly in advance throughout the term of the policy or until earlier death.

In the first policy year, 25% of the premium is allocated to the policyholder's fund, followed by 102.5% in the second and subsequent years. The units are subject to a bid-offer spread of 5% and an annual management charge of 1% of the bid value of units is deducted at the end of each policy year. Management charges are deducted from the unit fund before death, surrender and maturity benefits are paid.

If the policyholder dies during the term of the policy, the death benefit of $3000 or the bid value of the units, whichever is higher, is payable at the end of the policy year of death. The policyholder may surrender the policy only at the end of each policy year. On surrender, the bid value of the units is payable at the end of the policy year of exit. On maturity, 110% of the bid value of the units is payable. The company uses the following assumptions in carrying out profit tests of this contract:

Rate of growth on assets in the policyholder's fund:	6.5% per year
Rate of interest on insurer's fund cash flows:	5.5% per year
Survival model:	Standard Ultimate Survival Model
Initial expenses:	$150
Renewal expenses:	$65 per year on the second and subsequent premium dates
Initial commission:	10% of first premium
Renewal commission:	2.5% of the second and subsequent years' premiums
Risk discount rate:	8.5% per year
Surrenders:	10% of policies in force at the end of each of the first three years.

(a) Calculate the profit margin for the policy on the assumption that the company does not hold reserves.

(b) (i) Explain briefly why it would be appropriate to establish reserves for this policy.

(ii) Calculate the effect on the profit margin of a reserve requirement of $400 at the start of the second, third and fourth years, and $375 at the start of the fifth year. There is no initial reserve requirement.

(c) An actuary has suggested the profit test should be stochastic, and has generated a set of random accumulation factors for the policyholder's funds. The first stochastic scenario of annual accumulation factors for each of the five years is generated under the assumption that the accumulation factors are lognormally distributed with parameters $\mu = 0.07$ and $\sigma^2 = 0.2^2$. Using the random standard normal deviates given below, conduct the profit test using your simulated accumulation factors, and hence calculate the profit margin, allowing for the reserves as in (b):

$$-0.71873, \quad -1.09365, \quad 0.08851, \quad 0.67706, \quad 1.10300.$$

Answers to selected exercises

14.1 (a) 0.37040
   (b) $107.87
   (d) $19.54
   (e) (i) $3.46
      (ii) $24.83
14.2 (a) $3739.59
   (b) Based on one set of 500 projections

           (i) 0.528, (0.484, 0.572)
          (ii) 0.519
         (iii) 0.488, (0.444, 0.532)
14.3 (a) (3.00, 6.14, 9.44, 12.88, 16.50)'
      (b) (0.27, 1.37, 2.77, 4.33, 5.76)'
      (e)   (i) 0.114
           (ii) $80.50
14.4 (a) 0.054
      (b) (0.036, 0.072)
      (c) $17.30
      (d) $21.46
14.5 (a) 1.56%
      (b) (ii) Reduces to 0.51%
      (c) −1.43%

15

Option pricing

15.1 Summary

In this chapter we review the basic financial mathematics behind option pricing. First, we discuss the no-arbitrage assumption, which is the foundation for all modern financial mathematics. We present the binomial model of option pricing, and illustrate the principles of the risk neutral and real world measures, and of pricing by replication.

We discuss the Black–Scholes–Merton option pricing formula, and, in particular, demonstrate how it may be used both for pricing and risk management.

15.2 Introduction

In Section 14.4 we discussed the problem of non-diversifiable risk in connection with equity-linked insurance policies. A methodology for managing this risk, stochastic pricing and reserving, was set out in Sections 14.5 and 14.6. However, as we explained there, this methodology is not entirely satisfactory since it often requires the insurer to set aside large amounts of capital as reserves to provide some protection against adverse experience. At the end of the contract, the capital may not be needed, but having to maintain large reserves is expensive for the insurer. If experience *is* adverse, there is no assurance that reserves will be sufficient.

Since the non-diversifiable risks in equity-linked contracts and some pension plans typically arise from financial guarantees on maturity or death, and since these guarantees are very similar to the guarantees in exchange traded financial options, we can use the Black–Scholes–Merton theory of option pricing to price and actively manage these risks. When a financial guarantee is a part of the benefits under an insurance policy, we call it an **embedded option**.

There are several reasons why it is very helpful for an insurance company to understand option pricing and financial engineering techniques. The insurer may buy options from a third party such as a bank or a reinsurer to offset the embedded options in their liabilities; a good knowledge of derivative pricing will be useful in the negotiations. Also, by understanding financial engineering methods an insurer can make better risk management decisions. In particular, when an option is embedded in an insurance policy, the insurer must make an informed decision whether to hedge the products in-house or subcontract the task to a third party.

There are many different types of financial guarantees in insurance contracts. This chapter contains sufficient introductory material on financial engineering to enable us to study in Chapter 16 the valuation and hedging of options embedded within insurance policies that can be viewed as relatively straightforward European put or call options.

15.3 The 'no-arbitrage' assumption

The 'no-arbitrage' assumption is the foundation of modern valuation methods in financial mathematics. The assumption is more colloquially known as the 'no free lunch' assumption, and states quite simply that you cannot get something for nothing.

An **arbitrage** opportunity exists if an investor can construct a portfolio that costs zero at inception and generates positive profits with a non-zero probability in the future, with no possibility of incurring a loss at any future time.

If we assume that there are no arbitrage opportunities in a market, then it follows that **any two securities or combinations of securities that give exactly the same payments must have the same price**. For example, consider two assets priced at $A and $B which produce the same future cash flows. If $A \neq B$, then an investor could buy the asset with the lower price and sell the more expensive one. The cash flows purchased at the lower price would exactly match the cash flows sold, so the investor would make a risk free profit of the difference between A and B.

The no-arbitrage assumption is very simple and very powerful. It enables us to find the price of complex financial instruments by 'replicating' the payoffs. Replication is a crucial part of the framework. This means that if we can construct a portfolio of assets with exactly the same payments as the investment in which we are interested, then the price of the investment must be the same as the price of the '**replicating portfolio**'.

For example, suppose an insurer incurs a liability, under which it must deliver the price of one share in Superior Life Insurance Company in one year's time, and the insurer wishes to value this liability. The traditional way to value this might be by constructing a probability distribution for the future value – suppose the current value is $400 and the insurer assumes the share price in one year's time will follow a lognormal distribution, with parameters $\mu = 6.07$ and $\sigma^2 = 0.16^2$. Then the mean value of the share price in one year's time is $e^{\mu + \sigma^2/2} = \$438.25$.

The next step is to discount to current values, at, say 6% per year (perhaps using the long-term bond yield), to give a present value of \$413.45.

So we have a value for the liability, with an implicit risk management plan of putting the \$413.45 in a bond, which in one year will pay \$438.25, which may or may not be sufficient to buy the share to deliver to the creditor. It will almost surely be either too much or not enough.

A better approach is to replicate the payoff, and value the cost of replication. In this simple case, that means holding a replicating portfolio of one share in Superior Life Insurance Company. The cost of this now is \$400. In one year, the portfolio is exactly sufficient to pay the creditor, whatever the outcome. So, since it costs \$400 to replicate the payoff, that is how much the liability is worth. It cannot be worth \$413.45 – that would allow the company to sell the liability for \$413.45, and replicate it for \$400, giving a risk free profit (or arbitrage) of \$13.45.

Replication does not require a model; we have eliminated the uncertainty in the payoff, and we implicitly have a risk management strategy – buy the share and hold it until the liability falls due.

Although this is an extreme example, the same argument will be applied in this chapter and the next, even when finding the replicating portfolio is a more complicated process.

In practice, in most securities markets, arbitrage opportunities arise from time to time and are very quickly eliminated as investors spot them and trade on them. Since they exist only for very short periods, assuming that they do not exist at all is sufficiently close to reality for most purposes.

15.4 Options

Options are very important financial contracts, with billions of dollars of trades in options daily around the world. In this section we introduce the language of options and explain how some option contracts operate. European options are perhaps the most straightforward type of options, and the most basic forms of these are a **European call option** and a **European put option**.

The holder of a European call option on a stock has the right (but not the obligation) to buy an agreed quantity of that stock at a fixed price, known as the **strike price**, at a fixed date, known as the **expiry** or **maturity** date of the contract.

Let S_t denote the price of the stock at time t. The holder of a European call option on this stock with strike price K and maturity date T would exercise the option only if $S_T > K$, in which case the option is worth $S_T - K$ to the option holder at the maturity date. The option would not be exercised at the maturity date in the case when $S_T < K$, since the stock could then be bought for a lower price in the market at that time. Thus, the payoff at time T under the option is

$$(S_T - K)^+ = \max(S_T - K, 0).$$

The holder of a European put option on a stock has the right (but not the obligation) to sell an agreed quantity of that stock at a fixed strike price, at the maturity date of the contract. The holder of a European put option would exercise the option only if $S_T < K$, since the holder of the option could sell the stock at time T for K then buy the stock at the lower price of S_T in the market and hence make a profit of $K - S_T$. In this case the option is worth $K - S_T$ to the option holder at the maturity date. The option would not be exercised at the maturity date in the case when $S_T > K$, since the option holder would then be selling stock at a lower price than could be obtained by selling it in the market. Thus, the payoff at time T under a European put option is

$$(K - S_T)^+ = \max(K - S_T, 0).$$

In making all of the above statements, we are assuming that people act rationally when they exercise options. We can think of options as providing guarantees on prices. For example, a call option guarantees that the holder of the option pays no more than the strike price to buy the underlying stock at the maturity date.

American options are defined similarly, except that the option holder has the right to exercise the option at any time before the maturity date. The names 'European' and 'American' are historical conventions, and do not signify where these options are sold – both European and American options are sold worldwide. In this book we are concerned only with European options which are significantly more straightforward to price than American options. Many of the options embedded in life insurance contracts are European-style.

If at any time t prior to the maturity date the stock price S_t is such that the option would mature with a non-zero value if the stock price did not change, we say that the option is 'in-the-money'; so, a call option is in-the-money when $S_t > K$, and a put option is in-the-money when $K > S_t$. When $K = S_t$, or even when K is close to S_t, we say the option is 'at-the-money'. Otherwise it is 'out-of-the-money'.

15.5 The binomial option pricing model

15.5.1 Assumptions

Throughout Section 15.5 we use the no-arbitrage principle together with a simple discrete time model of a stock price process called the binomial model to price options.

Although the binomial model is simple, and not very realistic, it is useful because the techniques we describe below carry through to more complicated models for a stock price process.

We make the following assumptions.

- There is a frictionless financial market in which there exists a risk free asset (such as a zero-coupon bond) and a risky asset, which we assume here to be a stock. The market is free of arbitrage.
- The financial market is modelled in discrete time. Trades occur only at specified time points. Changes in asset prices and the exercise date for an option can occur only at these same dates.
- In each unit of time the stock price either moves up by a predetermined amount or moves down by a predetermined amount. This means there are just two possible states one period later if we start at a given time and price.
- Investors can buy and sell assets without cost. These trades do not impact the prices.
- Investors can *short sell* assets, so that they can hold a negative amount of an asset. This is achieved by selling an asset they do not own, so the investor 'owes' the asset to the lender. We say that an investor is *long* in an asset if the investor has a positive holding of the asset, and is *short* in the asset if the investor has a negative holding.

We start by considering the pricing of an option over a single time period. We then extend this to two time periods.

15.5.2 Pricing over a single time period

To illustrate ideas numerically, consider a stock whose current price is $100 and whose price at time $t = 1$ will be either $105 or $90. We assume that the continuously compounded risk free rate of interest is $r = 0.03$ per unit of time. Note that we must have

$$90 < 100e^r < 105$$

since otherwise arbitrage is possible. To see this, suppose $100e^r > 105$. In this case an investor could receive $100 by short selling one unit of stock at time $t = 0$ and invest this for one unit of time at the risk free rate of interest. At time $t = 1$ the investor would then have $\$100e^r$, part of which would be used to buy one unit of stock in the market to wipe out the negative holding, leaving a profit of either $\$(100e^r - 105)$ or $\$(100e^r - 90)$, both of which are positive. Similarly, if $100e^r < 90$ (which means a negative risk free rate) selling the risk free asset short and buying the stock will generate an arbitrage.

Now, consider a put option on this stock which matures at time $t = 1$ with a strike price of $K = \$100$. The holder of this option will exercise the option at time $t = 1$ only if the stock price goes down, since by exercising the option the option holder will get $\$100$ for a stock worth $\$90$. As we are assuming that there are no trading costs in buying and selling stocks, the option holder could use the sale price of $\$100$ to buy stock at $\$90$ at time $t = 1$ and make a profit of $\$10$.

The seller of the put option will have no liability at time $t = 1$ if the stock price rises, since the option holder will not sell a stock for $\$100$ when it is worth $\$105$ in the market. However, if the stock price falls, the seller of the put option has a liability of $\$10$.

We use the concept of replication to price this put option. This means that we look for a portfolio of assets at time $t = 0$ that will exactly match the payoff under the put option at time $t = 1$. Since our market comprises only the risk free asset and the stock, any portfolio at time $t = 0$ must consist of some amount, say $\$a$, in the risk free asset and some amount, $\$100b$, in the stock (so that b units of stock are purchased). Then at time $t = 1$, the portfolio is worth

$$ae^r + 105b$$

if the stock price goes up, and is worth

$$ae^r + 90b$$

if the stock price goes down. If this portfolio replicates the payoff under the put option, then the portfolio must be worth 0 at time $t = 1$ if the stock price goes up, and $\$10$ at time $t = 1$ if the stock price goes down. To achieve this we require that

$$ae^r + 105b = 0,$$
$$ae^r + 90b = 10.$$

Solving these equations we obtain $b = -2/3$ and $a = 67.9312$. We have shown that a portfolio consisting of $\$67.9312$ of the risk free asset and a short holding of $-2/3$ units of stock exactly matches the payoff under the put option at time $t = 1$, regardless of the stock price at time $t = 1$. This portfolio is called the **replicating**, or **hedge**, portfolio.

The no-arbitrage principle tells us that if the put option and the replicating portfolio have the same value at time $t = 1$, they must have the same value at time $t = 0$, and this then must be the price of the option, which is

$$a + 100b = \$1.26.$$

We can generalize the above arguments to the case when the stock price at time $t = 0$ is S_0, the stock price at time $t = 1$ is $u S_0$ if the stock price goes up and $d S_0$ if the stock price goes down, and the strike price for the put option is K. We note here that under the no-arbitrage assumption, we must have $d S_0 < S_0 e^r < u S_0$. Similarly, we must also have $d S_0 < K < u S_0$ for a contract to be feasible.

The hedge portfolio consists of $\$a$ in the risk free asset and $\$b S_0$ in stock. Since the payoff at time $t = 1$ from this portfolio replicates the option payoff, we must have

$$ae^r + bu S_0 = 0,$$
$$ae^r + bd S_0 = K - d S_0$$

giving

$$a = \frac{ue^{-r}(K - d S_0)}{u - d} \quad \text{and} \quad b = \frac{d S_0 - K}{S_0(u - d)}.$$

The option price at time 0 is $a + b S_0$, the value of the hedge portfolio, which we can write as

$$e^{-r}q (K - d S_0) \tag{15.1}$$

where

$$q = \frac{u - e^r}{u - d}. \tag{15.2}$$

Note that, from our earlier assumptions,

$$0 < q < 1.$$

An interesting feature of expression (15.1) for the price of the put option is that, if we were to treat q as the probability of a downward movement in the stock price and $1 - q$ as the probability of an upward movement, then formula (15.1) could be thought of as the discounted value of the expected payoff under the option. If the stock price moves down, the payoff is $K - d S_0$, with discounted value $e^{-r}(K - d S_0)$. If q were the probability of a downward movement in the stock price, then $qe^{-r}(K - d S_0)$ would be the EPV of the option payoff. Recall that these parameters, q and $1 - q$, are not the true 'up' and 'down' probabilities. In fact, nowhere in our determination of the price of the put option have we needed to know the probabilities of the stock price moving up or down. The parameter q comes from the binomial framework, but it is not the 'real' probability of a downward movement; it is just convenient to treat it as such, as it allows us to use the conventions and notation of probability. It is important to remember though that we have not used a probabilistic argument here, we have used instead a replication argument.

It turns out that the price of an option in the binomial framework can *always* be expressed as the discounted value of the option's 'expected' payoff using the artificial probabilities of upward and downward price movements, $1 - q$ and q, respectively. The following example demonstrates this for a general payoff.

Example 15.1 Consider an option over one time period which has a payoff C_u if the stock price at the end of the period is $u S_0$, and has a payoff C_d if the stock price at the end of the period is $d S_0$. Show that the option price is

$$e^{-r} \left(C_u (1 - q) + C_d q \right)$$

where q is given by formula (15.2).

Solution 15.1 We construct the replicating portfolio which consists of $\$a$ in the risk-free asset and $\$b S_0$ in stock so that

$$ae^r + bu S_0 = C_u,$$

$$ae^r + bd S_0 = C_d,$$

giving

$$b = \frac{C_u - C_d}{(u - d) S_0}$$

and

$$a = e^{-r} \left(C_u - u \frac{C_u - C_d}{u - d} \right)$$

$$= e^{-r} \left(\frac{u}{u - d} C_d - \frac{d}{u - d} C_u \right).$$

Hence the option price is

$$a + b S_0 = e^{-r} \left(\frac{u}{u - d} C_d - \frac{d}{u - d} C_u \right) + \frac{C_u - C_d}{u - d}$$

$$= C_u \left(\frac{1 - de^{-r}}{u - d} \right) + C_d \left(\frac{ue^{-r} - 1}{u - d} \right)$$

$$= e^{-r} \left(C_u \left(\frac{e^r - d}{u - d} \right) + C_d \left(\frac{u - e^r}{u - d} \right) \right)$$

$$= e^{-r} \left(C_u (1 - q) + C_d q \right). \qquad \square$$

In the above example, if we treat q as the probability that the stock price at time $t = 1$ is $d S_0$, then the expected payoff under the option at time $t = 1$ is

$$C_u(1 - q) + C_d \, q,$$

and so the option price is the discounted expected payoff. Note that q has not been defined as the probability that the stock price is equal to $d S_0$ at time $t = 1$, and, in general, will not be equal to this probability. We emphasize that the probability q is an artificial construct, but a very useful one.

Under the binomial framework that we use here, there is some real probability that the stock price moves down or up. We have not needed to identify it here. The true distribution is referred to by different names, the **physical measure**, the **real world measure**, the **subjective measure** or **nature's measure**. In the language of probability theory, it is called the **P-measure**. The artificial distribution that arises in our pricing of options is called the **risk neutral measure**, and in the language of probability theory is called the **Q-measure**. The term 'measure' can be thought of as interchangeable with 'probability distribution'. In what follows, we use E^Q to denote expectation with respect to the Q-measure. The Q-measure is called the risk neutral measure since, under the Q-measure, the expected return on every asset in the market (risky or not) is equal to the risk-free rate of interest, as if investors in this hypothetical world were neutral as to the risk in the assets. We know that in the real world investors require extra expected return for extra risk. We demonstrate risk neutrality in the following example.

Example 15.2 Show that if S_1 denotes the stock price at time $t = 1$, then under our model $\mathrm{E}^Q[e^{-r} S_1] = S_0$.

Solution 15.2 Under the Q-measure,

$$S_1 = \begin{cases} u S_0 & \text{with probability } 1 - q, \\ d S_0 & \text{with probability } q. \end{cases}$$

Then

$$\mathrm{E}^Q[e^{-r} S_1] = e^{-r} \left((1 - q) u S_0 + q d S_0 \right)$$
$$= e^{-r} \left(\left(\frac{e^r - d}{u - d} \right) u S_0 + \left(\frac{u - e^r}{u - d} \right) d S_0 \right)$$
$$= S_0.$$

□

The result in Example 15.2 shows that under the risk neutral measure, the stock price at time $t = 0$ is the EPV under the Q-measure of the stock price at time $t = 1$. We also see that the expected accumulation factor of the stock price over a unit time interval is e^r, the same as the risk free accumulation factor. Under the P-measure we expect the accumulation factor to exceed e^r on average, as a reward for the extra risk.

15.5.3 Pricing over two time periods

In the previous section we considered a single period of time and priced the option by finding the replicating portfolio at time $t = 0$. We now extend this idea to pricing an option over two time periods. This involves the idea of **dynamic hedging**, which we introduce by extending the numerical example of the previous section.

Let us now assume that in each of our two time periods, the stock price can either increase by 5% of its value at the start of the time period, or decrease by 10% of its value. We assume that the stock price movement in the second time period is independent of the movement in the first time period.

As before, we consider a put option with strike price $100, but this time the exercise date is at the end of the second time period. As illustrated in Figure 15.1, the stock price at time $t = 2$ is $110.25 if the stock price moves up in each time period, $94.50 if the stock price moves up once and down once, and $81.00 if the stock price moves down in each time period. This means that the put option will be exercised if at time $t = 2$ the stock price is $94.50 or $81.00.

In order to price the option, we use the same replication argument as in the previous section, but now we must work backwards from time $t = 2$. Suppose first that at time $t = 1$ the stock price is $105. We can establish a portfolio at time $t = 1$ that replicates the payoff under the option at time $t = 2$. Suppose this portfolio contains $\$a_u$ of the risk free asset and b_u units of stock, so that the replicating portfolio is worth $\$(a_u + 105b_u)$. Then at time $t = 2$, the value of the portfolio should be 0 if the stock price moves up in the second time period since the option will not be exercised, and the value should be $5.50 if the stock price moves down in the second time period since the option will be exercised in this case. The equations that determine a_u and b_u are

$$a_u e^r + 110.25b_u = 0,$$
$$a_u e^r + 94.5b_u = 5.50,$$

giving $b_u = -0.3492$ and $a_u = 37.3622$. This shows that the replicating portfolio at time $t = 1$, if the stock price at that time is 105, has value $P_u = \$0.70$.

Similarly, if at time $t = 1$ the stock price is $90, we can find the replicating portfolio whose value at time $t = 1$ is $\$(a_d + 90b_d)$, where the equations that determine a_d and b_d are

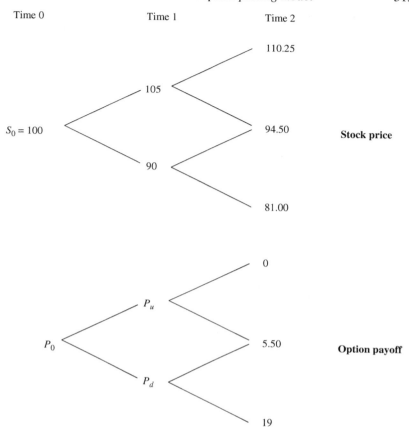

Figure 15.1 Two-period binomial model.

$$a_d e^r + 94.5 b_d = 5.50,$$
$$a_d e^r + 81 b_d = 19,$$

since if the stock price rises to \$94.50, the payoff under the put option is \$5.50, and if the stock price falls to \$81, the payoff under the option is \$19. Solving these two equations we find that $b_d = -1$ and $a_d = 97.0446$. Thus, the replicating portfolio at time $t = 1$, if the stock price at that time is \$90, has value $P_d = \$7.04$.

We now move back to time $t = 0$. At this time point we want to find a portfolio that replicates the possible amounts required at time $t = 1$, namely \$0.70 if the stock price goes up to \$105 in the first time period, and \$7.04 if it goes down to \$90. This portfolio consists of \$$a$ in the risk free asset and b units of stock, so that the equations that determine a and b are

$$ae^r + 105b = 0.70,$$
$$ae^r + 90b = 7.04,$$

giving $b = -0.4233$ and $a = 43.8049$. The replicating portfolio has value P_0 at time $t = 0$, where

$$P_0 = a + 100b = \$1.48$$

and, by the no-arbitrage principle, this is the price of the option.

There are two important points to note about the above analysis. The first is a point we noted about option pricing over a single period – we do not need to know the true probabilities of the stock price moving up or down in any time period in order to find the option price. The second point is that the replicating portfolio is **self-financing**. The initial portfolio of \$43.80 in the risk free asset and a short holding of -0.4233 units of stock is exactly sufficient to provide the replicating portfolio at time $t = 1$ regardless of the stock price movement in the first time period. The replicating portfolio at time $t = 1$ then matches exactly the option payoff at time $t = 2$. Thus, once the initial portfolio has been established, no further injection of funds is required to match the option payoff at time $t = 2$.

What we have done in this process is an example of dynamic hedging. At time $t = 1$ we established what portfolios were required to replicate the possible payoffs at time $t = 2$, then at time $t = 0$ we worked out what portfolio was required to provide the portfolio values required at time $t = 1$. This process works for any number of steps, but if there is a large number of time periods it is a time-consuming process to work backwards through time to construct all the hedging strategies. However, if all we want to work out is the option price, the result we saw for a single time period, that the option price is the discounted value of the expected payoff at the expiry date under the Q-measure, also holds when we are dealing with multiple time periods.

In our analysis we have $u = 1.05$, $d = 0.9$ and $r = 0.03$. From formula (15.2), the probability of a downward movement in the stock price under the Q-measure is

$$q = \frac{1.05 - e^{0.03}}{1.05 - 0.9} = 0.1303,$$

and so the expected payoff at the expiry date is

$$19q^2 + 5.5 \times 2(1 - q)q = \$1.5962.$$

This gives the option price as

$$1.5962e^{-0.06} = \$1.48.$$

15.5.4 Summary of the binomial model option pricing technique

- We use the principle of replication; we construct a portfolio that replicates the option's payoff at maturity. The value of the option is the cost of purchasing the replicating (or hedge) portfolio.

- We use dynamic hedging – replication requires us to rebalance the portfolio at each time step according to the movement in the stock price in the previous time step.

- We do not use any argument involving the true probabilities of upward or downward movements in the stock price. However, there are important links between the real world (P-measure) model and the risk neutral (Q-measure) model. We started by assuming a two-point distribution for the stock price after a single time period in the real world. From this we showed that in the risk neutral world the stock price after a single time period also has a two-point distribution with the same possible values, uS_0 and dS_0, but the probabilities of moving up or down are not linked to those of the real world model.

- Our valuation can be written in the form of an EPV, using artificial probabilities that are determined by the possible changes in the stock price. This artificial distribution is called the risk neutral measure because the mean accumulation of a unit of stock under this distribution is exactly the accumulated value of a unit investment in the risk free asset. Thus, an investor would be indifferent between investment in the risk free asset and investment in the stock, under the risk neutral measure.

The binomial model option pricing framework is clearly not very realistic, but we can make it more flexible by increasing the number of steps in a unit of time, as discussed below. If we do this, the binomial model converges to the Black–Scholes–Merton model, which is described in the following section.

15.6 The Black–Scholes–Merton model

15.6.1 The model

Under the Black–Scholes–Merton model, we make the following assumptions.

- The market consists of zero-coupon bonds (the risk free asset) and stocks (the risky asset).

- The stock does not pay any dividends, or, equivalently, any dividends are immediately reinvested in the stock. This assumption simplifies the presentation but can easily be relaxed if necessary.
- Portfolios can be rebalanced (that is, stocks and bonds can be bought and sold) in continuous time. In the two-period binomial example we showed how the replicating portfolio was rebalanced (costlessly) after the first time unit. In the continuous time model the stock price moves are continuous, so the rebalancing is (at least in principle) continuous.
- There are no transaction costs associated with trading the stocks and bonds.
- The continuously compounded risk free rate of interest, r per unit time, is constant and the yield curve is flat.
- Stocks and bonds can be bought or sold in any quantities, positive or negative; we are not restricted to integer units of stock, for example. Selling or buying can be transacted at any time without restrictions on the amounts available, and the amount bought or sold does not affect the price.
- In the real world, the stock price, denoted S_t at time t, follows a continuous time lognormal process with some parameters μ and σ^2. This process, also called geometric Brownian motion, is the continuous time version of the lognormal model for one year accumulation factors introduced in Chapter 14.

Clearly these are not realistic assumptions. Continuous rebalancing is not feasible, and although major financial institutions like insurance companies can buy and sell assets cheaply, transactions costs will arise. We also know that yield curves are rarely flat. Despite all this, the Black–Scholes–Merton model works remarkably well, both for determining the price of options and for determining risk management strategies. The Black–Scholes–Merton theory is extremely powerful and has revolutionized risk management for non-diversifiable financial risks.

A lognormal stochastic process with parameters μ and σ has the following characteristics.

- Over any fixed time interval, say $(t, t + \tau)$ where $\tau > 0$, the stock price accumulation factor, $S_{t+\tau}/S_t$, has a lognormal distribution with parameters $\mu\tau$ and $\sigma^2\tau$, so that

$$\frac{S_{t+\tau}}{S_t} \sim_P LN(\mu\tau, \sigma^2\tau), \tag{15.3}$$

which implies that

$$\log\frac{S_{t+\tau}}{S_t} \sim_P N(\mu\tau, \sigma^2\tau).$$

We have added the subscript P as a reminder that these statements refer to the real world, or P-measure, model. Our choice of parameters μ and σ^2 here uses the standard statistical parameterizations. Some authors, particularly in financial mathematics, use the same σ, but use a different location parameter μ', say, such that $\mu' = \mu + \sigma^2/2$. It is important to check what μ represents when it is used as a parameter of a lognormal distribution.

We call $\log(S_{t+\tau}/S_t)$ the log-return on the stock the time period $(t, t+\tau)$. The parameter μ is the mean log-return over a unit of time, and σ is the standard deviation of the log-return over a unit of time. We call σ the volatility, and it is common for the unit of time to be one year so that these parameters are expressed as annual rates. Some information on the lognormal distribution is given in Appendix A.

- Stock price accumulation factors over non-overlapping time intervals are independent of each other. (This is the same as in the binomial model, where the stock price movement in any time interval is independent of the movement in any other time interval.) Thus, if S_u/S_t and S_w/S_v represent the accumulation factors over the time intervals (t, u) and (v, w) where $t < u \leq v < w$, then these accumulation factors are independent of each other.

The lognormal process assumed in the Black–Scholes–Merton model can be derived as the continuous time limit, as the number of steps increases, of the binomial model of the previous sections. The proof requires mathematics beyond the scope of this book, but we give some references in Section 15.7 for interested readers.

15.6.2 The Black–Scholes–Merton option pricing formula

Under the Black–Scholes–Merton model assumptions we have the following important results.

- There is a unique risk neutral distribution, or Q-measure, for the stock price process, under which the stock price process, $\{S_t\}_{t \geq 0}$, is a lognormal process with parameters $r - \sigma^2/2$ and σ^2.
- For any European option on the stock, with payoff function $h(S_T)$ at maturity date T, the value of the option at time $t \leq T$ denoted $v(t)$, can be found as the expected present value of the payoff under the risk neutral distribution (Q-measure)

$$\boxed{v(t) = E_t^Q \left[e^{-r(T-t)} h(S_T) \right],} \tag{15.4}$$

where E_t^Q denotes expectation using the risk neutral (or Q) measure, using all the information available up to time t. This means, in particular, that valuation at time t assumes knowledge of the stock price at time t.

Important points to note about this result are:

- Over any fixed time interval, say $(t, t + \tau)$ where $\tau > 0$, the stock price accumulation factor, $S_{t+\tau}/S_t$, has a lognormal distribution in the risk neutral world with parameters $(r - \sigma^2/2)\tau$ and $\sigma^2\tau$, so that

$$\frac{S_{t+\tau}}{S_t} \sim_Q LN((r - \sigma^2/2)\tau, \sigma^2\tau), \qquad (15.5)$$

  which implies that

$$\log \frac{S_{t+\tau}}{S_t} \sim_Q N((r - \sigma^2/2)\tau, \sigma^2\tau).$$

  We have added the subscript Q as a reminder that these statements refer to the risk neutral, or Q-measure model.

- The expected Q-measure present value (at rate r per year) of the future stock price, $S_{t+\tau}$, is the stock price now, S_t. This follows from the previous point since

$$E_t^Q[S_{t+\tau}/S_t] = \exp\left\{(r - \sigma^2/2)\tau + \tau\sigma^2/2\right\} = e^{r\tau}.$$

  This is the result within the Black–Scholes–Merton framework which corresponds to the result in Example 15.2 for the binomial model.

- The Q-measure is related to the corresponding P-measure in two ways.
- Under the Q-measure, the stock price follows a lognormal process, as it does in the real world.
- The volatility parameter, σ, is the same for both measures.
- The first of these connections should not surprise us since the real world model, the lognormal process, can be regarded as the limit of a binomial process, for which, as we have seen in Section 15.5, the corresponding risk neutral model is also binomial; the limit as the number of steps increases in the (risk neutral) binomial model is then also a lognormal process. The second connection does not have any simple explanation. Note that the parameter μ, the mean log-return per unit time for the P-measure, does not appear in the specification of the Q-measure. This should not surprise us: the real world probabilities of upward and downward movements in the binomial model did not appear in the corresponding Q-measure probability, q.
- Formula (15.4) is the continuous-time extension of the same result for the single period binomial model (Example 15.1) and the two-period binomial model (Section 15.5.3). In both the binomial and Black–Scholes–Merton

models, we take the expectation under the Q-measure of the payoff discounted at the risk free force of interest.

- A mathematical derivation of the Q-measure and of formula (15.4) is beyond the scope of this book. Interested readers should consult the references in Section 15.7.

Now consider the particular case of a European call option with strike price K. The option price at time t is $c(t)$, where

$$c(t) = E_t^Q \left[e^{-r(T-t)} (S_T - K)^+ \right].$$
(15.6)

To evaluate this price, first we write it as

$$c(t) = e^{-r(T-t)} S_t E_t^Q \left[(S_T/S_t - K/S_t)^+ \right].$$

Now note that, under the Q-measure,

$$S_T/S_t \sim LN((r - \sigma^2/2)(T - t), \sigma^2(T - t)).$$

So, letting f and F denote the lognormal probability density function and distribution function, respectively, of S_T/S_t, under the Q-measure, we have

$$c(t) = e^{-r(T-t)} S_t \int_{K/S_t}^{\infty} (x - K/S_t) f(x) \, dx$$

$$= e^{-r(T-t)} S_t \left(\int_{K/S_t}^{\infty} x f(x) \, dx - \frac{K}{S_t} (1 - F(K/S_t)) \right).$$
(15.7)

In Appendix A we derive the formula

$$\int_0^a x f(x) dx = \exp\{\mu + \sigma^2/2\} \, \Phi \left(\frac{\log a - \mu - \sigma^2}{\sigma} \right)$$

for a lognormal random variable with parameters μ and σ^2, where Φ denotes the standard normal distribution function. Since the mean of this random variable is

$$\int_0^\infty x f(x) dx = \exp\{\mu + \sigma^2/2\},$$

we have

$$\int_a^\infty x f(x) dx = \exp\{\mu + \sigma^2/2\} \left(1 - \Phi \left(\frac{\log a - \mu - \sigma^2}{\sigma} \right) \right)$$

$$= \exp\{\mu + \sigma^2/2\} \, \Phi \left(\frac{-\log a + \mu + \sigma^2}{\sigma} \right).$$

Applying this to formula (15.7) for $c(t)$ gives

$$c(t) = e^{-r(T-t)} S_t \, e^{r(T-t)} \, \Phi \left(\frac{-\log(K/S_t) + (r - \sigma^2/2)(T-t) + \sigma^2(T-t)}{\sigma\sqrt{T-t}} \right)$$

$$- e^{-r(T-t)} K \left(1 - \Phi \left(\frac{\log(K/S_t) - (r - \sigma^2/2)(T-t)}{\sigma\sqrt{T-t}} \right) \right)$$

$$= S_t \, \Phi \left(\frac{\log(S_t/K) + (r + \sigma^2/2)(T-t)}{\sigma\sqrt{T-t}} \right)$$

$$- e^{-r(T-t)} K \, \Phi \left(\frac{\log(S_t/K) + (r - \sigma^2/2)(T-t)}{\sigma\sqrt{T-t}} \right).$$

This is the Black–Scholes formula for the price of a call option, and is usually written as

$$\boxed{c(t) = S_t \Phi\left(d_1(t)\right) - K e^{-r(T-t)} \Phi\left(d_2(t)\right),} \qquad (15.8)$$

where

$$\boxed{d_1(t) = \frac{\log(S_t/K) + (r + \sigma^2/2)(T-t)}{\sigma\sqrt{T-t}} \quad \text{and} \quad d_2(t) = d_1(t) - \sigma\sqrt{T-t}.}$$

$$(15.9)$$

Since the stock price S_t appears (explicitly) only in the first term of formula (15.8) and r appears only in the second term, this formula *suggests* that the replicating portfolio at time t for the call option comprises

- $\Phi\left(d_1(t)\right)$ units of the stock, with total value at time t

$$S_t \, \Phi\left(d_1(t)\right),$$

  plus
- a **short** holding of $\Phi\left(d_2(t)\right)$ units of zero-coupon bonds with face value K, maturing at time T, with a value at time t of

$$-K e^{-r(T-t)} \Phi\left(d_2(t)\right).$$

Indeed, this **is** the self-financing replicating portfolio required at time t. We note though that the derivation is not quite as simple as it looks, as $\Phi\left(d_1(t)\right)$ and $\Phi\left(d_2(t)\right)$ both depend on the current stock price and time.

If the strike price is very small relative to the stock price we see that $\Phi\left(d_1(t)\right)$ tends to one and $\Phi\left(d_2(t)\right)$ tends to zero. The replicating portfolio tends to a long position in the stock and zero in the bond.

For a European put option, with strike price K, the option price at time t is $p(t)$, where

$$p(t) = \mathrm{E}_t^Q \left[e^{-r(T-t)} (K - S_T)^+ \right],$$

which, after working through the integration, becomes the Black–Scholes put option formula

$$p(t) = Ke^{-r(T-t)}\Phi(-d_2(t)) - S_t\Phi(-d_1(t)),$$ (15.10)

where $d_1(t)$ and $d_2(t)$ are defined as before.

The replicating portfolio for the put option comprises

- $\Phi(-d_2(t))$ units of zero-coupon bonds with face value K, maturing at time T, with value at time t

$$Ke^{-r(T-t)}\Phi(-d_2(t)),$$

plus

- a **short** holding of $\Phi(-d_1(t))$ units of the stock, with total value at time t

$$-S_t\Phi(-d_1(t)).$$

For the European call and put options, we can show that

$$S_t\frac{d}{dS_t}c(t) = S_t\Phi(d_1(t)) \quad \text{and} \quad S_t\frac{d}{dS_t}p(t) = -S_t\Phi(-d_1(t)).$$

You are asked to prove the first of these formulae as Exercise 15.1. These two formulae show that, for these options, the replicating portfolio has a portion $S_t\,dv(t)/dS_t$ invested in the stock, and hence a portion $v(t) - S_t\,dv(t)/dS_t$ invested in the bond, where $v(t)$ is the value of the option at time t.

This result holds generally for any option valued under the Black–Scholes–Merton framework. The quantity $dv(t)/dS_t$ is known as the **delta** of the option at time t. The portfolio is the **delta hedge**.

Example 15.3 Let $p(t)$ and $c(t)$ be the prices at time t for a European put and call, respectively, both with strike price K and remaining term to maturity $T - t$.

(a) Use formulae (15.8) and (15.10) to show that, using the Black–Scholes–Merton framework,

$$c(t) + Ke^{-r(T-t)} = p(t) + S_t.$$ (15.11)

(b) Use a no-arbitrage argument to show that formula (15.11) holds *whatever the model for stock price movements between times t and T*.

Solution 15.3 (a) From formulae (15.8) and (15.10), and using the fact that $\Phi(z) = 1 - \Phi(-z)$ for any z, we have

$$
\begin{aligned}
c(t) &= S_t \, \Phi(d_1(t)) - K e^{-r(T-t)} \, \Phi(d_2(t)) \\
&= S_t (1 - \Phi(-d_1(t))) - K e^{-r(T-t)} (1 - \Phi(-d_2(t))) \\
&= S_t - K e^{-r(T-t)} + p(t)
\end{aligned}
$$

which proves (15.11).

(b) To prove this result without specifying a model for stock price movements, consider two portfolios held at time t. The first comprises the call option plus a zero-coupon bond with face value K maturing at time T; the second comprises the put option plus one unit of the stock. These two portfolios have current values

$$
c(t) + K \, e^{-r(T-t)} \quad \text{and} \quad p(t) + S_t,
$$

respectively. At time T the first portfolio will be worth K if $S_T \leq K$, since the call option will then be worthless and the bond will pay K, and it will be worth S_T if $S_T > K$, since then the call option would be exercised and the proceeds from the bond would be used to purchase one unit of stock. Now consider the second portfolio at time T. This will be worth K if $S_T \leq K$, since the put option would be exercised and the stock would be sold at the exercise price, K, and it will be worth S_T if $S_T > K$, since the put option will then be worthless and the stock will be worth S_T. Since the two portfolios have the same payoff at time T under all circumstances, they must have the same value at all other times, in particular at time t. This gives equation (15.11).

This important result is known as **put–call parity**. $\qquad\square$

Example 15.4 An insurer offers a two-year contract with a guarantee under which the policyholder invests a premium of \$1000. The insurer keeps 3% of the premium to cover all expenses, then invests the remainder in a mutual fund. (A mutual fund is an investment that comprises a diverse portfolio of stocks and bonds. In the UK similar products are called unit trusts or investment trusts.) The mutual fund investment value is assumed to follow a lognormal process, with parameters $\mu = 0.085$ and $\sigma^2 = 0.2^2$ per year. The mutual fund does not pay out dividends; any dividends received from the underlying portfolio are reinvested. The risk free rate of interest is 5% per year compounded continuously. The insurer guarantees that the payout at the maturity date will not be less than the original \$1000 investment.

(a) Show that the 3% expense loading is not sufficient to fund the guarantee.

(b) Calculate the real world probability that the guarantee applies at the maturity date.

(c) Calculate the expense loading that would be exactly sufficient to fund the guarantee.

Solution 15.4 (a) The policyholder has, through the insurer, invested $970 in the mutual fund. This will accumulate over the two years of the contract to some random amount, S_2, say. If $S_2 < \$1000$ then the insurer's guarantee bites, and the insurer must make up the difference. In other words, the policyholder has the right at the maturity date to receive a price of $1000 from the insurer for the mutual fund stocks. This is a two-year put option, with payoff at time $T = 2$ of

$$(1\,000 - S_2)^+.$$

If the mutual fund stocks are worth more than $1000, then the policyholder just takes the proceeds and the insurer has no further liability.

In terms of option pricing, we have a strike price $K = \$1000$, a mutual fund stock price at time $t = 0$ of $S_0 = \$970$, and a risk free rate of interest of 5%. So the price of the put option at inception is

$$p(0) = Ke^{-rT}\Phi(-d_2(0)) - S_0\Phi(-d_1(0))$$

where

$$d_1(0) = \frac{\log(S_0/K) + (r + \sigma^2/2)T}{\sigma\sqrt{T}} = 0.3873 \Rightarrow \Phi(-d_1(0)) = 0.3493,$$

$$d_2(0) = d_1(0) - \sigma\sqrt{T} = 0.1044 \Rightarrow \Phi(-d_2(0)) = 0.4584,$$

giving

$$p(0) = 414.786 - 338.794 = \$75.99.$$

So the 3% expense charge, $30, is insufficient to fund the guarantee cost. The cost of the guarantee is actually 7.599% of the initial investment. However, if we actually set 7.599% as the expense loading, the price of the guarantee would be even greater, as we would invest less money in the mutual fund at inception whilst keeping the same strike price.

(b) The real world distribution of S_2/S_0 is $LN(2\mu,\,2\sigma^2)$. This means that

$$\log(S_2/S_0) \sim N(2\mu,\,2\sigma^2),$$

which implies that

$$\log S_2 \sim N(\log S_0 + 2\mu,\,2\sigma^2).$$

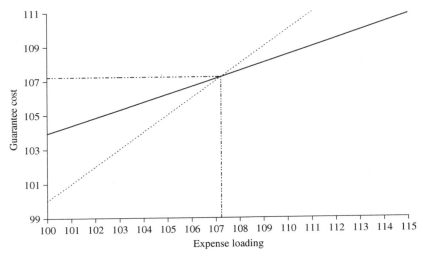

Figure 15.2 Expense loading plotted against guarantee cost for Example 15.4.

Then

$$S_2 \sim LN(\log S_0 + 2\mu, \ 2\sigma^2),$$

which implies that

$$\Pr[S_2 < 1000] = \Phi\left(\frac{\log 1000 - \log S_0 - 2\mu}{\sqrt{2}\sigma}\right) = 0.311.$$

That is, the probability of a payoff under the guarantee is 0.311.

(c) Increasing the expense loading increases the cost of the guarantee, and there is no analytic method to find the expense loading, E, which pays for the guarantee with an initial investment of $(1000 - E)$. Figure 15.2 shows a plot of the expense loading against the cost of the guarantee (shown as a solid line). Where this line crosses the line $x = y$ (shown as a dotted line) we have a solution. From this plot we see that the solution is around 10.72% (i.e. the expense loading is around $107.2). Alternatively, Excel Solver gives the solution that an expense loading of 10.723% exactly funds the resulting guarantee.   □

Finding the price is only the first step in the process. The beauty of the Black–Scholes–Merton approach is that it gives not only the price but also directs us in what we can do with the price to manage the guarantee risk. In part (a) of Example 15.4, the guarantee payoff can be replicated by investing $414.79 in two-year zero-coupon bonds and short selling $338.79 of the mutual fund stock, with a net cost of $75.99. If we continuously rebalance such that at any time t the bond position has value $1\,000e^{-r(2-t)}\Phi(-d_2(t))$ and the short stock position has value $-S_t\Phi(-d_1(t))$, then this will exactly pay off the guarantee liability at the maturity date.

In practice, continuous rebalancing is impossible. Rebalancing at discrete intervals is possible but introduces some additional cash flows, and in the next example we explore this issue.

Example 15.5 Let us continue Example 15.4 above, where an insurer has issued a guarantee which matures in two years. The initial investment (net of expenses) is $970 and the maturity guarantee is $1000.

In Table 15.1 you are given the monthly values for the underlying mutual fund stock price for the two-year period, assuming a starting price of $970.

Assume, as in Example 15.4, that the continuously compounded risk free rate, r, is 5% per year. Determine the cash flows arising assuming that the insurer

(a) invests the entire option cost in the risk free asset,
(b) invests the entire option cost in the mutual fund asset,
(c) allocates the initial option cost to bonds and the mutual fund at the outset, according to the Black–Scholes–Merton model, that is $414.79 to zero-coupon bonds and $-$338.79 to the mutual fund shares, and then
  (i) never subsequently rebalances the portfolio
  (ii) rebalances only once, at the end of the first year
  (iii) rebalances at the end of each month.

Solution 15.5 We note that the guarantee ends in-the-money, with a liability under the put option of $(1000 - 766.66) = $233.34 at the maturity date.

(a) If the option cost is invested in the risk free asset, it accumulates to $75.99e^{2r} = $83.98. This leaves a shortfall at maturity of

$$\$(233.34 - 83.98) = \$149.36.$$

(b) If the option cost is invested in the mutual fund asset, it will accumulate to $75.99 \times (766.66/970) = $60.06 leaving a shortfall at maturity of $173.28.

(c) (i) If the insurer invests in the initial hedge portfolio, but never rebalances,
   - the bond part of the hedge accumulates at the risk free rate for the whole two-year period to an end value of $458.41;
   - the stock part of the hedge accumulates in proportion to the mutual fund share price, with final value
     $-338.79 \times (766.66/970) = -\$267.77$; and

Table 15.1 *Table of mutual
fund stock prices for
Example 15.5.*

Time, t (months)	S_t $
0	970.00
1	950.07
2	959.99
3	940.93
4	921.06
5	967.25
6	1045.15
7	1007.59
8	945.97
9	913.77
10	932.99
11	951.11
12	906.11
13	824.86
14	831.08
15	797.99
16	785.86
17	724.36
18	707.43
19	713.87
20	715.14
21	690.74
22	675.80
23	699.71
24	766.66

- the hedge portfolio value at maturity is then worth $458.41 - 267.77$ = \$190.64, which means that the insurer is liable for an additional cash flow at maturity of \$42.70, as the hedge portfolio value is less than the option guarantee cost. In this case the total cost of the guarantee is the initial hedge cost of \$75.99 plus a final balancing payment of \$42.70.

(ii) If the insurer rebalances only once, at the end of the first year, the value of the initial hedge portfolio at that time is

Bonds: $414.79e^r = \$436.05.$

Mutual fund: $-338.79\,(906.11/970) = -\$316.48.$

So the value of the hedge portfolio immediately before rebalancing is $119.57.

The rebalanced hedge is found from formula (15.10) with $t = 1$ year as

$$p(1) = Ke^{-r(2-1)}\Phi(-d_2(1)) - S_1\Phi(-d_1(1))$$
$$= 603.26 - 504.56$$
$$= 98.70.$$

This means there is a cash flow of $(119.57 - 98.70) = \$20.87$ back to the insurer, as the value of the initial hedge more than pays for the rebalanced hedge.

We now track the new hedge through to the maturity date.

Bonds: $603.26e^r = \$634.19.$

Mutual fund: $-504.56 \times (766.66/906.11)$
$$= -\$426.91.$$

Total hedge portfolio value: $207.28.

We need $233.34 to pay the guarantee liability, so the insurer is liable for an additional cash flow of $26.06.

So, in tabular form we have the following cash flows, where a positive value is a cash flow out and negative value is a cash flow back to the insurer.

Time (years)	Value of hedge brought forward	Cost of new hedge	Final guarantee cost	Net cash flow $
0	0	75.99	–	75.99
1	119.57	98.70	–	−20.87
2	207.28	–	233.34	26.06

(iii) Here, we repeat the exercise in (b) but we now accumulate and rebalance each month. The results are given in Table 15.2. The second, third and fourth columns show the bond part, the mutual fund part and the total cost of the hedge required at the start of each month. In the final month, the total reflects the cost of the guarantee payoff. The fifth column shows the value of the hedge brought forward, and the difference between the new hedge cost and the hedge brought forward is the cash flow required at that time.

Table 15.2 *Cash flow calculations for Example 15.5.*

Time	New hedge portfolio			Old hedge	Net cash flow
(months)	Bonds	Mutual Fund	Total	brought forward	$
0	414.79	−338.79	75.99	0.00	75.99
1	446.09	−363.17	82.92	84.68	−1.76
2	437.17	−358.37	78.80	80.99	−2.19
3	469.69	−383.83	85.86	87.74	−1.88
4	505.72	−411.67	94.05	95.93	−1.88
5	441.15	−366.59	74.56	75.52	−0.96
6	332.07	−283.53	48.54	46.88	1.66
7	388.22	−329.43	58.79	60.11	−1.33
8	492.86	−411.51	81.35	80.56	0.79
9	557.18	−461.25	95.94	97.41	−1.48
10	531.28	−445.30	85.97	88.56	−2.59
11	505.60	−428.81	76.78	79.54	−2.76
12	603.26	−504.56	98.70	99.18	−0.48
13	769.54	−617.58	151.96	146.46	5.50
14	776.58	−628.41	148.17	150.52	−2.35
15	847.22	−671.33	175.88	176.43	−0.55
16	882.11	−693.88	188.22	189.62	−1.40
17	948.97	−700.74	248.24	246.21	2.03
18	965.94	−697.59	268.35	268.58	−0.23
19	973.54	−707.77	265.76	266.03	−0.27
20	981.09	−712.67	268.42	268.57	−0.15
21	987.44	−690.59	296.84	296.83	0.01
22	991.70	−675.80	315.90	315.90	0.00
23	995.84	−699.71	296.13	296.13	0.00
24			233.34	233.34	0.00

We see how the rebalancing frequency affects the cash flows; with a monthly rebalancing frequency, all the cash flows required are relatively small, after the initial hedge cost. The fact that these cash flows are non-zero indicates that the original hedge is not self-financing with monthly rebalancing. However, the amounts are small, demonstrating that if the insurer follows this rebalancing strategy, there is little additional cost involved after the initial hedge cost, even though the final guarantee payout is substantial. The total of the additional cash flows after the initial hedge cost is −$12.26 in this case. It can be shown that the expected value of the additional cash flows using the P-measure is zero.   □

This example demonstrates that in this case, where the option matures in-the-money, the dynamic hedge is remarkably efficient at converging to the payoff with only small adjustments required each month. If we were to rebalance more frequently still, the rebalancing cash flows would converge to zero. In practice, many hedge portfolios are rebalanced daily or even several times a day.

Of course, this guarantee might well end up out-of-the-money, in which case the hedge portfolio would be worth nothing at the maturity date, and the insurer would lose the cost of establishing the hedge portfolio in the first place. The hedge is a form of insurance, and, as with all insurance, there is a cost even when there is no claim.

15.7 Notes and further reading

This chapter offers a very brief introduction to an important and exciting area. For a much more comprehensive introduction, see for example Hull (2011) or McDonald (2009). For a description of the history of options and option pricing, see Boyle and Boyle (2001).

The proof that the binomial model converges to the lognormal model as the time unit, h, tends to zero is somewhat technical. The original proof is given in Cox *et al.* (1979); another method is in Hsia (1983).

We assumed from Section 15.6.1 onwards that the stock did not pay any dividends. Adapting the model and results for dividends is explained in Hull (2011) and McDonald (2009).

15.8 Exercises

Exercise 15.1 Let $c(t)$ denote the price of a call option on a non-dividend paying stock, using equation (15.6). Show that

$$\frac{dc(t)}{dS_t} = \Phi(d_1(t)).$$

Hint: remember that $d_1(t)$ is a function of S_t.

Exercise 15.2 (a) Show that, under the binomial model of Section 15.5,

$$E^Q[S_n] = S_0 \, e^{rn}.$$

(b) Show that, under the Black–Scholes–Merton model,

$$E^Q[S_n] = S_0 \, e^{rn}.$$

Exercise 15.3 A binomial model for a non-dividend paying security with price S_t at time t is as follows:

$$S_0 = 100,$$

$$S_{t+1} = \begin{cases} 1.1S_t & \text{if the stock price rises,} \\ 0.9S_t & \text{if the stock price falls.} \end{cases}$$

Zero-coupon bonds are available for all integer durations, with a risk free rate of interest of 6% per time period compounded continuously.

A derivative security pays $20 at a specified maturity date if the stock price has increased from the start value, and pays $0 if the stock price is at or below the start value at maturity.

(a) Find the price and the replicating portfolio for the option assuming it is issued at $t = 0$ and matures at $t = 1$.

(b) Now assume the option is issued at $t = 0$ and matures at $t = 2$. Find the price and the replicating portfolio at $t = 0$ and at $t = 1$.

Exercise 15.4 Consider a two-period binomial model for a non-dividend paying security with price S_t at time t, where $S_0 = 1.0$,

$$S_{t+1} = \begin{cases} 1.2 S_t & \text{if the stock price rises,} \\ 0.95 S_t & \text{if the stock price falls.} \end{cases}$$

At time $t = 2$ option A pays $3 if the stock price has risen twice, $2 if it has risen once and fallen once and $1 if it has fallen twice.

At time $t = 2$ option B pays $1 if the stock price has risen twice, $2 if it has risen once and fallen once and $3 if it has fallen twice.

The risk free force of interest is 4.879% per period. You are given that the true probability that the price rises each period is 0.5.

(a) Calculate the EPV (under the P-measure) of option A and show that it is the same as the EPV of option B.

(b) Calculate the price of option A and show that it is different from the price of option B.

(c) Comment on why the prices differ even though the expected payout is the same.

Exercise 15.5 A stock is currently priced at $400. The price of a six-month European call option with a strike price of $420 is $41. The risk free rate of interest is 7% per year, compounded continuously.

Assume the Black–Scholes–Merton pricing formula applies.

(a) Calculate the current price of a six-month European put option with the same exercise price. State the assumptions you make in the calculation.

(b) Estimate the implied volatility of the stock.

(c) Calculate the delta of the option.

(d) Find the hedging portfolio of stock and risk-free zero-coupon bonds that a writer of 10 000 units of the call option should hold.

Exercise 15.6 A binomial model for a non-dividend paying security with price S_t at time t is as follows: the price at time $t + 1$ is either $1.25\,S_t$ or $0.8\,S_t$. The risk free rate of interest is 10% per time unit effective.

(a) Calculate the risk neutral probability measure for this model.

 The value of S_0 is 100. A derivative security with price D_t at time t pays the following returns at time 2:

$$D_2 = \begin{cases} 1 & \text{if } S_2 = 156.25, \\ 2 & \text{if } S_2 = 100, \\ 0 & \text{if } S_2 = 64. \end{cases}$$

(b) Determine D_1 when $S_1 = 125$ and when $S_1 = 80$ and hence calculate the value of D_0.

(c) Derive the corresponding hedging strategy, i.e. the combination of the underlying security and the risk free asset required to hedge an investment in the derivative security.

(d) Comment on your answer to (c) in the light of your answer to (b).

Exercise 15.7 A non-dividend paying stock has a current price of $8.00. In any unit of time $(t, t+1)$ the price of the stock either increases by 25% or decreases by 20%. $1 held in cash between times t and $t + 1$ receives interest to become $1.04 at time $t + 1$. The stock price after t time units is denoted by S_t.

(a) Calculate the risk neutral probability measure for the model.

(b) Calculate the price (at time $t = 0$) of a derivative contract written on the stock with expiry date $t = 2$ which pays $10.00 if and only if S_2 is not $8.00 (and otherwise pays 0).

Answers to selected exercises

15.3 (a) $15.24
    (b) $11.61
15.4 (a) $1.81
    (b) Option A: $1.633,   Option B: $1.995
15.5 (a) $46.55
    (b) 38.6%
    (c) 53.42%
    (d) Long 5342.5 shares of stock and short 17 270 bonds, where each bond is worth $100 at time zero
15.6 (a) $\frac{2}{3}$ (increase), $\frac{1}{3}$ (decrease)
    (b) $D_0 = 1.1019$
15.7 (a) 0.5333 (increase),   0.4667 (decrease)
    (b) $4.6433

16

Embedded options

16.1 Summary

In this chapter we describe financial options embedded in insurance contracts, focusing in particular on the most straightforward options which appear as guaranteed minimum death and maturity options in equity-linked life insurance policies effected by a single premium. We investigate pricing, valuation and risk management for these guarantees, performing our analysis under the Black–Scholes–Merton framework described in Chapter 15.

16.2 Introduction

The guaranteed minimum payments under an equity-linked contract usually represent a relatively minor aspect of the total payout under the policy, because the guarantees are designed to apply only in the most extreme situation of very poor returns on the policyholders' funds. Nevertheless, these guarantees are not negligible – failure to manage the risk from apparently innocuous guarantees has led to significant financial problems for some insurers.

In Chapter 14 we described profit testing of equity-linked contracts with guarantees, where the only risk management involved was a passive strategy of holding capital reserves in case the experience is adverse – or, even worse, holding no capital in the expectation that the guarantee will never apply. However, in the case when the equity-linked contract incorporates financial guarantees that are essentially the same as the financial options discussed in Chapter 15, we can use the more sophisticated techniques of Chapter 15 to price and manage the risks associated with the guarantees. These techniques are preferable to those of Chapter 14 because they mitigate the risk that the insurer will have insufficient funds to pay for the guarantees when necessary.

To show how the guarantees can be viewed as options, recall Example 14.2, where we described an equity-linked insurance contract, paid for with a single premium P, with a guaranteed minimum maturity benefit (GMMB) and a guaranteed minimum death benefit (GMDB). Consider, for now, the GMMB only. After some expense deductions a single premium is invested in an equity fund, or perhaps a mixed equity/bond fund. The fund value is variable, moving up and down with the underlying assets. At maturity, the insurer promises to pay the greater of the actual fund value and the original premium amount.

Let F_t denote the value of the policyholder's fund at time t. Suppose that, as in Example 14.2, the benefit for policies still in force at the maturity date, say at time n (the term is $n = 5$ years in Example 14.2, but more typically it would be 10 years or longer) is $\max(P, F_n)$. As the policyholder's fund contributes the amount F_n, the insurer's additional liability is $h(n)$, where

$$h(n) = \max(P - F_n, 0).$$

The total benefit paid for such a contract in force at the maturity date is

$$F_n + h(n).$$

Recognizing that the fund value process $\{F_t\}_{t \geq 0}$ may be considered analogous to a stock price process, and that P is a fixed, known amount, the guarantee payoff $h(n)$ is identical to the payoff under an n-year European put option with strike price P, as described in Section 15.4. So, while in Chapter 14 we modelled this contract with cash flow projection, we have a more appropriate technique for pricing and valuation from Chapter 15, using the Black–Scholes–Merton framework.

Similarly, the guaranteed minimum death benefit in an equity-linked insurance contract offers a payoff that can be viewed as an option – often a put option similar to that under a GMMB.

There are a few differences between the options embedded in equity-linked contracts and standard options traded in markets. Two important differences are as follows.

(1) The options embedded in equity-linked contracts have random terms to maturity. If the policyholder surrenders the contract, or dies, before the expiry date, the GMMB will never be paid. The GMDB expires on the death of the policyholder, if that occurs during the term of the contract.

(2) The options embedded in equity-linked contracts depend on the value of the policyholder's fund at death or maturity. The underlying risky asset

process represents the value of a traded stock or stock index. The fund value at time t, F_t, is related to the risky asset price, S_t, since we assume the policyholder's fund is invested in a fund with returns following traded stocks, but with the important difference that regular management charges are being deducted from the policyholder's fund.

These differences mean that we must adapt the Black–Scholes–Merton theory of Chapter 15 in order to apply it to equity-linked insurance.

Throughout this chapter we consider equity-linked contracts paid for by a single premium, P, which, after the deduction of any initial charges, is invested in the policyholder's fund. This fund, before allowing for the deduction of any management charges, earns returns following the underlying stock price process, $\{S_t\}_{t\geq0}$. We make all the assumptions in Section 15.6.1 relating to the Black–Scholes–Merton framework. In particular, we assume the stock price process is a lognormal process with volatility σ per year, and also that there is a risk free rate of interest, r per year, continuously compounded.

16.3 Guaranteed minimum maturity benefit

16.3.1 Pricing

From Chapter 15 we know that the price of an option is the EPV of the payoff under the risk neutral probability distribution, discounting at the risk free rate. Suppose a GMMB under a single premium contract guarantees that the payout at maturity, n years after the issue date of the contract, will be at least equal to the single premium, P. Then the option payoff, as mentioned above, is $h(n) = \max(P - F_n, 0)$, because the remainder of the benefit, F_n, will be paid from the policyholder's fund. This payoff is conditional on the policy remaining in force until the maturity date. In order to price the guarantee we assume that the survival of a policyholder for n years, taking account of mortality and lapses, is independent of the fund value process and is a diversifiable risk. For simplicity here we ignore surrenders and assume all policyholders are aged x at the commencement of their policies, and are all subject to the same survival model. Under these assumptions, the probability that a policy will still be in force at the end of the term is $_n p_x$.

Consider the situation at the issue of the contract. If the policyholder does not survive n years, the GMMB does not apply at time n, and so the insurer does not need to fund the guarantee in this case. If the policyholder does survive n years, the GMMB does apply at time n, and we know that the amount required at the issue of the contract to fund this guarantee is

$$\mathrm{E}_0^Q\left[e^{-rn}\left(P - F_n\right)^+\right].$$

Thus, the expected amount (with respect to survival) required by the insurer at the time of issue *per contract issued* is $\pi(0)$, where

$$\pi(0) = {}_n p_x \, \mathrm{E}_0^Q \left[e^{-rn} \, (P - F_n)^+ \right].$$

Note that we are adopting a mixture of two different methodologies here. The non-diversifiable risk from the stock price process, which channels through to F_n, is priced using the methodology of Chapter 15, whereas the mortality risk, which we have assumed to be diversifiable, is priced using the expected value principle.

Suppose that the total initial expenses are a proportion e of the single premium, and the management charge is a proportion m of the policyholder's fund, deducted at the start of each year after the first. Then

$$F_n = P(1 - e)(1 - m)^{n-1} \frac{S_n}{S_0}.$$

Since we are interested in the relative increase in S_t, we can assume $S_0 = 1$ without any loss of generality. (We interpret the stock price process $\{S_t\}_{t \geq 0}$ as an index for the fund assets; as an index, we can arbitrarily set S_0 to any convenient value.) Then

$$F_n = P(1 - e)(1 - m)^{n-1} S_n.$$

The value of the guarantee can be written

$$\pi(0) = {}_n p_x \, \mathrm{E}_0^Q \left[e^{-rn} (P - P(1 - e)(1 - m)^{n-1} S_n)^+ \right]$$

$$= P \, {}_n p_x \, \mathrm{E}_0^Q \left[e^{-rn} \left(1 - (1 - e)(1 - m)^{n-1} S_n \right)^+ \right]$$

$$= P \, {}_n p_x \, \xi \, \mathrm{E}_0^Q \left[e^{-rn} \left(\xi^{-1} - S_n \right)^+ \right]$$

where the expense factor $\xi = (1 - e)(1 - m)^{n-1}$ is a constant. We can now apply formula (15.10) for the price of a put option, setting the strike price for the option, $K = \xi^{-1}$. Then the price at the issue date of a GMMB, guaranteeing a return of at least the premium P, is

$$\pi(0) = P \, {}_n p_x \, \xi \, \left(\xi^{-1} e^{-rn} \Phi(-d_2(0)) - \Phi(-d_1(0)) \right) \qquad (16.1)$$

$$= P \, {}_n p_x \, \left(e^{-rn} \Phi(-d_2(0)) - \xi \Phi(-d_1(0)) \right)$$

where

$$d_1(0) = \frac{\log(\xi) + (r + \sigma^2/2)n}{\sigma \sqrt{n}}$$

and

$$d_2(0) = d_1(0) - \sigma \sqrt{n}.$$

The return of premium guarantee is a common design for a GMMB, but many other designs are sold. Any guarantee can be viewed as a financial option. Suppose $h(n)$ denotes a general payoff function for a GMMB when it matures at time n years. In equation (16.1) the payoff function is $h(n) = (P - F_n)^+$. In other cases when the only random quantity in the payoff function is the fund value at maturity, we can use exactly the same approach as in equation (16.1), so that the value of the GMMB is always

$$\pi(0) = {}_n p_x \, \mathrm{E}_0^Q \left[e^{-rn} h(n) \right].$$

Example 16.1 Consider a 10-year equity-linked contract issued to a life aged 60, with a single premium of $P = \$10\,000$. After a deduction of 3% for initial expenses, the premium is invested in an equity fund. An annual management charge of 0.5% is deducted from the fund at the start of every year except the first.

The contract carries a guarantee that the maturity benefit will not be less than the single premium, P.

The risk free rate of interest is 5% per year, continuously compounded, and stock price volatility is 25% per year.

(a) Calculate the cost at issue of the GMMB as a percentage of the single premium, assuming there are no lapses and that the survival model is Makeham's law with $A = 0.0001$, $B = 0.00035$ and $c = 1.075$.
(b) Now suppose that, allowing for mortality and lapses, the insurer expects only 55% of policyholders to maintain their policies to maturity. Calculate the revised cost at issue of the GMMB as a percentage of the single premium, commenting on any additional assumptions required.

Solution 16.1 (a) With $n = 10$ we have

$$\xi = (1 - 0.03)(1 - 0.005)^9 = 0.927213,$$

$$d_1(0) = \frac{\log \xi + (r + \sigma^2/2)n}{\sigma \sqrt{n}} = 0.932148,$$

$$d_2(0) = d_1(0) - \sigma \sqrt{n} = 0.141579,$$

$$\mathrm{E}_0^Q \left[e^{-10r} h(10) \right] = 0.106275 \, P$$

and

$${}_{10} p_{60} = 0.673958,$$

so that

$$\pi(0) = 0.0716P.$$

That is, the option cost, assuming no lapses, is 7.16% of the single premium.

(b) If we assume that precisely 55% of policies issued reach maturity, the option value per policy issued is reduced to

$$0.55\, \mathrm{E}_0^Q \left[e^{-10r} h(10) \right] = 0.55 \times 0.106275 P$$

which is 5.85% of the single premium.

The assumption that 55% of policies reach maturity is reasonable if we assume that survival, allowing for mortality and lapses, is a diversifiable risk which is independent of the stock price process. In practice, lapse rates may depend on the fund's performance so that this assumption may not be reasonable. □

16.3.2 *Reserving*

We have already defined the reserve for an insurance contract as the capital set aside during the term of a policy to meet future obligations under the policy. In Chapter 14 we demonstrated a method of reserving for financial guarantees using a stochastic projection of the net present value of future outgo minus income, where we set the reserve to provide adequate resources in the event that investment experience for the portfolio was adverse.

Using the Black–Scholes–Merton approach, the value of the guarantee is interpreted as the value of the portfolio of assets that hedges, or replicates, the payoff under the guarantee. The insurer may use the cost of the guarantee to purchase appropriate options from another financial institution. If the mortality and lapse experiences follow the basis assumptions, the payoffs from the options will be precisely the amounts required for the guarantee payments. There is usually no need to hold further reserves since any reserve would cover only the future net expenses of maintaining the contract, which are, usually, fully defrayed by the future management charge income.

Increasingly, insurers are hedging their own guarantees. This should be less expensive than buying options from a third party, but requires the insurer to have the necessary expertise in financial risk management. When the insurer retains the risk, the contribution to the policy reserve for the guarantee will be the cost of maintaining the replicating portfolio. We saw in Chapter 15 that the cost of the replicating portfolio at some time t, before an option matures, is the price of the option at time t.

Suppose we consider the GMMB from Section 16.3.1, where the guarantee liability for the insurer at maturity, time n, is $(P - F_n)^+$, and where the issue price was $\pi(0)$ from equation (16.1). The contribution to the reserve at time t, where $0 \le t \le n$, for the GMMB, assuming the contract is still in force at time t, is the value at t of the option, which is

$$\pi(t) = P \, _{n-t}p_{x+t} \left(e^{-r(n-t)}\Phi(-d_2(t)) - \xi S_t \Phi(-d_1(t)) \right)$$

where

$$d_1(t) = \frac{\log(\xi \, S_t) + (r + \sigma^2/2)(n - t)}{\sigma\sqrt{n - t}} \quad \text{and} \quad d_2(t) = d_1(t) - \sigma\sqrt{n - t}.$$

Note here that the expense factor $\xi = (1 - e)(1 - m)^{n-1}$ does not depend on t, but the reserve at time t does depend on the stock price at time t, S_t.

For a more general GMMB, with payoff $h(n)$ on survival to time n, the contribution to the reserve is

$$\pi(t) = \, _{n-t}p_{x+t} \, \mathrm{E}_t^Q \left[e^{-r(n-t)} h(n) \right],$$

where E_t^Q denotes the expectation at time t with respect to the Q-measure. In particular, E_t^Q assumes knowledge of the stock price process at t, S_t.

In principle, the hedge for the maturity guarantee will (under the basis assumptions) exactly pay off the guarantee liability, so there should be no need to apply stochastic reserving methods. In practice though, it is not possible to hedge the guarantee perfectly, as the assumptions of the Black–Scholes–Merton formula do not apply exactly. The insurer may hold an additional reserve over and above the hedge cost to allow for unhedgeable risk and for the risk that lapses, mortality and volatility do not exactly follow the basis assumptions. Determining an appropriate reserve for the unhedgeable risk is beyond the scope of this book, but could be based on the stochastic methodology described in Chapter 14.

Example 16.2 Assume that the policy in Example 16.1 is still in force six years after it was issued to a life aged 60. Assuming there are no lapses, calculate the contribution to the reserve from the GMMB at this time given that, since the policy was purchased, the value of the stock has

(a) increased by 45%, and
(b) increased by 5%.

Solution 16.2 (a) Recall that in the option valuation we have assumed that the return on the fund, before management charge deductions, is modelled by the index $\{S_t\}_{t\ge 0}$, where $S_0 = 1$. We are given that $S_6 = 1.45$. Then

$$\pi(6) = P \, _4p_{66} \left(e^{-4r}\Phi(-d_2(6)) - \xi S_6 \Phi(-d_1(6)) \right)$$

where

$$d_1(t) = \frac{\log(\xi\, S_t) + (r + \sigma^2/2)(10 - t)}{\sigma\sqrt{10 - t}} \quad \text{and} \quad d_2(t) = d_1(t) - \sigma\sqrt{10 - t},$$

and $\xi = 0.927213$ as in Example 16.1. So

$$d_1(6) = 1.241983,$$
$$d_2(6) = 0.741983,$$
$$_4p_{66} = 0.824935$$

and hence

$$\pi(6) = 0.035892P = \$358.92.$$

(b) For $S_6 = 1.05$ we have $\pi(6) = \$905.39$.

A lower current fund value means that the guarantee is more likely to mature in-the-money and so a larger reserve is required. □

16.4 Guaranteed minimum death benefit

16.4.1 Pricing

Not all equity-linked insurance policies carry GMMBs, but most carry GMDBs of some kind to distinguish them from regular investment products. The most common guarantees on death are a fixed or an increasing minimum death benefit. In Canada, for example, contracts typically offer a minimum death benefit of the total amount of premiums paid. In the USA, the guaranteed minimum payout on death might be the accumulation at some fixed rate of interest of all premiums paid. In the UK, the benefit might be the greater of the total amount of premiums paid and, say, 101% of the policyholder's fund.

We approach GMDBs in the same way as we approached GMMBs. Consider an n-year policy issued to a life aged x under which the payoff under the GMDB is $h(t)$ if the life dies at age $x + t$, where $t < n$. If the insurer knew at the issue of the policy that the life would die at age $x + t$, the insurer could cover the guarantee by setting aside

$$v(0, t) = \mathrm{E}_0^Q\left[e^{-rt}\, h(t)\right]$$

at the issue date, where Q is again the risk neutral measure for the stock price process that underlies the policyholder's fund.

We know from Chapter 2 that the probability density associated with death at age $x + t$ for a life now aged x is $_t p_x \mu_{x+t}$, and so the amount that should be set aside to cover the GMDB, denoted $\pi(0)$, is found by averaging over the possible ages at death, $x + t$, so that

$$\pi(0) = \int_0^n v(0, t) {}_t p_x \mu_{x+t} \, dt. \tag{16.2}$$

If the death benefit is payable at the end of the month of death rather than immediately, the value of the guarantee becomes

$$\pi(0) = \sum_{j=1}^{12n} v(0, j/12) \; {}_{\frac{j-1}{12}} \big| {}_{\frac{1}{12}} q_x. \tag{16.3}$$

Notice that (16.2) and (16.3) are similar to formulae we have met in earlier chapters. For example, the EPV of a term insurance benefit of S payable immediately on the death within n years of a life currently aged x is

$$\int_0^n S v^t \; {}_t p_x \mu_{x+t} \, dt. \tag{16.4}$$

There are similarities and differences between (16.2) and (16.4). In each expression we are finding the expected amount required at time 0 to provide a death benefit (and in each case we require 0 at time n with probability ${}_n p_x$). In expression (16.4) the amount required if death occurs at time t is the present value of the payment at time t, namely $S v^t$, whereas in expression (16.2) $v(0, t)$ is the amount required at time 0 in order to replicate the (possible) payment at time t.

Example 16.3 An insurer issues a five-year equity-linked insurance policy to a life aged 60. A single premium of $P = \$10\,000$ is invested in an equity fund. Management charges of 0.25% are deducted at the start of each month. At the end of the month of death before age 65, the death benefit is the accumulated amount of the investment with a GMDB equal to the accumulated amount of the single premium, with interest at 5% per year compounded continuously.

Calculate the value of the guarantee on the following basis.

- Survival model: Makeham's law with $A = 0.0001$, $B = 0.00035$ and $c = 1.075$
- Risk free rate of interest: 5% per year, continuously compounded
- Volatility: 25% per year

Solution 16.3 As in previous examples, let $\{S_t\}_{t \geq 0}$ be an index of prices for the equity fund, with $S_0 = 1$, and let $m = 0.0025$ denote the monthly management charge. Then the payoff if death occurs in the month from time $k - \frac{1}{12}$ to k, for $k = \frac{1}{12}, \frac{2}{12}, \ldots, \frac{60}{12}$, is

$$h(k) = \max(P e^{0.05k} - F_k, 0)$$

where

$$F_k = P \, S_k \, (1 - m)^{12k},$$

so that

$$h(k) = P(1 - m)^{12k} \max \left(\frac{e^{0.05k}}{(1 - m)^{12k}} - S_k, 0 \right).$$

For any value of k ($k = \frac{1}{12}, \frac{2}{12}, \ldots, \frac{60}{12}$), the payoff is a multiple of the payoff under a put option with strike price $e^{0.05k}/(1 - m)^{12k}$. Before applying formula (15.10) to value this option, it is convenient to extend the notation for $d_1(t)$ and $d_2(t)$ in formula (15.9) to include the maturity date, so we now write these as $d_1(t, T)$ and $d_2(t, T)$ where T is the maturity date.

We can now apply formula (15.10) with strike price $e^{0.05k}/(1 - m)^{12k}$, which we discount at the risk free rate of $r = 0.05$, to obtain the first term in formula (15.10) as $\Phi(-d_2(0, k))/(1 - m)^{12k}$. Thus, if $v(0, k)$ denotes the value at time 0 of the guarantee at time k, then

$$v(0, k) = P(1 - m)^{12k} \left(\frac{\Phi(-d_2(0, k))}{(1 - m)^{12k}} - S_0 \Phi(-d_1(0, k)) \right)$$

$$= P \left(\Phi(-d_2(0, k)) - (1 - m)^{12k} \Phi(-d_1(0, k)) \right)$$

where, from (15.9),

$$d_1(0, k) = \frac{\log((1 - m)^k / e^{0.05k}) + (r + \sigma^2/2) k}{\sigma \sqrt{k}} \quad \text{and} \quad d_2(0, k) = d_1(0, k) - \sigma \sqrt{k},$$

with $\sigma = 0.25$.

Table 16.1 shows selected values from a spreadsheet containing deferred mortality probabilities and option prices for each possible month of death. Using these values in formula (16.3), the value of this GMDB is 2.7838% of the single premium, or \$278.38. □

16.4.2 Reserving

We now apply the approach of the previous section to reserving for a GMDB on the assumption that the insurer is internally hedging. Consider a policy issued to a life aged x with a term of n years and with a GMDB which is payable immediately on death if death occurs at time s where $0 < s < n$. Suppose that the payoff function under the guarantee at time s is $h(s)$. Let $v(t, s)$ denote the price at time t for an option with payoff $h(s)$ at time s, where $0 \leq t \leq s$, assuming the policyholder dies at age $x + s$. Then

$$v(t, s) = \mathrm{E}_t^Q \left[e^{-r(s-t)} h(s) \right].$$

Table 16.1 *Spreadsheet excerpt for the GMDB in Example 16.3.*

k (years)	$d_1(0, k)$	$d_2(0, k)$	$v(0, k)$	$\frac{k-1}{12}\vert\frac{1}{12}q_x$
1/12	0.001400	−0.070769	300.16	0.002248
2/12	0.001980	−0.100082	431.43	0.002257
3/12	0.002425	−0.122575	534.79	0.002265
4/12	0.002800	−0.141538	623.65	0.002273
5/12	0.003130	−0.158244	703.20	0.002282
6/12	0.003429	−0.173347	776.12	0.002290
7/12	0.003704	−0.187237	843.99	0.002299
$\vdots$	$\vdots$	$\vdots$	$\vdots$	$\vdots$
56/12	0.010477	−0.529585	2708.30	0.002702
57/12	0.010570	−0.534293	2735.70	0.002709
58/12	0.010662	−0.538959	2762.88	0.002717
59/12	0.010754	−0.543585	2789.86	0.002725
60/12	0.010844	−0.548173	2816.63	0.002732

Hence, the value of the GMDB for a policy in force at time t $(< n)$ is $\pi(t)$, where

$$\pi(t) = \int_t^n v(t, s)\, _{s-t}p_{x+t}\, \mu_{x+s}\, ds$$

$$= \int_0^{n-t} v(t, w+t)\, _w p_{x+t}\, \mu_{x+t+w}\, dw,$$

when the benefit is paid immediately on death, and

$$\pi(t) = \sum_{j=1}^{12(n-t)} v(t, t+j/12)\, _{\frac{j-1}{12}}\vert_{\frac{1}{12}}q_{x+t},$$

when the benefit is paid at the end of the month of death.

Example 16.4 Assume that the policy in Example 16.3 is still in force three years and six months after the issue date. Calculate the contribution of the GMDB to the reserve if the stock price index of the underlying fund assets

(a) has grown by 50% since inception, so that $S_{3.5} = 1.5$, and
(b) is the same as the initial value, so that $S_{3.5} = 1.0$.

Solution 16.4 Following the solution to Example 16.3, the strike price for an option expiring at time s is $e^{0.05s}/(1-m)^{12s}$. Since we are valuing the option at time $t < s$, the time to expiry is now $s - t$. Thus, applying formula (15.10) we have

$$v(t, s) = P(1 - m)^{12s} \left(\frac{e^{0.05s} e^{-0.05(s-t)}}{(1 - m)^{12s}} \Phi(-d_2(t, s)) - S_t \Phi(-d_1(t, s)) \right)$$

$$= P \left(e^{0.05t} \Phi(-d_2(t, s)) - S_t (1 - m)^{12s} \Phi(-d_1(t, s)) \right)$$

where

$$d_1(t, s) = \frac{\log(S_t(1 - m)^{12s}/e^{0.05s}) + (r + \sigma^2/2)(s - t)}{\sigma \sqrt{s - t}}$$

and

$$d_2(t, s) = d_1(t, s) - \sigma \sqrt{s - t}.$$

For the valuation at time $t = 3.5$, we calculate $v(3.5, s)$ for $s = 3\frac{7}{12}$, $3\frac{8}{12}$, $3\frac{7}{12}$, $3\frac{9}{12}, \ldots, 5$ and multiply each value by the mortality probability, $_{s-t-\frac{1}{12}}|_{\frac{1}{12}}q_{63.5}$. The resulting valuation is

(a) \$30.55 when $S_{3.5} = 1.5$, and
(b) \$172.05 when $S_{3.5} = 1.0$.   □

Example 16.5 An insurer offers a 10-year equity-linked policy with a single premium. An initial expense deduction of 4% of the premium is made, and the remainder of the premium is invested in an equity fund. Management charges are deducted daily from the policyholder's account at a rate of 0.6% per year. On death before the policy matures a death benefit of 110% of the fund value is paid. There is no guaranteed minimum maturity benefit.

(a) Calculate the price at issue of the excess amount of the death benefit over the fund value at the date of death for a life aged 55 at the purchase date, as a percentage of the single premium.
(b) Calculate the value of the excess amount of the death benefit over the fund value at the date of death six years after the issue date, as a percentage of the policyholder's fund at that date. You are given that the policy is still in force at the valuation date.

Basis:

• Survival model: Makeham's law, with $A = 0.0001$, $B = 0.00035$ and $c = 1.075$
• Risk free rate of interest: 5% per year, continuously compounded
• Volatility: 25% per year

Solution 16.5 (a) First, we note that the daily management charge can be treated as a continuous deduction from the fund, so that, for a unit premium,

$$F_t = 0.96e^{-0.006t} S_t.$$

Second, we note that the excess amount of the death benefit over the fund value at the date of death can be viewed as a GMDB equal to 10% of the fund value at the date of death. For a unit premium, the payoff function $h(s)$ if death occurs at time s, is

$$h(s) = 0.1 \, F_s = 0.096 \, e^{-0.006s} \, S_s.$$

The value at issue of the death benefit payable if the policyholder dies at time s is

$$v(0, s) = E_0^Q \left[e^{-rs} h(s) \right] = E_0^Q \left[e^{-rs} \, 0.096 \, e^{-0.006s} \, S_s \right].$$

In the previous chapter we saw that under the risk neutral measure the EPV of a stock price at a future point in time is the stock price now. Thus

$$E_0^Q \left[e^{-rs} \, S_s \right] = S_0.$$

Since $S_0 = 1$, we have

$$v(0, s) = S_0 \times 0.096 \, e^{-0.006s} = 0.096 \, e^{-0.006s}.$$

The GMDB value at issue is then

$$\pi(0) = \int_0^{10} v(0, s) \, _s p_{55} \, \mu_{55+s} \, ds$$

$$= 0.096 \int_0^{10} e^{-0.006s} \, _s p_{55} \, \mu_{55+s} \, ds$$

$$= 0.096 \, \bar{A}^{\,1}_{55:\overline{10}|\delta=0.6\%} \tag{16.5}$$

$$= 0.02236.$$

So the value of the GMDB at the inception of the policy is 2.24% of the single premium.

(b) The value at time $t < s$ of the option that would be needed to fund the GMDB if the policyholder were to die at time s, given that the policy is in force at t, is, for a unit premium,

$$v(t, s) = E_t^Q \left[e^{-r(s-t)} h(s) \right] = 0.1 \times 0.96 S_t \, e^{-0.006s}.$$

The total contribution to the reserve for the GMDB for a policy still in force at time t, with original premium P, is then

$$\pi(t) = P \int_0^{10-t} v(t, w + t)\; _w p_{55+t}\; \mu_{55+t+w}\, dw$$

$$= 0.096 P\; S_t \int_0^{10-t} e^{-0.006(w+t)}\; _w p_{55+t}\; \mu_{55+t+w}\, dw$$

$$= 0.096\; P\; S_t\; e^{-0.006t} \int_0^{10-t} e^{-0.006 w}\; _w p_{55+t}\; \mu_{55+t+w}\, dw$$

$$= 0.096\; P\; S_t\; e^{-0.006t}\; \bar{A}^{\,1}_{55+t:\overline{10-t}|\delta=0.6\%}.$$

So, at time $t = 6$, given that the policy is still in force, the contribution to the reserve from the GMDB, per unit premium, is

$$\pi(6) = 0.096\; P\; S_6\; e^{-0.006\times 6}\; \bar{A}^{\,1}_{64:\overline{4}|\delta=0.6\%}$$

$$= 0.096\; P\; S_6\; e^{-0.036} \times 0.12403.$$

The fund value at time $t = 6$ is

$$F_6 = 0.96\; P\; S_6 \times e^{-0.036},$$

and so the reserve, as a proportion of the fund value, is

$$\frac{0.096\; P\; S_6\; e^{-0.036}\; \bar{A}^{\,1}_{61:\overline{4}|\delta=0.6\%}}{0.96\; P\; S_6\; e^{-0.036}} = 0.1\bar{A}^{\,1}_{61:\overline{4}|\delta=0.6\%} = 0.0124.$$

That is, the GMDB reserve would be 1.24% of the policyholder's fund value. $\square$

16.5 Pricing methods for embedded options

In discussing pricing above, we have expressed the price of a GMMB and a GMDB as a percentage of the initial premium. This is appropriate if the option is funded by a deduction from the premium at the inception of the policy. That is, the price of the option would come from the initial deduction of eP in the notation of Section 16.3.1 above. This sum could then be invested in the hedge portfolio for the option.

A relatively large expense deduction at inception, called a **front-end load**, is common for UK policies, but less common in North America. A more common expense loading in North America is a management charge, applied as a regular percentage deduction from the policyholder's fund.

If the guarantee is to be funded through a regular management charge, rather than a deduction from the single premium as in Sections 16.3.1 and 16.4.1, we need a way to express the cost in terms of this charge.

Consider a single premium equity-linked policy with a term of n years issued to a life aged x. We assume, for simplicity, that there are no lapses and no initial expenses, so that $e = 0$ in the notation of Section 16.3.1. Also, we assume that mortality is a diversifiable risk which is independent of the stock price process.

Let $\pi(0)$ denote the cost at inception of the guarantees embedded in the policy, as derived in Sections 16.3.1 and 16.4.1. Suppose these guarantees consist of a payment of amount $h(t)$ if the life dies at time t ($< n$) and a payment $h(n)$ if the life survives to the end of the term. The value of each of these guarantees is

$$E_0^Q[h(t)\, e^{-rt}]$$

given that the life does die at time t, and

$$E_0^Q[h(n)\, e^{-rn}]$$

given that the life does survive to time n. Allowing for the probabilities of death and survivorship, we have

$$\pi(0) = \int_0^n E_0^Q[h(t)\, e^{-rt}]\, {}_tp_x\, \mu_{x+t}\, dt + {}_np_x\, E_0^Q[h(n)\, e^{-rn}].$$

We interpret $\pi(0)$ as the cost at time 0 of setting up the replicating portfolios to pay the guarantees.

Let c denote the component of the management charge that is required to fund the guarantees from a total (fixed) management charge of m ($> c$) per year. We call c the **risk premium** for the guarantees.

Assume that the management charge is deducted daily, which we treat as a continuous deduction. With these assumptions, the fund value at time t for a policy still in force at that time, F_t, can be written

$$F_t = P\, S_t\, e^{-mt}.$$

Hence, the risk premium received in the time interval t to $t + dt$ for a policy still in force is (loosely) $c\, P\, S_t\, e^{-mt}\, dt$. Ignoring survivorship for the moment, the value at time 0 of this payment can be calculated as the cost of setting up a replicating portfolio which will pay this amount at time t. This cost is $c\, P\, e^{-mt}\, dt$ since an investment of this amount at time 0 in the stock will accumulate to $c\, P\, S_t\, e^{-mt}\, dt$ at time t (recall that $S_0 = 1$). Allowing for survivorship, the value at time 0 of the risk premium received in the time interval t to

$t + dt$ is $c\,P\,e^{-mt}\,dt\,{}_tp_x$ and so the value at time 0 of the total risk premiums to be received is

$$\int_0^n c\,P\,e^{-mt}\,{}_tp_x\,dt = c\,P\,\bar{a}_{x:\overline{n}|\delta=m}.$$

The risk premium c is chosen so that the value to the insurer of the risk premiums to be received is equal to the cost at time 0 of setting up the replicating portfolios to pay the guarantees, so that

$$c = \pi(0)/(P\,\bar{a}_{x:\overline{n}|\delta=m}).$$

Calculating c from this formula is a slightly circular process. The risk premium c is a component of the total management charge m, but we need to know m to calculate the right-hand side of this equation for c. In practice, we may need to iterate through the calculations a few times to determine the value of c. In some cases there may be no solution. For example, increasing the total management charge m may increase the cost of the guarantees, therefore requiring a higher value for the risk premium c, which may in turn require a higher value for m.

If the management charge is deducted less frequently, say annually in advance, we can use the same principles as above to derive the value of the risk premiums. The cost at time 0 of setting up the replicating portfolios which will provide exactly for the guarantees is still $\pi(0)$. Ignoring survivorship, the amount of the risk premium to be received at time t ($t = 0, 1, \ldots, n-1$) is $c\,F_t = c\,P\,(1-m)^t\,S_t$ and the value of this at time 0 is $c\,P\,(1-m)^t$. Allowing for survivorship, this value is $c\,P\,(1-m)^t\,{}_tp_x$ and so the value at time 0 of all the risk premiums to be received is

$$\sum_{t=0}^{n-1} {}_tp_x\,c\,P\,(1-m)^t = c\,P\,\ddot{a}_{x:\overline{n}|i^*}$$

where

$$i^* = m/(1-m) \quad \text{so that} \quad 1/(1+i^*) = 1 - m.$$

Example 16.6 In Example 16.3 the monthly management charge, m, was 0.25% of the fund value and the GMDB option price was determined to be 2.7838% of the single premium.

You are given that 0.20% per month is allocated to commission and administrative expenses. Determine whether the remaining 0.05% per month is sufficient to cover the risk premium for the option.

Use the same basis as in Example 16.3.

Solution 16.6 The risk neutral value of the risk premium of c per month is

$$E_0^Q \left[c F_0 + c F_{1/12} e^{-r/12} \, _{1/12}p_{60} + \cdots + c F_{59/12} e^{-59r/12} \, _{59/12}p_{60} \right]$$

$$= c P S_0 \left(1 + (1-m) \, _{1/12}p_{60} + (1-m)^2 \, _{2/12}p_{60} + \cdots + (1-m)^{59} \, _{59/12}p_{60} \right)$$

$$= 12 c P S_0 \, \ddot{a}^{(12)}_{60:\overline{5}|}$$

where the annuity interest rate is i such that

$$v_i^{1/12} = (1-m) \Rightarrow i = (1-m)^{-12} - 1 = 3.0493\% \text{ per year.}$$

The annuity value is 4.32662, so the value of the risk premium of 0.05% per month is \$259.60.

The value of the guarantee at the inception date, from Example 16.3, is \$278.38 so the risk premium of 0.05% per month is not sufficient to pay for the guarantee. The insurer needs to revise the pricing structure for this product. $\square$

16.6 Risk management

The option prices derived in this chapter are the cost of either buying the appropriate options in the market, or internally hedging the options. If the insurer does not plan to purchase or hedge the options, then the price or reserve amount calculated may be inadequate. It would be inappropriate to charge an option premium using the Black–Scholes–Merton framework, and then invest the premium in bonds or stocks with no consideration of the dynamic hedging implicit in the calculation of the cost. Thus, the decision to use Black–Scholes–Merton pricing carries with it the consequential decision either to buy the options or to hedge using the Black–Scholes–Merton framework.

Under the assumptions of the Black–Scholes–Merton model, and provided the mortality and lapse experience is as assumed, the hedge portfolio will mature to the precise cost of the guarantee. In reality the match will not be exact but will usually be very close. So hedging is a form of risk mitigation. Choosing not to hedge may be a very risky strategy – with associated probabilities of severe losses. Generally, if the risk is not hedged, the reserves required using the stochastic techniques of Chapter 14 will be considerably greater than the hedge costs.

One of the reasons why the hedge portfolio will not exactly meet the cost of the guarantee is that under the Black–Scholes–Merton assumptions, the hedge portfolio should be continuously rebalanced. In reality, the rebalancing will be less frequent. A large portfolio might be rebalanced daily, a smaller one at weekly or even monthly intervals.

If the hedge portfolio is rebalanced at discrete points in time (e.g. monthly), there will be small costs (positive or negative) incurred as the previous hedge portfolio is adjusted to create the new hedge portfolio. See Example 15.5.

The hedge portfolio value required at time t for an n-year GMMB is, from Section 16.3.2,

$$\pi(t) = {}_{n-t}p_{x+t}\, E^Q_t [e^{-r(n-t)}\, h(n)] = {}_{n-t}p_{x+t}\, v(t, n)$$

where, as above, $v(t, n)$ is the value at time t of the option maturing at time n, unconditional on the policyholder's survival.

The hedge portfolio is invested partly in zero-coupon bonds, maturing at time n, and partly (in fact, a negative amount, i.e. a short sale) in stocks. The value of the stock part of the hedge portfolio is

$$_{n-t}p_{x+t} \left(\frac{d}{dS_t} v(t, n) S_t \right)$$

and the value of the zero-coupon bond part of the hedge portfolio is

$$\pi(t) - {}_{n-t}p_{x+t} \left(\frac{d}{dS_t} v(t, n) S_t \right).$$

For a GMDB, the approach is identical, but the option value is a weighted average of options of all possible maturity dates, so the hedge portfolio is a mixture of zero-coupon bonds of all possible maturity dates, and (short positions in) stocks. For example, when the benefit is payable immediately on death, the value at time t of the option is $\pi(t)$, where

$$\pi(t) = \int_0^{n-t} v(t, w+t)\, {}_w p_{x+t}\, \mu_{x+t+w}\, dw.$$

The stock part of the hedge portfolio has value

$$\int_0^{n-t} S_t \left(\frac{d}{dS_t} v(t, w+t) \right) {}_w p_{x+t}\, \mu_{x+t+w}\, dw.$$

The value of the bond part of the hedge portfolio is the difference between $\pi(t)$ and the value of the stock part, so that the amount invested in a w-year zero-coupon bond at time t is (loosely)

$$\left(v(t, t+w) - S_t \frac{d}{dS_t} v(t, t+w) \right) {}_w p_{x+t}\, \mu_{x+t+w}\, dw.$$

The hedge strategy described in this section, which is called a delta-hedge, uses only zero-coupon bonds and stocks to replicate the guarantee payoff. More complex strategies are also possible, bringing options and futures into the hedge, but these are beyond the scope of this book.

The Black–Scholes–Merton valuation can be interpreted as a **market-consistent valuation**, by which we mean that the option sold in the financial markets as a stand alone product (rather than embedded in life insurance) would have the same value. Many jurisdictions are moving towards market consistent valuation for accounting purposes, even where the insurers do not use hedging.

16.7 Emerging costs

Whether the insurer is hedging internally or buying the options to hedge, the profit testing of an equity-linked policy proceeds as described in Chapter 14. The insurer might profit test deterministically, using best estimate scenarios, and then stress test using different scenarios, or might test stochastically, using Monte Carlo simulation to generate the scenarios for the increase in the stock prices in the policyholder's fund. In this section, we first explore deterministic profit testing, and then discuss how to make the profit test stochastic.

The cash flow projection depends on the projected fund values. Suppose we are projecting the emerging cash flows for a single premium equity-linked policy with a term of n years and with a GMDB and/or a GMMB, for a given stock price scenario. We assume all cash flows occur at intervals of $1/m$ years.

Assuming the insurer hedges the options internally, the income to and outgo from the insurer's fund for this contract arise as follows:

Income: + Initial front-end-load expense deduction.

+ Regular management charge income.

+ Investment return on income over the $1/m$ year period.

Outgo: − Expenses.

− Initial hedge cost, at $t = 0$.

− After the first month, the hedge portfolio needs to be rebalanced; the cost is the difference between the hedge value brought forward and the hedge required to be carried forward.

− If the policyholder dies, there may be a GMDB liability.

− If the policyholder survives to maturity, there may be a GMMB liability.

The part of this that differs from Chapter 14 is the cost of rebalancing the hedge portfolio. In Example 15.5, for a standard put option, we looked at calculating rebalancing errors for a hedge portfolio adjusted monthly. The hedge portfolio adjustment in this chapter follows the same principles, but with the complication that the option is contingent on survival. As in Example 15.5, we assume that the hedge portfolio value is invested in a delta hedge. If rebalancing is continuous (in practice, one or more times daily), then the hedge adjustment will be (in practice, close to) zero, and the emerging guarantee cost will be zero given that the experience in terms of stock price movements and survival is in accordance with the models used. Under the model assumptions, the hedge is self-financing and exactly meets the guarantee costs. Also, if the hedge cost is used to buy options in the market, there will be no hedge adjustment cost and no guarantee cost once the options are purchased.

If the rebalancing takes place every $1/m$ years, then we need to model the rebalancing costs. We break the hedge portfolio down into the stock part, assumed to be invested in the underlying index $\{S_t\}_{t\geq 0}$, and the bond part, invested in a portfolio of zero-coupon bonds. Suppose the values of these two parts are $\Psi_t S_t$ and Υ_t, respectively, so that

$$\pi(t) = \Upsilon_t + \Psi_t S_t.$$

Then $1/m$ years later, the bond part of the hedge portfolio has appreciated by a factor $e^{r/m}$ and the stock part by a factor $S_{t+1/m}/S_t$. This means that, before rebalancing, the value of the hedge portfolio is, say, $\pi^{bf}(t + \frac{1}{m})$, where

$$\pi^{bf}(t + \tfrac{1}{m}) = \Upsilon_t e^{r/m} + \Psi_t S_{t+1/m}.$$

The rebalanced hedge portfolio required at time $t + 1/m$ has value $\pi(t + \frac{1}{m})$, but is required only if the policyholder survives. If the policyholder dies, the guarantee payoff is $h(t + \frac{1}{m})$. So the total cost at time $t + 1/m$ of rebalancing the hedge, given that the policy was in force at time t, is

$$\pi(t + \tfrac{1}{m}) \,_{\frac{1}{m}}p_{x+t} - \pi^{bf}(t + \tfrac{1}{m})$$

and the cost of the GMDB is

$$h(t + \tfrac{1}{m}) \,_{\frac{1}{m}}q_{x+t}.$$

Note that these formulae need to be adjusted for the costs at the final maturity date, n: $\pi(n)$ is zero since there is no longer any need to set up a hedge portfolio, and the cost of the GMMB is $h(n) \,_{\frac{1}{m}}p_{x+n-\frac{1}{m}}$.

If lapses are explicitly allowed for, then the mortality probability would be replaced by an in-force survival probability.

In the following example, all of the concepts introduced in this chapter are illustrated as we work through the process of pricing and profit testing an equity-linked contract with both a GMDB and a GMMB.

Example 16.7 An insurer issues a five-year equity-linked policy to a life aged 60. The single premium is $P = \$1\,000\,000$. The benefit on maturity or death is a return of the policyholder's fund, subject to a minimum of the initial premium.

The death benefit is paid at the end of the month of death and is based on the fund value at that time.

Management charges of 0.3% per month are deducted from the fund at the start of each month.

(a) Calculate the monthly risk premium (as part of the overall management charge) required to fund the guarantees, assuming
  (i) volatility is 25% per year, and
  (ii) volatility is 20% per year.

Basis:

Survival model:	Makeham's law with $A = 0.0001$, $B = 0.00035$ and $c = 1.075$
Lapses:	None
Risk free rate of interest:	5% per year, continuously compounded

(b) The insurer is considering purchasing options to hedge the guarantees in the market; in this case the price for the options would be based on the 25% volatility assumption. Assuming that the monthly risk premium based on the 25% volatility assumption is used to purchase the options for the GMDB and GMMB liabilities, profit test the contract for the two stock price scenarios below, using a risk discount rate of 10% per year effective, and using monthly time intervals. Use the basis from part (a), assuming, additionally, that expenses incurred at the start of each month are 0.01% of the fund, after deducting the management charge, plus $20. The two stock price scenarios are
  (i) stock prices in the policyholder's fund increase each month by 0.65%, and
  (ii) stock prices in the policyholder's fund decrease each month by 0.05%.

(c) The alternative strategy for the insurer is to hedge internally. Calculate all the cash flows to and from the insurer's fund at times 0, $\frac{1}{12}$ and $\frac{2}{12}$ per policy issued for the following stock price scenarios
  (i)   stock prices in the policyholder's fund increase each month by 0.65%,
  (ii) stock prices in the policyholder's fund decrease each month by 0.05%, and
  (iii) $S_{\frac{1}{12}} = 1.0065$, $S_{\frac{2}{12}} = 0.9995$.

Assume that

the hedge cost is based on the 20% volatility assumption,

the hedge portfolio is rebalanced monthly,

expenses incurred at the start of each month are 0.025% of the fund, after deducting the management charge, and the insurer holds no additional reserves apart from the hedge portfolio for the options.

Solution 16.7 (a) The payoff function, $h(t)$, for $t = \frac{1}{12}, \frac{2}{12}, \ldots, \frac{59}{12}, \frac{60}{12}$, is

$$h(t) = (P - F_t)^+$$

where

$$F_t = P\, S_t\, (1-m)^{12t}$$

and $m = 0.003$. Let $v(t, s)$ denote the value at t of the option given that it matures at s $(> t)$. Then

$$v(t, s) = E_t^Q \left[e^{-r(s-t)} h(s) \right]$$

$$= E_t^Q \left[e^{-r(s-t)} \left(P - P\, S_s(1-m)^{12s} \right)^+ \right]$$

$$= P \left(e^{-r(s-t)} \Phi(-d_2(t, s)) - S_t (1-m)^{12s} \Phi(-d_1(t, s)) \right)$$

where

$$d_1(t, s) = \frac{\log(S_t(1-m)^{12s}) + (r + \sigma^2/2)(s - t)}{\sigma \sqrt{s - t}}$$

and

$$d_2(t, s) = d_1(t, s) - \sigma \sqrt{s - t}.$$

The option price at issue is

$$\pi(0) = v\left(0, \tfrac{1}{12}\right) \tfrac{1}{12} q_x + v\left(0, \tfrac{2}{12}\right) \tfrac{1}{12} |_{\tfrac{1}{12}} q_x + v\left(0, \tfrac{3}{12}\right) \tfrac{2}{12} |_{\tfrac{1}{12}} q_x + \cdots$$
$$+ v\left(0, \tfrac{60}{12}\right) \tfrac{59}{12} |_{\tfrac{1}{12}} q_x + v\left(0, \tfrac{60}{12}\right) \tfrac{60}{12} p_x.$$

This gives the option price as

(i) $0.145977\, P$ for $\sigma = 0.25$ per year, and

(ii) $0.112710\, P$ for $\sigma = 0.20$ per year.

Next, we convert the premium to a regular charge on the fund, c, using

$$\pi(0) = 12\, c\, P\, \ddot{a}_{\overline{60:5}|}^{(12)}$$

where the interest rate for the annuity is $i = (1-m)^{-12} - 1 = 3.6712\%$, which gives $\ddot{a}_{\overline{60:5}|}^{(12)} = 4.26658$. The charge on the fund is then

(i) $c = 0.00285$ for $\sigma = 0.25$, and

(ii) $c = 0.00220$ for $\sigma = 0.20$.

(b) Following the convention of Chapter 14, we use the stock price scenarios to project the policyholder's fund value assuming that the policy stays in force throughout the five-year term of the contract. From this projection we can project the management charge income to the insurer's fund at the start of each month. Outgo at the start of the month comprises the risk premium for the option (which is paid to the option provider), and the expenses.

The steps in this calculation are as follows. At time $t = k/12$, where $k = 0, 1, \ldots, 59$, assuming the policy is still in force:

- The policyholder's fund, just before the deduction of the management charge, is F_t, where

$$F_t = P \, (1 + g)^k \, (1 - 0.003)^k$$

and g is the rate of growth of the stock price.

- The amount transferred to the insurer's fund in respect of the management charge is

$$0.003 \, F_t.$$

- The insurer's expenses, excluding the risk premium, are

$$0.0001 \, (1 - 0.003) \, F_t + 20.$$

- The risk premium is

$$0.00285 \, (1 - 0.003) \, F_t.$$

- The profit to the insurer is

$$\mathrm{Pr}_t = (0.003 - (1 - 0.003)(0.0001 + 0.00285)) \, F_t - 20.$$

- The profit to the insurer, allowing for survivorship to time t, is

$$\Pi_t = {}_t p_{60} \, ((0.003 - (1 - 0.003)(0.0001 + 0.00285)) \, F_t - 20).$$

- The net present value of the profit using a risk discount rate of 10% per year is

$$\mathrm{NPV} = \sum_{k=0}^{59} \Pi_{\frac{k}{12}} \, 1.1^{-\frac{k}{12}}.$$

Because the insurer is buying the options, there is no outgo for the insurer in respect of the guarantees on death or maturity – the purchased options are assumed to cover any liability. As there is no residual liability for the insurer for the contract, there is no need to hold reserves. There are no end-of-month cash flows, so we calculate the profit vector using cash flows at the start of the month. Hence, Pr_t is the profit to the insurer at

Table 16.2 *Profit test for Example 16.7 part (b), first stock price scenario.*

Time, t (months)	Management charge	Expenses	Risk premium	Pr_t	$_{t/12}p_{60}$	Π_t
0	3000.00	119.70	2842.63	37.67	1	37.67
1	3010.44	120.05	2852.52	37.87	0.99775	37.79
2	3020.92	120.40	2862.45	38.08	0.99550	37.90
$\vdots$	$\vdots$	$\vdots$	$\vdots$	$\vdots$	$\vdots$	
58	3669.78	141.96	3477.27	50.55	0.85582	43.26
59	3682.55	142.38	3489.37	50.79	0.85309	43.33

time t, assuming the policy is in force at that time, and Π_t is the profit at time t assuming only that the policy was in force at time 0.

Some of the calculations for the scenario where the stock price grows at 0.65% per month are presented in Table 16.2.

The net present value for this contract, using the 10% risk discount rate and the first stock price scenario, is $1940.11.

The second stock price scenario, with stock prices falling by 0.05% each month, gives an NPV of $1463.93.

(c) The items of cash flow for the insurer's fund at times 0, $\frac{1}{12}$ and $\frac{2}{12}$, per policy issued, are shown in Table 16.3. The individual items are as follows:

Income: the management charge (1).

Outgo:

the insurer's expenses (2),

the amount, if any, needed to increase death or maturity benefits to the guaranteed amount (3),

the amount needed to set up, or rebalance, the hedge portfolio (4), and the net cash flow (5), calculated as

$$(5) = (1) - (2) - (3) - (4).$$

The individual cash flows at time t, per policy issued, are calculated as follows.

(1) Management charge

$$_tp_{60}\, P\, S_t \times 0.997^{12t} \times 0.003.$$

(2) Expenses

$$_tp_{60}\, P\, S_t \times 0.997^{12t+1} \times 0.00025.$$

(3) Death benefit (for $t > 0$)

$$(_{t-\frac{1}{12}}p_{60} - _tp_{60})\, P(1 - S_t \times 0.997^{12t})^+.$$

Table 16.3 *Cash flows for Example 16.7 part (c).*

Time, t	Scenario	Management charge (1)	Expenses (2)	GMDB and GMMB (3)	Cost of hedge (4)	Net cash flow (5)
0	(i)	3000	249.25	0	112 709.54	$-109\,958.79$
	(ii)	3000	249.25	0	112 709.54	$-109\,958.79$
	(iii)	3000	249.25	0	112 709.54	$-109\,958.79$
$\frac{1}{12}$	(i)	3003.67	249.56	0	-1380.84	4134.96
	(ii)	2982.78	247.82	7.87	-1380.40	4107.50
	(iii)	3003.67	249.56	0	-1380.84	4134.96
$\frac{2}{12}$	(i)	3007.31	249.86	0	-1388.47	4145.92
	(ii)	2965.63	246.39	15.76	-1394.21	4097.68
	(iii)	2967.11	246.52	14.64	$-1\,352.25$	4058.20

(4) The cost of setting up the hedge portfolio at time 0 is the same for each stock price scenario and is equal to $10^6 \, \pi(0)$. At time $t = \frac{1}{12}$ the value of the hedge portfolio is

$$(\Upsilon_0 \, e^{0.05/12} + \Psi_0 \, S_{\frac{1}{12}}).$$

The cost of setting up the new hedge portfolio for each policy still in force is $\pi(\frac{1}{12})$. Hence, the net cost of rebalancing the hedge portfolio at this time per policy originally issued is

$$\left(\tfrac{1}{12} p_{60} \, \pi(1/12) - (\Upsilon_0 \, e^{0.05/12} + \Psi_0 \, S_{\frac{1}{12}}) \right).$$

Similarly, the net cost of rebalancing the hedge portfolio at time $\frac{2}{12}$ per policy originally issued is

$$\left(\tfrac{2}{12} p_{60} \, \pi(2/12) - \tfrac{1}{12} p_{60} \left(\Upsilon_{\frac{1}{12}} \, e^{0.05/12} + \Psi_{\frac{1}{12}} \, S_{\frac{2}{12}} \right) \right).$$

The values of $\pi(t)$, Υ_t and $\Psi_t \, S_t$ are shown in Table 16.4. $\quad\square$

We note several important points about this example.

(1) Stock price scenarios (i) and (ii) used in parts (b) and (c) are not realistic, and lead to unrealistic figures for the NPV. This is particularly true for the internal hedging case, part (c). The NPV values for scenarios (i) and (ii), assuming internal hedging and a risk discount rate of 10% per year, can

Table 16.4 *Hedge portfolios for Example 16.7 part(c).*

Time		Investment scenario		
t		(i)	(ii)	(iii)
0	$\pi(t)$	112 710	112 710	112 710
	Υ_t	417 174	417 174	417 174
	$\Psi_t\, S_t$	−304 465	−304 465	−304 465
$\frac{1}{12}$	$\pi(t)$	111 342	113 478	111 342
	Υ_t	415 700	421 369	415 700
	$\Psi_t\, S_t$	−304 358	−307 891	−304 358
$\frac{2}{12}$	$\pi(t)$	109 956	114 253	114 097
	Υ_t	414 172	425 626	425 216
	$\Psi_t\, S_t$	−304 216	−311 373	−311 119

be shown to be $99\,944$ and $73\,584$, respectively. If the lognormal model for stock prices is appropriate, then the expected present value (under the P-measure) of the hedge rebalancing costs will be close to zero. Under both scenarios (i) and (ii) in Example 16.7 the present value is significant and negative, meaning that the hedge portfolio value brought forward each month is more than sufficient to pay for the guarantee and new hedge portfolio at the month end. This is because more realistic scenarios involve far more substantial swings in stock price values, and it is these that generate positive hedge portfolio rebalancing costs.

(2) The comment above is more clearly illustrated when the profit test is used with stochastic stock price scenarios. In the table below we show some summary statistics for 500 simulations of the NPV for part (c), again calculated using a risk discount rate of 10% per year. The stock price scenarios were generated using a lognormal model, with parameters $\mu = 8\%$ per year, and volatility $\sigma = 0.20$ per year.

Mean NPV	Standard deviation	5% quantile	50% quantile	95% quantile
$31\,684	$37\,332	−$23\,447	$28\,205	$99\,861

We note that the NPV value for scenario (i) falls outside the 90% confidence interval for the net present value generated by stochastic simulation. This is because this scenario is highly unrepresentative of the true stock price process. Over-reliance on deterministic scenarios can lead to poor risk management.

(3) If we run a stochastic profit test under part (b), where the option is purchased in the market, the variability of simulated NPVs is very small. The

net management charge income is small, and the variability arising from the guarantee cost has been passed on to the option provider. The mean NPV over 500 simulations is approximately $2137, and the standard deviation of the NPV is approximately $766, assuming the same parameters for the stock price process as for (c) above.

(4) If we neither hedge nor reserve for this option, and instead use the methods from Chapter 14, the two deterministic scenarios give little indication of the variability of the net present value. Using the first scenario (increasing prices) generates a NPV of $137053 and using the second gives $2381. Using stochastic simulation generates a mean NPV of around $100000 with a 5% quantile of approximately −$123000.

16.8 Notes and further reading

There is a wealth of literature on pricing and hedging embedded options. Hardy (2003) gives some examples and information on practical ways to manage the risks. The options illustrated here are relatively straightforward. Much more convoluted options are sold, particularly in association with variable annuity policies. For example, a guaranteed minimum withdrawal benefit allows the policyholder the right to withdraw some proportion of the premium for a fixed time, even if the fund is exhausted. Also, the guarantee may specify that after an introductory period, the policyholder could withdraw 5% of the initial premium per year for 20 years. Other complicating features include resets where the policyholder has the right to set the guarantee at the current fund value at certain times during the contract. New variants are being created regularly, reflecting the strong interest in these products in the market.

In Section 16.2 we noted three differences between options embedded in insurance policies and standard options commonly traded in financial markets. The first was the life contingent nature of the benefit and the second was the fact that the option is based on the fund value rather than the underlying stocks. Both of these issues have been addressed in this chapter. The third issue is the fact that embedded options are generally much longer term than traded options. One of the implications is that the standard models for short-term options may not be appropriate over longer terms. The most important area of concern here is the lognormal model for stock prices. There is considerable empirical evidence that the lognormal model is not a good fit for stock prices in the long run. This issue is not discussed further here, but is important for a more advanced treatment of equity-linked insurance risk management. Sources for further information include Hardy (2003) and Møller (1998).

The first applications of modern financial mathematics to equity-linked insurance can be found in Brennan and Schwartz (1976) and Boyle and Schwartz (1977).

In some countries annual premium equity-linked contracts are common. We have not discussed these in this chapter, as the valuation and risk management is more complicated and requires more advanced financial mathematics. Bacinello (2003) discusses an Italian style annual premium policy.

Ledlie *et al.* (2008) give an introduction to some of the issues around equity-linked insurance, including a discussion of a guaranteed minimum income benefit, another more complex embedded option.

16.9 Exercises

Exercise 16.1 An insurer is designing a 10-year single premium variable annuity policy with a guaranteed maturity benefit of 85% of the single premium.

(a) Calculate the value of the GMMB at the issue date for a single premium of $100.
(b) Calculate the value of the GMMB as a regular annual deduction from the fund.
(c) Calculate the value of the GMMB two years after issue, assuming that the policy is still in force, and that the underlying stock prices have decreased by 5% since inception.

Basis and policy information:

Age at issue:	60
Front-end expense loading:	2%
Annual management charge:	2% at each year end (including the first)
Survival model:	Standard Ultimate Survival Model
Lapses:	5% at each year end except the final year
Risk free rate:	4% per year, continuously compounded
Volatility:	20% per year

Exercise 16.2 An insurer issues a 10-year equity-linked insurance policy to a life aged 60. A single premium of $10 000 is invested in an equity fund. Management charges at a rate of 3% per year are deducted daily. At the end of the month of death before age 70, the death benefit is 105% of the policyholder's fund subject to a minimum of the initial premium.

(a) Calculate the price of the death benefit at issue.
(b) Express the cost of the death benefit as a continuous charge on the fund.

Basis:

Survival model:	Standard Ultimate Survival Model
Risk free rate:	4% per year, continuously compounded
Volatility:	25% per year
Lapses:	None

Exercise 16.3 An insurer issues a 10-year variable annuity policy. Assume an investor deposits a single premium of $100 000. The policy carries a guaranteed minimum maturity benefit of 100% of the premium.

(a) Calculate the probability that the guaranteed minimum maturity benefit will mature in-the-money (i.e. the probability that the fund at the maturity date is worth less than 100% of the single premium) under the P-measure.
(b) Calculate the probability that the guaranteed minimum maturity benefit will mature in-the-money under the Q-measure.
(c) Calculate the EPV of the option payoff under the P-measure, discounting at the risk free rate.
(d) Calculate the price of the option.
(e) A colleague has suggested the value of the option should be the EPV of the guarantee under the P-measure, analogous to the value of term insurance liabilities. Explain why this value would not be suitable.
(f) For options that are complicated to value analytically we can use Monte Carlo simulation to find the value. We simulate the payoff under the risk neutral measure, discount at the risk free rate and take the mean value to estimate the Q-measure expectation. Use Monte Carlo simulation to estimate the value of this option with 1000 scenarios, and comment on the accuracy of your estimate.

Basis:

Survival model:	No mortality
Stock price appreciation:	Lognormally distributed, with $\mu = 0.08$ per year, $\sigma = 0.25$ per year
Risk free rate of interest:	4% per year, continuously compounded
Management charges:	3% of the fund per year, in advance

Exercise 16.4 An insurer issues a single premium variable annuity contract with a 10-year term. There is a guaranteed minimum maturity benefit equal to the initial premium of $100.

After five years the policyholder's fund value has increased to 110% of the initial premium. The insurer offers the policyholder a reset option, under which

Table 16.5 *Single scenario of stock prices for stochastic profit test for Exercise 16.5.*

t	S_t	t	S_t	t	S_t	t	S_t	t	S_t
0	1.00000								
1	0.95449	13	0.92420	25	1.09292	37	1.09203	49	1.34578
2	0.96745	14	0.95545	26	1.17395	38	1.10988	50	1.42368
3	0.97371	15	1.02563	27	1.27355	39	1.05115	51	1.50309
4	1.01158	16	1.13167	28	1.32486	40	1.05659	52	1.63410
5	1.01181	17	1.25234	29	1.31999	41	1.18018	53	1.45134
6	0.93137	18	1.10877	30	1.24565	42	1.20185	54	1.46399
7	0.98733	19	1.10038	31	1.20481	43	1.34264	55	1.40476
8	0.89062	20	0.99481	32	1.18405	44	1.37309	56	1.44512
9	0.91293	21	1.04213	33	1.23876	45	1.39327	57	1.39672
10	0.90374	22	1.07980	34	1.15140	46	1.40633	58	1.30130
11	0.88248	23	1.14174	35	1.09478	47	1.41652	59	1.25762
12	0.92712	24	1.12324	36	1.03564	48	1.43076	60	1.19427

the policyholder may reset the guarantee to the current fund level, in which case the remaining term of the policy will be increased to 10 years.

(a) Determine which of the original guarantee and the reset guarantee has greater value at the reset date.

(b) Determine the threshold value for F_5 (i.e. the fund at time 5) at which the option to reset becomes more valuable than the original option.

Basis:

Survival model:	No mortality
Volatility:	$\sigma = 0.18$ per year
Risk free rate of interest:	5% per year, continuously compounded
Management charges:	1% of the fund per year, in advance
Front-end-load charge:	3%

Exercise 16.5 An insurer issues a five-year single premium equity-linked insurance policy to (60) with guaranteed minimum maturity benefit of 100% of the initial premium. The premium is $100 000. Management fees of 0.25% of the fund are deducted at the start of each month.

(a) Verify that the guarantee cost expressed as a monthly deduction is 0.19% of the fund.

(b) The actuary is profit testing this contract using a stochastic profit test. The actuary first works out the hedge rebalancing cost each month then inserts that into the profit test.

 The stock price figures in Table 16.5 represent one randomly generated scenario. The table shows the stock price index values for each month in the 60-month scenario.

Table 16.6 *Hedge rebalance table for Exercise 16.5, in $100 000s.*

Time (months)	S_t	Option cost at t	Stock part of hedge at t	Bond part of hedge at t	Hedge b/f	Hedging Rebalance cost
0	1.00000	10.540	−27.585	38.125	–	–
1	0.95449	11.931	−29.737	41.668	11.955	−0.024
2	0.96745	11.592	−29.528	41.120	11.701	−0.109
⋮		⋮	⋮	⋮	⋮	⋮
59	1.25762	0.200	−7.658	7.858	0.526	−0.326
60	1.19427	0.000	–	–	0.619	−0.619

Table 16.7 *Profit test table for Exercise 16.5, in $s.*

Time, t (months)	F_t	Management costs	Expenses	Hedge costs	Pr_t
0	100 000.00	250.00	1000.00	10 540.21	−11 290.21
1	95 210.38	238.03	61.89	−23.99	200.13
2	96 261.88	240.65	62.57	−109.16	287.24
⋮					

(i) Table 16.6 shows the first two rows of the hedge rebalancing cost table. Use the stock price scenario in Table 16.5 to complete this table. Calculate the present value of the hedge rebalance costs at an effective rate of interest of 5% per year.

(ii) Table 16.7 shows the first two rows of the profit test for this scenario. The insurer uses the full cost of the option at the start of the contract to pay for the hedge portfolio.

Complete the profit test and determine the profit margin (NPV as a percentage of the single premium) for this scenario.

(iii) State with reasons whether you would expect this contract to be profitable, on average, over a large number of simulations.

Basis for hedging and profit test calculations:

Survival:	Standard Ultimate Survival Model
Lapses:	None
Risk free rate:	5% per year, continuously compounded
Volatility:	20% per year
Incurred expenses – initial:	1% of the premium

| Incurred expenses – renewal: | 0.065% of the fund before management charge deduction, monthly in advance from the second month |
| Risk discount rate: | 10% per year |

Answers to selected exercises

16.1 (a) $4.61
    (b) 0.68%
    (c) $6.08

16.2 (a) $107.75
    (b) 0.13%

16.3 (a) 0.26545
    (b) 0.60819
    (c) $6033
    (d) $18 429

16.4 (a) The original option value is $4.85 and the reset option value is $6.46.
    (b) At $F_5 = 103.4$ both options have value $6.07.

16.5 (b) (i) The PV of rebalancing costs is $-\$1092.35$
       (ii) -1.23%
     (iii) We note that the initial hedge cost converts to a monthly outgo of 0.19% of the fund; adding the monthly incurred expenses, this comes to 0.255%, compared with income of 0.25% of the fund. Overall we would not expect this contract to be profitable on these terms.

Appendix A
Probability theory

A.1 Probability distributions

In this appendix we give a very brief description of the probability distributions used in this book. Derivations of the results quoted in this appendix can be found in standard introductory textbooks on probability theory.

A.1.1 Binomial distribution

If a random variable X has a binomial distribution with parameters n and p, where n is a positive integer and $0 < p < 1$, then its probability function is

$$\Pr[X = x] = \binom{n}{x} p^x (1 - p)^{n-x}$$

for $x = 0, 1, 2, \ldots, n$. This distribution has mean np and variance $np(1 - p)$, and we write $X \sim B(n, p)$.

The moment generating function is

$$M_X(t) = (pe^t + 1 - p)^n. \tag{A.1}$$

A.1.2 Uniform distribution

If a random variable X has a uniform distribution on the interval (a, b), then it has distribution function

$$\Pr[X \le x] = \frac{x - a}{b - a}$$

for $a \le x \le b$, and has probability density function

$$f(x) = \frac{1}{b - a}$$

for $a < x < b$. This distribution has mean $(a+b)/2$ and variance $(b-a)^2/12$, and we write $X \sim U(a, b)$.

A.1.3 Normal distribution

If a random variable X has a normal distribution with parameters μ and σ^2 then its probability density function is

$$f(x) = \frac{1}{\sigma\sqrt{2\pi}} \exp\left\{\frac{-(x-\mu)^2}{2\sigma^2}\right\}$$

for $-\infty < x < \infty$, where $-\infty < \mu < \infty$ and $\sigma > 0$. This distribution has mean μ and variance σ^2, and we write $X \sim N(\mu, \sigma^2)$.

The random variable Z defined by the transformation $Z = (X - \mu)/\sigma$ has mean 0 and variance 1 and is said to have the standard normal distribution. A common notation is $\Pr[Z \leq z] = \Phi(z)$, and as the probability density function is symmetric about 0, $\Phi(z) = 1 - \Phi(-z)$.

The traditional approach to computing probabilities for a normal random variable is to use the relationship

$$\Pr[X \leq x] = \Pr[Z \leq (x - \mu)/\sigma]$$

and to find the right-hand side from tables of the standard normal distribution, or from an approximation such as

$$\Phi(x) \approx 1 - \tfrac{1}{2}\left(1 + a_1 x + a_2 x^2 + a_3 x^3 + a_4 x^4 + a_5 x^5 + a_6 x^6\right)^{-16}$$

for $x \geq 0$ where

$$a_1 = 0.0498673470, \qquad a_4 = 0.0000380036,$$
$$a_2 = 0.0211410061, \qquad a_5 = 0.0000488906,$$
$$a_3 = 0.0032776263, \qquad a_6 = 0.0000053830.$$

The absolute value of the error in this approximation is less than 1.5×10^{-7}.

There are plenty of software packages that compute values of the normal distribution function. For example, in Excel we can find $\Pr[X \leq x]$ from the NORM.DIST command as

$$= \text{NORM.DIST}(x, \mu, \sigma, \text{TRUE})$$

where the value TRUE for the final parameter indicates that we want to obtain the distribution function. (Changing this parameter to FALSE gives the value of the probability density function at x.)

Similarly we can find percentiles of a normal distribution using either approximations or software. Suppose we want to find the value x_p such that $\Pr[Z > x_p] = p$ where $Z \sim N(0, 1)$ and $0 < p \le 0.5$. We can find this approximately as

$$x_p = t - \frac{a_0 + a_1 t + a_2 t^2}{1 + d_1 t + d_2 t^2 + d_3 t^3}$$

where $t = \sqrt{\log(1/p^2)}$ and

$$
\begin{aligned}
a_0 &= 2.515517, & d_1 &= 1.432788, \\
a_1 &= 0.802853, & d_2 &= 0.189269, \\
a_2 &= 0.010328, & d_3 &= 0.001308.
\end{aligned}
$$

The absolute value of the error in this approximation is less than 4.5×10^{-4}. Using the symmetry of the normal distribution we can deal with the case $p > 0.5$, but in practical actuarial applications this case rarely arises.

In Excel, we use the NORM.INV command to find percentiles. Specifically, we can find x such that $\Pr[X \le x] = p$ using

$$= \text{NORM.INV}(p, \mu, \sigma).$$

A.1.4 Lognormal distribution

If a random variable X has a lognormal distribution with parameters μ and σ^2 then its probability density function is

$$f(x) = \frac{1}{x\sigma\sqrt{2\pi}} \exp\left\{ \frac{-(\log x - \mu)^2}{2\sigma^2} \right\}$$

for $x > 0$, where $-\infty < \mu < \infty$ and $\sigma > 0$. This distribution has mean $\exp\{\mu + \sigma^2/2\}$ and variance $\exp\{2\mu + \sigma^2\}(\exp\{\sigma^2\} - 1)$, and we write $X \sim LN(\mu, \sigma^2)$.

We can calculate probabilities as follows. We know that

$$\Pr[X \le x] = \int_0^x \frac{1}{y\sigma\sqrt{2\pi}} \exp\left\{ \frac{-(\log y - \mu)^2}{2\sigma^2} \right\} dy.$$

Now substitute $z = \log y$, so that the range of the integral changes to $(-\infty, \log x)$, with $dz = dy/y$. Then

$$\Pr[X \le x] = \int_{-\infty}^{\log x} \frac{1}{\sigma\sqrt{2\pi}} \exp\left\{ \frac{-(z-\mu)^2}{2\sigma^2} \right\} dz$$

$$= \int_{-\infty}^{(\log x - \mu)/\sigma} \frac{1}{\sqrt{2\pi}} \exp\{-t^2/2\} dt$$

$$= \Pr\left[Z \le \frac{\log x - \mu}{\sigma} \right]$$

$$= \Phi\left(\frac{\log x - \mu}{\sigma} \right),$$

where Z has a standard normal distribution. Thus, we can compute probabilities for a lognormally distributed random variable from the standard normal distribution.

The above argument also shows that if $X \sim LN(\mu, \sigma^2)$, then $\log X \sim N(\mu, \sigma^2)$.

In Chapters 14 and 15 we used the result that if $X \sim LN(\mu, \sigma^2)$ then

$$\int_0^a x\, f(x)dx = \exp\{\mu + \sigma^2/2\} \Phi\left(\frac{\log a - \mu - \sigma^2}{\sigma} \right). \qquad (A.2)$$

To show this, we first note that

$$\int_0^a x\, f(x)dx = \int_0^a \frac{1}{\sigma\sqrt{2\pi}} \exp\left\{ \frac{-(\log x - \mu)^2}{2\sigma^2} \right\} dx,$$

and the substitution $z = \log x$ gives

$$\int_0^a x\, f(x)dx = \int_{-\infty}^{\log a} \frac{1}{\sigma\sqrt{2\pi}} \exp\left\{ \frac{-(z-\mu)^2}{2\sigma^2} \right\} \exp\{z\}dz.$$

Combining the exponential terms, the exponent becomes

$$z - \frac{(z-\mu)^2}{2\sigma^2} = \frac{-1}{2\sigma^2}\left(z^2 - 2\mu z + \mu^2 - 2\sigma^2 z \right)$$

$$= \frac{-1}{2\sigma^2}\left(z^2 - 2(\mu + \sigma^2)z + \mu^2 \right)$$

$$= \frac{-1}{2\sigma^2}\left(z^2 - 2(\mu + \sigma^2)z + (\mu + \sigma^2)^2 + \mu^2 - (\mu + \sigma^2)^2 \right)$$

$$= \frac{-1}{2\sigma^2}\left((z - (\mu + \sigma^2))^2 - 2\mu\sigma^2 - \sigma^4 \right)$$

$$= \frac{-(z - (\mu + \sigma^2))^2}{2\sigma^2} + \mu + \frac{\sigma^2}{2}.$$

This technique is known as 'completing the square' and is very useful in problems involving normal or lognormal random variables. We can now write

$$\int_0^a x\, f(x)\,dx = \int_{-\infty}^{\log a} \frac{1}{\sigma\sqrt{2\pi}} \exp\left\{ \frac{-\left(z-(\mu+\sigma^2)\right)^2}{2\sigma^2} \right\} \exp\left\{ \mu + \frac{\sigma^2}{2} \right\} dz$$

$$= \exp\left\{ \mu + \frac{\sigma^2}{2} \right\} \int_{-\infty}^{\log a} \frac{1}{\sigma\sqrt{2\pi}} \exp\left\{ \frac{-\left(z-(\mu+\sigma^2)\right)^2}{2\sigma^2} \right\} dz.$$

Now the integrand is the probability density function of a normal random variable with mean $\mu + \sigma^2$ and variance σ^2, and so

$$\int_{-\infty}^{\log a} \frac{1}{\sigma\sqrt{2\pi}} \exp\left\{ \frac{-\left(z-(\mu+\sigma^2)\right)^2}{2\sigma^2} \right\} dz = \Phi\left(\frac{\log a - \mu - \sigma^2}{\sigma} \right),$$

giving formula (A.2). We note that

$$\lim_{a\to\infty} \Phi\left(\frac{\log a - \mu - \sigma^2}{\sigma} \right) = 1,$$

and from this result and formula (A.2) we see that the mean of the lognormal distribution with parameters μ and σ^2 is

$$\exp\left\{ \mu + \frac{\sigma^2}{2} \right\}.$$

A.2 The central limit theorem

The central limit theorem is a very important result in probability theory. Suppose that $X_1, X_2, X_3, \dots$ is a sequence of independent and identically distributed random variables, each having mean μ and variance σ^2. Now define the sum $S_n = \sum_{i=1}^{n} X_i$ so that $E[S_n] = n\mu$ and $V[S_n] = n\sigma^2$. The central limit theorem states that

$$\lim_{n\to\infty} \Pr\left[\frac{S_n - n\mu}{\sigma\sqrt{n}} \le x \right] = \Phi(x)$$

where Φ is the standard normal distribution function.

The central limit theorem can be used to justify approximating the distribution of a (finite) sum of independent and identically distributed random variables by a normal distribution. For example, suppose that each X_i has a Bernoulli distribution (i.e. a $B(1, p)$ distribution). Then using moment generating functions we see that the distribution of S_n is $B(n, p)$ since

$$E[\exp\{t\,S_n\}] = E[\exp\{t\,(X_1 + X_2 + \cdots + X_n)\}]$$

$$= \prod_{i=1}^{n} E[\exp\{t\,X_i\}]$$

$$= \prod_{i=1}^{n}(pe^t + 1 - p)$$

$$= (pe^t + 1 - p)^n.$$

(Here we have used in order: independence, identical distribution and formula (A.1) with $n = 1$.) The uniqueness of moment generating functions tells us that $S_n \sim B(n, p)$. Thus we can think of a binomial random variable as the sum of Bernoulli random variables, and, provided the number of variables being summed is large, we can approximate the distribution of this sum by a normal distribution.

A.3 Functions of a random variable

In many places in this book we have considered functions of a random variable. For example, in Chapter 4 we considered v^{T_x} where T_x is a random variable representing future lifetime. We have also evaluated the expected value and higher moments of functions of a random variable. Here, we briefly review the theory that we have applied, considering separately random variables that follow discrete, continuous and mixed distributions. We quote results only, giving references for these results in Section A.5.

A.3.1 Discrete random variables

We first consider a discrete random variable, X, with probability function $\Pr[X = x]$ for $x = 0, 1, 2, \ldots$. Let g be a function and let $Y = g(X)$, so that the possible values for Y are $g(0), g(1), g(2), \ldots$. Then for $x = 0, 1, 2, \ldots$, Y takes the value $g(x)$ if X takes the value x. Thus,

$$\Pr[Y = g(x)] = \Pr[X = x],$$

and so

$$E[Y] = \sum_{x=0}^{\infty} g(x)\Pr[Y = g(x)] = \sum_{x=0}^{\infty} g(x)\Pr[X = x]. \tag{A.3}$$

Thus, we can compute E[Y] in terms of the probability function of X. Higher moments are similarly computed. For $r = 1, 2, 3, \ldots$ we have

$$E[Y^r] = \sum_{x=0}^{\infty} g(x)^r \Pr[X = x].$$

For example, suppose that X has probability function

$$\Pr[X = x] = pq^{x-1}$$

for $x = 1, 2, 3, \ldots$, and define $Y = v^X$ where $0 < v < 1$. Then $g(x) = v^x$ and

$$E[Y^r] = \sum_{x=1}^{\infty} v^{xr} pq^{x-1} = \frac{pv^r}{1 - qv^r}.$$

A.3.2 *Continuous random variables*

We next consider the situation of a continuous random variable, X, distributed on $(0, \infty)$ with probability density function $f(x)$ for $x > 0$. Consider a function g, let g^{-1} denote the inverse of this function, and define $Y = g(X)$. Then we can compute the expected value of Y as

$$E[Y] = E[g(X)] = \int_0^{\infty} g(x) f(x) dx. \qquad (A.4)$$

As in the case of discrete random variables, the expected value of Y can be found without explicitly stating the distribution of Y, and higher moments can be found similarly. Note the analogy with equation (A.3) – probability function has been replaced by probability density function, and summation by integration.

It can be shown that Y has a probability density function, which we denote h, given by

$$h(y) = f\left(g^{-1}(y)\right) \left| \frac{d}{dy} g^{-1}(y) \right| \qquad (A.5)$$

provided that g is a monotone function. However, formula (A.4) allows us to compute the expected value of Y without finding its probability density function.

For example, suppose that X has an exponential distribution with parameter λ. Now define $Y = e^{-\delta X}$, where $\delta > 0$. Then by formula (A.4) with $g(y) = e^{-\delta y}$,

$$E[Y] = \int_0^{\infty} e^{-\delta y} \lambda e^{-\lambda y} dy = \frac{\lambda}{\lambda + \delta}.$$

The alternative (and more complicated) approach to finding E[Y] is to first identify the distribution of Y, then find its mean. To follow this approach, we first note that if $g(y) = e^{-\delta y}$, then $g^{-1}(y) = (-1/\delta) \log y$ and so

$$\frac{d}{dy} g^{-1}(y) = \frac{-1}{\delta y}.$$

By formula (A.5), Y has probability density function $h(y)$, which is defined for $0 < y < 1$ (since $X > 0$ implies that $0 < e^{-\delta X} < 1$ as $\delta > 0$), with

$$h(y) = \lambda \exp\{(\lambda/\delta) \log y\} \frac{1}{\delta y}$$

$$= \frac{\lambda}{\delta} y^{(\lambda/\delta)-1}.$$

Thus

$$\mathrm{E}[Y] = \int_0^1 y h(y) dy = \frac{\lambda}{\delta} \int_0^1 y^{\lambda/\delta} dy = \frac{\lambda}{\delta} \frac{y^{(\lambda/\delta)+1}}{(\lambda/\delta)+1} \Bigg|_0^1 = \frac{\lambda}{\lambda+\delta}.$$

We could also have evaluated this integral by noting that Y has a beta distribution with parameters λ/δ and 1. In any event, the key point is that a function of a random variable is itself a random variable with its own distribution, but because of formula (A.4) it is not necessary to find this distribution to evaluate its moments.

A.3.3 Mixed random variables

Most of the mixed random variables we have encountered in this book have a probability density function over an interval and a mass of probability at one point only. For example, under an endowment insurance with term n years, there is probability density associated with payment of the sum insured at time t for $0 < t < n$, and a mass of probability associated with payment at time n. In that situation we defined the random variable (see Section 4.4.7)

$$Z = \begin{cases} v^{T_x} & \text{if } T_x < n, \\ v^n & \text{if } T_x \geq n. \end{cases}$$

More generally, suppose that X is a random variable with probability density function f over some interval (or possibly intervals) which we denote by $\mathcal{I}$, and has masses of probability, $\Pr[X = x_i]$, at points $x_1, x_2, x_3, \ldots$. Then if we define $Y = g(X)$, we have

$$\mathrm{E}[Y] = \int_{\mathcal{I}} g(x) f(x) dx + \sum_i g(x_i) \Pr[X = x_i].$$

For example, suppose that $\Pr[X \leq x] = 1 - e^{-\lambda x}$ for $0 < x < n$, and $\Pr[X = n] = e^{-\lambda n}$. Then X has probability density function $f(x) = \lambda e^{-\lambda x}$ for $0 < x < n$, and has a mass of probability of amount $e^{-\lambda n}$ at n. If we define $Y = e^{-\delta X}$, then

$$
\begin{aligned}
\mathrm{E}[Y] &= \int_0^n e^{-\delta x} \lambda e^{-\lambda x} + e^{-\delta n} e^{-\lambda n} \\
&= \frac{\lambda}{\lambda + \delta} \left(1 - e^{-(\lambda+\delta)n} \right) + e^{-(\lambda+\delta)n} \\
&= \frac{1}{\lambda + \delta} \left(\lambda + \delta e^{-(\lambda+\delta)n} \right).
\end{aligned}
$$

A.4 Conditional expectation and conditional variance

Consider two random variables X and Y whose first two moments exist. We can find the mean and variance of Y in terms of the conditional mean and variance of Y given X. In particular,

$$
\mathrm{E}[Y] = \mathrm{E}\left[\mathrm{E}[Y|X]\right] \tag{A.6}
$$

and

$$
\mathrm{V}[Y] = \mathrm{E}\left[\mathrm{V}[Y|X]\right] + \mathrm{V}[\mathrm{E}[Y|X]]. \tag{A.7}
$$

These formulae hold generally, but to prove them we restrict ourselves here to the situation when both X and Y are discrete random variables. Consider first expression (A.6). We note that for a function g of X and Y, we have

$$
\mathrm{E}[g(X, Y)] = \sum_x \sum_y g(x, y) \Pr[X = x, Y = y] \tag{A.8}
$$

(this is just the bivariate version of formula (A.3)). By the rules of conditional probability,

$$
\Pr[X = x, Y = y] = \Pr[Y = y | X = x] \Pr[X = x]. \tag{A.9}
$$

Then setting $g(X, Y) = Y$ and using (A.8) and (A.9) we obtain

$$
\begin{aligned}
\mathrm{E}[Y] &= \sum_x \sum_y y \Pr[Y = y | X = x] \Pr[X = x] \\
&= \sum_x \Pr[X = x] \sum_y y \Pr[Y = y | X = x] \\
&= \sum_x \Pr[X = x] \mathrm{E}[Y | X = x] \\
&= \mathrm{E}\left[\mathrm{E}[Y|X]\right].
\end{aligned}
$$

To obtain formula (A.7) we have

$$
\begin{aligned}
V[Y] &= E[Y^2] - E[Y]^2 \\
&= E[E[Y^2|X]] - E[Y]^2 \\
&= E\left[V[Y|X] + E[Y|X]^2\right] - E[Y]^2 \\
&= E[V[Y|X]] + E\left[E[Y|X]^2\right] - E[E[Y|X]]^2 \\
&= E[V[Y|X]] + V[E[Y|X]].
\end{aligned}
$$

A.5 Notes and further reading

Further details on the probability theory contained in this appendix can be found in texts such as Grimmett and Welsh (1986) and Hogg and Tanis (2009). The approximations for the standard normal distribution can be found in Abramovitz and Stegun (1965).

Appendix B

Numerical techniques

B.1 Numerical integration

In this section we illustrate two methods of numerical integration. The first, the trapezium rule, has the advantage of simplicity, but its main disadvantage is the amount of computation involved for the method to be very accurate. The second, repeated Simpson's rule, is not quite as straightforward, but is usually more accurate. We now outline each method, and give numerical illustrations of both. Further details can be found in the references in Section B.3.

Our aim in the next two sections is to evaluate numerically

$$I = \int_a^b f(x)dx$$

for some function f.

B.1.1 The trapezium rule

Under the trapezium rule, the interval (a, b) is split into n intervals, each of length $h = (b - a)/n$. Thus, we can write I as

$$I = \int_a^{a+h} f(x)dx + \int_{a+h}^{a+2h} f(x)dx + \ldots + \int_{a+(n-1)h}^{a+nh} f(x)dx$$

$$= \sum_{j=0}^{n-1} \int_{a+jh}^{a+(j+1)h} f(x)dx.$$

We obtain the value of I under the trapezium rule by assuming that f is a linear function in each interval so that under this assumption

Table B.1 *Values of I^* under the trapezium rule.*

n	I^*
20	12.64504
40	12.64307
80	12.64258
160	12.64245
320	12.64242

$$\int_{a+jh}^{a+(j+1)h} f(x)dx = \tfrac{h}{2}\left(f(a+jh) + f(a+(j+1)h)\right),$$

and hence

$$I = h\left(\tfrac{1}{2}f(a) + f(a+h) + f(a+2h) + \cdots + f(a+(n-1)h) + \tfrac{1}{2}f(b)\right)$$
$$= h\left(\tfrac{1}{2}f(a) + \sum_{j=1}^{n-1} f(a+jh) + \tfrac{1}{2}f(b)\right).$$

To illustrate the application of the trapezium rule, consider

$$I^* = \int_0^{20} e^{-0.05x}dx.$$

We have chosen this integral as we can evaluate it exactly as

$$I^* = \frac{1}{0.05}\left(1 - e^{-0.05 \times 20}\right) = 12.64241,$$

and hence we can compare evaluation by numerical integration with the true value. We have $a = 0$ and $b = 20$, and for our numerical illustration we have set $n = 20, 40, 80, 160$ and 320, so that the values of h are $1, 0.5, 0.25, 0.125$ and 0.0625. Table B.1 shows the results. We see that in this example we need a small value of h to obtain an answer that is correct to four decimal places, but we note that the percentage error is small in all cases.

B.1.2 Repeated Simpson's rule

This rule is based on Simpson's rule which gives the following approximation:

$$\int_a^{a+2h} f(x)dx \approx \tfrac{h}{3}\left(f(a) + 4f(a+h) + f(a+2h)\right).$$

This approximation arises by approximating the function f by a quadratic function that goes through the three points $(a, f(a))$, $(a+h, f(a+h))$ and

Table B.2 *Values of I^* under*
repeated Simpson's rule.

n	I^*
10	12.6424116
20	12.6424112
40	12.6424112

$(a + 2h, f(a + 2h))$. Repeated application of this result leads to the repeated Simpson's rule, namely

$$\int_a^b f(x)dx \approx h/3 \left(f(a) + 4\sum_{j=1}^{n} f(a + (2j - 1)h) + 2\sum_{j=1}^{n-1} f(a + 2jh) + f(b) \right)$$

where $h = (b - a)/2n$.

Let us again consider

$$I^* = \int_0^{20} e^{-0.05x}\, dx.$$

To seven decimal places, $I^* = 12.6424112$ and Table B.2 shows numerical values for I^* when $n = 10$, 20 and 40.

We see from Table B.2 that the calculations are considerably more accurate than under the trapezium rule. The reason for this is that the error in applying the trapezium rule is

$$\frac{(b - a)^3}{12n^2} f''(c)$$

for some c, where $a < c < b$, whilst under repeated Simpson's rule the error is

$$\frac{(b - a)^5}{2880n^4} f^{(4)}(c)$$

for some c, where $a < c < b$.

B.1.3 Integrals over an infinite interval

*********** Many situations arise under which we have to find the numerical value of an integral over the interval $(0, \infty)$. For example, we saw in Chapter 2 that the complete expectation of life is given by

$$\overset{\circ}{e}_x = \int_0^{\infty} {}_t p_x\, dt.$$

Table B.3 *Values of I_m.*

m	I_m
60	34.67970
70	34.75059
80	34.75155
90	34.75155
100	34.75155

To evaluate such integrals numerically, it usually suffices to take a pragmatic approach. For example, looking at the integrand in the above expression, we might say that the probability of a life aged x surviving a further $120 - x$ years is very small, and so we might replace the upper limit of integration by $120-x$, and perform numerical integration over the finite interval $(0, 120 - x)$. We could then assess our answer by considering a wider interval, say $(0, 130 - x)$.

To illustrate this idea, consider the following integral from Section 2.6.2 where we computed $\overset{\circ}{e}_x$ for a range of values for x in Table 2.2. Table B.3 shows values of

$$I_m = \int_0^m {}_t p_{40} \, dt$$

for a range of values for m. These values have been calculated using repeated Simpson's rule. We set $n = 120$ for $m = 60$, then changed the value of n for each subsequent value of m in such a way that the value of h was unchanged. For example, with $m = 70$, setting $n = 140$ results in $h = 0.25$, which is the same value of h obtained when $m = 60$ and $n = 120$. This maintains consistency between successive calculations of I_m values. For example,

$$I_{70} = I_{60} + \int_{60}^{70} {}_t p_{40} \, dt,$$

and setting $n = 140$ to compute I_{70} then gives the value we computed for I_{60} with $n = 120$. From this table our conclusion is that, to five decimal places, $\overset{\circ}{e}_{40} = 34.75155$.

B.2 Woolhouse's formula

Woolhouse's formula was used in Chapter 5. Here we give an indication of how this formula arises. We use the Euler–Maclaurin formula which is concerned with numerical integration. This formula gives a series expansion for the integral of a function, assuming that the function is differentiable a certain number of times. For a function f, the Euler–Maclaurin formula can be written as

$$\int_a^b f(x)\, dx = h \left(\sum_{i=0}^{N} f(a+ih) - \frac{1}{2} \left(f(a) + f(b) \right) \right)$$

$$+ \frac{h^2}{12} \left(f'(a) - f'(b) \right) - \frac{h^4}{720} \left(f'''(a) - f'''(b) \right) + \cdots, \quad \text{(B.1)}$$

where $h = (b-a)/N$, N is an integer, and the terms we have omitted involve higher derivatives of f. We shall apply this formula twice, in each case ignoring third and higher order derivatives of f.

First, setting $a = 0$ and $b = N = n$ (so that $h = 1$), the right-hand side of (B.1) is

$$\sum_{i=0}^{n} f(i) - \tfrac{1}{2} \left(f(0) + f(n) \right) + \tfrac{1}{12} \left(f'(0) - f'(n) \right). \quad \text{(B.2)}$$

Second, setting $a = 0$, $b = n$ and $N = mn$ for some integer $m > 1$ (so that $h = 1/m$), the right-hand side of (B.1) is

$$\frac{1}{m} \left(\sum_{i=0}^{mn} f(i/m) - \tfrac{1}{2} \left(f(0) + f(n) \right) \right) + \frac{1}{12m^2} \left(f'(0) - f'(n) \right). \quad \text{(B.3)}$$

As each of (B.2) and (B.3) approximates the same quantity, we can obtain an approximation to $\frac{1}{m} \sum_{i=0}^{mn} f(i/m)$ by equating them, so that

$$\frac{1}{m} \sum_{i=0}^{mn} f(i/m)$$

$$\approx \sum_{i=0}^{n} f(i) - \frac{m-1}{2m} \left(f(0) + f(n) \right) + \frac{m^2 - 1}{12m^2} \left(f'(0) - f'(n) \right). \quad \text{(B.4)}$$

The right-hand side of formula (B.4) gives the first three terms of Woolhouse's formula, and in actuarial applications it usually suffices to apply only these terms.

B.3 Notes and further reading

A list of numerical integration methods is given in Abramovitz and Stegun (1965). Details of the derivation of the trapezium rule and repeated Simpson's rule can be found in standard texts on numerical methods such as Burden and Fairs (2010) and Ralston and Rabinowitz (2001).

Appendix C
Simulation

C.1 The inverse transform method

The inverse transform method allows us to simulate observations of a random variable, X, when we have a uniform $U(0, 1)$ random number generator available.

The method states that if $F(x) = \Pr[X \leq x]$ and u is a random drawing from the $U(0, 1)$ distribution, then

$$x = F^{-1}(u)$$

is our simulated value of X.

The result follows for the following reason: if $U \sim U(0, 1)$, then $F^{-1}(U)$ has the same distribution as X. To show this, we assume for simplicity that the distribution function F is continuous – this is not essential for the method, it just gives a simpler proof. First, we note that as the distribution function F is continuous, it is a monotonic increasing function. Next, we know from the properties of the uniform distribution on $(0, 1)$ that for $0 \leq y \leq 1$,

$$\Pr[U \leq y] = y.$$

Now let $\tilde{X} = F^{-1}(U)$. Then

$$\Pr[\tilde{X} \leq x] = \Pr[F^{-1}(U) \leq x]$$

$$= \Pr[U \leq F(x)]$$

since F is a monotonic increasing function. As $\Pr[U \leq F(x)] = F(x)$, we have

$$\Pr[\tilde{X} \leq x] = F(x) = \Pr[X \leq x]$$

which shows that $\tilde{X}$ and X have the same distribution function.

Example C.1 Simulate three values from an exponential distribution with mean 100 using the three random drawings

$$u_1 = 0.1254, \quad u_2 = 0.4529, \quad u_3 = 0.7548,$$

from the $U(0, 1)$ distribution.

Solution C.1 Let F denote the distribution function of an exponentially distributed random variable with mean 100, so that

$$F(x) = 1 - \exp\{-x/100\}.$$

Then setting $u = F^{-1}(x)$ gives

$$x = -100 \log(1 - u),$$

and hence our three simulated values from this exponential distribution are

$$-100 \log 0.8746 = 13.399,$$
$$-100 \log 0.5471 = 60.312,$$
$$-100 \log 0.2452 = 140.57.$$

□

C.2 Simulation from a normal distribution

In Chapters 11 and 14 we used Excel to generate random numbers from a normal distribution. In many situations, for example if we wish to create a large number of simulations of an insurance portfolio over a long time period, it is much more effective in terms of computing time to use a programming language rather than a spreadsheet. Most programming languages do not have an in-built function to generate random numbers from a normal distribution, but do have a random number generator, that is they have an in-built function to generate (pseudo-)random numbers from the $U(0, 1)$ distribution.

   Without going into details, we now state the two most common approaches to simulating values from a standard normal distribution. The detail behind these 'recipes' can be found in the references in Section C.3.

C.2.1 The Box–Muller method

The Box–Muller method is to first simulate two values, u_1 and u_2, from a $U(0, 1)$ distribution, then to compute the pair

$$x = \sqrt{-2 \log u_1} \ \cos(2\pi u_2)$$
$$y = \sqrt{-2 \log u_1} \ \sin(2\pi u_2)$$

which are random drawings from the standard normal distribution.

For example, if $u_1 = 0.643$ and $u_2 = 0.279$, we find that $x = -0.1703$ and $y = 0.9242$.

C.2.2 The polar method

From a computational point of view, the weakness of the Box–Muller method is that we have to compute trigonometric functions to apply it. This issue can be avoided by using the polar method which says that if u_1 and u_2 are as above, then set

$$v_1 = 2u_1 - 1,$$
$$v_2 = 2u_2 - 1,$$
$$s = v_1^2 + v_2^2.$$

If $s < 1$, we compute

$$x = v_1 \sqrt{\frac{-2 \log s}{s}},$$
$$y = v_2 \sqrt{\frac{-2 \log s}{s}}$$

which are random drawings from the standard normal distribution. However, should the computed value of s exceed 1, we discard the random drawings from the $U(0, 1)$ distribution and repeat the procedure until the computed value of s is less than 1.

For example, if $u_1 = 0.643$ and $u_2 = 0.279$, we find that $v_1 = 0.2860$, $v_2 = -0.4420$ and hence $s = 0.2772$. As the value of s is less than 1, we proceed to compute $x = 0.8703$ and $y = -1.3450$

C.3 Notes and further reading

Details of all the above methods can be found in standard texts on simulation, e.g. Ross (2006), or on probability theory, e.g. Borovkov (2003).

Appendix D

Tables

In this appendix we show tables of selected functions for the Standard Ultimate and Select Survival Models. These are used extensively throughout this book for examples and exercises.

The **Standard Ultimate Survival Model** follows Makeham's Law, parameterized as follows:

$$\mu_x = A + Bc^x \qquad \text{where } A = 0.00022, B = 2.7 \times 10^{-6}, c = 1.124. \tag{D.1}$$

The **Standard Select Survival Model** is defined as follows:

◇ The select period is two years.
◇ The ultimate part of the model is the Standard Ultimate Survival Model.
◇ For the select part of the model, for $0 \le s \le 2$,

$$\mu_{[x]+s} = 0.9^{2-s}\mu_{x+s}. \tag{D.2}$$

This model was introduced in Example 3.13.

We also present, for convenience of access, the pension service table derived and used for examples and exercises in Chapter 10.

Note that all the solutions to the examples and exercises in the text, and in the accompanying model solutions, were calculated directly from the models, not from these tables. Using these tables will introduce rounding errors, resulting in some small differences compared with the answers in the text.

The tables are designed to provide a convenient reference for readers, and to assist with exam preparation for exam candidates. However, there are many examples and exercises in the text that cannot be answered using these tables. It is recommended that readers create their own spreadsheets, which can be used when the parameters or interest rates required are different from those used here.

Table D.1 *Standard Select and Ultimate Survival Model.*

x	$l_{[x]}$	$l_{[x]+1}$	l_{x+2}	x + 2	x	$l_{[x]}$	$l_{[x]+1}$	l_{x+2}	x + 2
			100000.00	20	60	96568.13	96287.48	95940.60	62
			99975.04	21	61	96232.34	95920.27	95534.43	63
20	99995.08	99973.75	99949.71	22	62	95858.91	95511.80	95082.53	64
21	99970.04	99948.40	99923.98	23	63	95443.51	95057.36	94579.73	65
22	99944.63	99922.65	99897.79	24	64	94981.34	94551.72	94020.33	66
23	99918.81	99896.43	99871.08	25	65	94467.11	93989.16	93398.05	67
24	99892.52	99869.70	99843.80	26	66	93895.00	93363.38	92706.06	68
25	99865.69	99842.38	99815.86	27	67	93258.63	92667.50	91936.88	69
26	99838.28	99814.41	99787.20	28	68	92551.02	91894.03	91082.43	70
27	99810.20	99785.70	99757.71	29	69	91764.58	91034.84	90133.96	71
28	99781.36	99756.17	99727.29	30	70	90891.07	90081.15	89082.09	72
29	99751.69	99725.70	99695.83	31	71	89921.62	89023.56	87916.84	73
30	99721.06	99694.18	99663.20	32	72	88846.72	87852.03	86627.64	74
31	99689.36	99661.48	99629.26	33	73	87656.25	86555.99	85203.46	75
32	99656.47	99627.47	99593.83	34	74	86339.55	85124.37	83632.89	76
33	99622.23	99591.96	99556.75	35	75	84885.49	83545.75	81904.34	77
34	99586.47	99554.78	99517.80	36	76	83282.61	81808.54	80006.23	78
35	99549.01	99515.73	99476.75	37	77	81519.30	79901.17	77927.35	79
36	99509.64	99474.56	99433.34	38	78	79584.04	77812.44	75657.16	80
37	99468.12	99431.02	99387.29	39	79	77465.70	75531.88	73186.31	81
38	99424.18	99384.82	99338.26	40	80	75153.97	73050.22	70507.19	82
39	99377.52	99335.62	99285.88	41				67614.60	83
40	99327.82	99283.06	99229.76	42				64506.50	84
41	99274.69	99226.72	99169.41	43				61184.88	85
42	99217.72	99166.14	99104.33	44				57656.68	86
43	99156.42	99100.80	99033.94	45				53934.73	87
44	99090.27	99030.10	98957.57	46				50038.65	88
45	99018.67	98953.40	98874.50	47				45995.64	89
46	98940.96	98869.96	98783.91	48				41841.05	90
47	98856.38	98778.94	98684.88	49				37618.56	91
48	98764.09	98679.44	98576.37	50				33379.88	92
49	98663.15	98570.40	98457.24	51				29183.78	93
50	98552.51	98450.67	98326.19	52				25094.33	94
51	98430.98	98318.95	98181.77	53				21178.30	95
52	98297.24	98173.79	98022.38	54				17501.76	96
53	98149.81	98013.56	97846.20	55				14125.89	97
54	97987.03	97836.44	97651.21	56				11102.53	98
55	97807.07	97640.40	97435.17	57				8469.73	99
56	97607.84	97423.18	97195.56	58				6248.17	100
57	97387.05	97182.25	96929.59	59					
58	97142.13	96914.80	96634.14	60					
59	96870.22	96617.70	96305.75	61					

Appendix D. Tables

Table D.2 *Standard Select Survival Model, $i = 5\%$ per year.*

x	$\ddot{a}_{[x]}$	$A_{[x]}$	$^2A_{[x]}$	$_5E_{[x]}$	$_{10}E_{[x]}$	$_{20}E_{[x]}$	x
20	19.967	0.04918	0.00576	0.78255	0.61227	0.37441	20
21	19.921	0.05140	0.00610	0.78254	0.61223	0.37431	21
22	19.872	0.05373	0.00648	0.78252	0.61218	0.37419	22
23	19.820	0.05618	0.00689	0.78249	0.61213	0.37406	23
24	19.766	0.05874	0.00734	0.78247	0.61208	0.37392	24
25	19.710	0.06143	0.00783	0.78244	0.61201	0.37375	25
26	19.651	0.06424	0.00837	0.78241	0.61194	0.37356	26
27	19.589	0.06720	0.00895	0.78237	0.61186	0.37336	27
28	19.524	0.07029	0.00959	0.78233	0.61177	0.37312	28
29	19.456	0.07353	0.01028	0.78229	0.61167	0.37286	29
30	19.384	0.07693	0.01104	0.78224	0.61156	0.37256	30
31	19.310	0.08049	0.01186	0.78218	0.61143	0.37223	31
32	19.232	0.08421	0.01276	0.78211	0.61128	0.37186	32
33	19.150	0.08811	0.01373	0.78204	0.61112	0.37144	33
34	19.064	0.09220	0.01479	0.78196	0.61094	0.37097	34
35	18.974	0.09647	0.01594	0.78187	0.61074	0.37044	35
36	18.880	0.10094	0.01720	0.78176	0.61051	0.36985	36
37	18.782	0.10562	0.01856	0.78165	0.61025	0.36919	37
38	18.679	0.11051	0.02004	0.78152	0.60996	0.36844	38
39	18.572	0.11563	0.02164	0.78137	0.60963	0.36761	39
40	18.460	0.12097	0.02338	0.78121	0.60927	0.36667	40
41	18.342	0.12656	0.02527	0.78102	0.60886	0.36562	41
42	18.220	0.13240	0.02731	0.78082	0.60840	0.36444	42
43	18.092	0.13849	0.02952	0.78058	0.60788	0.36312	43
44	17.958	0.14485	0.03191	0.78032	0.60730	0.36165	44
45	17.819	0.15149	0.03450	0.78003	0.60664	0.35999	45
46	17.673	0.15841	0.03730	0.77970	0.60591	0.35815	46
47	17.522	0.16563	0.04032	0.77932	0.60509	0.35608	47
48	17.364	0.17314	0.04358	0.77891	0.60416	0.35377	48
49	17.200	0.18098	0.04709	0.77844	0.60313	0.35120	49

Table D.2 (*Cont.*)

x	$\ddot{a}_{[x]}$	$A_{[x]}$	$^2A_{[x]}$	$_5E_{[x]}$	$_{10}E_{[x]}$	$_{20}E_{[x]}$	x
50	17.028	0.18913	0.05087	0.77791	0.60196	0.34832	50
51	16.850	0.19761	0.05495	0.77732	0.60066	0.34512	51
52	16.665	0.20642	0.05933	0.77665	0.59919	0.34156	52
53	16.473	0.21558	0.06404	0.77591	0.59755	0.33760	53
54	16.273	0.22509	0.06909	0.77507	0.59572	0.33320	54
55	16.066	0.23496	0.07451	0.77413	0.59366	0.32832	55
56	15.851	0.24519	0.08031	0.77307	0.59135	0.32293	56
57	15.628	0.25579	0.08653	0.77189	0.58877	0.31697	57
58	15.398	0.26677	0.09317	0.77056	0.58588	0.31041	58
59	15.160	0.27811	0.10025	0.76907	0.58265	0.30319	59
60	14.913	0.28984	0.10781	0.76739	0.57904	0.29528	60
61	14.659	0.30194	0.11586	0.76552	0.57501	0.28663	61
62	14.397	0.31442	0.12441	0.76341	0.57051	0.27721	62
63	14.127	0.32727	0.13350	0.76105	0.56550	0.26700	63
64	13.850	0.34049	0.14313	0.75841	0.55992	0.25596	64
65	13.564	0.35407	0.15333	0.75545	0.55371	0.24411	65
66	13.272	0.36801	0.16411	0.75214	0.54682	0.23143	66
67	12.972	0.38230	0.17548	0.74844	0.53917	0.21797	67
68	12.665	0.39692	0.18746	0.74429	0.53070	0.20377	68
69	12.351	0.41186	0.20005	0.73966	0.52134	0.18891	69
70	12.031	0.42710	0.21326	0.73450	0.51102	0.17350	70
71	11.705	0.44262	0.22709	0.72873	0.49966	0.15767	71
72	11.374	0.45840	0.24154	0.72230	0.48719	0.14160	72
73	11.037	0.47442	0.25662	0.71515	0.47355	0.12548	73
74	10.696	0.49065	0.27229	0.70719	0.45867	0.10954	74
75	10.352	0.50706	0.28856	0.69835	0.44250	0.09403	75
76	10.004	0.52362	0.30541	0.68854	0.42501	0.07920	76
77	9.654	0.54029	0.32280	0.67768	0.40618	0.06531	77
78	9.302	0.55704	0.34072	0.66568	0.38600	0.05258	78
79	8.950	0.57382	0.35912	0.65245	0.36451	0.04121	79
80	8.597	0.59061	0.37797	0.63789	0.34179	0.03133	80

Table D.3 *Standard Ultimate Survival Model, i = 5% per year.*

x	$\ddot{a}_x$	A_x	^2A_x	$_5E_x$	$_{10}E_x$	$_{20}E_x$	x
20	19.966	0.04922	0.00580	0.78252	0.61224	0.37440	20
21	19.920	0.05144	0.00614	0.78250	0.61220	0.37429	21
22	19.871	0.05378	0.00652	0.78248	0.61215	0.37417	22
23	19.819	0.05622	0.00694	0.78245	0.61210	0.37404	23
24	19.765	0.05879	0.00739	0.78243	0.61205	0.37390	24
25	19.709	0.06147	0.00788	0.78240	0.61198	0.37373	25
26	19.650	0.06429	0.00841	0.78236	0.61191	0.37354	26
27	19.588	0.06725	0.00900	0.78233	0.61183	0.37334	27
28	19.523	0.07034	0.00964	0.78229	0.61174	0.37310	28
29	19.455	0.07359	0.01033	0.78224	0.61163	0.37284	29
30	19.383	0.07698	0.01109	0.78219	0.61152	0.37254	30
31	19.309	0.08054	0.01192	0.78213	0.61139	0.37221	31
32	19.230	0.08427	0.01281	0.78206	0.61124	0.37183	32
33	19.148	0.08817	0.01379	0.78199	0.61108	0.37141	33
34	19.063	0.09226	0.01486	0.78190	0.61090	0.37094	34
35	18.973	0.09653	0.01601	0.78181	0.61069	0.37041	35
36	18.879	0.10101	0.01727	0.78170	0.61046	0.36982	36
37	18.780	0.10569	0.01863	0.78158	0.61020	0.36915	37
38	18.678	0.11059	0.02012	0.78145	0.60990	0.36841	38
39	18.570	0.11571	0.02173	0.78130	0.60957	0.36757	39
40	18.458	0.12106	0.02347	0.78113	0.60920	0.36663	40
41	18.340	0.12665	0.02536	0.78094	0.60879	0.36558	41
42	18.218	0.13249	0.02741	0.78072	0.60832	0.36440	42
43	18.090	0.13859	0.02963	0.78048	0.60780	0.36307	43
44	17.956	0.14496	0.03203	0.78021	0.60721	0.36159	44
45	17.816	0.15161	0.03463	0.77991	0.60655	0.35994	45
46	17.671	0.15854	0.03744	0.77956	0.60581	0.35809	46
47	17.519	0.16577	0.04047	0.77918	0.60498	0.35601	47
48	17.361	0.17330	0.04374	0.77875	0.60404	0.35370	48
49	17.196	0.18114	0.04727	0.77827	0.60299	0.35112	49

Table D.3 (*Cont.*)

x	$\ddot{a}_x$	A_x	^2A_x	$_5E_x$	$_{10}E_x$	$_{20}E_x$	x
50	17.025	0.18931	0.05108	0.77772	0.60182	0.34824	50
51	16.846	0.19780	0.05517	0.77711	0.60050	0.34503	51
52	16.661	0.20664	0.05957	0.77643	0.59902	0.34146	52
53	16.468	0.21582	0.06430	0.77566	0.59736	0.33749	53
54	16.268	0.22535	0.06938	0.77479	0.59550	0.33308	54
55	16.060	0.23524	0.07483	0.77382	0.59342	0.32819	55
56	15.844	0.24550	0.08067	0.77273	0.59109	0.32279	56
57	15.621	0.25613	0.08692	0.77151	0.58848	0.31681	57
58	15.390	0.26714	0.09360	0.77014	0.58556	0.31024	58
59	15.151	0.27852	0.10073	0.76860	0.58229	0.30300	59
60	14.904	0.29028	0.10834	0.76687	0.57864	0.29508	60
61	14.649	0.30243	0.11644	0.76493	0.57457	0.28641	61
62	14.386	0.31495	0.12506	0.76276	0.57003	0.27698	62
63	14.115	0.32785	0.13421	0.76033	0.56496	0.26674	63
64	13.836	0.34113	0.14392	0.75760	0.55932	0.25569	64
65	13.550	0.35477	0.15420	0.75455	0.55305	0.24381	65
66	13.256	0.36878	0.16507	0.75114	0.54609	0.23112	66
67	12.954	0.38313	0.17654	0.74732	0.53836	0.21764	67
68	12.646	0.39783	0.18862	0.74305	0.52981	0.20343	68
69	12.330	0.41285	0.20133	0.73828	0.52036	0.18856	69
70	12.008	0.42818	0.21467	0.73295	0.50994	0.17313	70
71	11.680	0.44379	0.22864	0.72701	0.49848	0.15730	71
72	11.347	0.45968	0.24324	0.72039	0.48590	0.14122	72
73	11.008	0.47580	0.25847	0.71303	0.47215	0.12511	73
74	10.665	0.49215	0.27433	0.70483	0.45715	0.10918	74
75	10.318	0.50868	0.29079	0.69574	0.44085	0.09368	75
76	9.967	0.52536	0.30783	0.68566	0.42323	0.07887	76
77	9.614	0.54217	0.32544	0.67450	0.40427	0.06500	77
78	9.260	0.55906	0.34359	0.66217	0.38396	0.05230	78
79	8.904	0.57599	0.36224	0.64859	0.36235	0.04096	79
80	8.548	0.59293	0.38134	0.63365	0.33952	0.03113	80

Table D.4 *Pension plan service table.*

x	l_x	w_x	i_x	r_x	d_x	x	l_x	w_x	i_x	r_x	d_x
20	1 000 000	95 104	951	0	237	44	137 656	6 708	134	0	95
21	903 707	85 946	859	0	218	45	130 719	2 586	129	0	100
22	816 684	77 670	777	0	200	46	127 904	2 530	127	0	106
23	738 038	70 190	702	0	184	47	125 140	2 476	124	0	113
24	666 962	63 430	634	0	170	48	122 428	2 422	121	0	121
25	602 728	57 321	573	0	157	49	119 763	2 369	118	0	130
26	544 677	51 800	518	0	145	50	117 145	2 317	116	0	140
27	492 213	46 811	468	0	134	51	114 572	2 266	113	0	151
28	444 800	42 301	423	0	125	52	112 042	2 216	111	0	163
29	401 951	38 226	382	0	117	53	109 553	2 166	108	0	176
30	363 226	34 543	345	0	109	54	107 102	2 118	106	0	190
31	328 228	31 215	312	0	102	55	104 688	2 070	103	0	206
32	296 599	28 207	282	0	96	56	102 308	2 023	101	0	224
33	268 014	25 488	255	0	91	57	99 960	1 976	99	0	243
34	242 181	23 031	230	0	86	58	97 642	1 930	96	0	264
35	218 834	10 665	213	0	83	59	95 351	1 884	94	0	288
36	207 872	10 131	203	0	84	60^-	93 085	0	0	27 926	0
37	197 455	9 623	192	0	84	60^+	65 160	0	62	6 188	210
38	187 555	9 141	183	0	85	61	58 700	0	56	5 573	212
39	178 147	8 682	174	0	86	62	52 860	0	50	5 018	213
40	169 206	8 246	165	0	87	63	47 579	0	45	4 515	214
41	160 708	7 832	157	0	89	64	42 805	0	41	4 061	215
42	152 631	7 438	149	0	90	65^-	38 488	0	0	38 488	0
43	144 954	7 064	141	0	93						

References

Arias, E. (2004). *United States Life Tables, 2002*. National Vital Statistics Reports; Vol 53, No. 6. Hyattsville, Maryland: National Center for Health Statistics.

Abramowitz, M. and Stegun, I. A. (1965). *Handbook of Mathematical Functions*. New York: Dover.

Atkinson, D. B. and Dallas, J. W. (2000) *Life Insurance Products and Finance*. Itasca: Society of Actuaries.

Australian Government Actuary (2004). *Australian Life Tables 2000–02*. Canberra: Commonwealth of Australia.

Bacinello, A. R. (2003). Pricing guaranteed life insurance participating policies with annual premiums and surrender option. *North American Actuarial Journal* **7**, 3, 1–17.

Blake, D. (2006). *Pension Finance*. Chichester: John Wiley & Sons.

Borovkov, K. A. (2003). *Elements of Stochastic Modelling*. Singapore: World Scientific.

Bowers, N. L., Gerber, H. U., Hickman, J. C., Jones, D. A. and Nesbitt, C. J. (1997). *Actuarial Mathematics*, 2nd edition. Itasca: Society of Actuaries.

Boyle, P. P. and Boyle, F. P. (2001). *Derivatives: The Tools that Changed Finance*. London: Risk Books.

Boyle, P. P. and Schwartz, E. S. (1977). Equilibrium prices of guarantees under equity-linked contracts. *Journal of Risk and Insurance* **44**, 639–66.

Brennan, M. J. and Schwartz, E. S. (1976). The pricing of equity-linked life insurance policies with an asset value guarantee. *Journal of Financial Economics* **3**, 195–213.

Burden, R. L. and Faires, J. D. (2010). *Numerical Analysis*, 7th edition. Pacific Grove: Brooks/Cole.

Cairns, A. J. G. (2004). *Interest Rate Models*. New Jersey: Princeton University Press.

Cairns A. J. G., Blake, D., Dowd, K., Coughlan, G. D., Epstein, D., Ong, A. and Balevich, I. (2009). A quantitative comparison of stochastic mortality models using data from England and Wales and the United States. *North American Actuarial Journal* **13**, 1, 1–34.

CMI (1991). *Continuous Mortality Investigation Report*, Number 12. London and Edinburgh: The Institute of Actuaries and the Faculty of Actuaries.

CMI (2006). *The Graduation of the CMI 1999-2002 Mortality Experience: Final 00 Series Mortality Tables Assured Lives.* www.actuaries.org.uk/files/pdf/cmi/wp21/wp21.pdf.

Coleman, D. A. and Salt, J. (1992). *The British Population: Patterns, Trends, and Processes.* Oxford: Oxford University Press.

Cox, D. R. and Miller, H. D. (1965). *The Theory of Stochastic Processes.* London: Chapman and Hall.

Cox, J. C., Ross, S. A. and Rubinstein, M. (1979). Options pricing: a simplified approach. *Journal of Financial Economics* **7**, 229–63.

Dickson, D. C. M. (2006). Premiums and reserves for life insurance products. *Australian Actuarial Journal* **12**, 259–79.

Forfar, D. O., McCutcheon, J. J. and Wilkie, A. D. (1988). On graduation by mathematical formula. *Transactions of the Faculty of Actuaries* **41**, 97–269.

Glasserman, P. (2004). *Monte Carlo Methods in Financial Engineering.* New York: Springer-Verlag.

Gompertz, B. (1825). On the nature of the function expressive of the law of human mortality, and on a new mode of determining the value of life contingencies. *Philosophical Transactions of the Royal Society of London* **115**, 513–85.

Graham, R. L., Knuth, D. E. and Patashnik, O. (1994). *Concrete Mathematics*, 2nd edition. Upper Saddle River: Addison-Wesley.

Grimmett, G. and Welsh, D. J. A. (1986) *Probability: An Introduction.* Oxford: Oxford University Press.

Hardy, M. R. (2003). *Investment Guarantees: Modeling and Risk Management for Equity-Linked Life Insurance.* New York: John Wiley & Sons.

Hoem, J. M. (1983). The reticent trio: Some little–known early discoveries in insurance mathematics by L. H. F. Opperman, T. N. Thiele and J. P. Gram. *International Statistical Review* **51**, 213–21.

Hoem, J. M. (1988). New avenues in modelling life insurance and other insurance of persons. *Transactions of the XXIII International Congress of Actuaries*, Volume R, pp. 171–202.

Hogg, R. V. and Tanis, E. A. (2009). *Probability and Statistical Inference*, 8th edition. New York: Pearson.

Hsia, C.-C. (1983). On binomial option pricing. *The Journal of Financial Research* **6**, 41–46.

Hull, J. C. (2011). *Options, Futures and Other Derivatives*, 8th edition. Upper Saddle River: Prentice Hall.

Ji, M., Hardy, M. R. and Li, J. S.-H. (2011) Markovian approaches to joint-life mortality. *North American Actuarial Journal* **15**, 2, 357–376.

Ledlie, M. C., Corry, D. P., Finkelstein, G. S., Ritchie, A. J., Su, K. and Wilson, D. C. E. (2008). *Variable Annuities.* Presented to the Faculty of Actuaries, 17 March 2008, and to the Institute of Actuaries, 31 March 2008.

Lee, R. D., and Carter, L. R. (1992). Modeling and forecasting U.S. mortality. *Journal of the American Statistical Association* **87**, 659–675.

Li, J. S.-H., Hardy, M. R. and Tan, K. S. (2010). Developing mortality improvement formulae: the Canadian insured lives case study. *North American Actuarial Journal* **14**, 4, 381–399.

Macdonald, A. S. (1996). An actuarial survey of statistical models for decrement and transition data. I: multiple state, binomial and Poisson models. *British Actuarial Journal* **2**, 129–55.

Macdonald, A. S., Waters, H. R. and Wekwete, C. T. (2003a). The genetics of breast and ovarian cancer I: A model of family history. *Scandinavian Actuarial Journal*, 1–27.

Macdonald, A. S., Waters, H. R. and Wekwete, C. T. (2003b). The genetics of breast and ovarian cancer II: A model of critical illness insurance. *Scandinavian Actuarial Journal*, 28–50.

Makeham, W. M. (1860). On the law of mortality and the construction of annuity tables. *Journal of the Institute of Actuaries* **8**, 301–10.

McDonald, R. C. (2009). *Derivatives Markets*, 3rd edition. Upper Saddle River: Prentice Hall.

McGill, D. M., Brown, K. N., Haley, J. J., Schieber, S. J. and Warshawsky, M. J. (2010). *Fundamentals of Private Pensions*, 9th edition. New York: Oxford University Press.

Møller, T. (1998). Risk minimizing hedging strategies for unit-linked life insurance contracts. *ASTIN Bulletin* **28**, 17–47.

Neill, A. (1977). *Life Contingencies*. London: Heinemann.

Norberg, R. (1995). Differential equations for higher-order moments of present values in life insurance. *Insurance: Mathematics & Economics* **17**, 171–80.

Office for National Statistics (1997). *English Life Tables No. 15*. London: The Stationery Office.

Press, W. H., Teukolsy, S. A., Vetterling, W. T. and Flannery, B. P. (2007). *Numerical Recipes*, 3rd edition. New York: Cambridge University Press.

Ralston, A. and Rabinowitz, P. (2001). *A First Course in Numerical Analysis*, 2nd edition. New York: Dover.

Renn, D. F. (ed.) (1998). *Life, Death and Money*. Oxford: Blackwell.

Rolski, T., Schmidli, H., Schmidt, V. and Teugels, J. (1999). *Stochastic Processes for Insurance and Finance*. Chichester: John Wiley & Sons.

Ross, S. M. (1995). *Stochastic Processes*, 2nd edition. New York: John Wiley & Sons.

Ross, S. M. (2006). *Simulation*, 4th edition. Burlington: Elsevier Academic Press.

Svedrup, E. (1965). Estimates and test procedures in connection with stochastic models for deaths, recoveries and transfers between different states of health. *Scandinavian Actuarial Journal*, 184–211.

Waters, H. R. (1984). An approach to the study of multiple state models. *Journal of the Institute of Actuaries* **111**, 363–74.

Waters, H. R. and Wilkie, A. D. (1988). A short note on the construction of life tables and multiple decrement models. *Journal of the Institute of Actuaries* **114**, 569–80.

Willets, R. C., Gallop, A. P., Leandro, P. A., Lu, J. L. C., Macdonald, A. S., Miller, K. A., Richards, S. J., Robjohns, N., Ryan, J. P. and Waters, H. R. (2004). Longevity in the 21st century. *British Actuarial Journal* **10**, 685–832.

Woolhouse, W. S. B. (1869). On an improved theory of annuities and assurances. *Journal of the Institute of Actuaries* **15**, 95–125.

Index